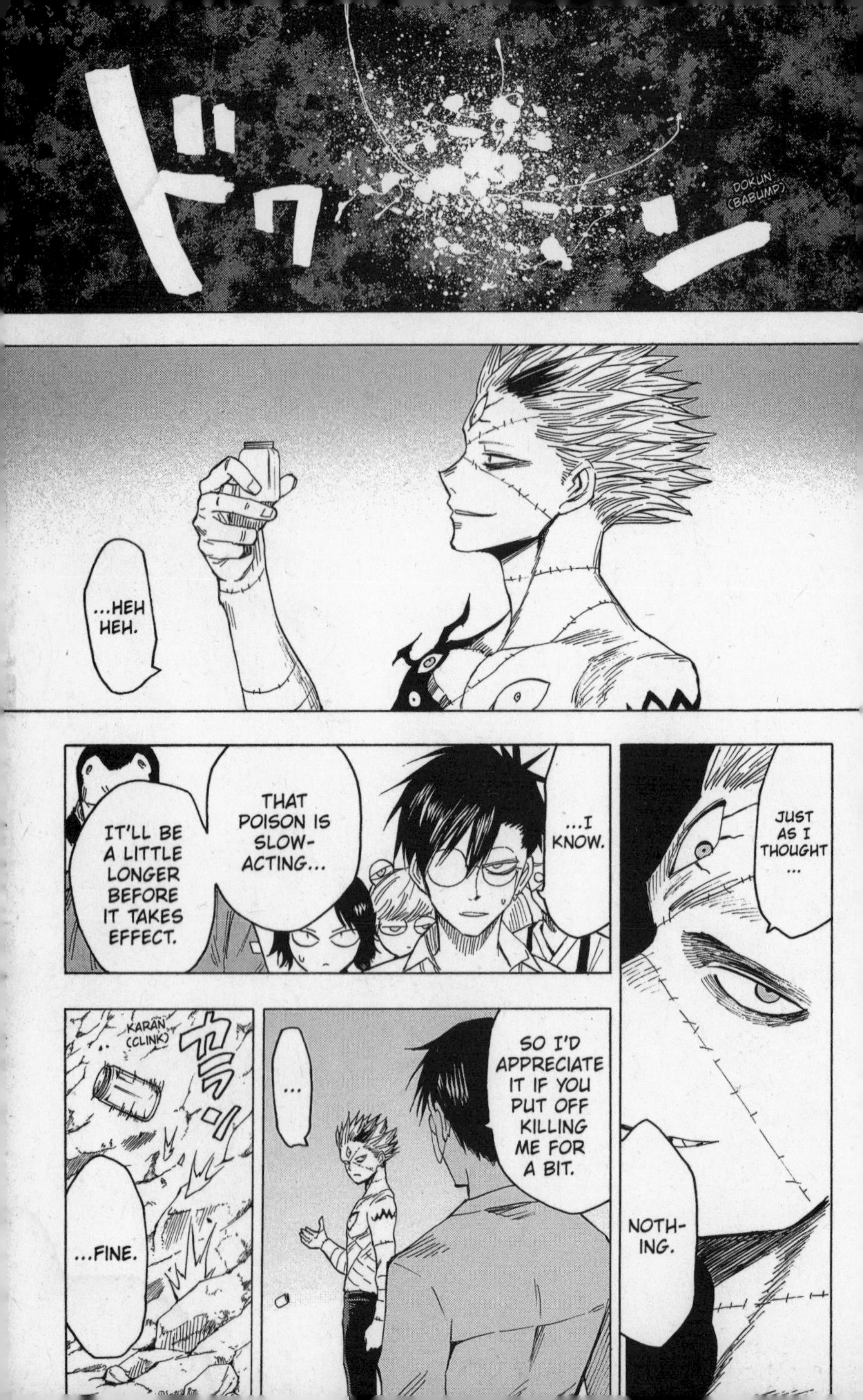
ドクン
DOKUN (BABUMP)
...HEH HEH.
JUST AS I THOUGHT...
NOTHING.
...I KNOW.
THAT POISON IS SLOW-ACTING...
IT'LL BE A LITTLE LONGER BEFORE IT TAKES EFFECT.
SO I'D APPRECIATE IT IF YOU PUT OFF KILLING ME FOR A BIT.
...
カラン
KARAN (CLINK)
...FINE.

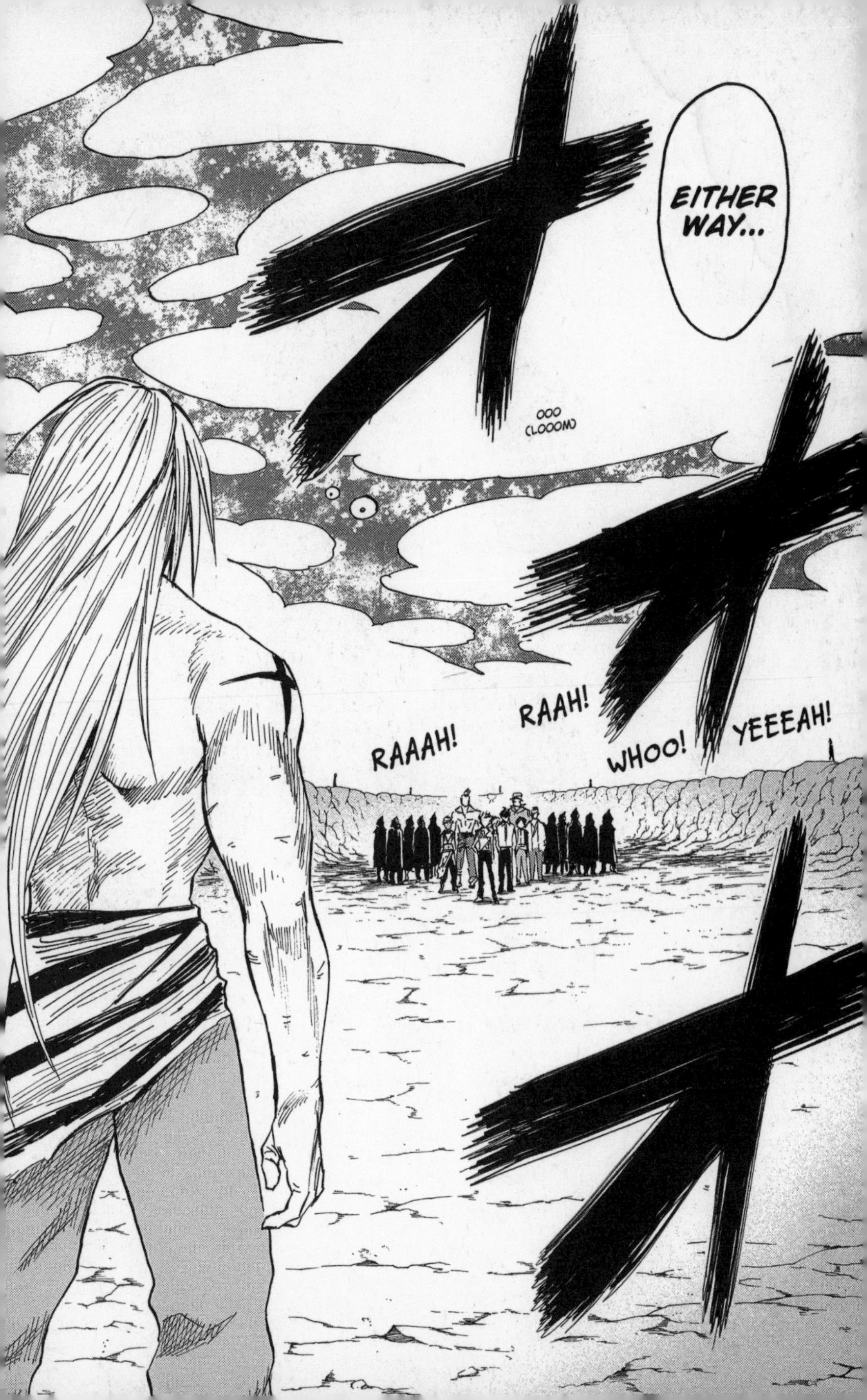
EITHER WAY...
OOO (LOOOM)
YEEEAH!
RAAH!
WHOO!
RAAAH!

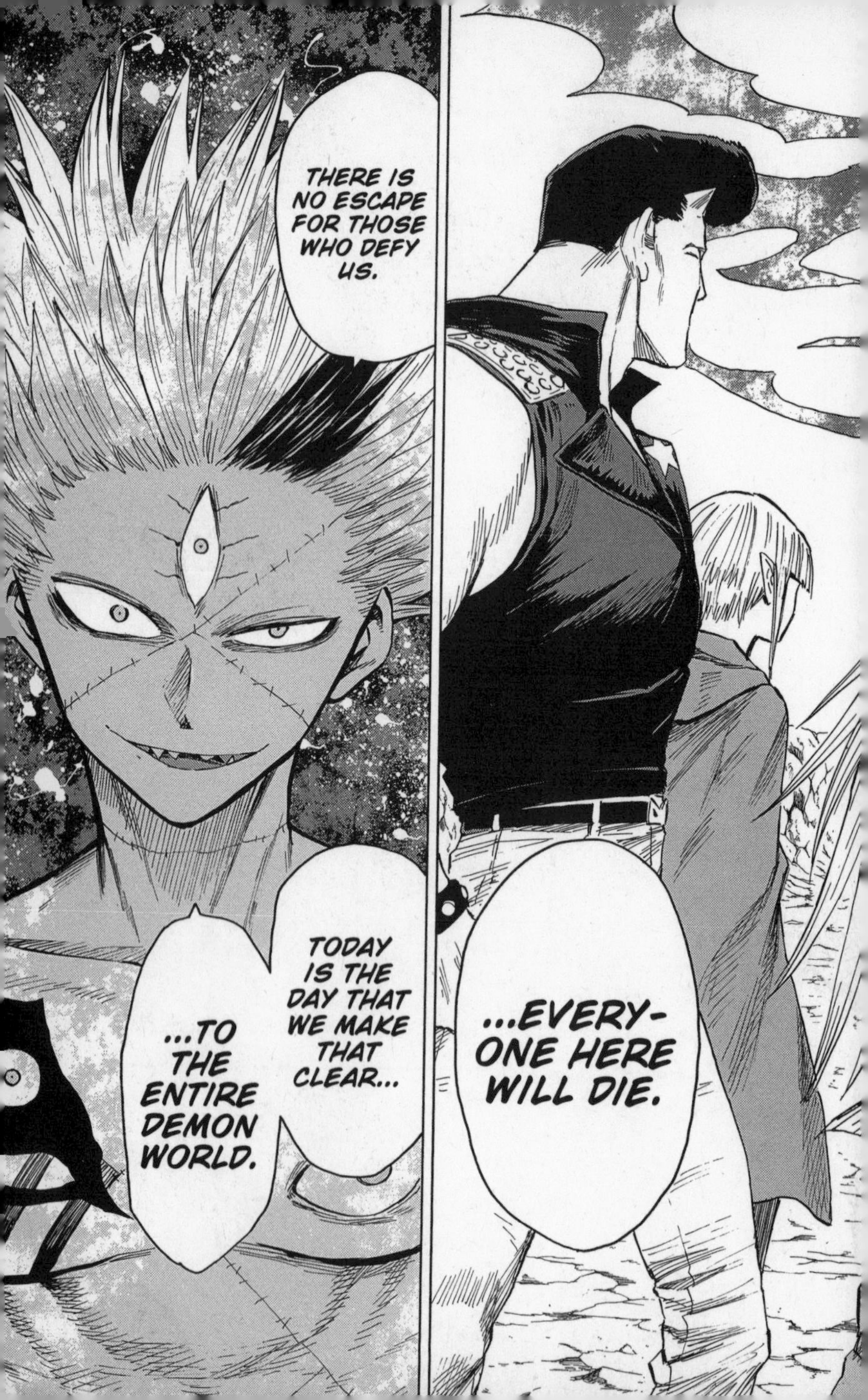
...EVERY-ONE HERE WILL DIE.
THERE IS NO ESCAPE FOR THOSE WHO DEFY US.
TODAY IS THE DAY THAT WE MAKE THAT CLEAR...
...TO THE ENTIRE DEMON WORLD.

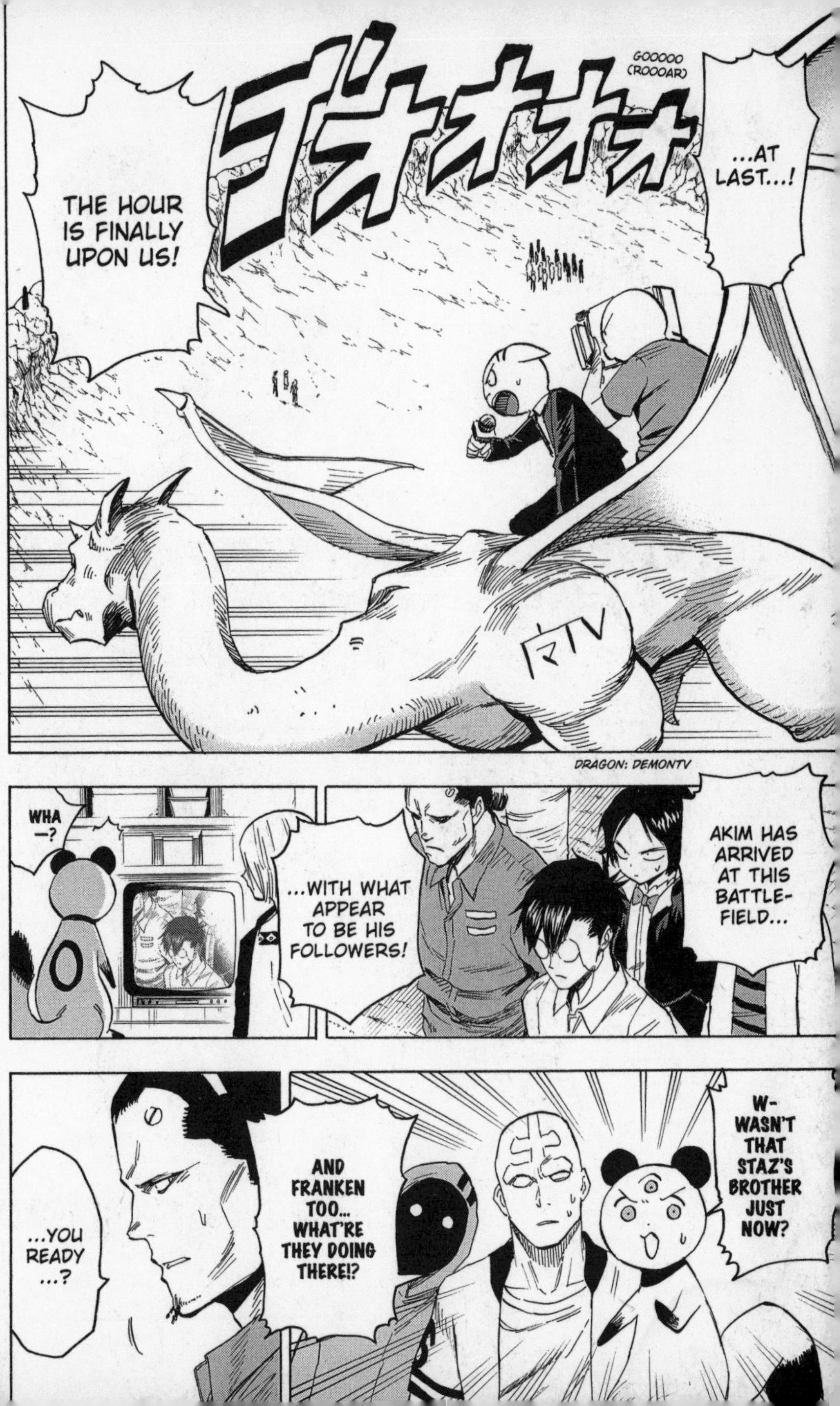
...AT LAST...!
GOOOOO (ROOOAR)
THE HOUR IS FINALLY UPON US!
DRAGON: DEMONTV
AKIM HAS ARRIVED AT THIS BATTLE-FIELD...
...WITH WHAT APPEAR TO BE HIS FOLLOWERS!
WHA—?
W-WASN'T THAT STAZ'S BROTHER JUST NOW?
AND FRANKEN TOO... WHAT'RE THEY DOING THERE!?
...YOU READY...?

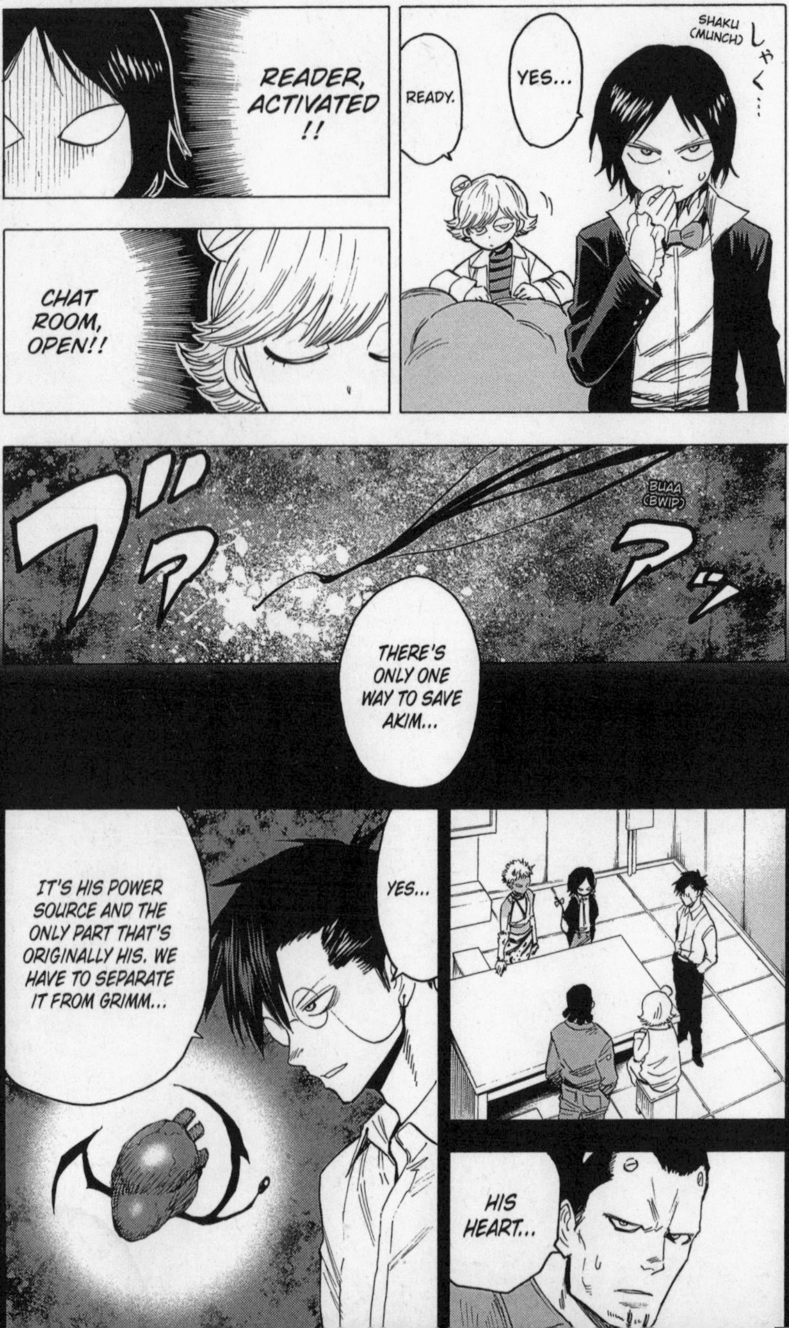
SHAKU (MUNCH) しゃく…
YES…
READY.
READER, ACTIVATED!!
CHAT ROOM, OPEN!!
BUAA (BWIP) ブァアッ
THERE'S ONLY ONE WAY TO SAVE AKIM…
HIS HEART…
YES…
IT'S HIS POWER SOURCE AND THE ONLY PART THAT'S ORIGINALLY HIS. WE HAVE TO SEPARATE IT FROM GRIMM…

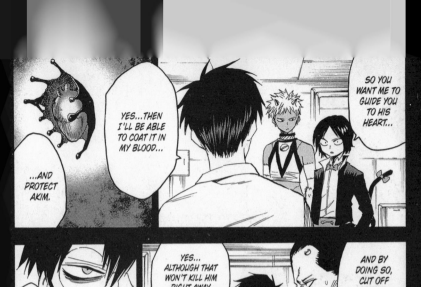

SO YOU WANT ME TO GUIDE YOU TO HIS HEART...

YES...THEN I'LL BE ABLE TO COAT IT IN MY BLOOD...

...AND PROTECT AKIM.

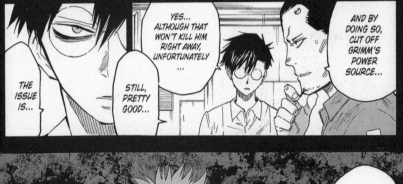

AND BY DOING SO, CUT OFF GRIMM'S POWER SOURCE...

YES... ALTHOUGH THAT WON'T KILL HIM RIGHT AWAY, UNFORTUNATELY ...

STILL, PRETTY GOOD...

THE ISSUE IS...

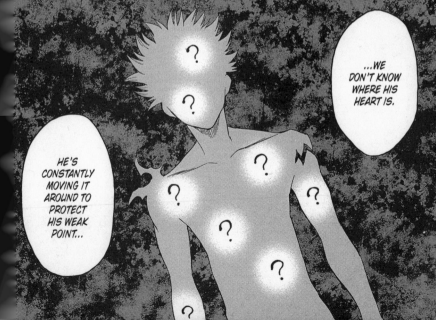

...WE DON'T KNOW WHERE HIS HEART IS.

HE'S CONSTANTLY MOVING IT AROUND TO PROTECT HIS WEAK POINT...

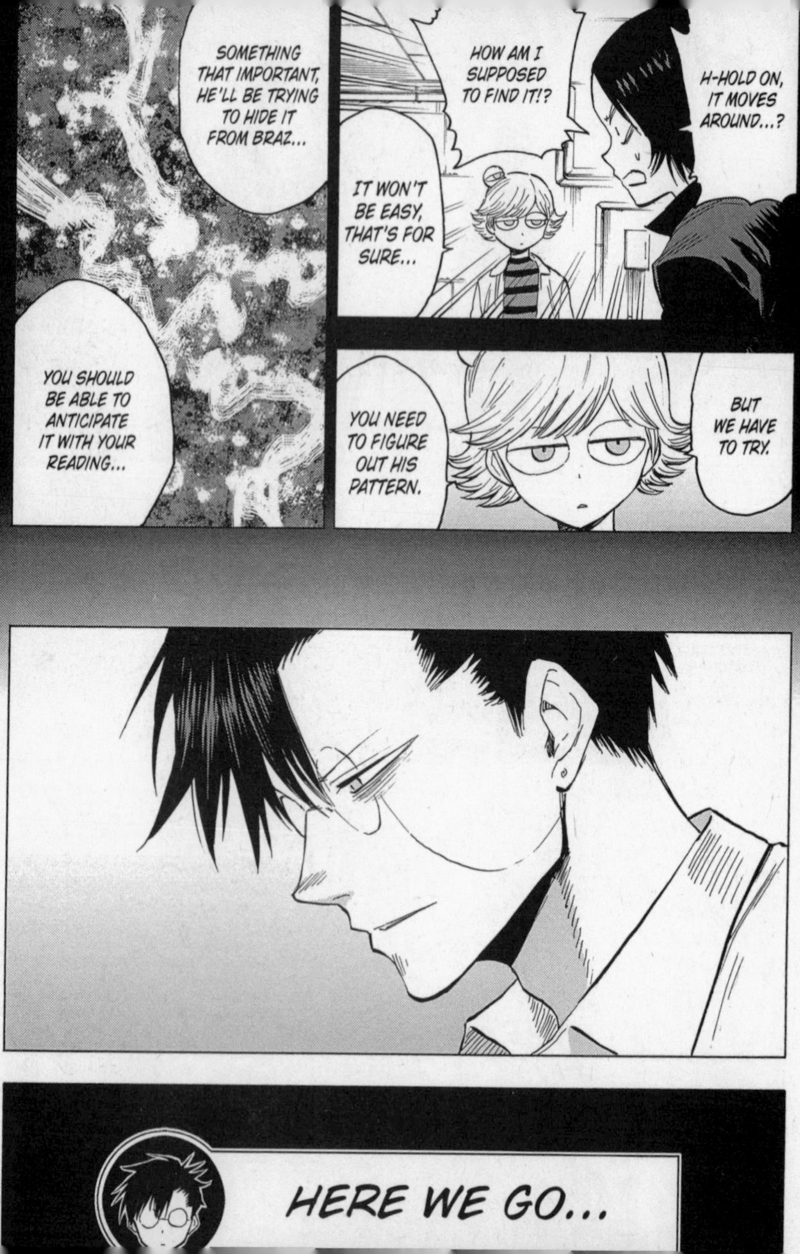
H-HOLD ON, IT MOVES AROUND...?
HOW AM I SUPPOSED TO FIND IT!?
IT WON'T BE EASY, THAT'S FOR SURE...
BUT WE HAVE TO TRY.
YOU NEED TO FIGURE OUT HIS PATTERN.
SOMETHING THAT IMPORTANT, HE'LL BE TRYING TO HIDE IT FROM BRAZ...
YOU SHOULD BE ABLE TO ANTICIPATE IT WITH YOUR READING...
HERE WE GO...

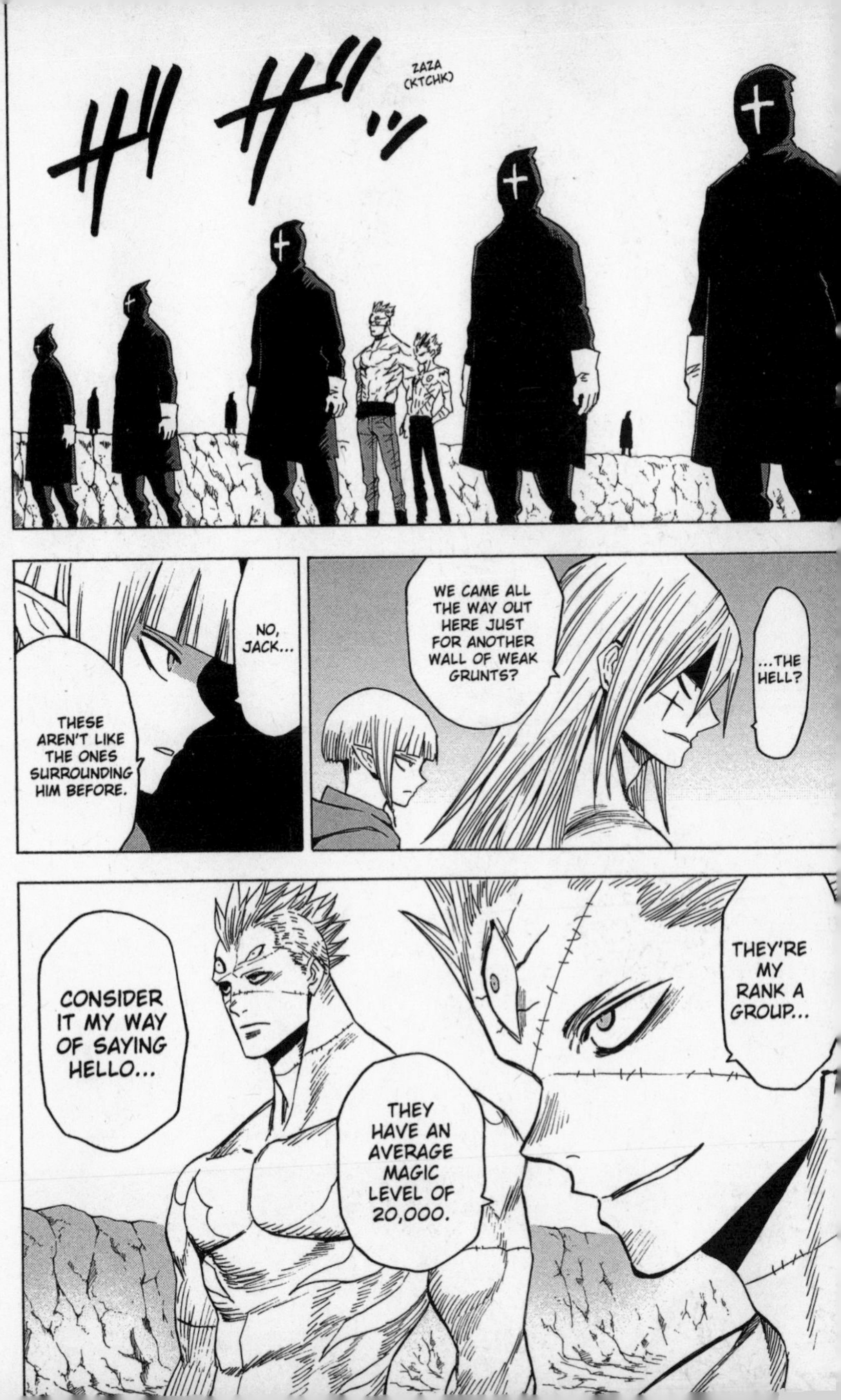
ZAZA (KTCHK)
...THE HELL?
WE CAME ALL THE WAY OUT HERE JUST FOR ANOTHER WALL OF WEAK GRUNTS?
NO, JACK...
THESE AREN'T LIKE THE ONES SURROUNDING HIM BEFORE.
THEY'RE MY RANK A GROUP...
THEY HAVE AN AVERAGE MAGIC LEVEL OF 20,000.
CONSIDER IT MY WAY OF SAYING HELLO...

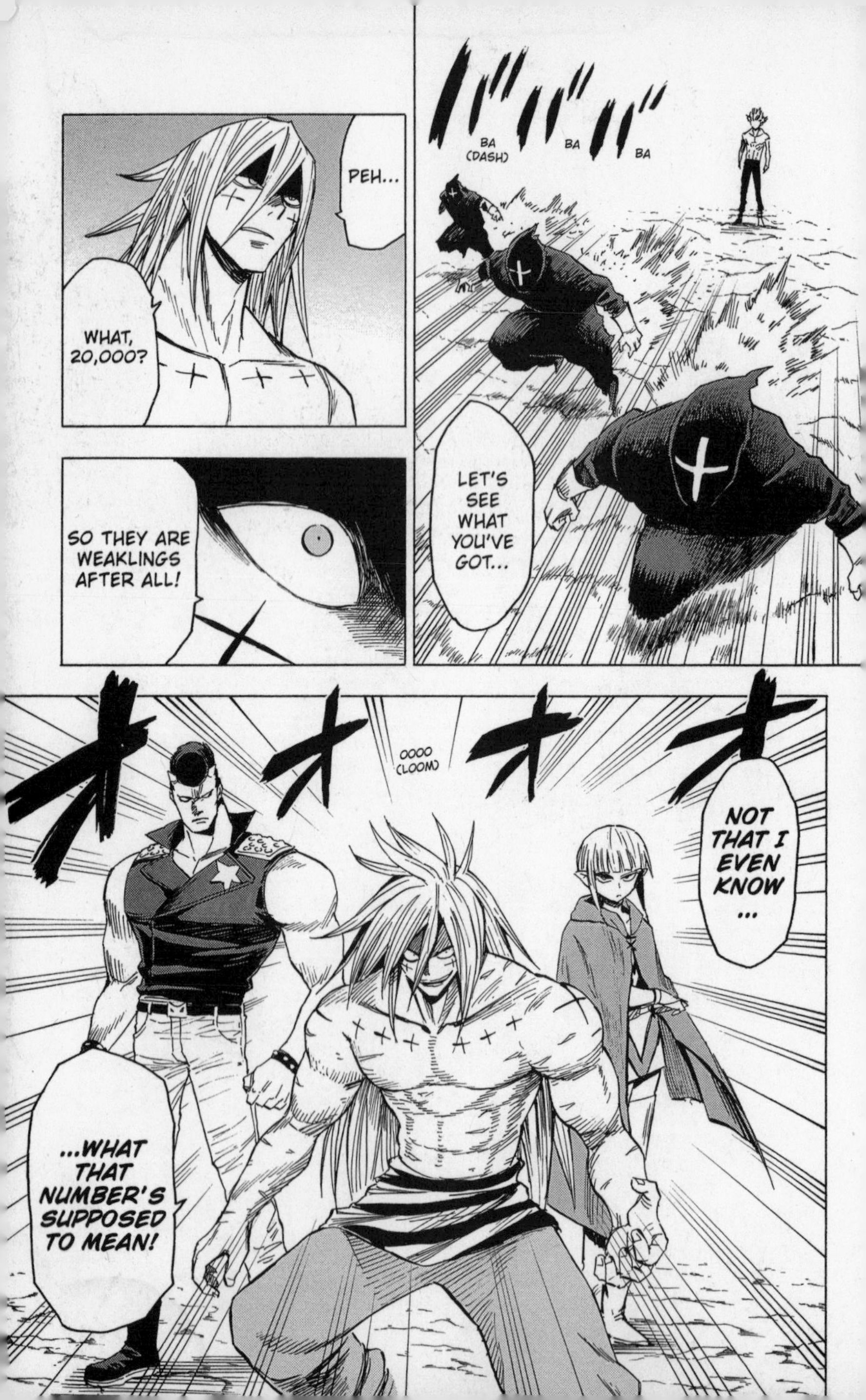
BA (DASH) BA BA
LET'S SEE WHAT YOU'VE GOT...
PEH...
WHAT, 20,000?
SO THEY ARE WEAKLINGS AFTER ALL!
NOT THAT I EVEN KNOW...
OOOO (LOOM)
...WHAT THAT NUMBER'S SUPPOSED TO MEAN!

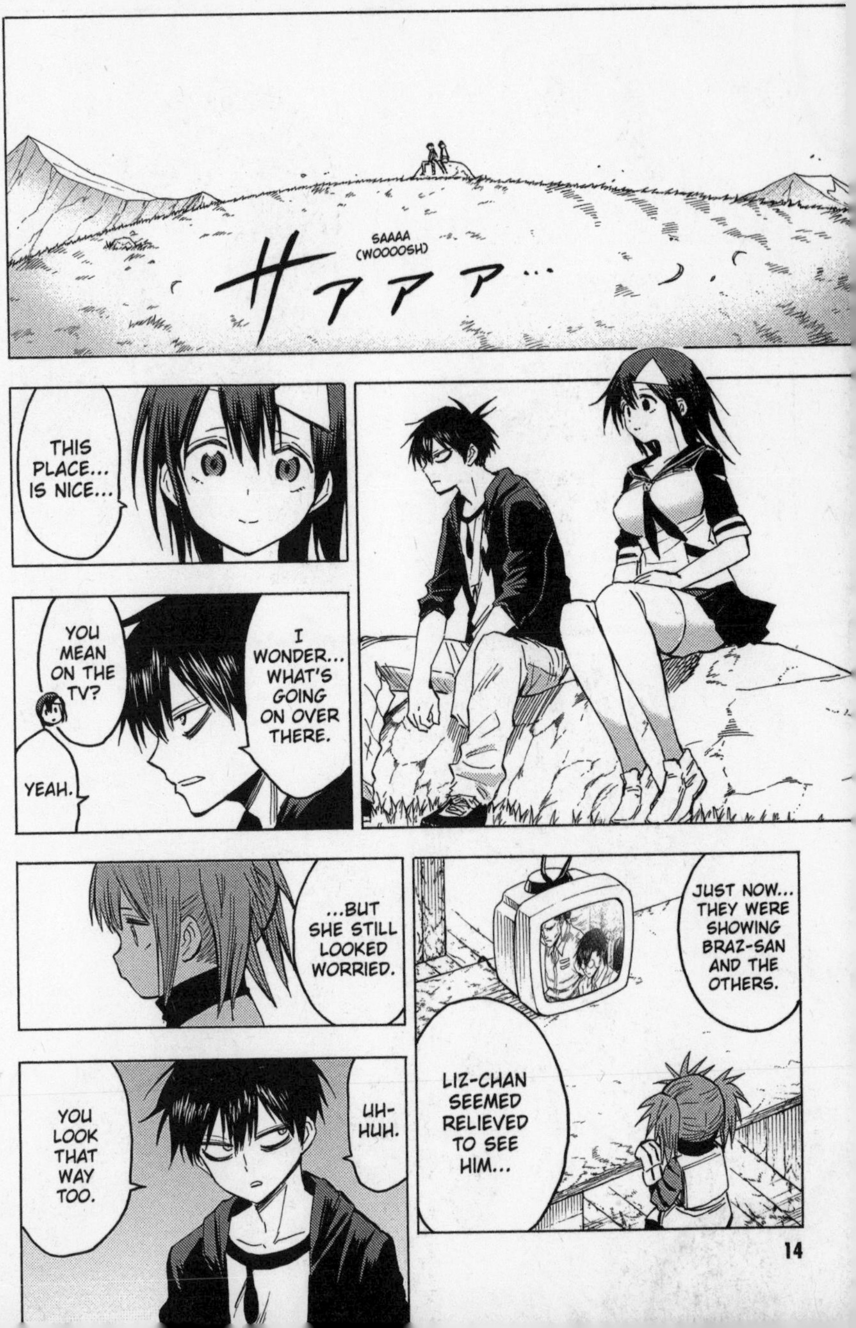
SAAAA (WOOOOSH)
サァアァ…
THIS PLACE... IS NICE...
I WONDER... WHAT'S GOING ON OVER THERE.
YOU MEAN ON THE TV?
YEAH.
JUST NOW... THEY WERE SHOWING BRAZ-SAN AND THE OTHERS.
LIZ-CHAN SEEMED RELIEVED TO SEE HIM...
...BUT SHE STILL LOOKED WORRIED.
UH-HUH.
YOU LOOK THAT WAY TOO.

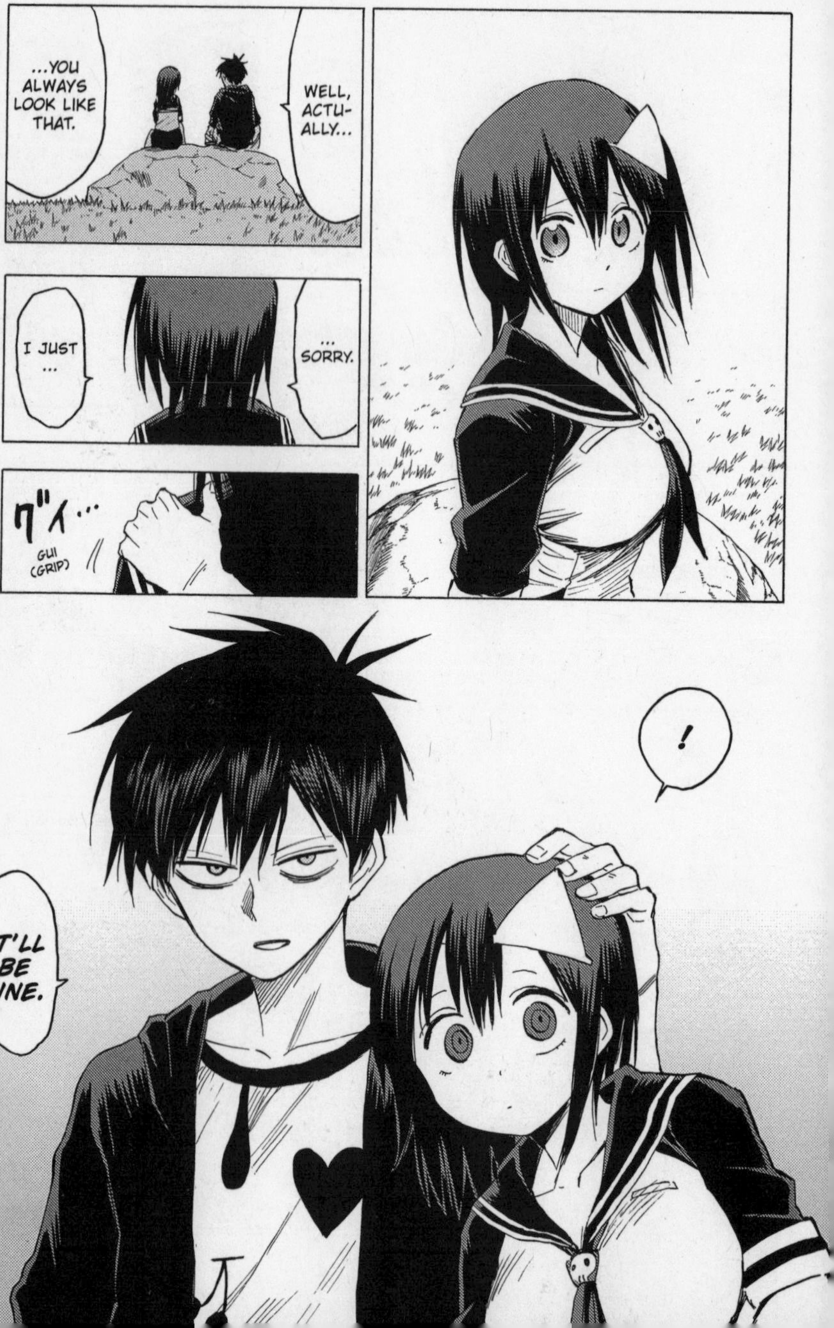
WELL, ACTUALLY...
...YOU ALWAYS LOOK LIKE THAT.
... SORRY.
I JUST ...
グイ…
GUI (GRIP)
!
IT'LL BE FINE.

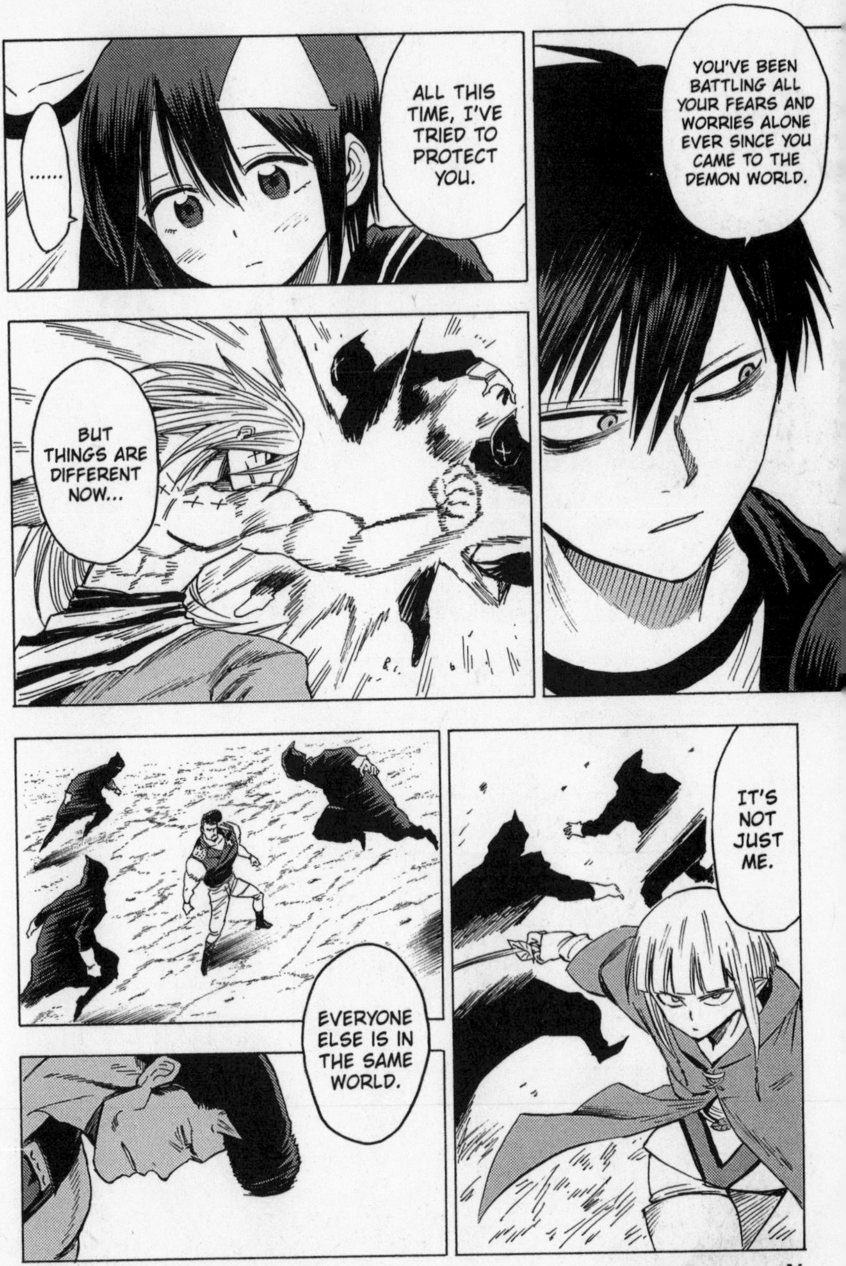
YOU'VE BEEN BATTLING ALL YOUR FEARS AND WORRIES ALONE EVER SINCE YOU CAME TO THE DEMON WORLD.
ALL THIS TIME, I'VE TRIED TO PROTECT YOU.
......
BUT THINGS ARE DIFFERENT NOW...
IT'S NOT JUST ME.
EVERYONE ELSE IS IN THE SAME WORLD.

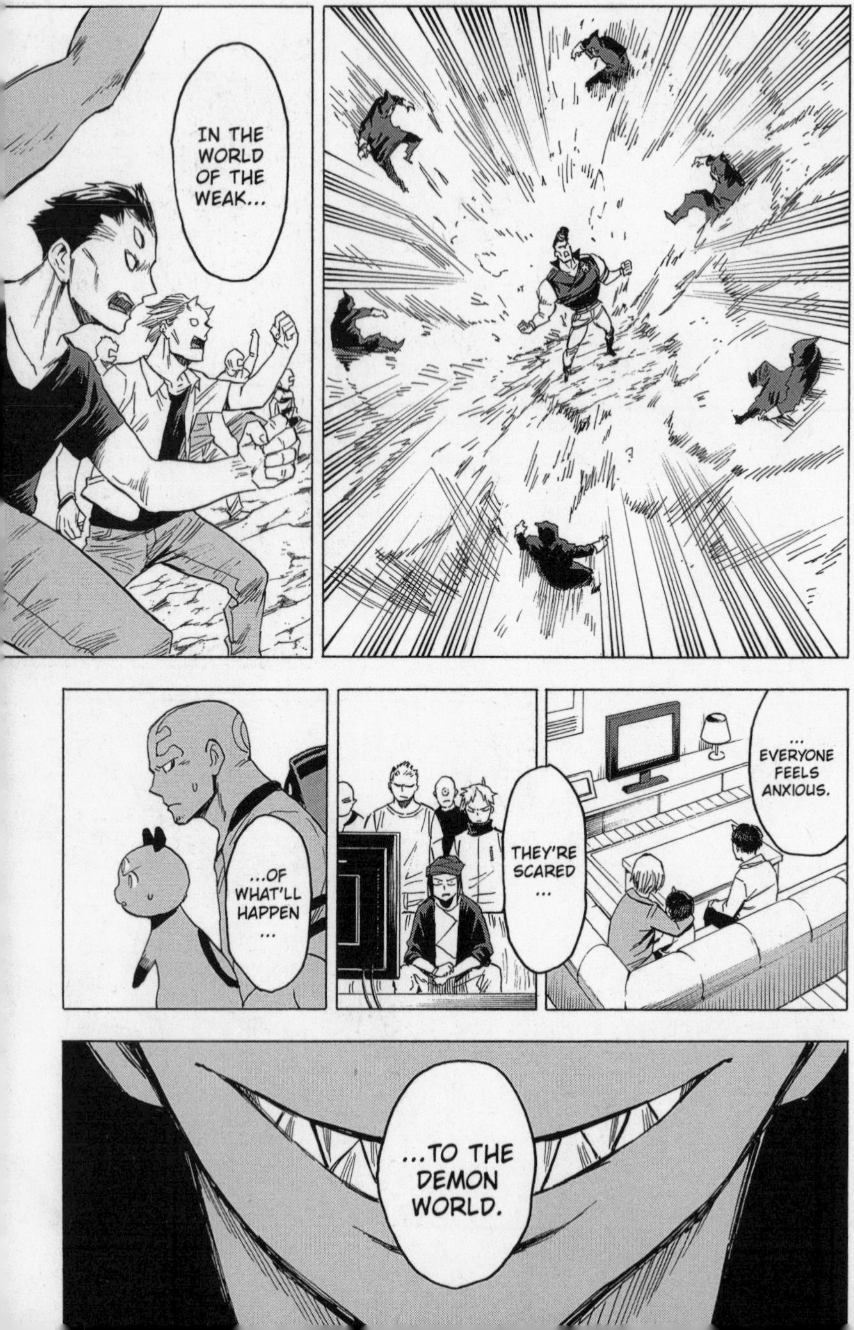
IN THE WORLD OF THE WEAK...
... EVERYONE FEELS ANXIOUS.
THEY'RE SCARED ...
...OF WHAT'LL HAPPEN ...
...TO THE DEMON WORLD.

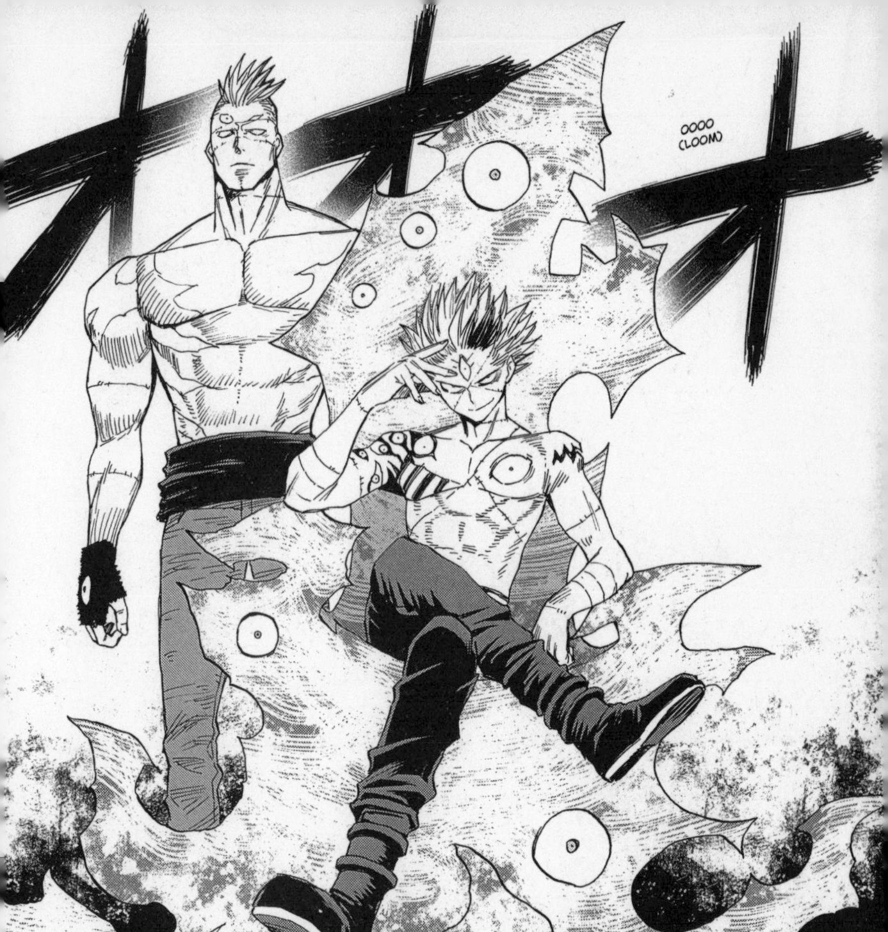
OOOO
(LOOM)
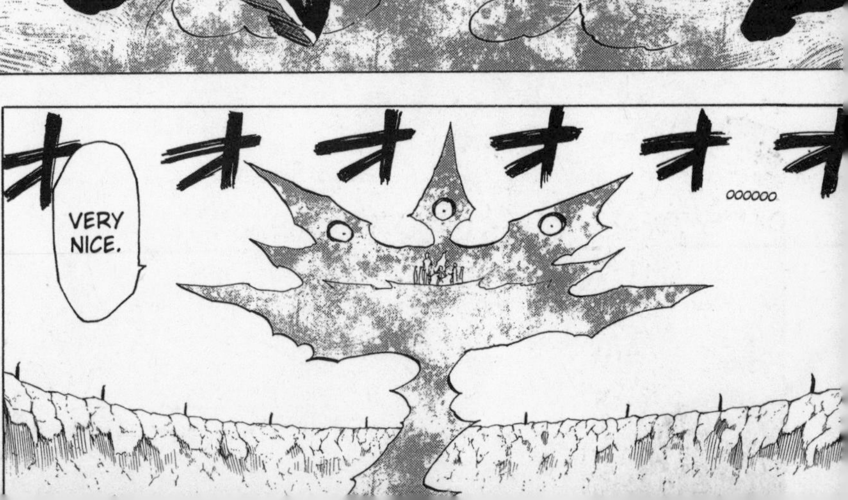
VERY NICE.
OOOOOO

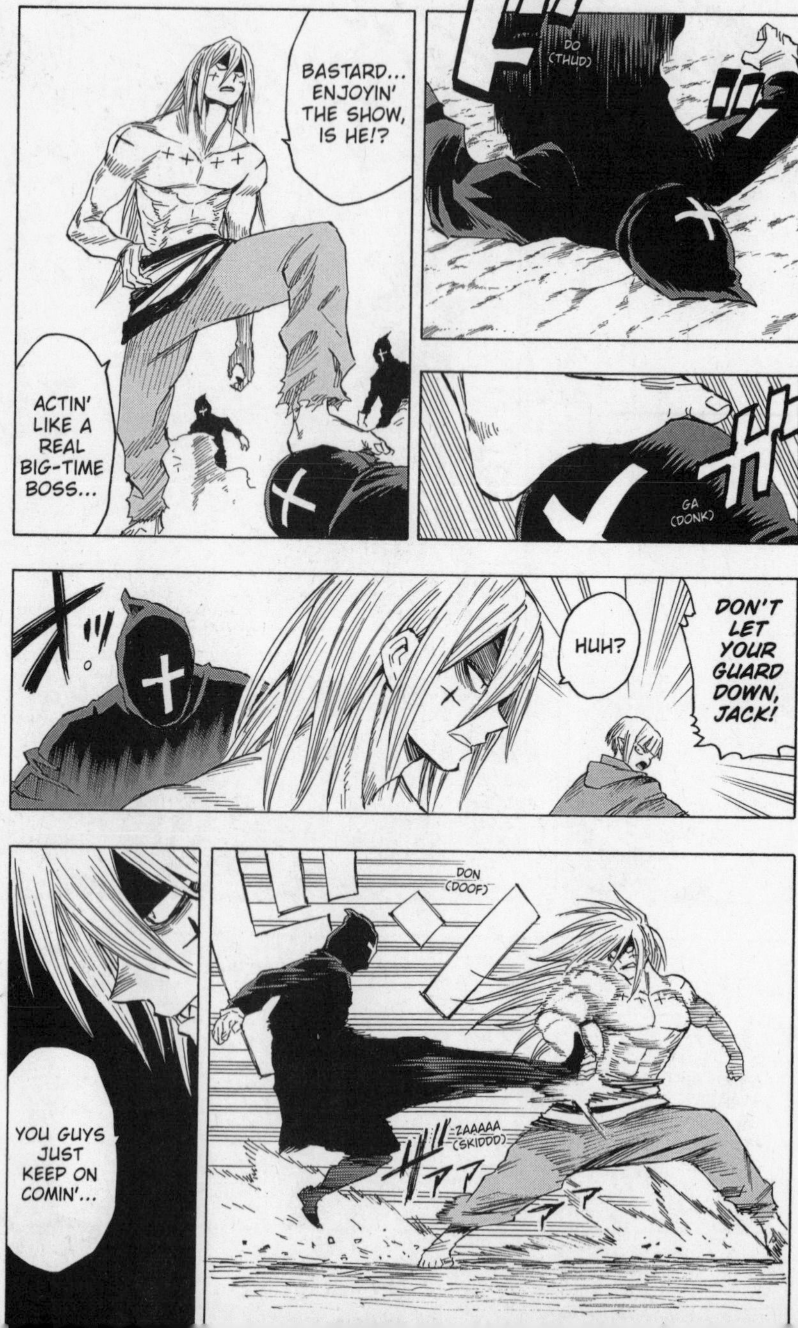
DO (THUD)
GA (DONK)
BASTARD... ENJOYIN' THE SHOW, IS HE!?
ACTIN' LIKE A REAL BIG-TIME BOSS...
DON'T LET YOUR GUARD DOWN, JACK!
HUH?
DON (DOOF)
ZAAAAA (SKIDDD)
YOU GUYS JUST KEEP ON COMIN'...

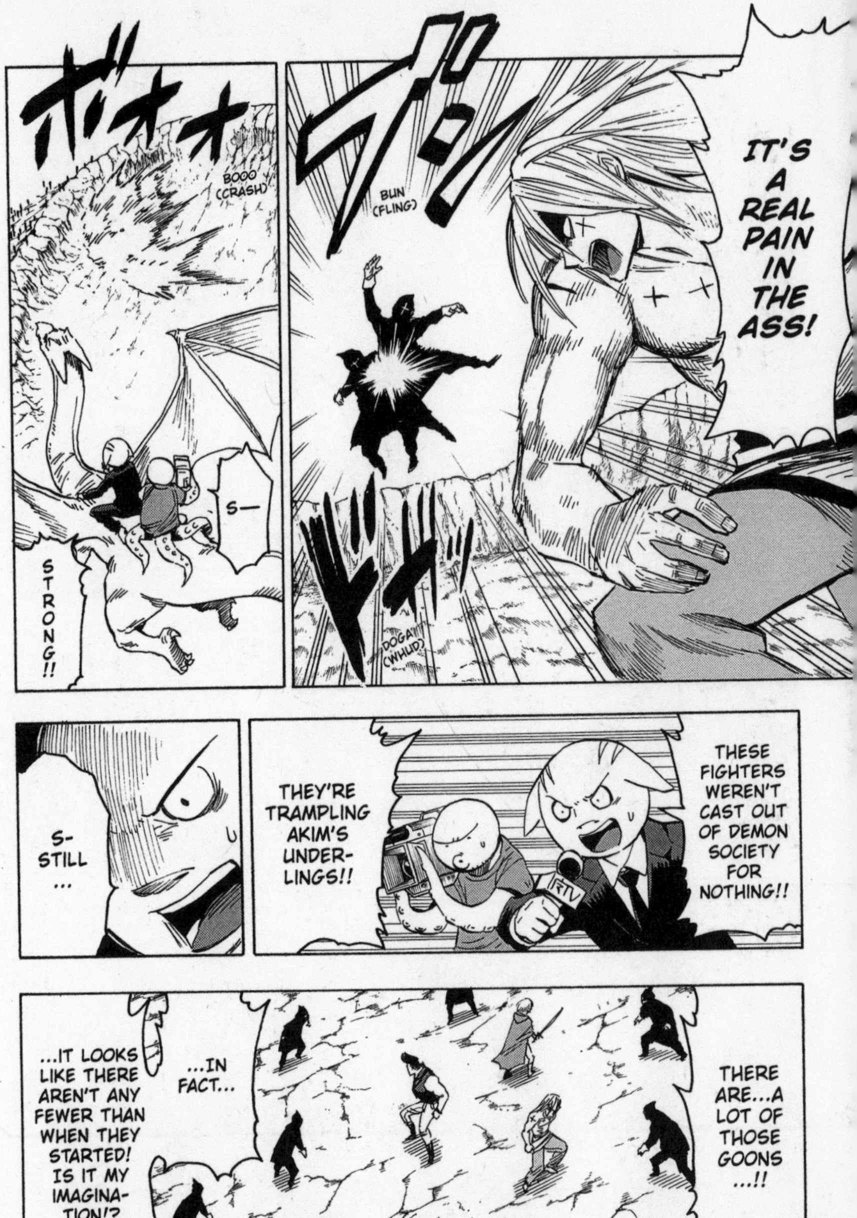
BUN (FLING)
IT'S A REAL PAIN IN THE ASS!
DOGA (WHUD)
BOOO (CRASH)
S—
STRONG!!
THESE FIGHTERS WEREN'T CAST OUT OF DEMON SOCIETY FOR NOTHING!!
THEY'RE TRAMPLING AKIM'S UNDER-LINGS!!
S-STILL...
THERE ARE...A LOT OF THOSE GOONS ...!!
...IN FACT...
...IT LOOKS LIKE THERE AREN'T ANY FEWER THAN WHEN THEY STARTED! IS IT MY IMAGINA-TION!?

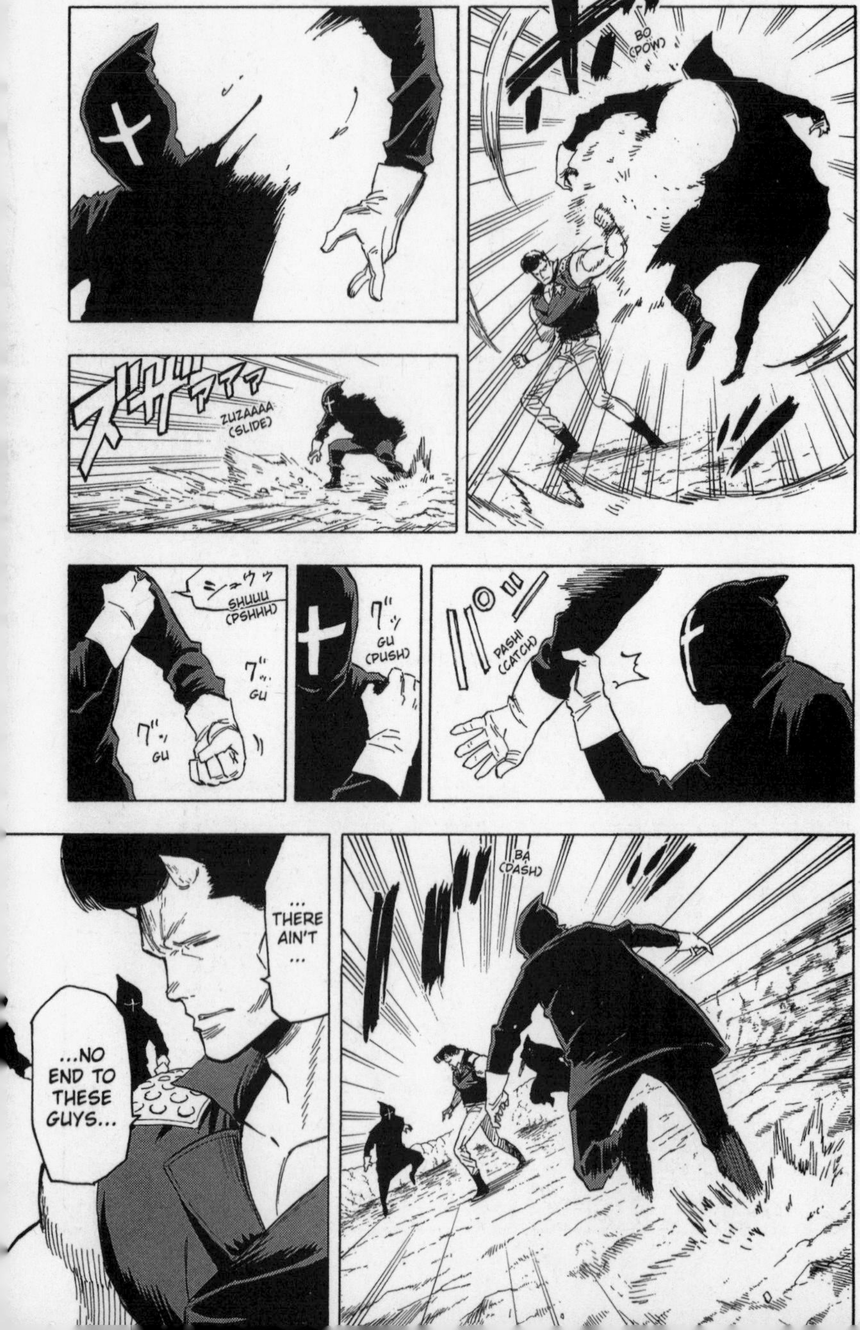
BO (POW)
ズザァァァ
ZUZAAAA (SLIDE)
PASHI (CATCH)
グッ
GU (PUSH)
シュウゥ
SHUUU (PSHHH)
グッ
GU
グッ
GU
BA (DASH)
... THERE AIN'T ...
...NO END TO THESE GUYS...

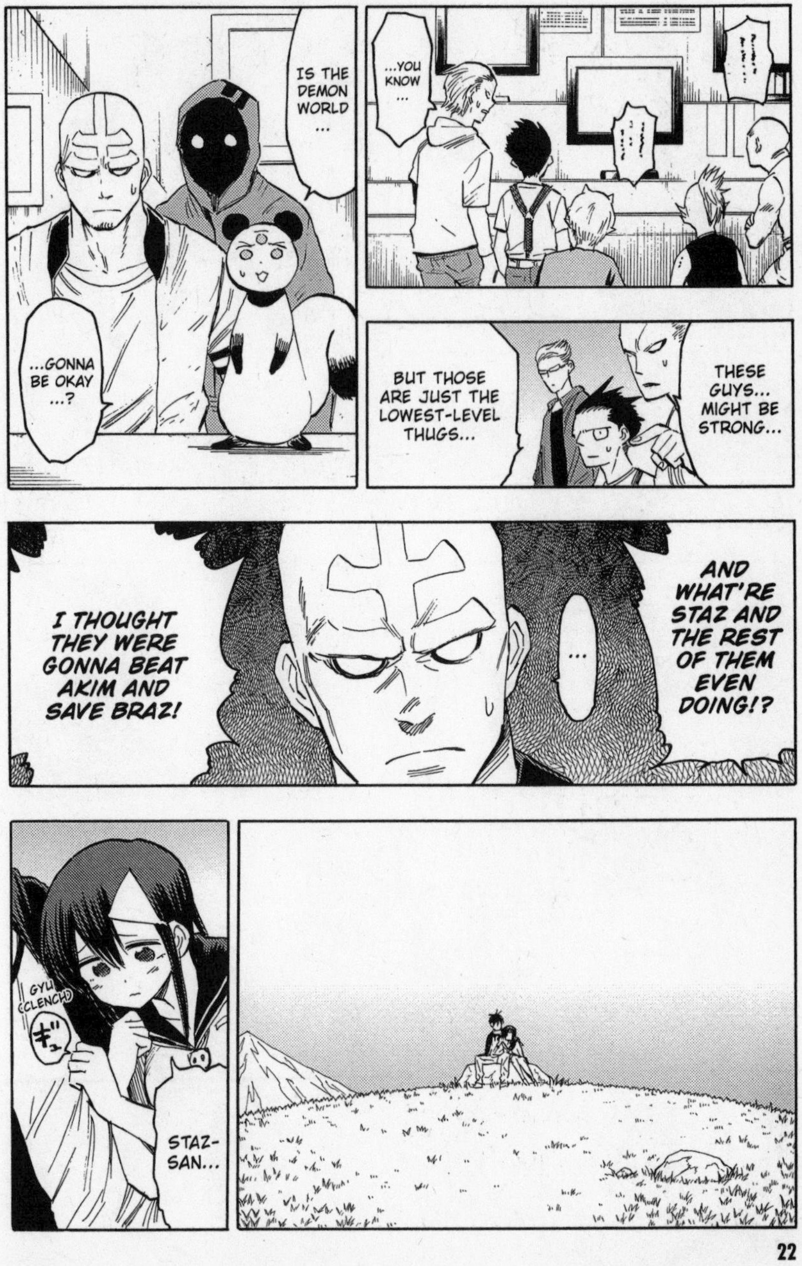
...YOU KNOW ...
THESE GUYS... MIGHT BE STRONG...
BUT THOSE ARE JUST THE LOWEST-LEVEL THUGS...
IS THE DEMON WORLD ...
...GONNA BE OKAY ...?
AND WHAT'RE STAZ AND THE REST OF THEM EVEN DOING!?
...
I THOUGHT THEY WERE GONNA BEAT AKIM AND SAVE BRAZ!
GYU (CLENCH)
ギュ
STAZ-SAN...

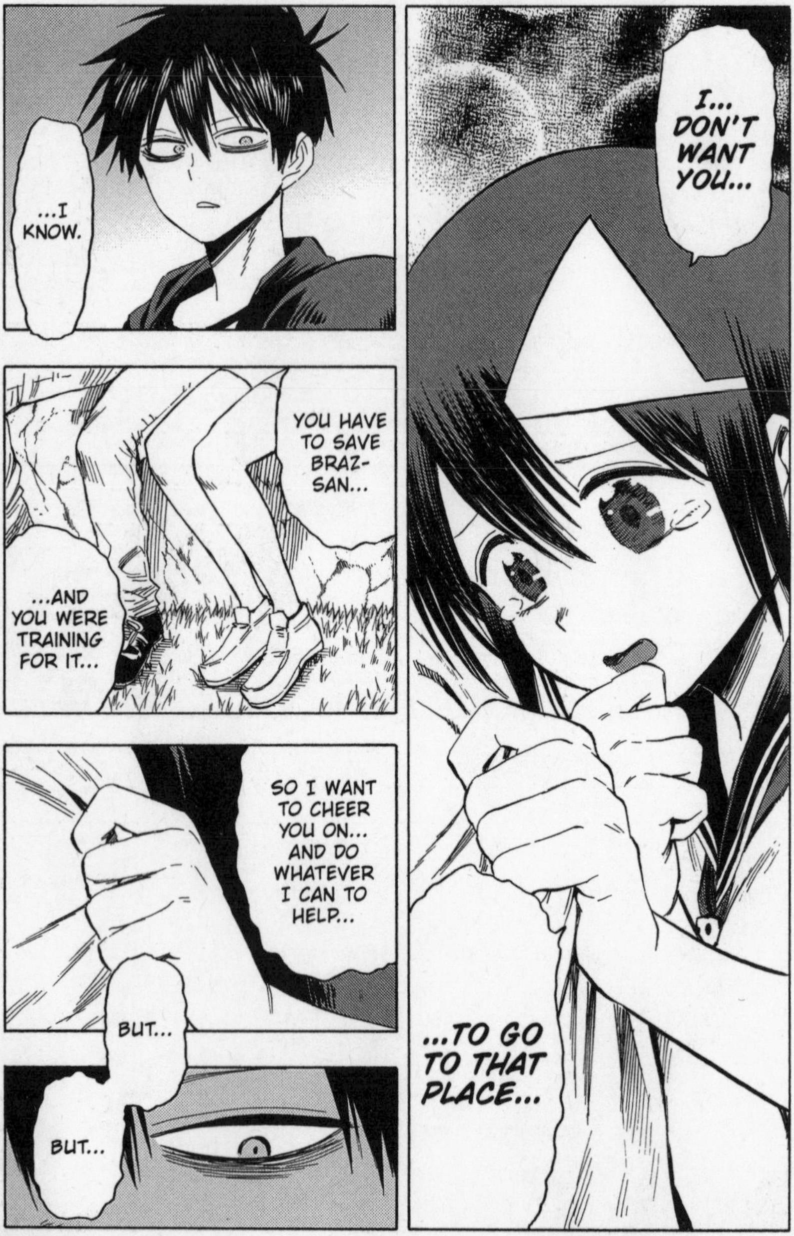
I... DON'T WANT YOU...
...TO GO TO THAT PLACE...
...I KNOW.
YOU HAVE TO SAVE BRAZ-SAN...
...AND YOU WERE TRAINING FOR IT...
SO I WANT TO CHEER YOU ON... AND DO WHATEVER I CAN TO HELP...
BUT...
BUT...

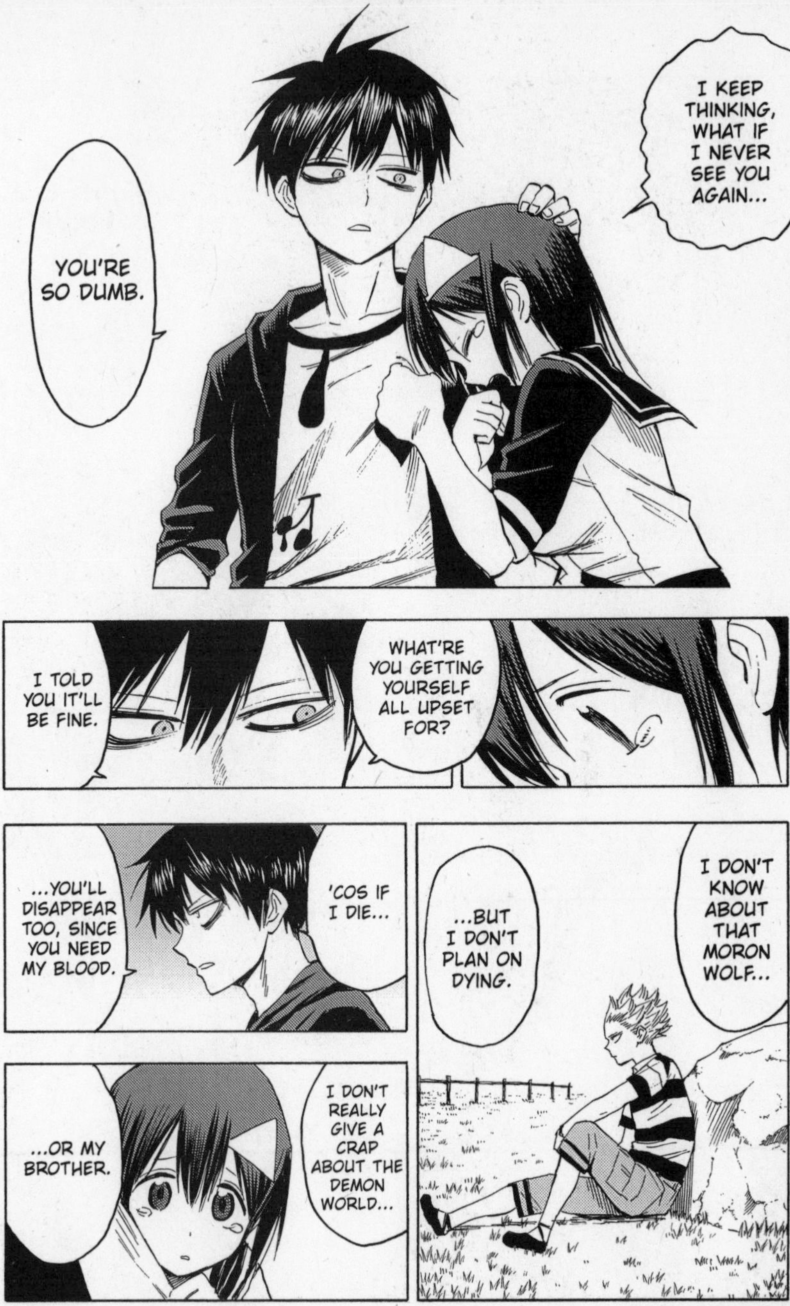
I KEEP THINKING, WHAT IF I NEVER SEE YOU AGAIN...
YOU'RE SO DUMB.
WHAT'RE YOU GETTING YOURSELF ALL UPSET FOR?
I TOLD YOU IT'LL BE FINE.
I DON'T KNOW ABOUT THAT MORON WOLF...
...BUT I DON'T PLAN ON DYING.
'COS IF I DIE...
...YOU'LL DISAPPEAR TOO, SINCE YOU NEED MY BLOOD.
I DON'T REALLY GIVE A CRAP ABOUT THE DEMON WORLD...
...OR MY BROTHER.

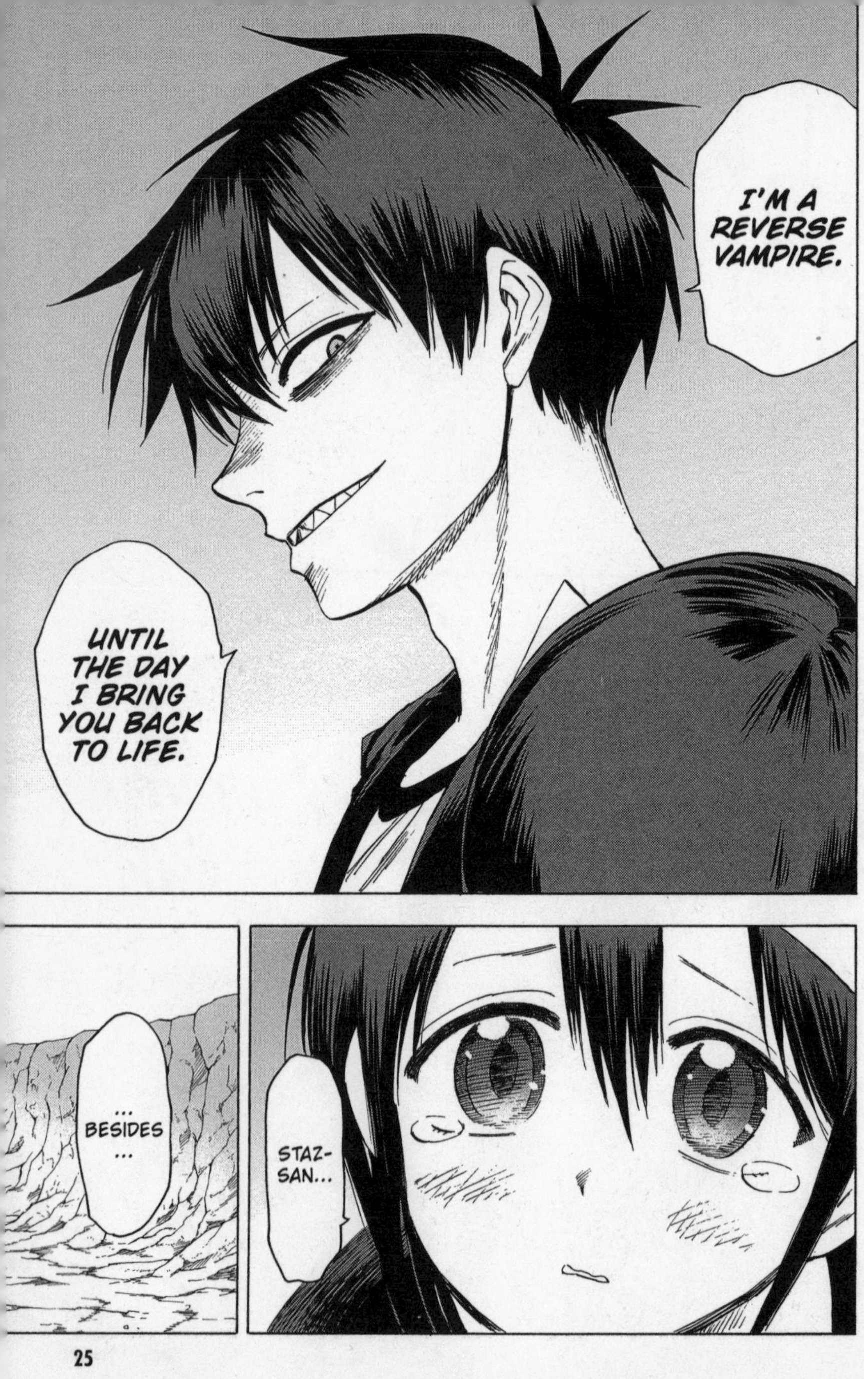
I'M A REVERSE VAMPIRE.
UNTIL THE DAY I BRING YOU BACK TO LIFE.
STAZ-SAN...
... BESIDES ...

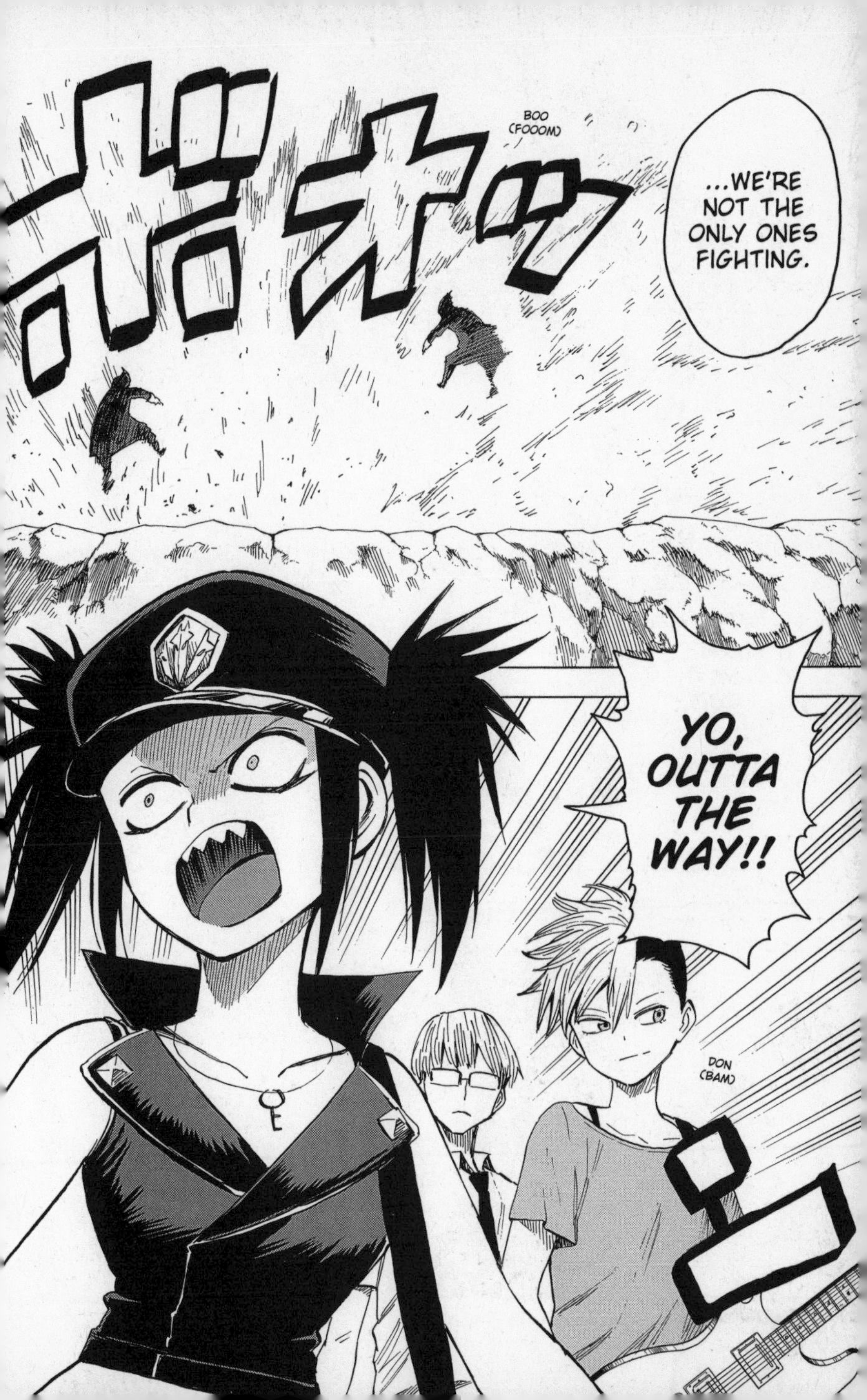
...WE'RE NOT THE ONLY ONES FIGHTING.
BOO (FOOOM)
YO, OUTTA THE WAY!!
DON (BAM)

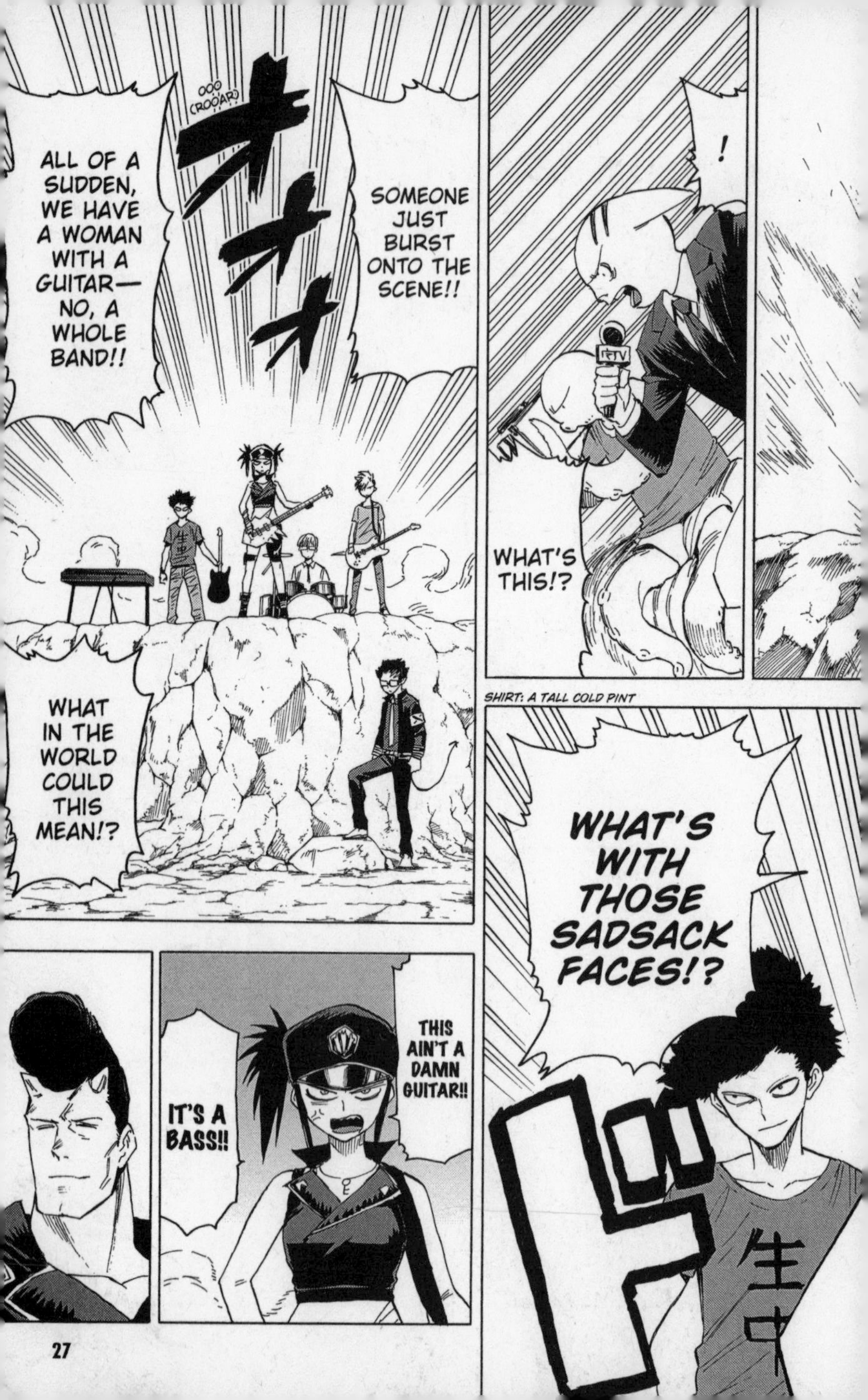
!
WHAT'S THIS!?
SOMEONE JUST BURST ONTO THE SCENE!!
OOO (ROOAR)
ALL OF A SUDDEN, WE HAVE A WOMAN WITH A GUITAR— NO, A WHOLE BAND!!
WHAT IN THE WORLD COULD THIS MEAN!?
SHIRT: A TALL COLD PINT
WHAT'S WITH THOSE SADSACK FACES!?
THIS AIN'T A DAMN GUITAR!!
IT'S A BASS!!

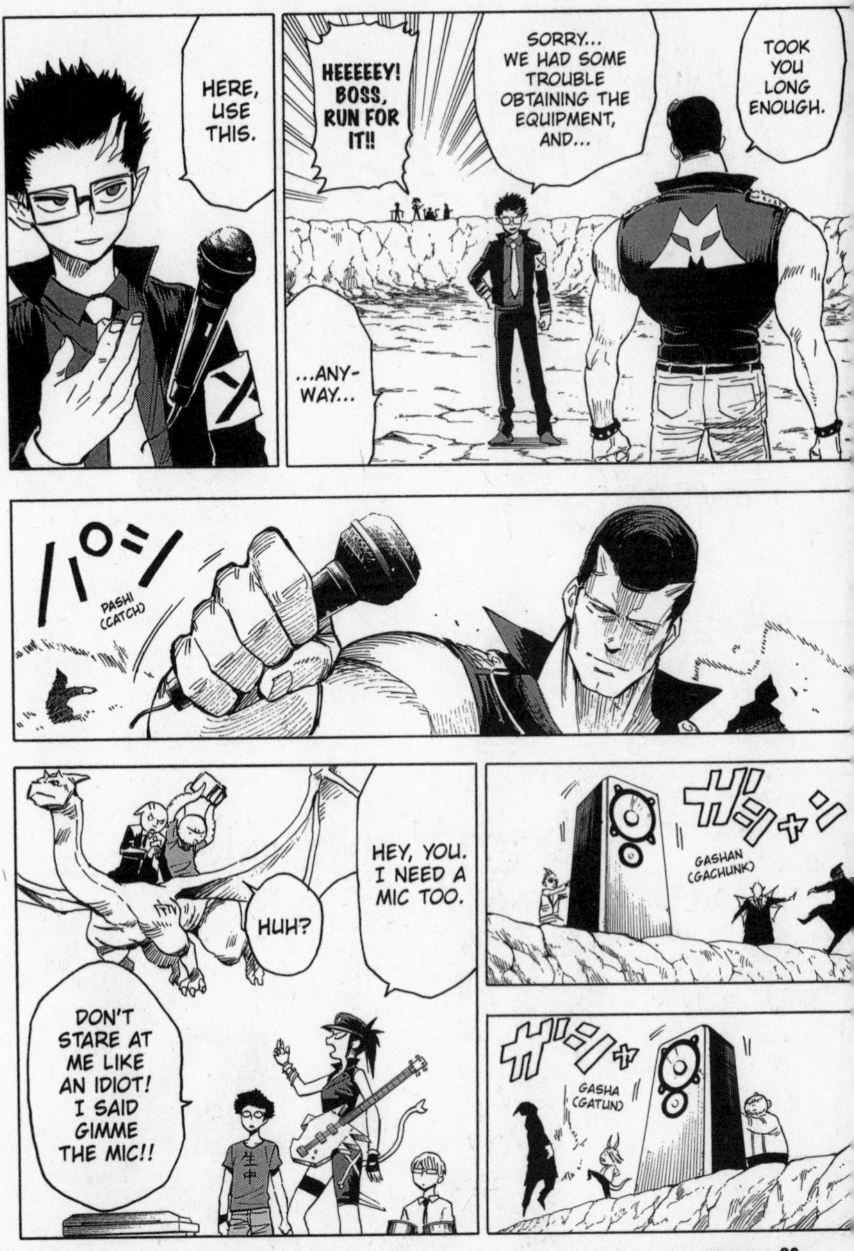
TOOK YOU LONG ENOUGH.
SORRY... WE HAD SOME TROUBLE OBTAINING THE EQUIPMENT, AND...
HEEEEEY! BOSS, RUN FOR IT!!
...ANY-WAY...
HERE, USE THIS.
パシ
PASHI (CATCH)
ガシャン
GASHAN (GACHUNK)
ガシャ
GASHA (GATUN)
HEY, YOU. I NEED A MIC TOO.
HUH?
DON'T STARE AT ME LIKE AN IDIOT! I SAID GIMME THE MIC!!

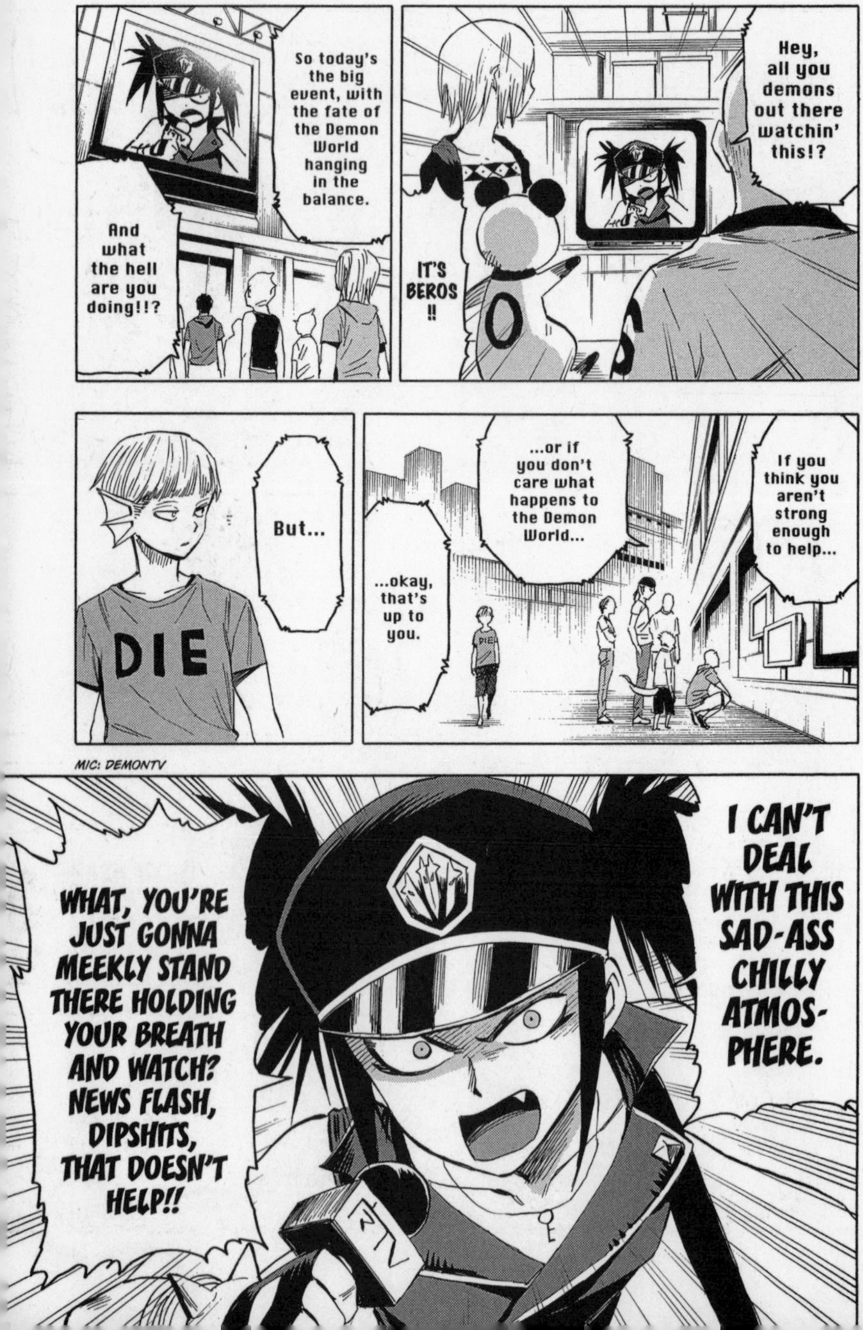
Hey, all you demons out there watchin' this!?
IT'S BEROS!!
So today's the big event, with the fate of the Demon World hanging in the balance.
And what the hell are you doing!!?
If you think you aren't strong enough to help...
...or if you don't care what happens to the Demon World...
...okay, that's up to you.
But...
DIE
MIC: DEMONTV
I CAN'T DEAL WITH THIS SAD-ASS CHILLY ATMOSPHERE.
WHAT, YOU'RE JUST GONNA MEEKLY STAND THERE HOLDING YOUR BREATH AND WATCH? NEWS FLASH, DIPSHITS, THAT DOESN'T HELP!!

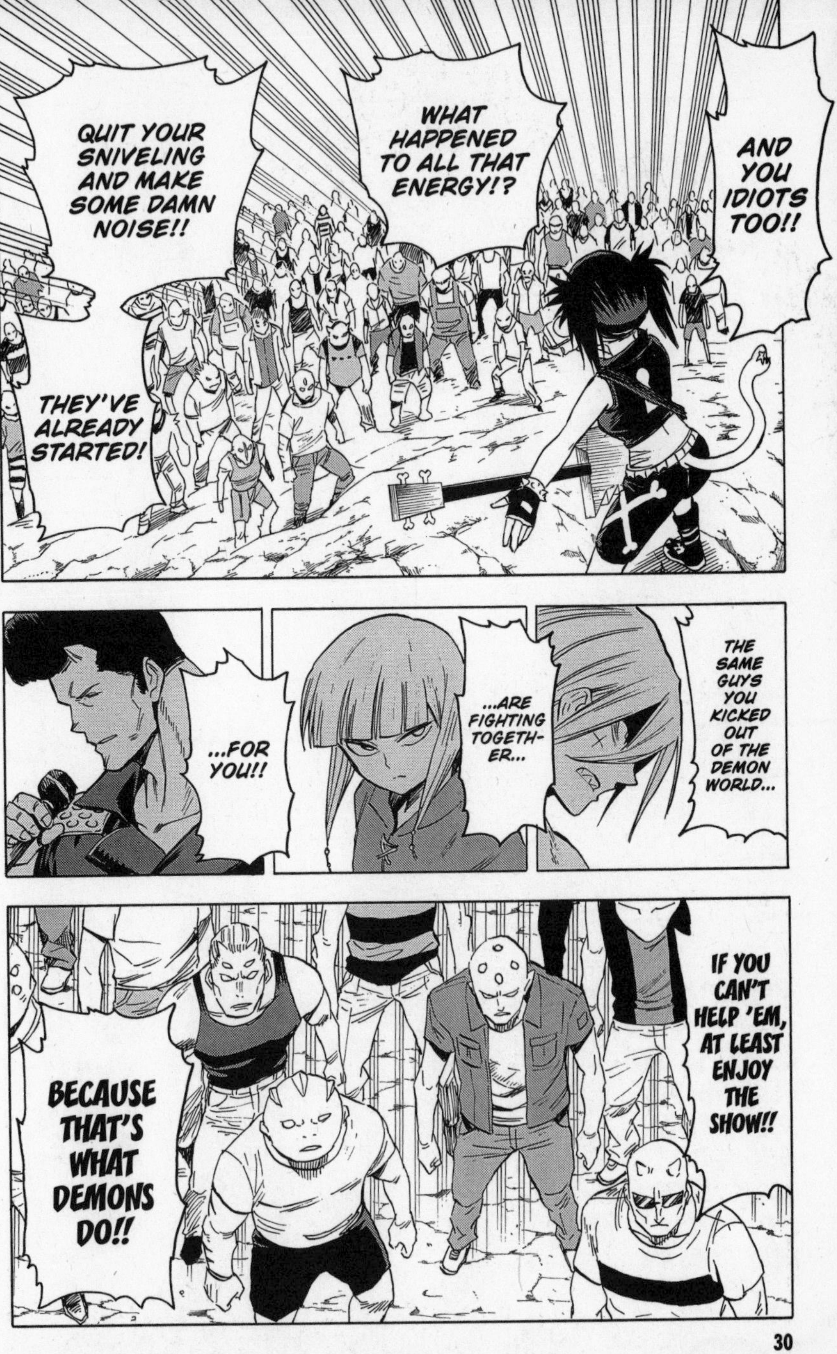
AND YOU IDIOTS TOO!!
WHAT HAPPENED TO ALL THAT ENERGY!?
QUIT YOUR SNIVELING AND MAKE SOME DAMN NOISE!!
THEY'VE ALREADY STARTED!
THE SAME GUYS YOU KICKED OUT OF THE DEMON WORLD...
...ARE FIGHTING TOGETH-ER...
...FOR YOU!!
IF YOU CAN'T HELP 'EM, AT LEAST ENJOY THE SHOW!!
BECAUSE THAT'S WHAT DEMONS DO!!

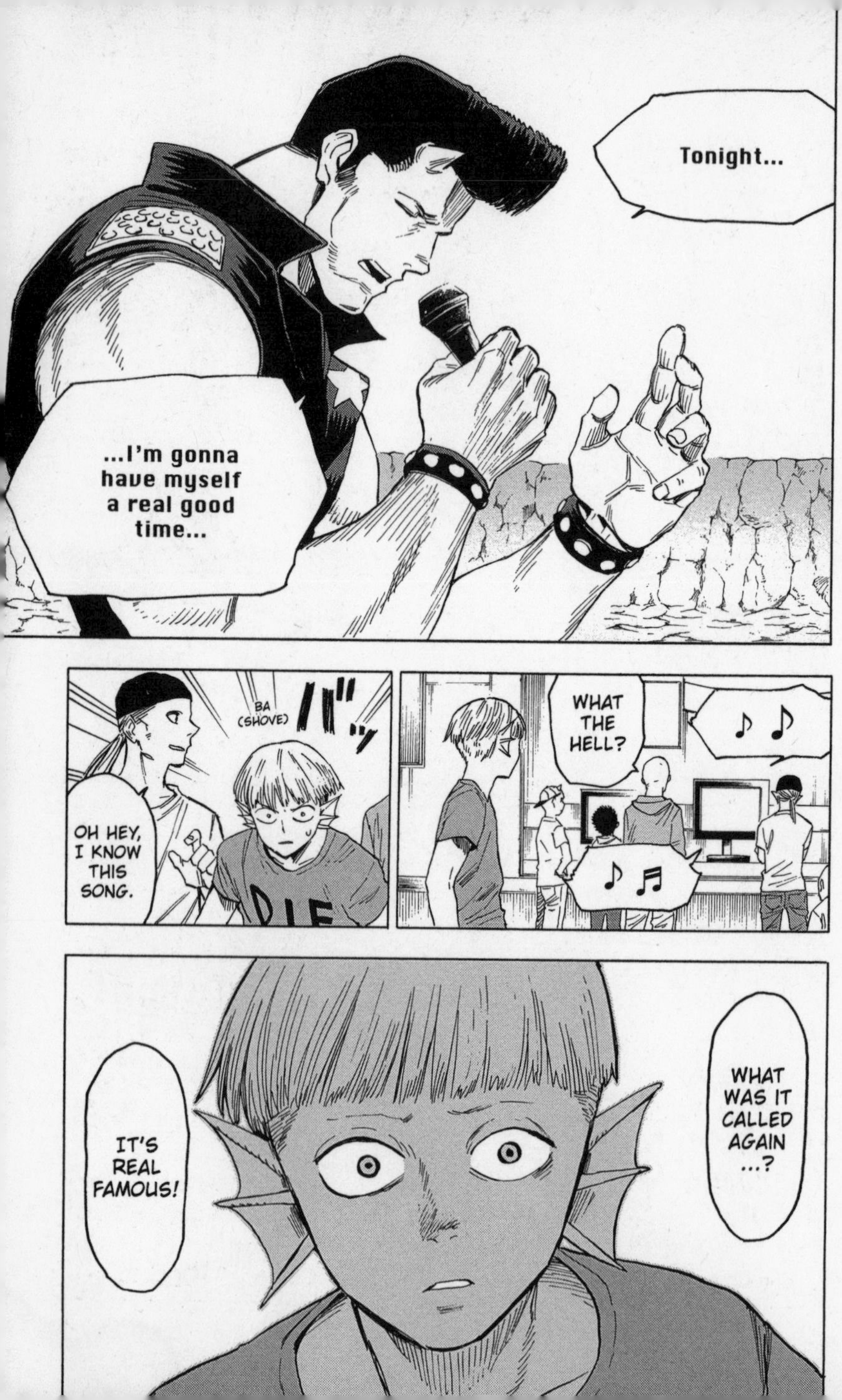
Tonight...
...I'm gonna have myself a real good time...
♪ ♪
WHAT THE HELL?
♪ ♬
バッ
BA (SHOVE)
OH HEY, I KNOW THIS SONG.
WHAT WAS IT CALLED AGAIN ...?
IT'S REAL FAMOUS!

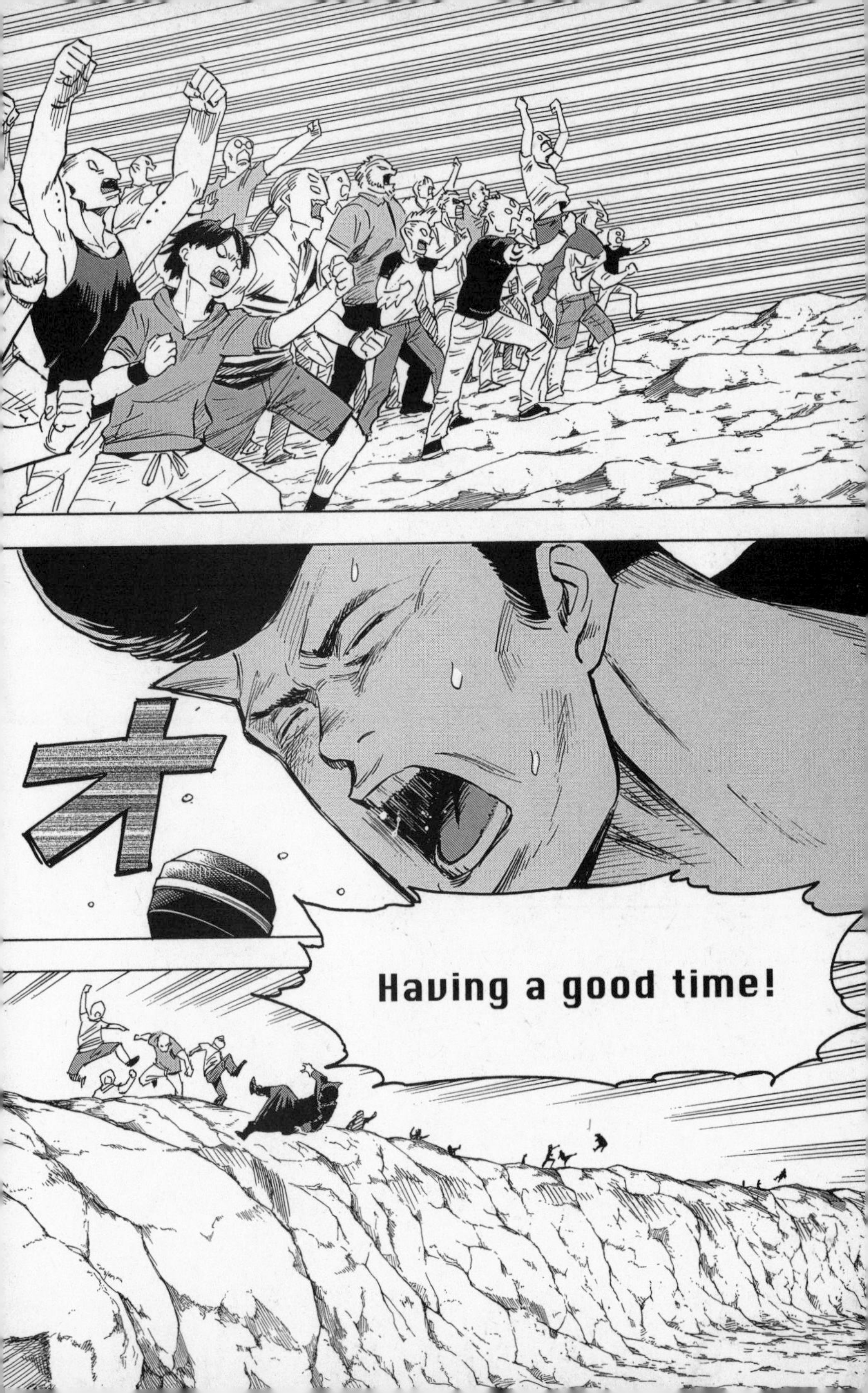
オ
Having a good time!

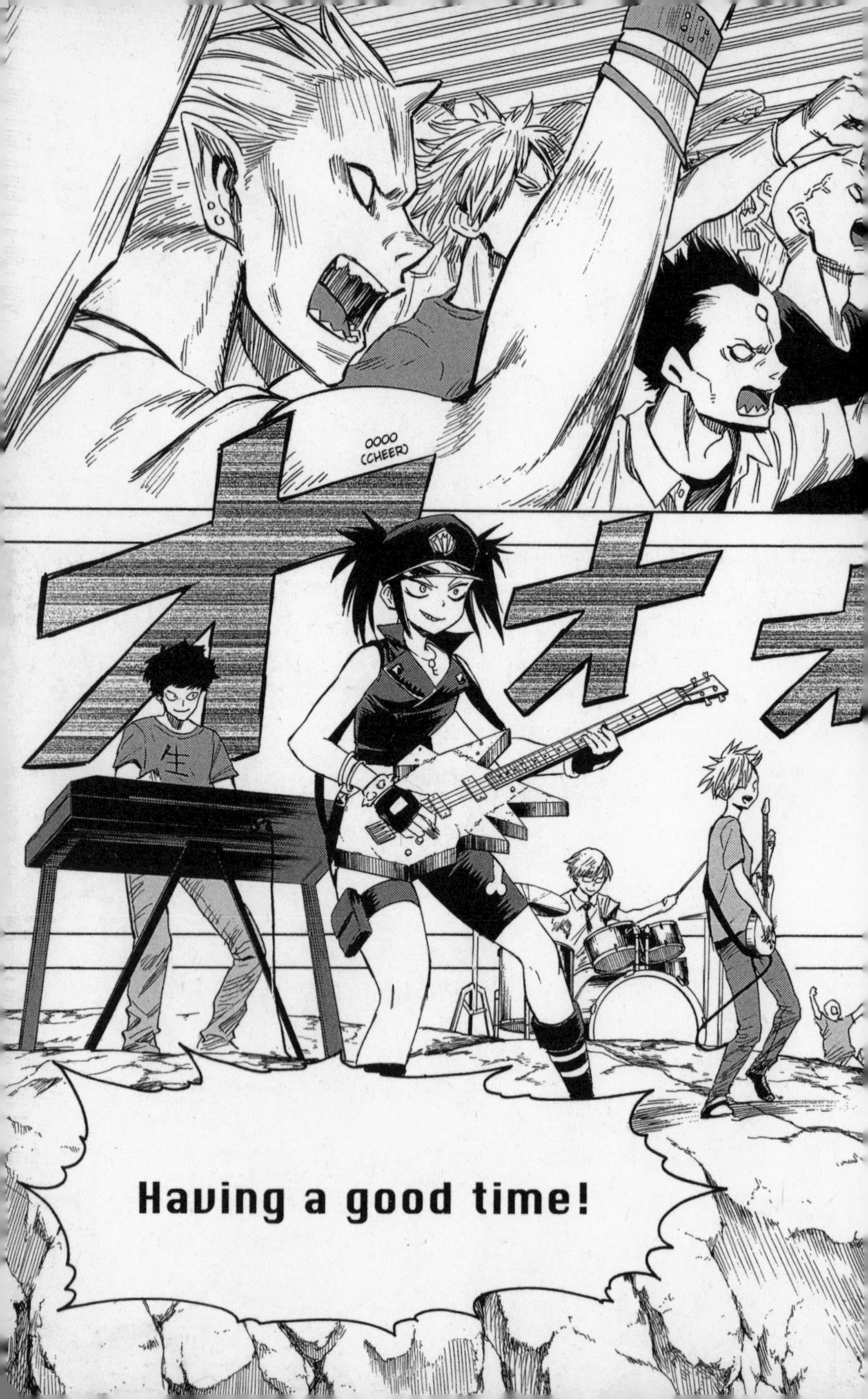
OOOO
(CHEER)
Having a good time!

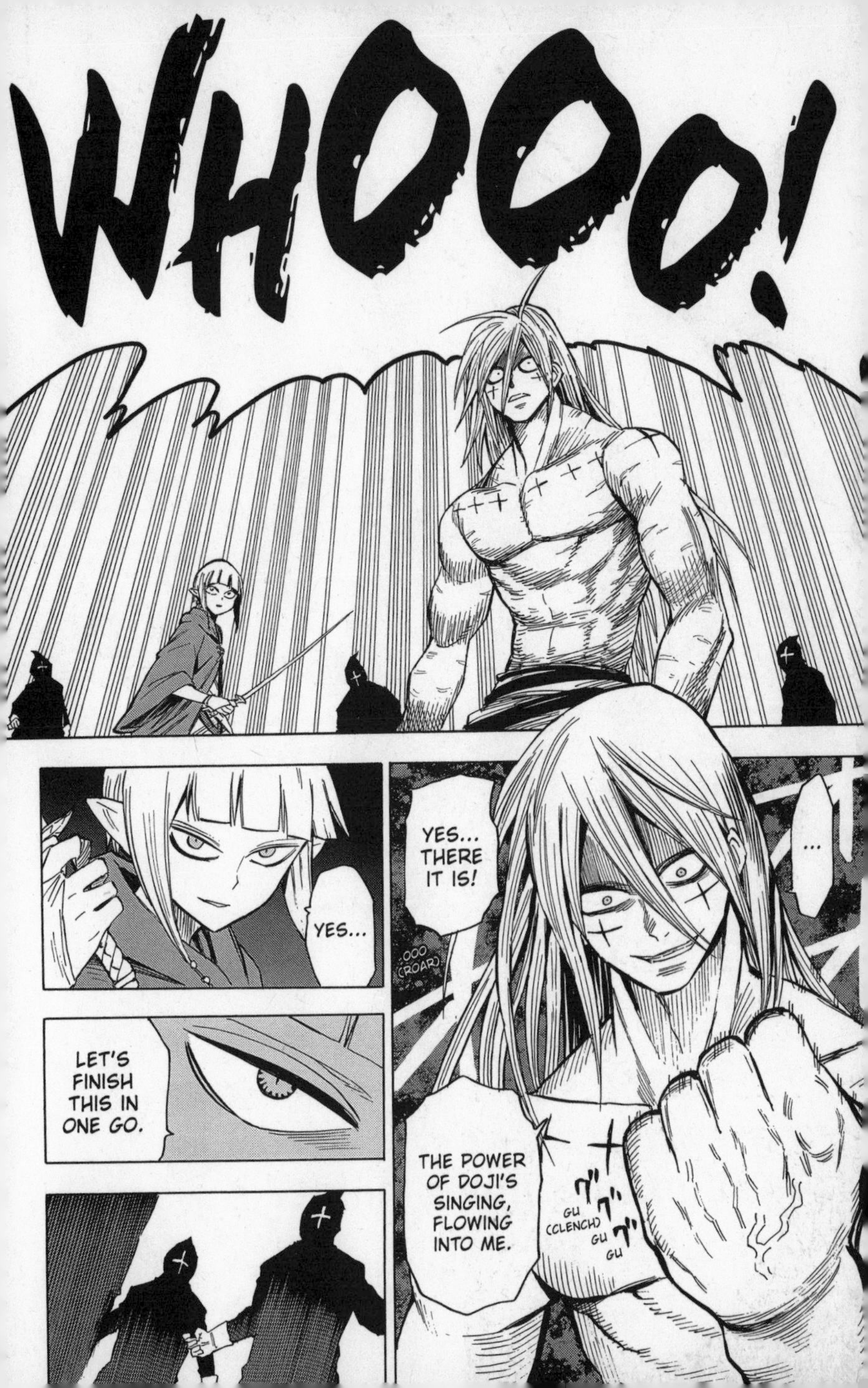
WHOOO!
...
YES... THERE IT IS!
OOO (ROAR)
GU (CLENCH) GU GU
THE POWER OF DOJI'S SINGING, FLOWING INTO ME.
YES...
LET'S FINISH THIS IN ONE GO.

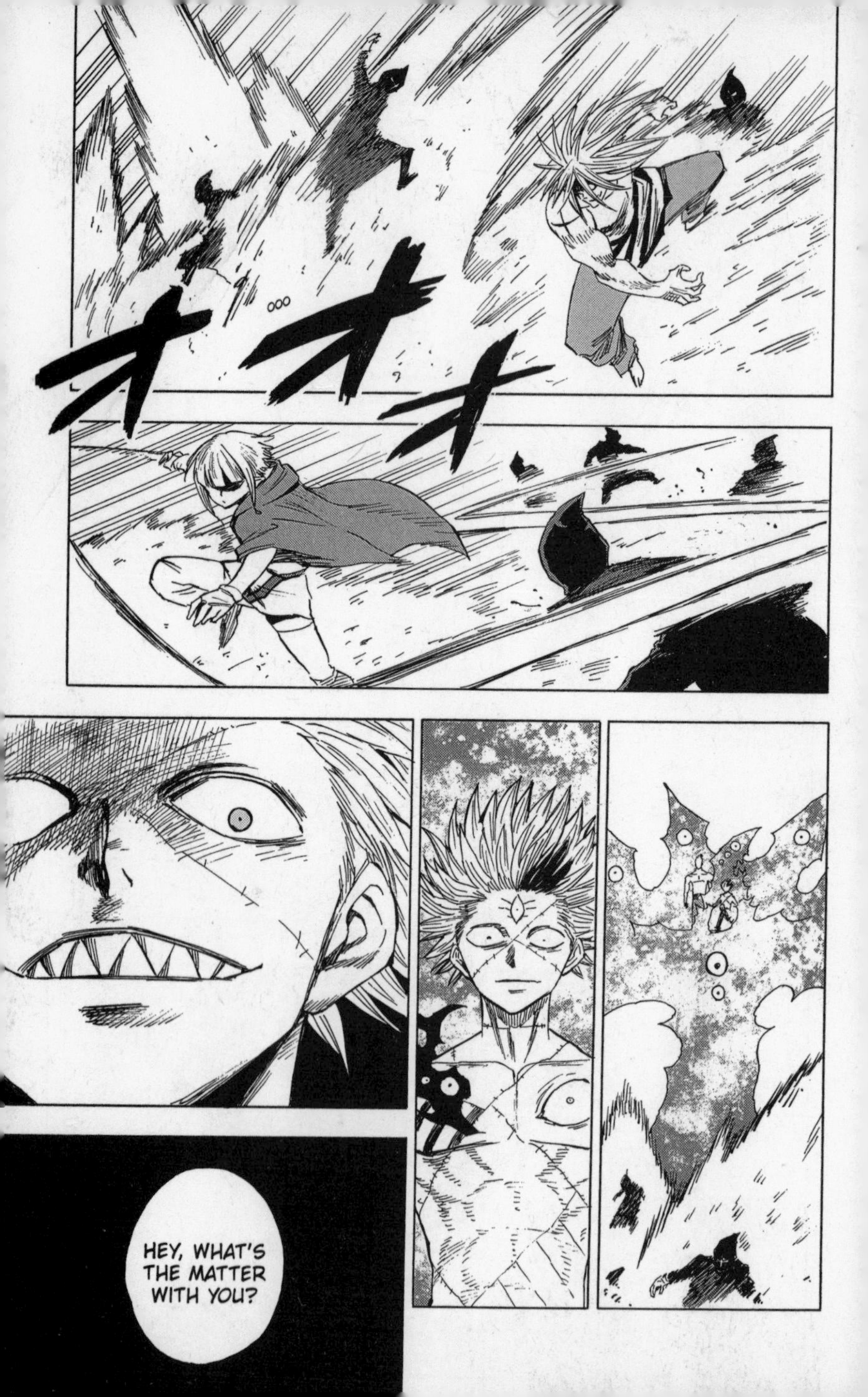
ooo
オオオ
HEY, WHAT'S THE MATTER WITH YOU?

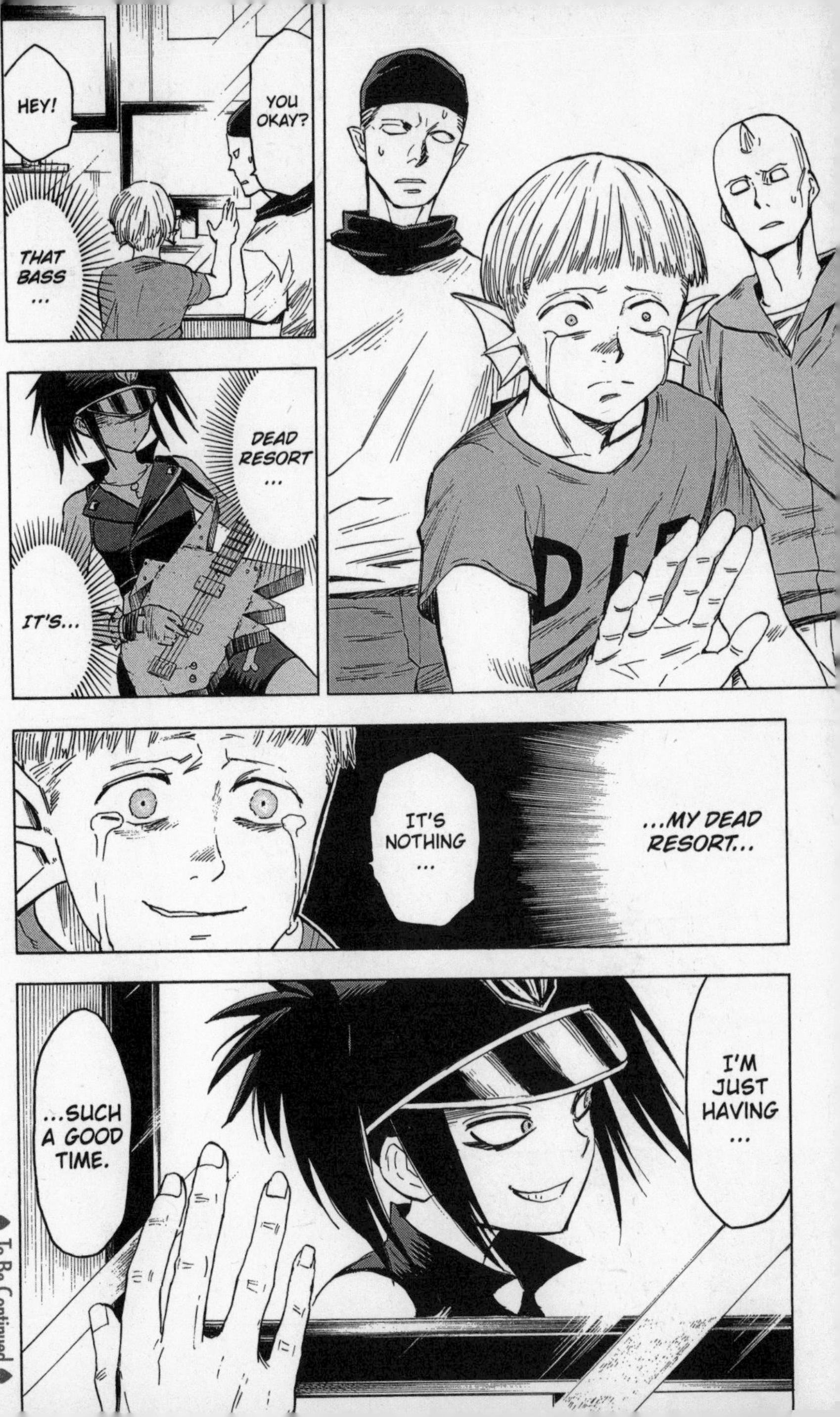
YOU OKAY?
HEY!
THAT BASS ...
DEAD RESORT ...
IT'S...
...MY DEAD RESORT...
IT'S NOTHING ...
I'M JUST HAVING ...
...SUCH A GOOD TIME.

♠ To Be Continued ♠

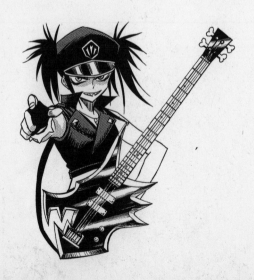

BLOOD LAD

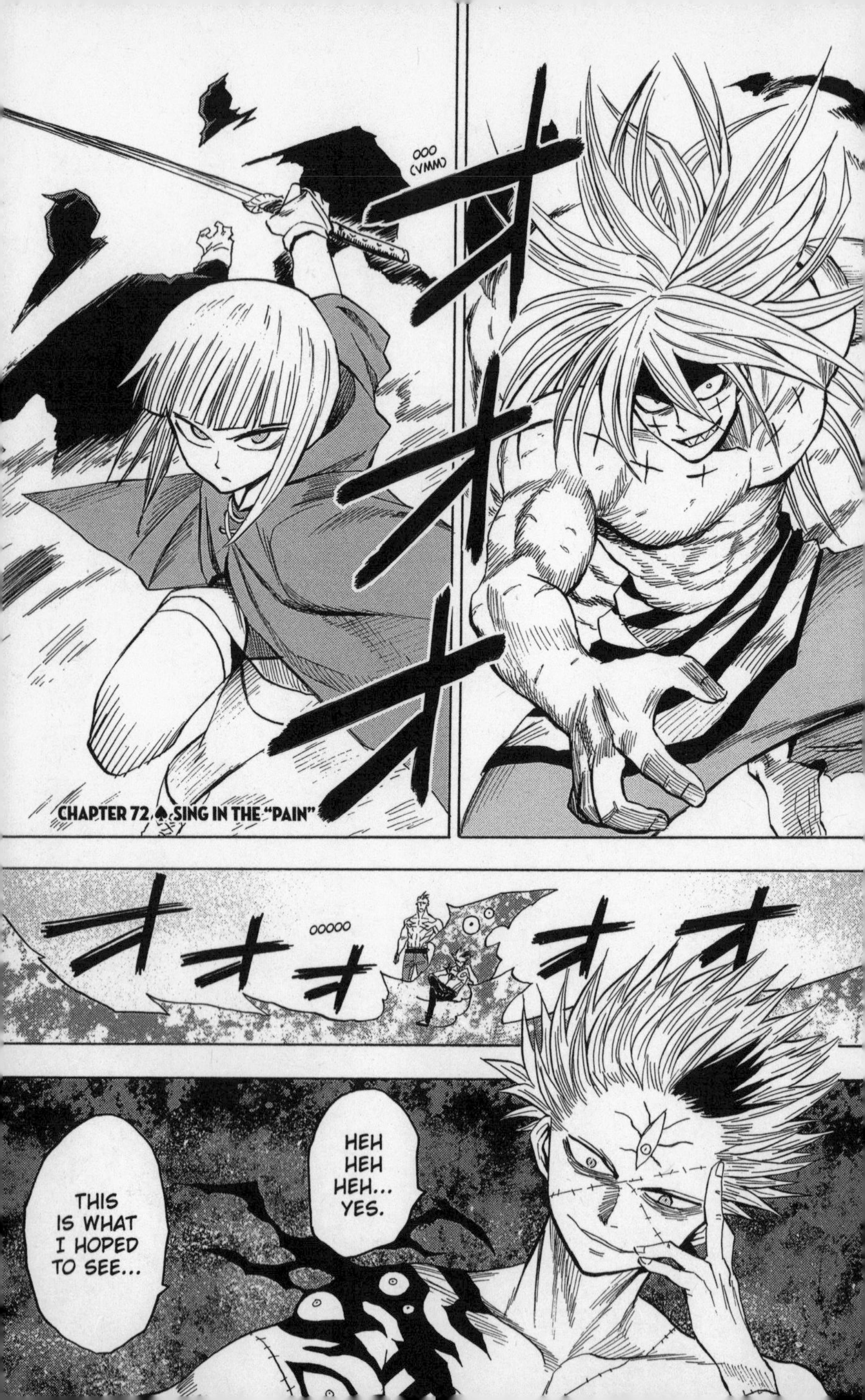
OOO (VMM)
CHAPTER 72 ♠ SING IN THE "PAIN"
OOOOO
HEH HEH HEH... YES.
THIS IS WHAT I HOPED TO SEE...

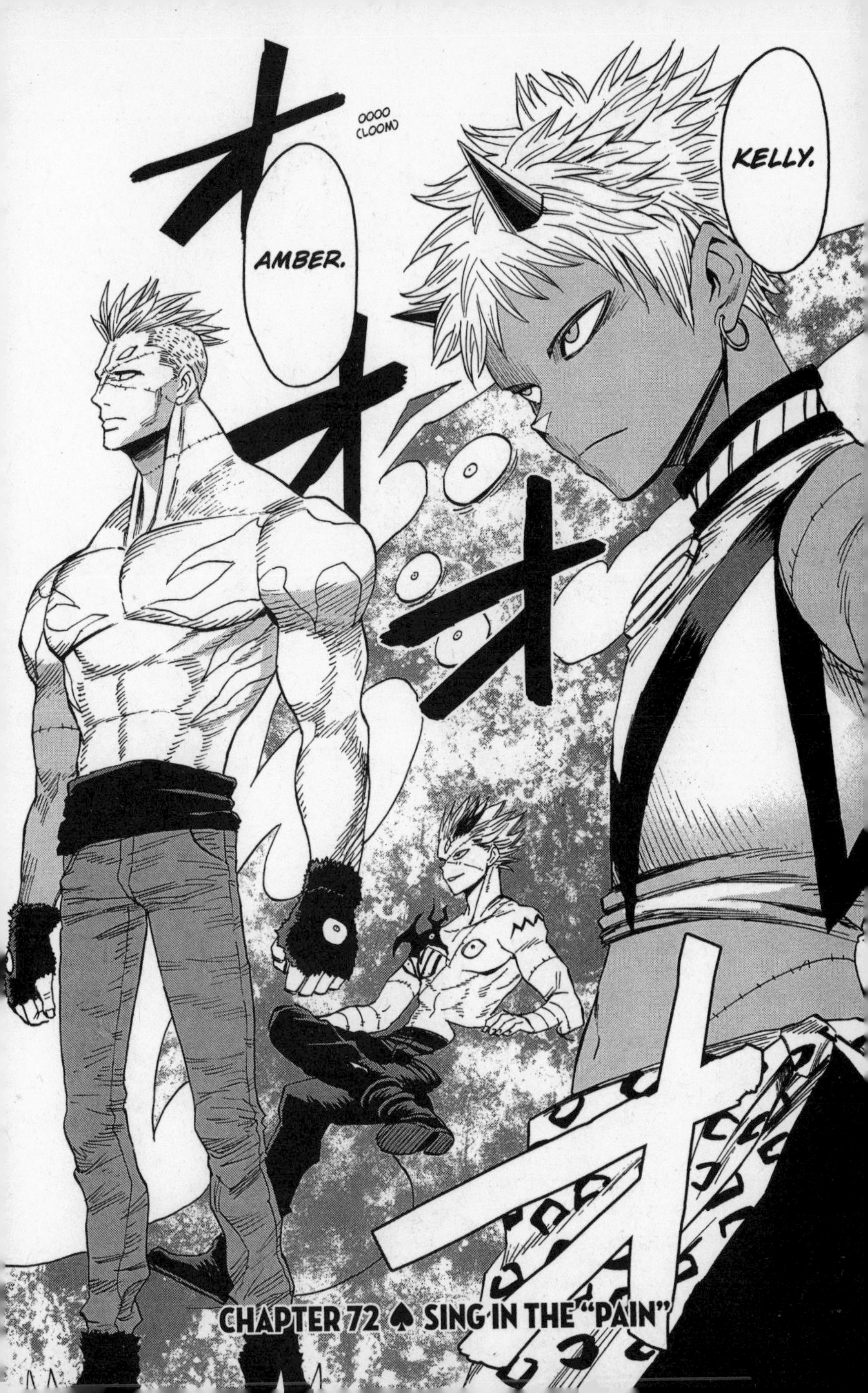
KELLY.
AMBER.
OOOO (LOOM)
CHAPTER 72 ♠ SING IN THE "PAIN"

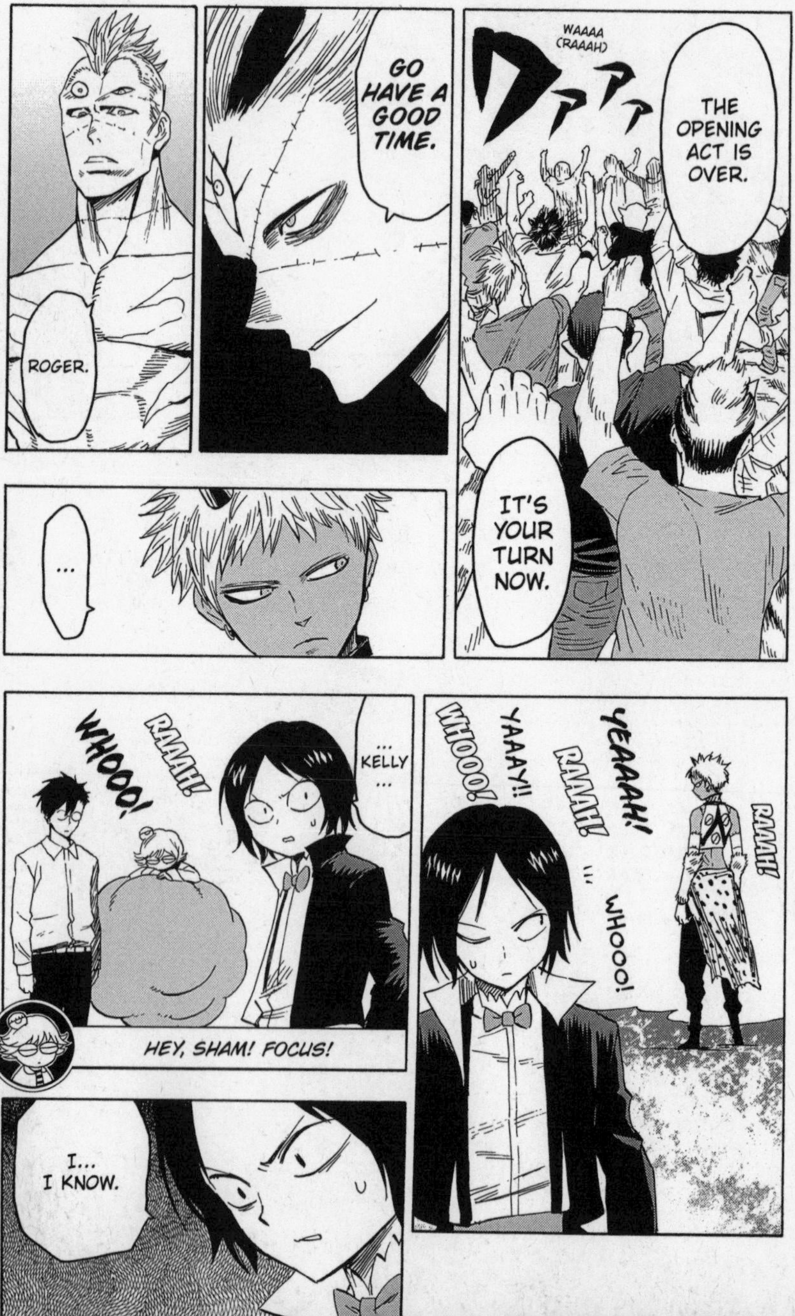
WAAAA (RAAAH)
THE OPENING ACT IS OVER.
IT'S YOUR TURN NOW.
GO HAVE A GOOD TIME.
ROGER.
...
YEAAAAH!
RAAAH!
YAAAY!!
WHOOOO!
!!
WHOOOO!
RAAAH!
...KELLY...
RAAAH!
WHOOOO!
HEY, SHAM! FOCUS!
I... I KNOW.

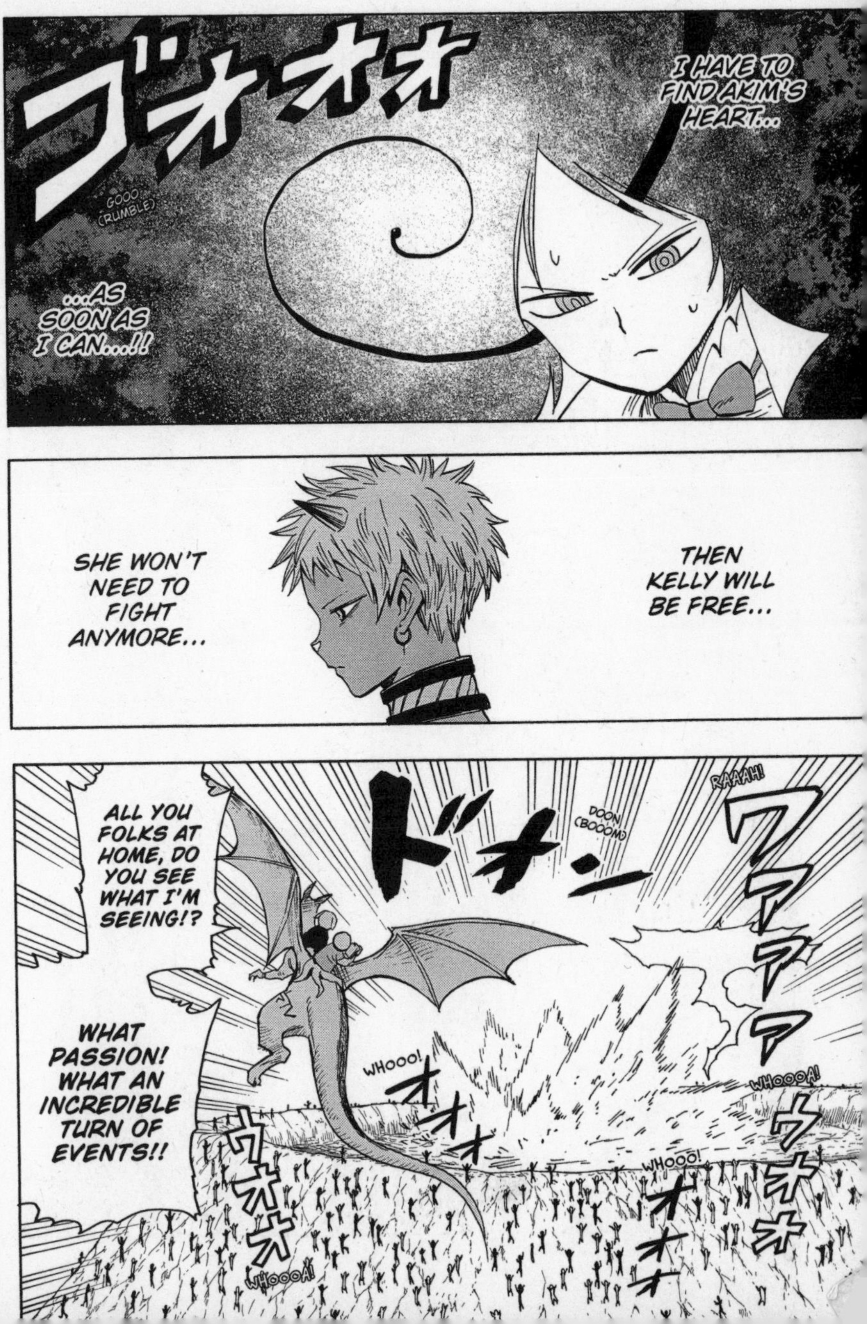
ゴオオオ
I HAVE TO FIND AKIM'S HEART...
GOOO (RUMBLE)
...AS SOON AS I CAN...!!
THEN KELLY WILL BE FREE...
SHE WON'T NEED TO FIGHT ANYMORE...
ワァァァ
RAAAH!
ドォン
DOON (BOOOM)
ALL YOU FOLKS AT HOME, DO YOU SEE WHAT I'M SEEING!?
ウオオ
WHOOOA!
オオオ
WHOOO!
WHAT PASSION! WHAT AN INCREDIBLE TURN OF EVENTS!!
オオオ
WHOOO!
ウオオ
WHOOOA!

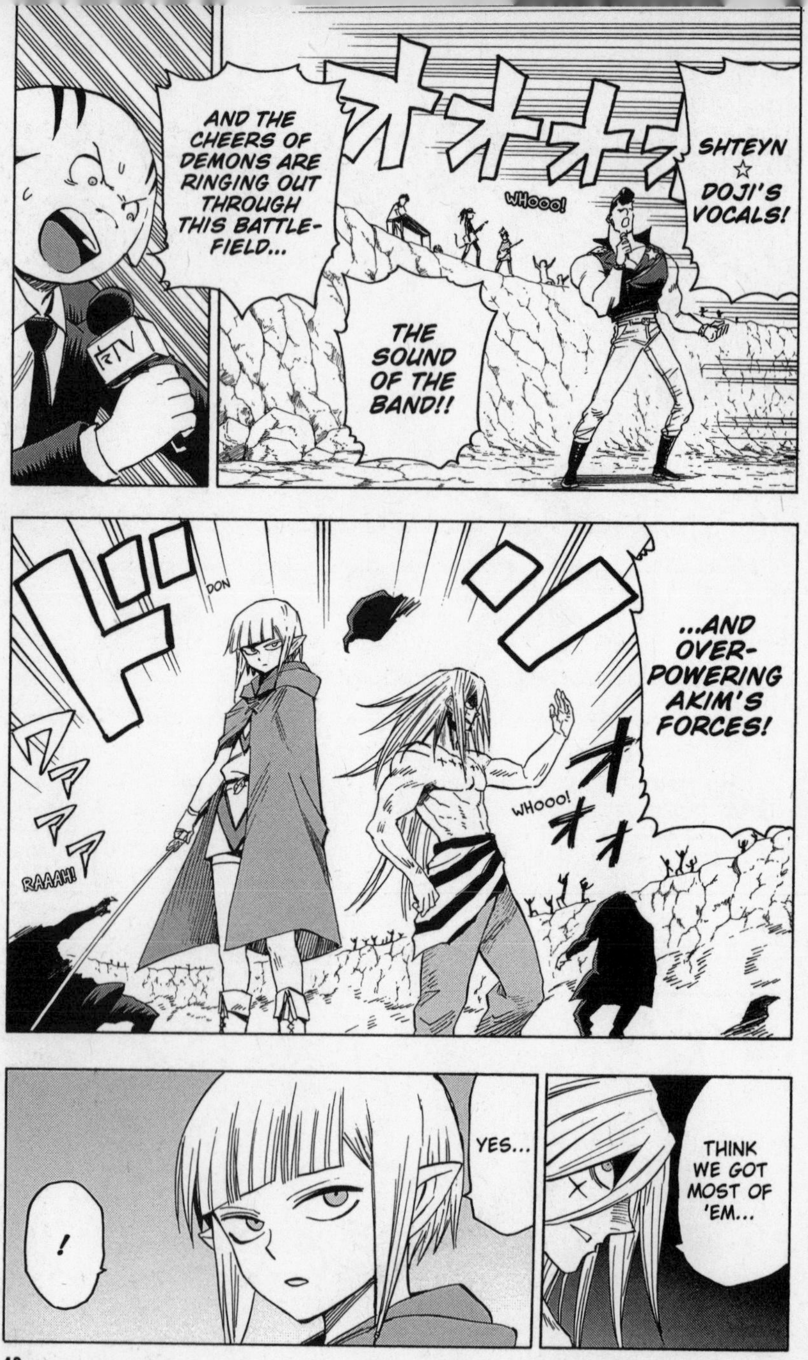
SHTEYN ☆ DOJI'S VOCALS!
WHOOO!
THE SOUND OF THE BAND!!
AND THE CHEERS OF DEMONS ARE RINGING OUT THROUGH THIS BATTLE-FIELD...
...AND OVER-POWERING AKIM'S FORCES!
DON
WHOOO!
RAAAH!
THINK WE GOT MOST OF 'EM...
YES...
!

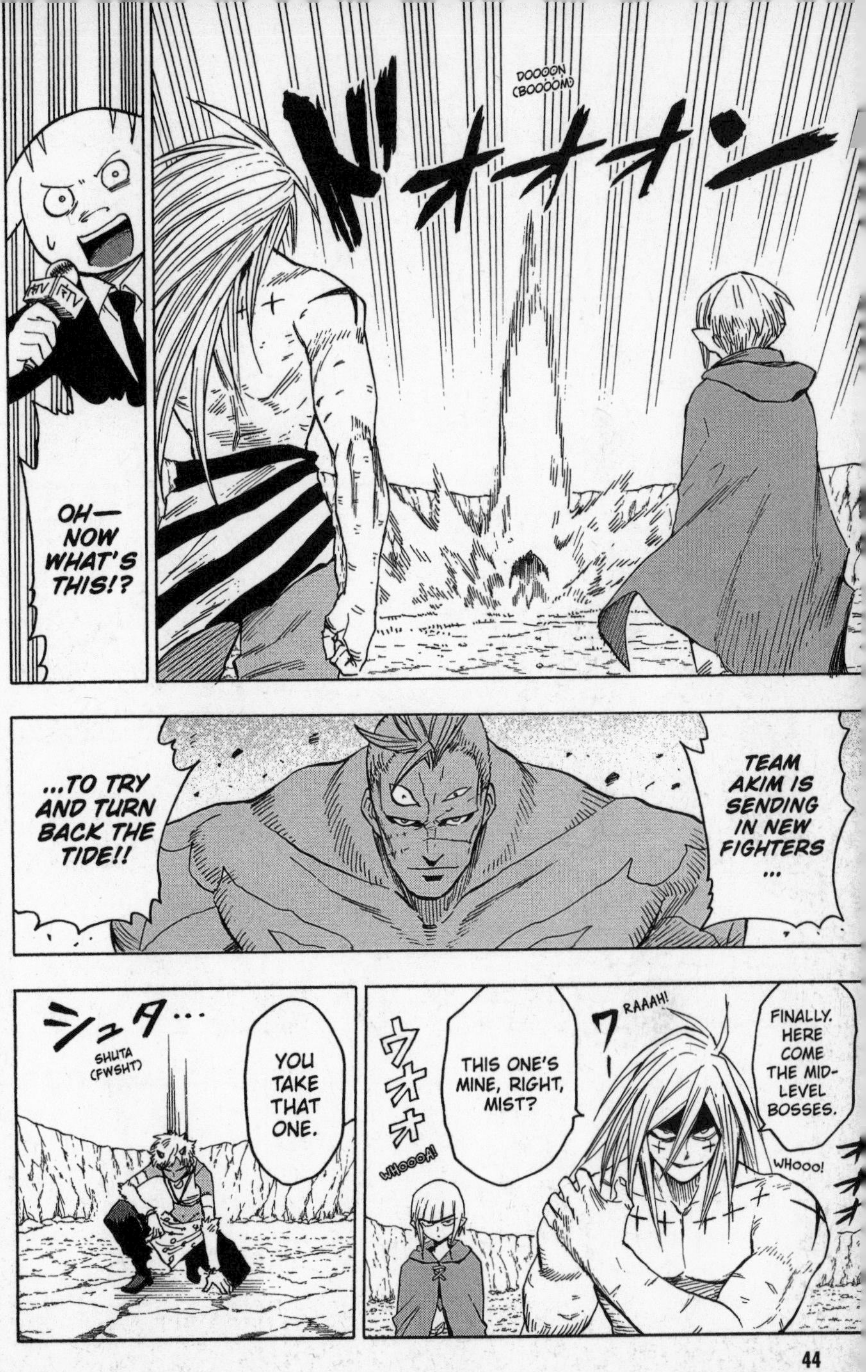
ドオオオン
DOOOON (BOOOOM)
OH— NOW WHAT'S THIS!?
TEAM AKIM IS SENDING IN NEW FIGHTERS ...
...TO TRY AND TURN BACK THE TIDE!!
FINALLY. HERE COME THE MID-LEVEL BOSSES.
WHOOO!
ワー
RAAAH!
THIS ONE'S MINE, RIGHT, MIST?
ウオオ
WHOOOA!
YOU TAKE THAT ONE.
シュタ...
SHUTA (FWSHT)

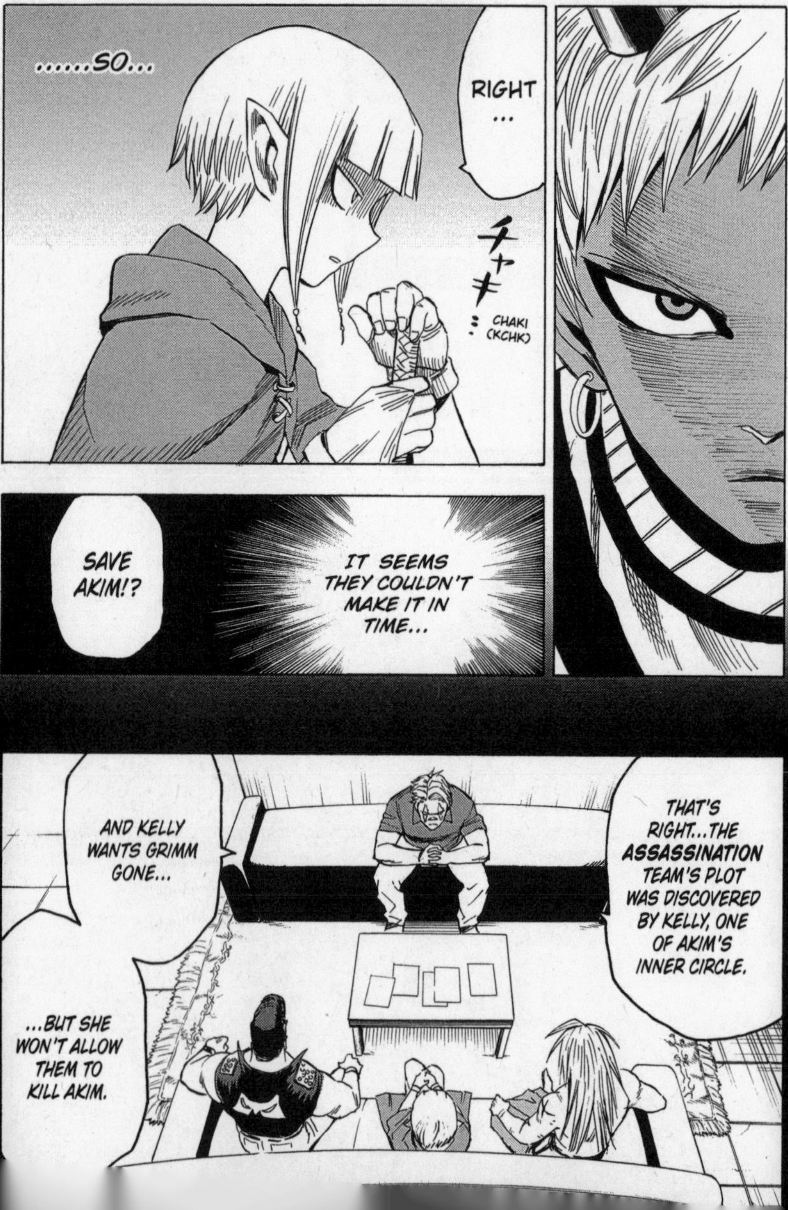
RIGHT ...
チャキ!!
CHAKI (KCHK)
......SO...
IT SEEMS THEY COULDN'T MAKE IT IN TIME...
SAVE AKIM!?
THAT'S RIGHT...THE ASSASSINATION TEAM'S PLOT WAS DISCOVERED BY KELLY, ONE OF AKIM'S INNER CIRCLE.
AND KELLY WANTS GRIMM GONE...
...BUT SHE WON'T ALLOW THEM TO KILL AKIM.

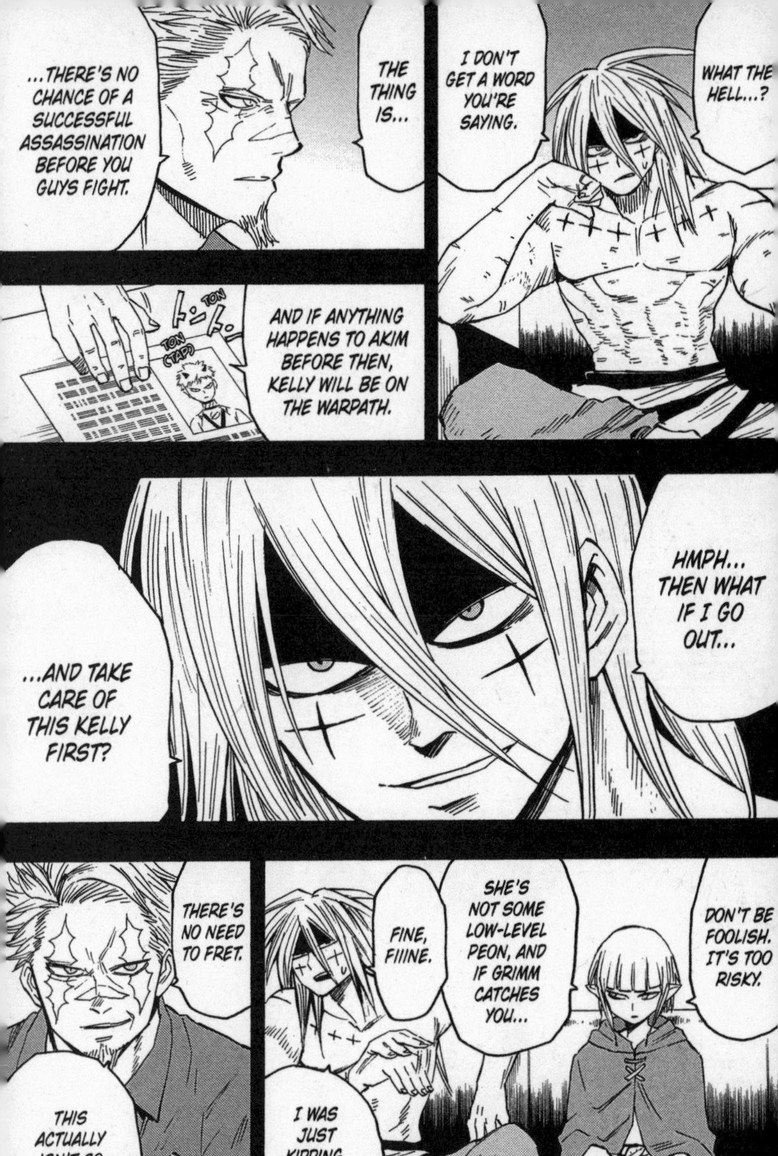
WHAT THE HELL...?
I DON'T GET A WORD YOU'RE SAYING.
THE THING IS...
...THERE'S NO CHANCE OF A SUCCESSFUL ASSASSINATION BEFORE YOU GUYS FIGHT.
AND IF ANYTHING HAPPENS TO AKIM BEFORE THEN, KELLY WILL BE ON THE WARPATH.
TON
TON (TAP)
HMPH... THEN WHAT IF I GO OUT...
...AND TAKE CARE OF THIS KELLY FIRST?
DON'T BE FOOLISH. IT'S TOO RISKY.
SHE'S NOT SOME LOW-LEVEL PEON, AND IF GRIMM CATCHES YOU...
FINE, FIIINE.
I WAS JUST KIDDING, OKAY? GEEZ.
THERE'S NO NEED TO FRET.
THIS ACTUALLY ISN'T SO BAD.

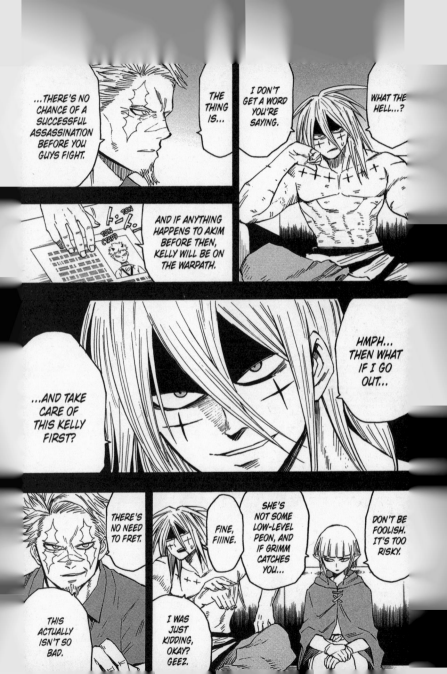

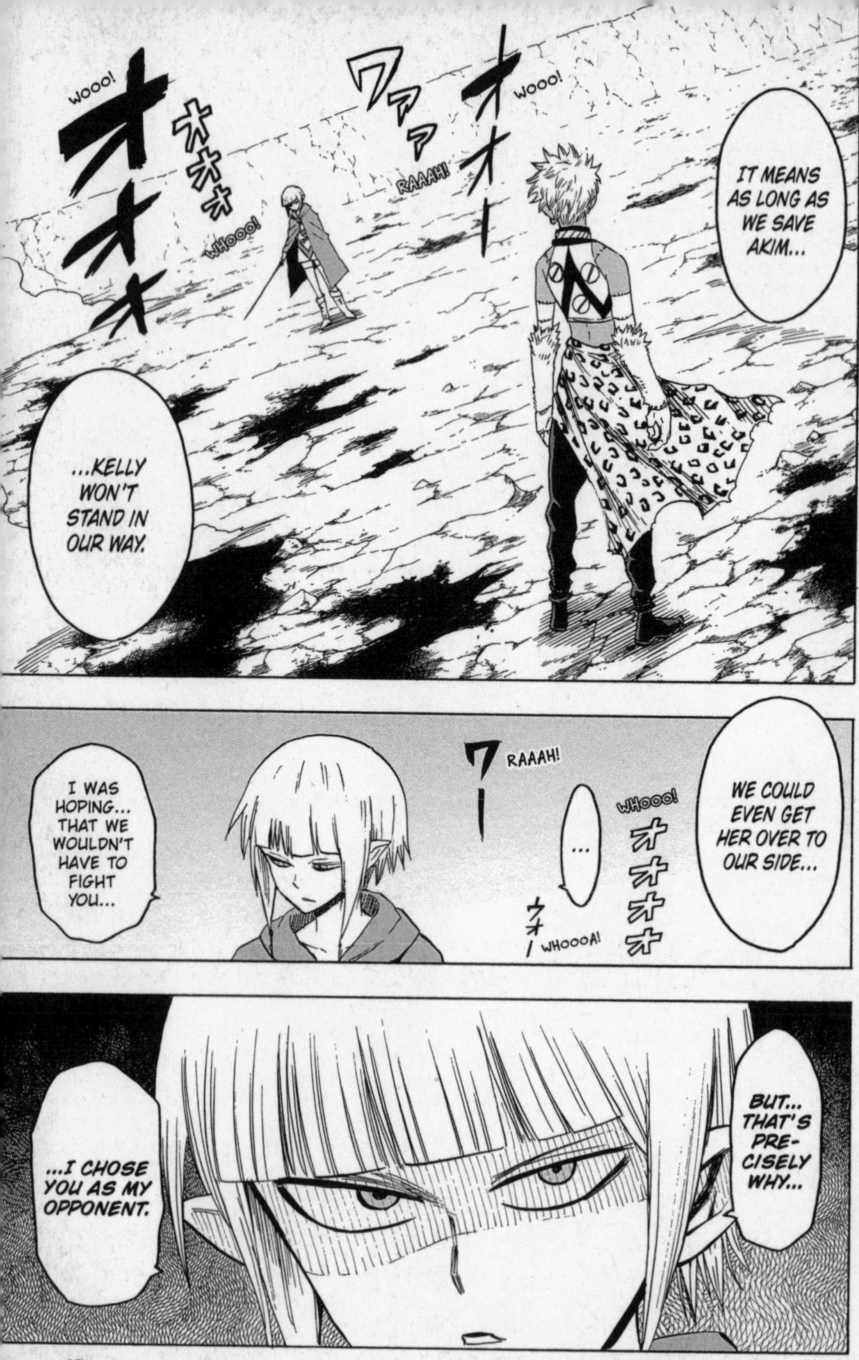
IT MEANS AS LONG AS WE SAVE AKIM...
オオー WOOO!
ワァァ RAAAH!
オオォ WHOOO!
WOOO! オオオ
...KELLY WON'T STAND IN OUR WAY.
WE COULD EVEN GET HER OVER TO OUR SIDE...
WHOOO! オオオオ
...
ウオー WHOOOA!
ワー RAAAH!
I WAS HOPING... THAT WE WOULDN'T HAVE TO FIGHT YOU...
BUT... THAT'S PRE-CISELY WHY...
...I CHOSE YOU AS MY OPPONENT.

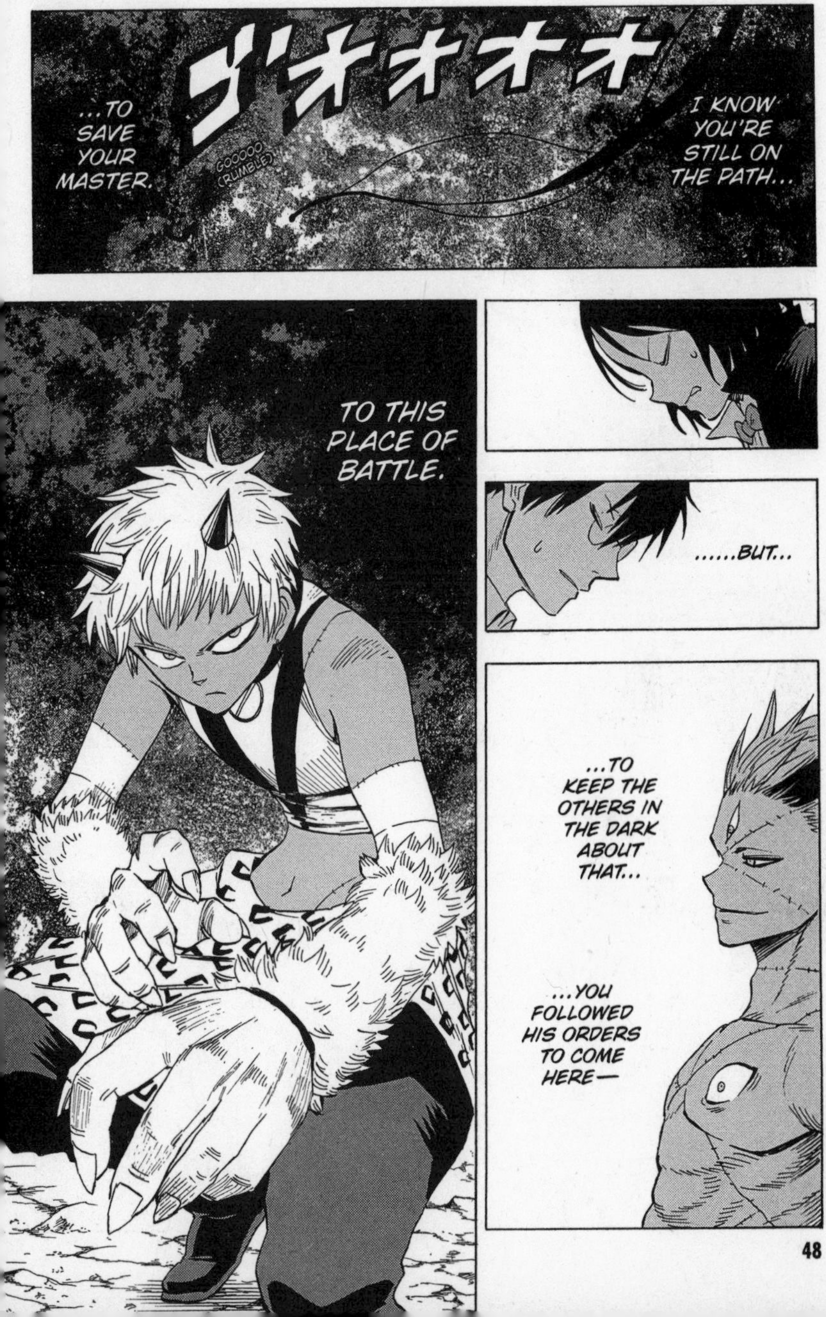
I KNOW YOU'RE STILL ON THE PATH...
ゴオオオオ
GOOOOO (RUMBLE)
...TO SAVE YOUR MASTER.
......BUT...
...TO KEEP THE OTHERS IN THE DARK ABOUT THAT...
...YOU FOLLOWED HIS ORDERS TO COME HERE—
TO THIS PLACE OF BATTLE.

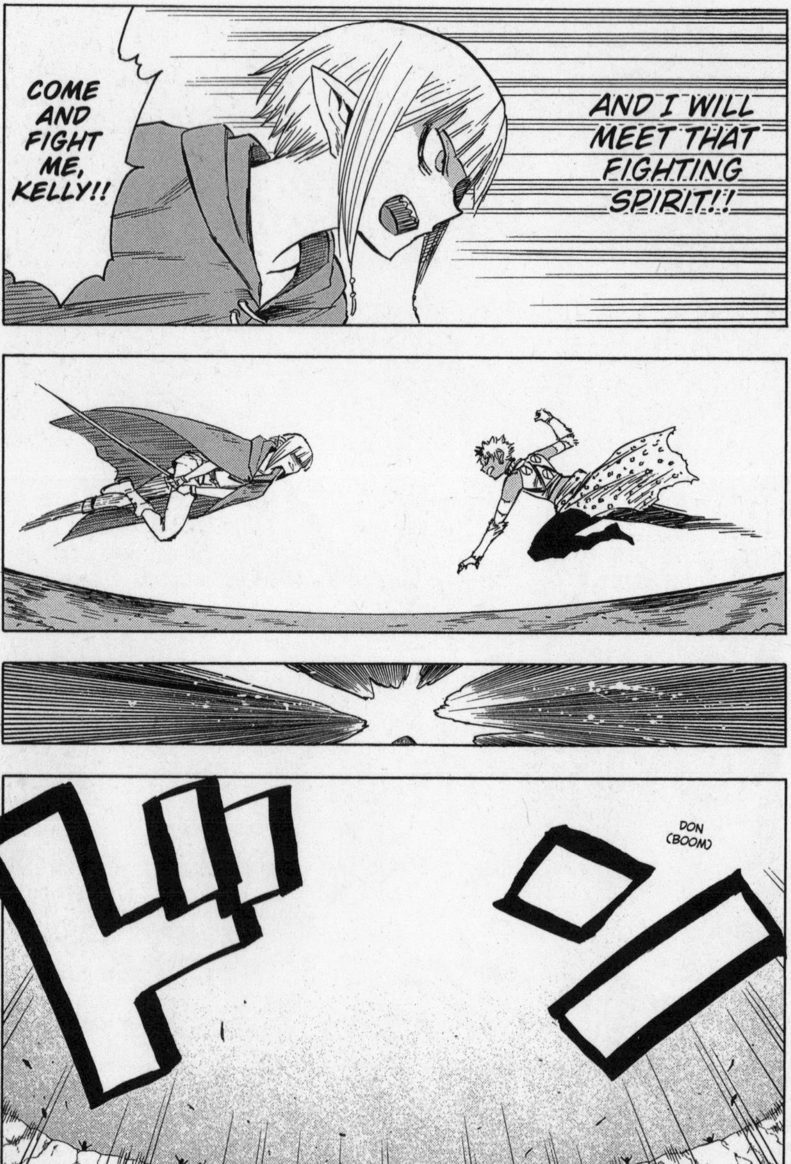
AND I WILL MEET THAT FIGHTING SPIRIT!!
COME AND FIGHT ME, KELLY!!
DON (BOOM)

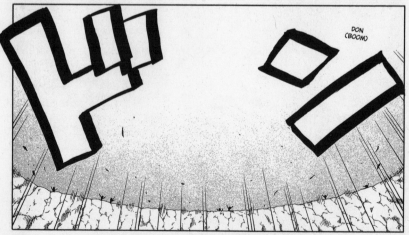

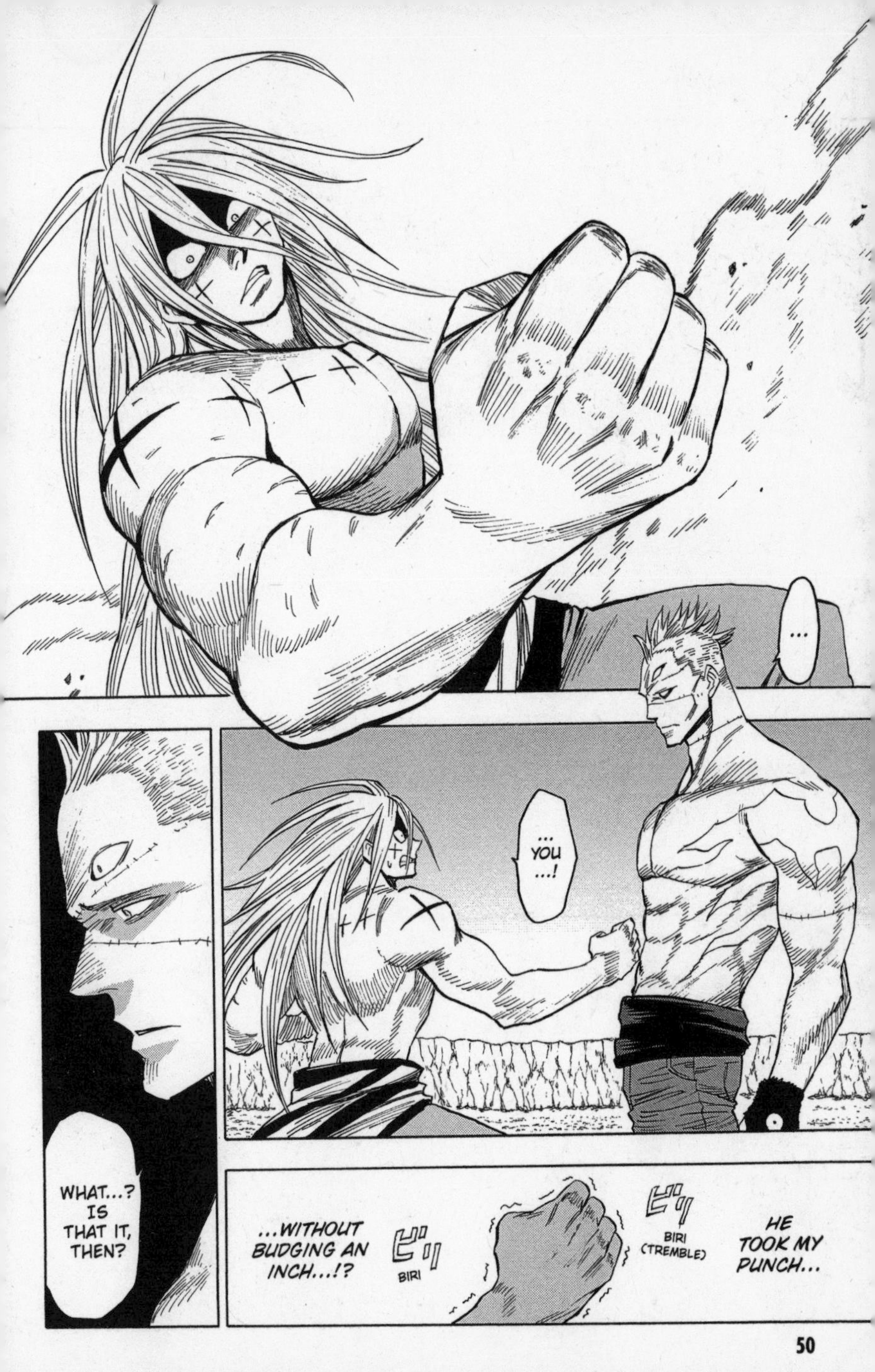
...
... YOU ...!
HE TOOK MY PUNCH...
ビリ
BIRI (TREMBLE)
...WITHOUT BUDGING AN INCH...!?
ビリ
BIRI
WHAT...? IS THAT IT, THEN?

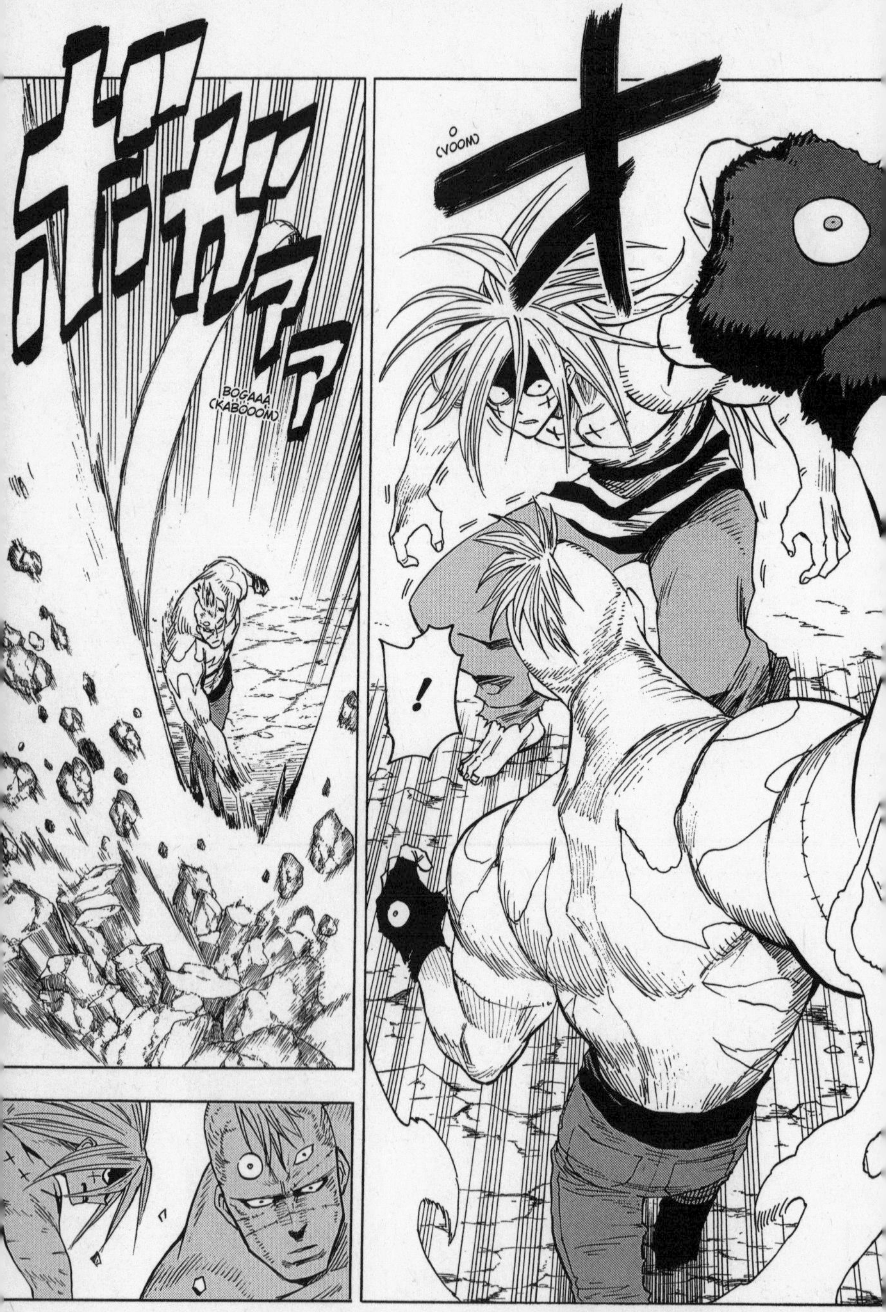
O
(VOOM)
!
BOGAAA
(KABOOOM)

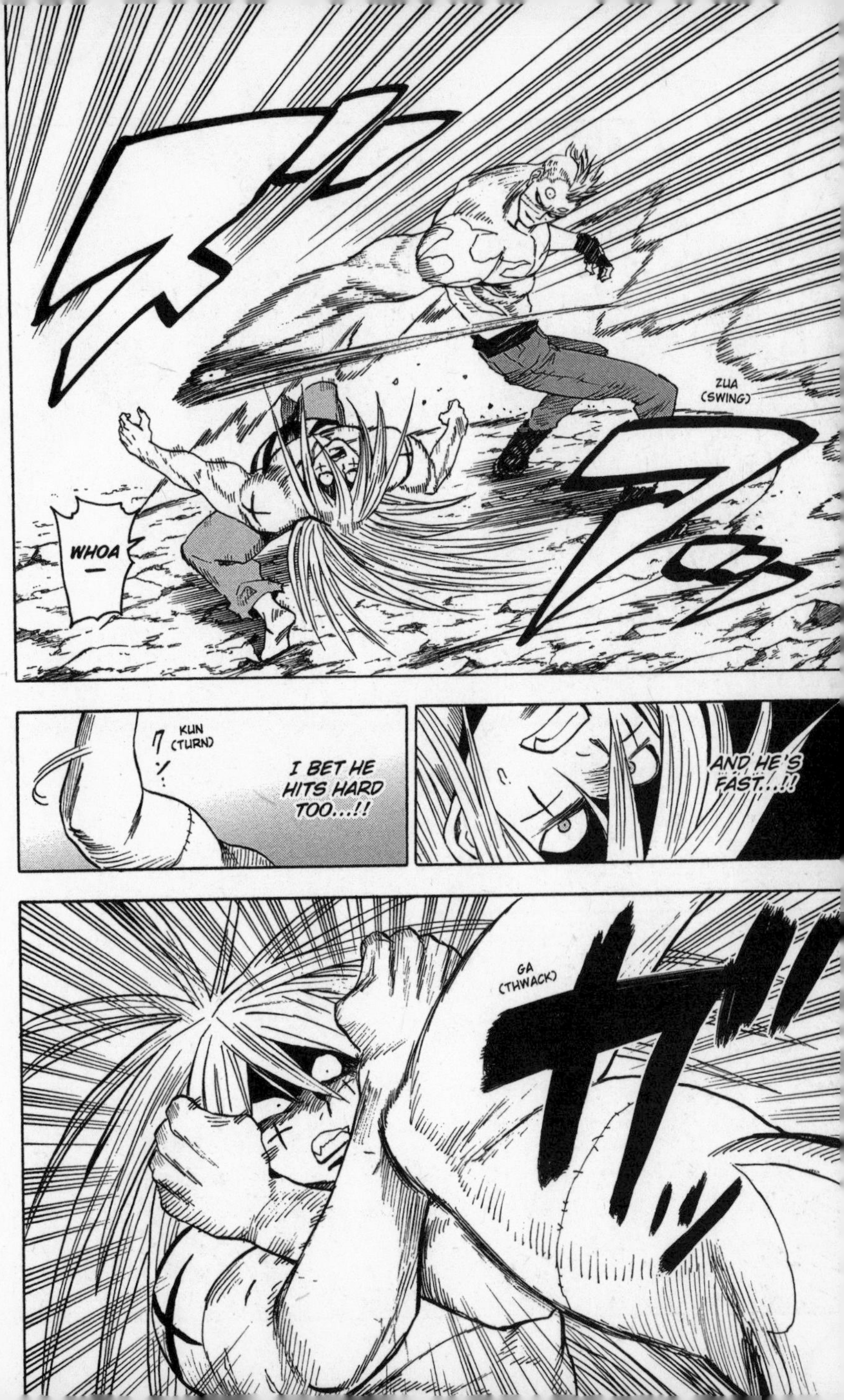
ZUA (SWING)
WHOA—
AND HE'S FAST...!!
KUN (TURN)
I BET HE HITS HARD TOO...!!
GA (THWACK)

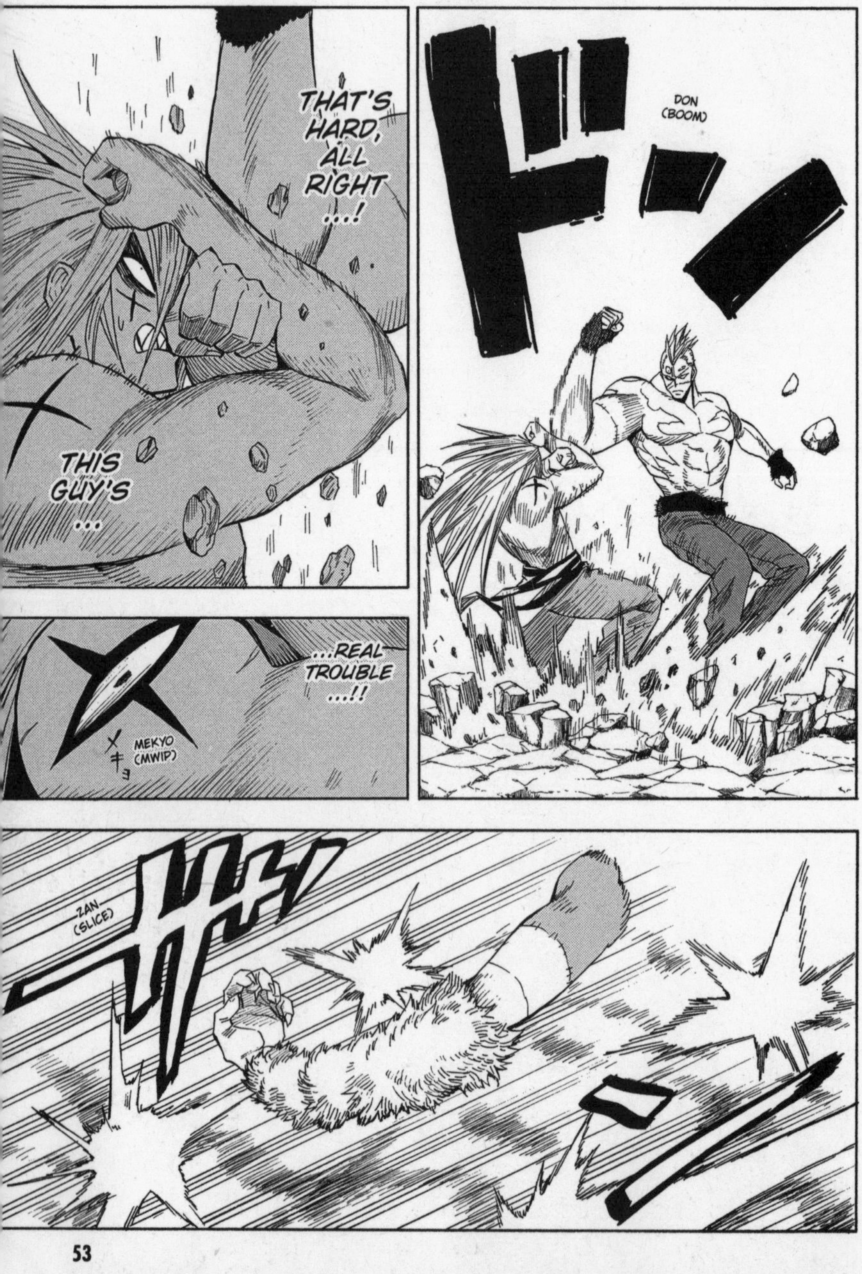
DON
(BOOM)
THAT'S HARD, ALL RIGHT ...!
THIS GUY'S ...
...REAL TROUBLE ...!!
MEKYO
(MWIP)
ZAN
(SLICE)

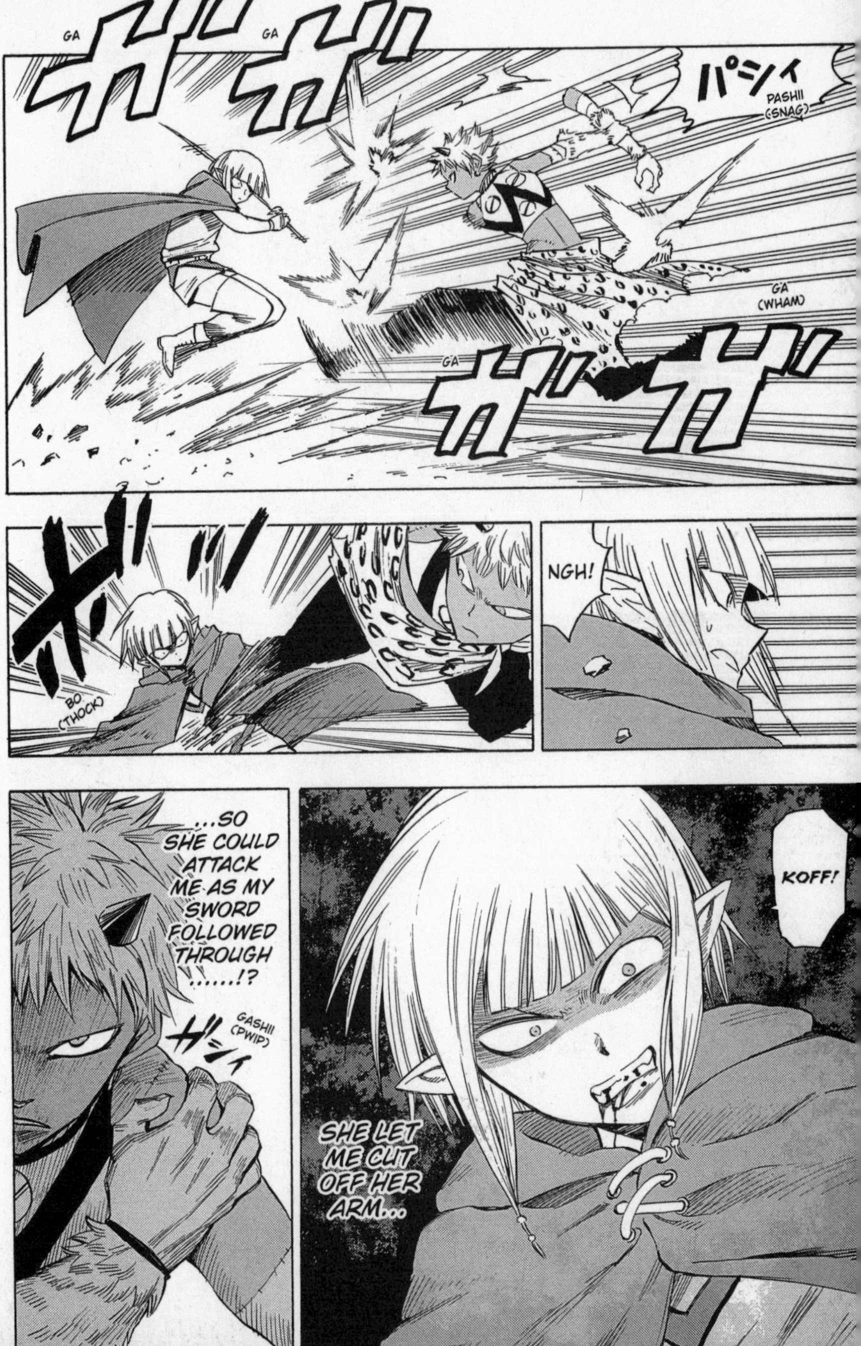
PASHII
(SNAG)
GA
GA
GA
(WHAM)
GA
NGH!
BO
(THOCK)
KOFF!
SHE LET ME CUT OFF HER ARM...
...SO SHE COULD ATTACK ME AS MY SWORD FOLLOWED THROUGH......!?
GASHII
(PWIP)

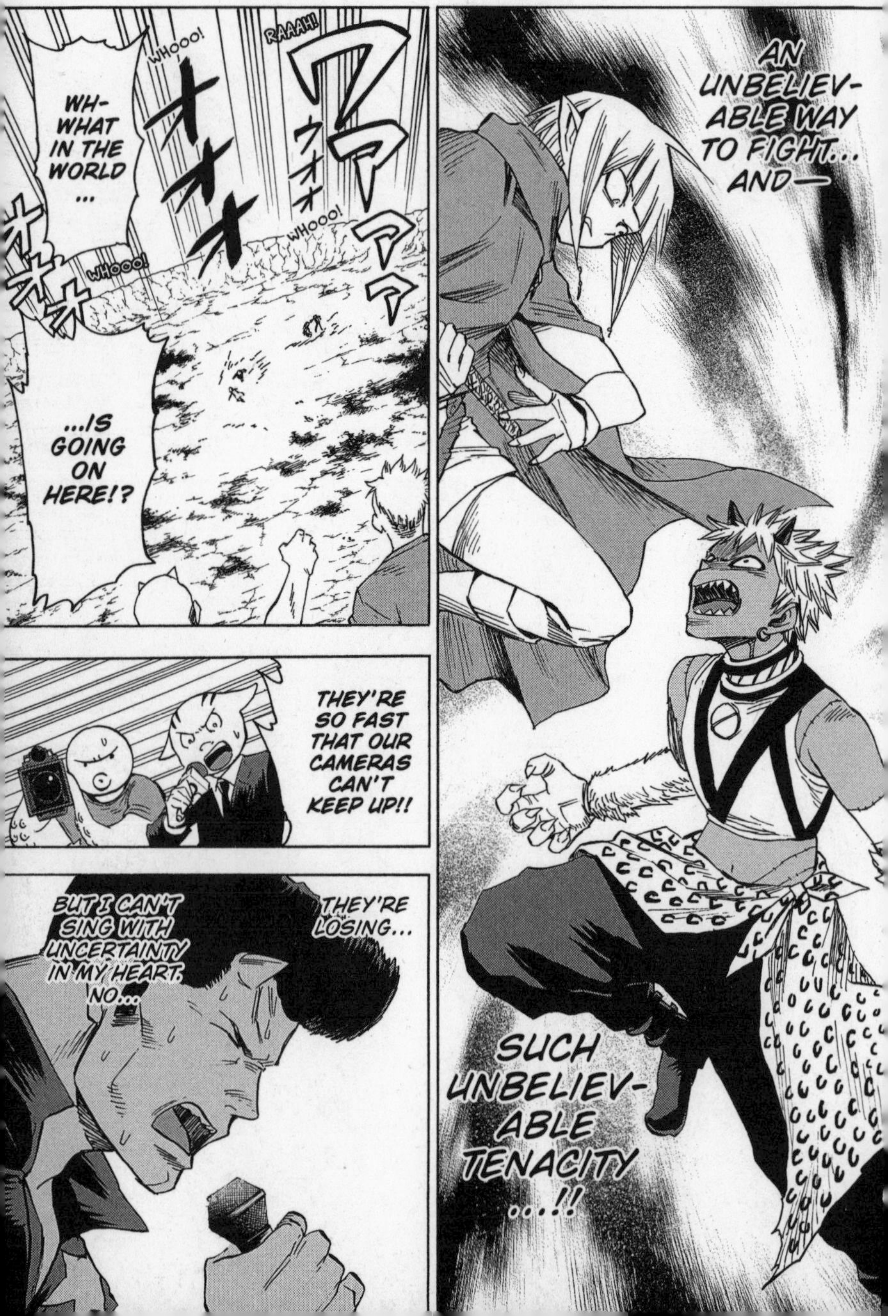
AN UNBELIEV-ABLE WAY TO FIGHT... AND—
SUCH UNBELIEV-ABLE TENACITY...!!
RAAAH!
WHOOO!
WH-WHAT IN THE WORLD...
WHOOO!
WHOOO!
...IS GOING ON HERE!?
THEY'RE SO FAST THAT OUR CAMERAS CAN'T KEEP UP!!
THEY'RE LOSING...
BUT I CAN'T SING WITH UNCERTAINTY IN MY HEART. NO...

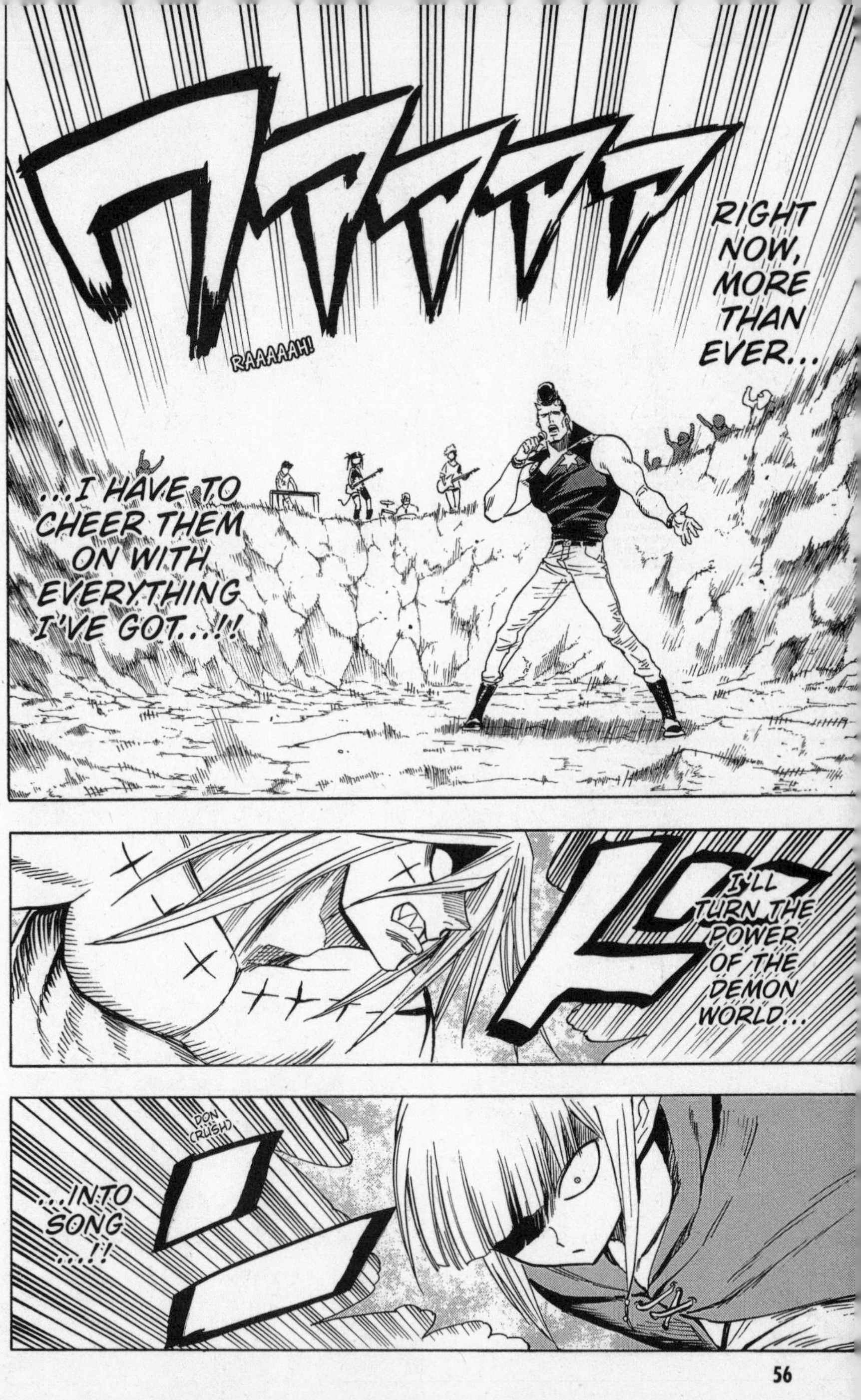
RIGHT NOW, MORE THAN EVER...
RAAAAAH!
...I HAVE TO CHEER THEM ON WITH EVERYTHING I'VE GOT...!!
I'LL TURN THE POWER OF THE DEMON WORLD...
DON (RUSH)
...INTO SONG ...!!

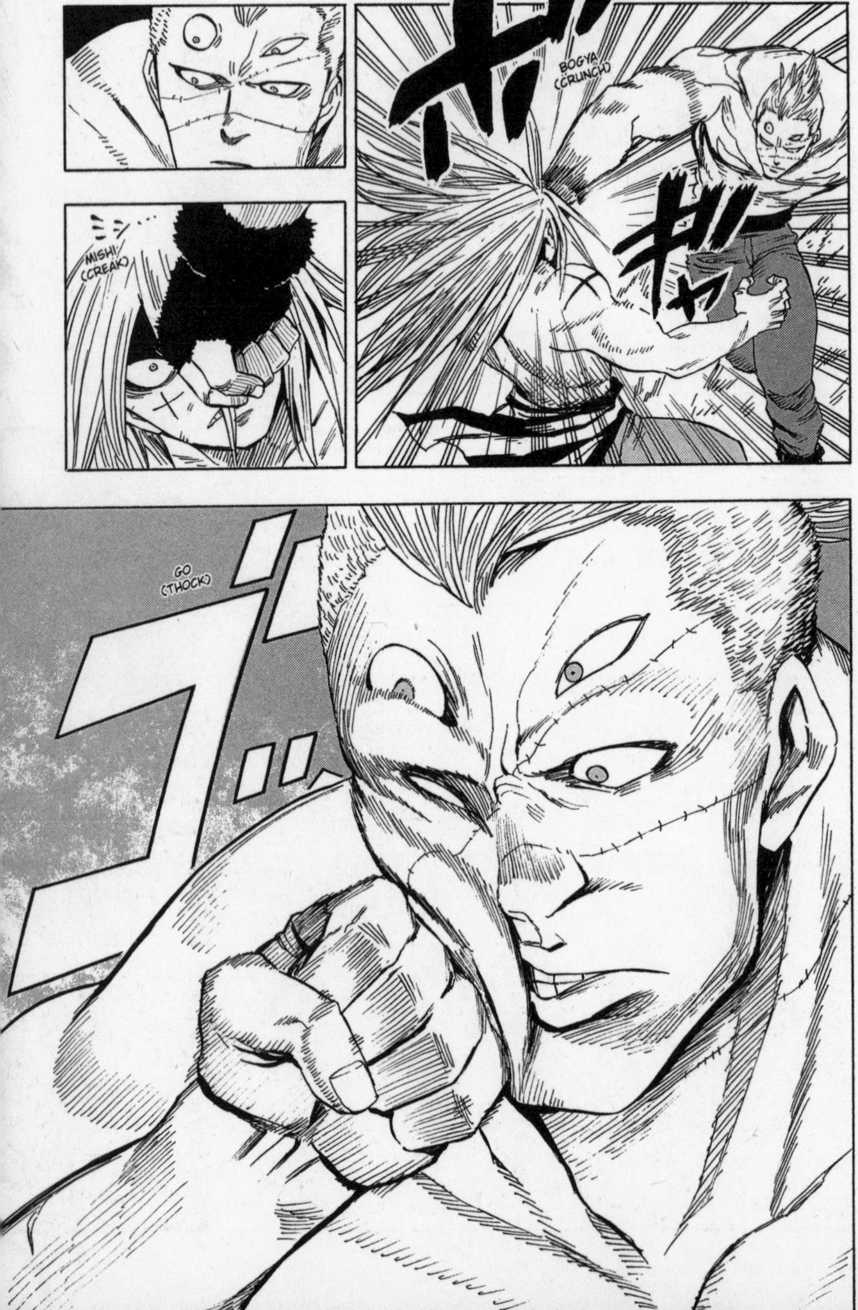

BOGYA (CRUNCH)
MISHI (CREAK)
GO (THOCK)

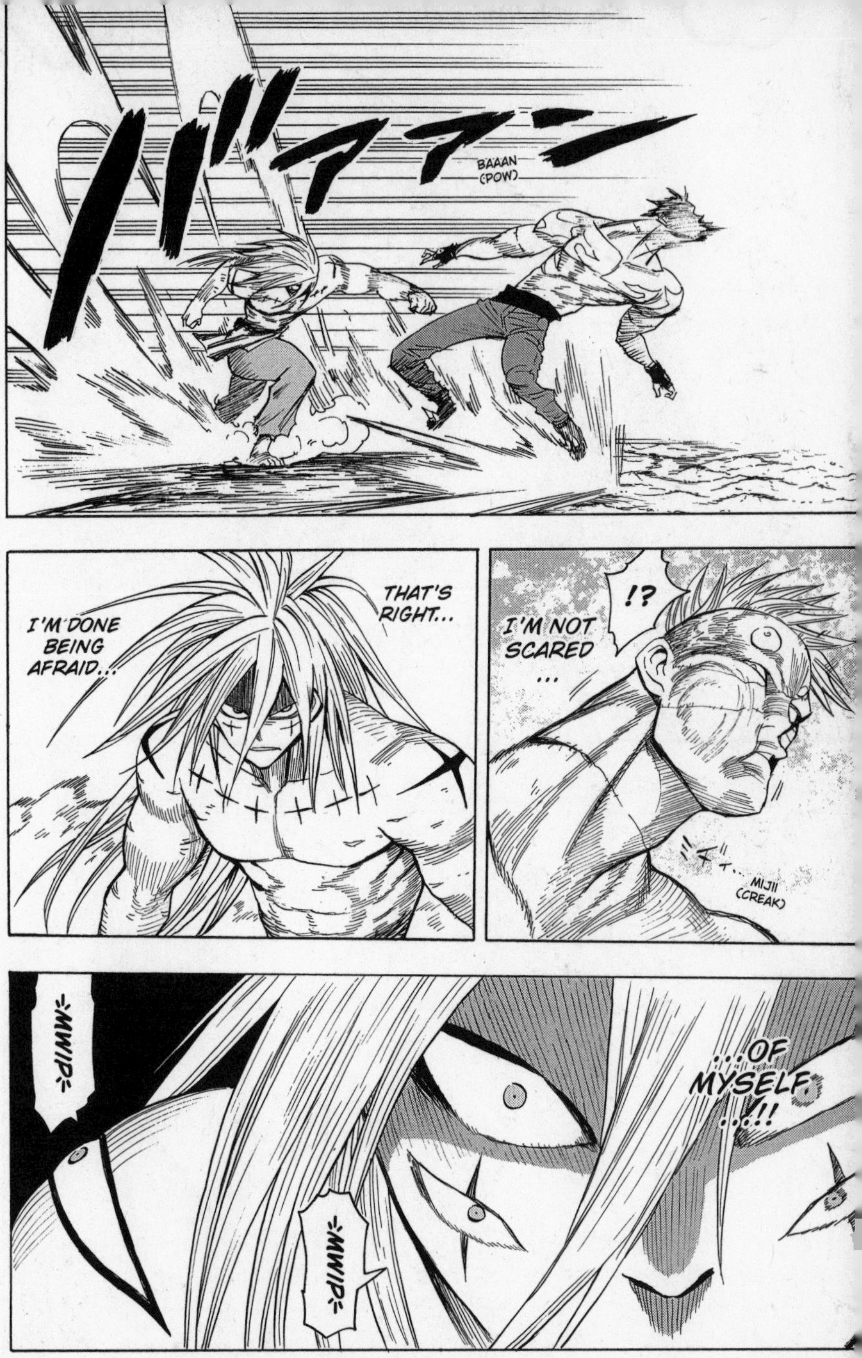
BAAAN (POW)
!?
I'M NOT SCARED ...
MIJII (CREAK)
THAT'S RIGHT...
I'M DONE BEING AFRAID...
...OF MYSELF ...!!
MWIP
MWIP

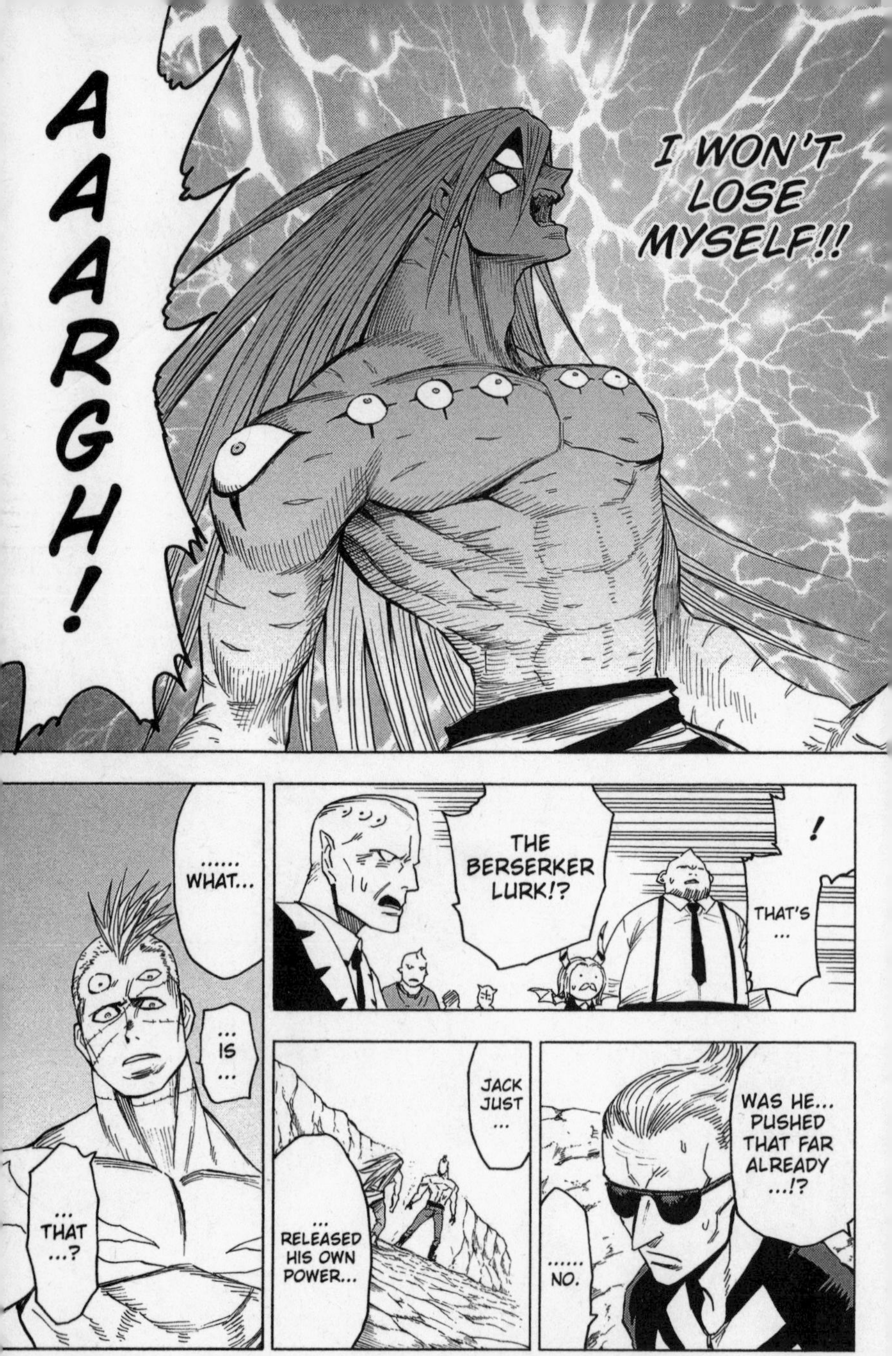
I WON'T LOSE MYSELF!!
AAAARGH!
!
THAT'S ...
THE BERSERKER LURK!?
WAS HE... PUSHED THAT FAR ALREADY ...!?
...... NO.
JACK JUST ...
... RELEASED HIS OWN POWER...
...... WHAT...
... IS ...
... THAT ...?

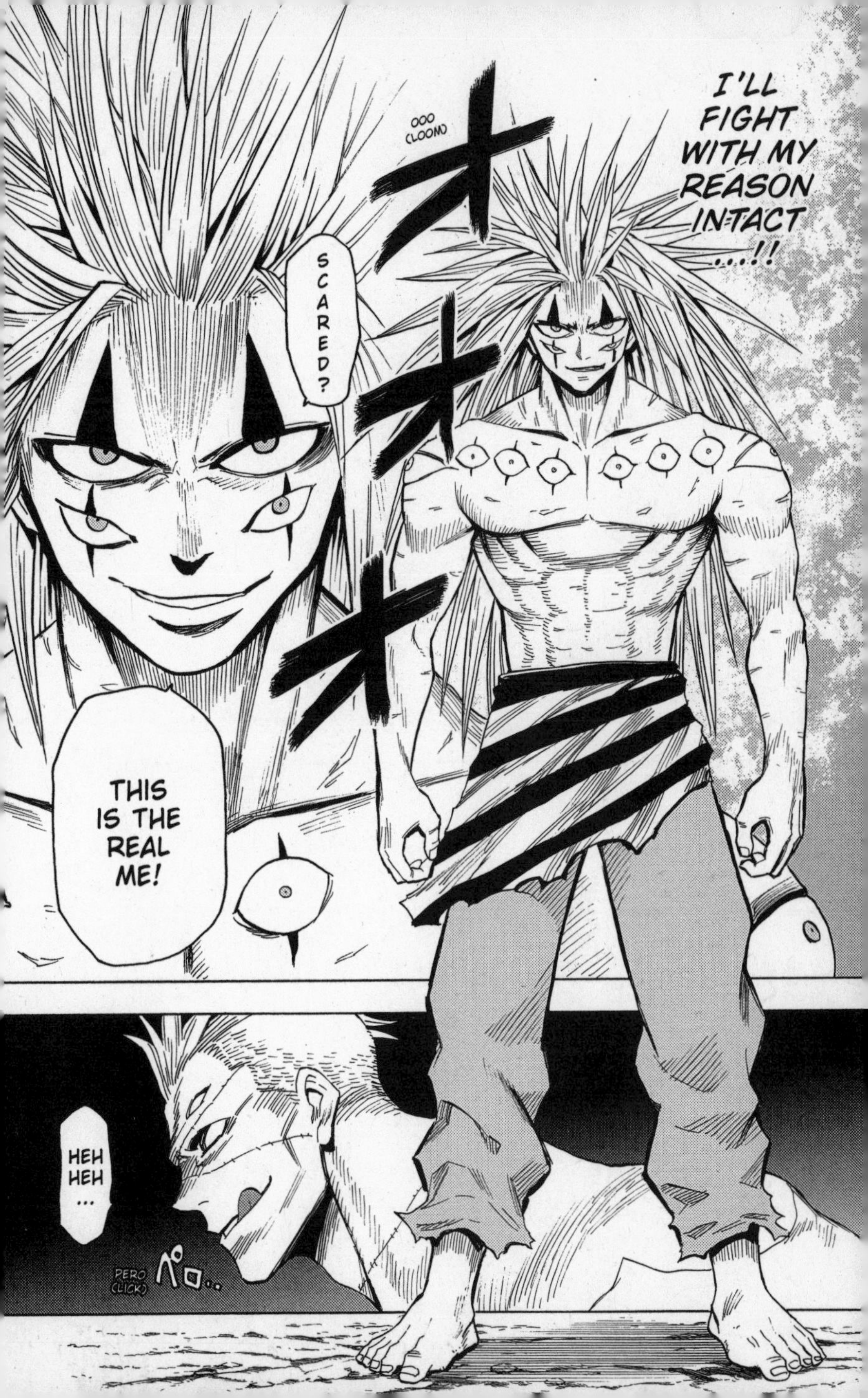
I'LL FIGHT WITH MY REASON INTACT ...!!
OOO (LOOM)
SCARED?
THIS IS THE REAL ME!
HEH HEH ...
PERO (CLICK)

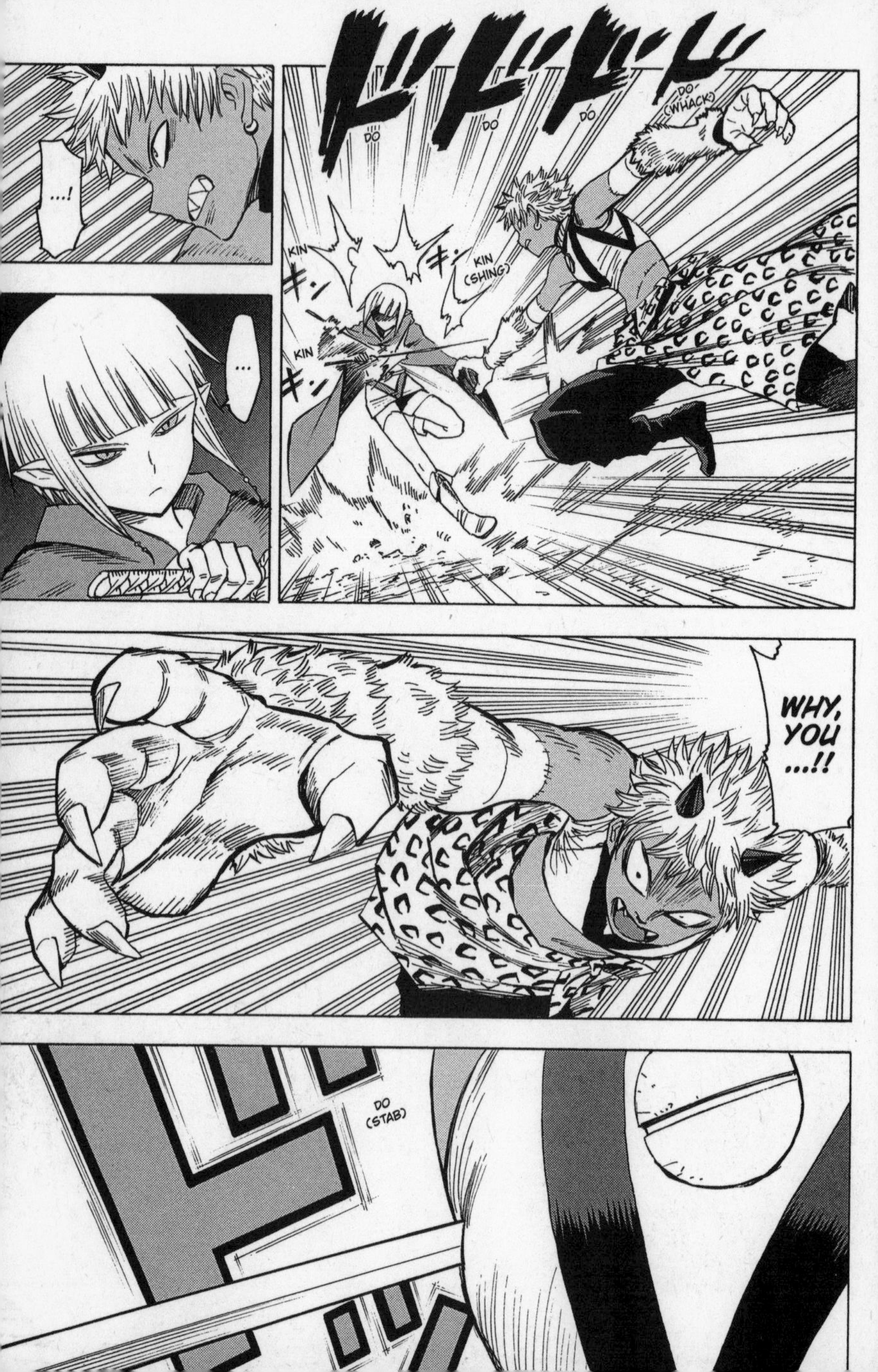

DO (WHACK)
DO
DO
DO
KIN (SHING)
KIN
KIN
...!
...
WHY, YOU ...!!
DO (STAB)

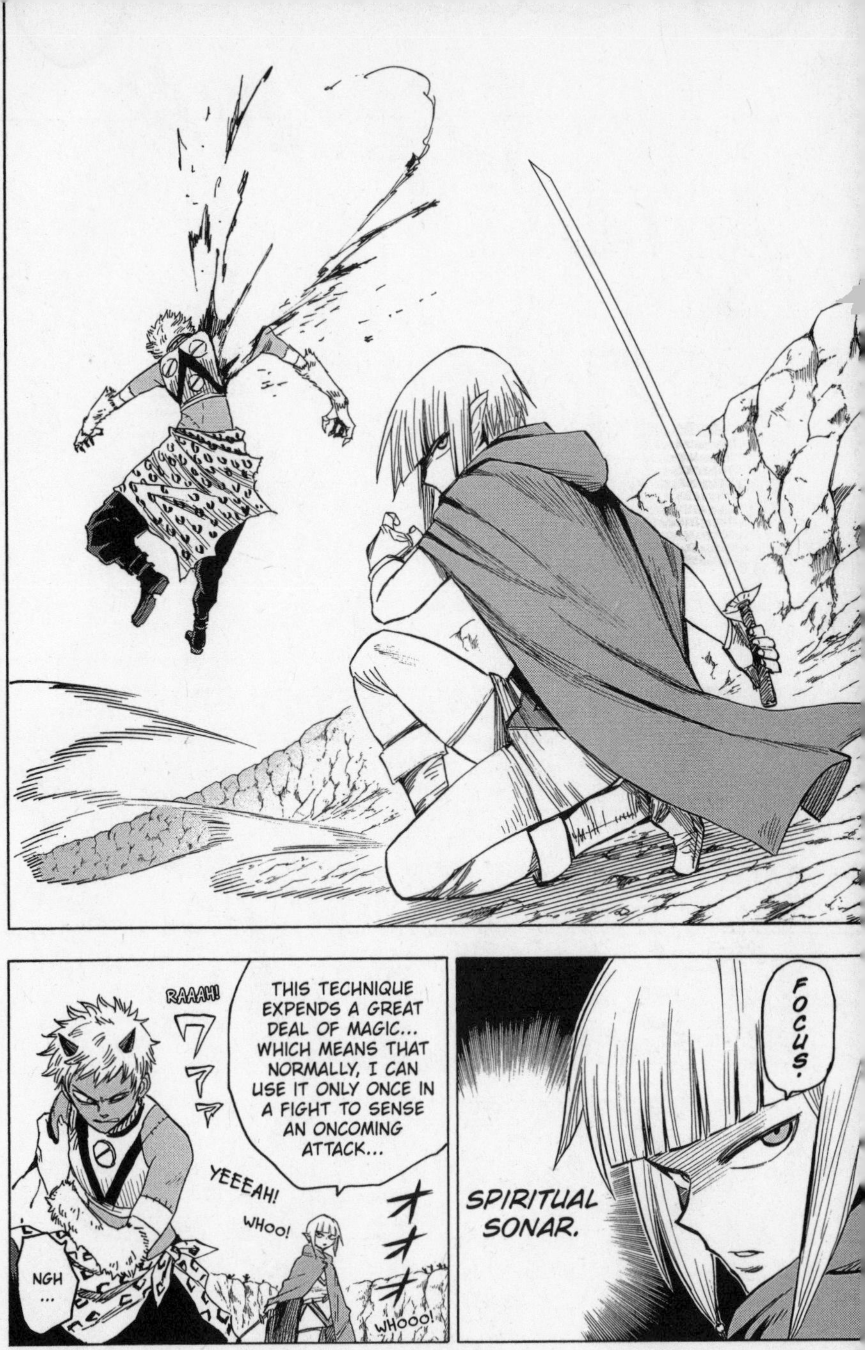
FOCUS.
SPIRITUAL SONAR.
THIS TECHNIQUE EXPENDS A GREAT DEAL OF MAGIC... WHICH MEANS THAT NORMALLY, I CAN USE IT ONLY ONCE IN A FIGHT TO SENSE AN ONCOMING ATTACK...
RAAAH!
YEEEAH!
WHOO!
WHOOO!
NGH ...

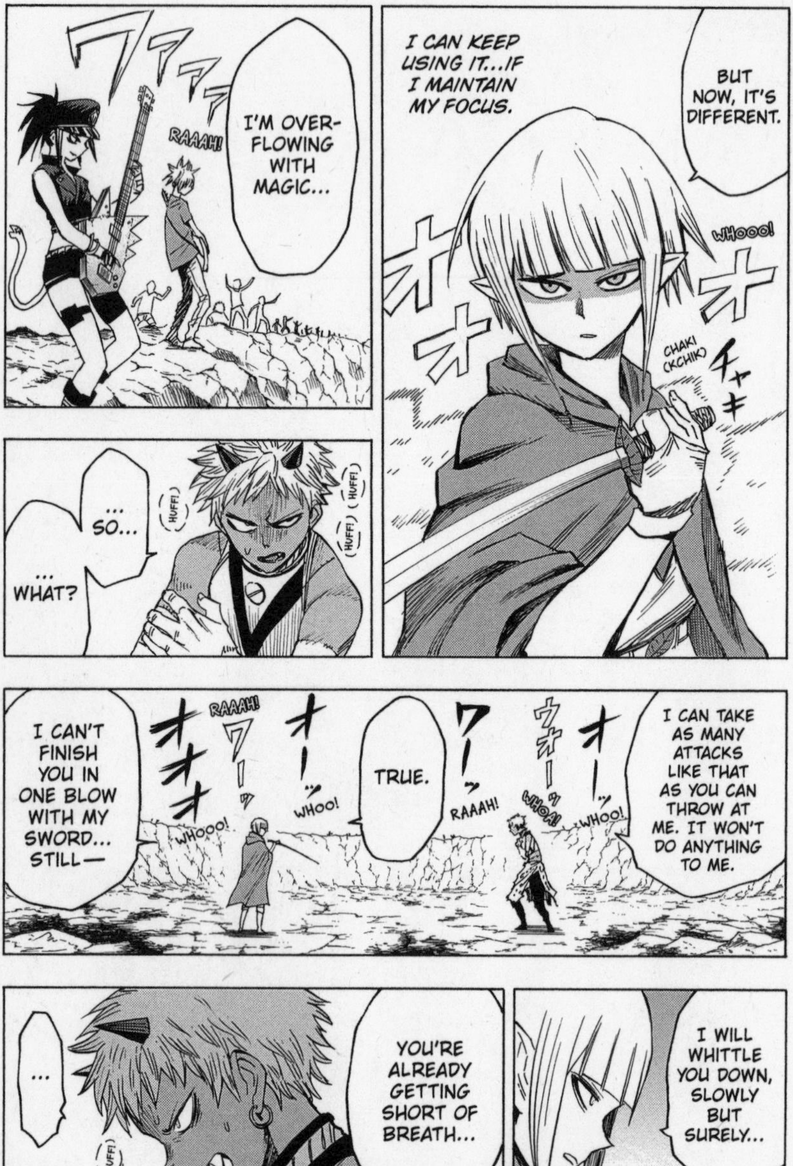
BUT NOW, IT'S DIFFERENT.
I CAN KEEP USING IT...IF I MAINTAIN MY FOCUS.
WHOOO!
CHAKI (KCHIK)
I'M OVER-FLOWING WITH MAGIC...
RAAAH!
(HUFF!) (HUFF!)
(HUFF!)
... SO...
... WHAT?
I CAN TAKE AS MANY ATTACKS LIKE THAT AS YOU CAN THROW AT ME. IT WON'T DO ANYTHING TO ME.
WHOO!
WHOA!
RAAAH!
TRUE.
WHOO!
RAAAH!
WHOOO!
I CAN'T FINISH YOU IN ONE BLOW WITH MY SWORD... STILL—
I WILL WHITTLE YOU DOWN, SLOWLY BUT SURELY...
YOU'RE ALREADY GETTING SHORT OF BREATH...
...
(HUFF!)
(HUFF!)
GIRI (GRIT)

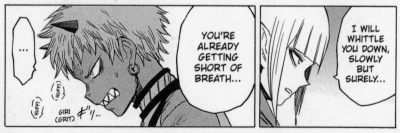

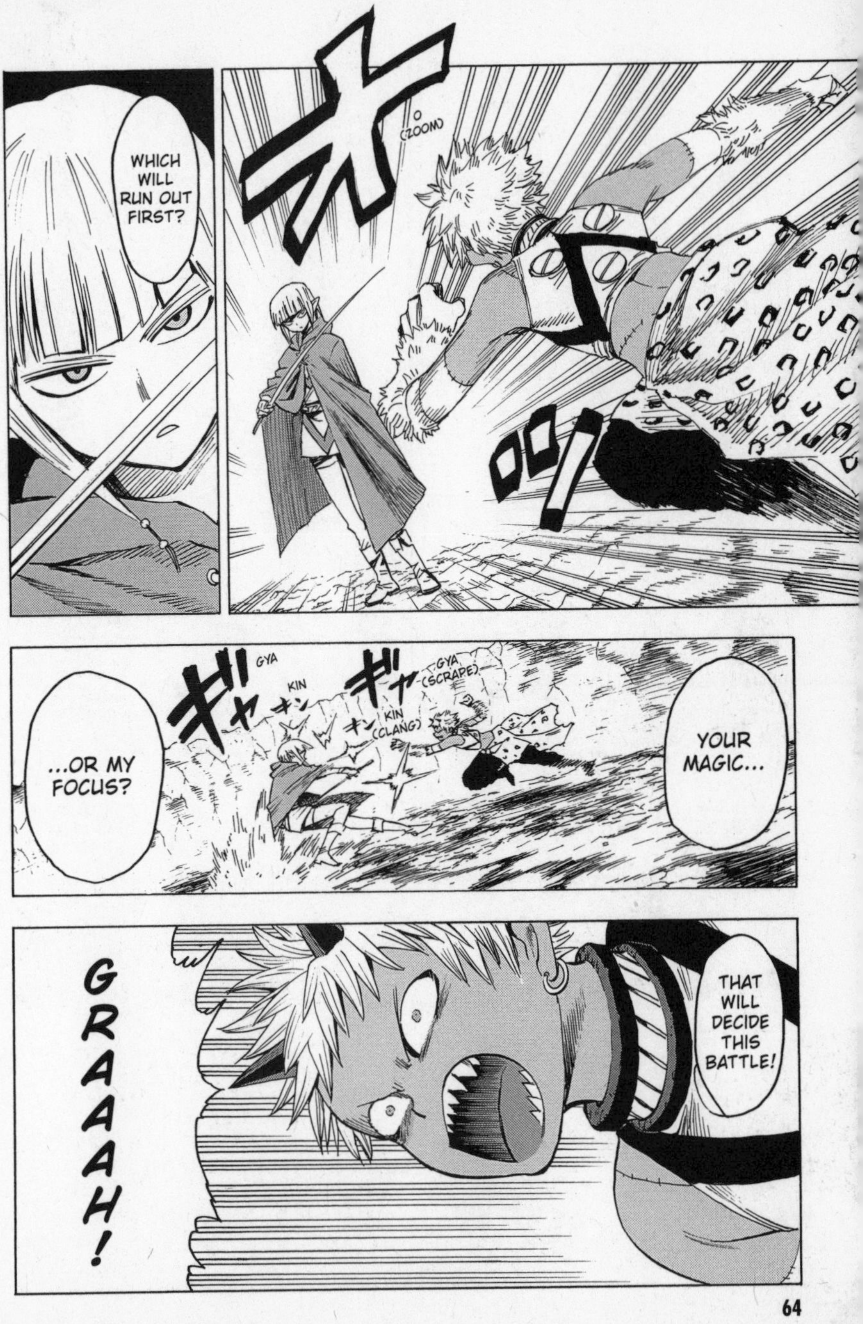
O (ZOOM)
WHICH WILL RUN OUT FIRST?
YOUR MAGIC...
GYA (SCRAPE)
KIN (CLANG)
GYA
KIN
...OR MY FOCUS?
THAT WILL DECIDE THIS BATTLE!
GRAAAH!

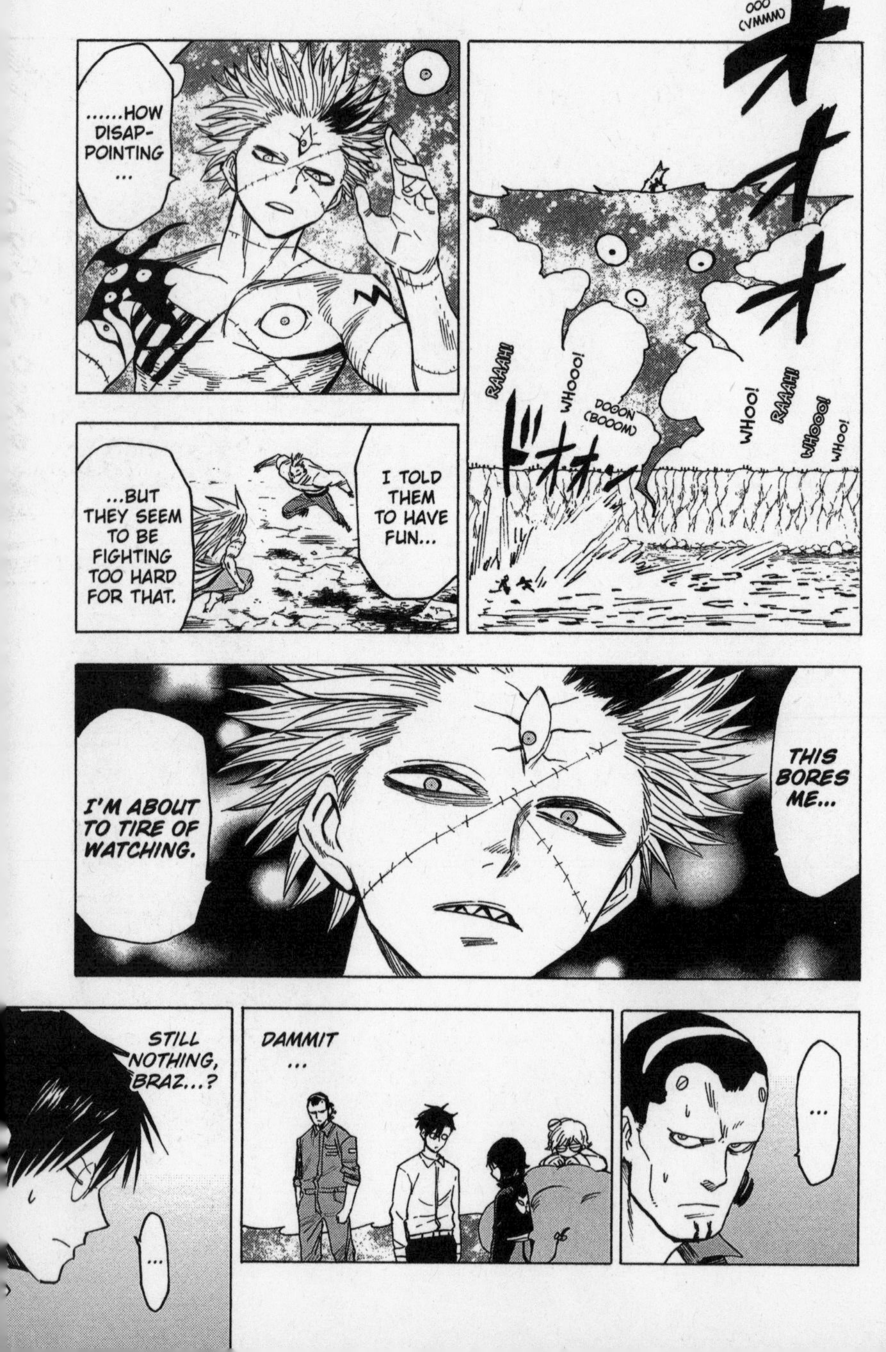

OOO (VMMM)
RAAAH!
WHOO!
DOOON (BOOOM)
WHOO!
RAAAH!
WHOOO!
WHOO!
......HOW DISAP-POINTING ...
I TOLD THEM TO HAVE FUN...
...BUT THEY SEEM TO BE FIGHTING TOO HARD FOR THAT.
THIS BORES ME...
I'M ABOUT TO TIRE OF WATCHING.
...
DAMMIT ...
STILL NOTHING, BRAZ...?
...

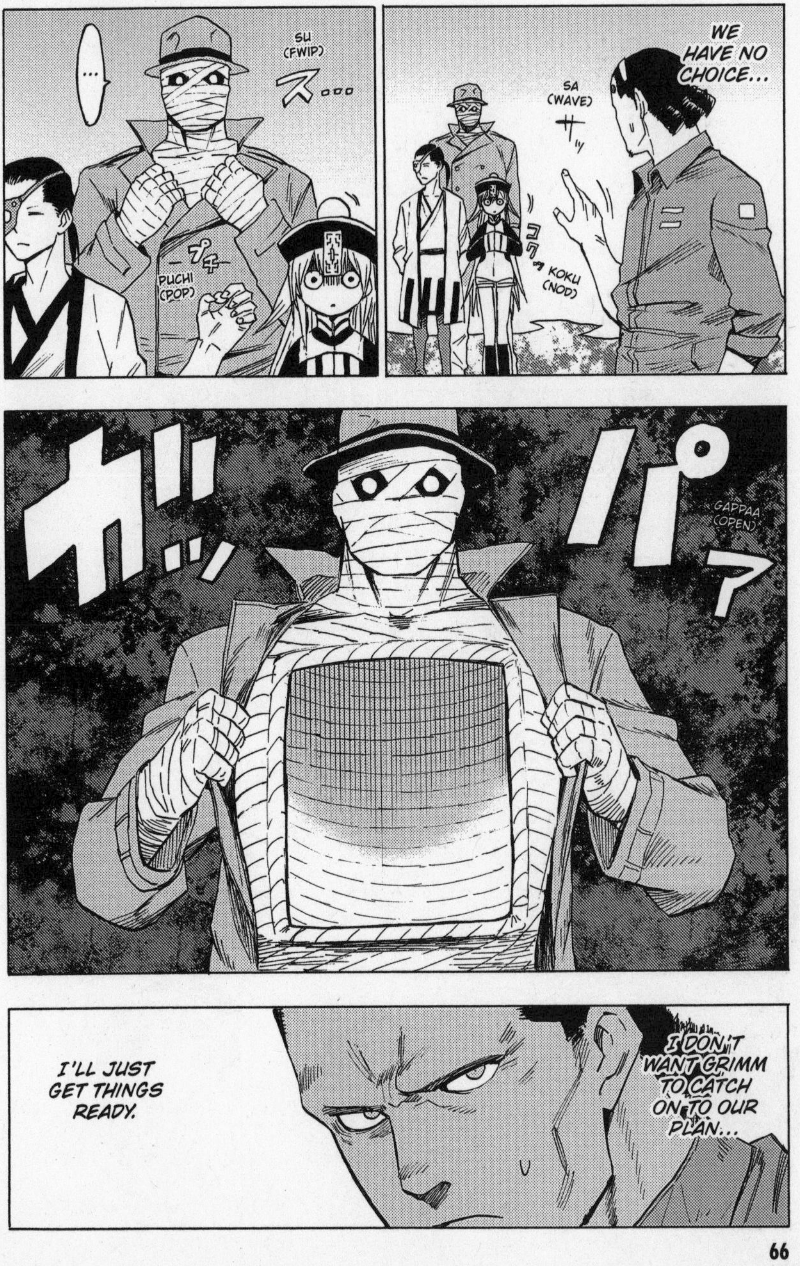
WE HAVE NO CHOICE...
SA (WAVE)
KOKU (NOD)
...
SU (FWIP)
PUCHI (POP)
GAPPAA (OPEN)
I DON'T WANT GRIMM TO CATCH ON TO OUR PLAN...
I'LL JUST GET THINGS READY.

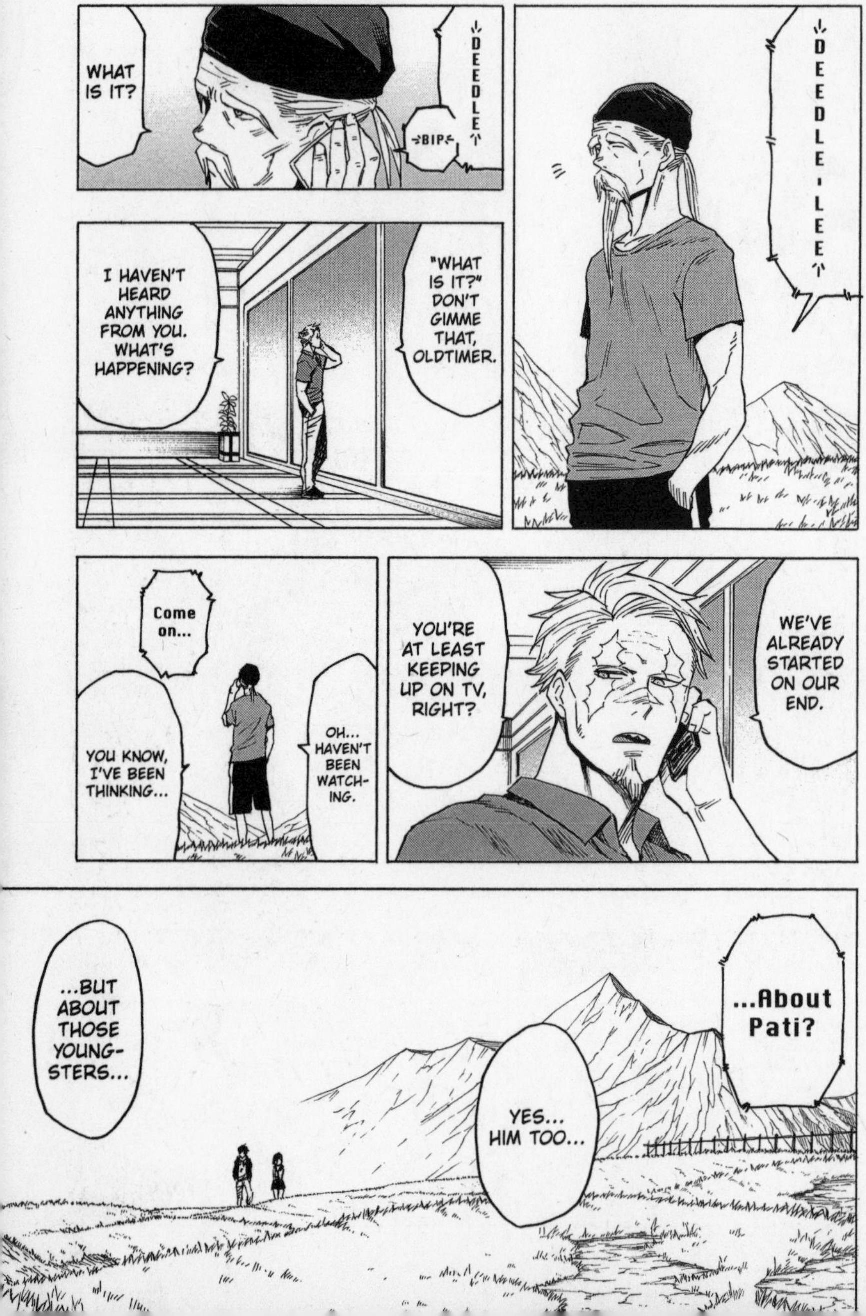
DEEDLE-LEE
DEEDLE
BIP
WHAT IS IT?
"WHAT IS IT?" DON'T GIMME THAT, OLDTIMER.
I HAVEN'T HEARD ANYTHING FROM YOU. WHAT'S HAPPENING?
WE'VE ALREADY STARTED ON OUR END.
YOU'RE AT LEAST KEEPING UP ON TV, RIGHT?
OH... HAVEN'T BEEN WATCHING.
Come on...
YOU KNOW, I'VE BEEN THINKING...
...About Pati?
YES... HIM TOO...
...BUT ABOUT THOSE YOUNGSTERS...

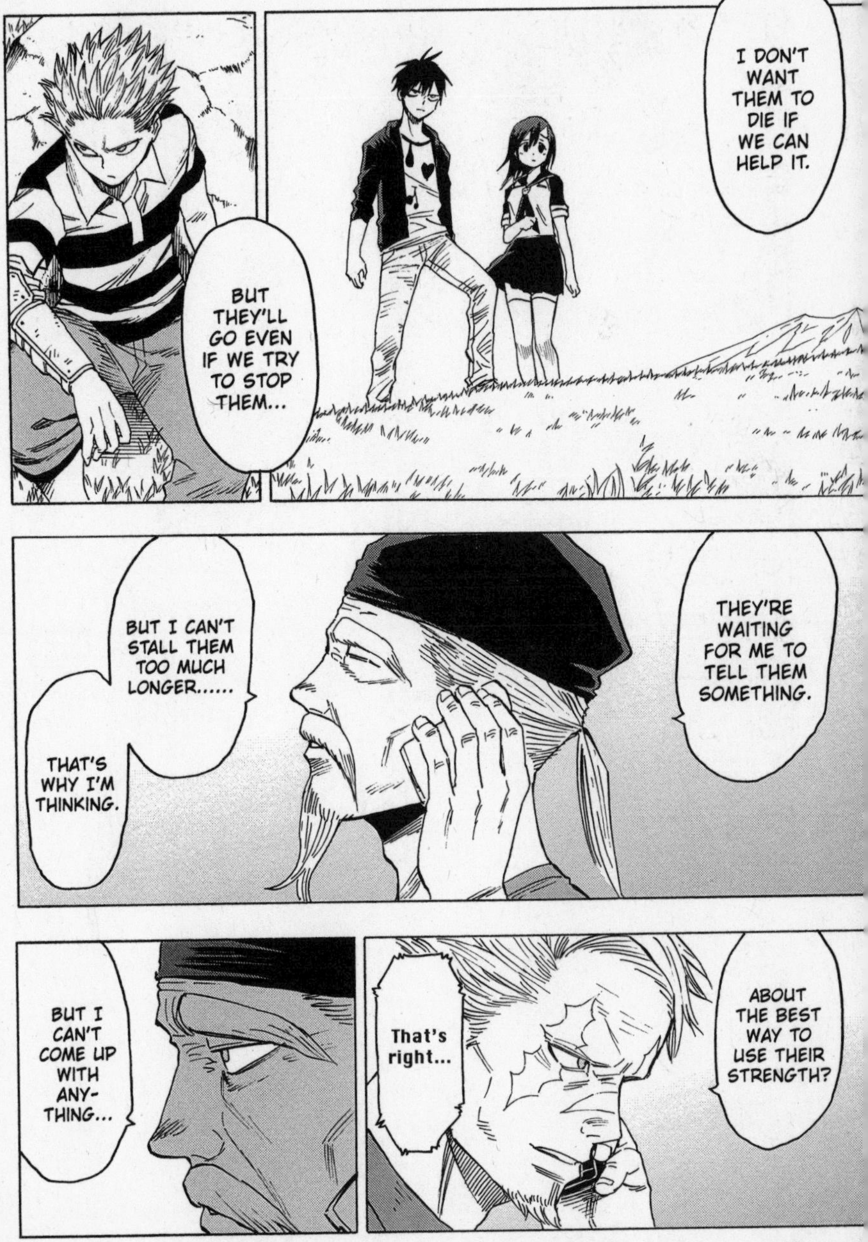
I DON'T WANT THEM TO DIE IF WE CAN HELP IT.
BUT THEY'LL GO EVEN IF WE TRY TO STOP THEM...
THEY'RE WAITING FOR ME TO TELL THEM SOMETHING.
BUT I CAN'T STALL THEM TOO MUCH LONGER......
THAT'S WHY I'M THINKING.
ABOUT THE BEST WAY TO USE THEIR STRENGTH?
That's right...
BUT I CAN'T COME UP WITH ANY-THING...

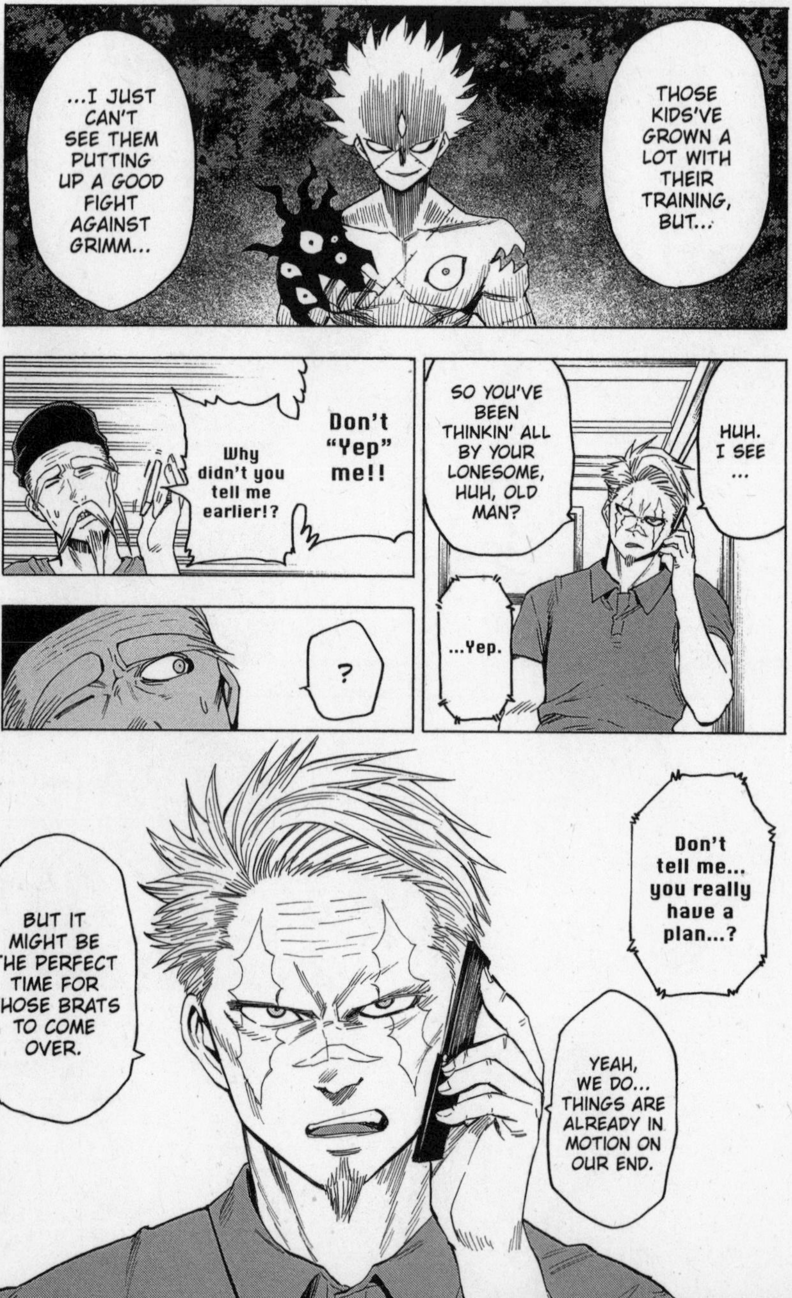
THOSE KIDS'VE GROWN A LOT WITH THEIR TRAINING, BUT...
...I JUST CAN'T SEE THEM PUTTING UP A GOOD FIGHT AGAINST GRIMM...
HUH. I SEE ...
SO YOU'VE BEEN THINKIN' ALL BY YOUR LONESOME, HUH, OLD MAN?
...Yep.
Don't "Yep" me!!
Why didn't you tell me earlier!?
?
Don't tell me... you really have a plan...?
YEAH, WE DO... THINGS ARE ALREADY IN MOTION ON OUR END.
BUT IT MIGHT BE THE PERFECT TIME FOR THOSE BRATS TO COME OVER.

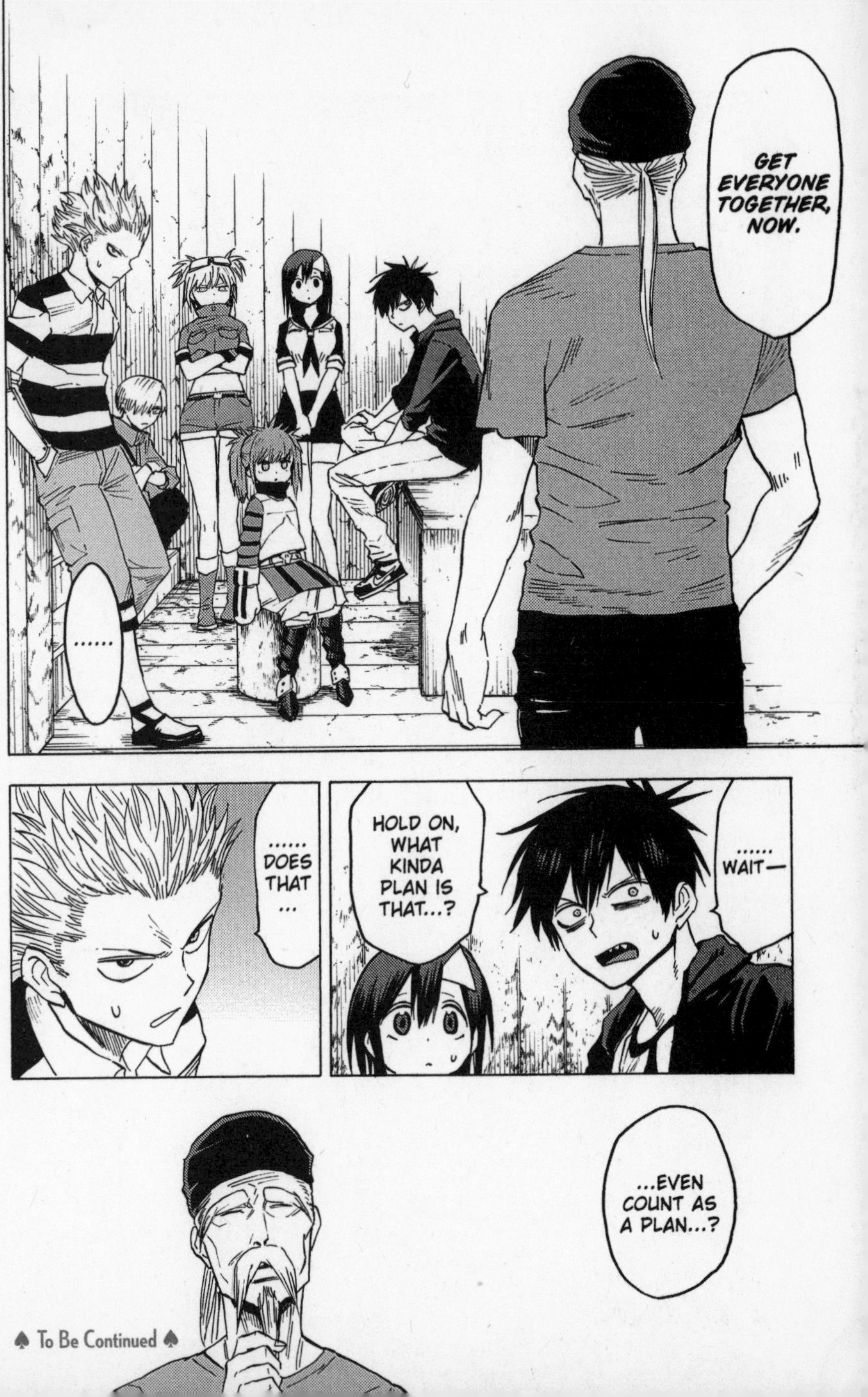
GET EVERYONE TOGETHER, NOW.
......
......WAIT—
HOLD ON, WHAT KINDA PLAN IS THAT...?
......DOES THAT ...
...EVEN COUNT AS A PLAN...?
♠ To Be Continued ♠

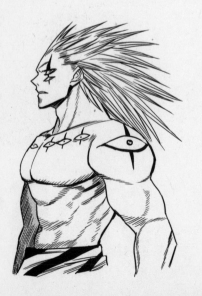

BLOOD LAD

# CHAPTER 73 ♠ "DEAD" IT BE

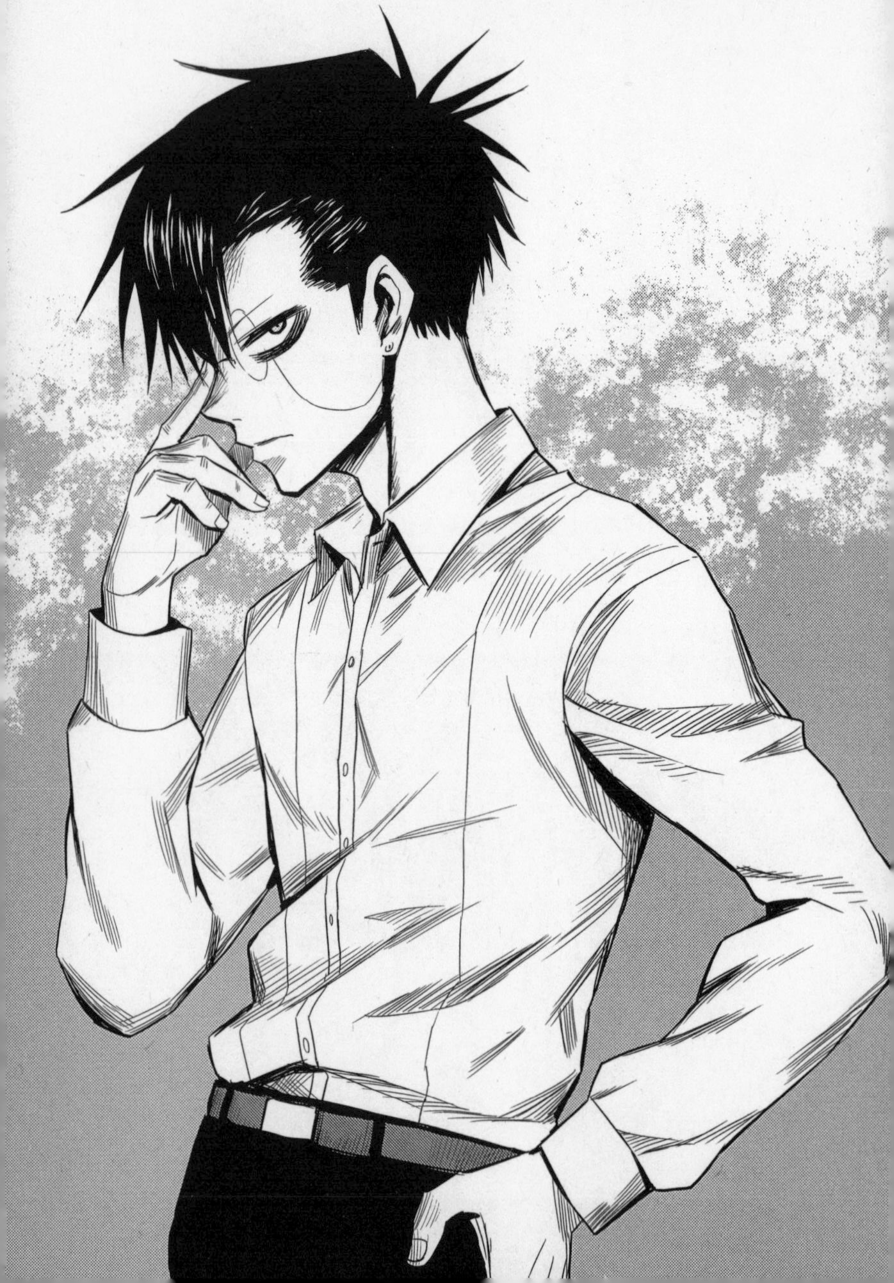

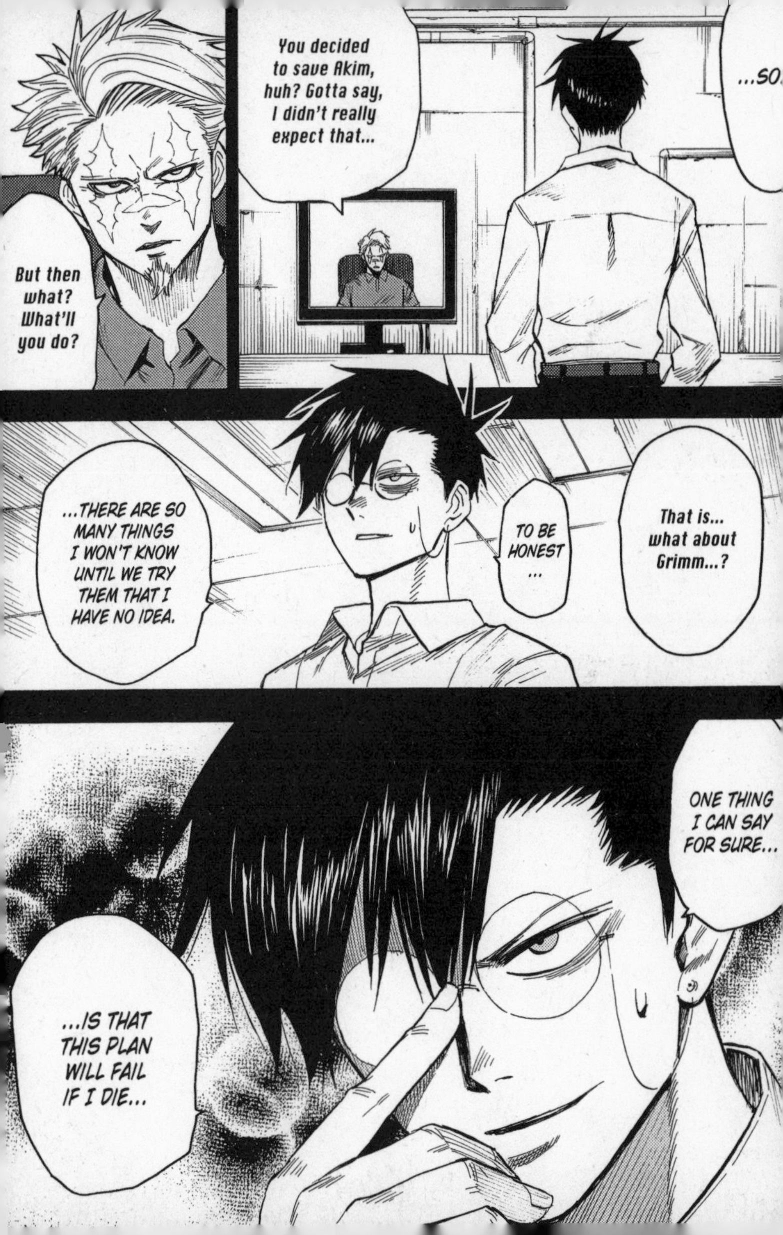
...SO
You decided to save Akim, huh? Gotta say, I didn't really expect that...
But then what? What'll you do?
That is... what about Grimm...?
TO BE HONEST ...
...THERE ARE SO MANY THINGS I WON'T KNOW UNTIL WE TRY THEM THAT I HAVE NO IDEA.
ONE THING I CAN SAY FOR SURE...
...IS THAT THIS PLAN WILL FAIL IF I DIE...

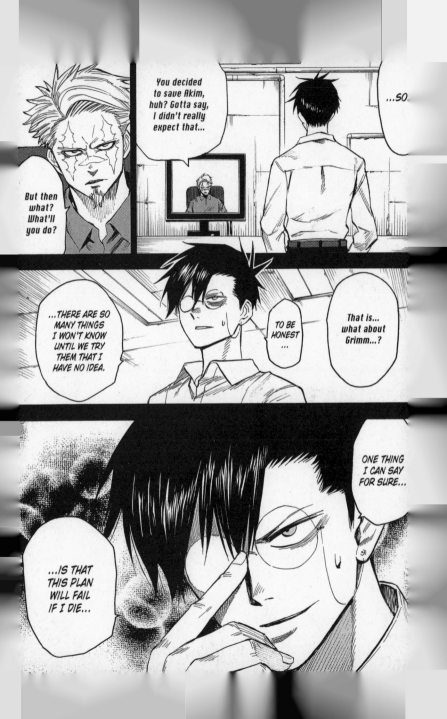

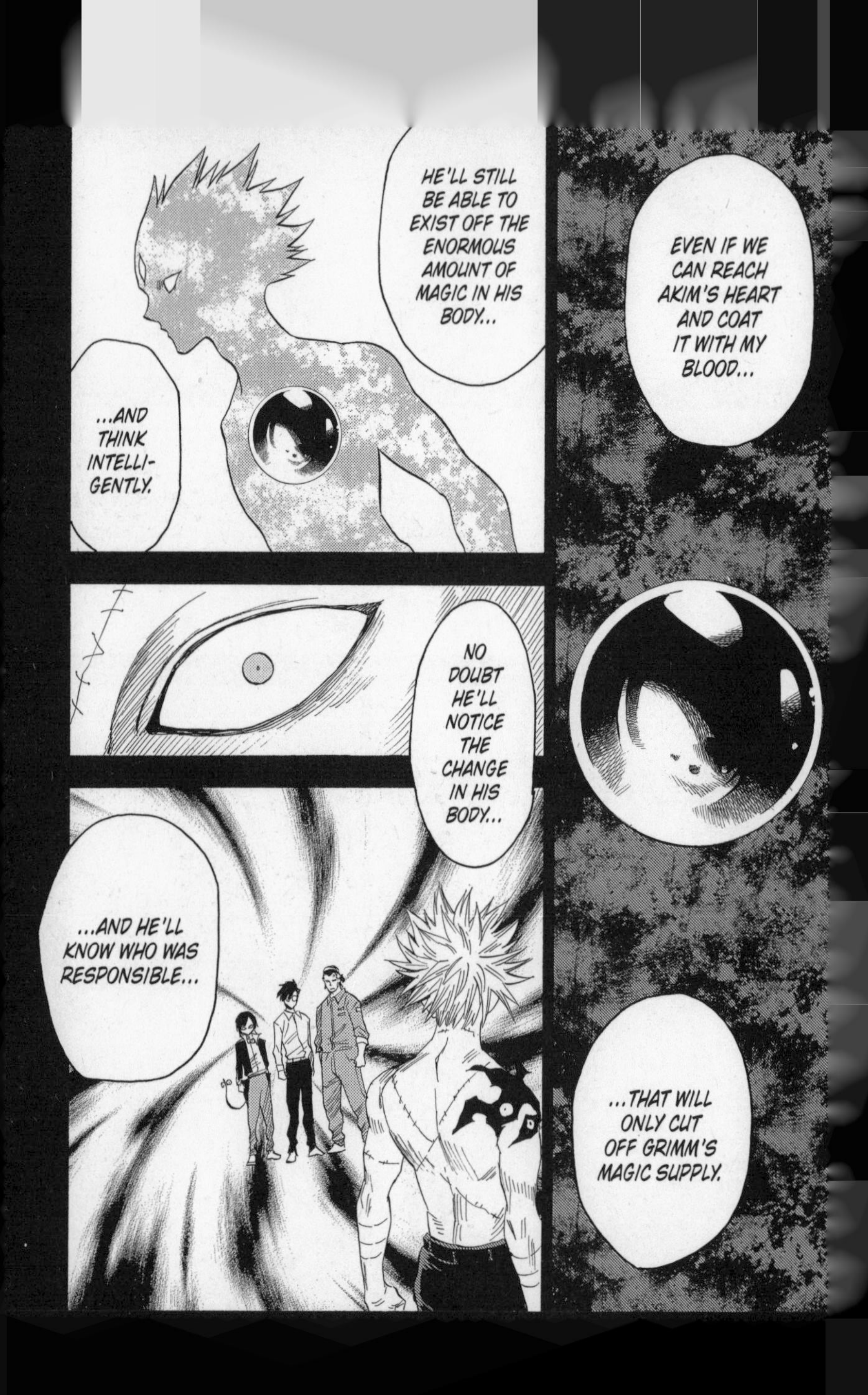
EVEN IF WE CAN REACH AKIM'S HEART AND COAT IT WITH MY BLOOD...
...THAT WILL ONLY CUT OFF GRIMM'S MAGIC SUPPLY.
HE'LL STILL BE ABLE TO EXIST OFF THE ENORMOUS AMOUNT OF MAGIC IN HIS BODY...
...AND THINK INTELLI-GENTLY.
NO DOUBT HE'LL NOTICE THE CHANGE IN HIS BODY...
...AND HE'LL KNOW WHO WAS RESPONSIBLE...

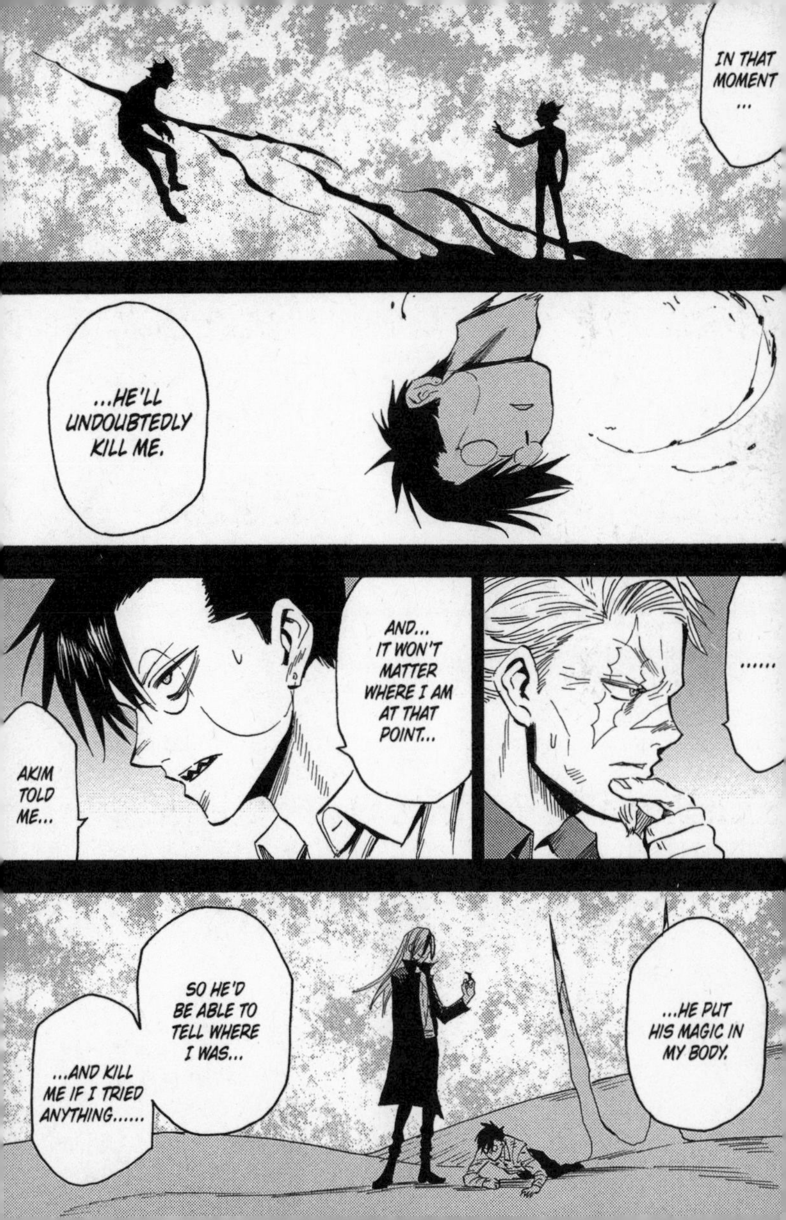
IN THAT MOMENT ...
...HE'LL UNDOUBTEDLY KILL ME.
......
AND... IT WON'T MATTER WHERE I AM AT THAT POINT...
AKIM TOLD ME...
...HE PUT HIS MAGIC IN MY BODY.
SO HE'D BE ABLE TO TELL WHERE I WAS...
...AND KILL ME IF I TRIED ANYTHING......

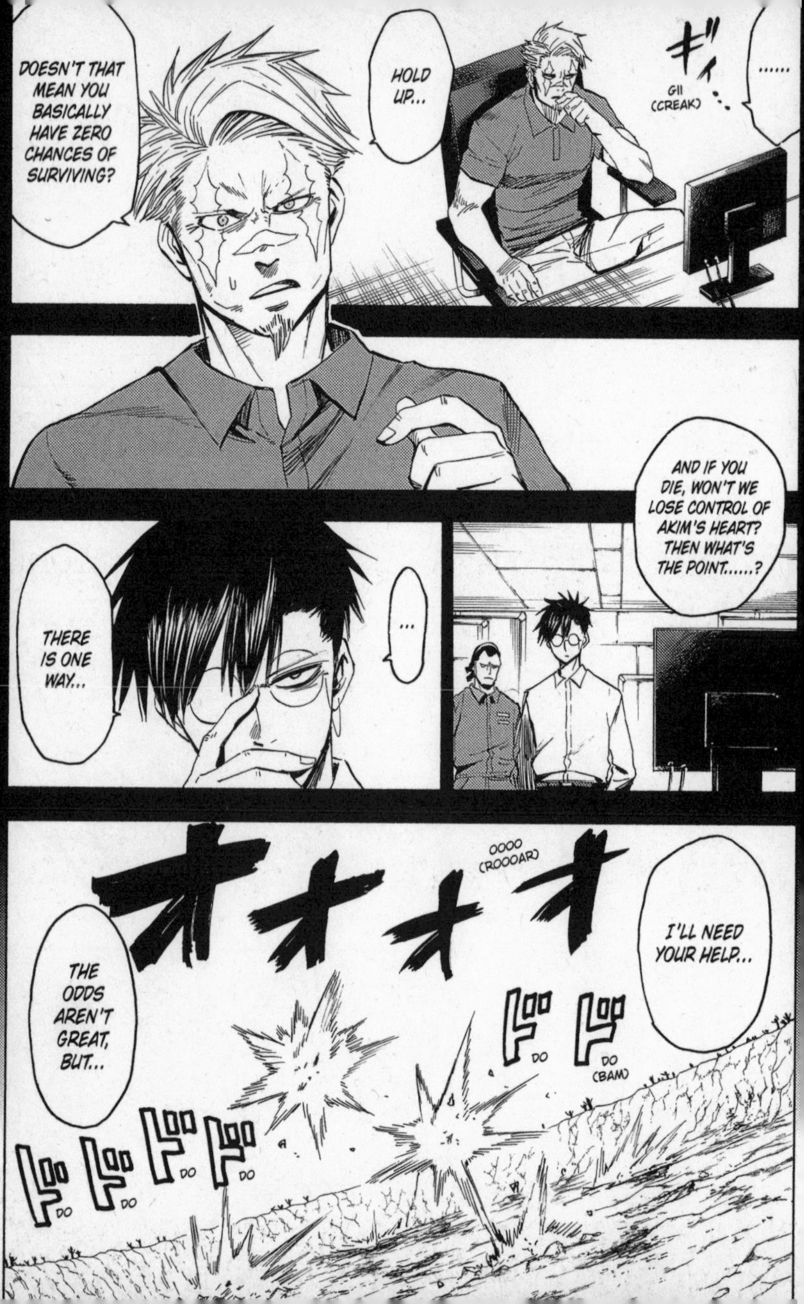

......
ギィ GII (CREAK)
HOLD UP...
DOESN'T THAT MEAN YOU BASICALLY HAVE ZERO CHANCES OF SURVIVING?
AND IF YOU DIE, WON'T WE LOSE CONTROL OF AKIM'S HEART? THEN WHAT'S THE POINT......?
...
THERE IS ONE WAY...
I'LL NEED YOUR HELP...
ド DO
ド DO (BAM)
オオオオ OOOO (ROOOAR)
THE ODDS AREN'T GREAT, BUT...
ド DO
ド DO
ド DO
ド DO

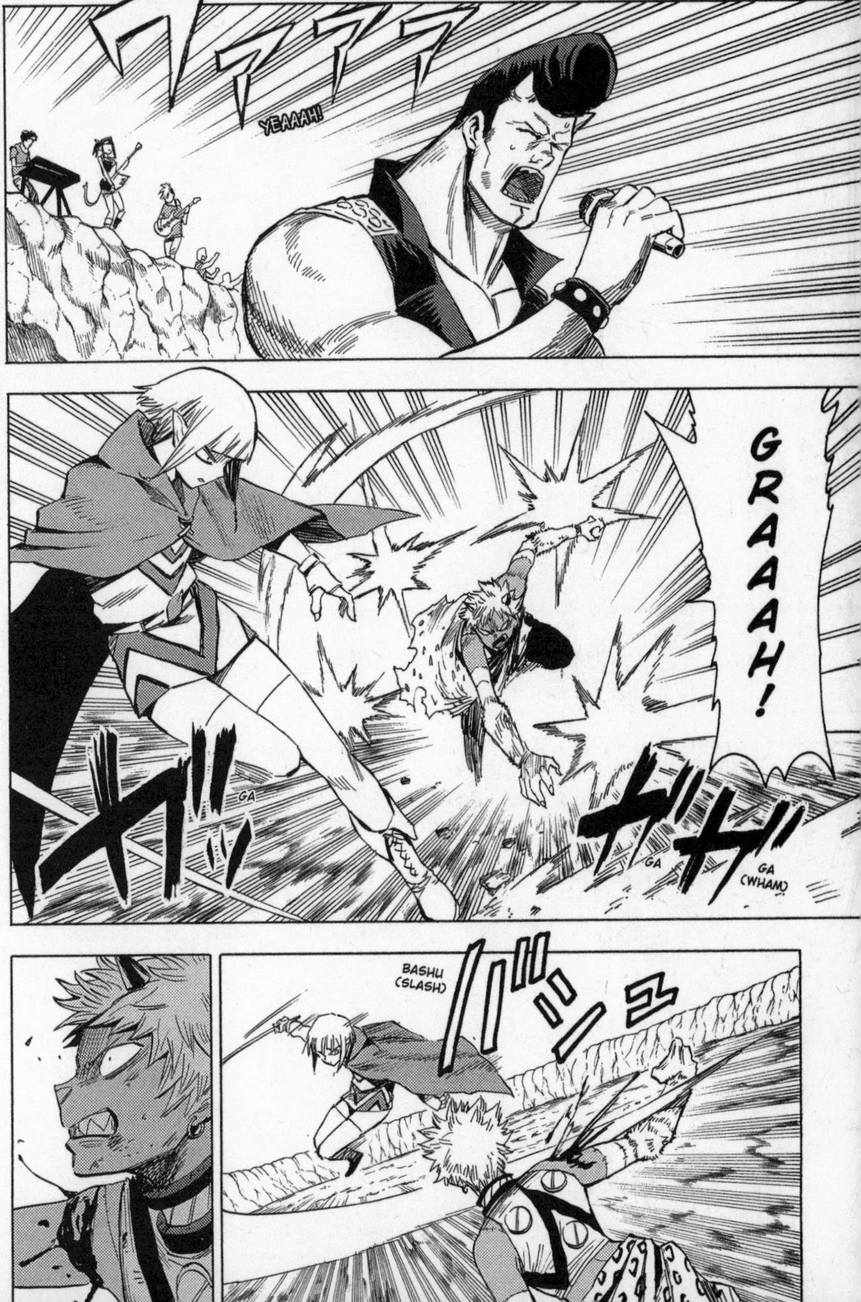
YEAAAH!
GRAAAAH!
GA
(WHAM)
GA
GA
BASHU
(SLASH)

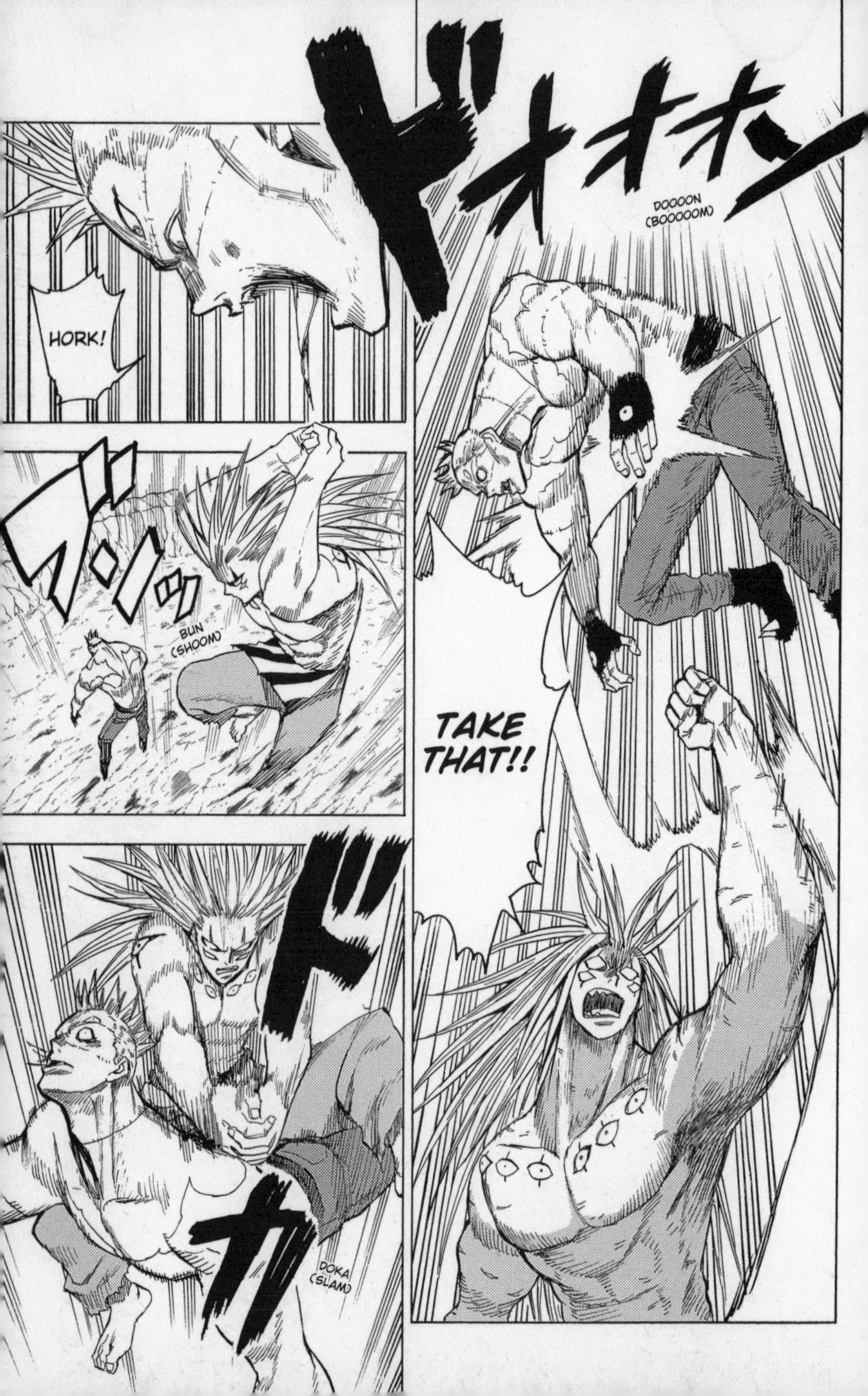
ドオオン
DOOOON
(BOOOOOM)
TAKE THAT!!
HORK!
BUN
(SHOOM)
ドガ
DOKA
(SLAM)

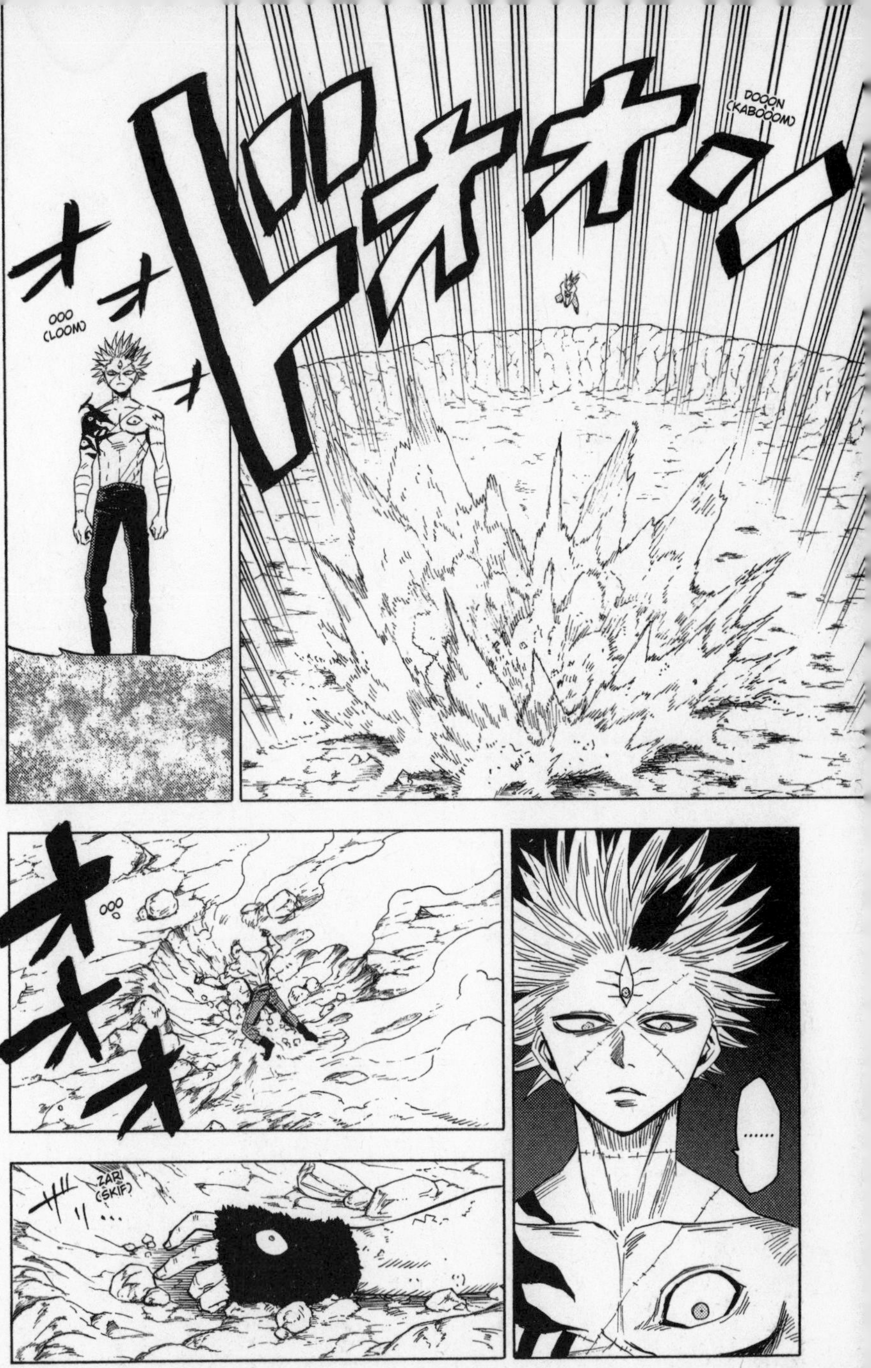
ドオオン
DOOON (KABOOOM)
オオオ
OOO (LOOM)
……
オオオ
OOO
ザリ…
ZARI (SKIF)

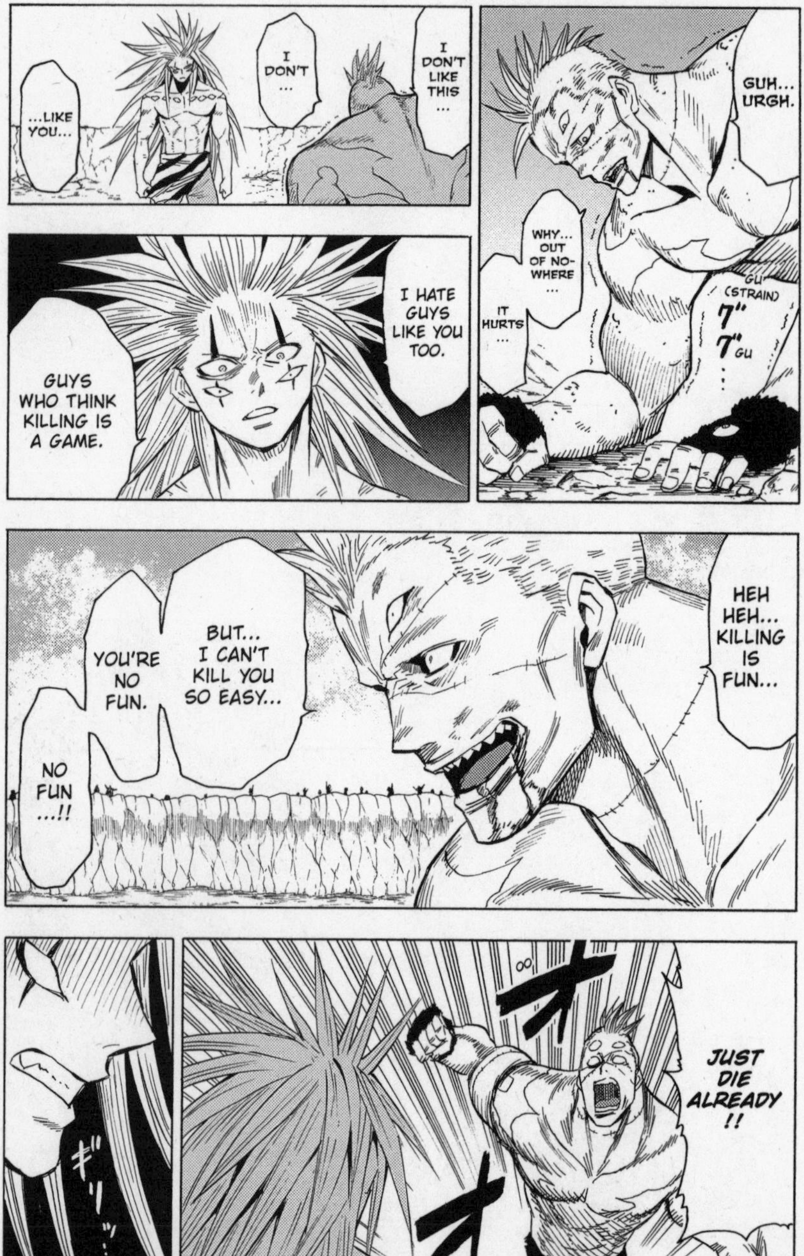
GUH... URGH.
WHY... OUT OF NO-WHERE...
IT HURTS...
GU (STRAIN)
GU...
I DON'T LIKE THIS...
I DON'T...
...LIKE YOU...
I HATE GUYS LIKE YOU TOO.
GUYS WHO THINK KILLING IS A GAME.
HEH HEH... KILLING IS FUN...
BUT... I CAN'T KILL YOU SO EASY...
YOU'RE NO FUN.
NO FUN...!!
JUST DIE ALREADY!!
GIRI (GRIT)

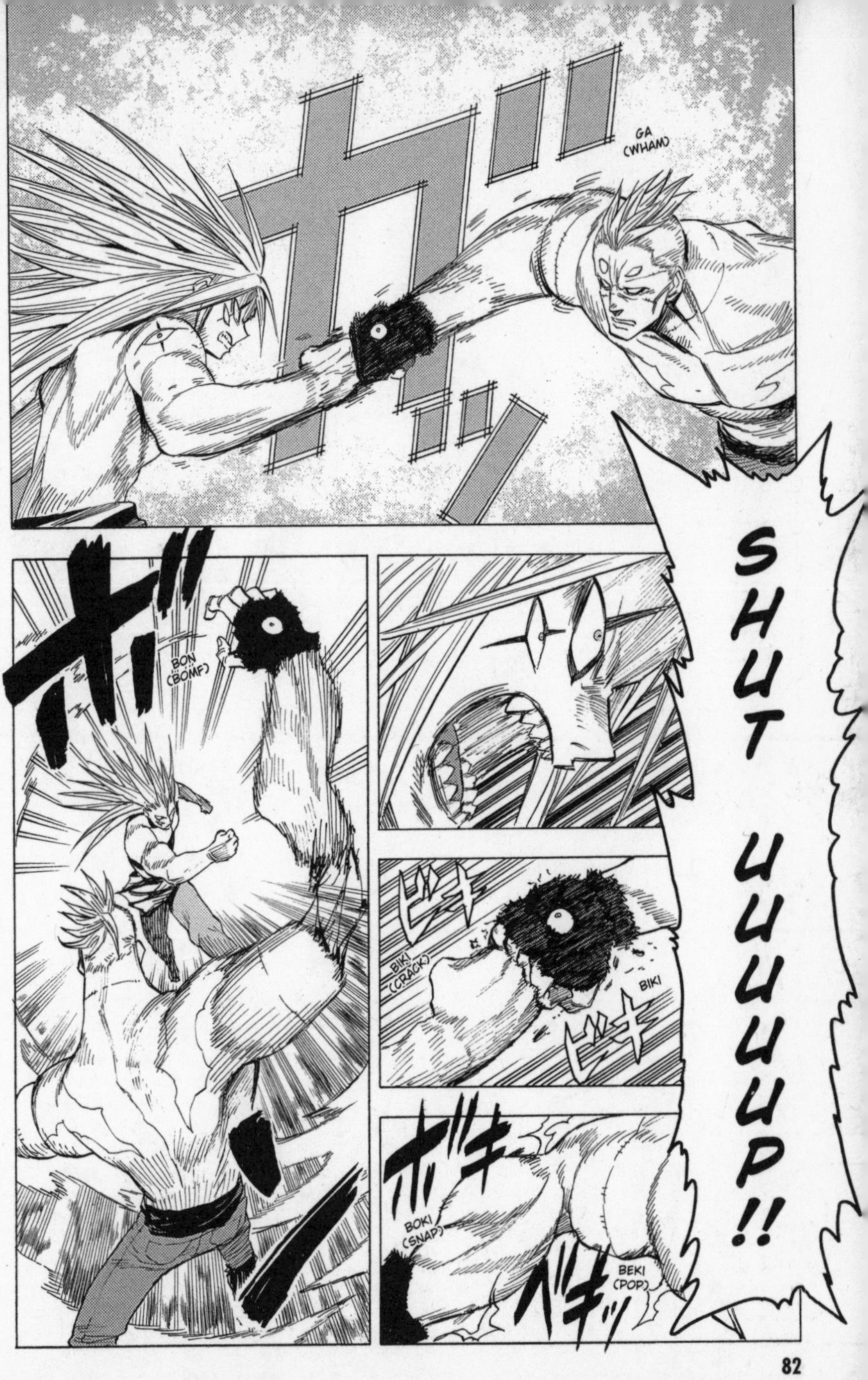

GA (WHAM)
SHUT UUUUUP!!
BIKI (CRACK)
BIKI
BOKI (SNAP)
BEKI (POP)
BON (BOMF)

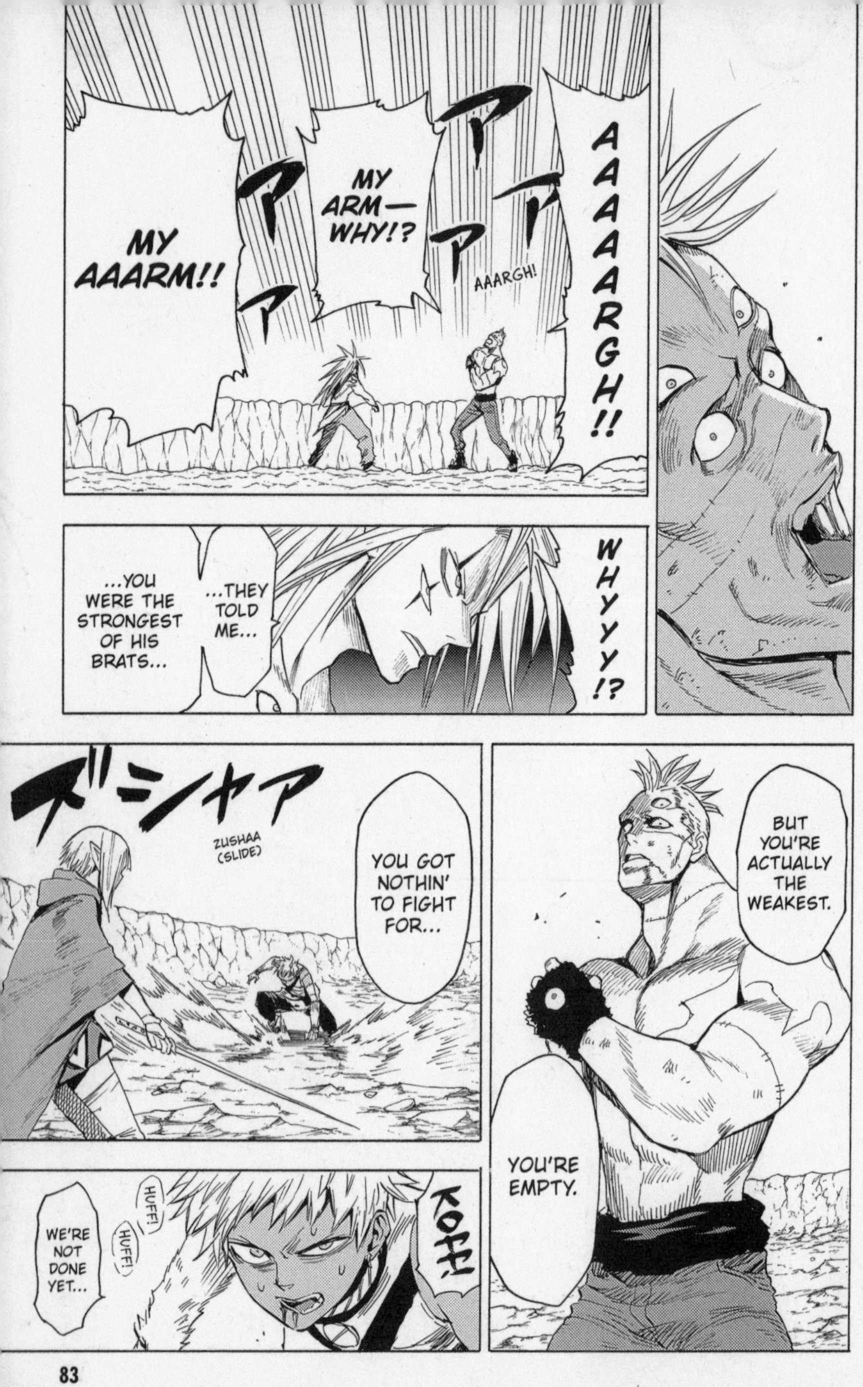
AAAAAARGH!!
WHYYYY!?
MY ARM—WHY!?
AAARGH!
MY AAARM!!
...THEY TOLD ME...
...YOU WERE THE STRONGEST OF HIS BRATS...
BUT YOU'RE ACTUALLY THE WEAKEST.
YOU'RE EMPTY.
ズシャア
ZUSHAA (SLIDE)
YOU GOT NOTHIN' TO FIGHT FOR...
KOF!
HUFF!
HUFF!
WE'RE NOT DONE YET...

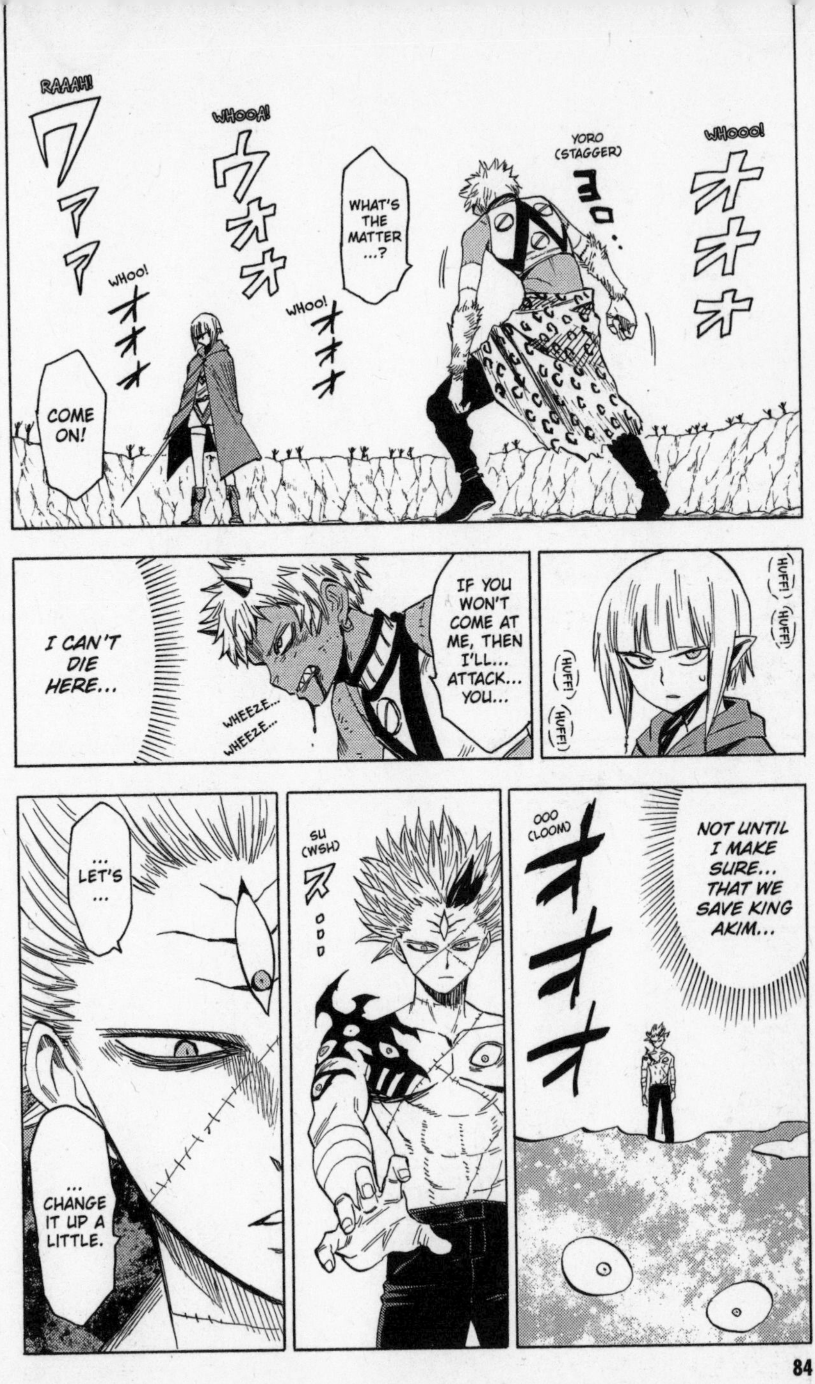
WHOOO!
オオオ
YORO (STAGGER)
ヨロ‥
WHAT'S THE MATTER ...?
WHOOA!
ウォォ
RAAAH!
ワァァ
WHOO!
オオオ
WHOO!
オオオ
COME ON!
HUFF!
HUFF!
HUFF!
HUFF!
IF YOU WON'T COME AT ME, THEN I'LL... ATTACK... YOU...
WHEEZE... WHEEZE...
I CAN'T DIE HERE...
NOT UNTIL I MAKE SURE... THAT WE SAVE KING AKIM...
OOO (LOOM)
オオオ
SU (WSH)
ス
... LET'S ...
... CHANGE IT UP A LITTLE.

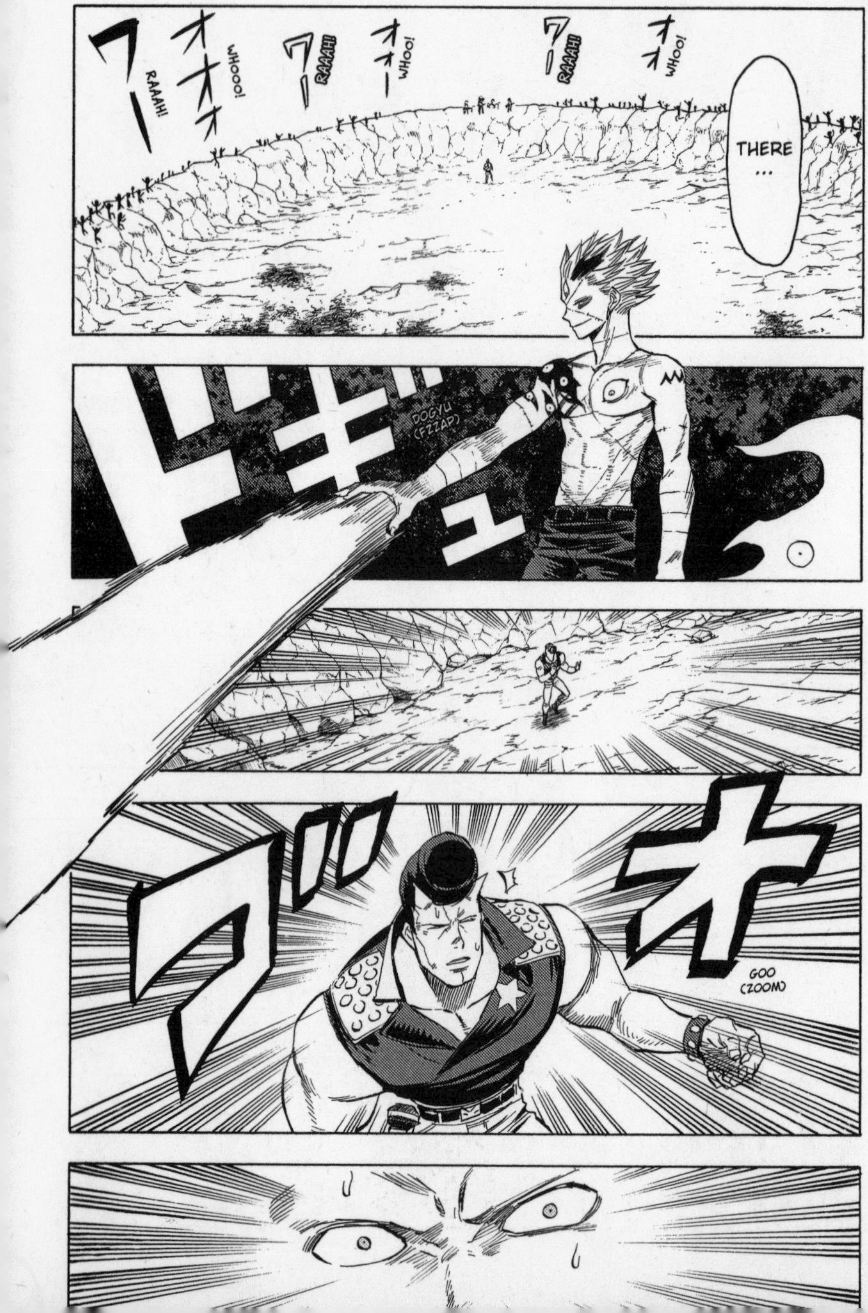
THERE ...
オオ
WHOO!
ワー
RAAAH!
オオー
WHOO!
ワー
RAAAH!
オオオ
WHOOO!
ワー
RAAAH!
ドギュ
DOGYU (FZZAP)
ゴオ
GOO (ZOOM)

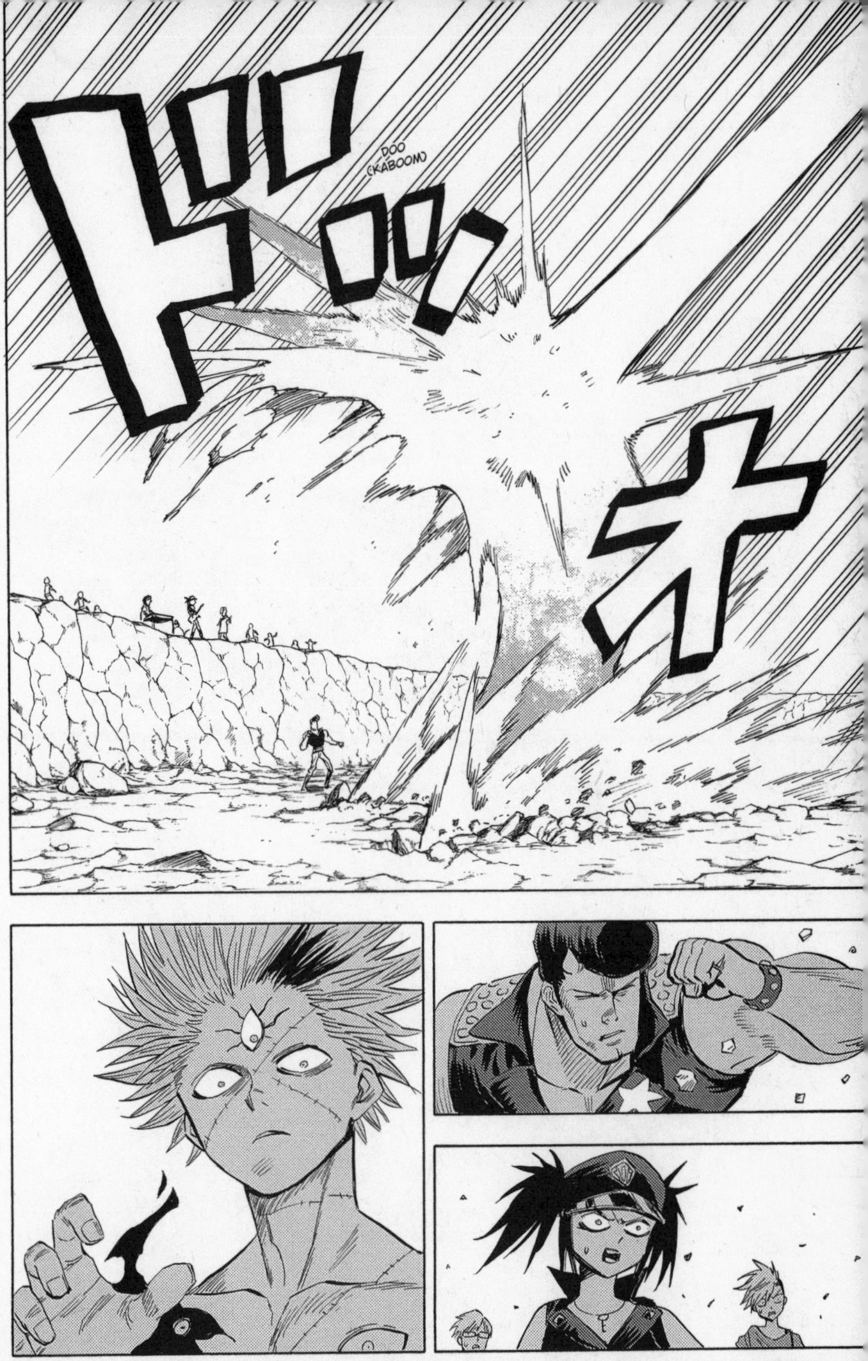
DOO (KABOOM)

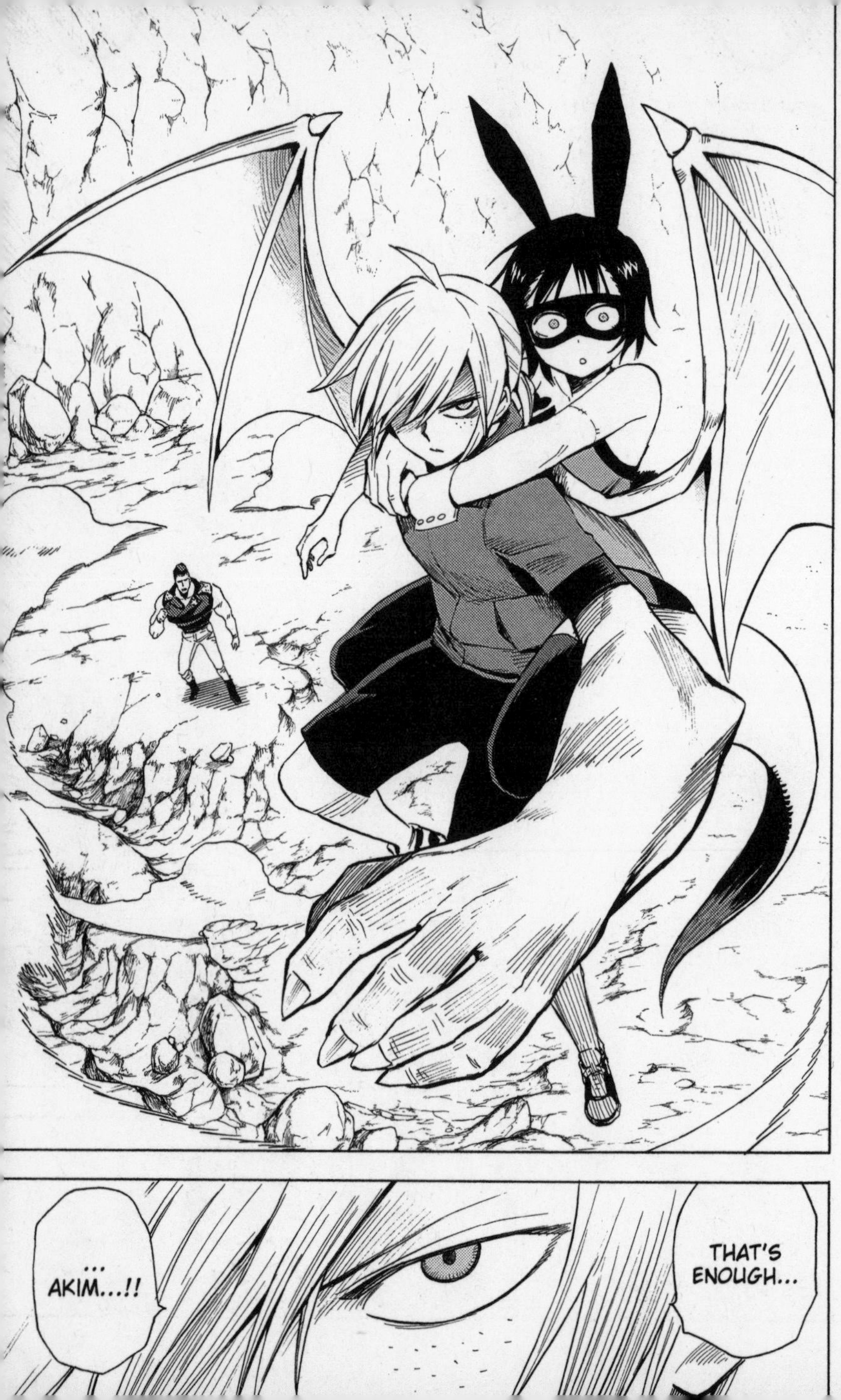
THAT'S ENOUGH...
... AKIM...!!

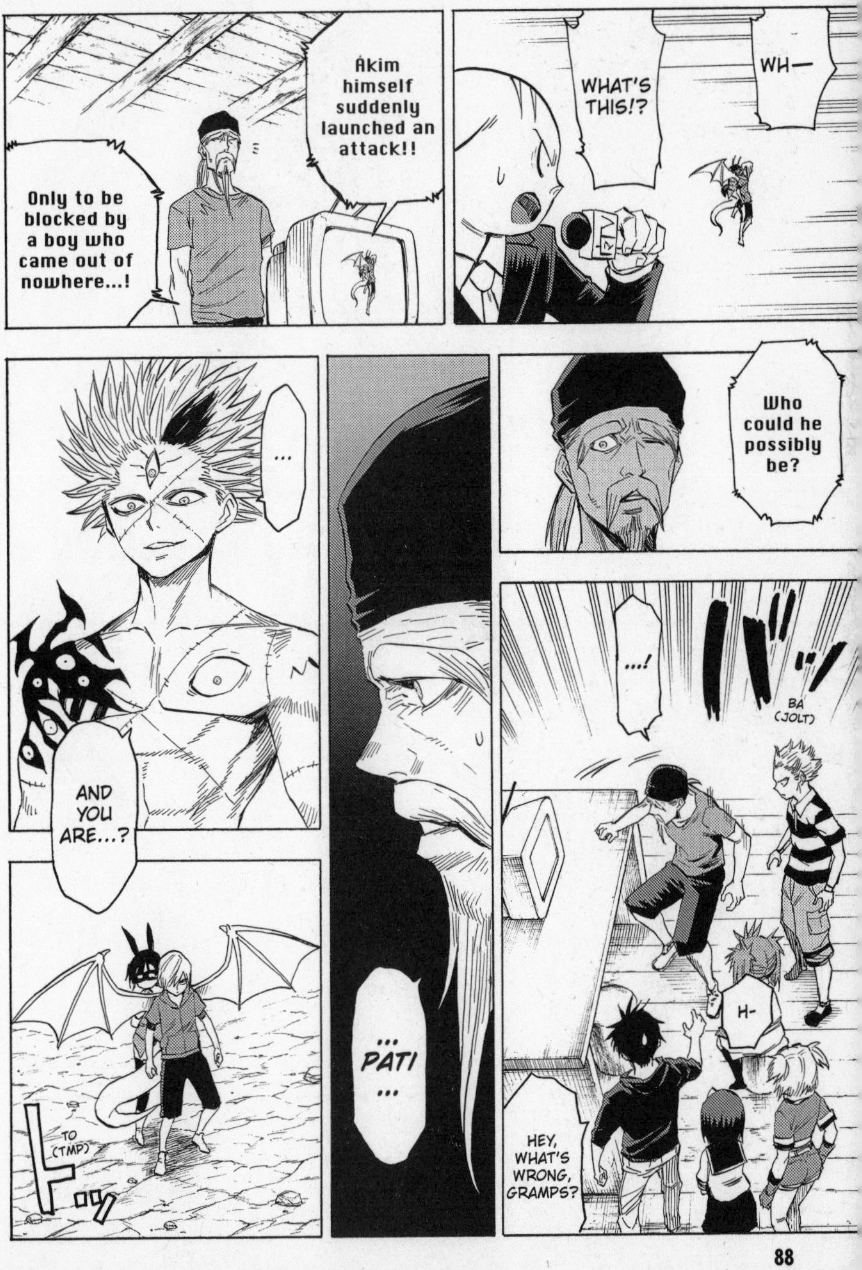
WH—
WHAT'S THIS!?
Akim himself suddenly launched an attack!!
Only to be blocked by a boy who came out of nowhere...!
Who could he possibly be?
...!
BA (JOLT)
H-
HEY, WHAT'S WRONG, GRAMPS?
...PATI...
...
AND YOU ARE...?
TO (TMP)

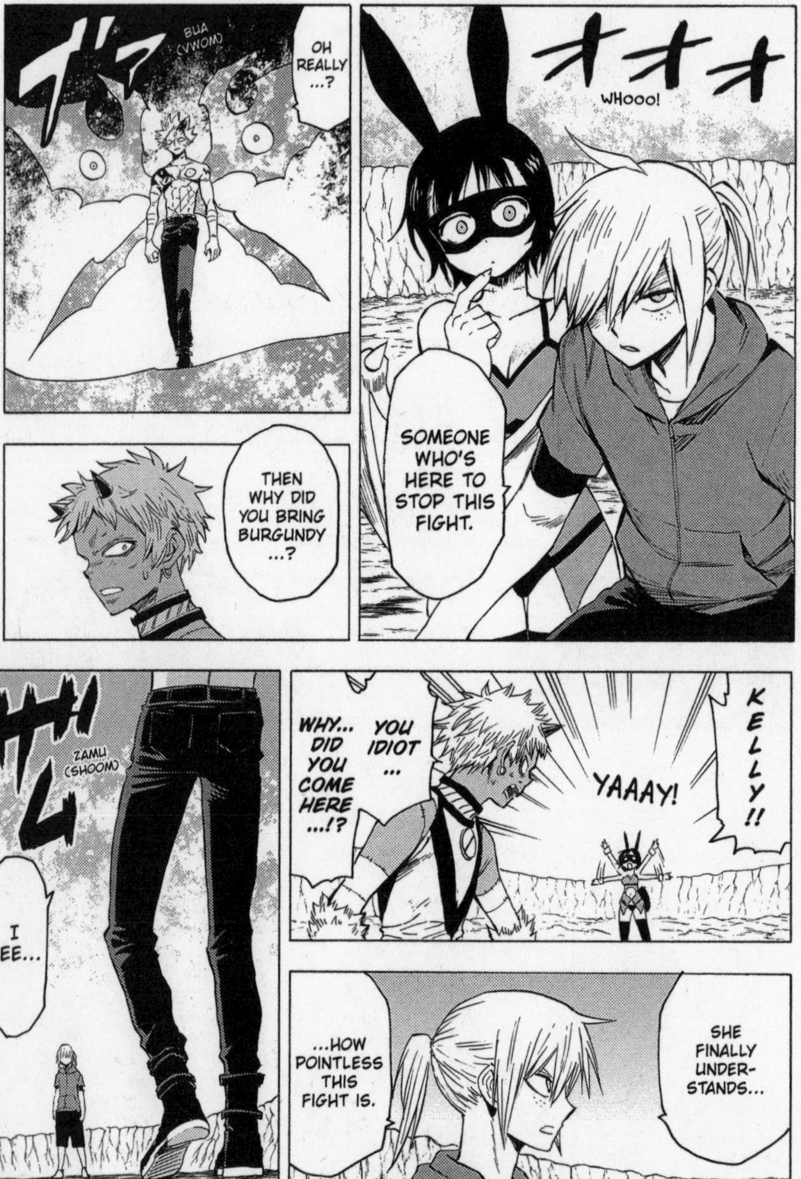
オオオ
WHOOO!
SOMEONE WHO'S HERE TO STOP THIS FIGHT.
BUA (VWOM)
OH REALLY ...?
THEN WHY DID YOU BRING BURGUNDY ...?
KELLY!!
YAAAY!
YOU IDIOT ...
WHY... DID YOU COME HERE ...!?
SHE FINALLY UNDER-STANDS...
...HOW POINTLESS THIS FIGHT IS.
ZAMU (SHOOM)
I SEE...

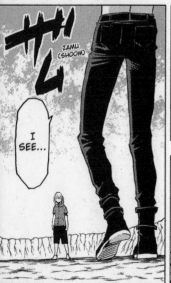

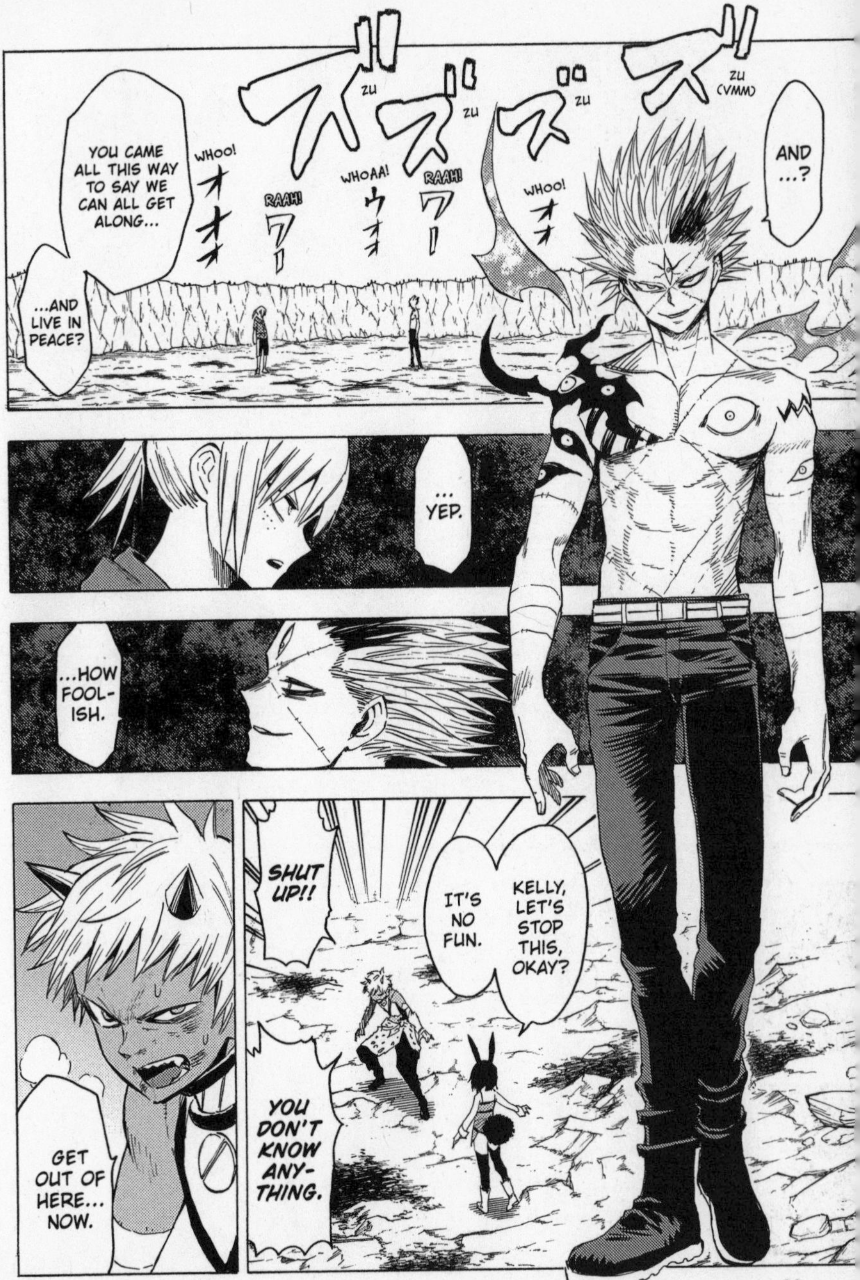
ZU (VMM)
ZU
ZU
ZU
AND ...?
WHOO!
RAAH!
WHOAA!
RAAH!
WHOO!
YOU CAME ALL THIS WAY TO SAY WE CAN ALL GET ALONG...
...AND LIVE IN PEACE?
... YEP.
...HOW FOOL-ISH.
KELLY, LET'S STOP THIS, OKAY?
IT'S NO FUN.
SHUT UP!!
YOU DON'T KNOW ANY-THING.
GET OUT OF HERE... NOW.

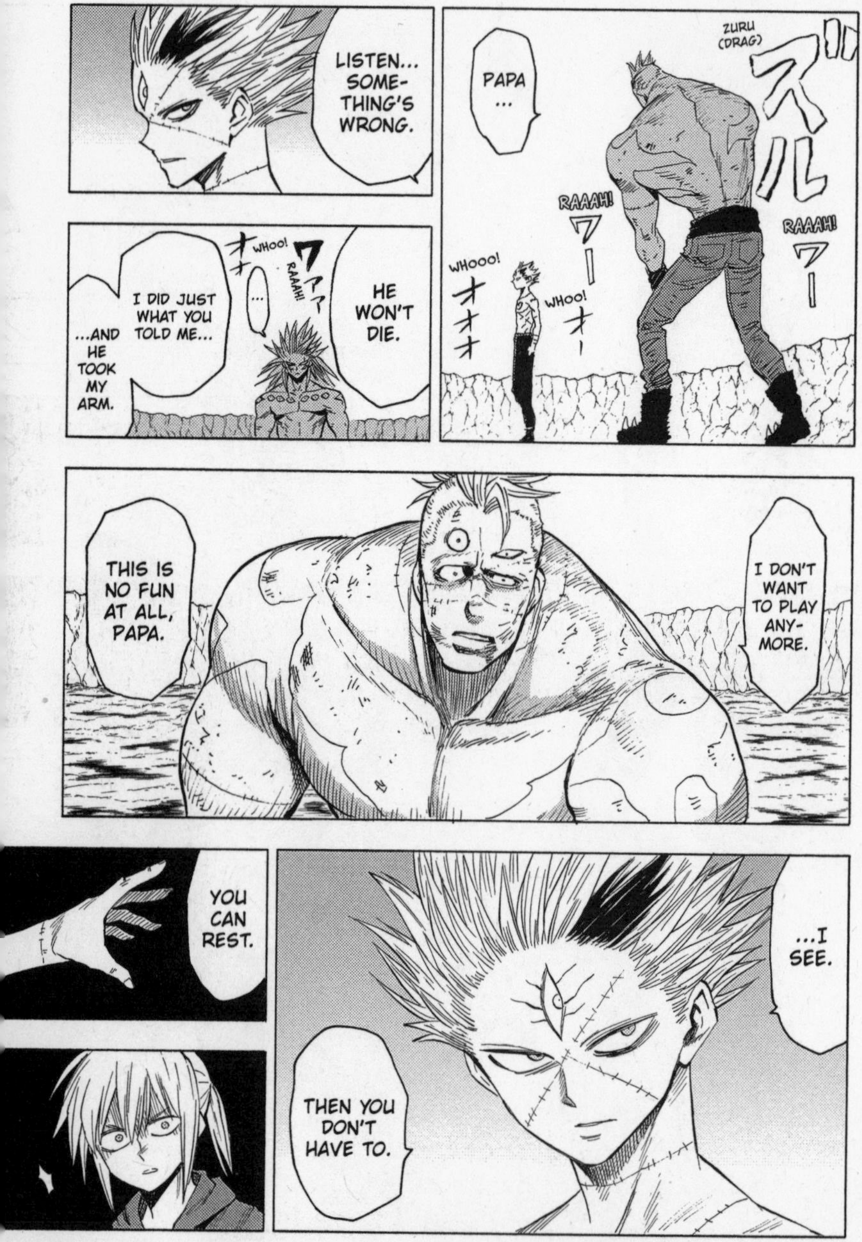
ZURU (DRAG)
ズル
PAPA ...
RAAAH!
ワー
RAAAH!
ワー
WHOOO!
オオオ
WHOO!
オー
LISTEN... SOME-THING'S WRONG.
HE WON'T DIE.
WHOO!
オオ
RAAAH!
ワアア
...
I DID JUST WHAT YOU TOLD ME...
...AND HE TOOK MY ARM.
I DON'T WANT TO PLAY ANY-MORE.
THIS IS NO FUN AT ALL, PAPA.
...I SEE.
THEN YOU DON'T HAVE TO.
YOU CAN REST.

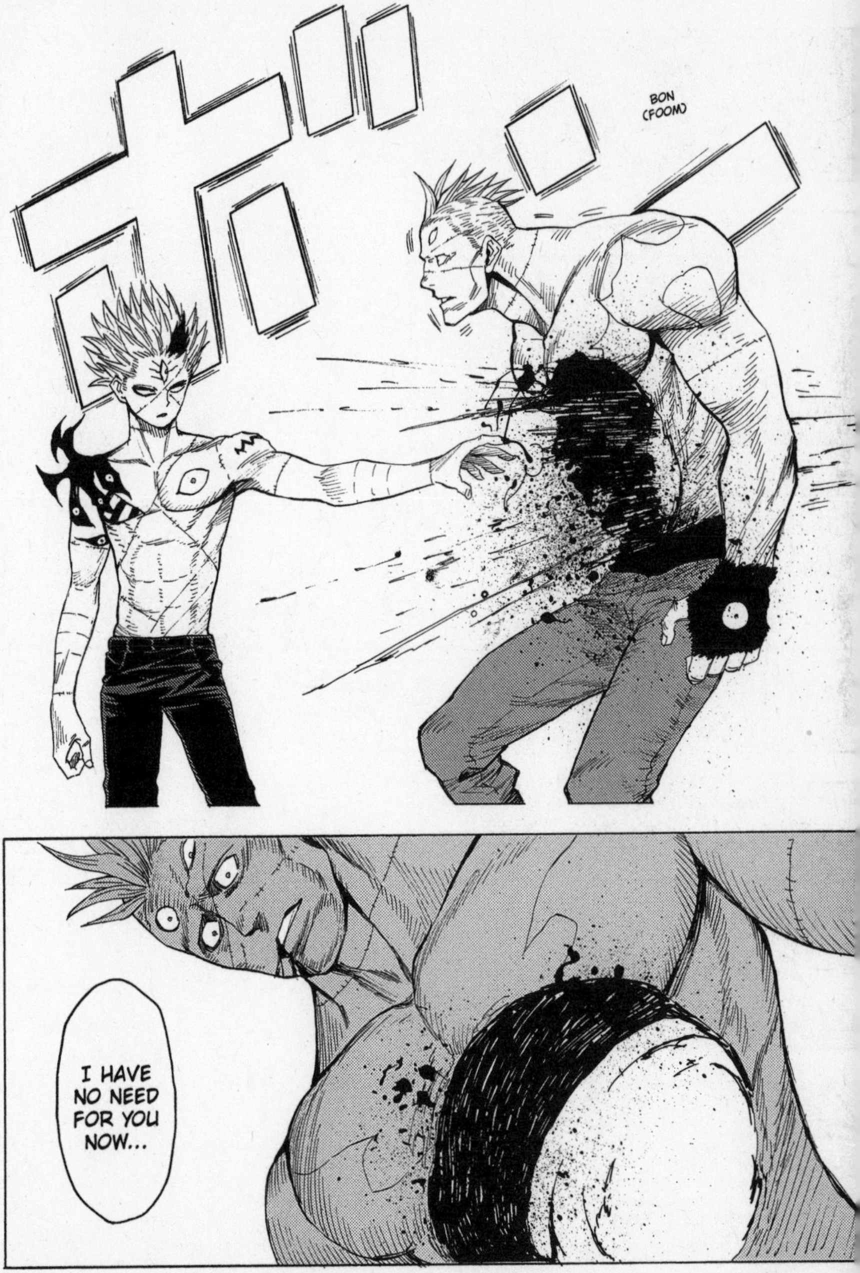
BON
(FOOM)
I HAVE NO NEED FOR YOU NOW...

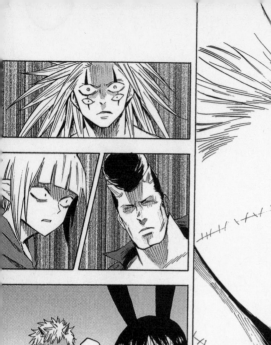

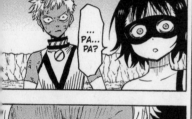

...PA... PA?

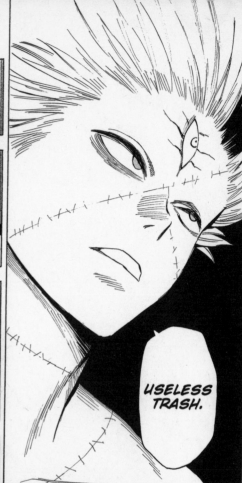

USELESS TRASH.

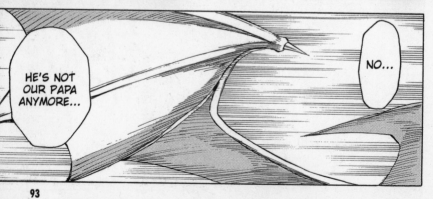

HE'S NOT OUR PAPA ANYMORE...

NO...

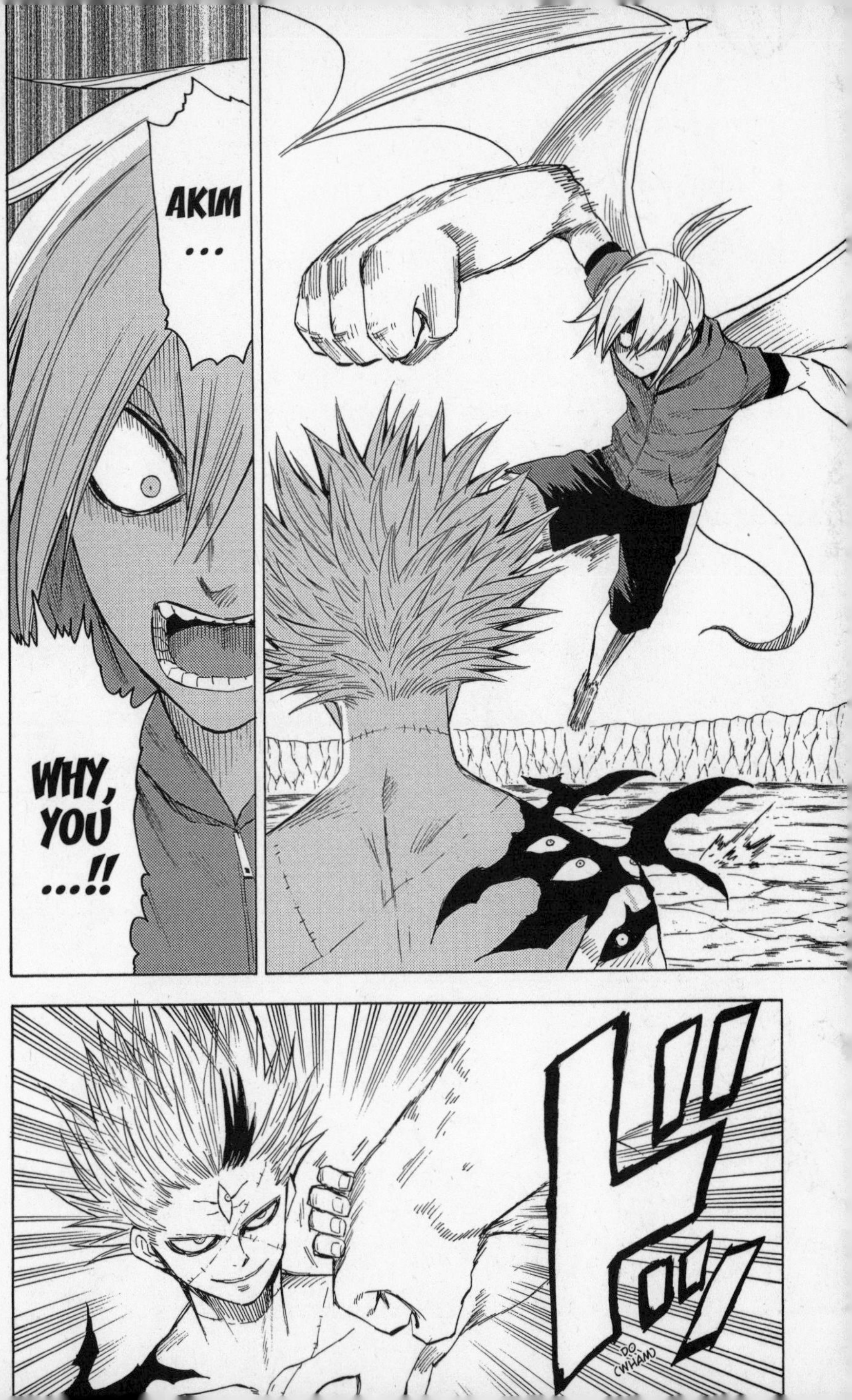
AKIM ...
WHY, YOU ...!!
DO (WHAM)

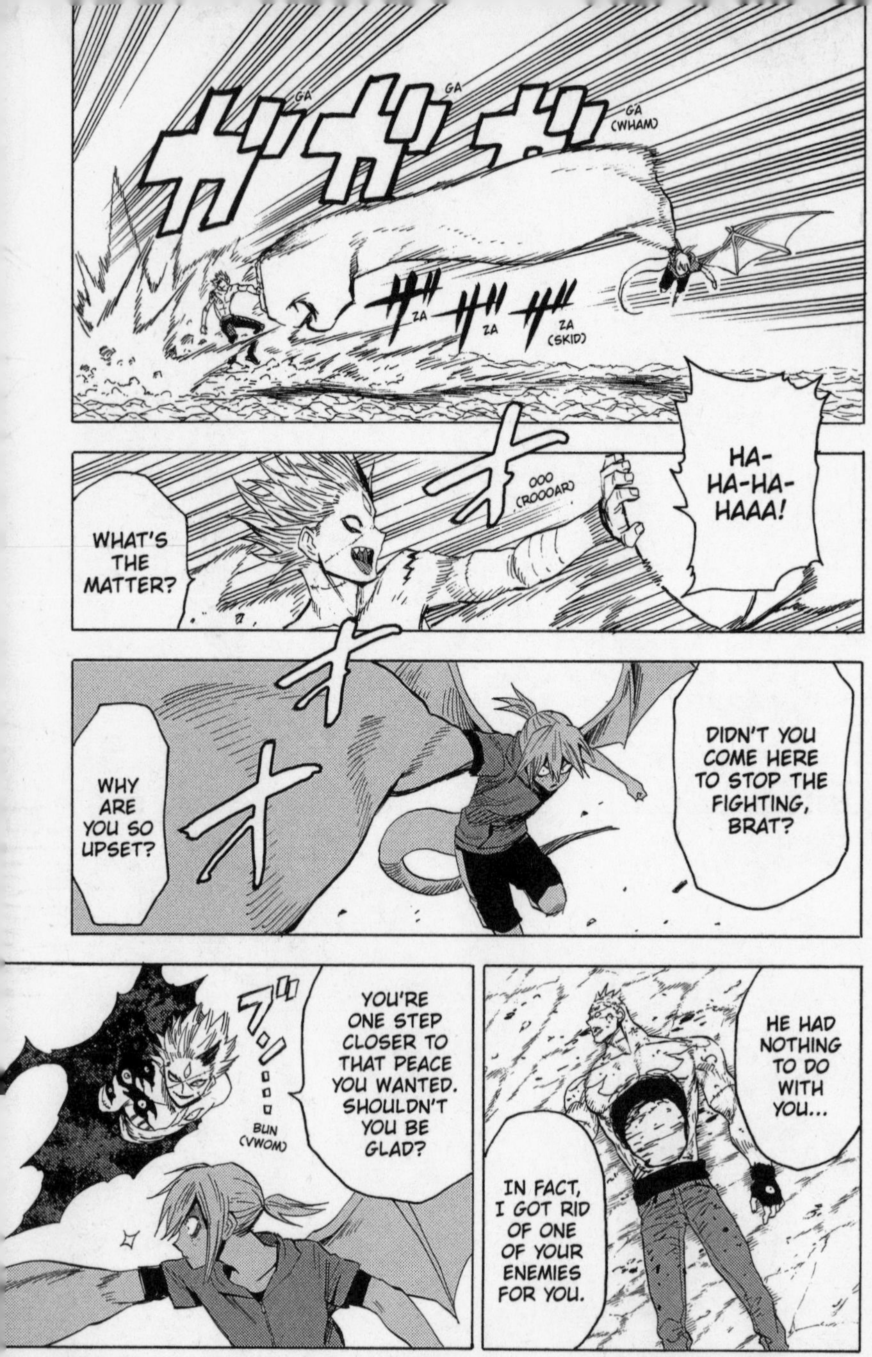
GA
GA
GA (WHAM)
ZA
ZA
ZA (SKID)
HA-HA-HA-HAAA!
OOO (ROOOAR)
WHAT'S THE MATTER?
DIDN'T YOU COME HERE TO STOP THE FIGHTING, BRAT?
WHY ARE YOU SO UPSET?
HE HAD NOTHING TO DO WITH YOU...
IN FACT, I GOT RID OF ONE OF YOUR ENEMIES FOR YOU.
YOU'RE ONE STEP CLOSER TO THAT PEACE YOU WANTED. SHOULDN'T YOU BE GLAD?
BUN (VWOM)

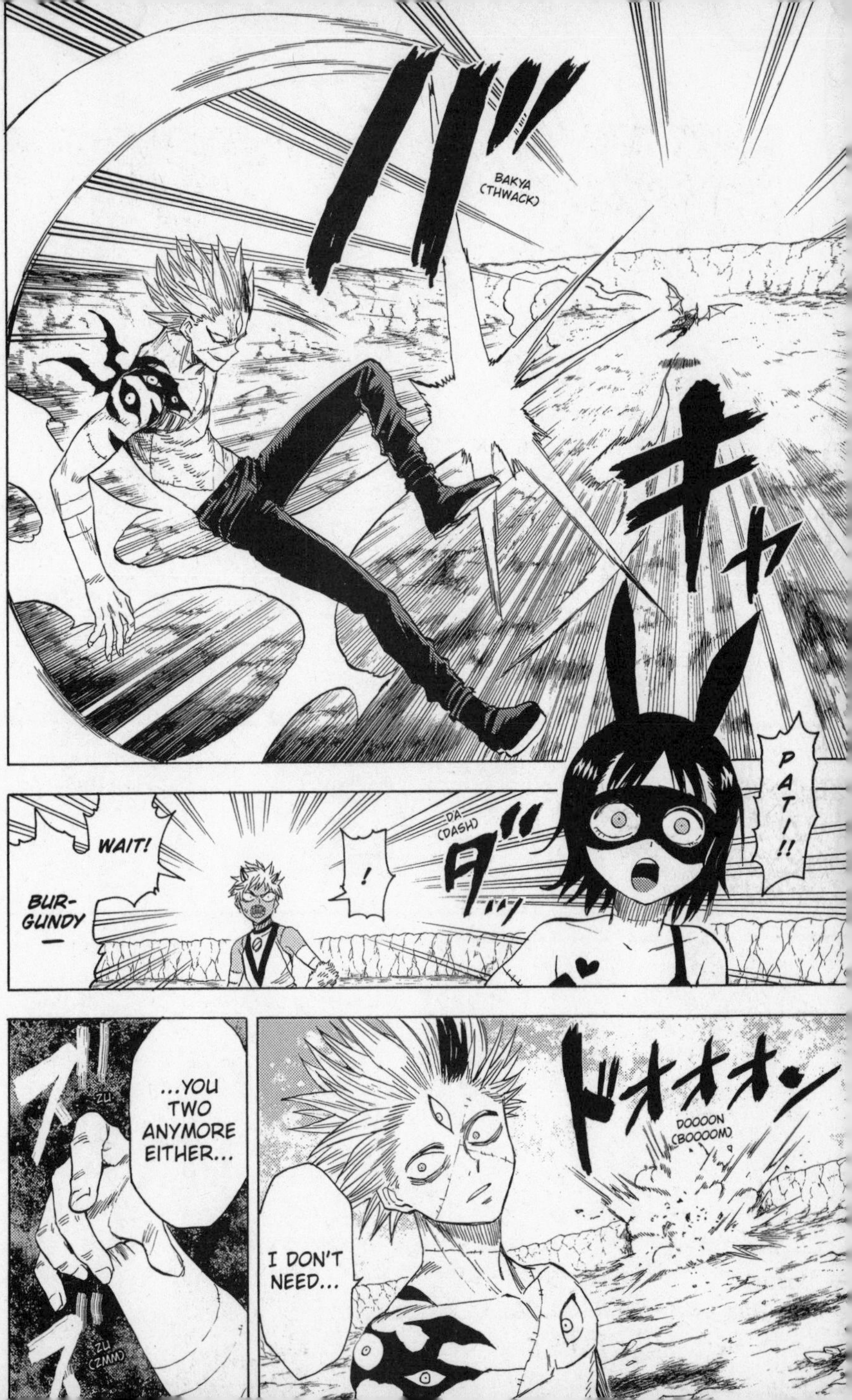
バキャ
BAKYA (THWACK)
PATI!!
ダッ
DA (DASH)
!
WAIT!
BUR-GUNDY —
ドオオオン
DOOOON (BOOOOM)
I DON'T NEED...
...YOU TWO ANYMORE EITHER...
ズ
ZU
ZU (ZMM)

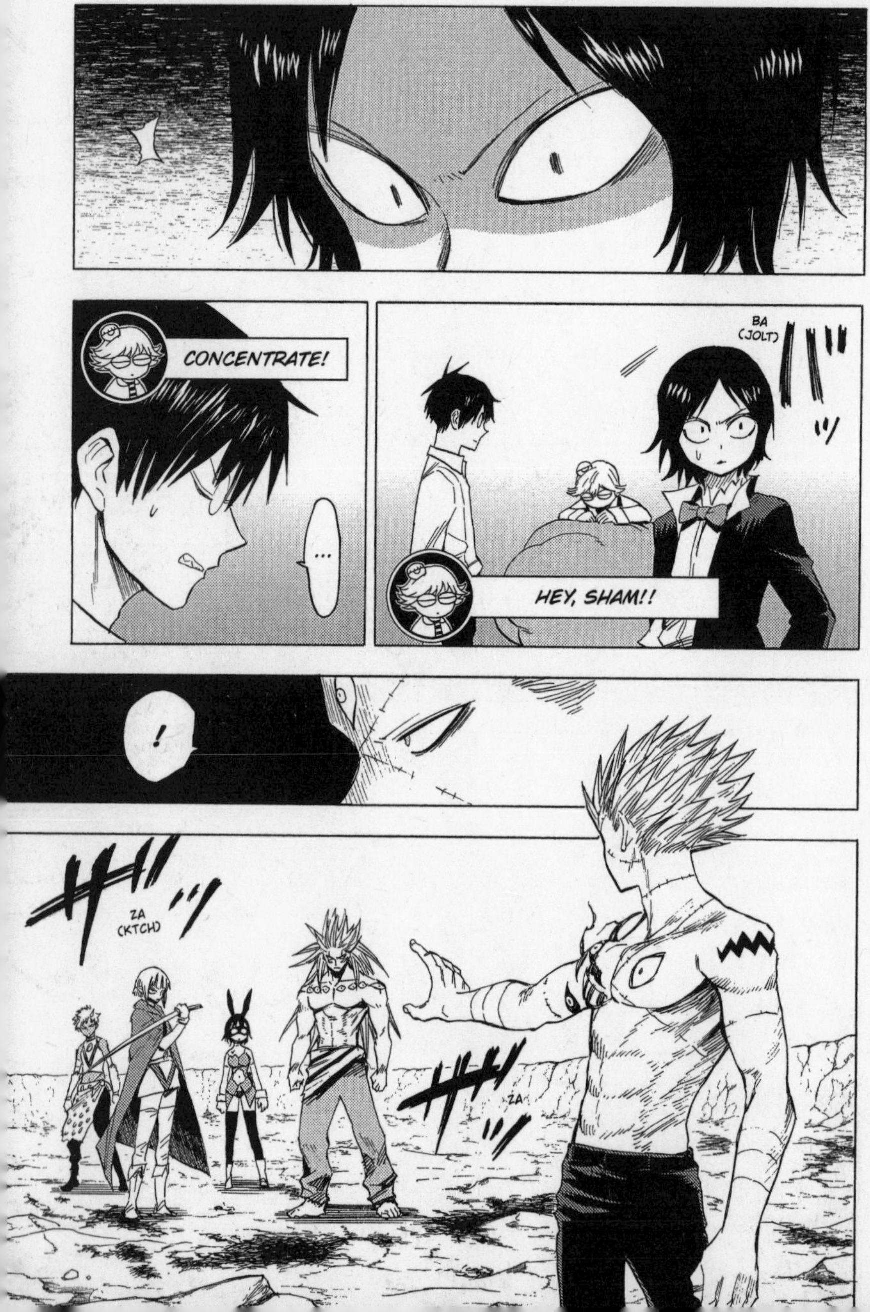
BA (JOLT)
HEY, SHAM!!
CONCENTRATE!
...
!
ZA
ZA (KTCH)

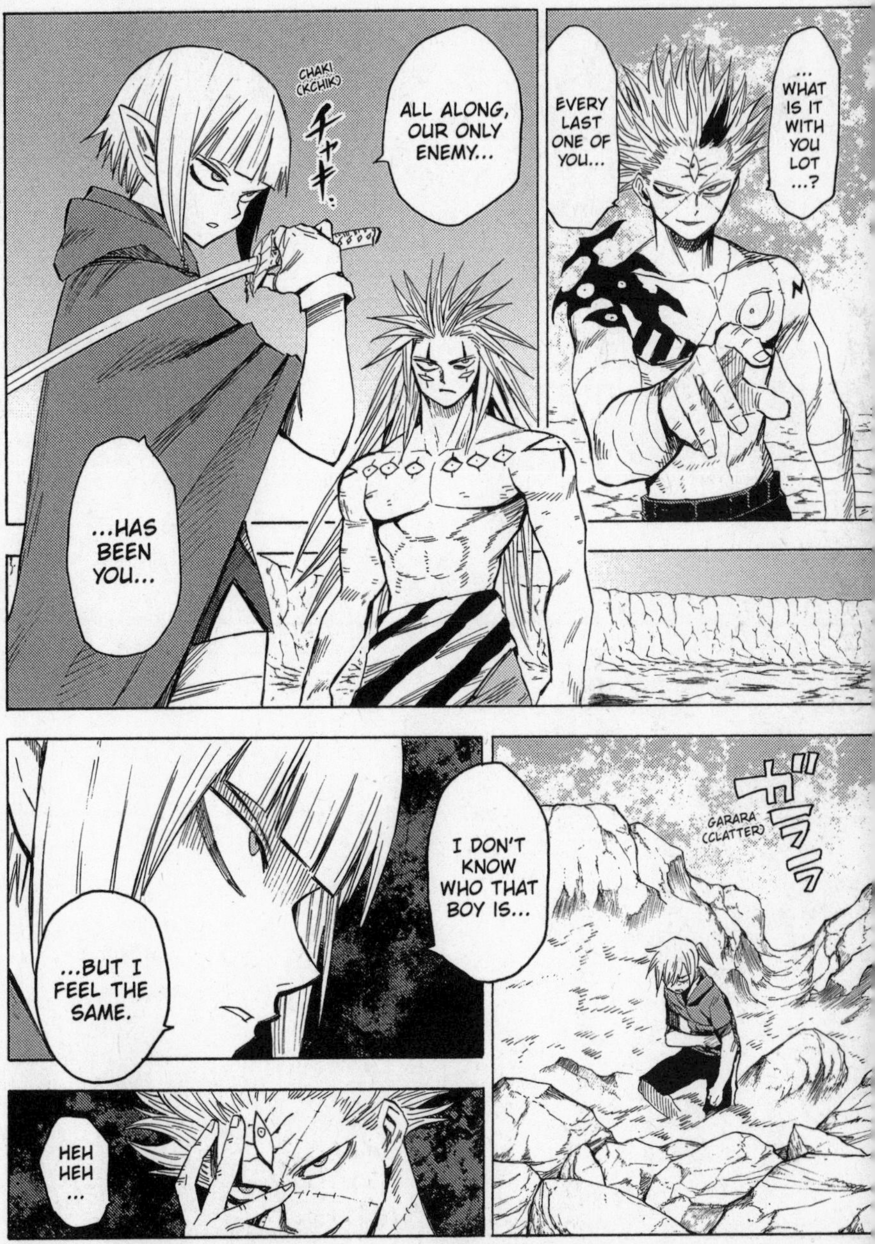
...WHAT IS IT WITH YOU LOT ...?
EVERY LAST ONE OF YOU...
CHAKI (KCHIK)
チャキ
ALL ALONG, OUR ONLY ENEMY...
...HAS BEEN YOU...
ガララ
GARARA (CLATTER)
I DON'T KNOW WHO THAT BOY IS...
...BUT I FEEL THE SAME.
HEH HEH ...

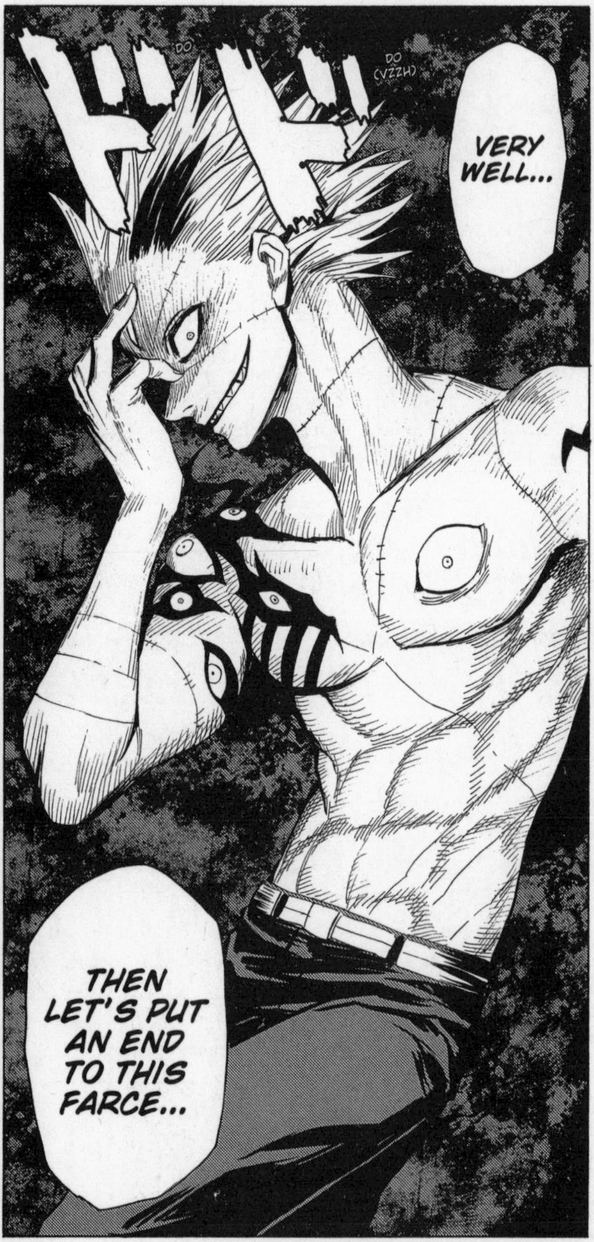
DO
DO (VZZH)
VERY WELL...
THEN LET'S PUT AN END TO THIS FARCE...

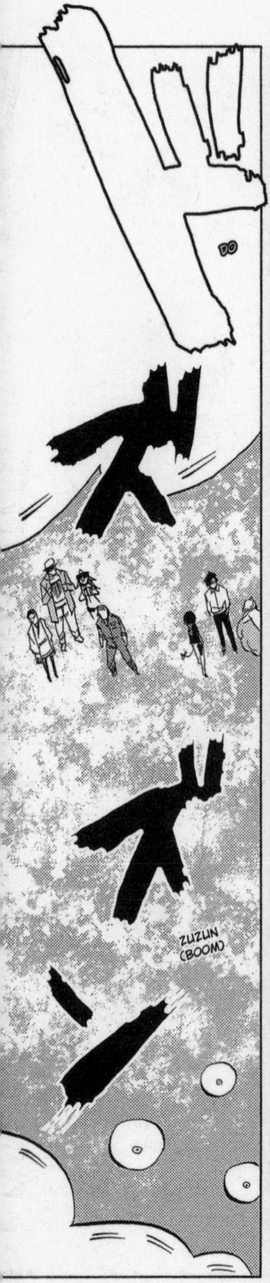
DO
ZUZUN (BOOM)

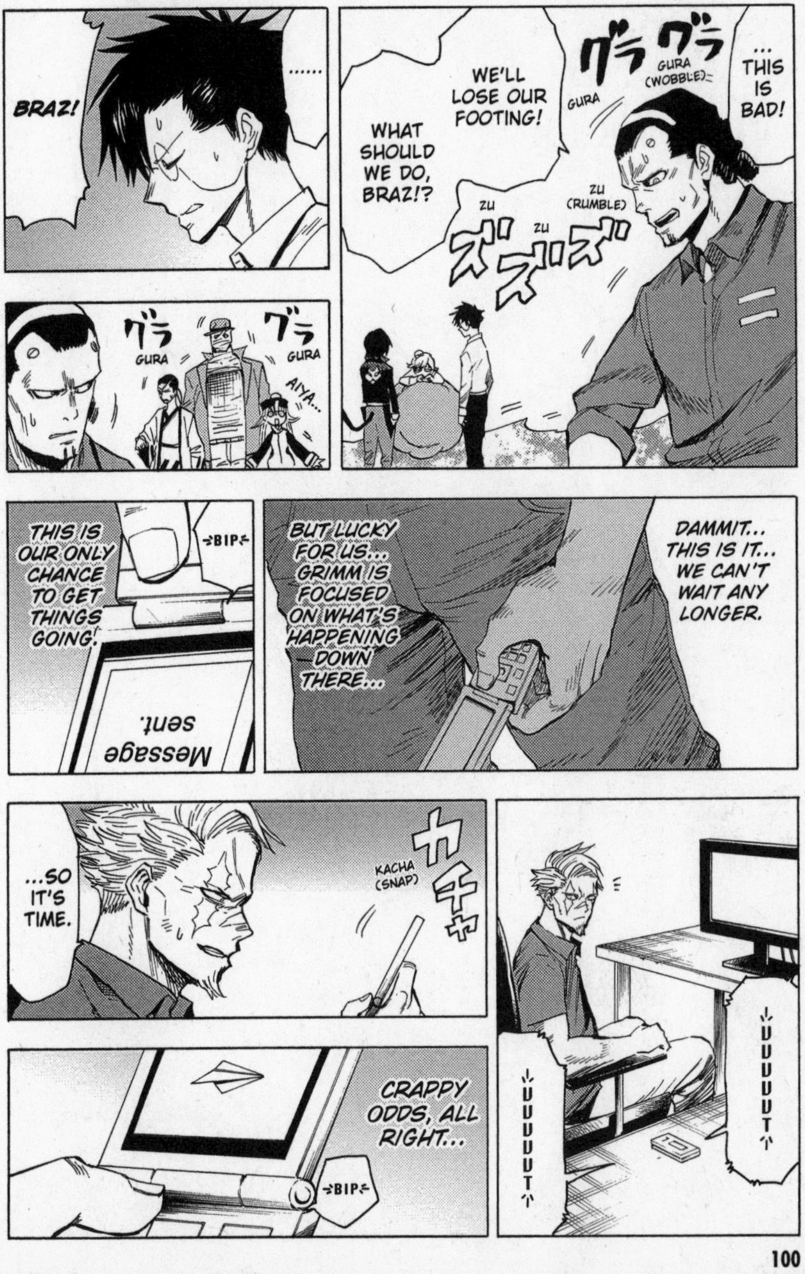
... THIS IS BAD!
グラ グラ
GURA (WOBBLE)
GURA
WE'LL LOSE OUR FOOTING!
WHAT SHOULD WE DO, BRAZ!?
ZU (RUMBLE)
ZU
ZU
ズズズ
......
BRAZ!
グラ GURA
グラ GURA
AIYA...
DAMMIT... THIS IS IT... WE CAN'T WAIT ANY LONGER.
BUT LUCKY FOR US... GRIMM IS FOCUSED ON WHAT'S HAPPENING DOWN THERE...
BIP
THIS IS OUR ONLY CHANCE TO GET THINGS GOING.
Message sent.
VUUUUUT
VUUUUUT
カチャ
KACHA (SNAP)
...SO IT'S TIME.
CRAPPY ODDS, ALL RIGHT...
BIP

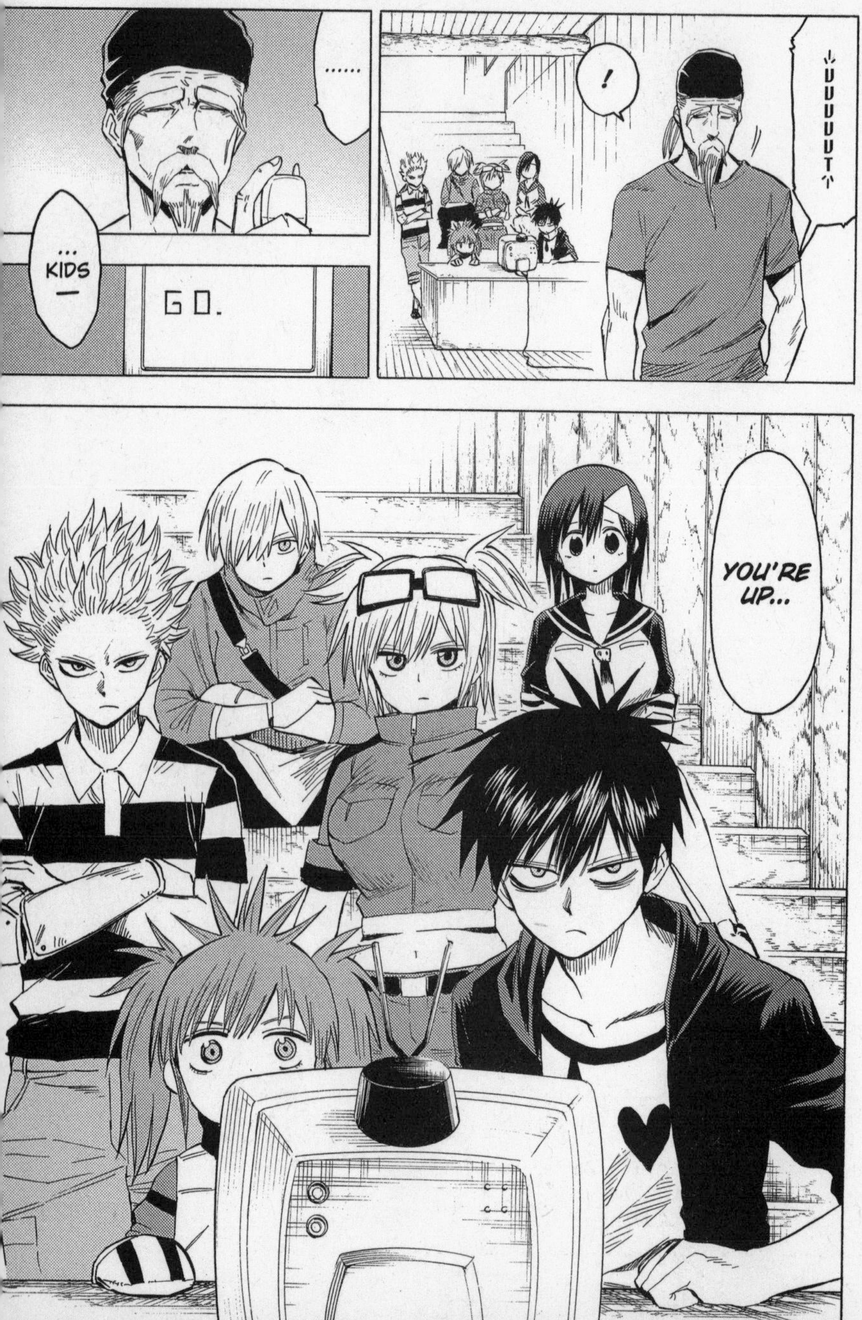
UUUUUT
!
......
... KIDS —
GO.
YOU'RE UP...

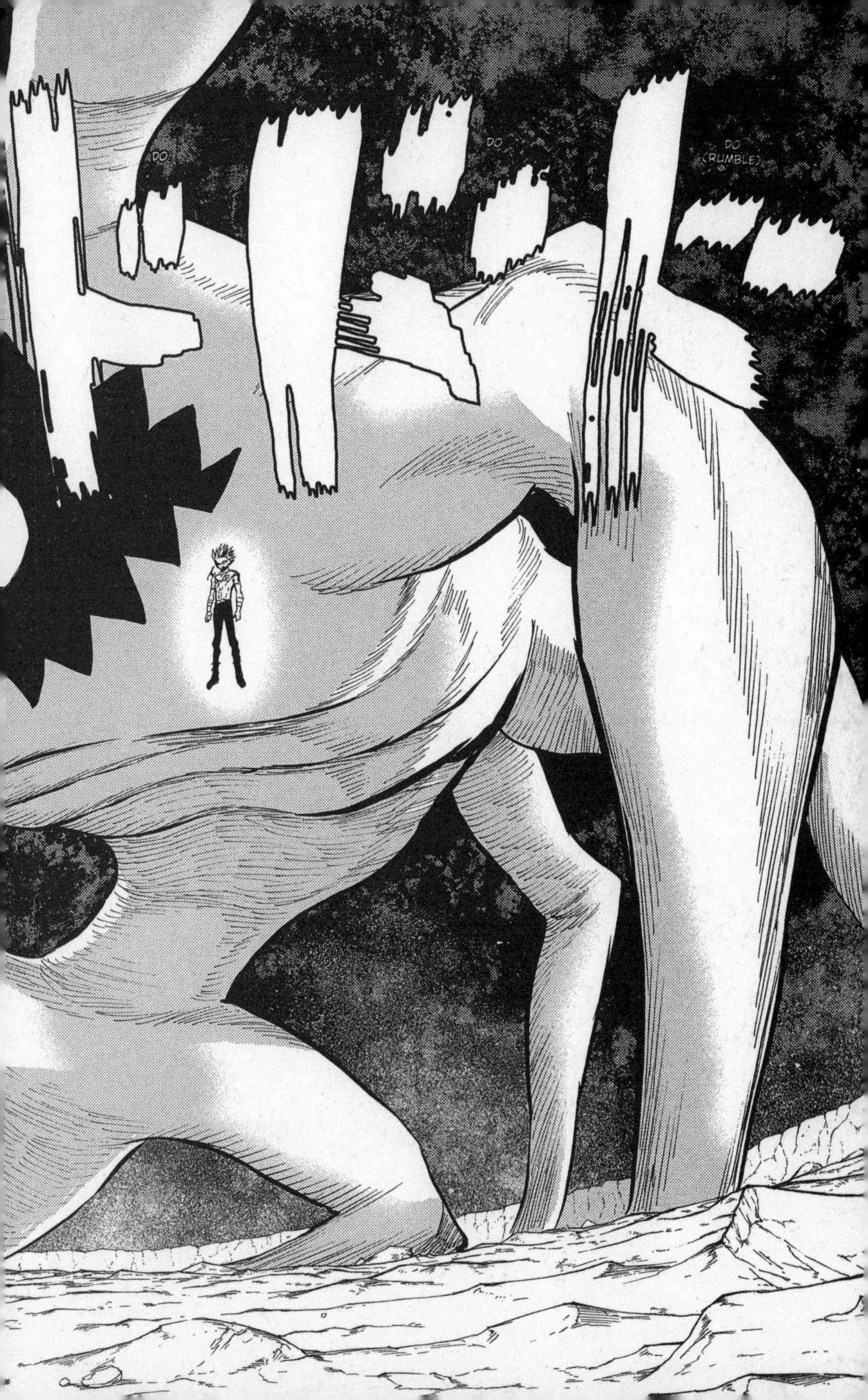
DO
DO
DO
(RUMBLE)

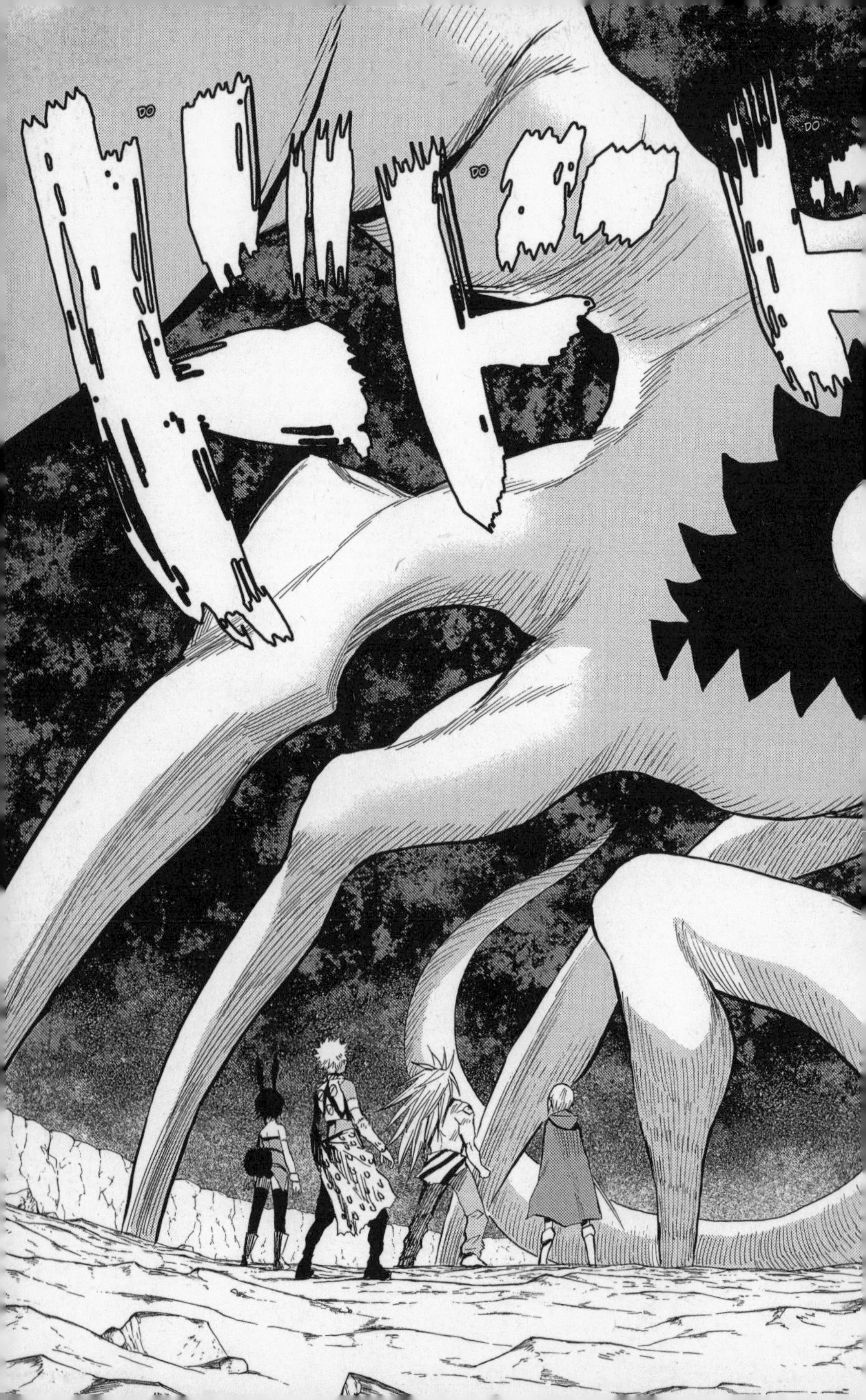
DO
DO
DO

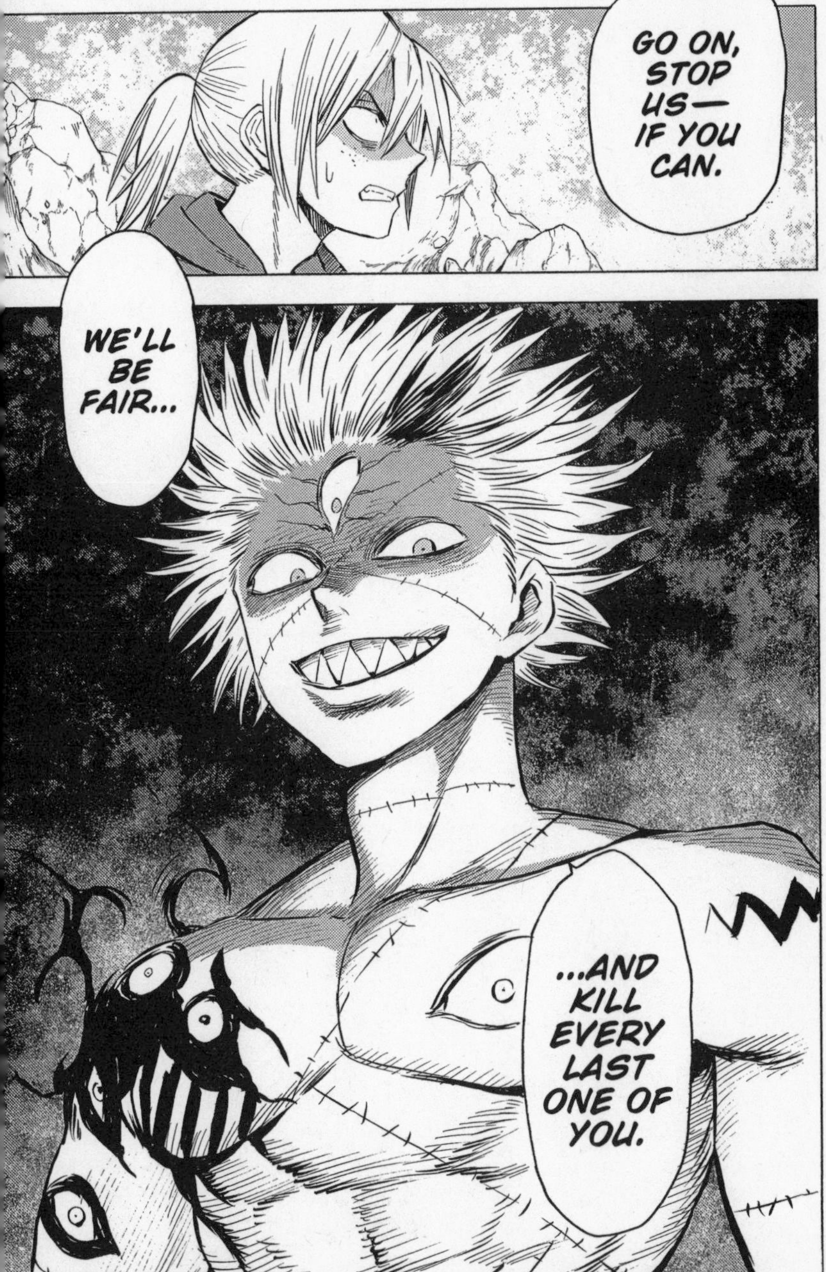
GO ON, STOP US— IF YOU CAN.
WE'LL BE FAIR...
...AND KILL EVERY LAST ONE OF YOU.
To Be Continued

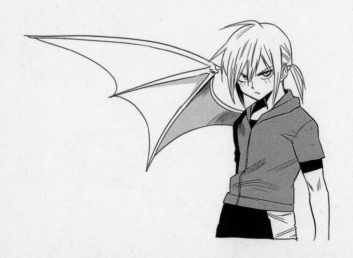

BLOOD LAD

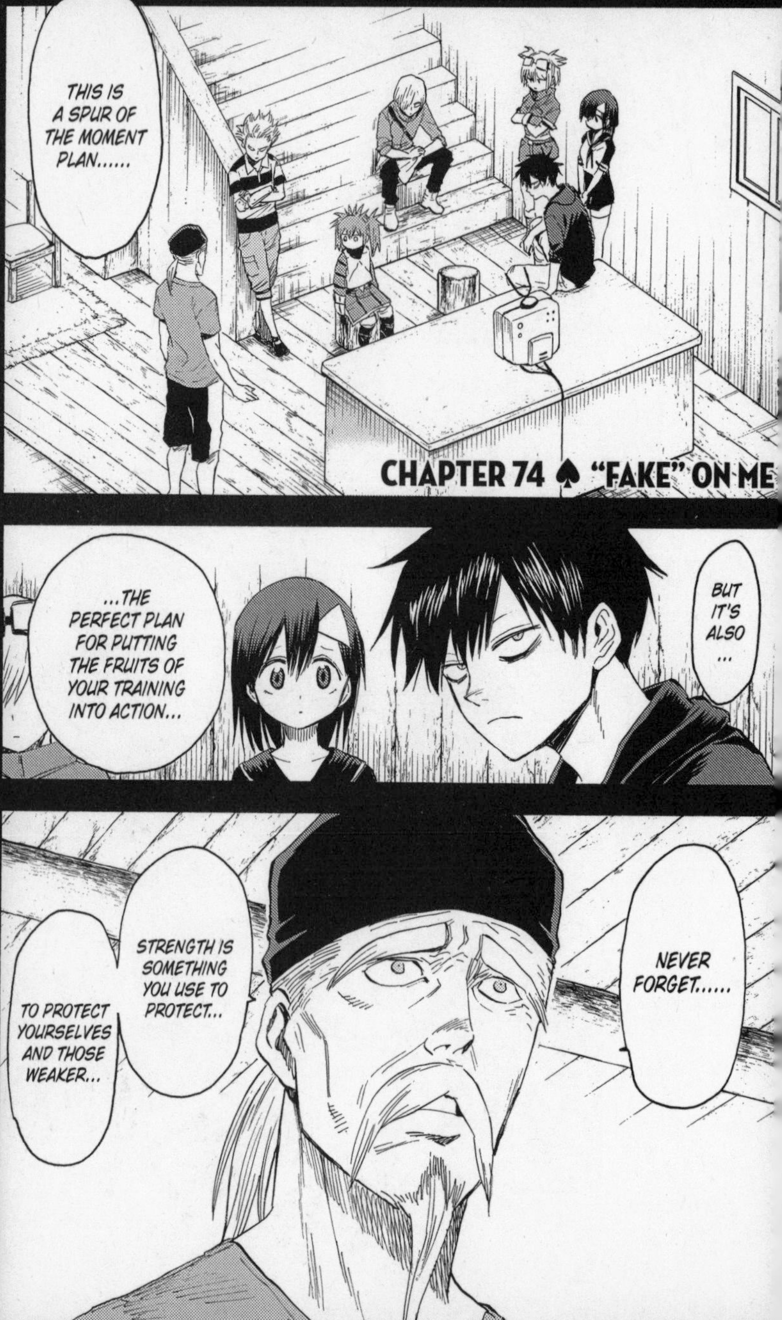
THIS IS A SPUR OF THE MOMENT PLAN......
CHAPTER 74 ♠ "FAKE" ON ME
BUT IT'S ALSO ...
...THE PERFECT PLAN FOR PUTTING THE FRUITS OF YOUR TRAINING INTO ACTION...
NEVER FORGET......
STRENGTH IS SOMETHING YOU USE TO PROTECT...
TO PROTECT YOURSELVES AND THOSE WEAKER...

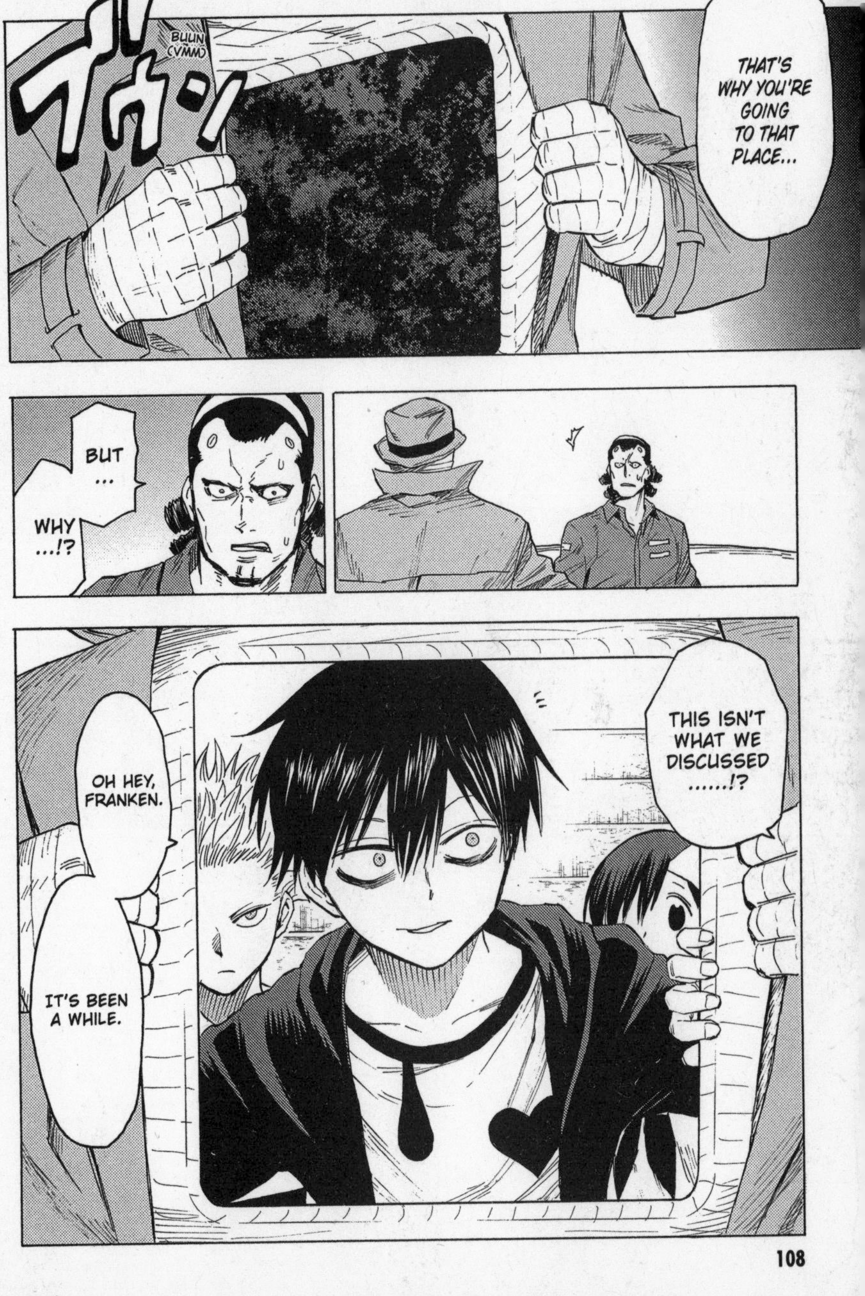
THAT'S WHY YOU'RE GOING TO THAT PLACE...
BUUN (VMM)
BUT ...
WHY ...!?
THIS ISN'T WHAT WE DISCUSSED ......!?
OH HEY, FRANKEN.
IT'S BEEN A WHILE.

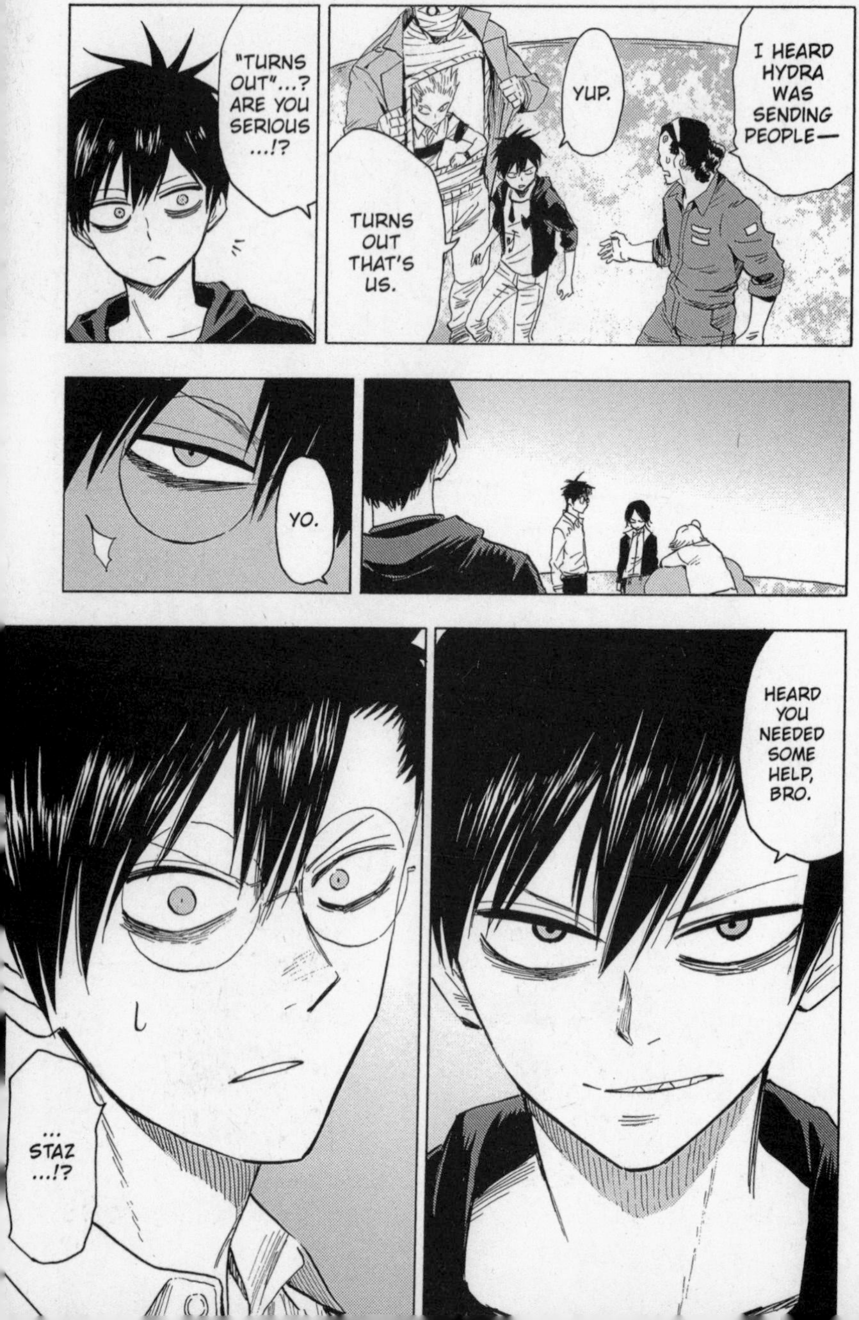
I HEARD HYDRA WAS SENDING PEOPLE—
YUP.
TURNS OUT THAT'S US.
"TURNS OUT"...? ARE YOU SERIOUS ...!?
YO.
HEARD YOU NEEDED SOME HELP, BRO.
... STAZ ...!?

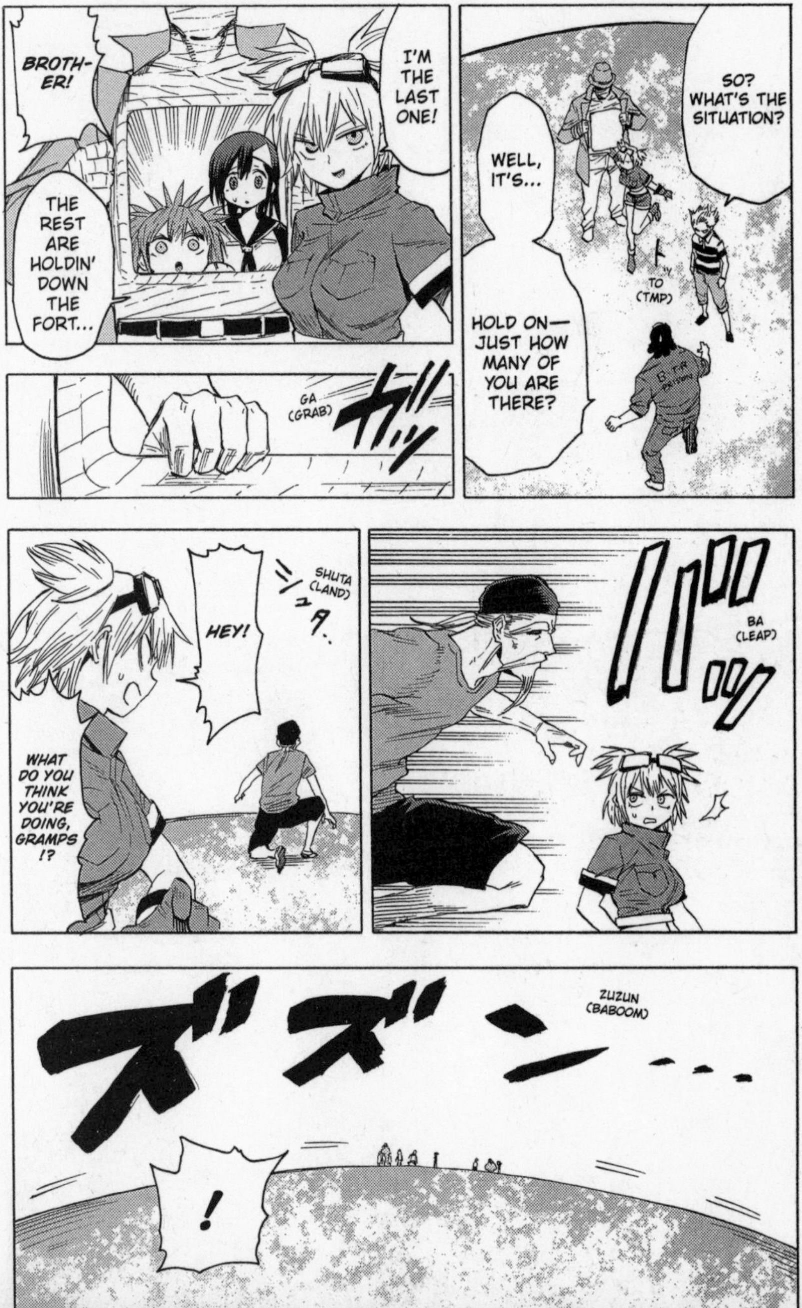
SO? WHAT'S THE SITUATION?
WELL, IT'S...
TO (TMP)
HOLD ON— JUST HOW MANY OF YOU ARE THERE?
I'M THE LAST ONE!
BROTHER!
THE REST ARE HOLDIN' DOWN THE FORT...
GA (GRAB)
BA (LEAP)
SHUTA (LAND)
HEY!
WHAT DO YOU THINK YOU'RE DOING, GRAMPS!?
ZUZUN (BABOOM)
!

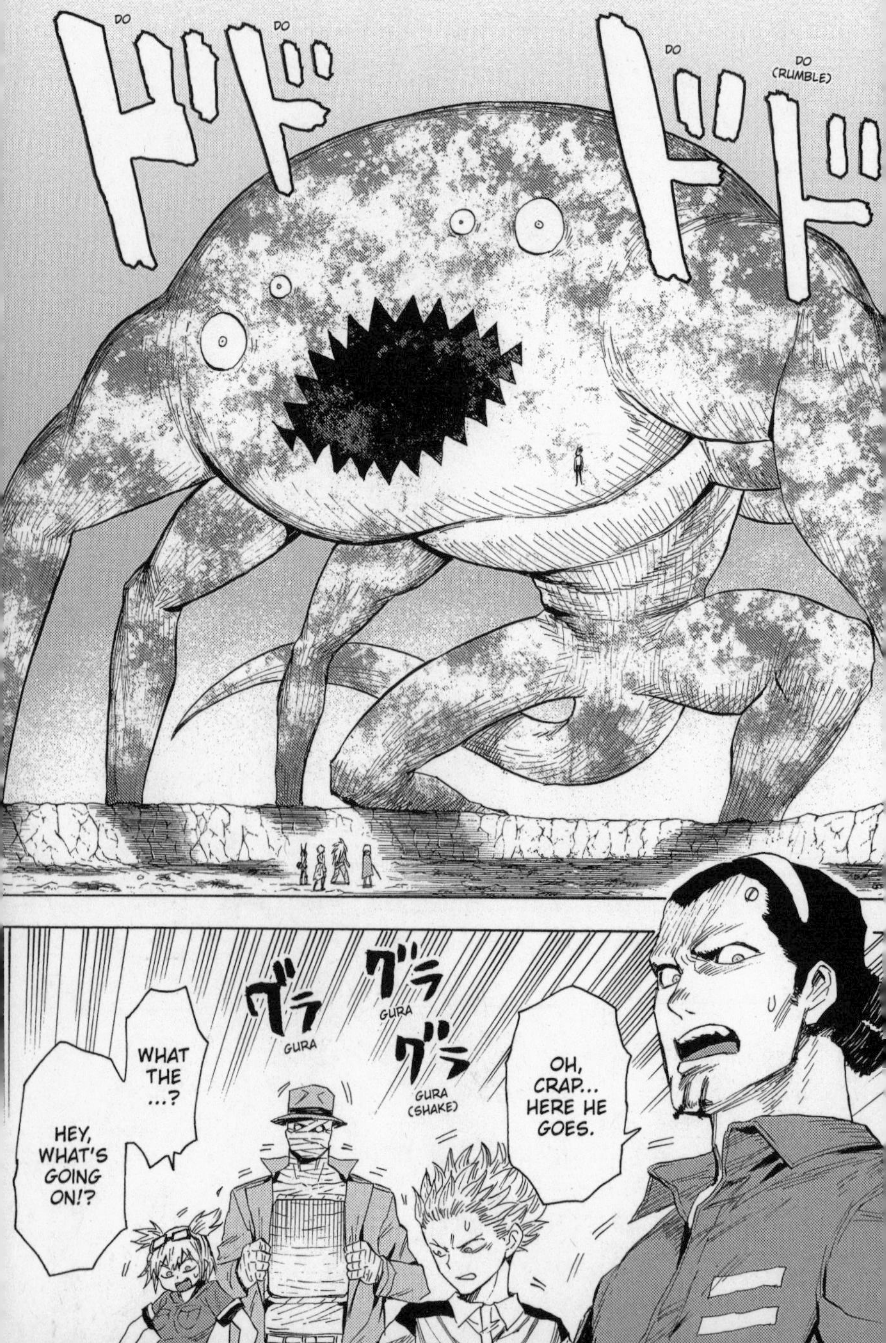
DO
DO (RUMBLE)
DO
DO
OH, CRAP... HERE HE GOES.
GURA
GURA (SHAKE)
GURA
WHAT THE ...?
HEY, WHAT'S GOING ON!?

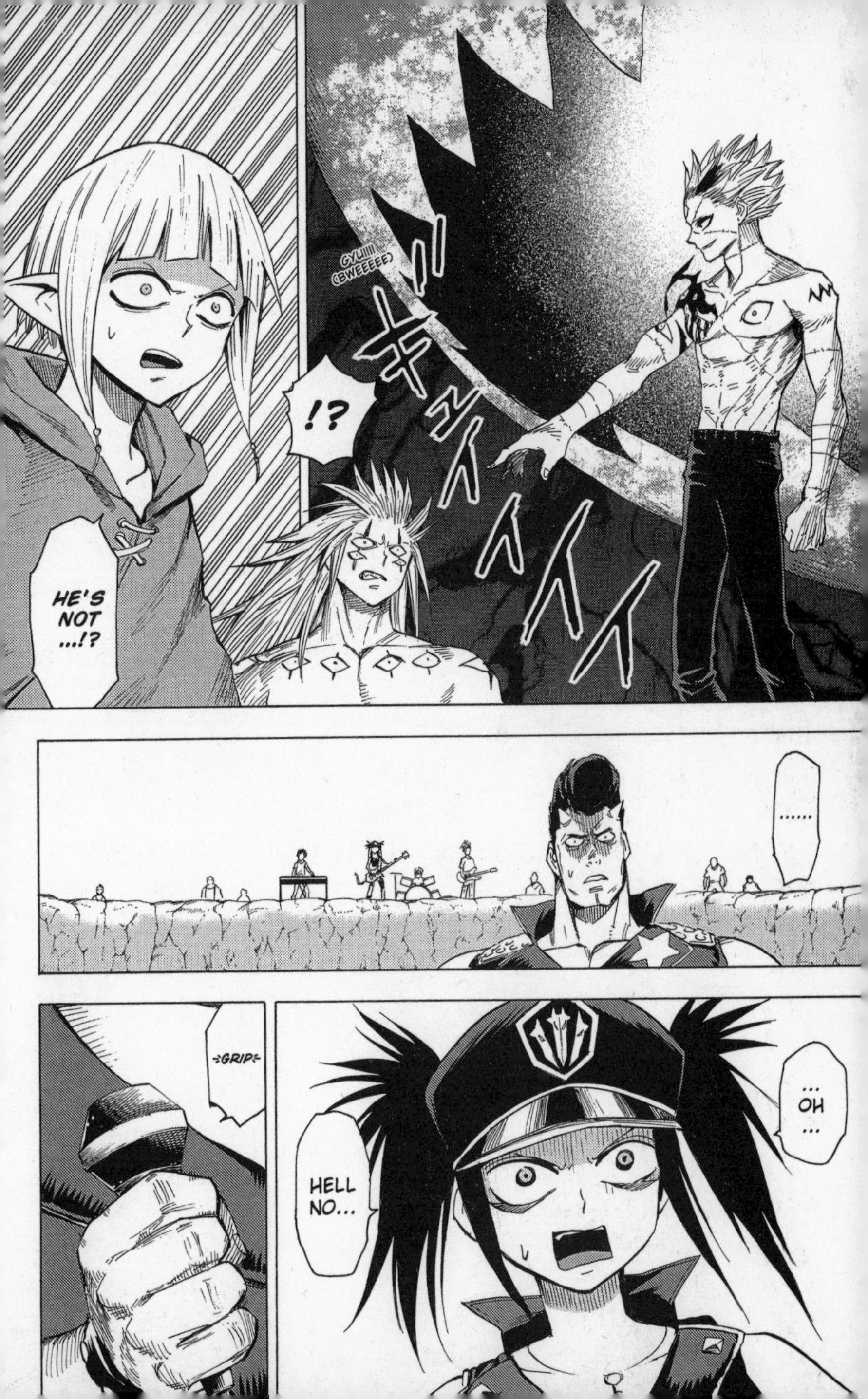
GYUIIIII
(BWEEEEEE)
!?
HE'S NOT ...!?
......
... OH ...
HELL NO...
-GRIP-

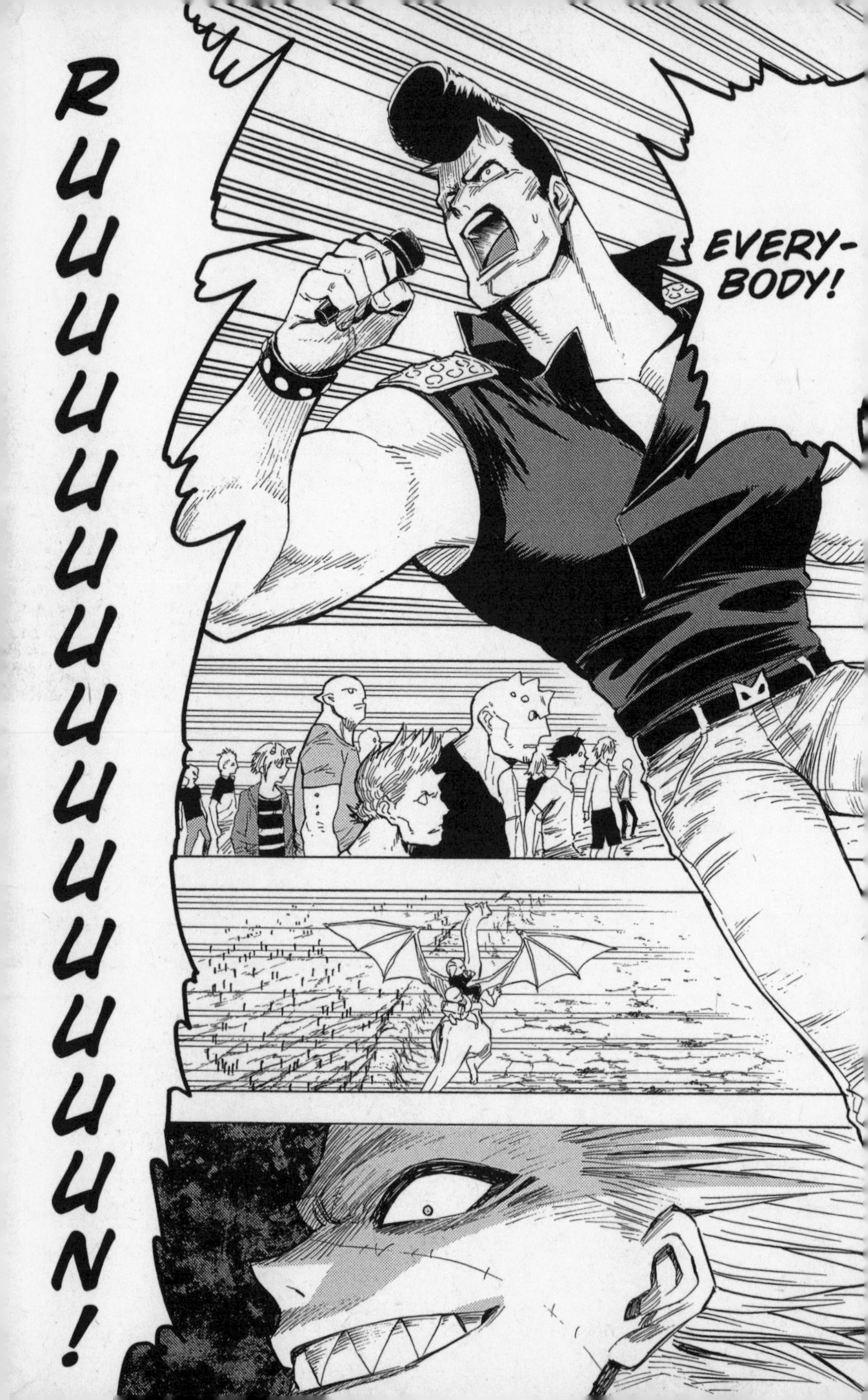
EVERY-BODY!
RUUUUUUUUUUUUUN!

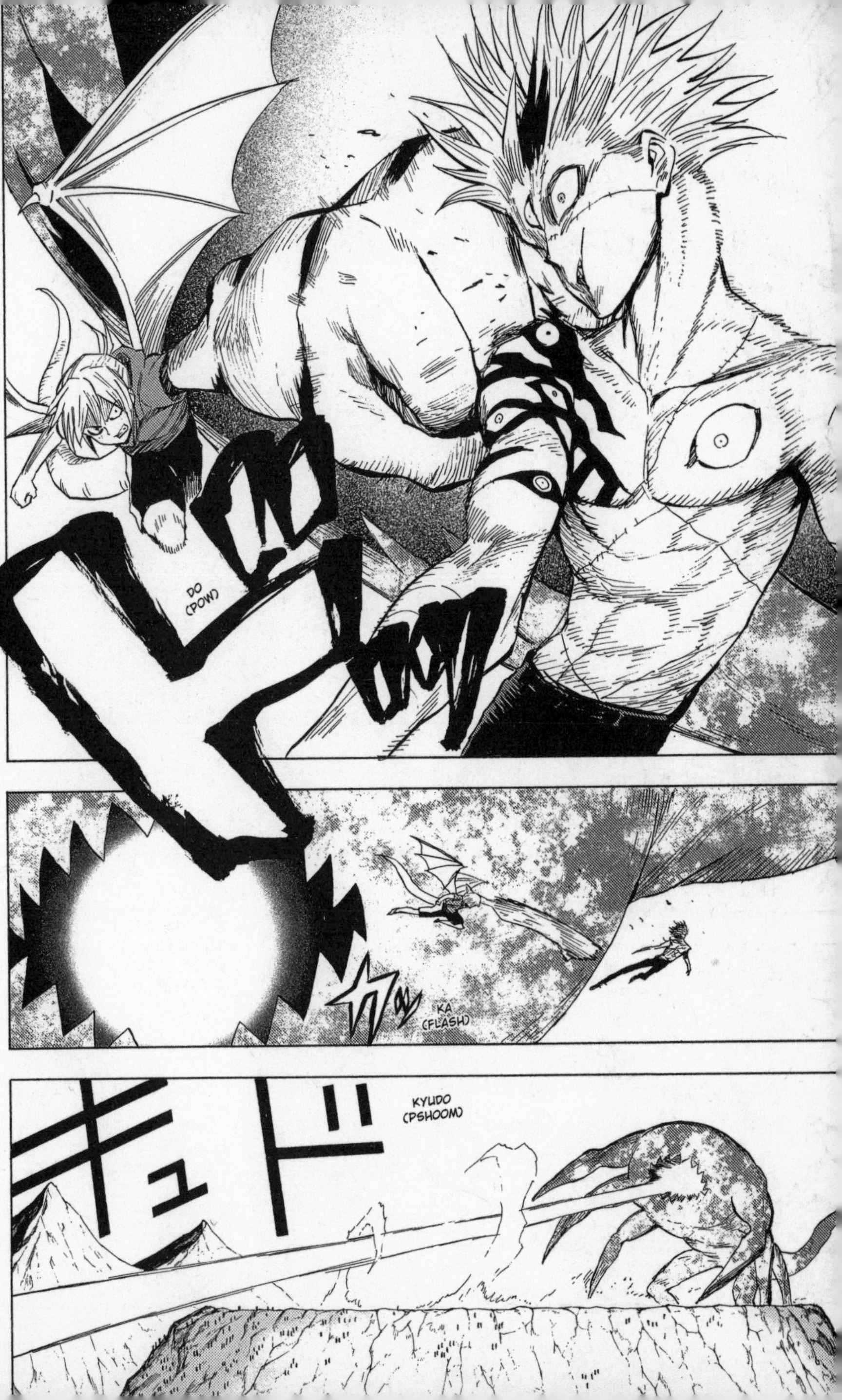
DO
(POW)
KA
(FLASH)
KYUDO
(PSHOOM)

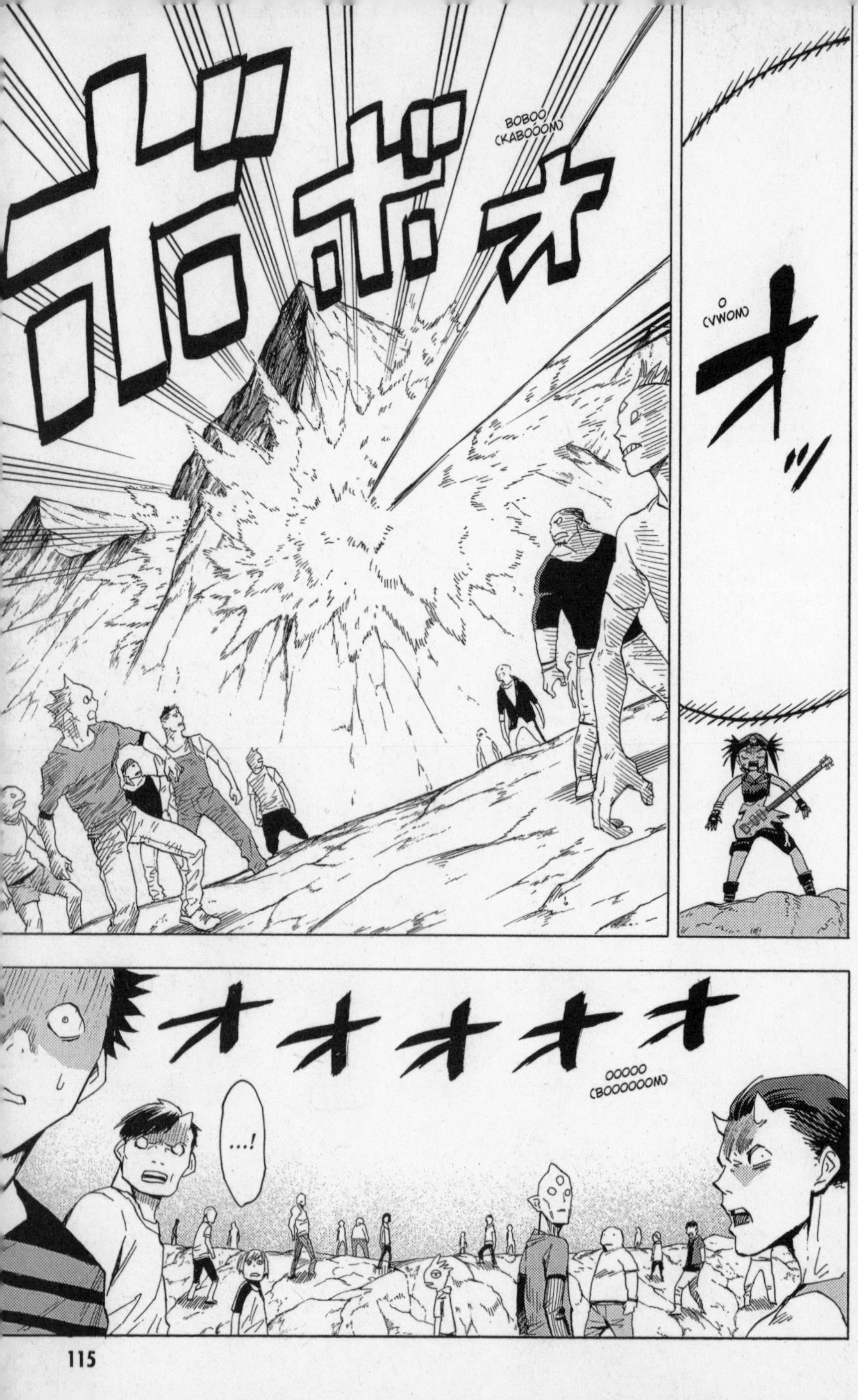

オッ
O (VWOM)
ボボオ
BOBOO (KABOOOM)
オオオオオ
OOOOO (BOOOOOOM)
...!

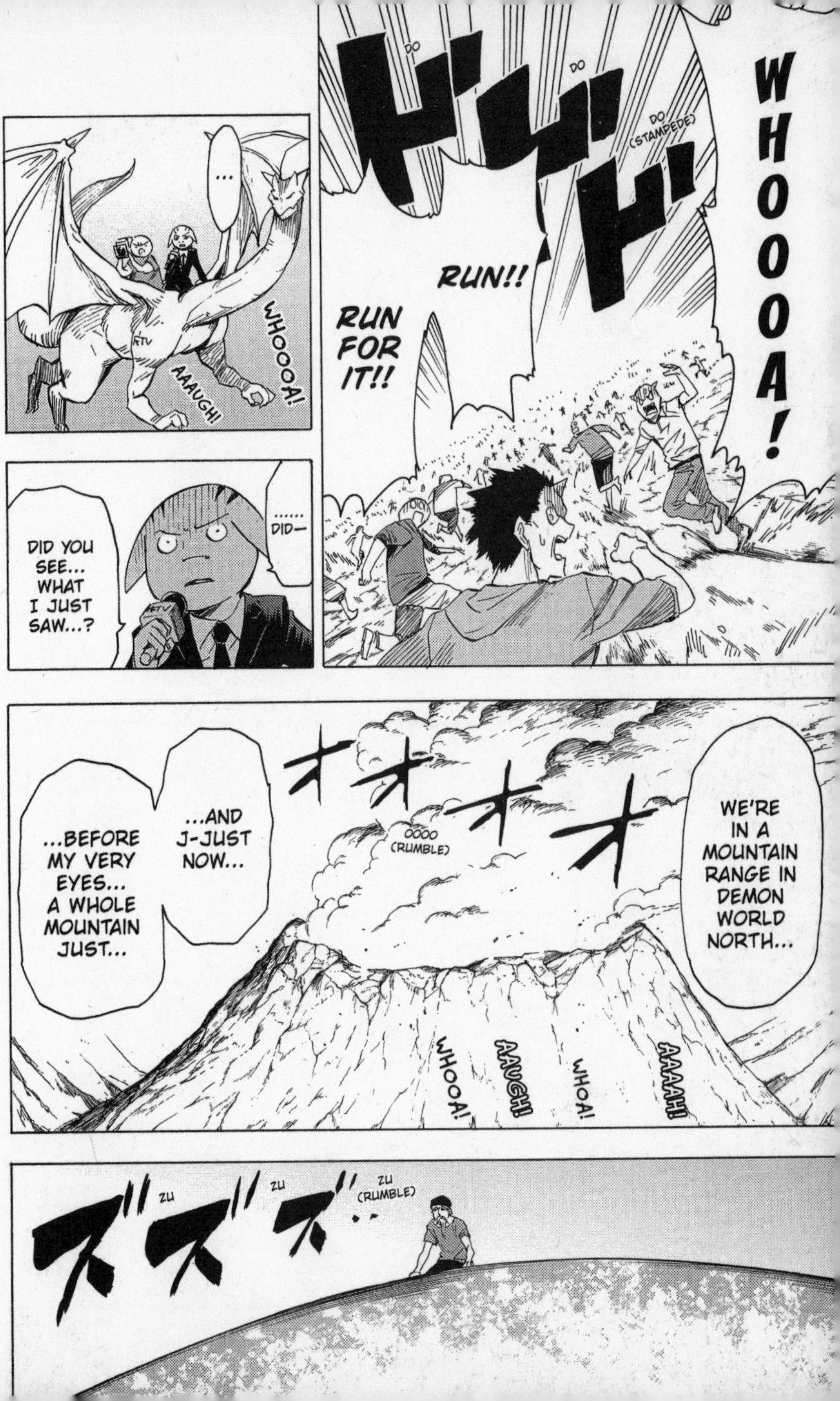

DO DO DO (STAMPEDE)
WHOOOOA!
RUN!!
RUN FOR IT!!
...
WHOOOOA!
AAAUGH!
......DID—
DID YOU SEE... WHAT I JUST SAW...?
WE'RE IN A MOUNTAIN RANGE IN DEMON WORLD NORTH...
OOOO (RUMBLE)
...AND J-JUST NOW...
...BEFORE MY VERY EYES... A WHOLE MOUNTAIN JUST...
AAAAH!
WHOA!
AAUGH!
WHOOA!
ZU ZU ZU (RUMBLE)

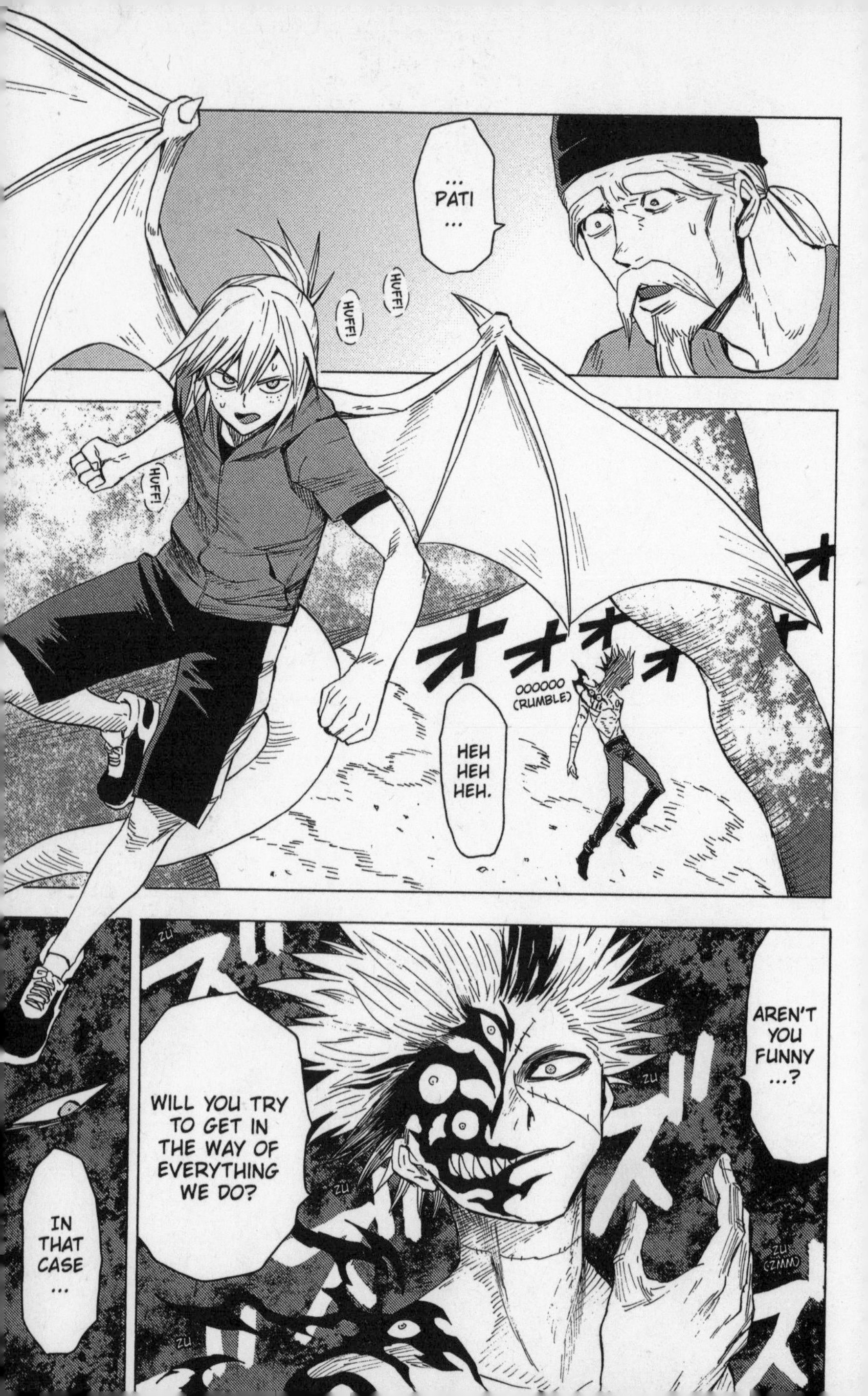
... PATI ...
HUFF! HUFF!
HUFF!
OOOOOO (RUMBLE)
HEH HEH HEH.
ZU
ARE'T YOU FUNNY ...?
WILL YOU TRY TO GET IN THE WAY OF EVERYTHING WE DO?
ZU (ZMM)
ZU
IN THAT CASE ...
ZU

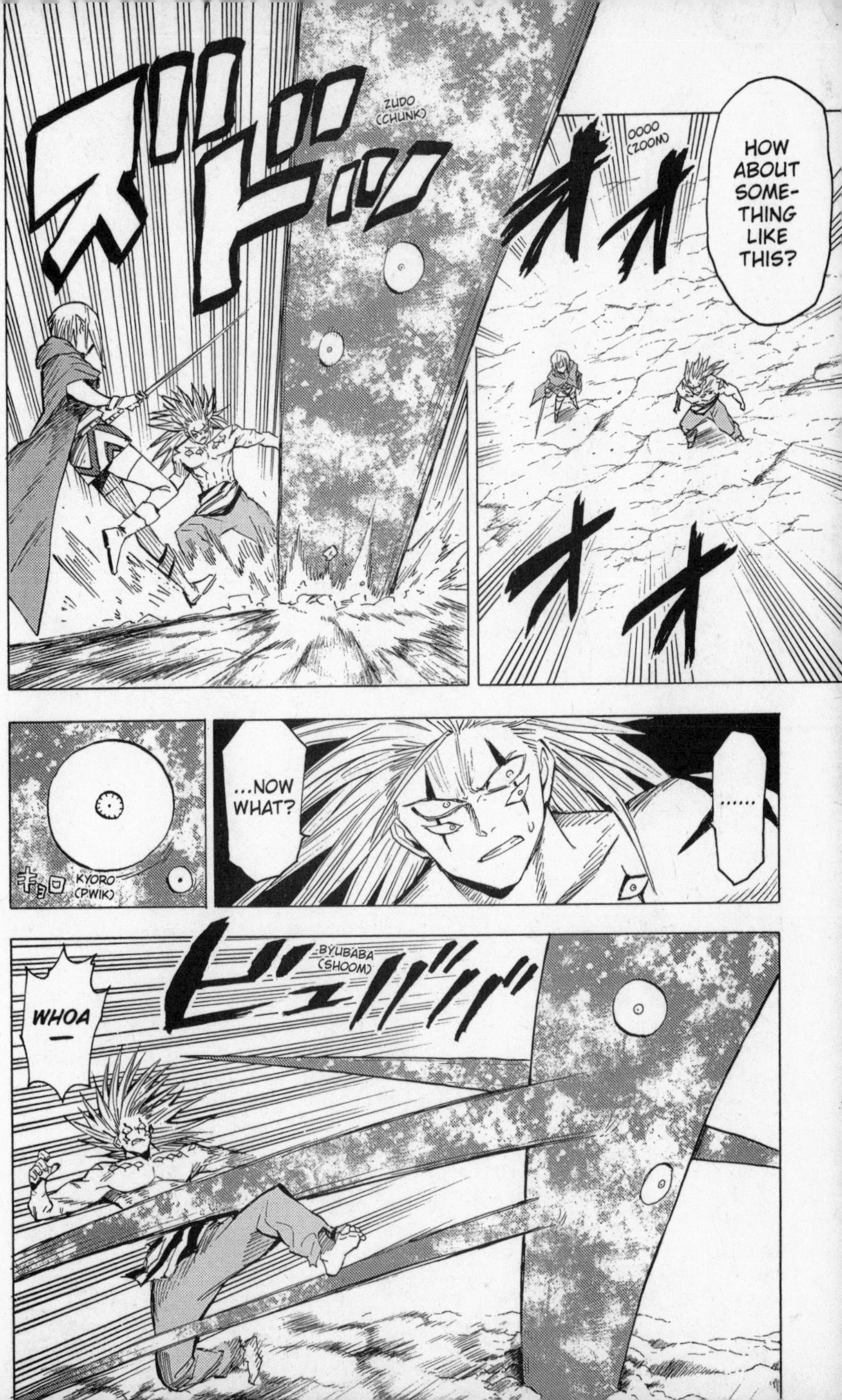
HOW ABOUT SOMETHING-THING LIKE THIS?
OOOO (ZOOM)
ZUDO (CHUNK)
......
...NOW WHAT?
KYORO (PWIK)
BYUBABA (SHOOM)
WHOA —

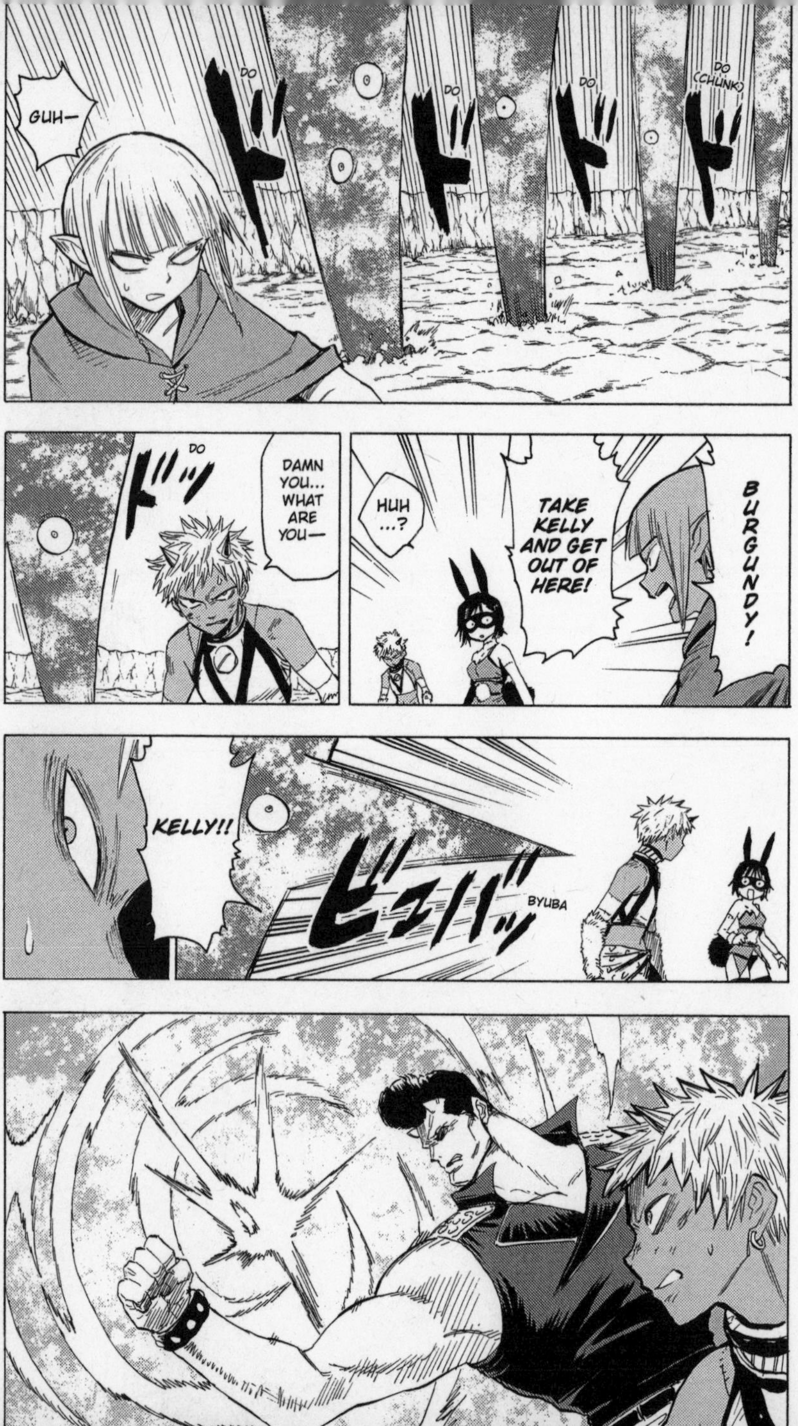
DO (CHUNK)
DO
DO
DO
GUH—
BURGUNDY!
TAKE KELLY AND GET OUT OF HERE!
HUH ...?
DAMN YOU... WHAT ARE YOU—
DO
KELLY!!
BYUBA

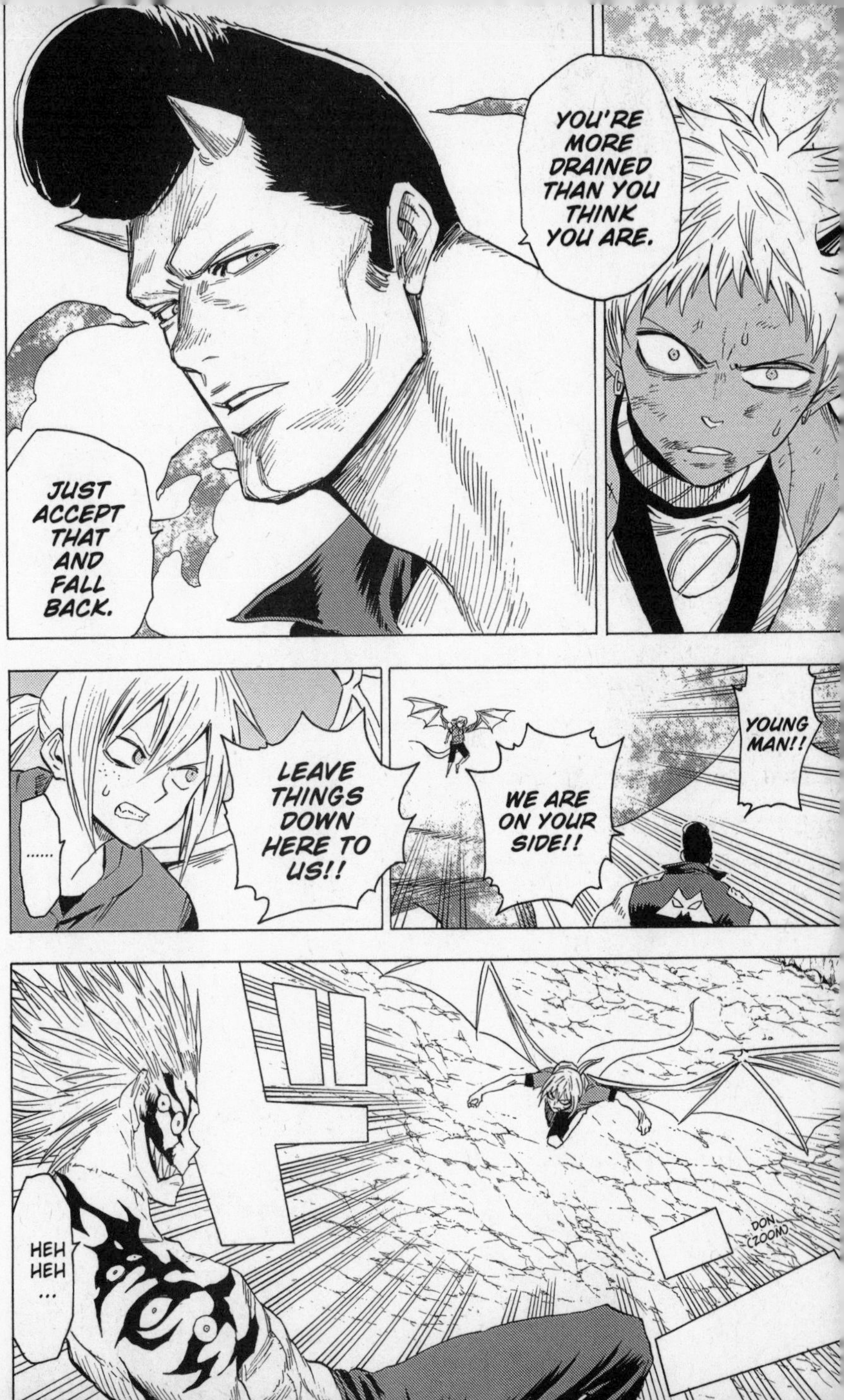
YOU'RE MORE DRAINED THAN YOU THINK YOU ARE.
JUST ACCEPT THAT AND FALL BACK.
YOUNG MAN!!
WE ARE ON YOUR SIDE!!
LEAVE THINGS DOWN HERE TO US!!
......
DON (ZOOM)
HEH HEH ...

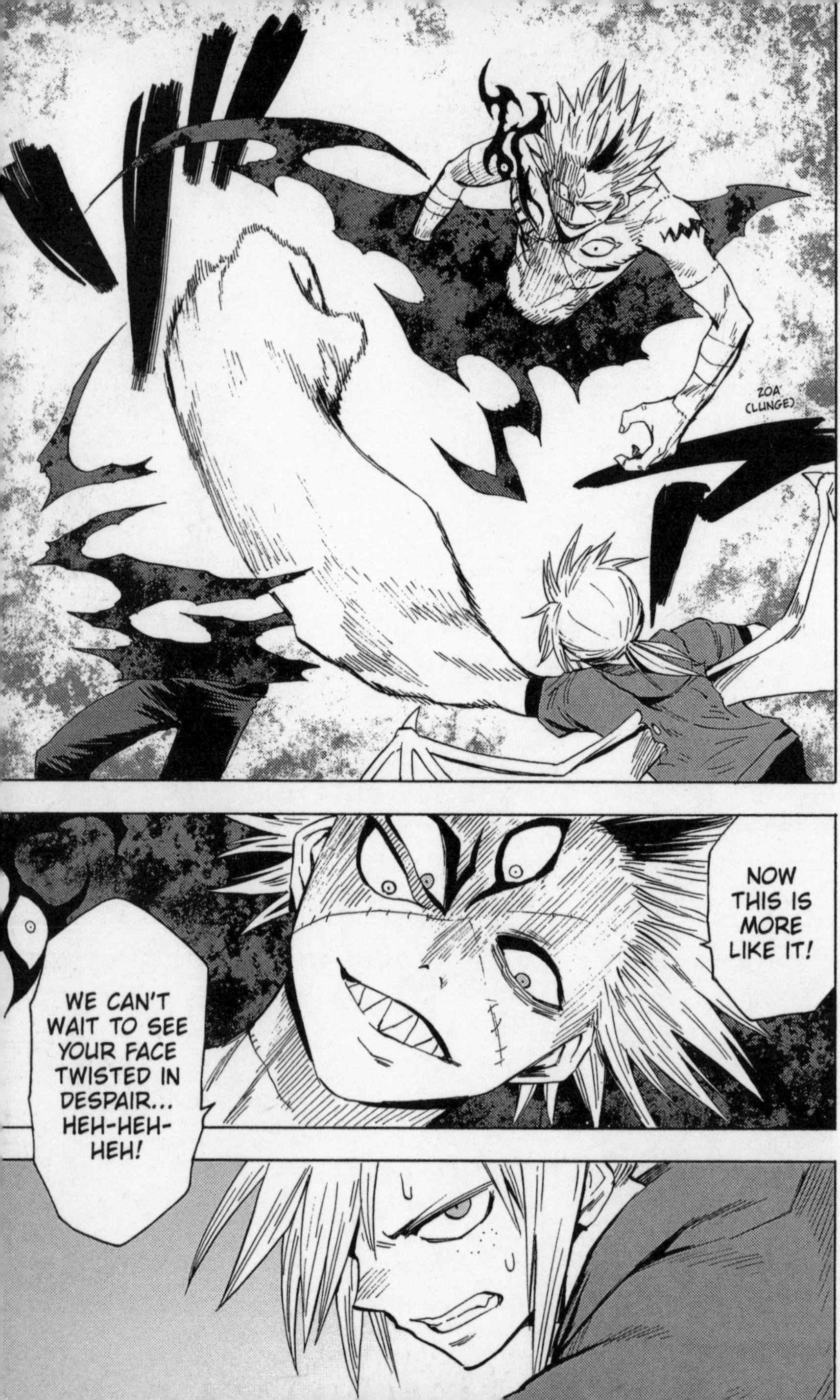
ZOA (LUNGE)
NOW THIS IS MORE LIKE IT!
WE CAN'T WAIT TO SEE YOUR FACE TWISTED IN DESPAIR... HEH-HEH-HEH!

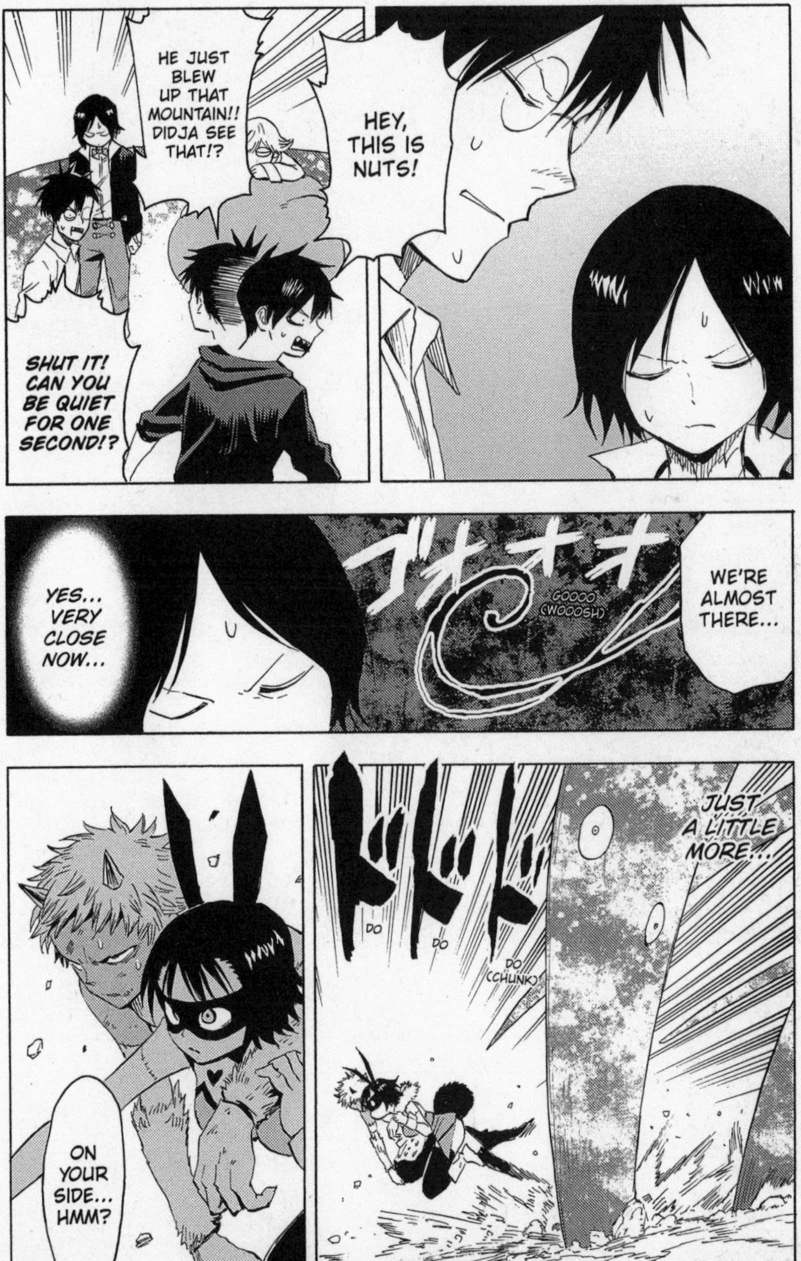
HEY, THIS IS NUTS!
HE JUST BLEW UP THAT MOUNTAIN!! DIDJA SEE THAT!?
SHUT IT! CAN YOU BE QUIET FOR ONE SECOND!?
WE'RE ALMOST THERE...
GOOOO (WOOOSH)
YES... VERY CLOSE NOW...
JUST A LITTLE MORE...
DO
DO
DO (CHUNK)
ON YOUR SIDE... HMM?

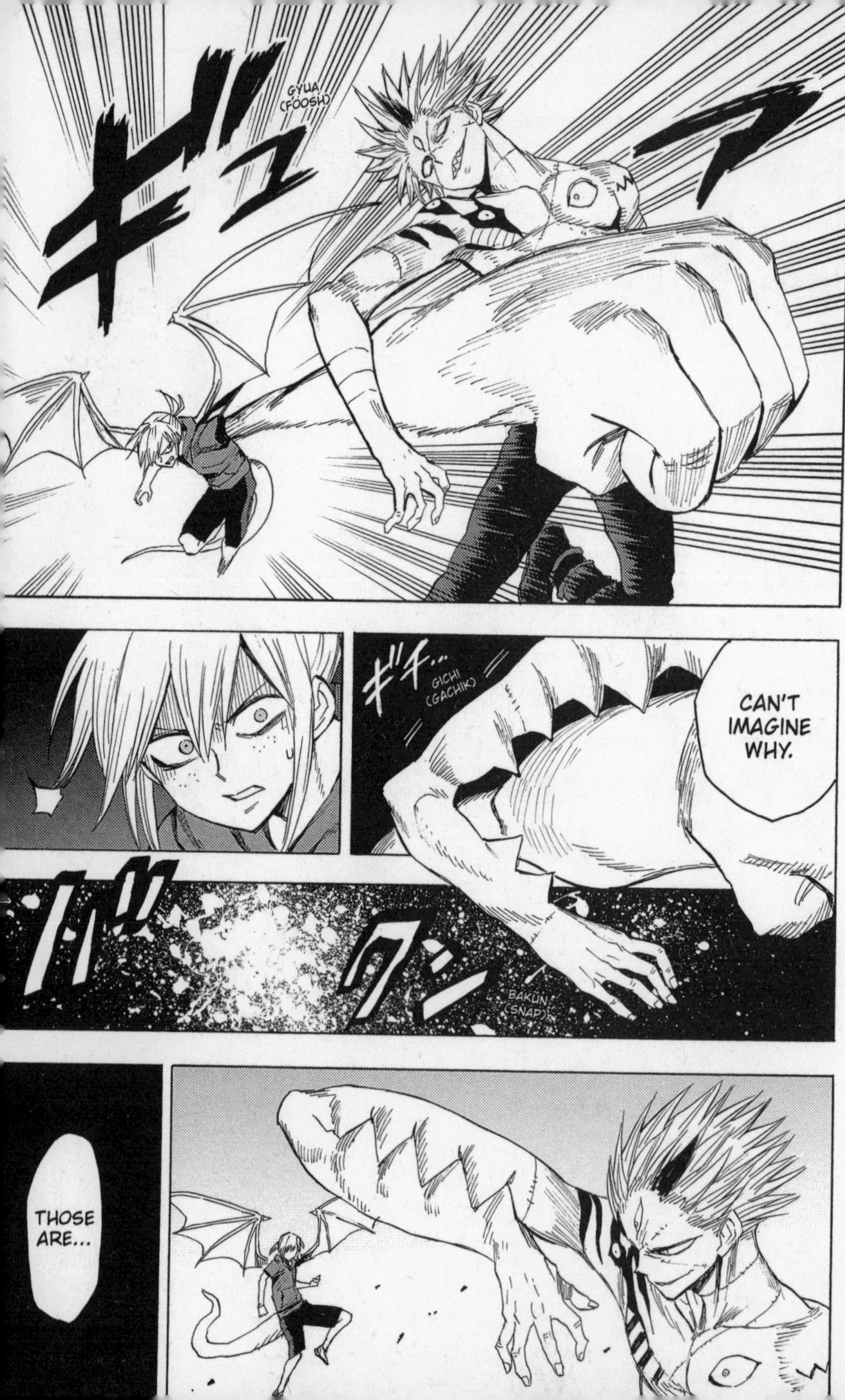

GYUA
(FOOSH)
CAN'T IMAGINE WHY.
GICHI
(GACHIK)
BAKUN
(SNAP)
THOSE ARE...

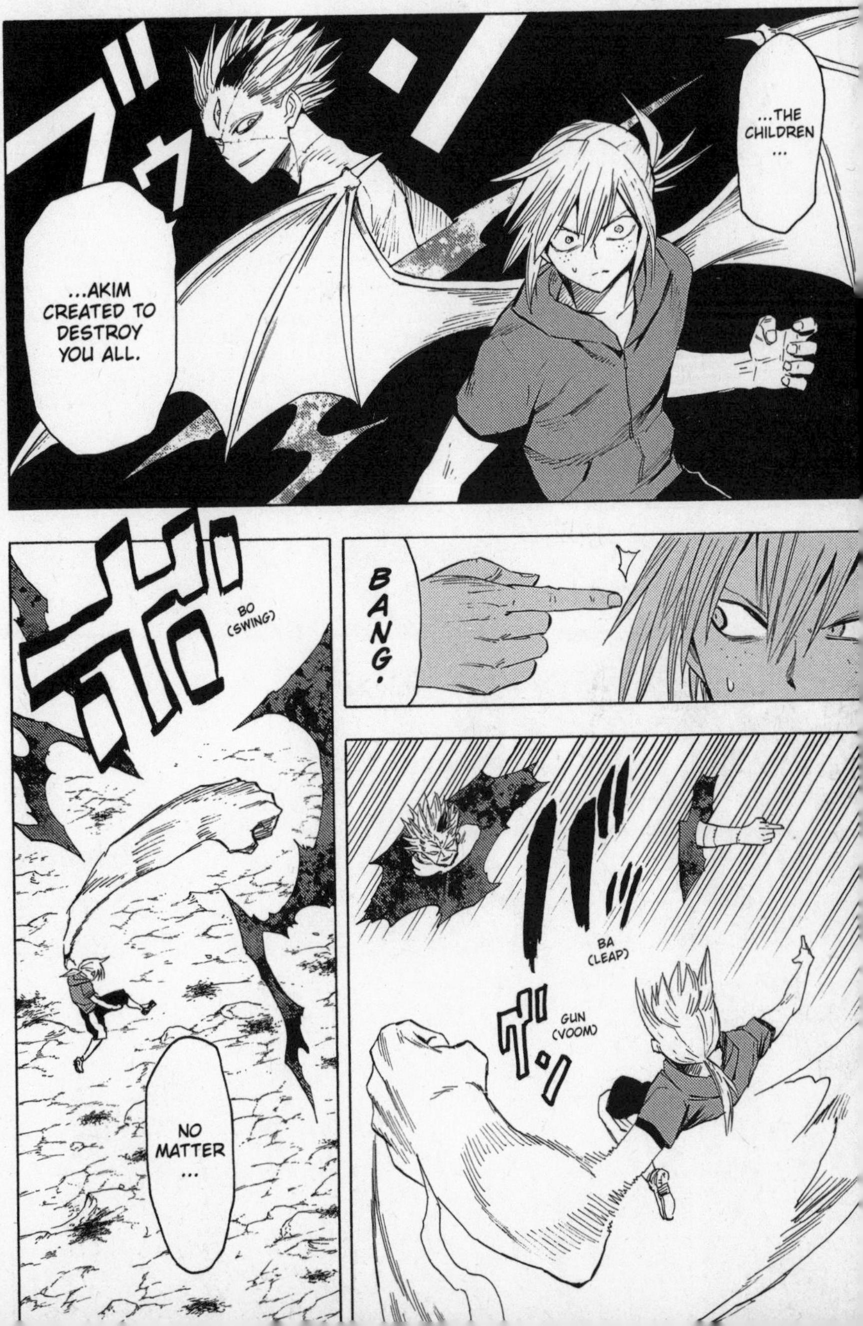
...THE CHILDREN ...
...AKIM CREATED TO DESTROY YOU ALL.
BANG.
BA (LEAP)
GUN (VOOM)
BO (SWING)
NO MATTER ...

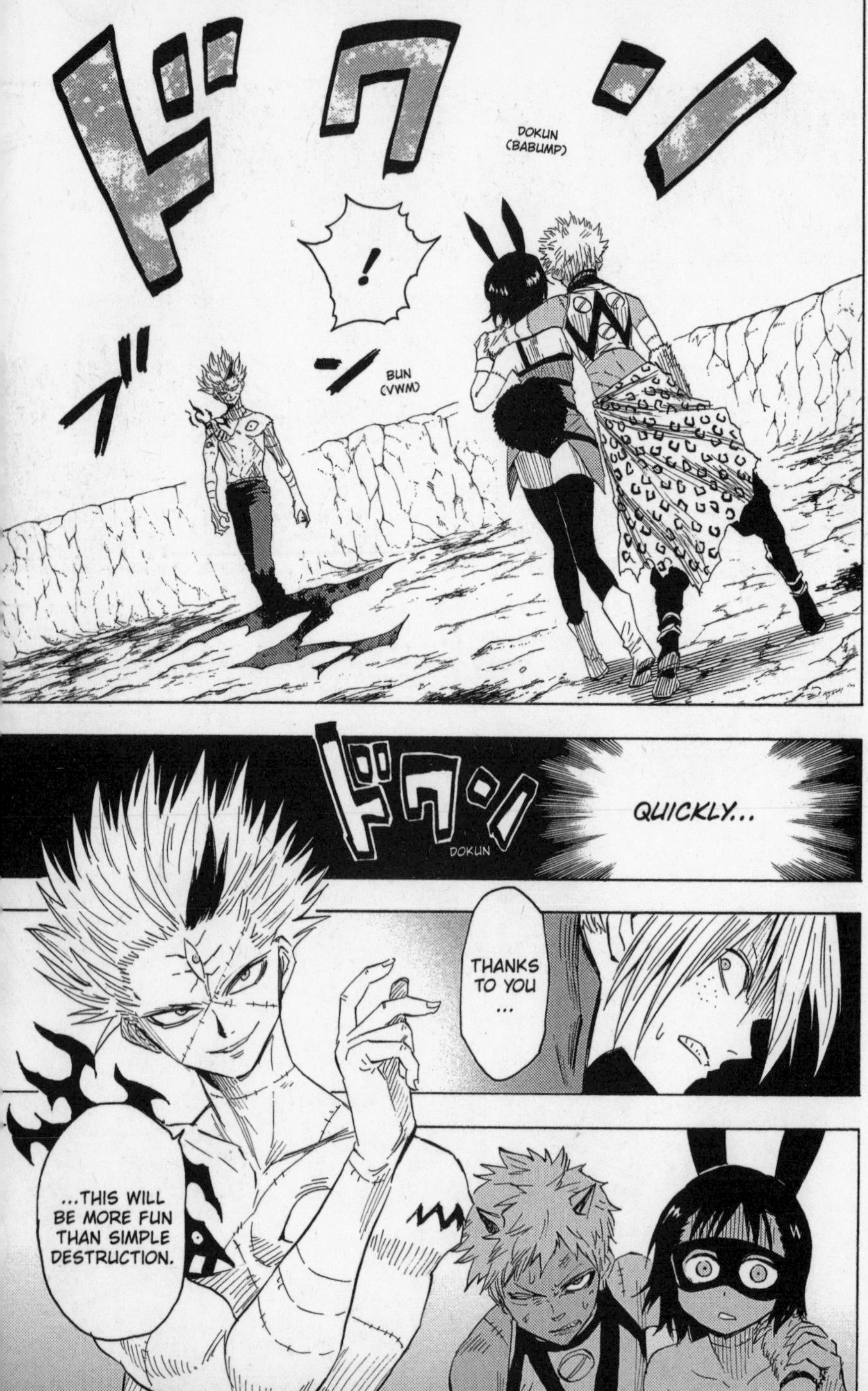
ドクン
DOKUN
(BABUMP)
!
ブン
BUN
(VWM)
QUICKLY...
ドクン
DOKUN
THANKS TO YOU ...
...THIS WILL BE MORE FUN THAN SIMPLE DESTRUCTION.

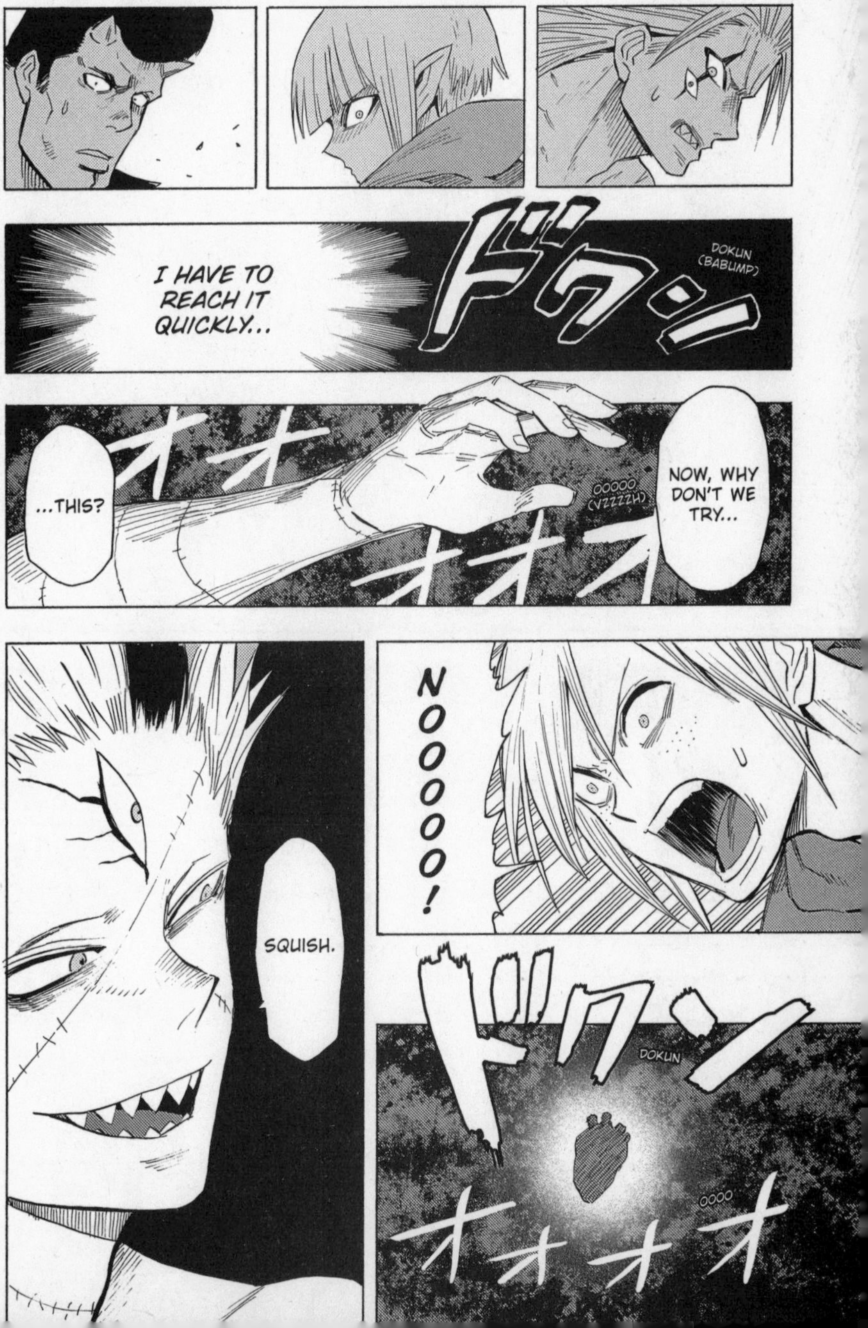
DOKUN (BABUMP)
I HAVE TO REACH IT QUICKLY...
NOW, WHY DON'T WE TRY...
OOOOO (VZZZZH)
...THIS?
NOOOOOO!
DOKUN
OOOO
SQUISH.

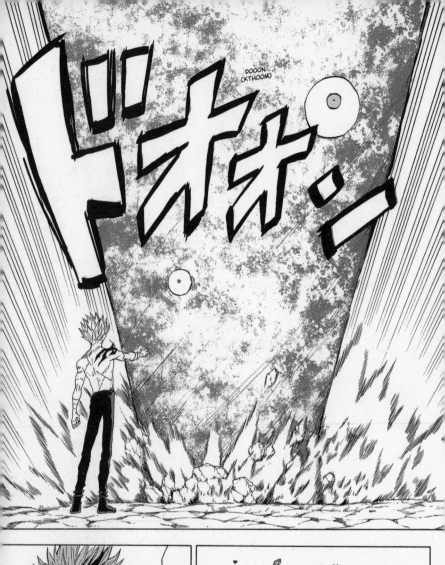

DOOON
(KTHOOM)

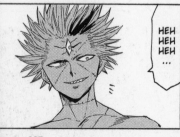

HEH
HEH
HEH
...

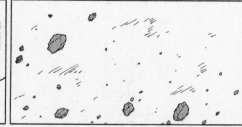

127

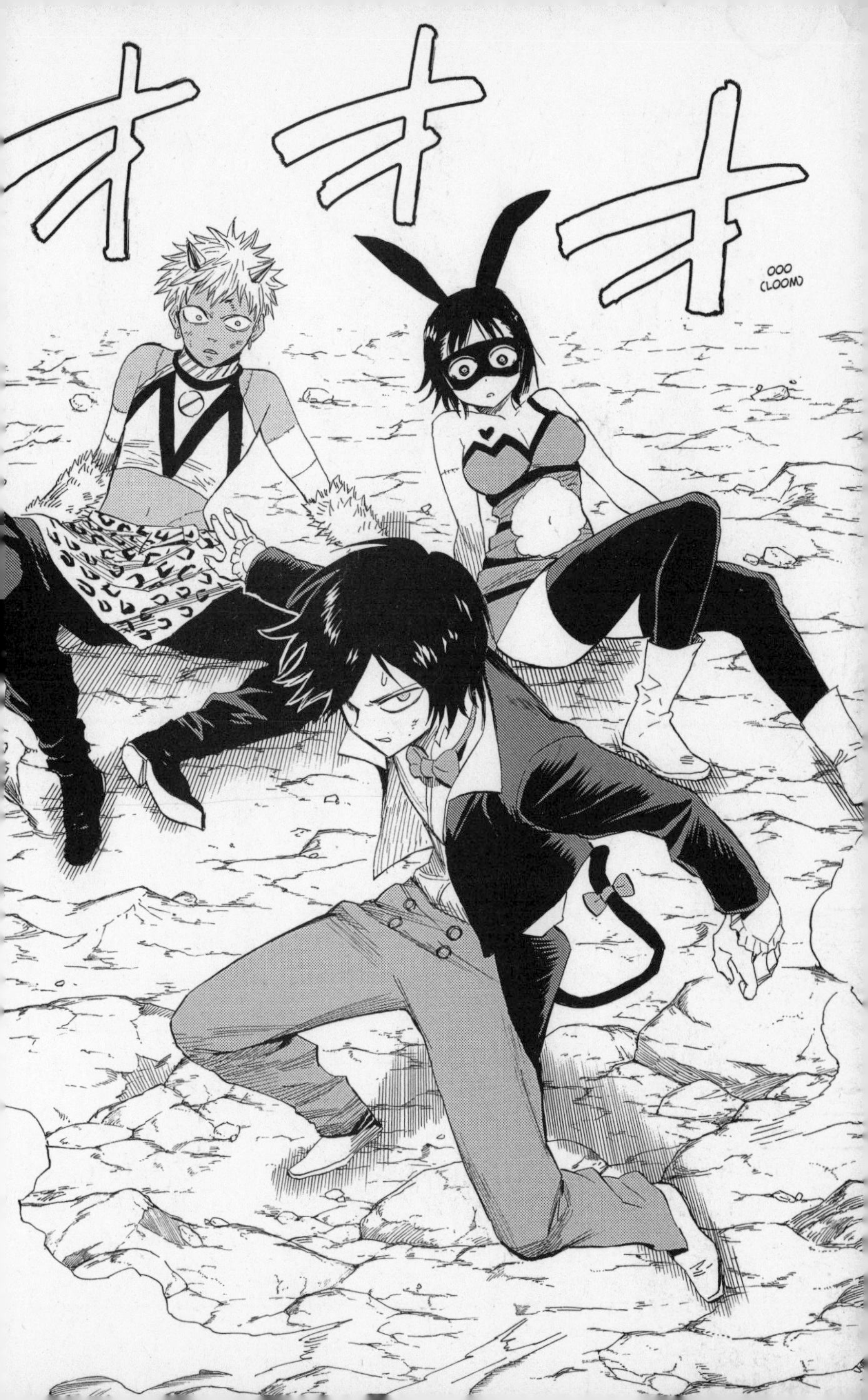
オオオ
OOO
(LOOM)

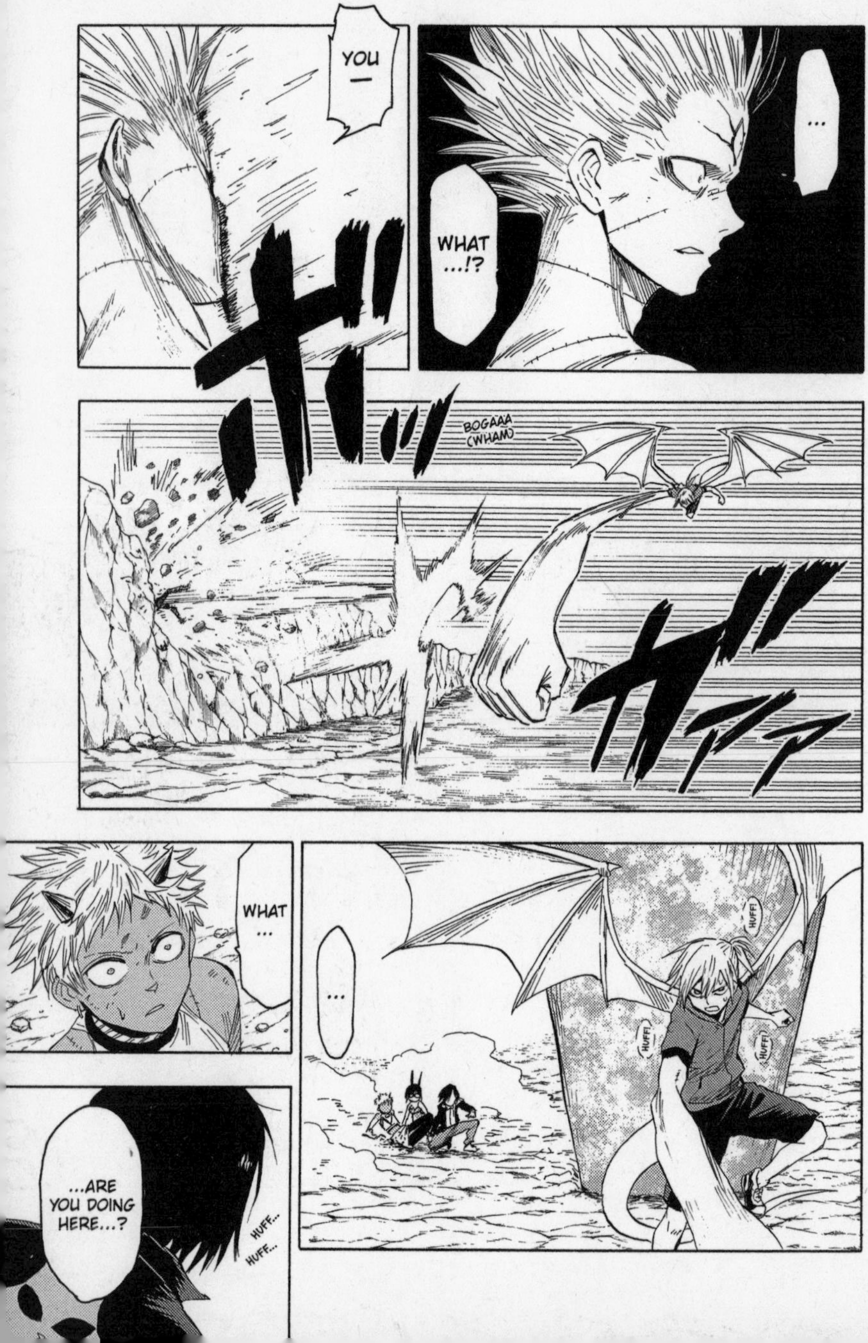
...
WHAT ...!?
YOU —
BOGAAA (WHAM)
...
HUFF!
HUFF!
HUFF!
WHAT ...
...ARE YOU DOING HERE...?
HUFF... HUFF...

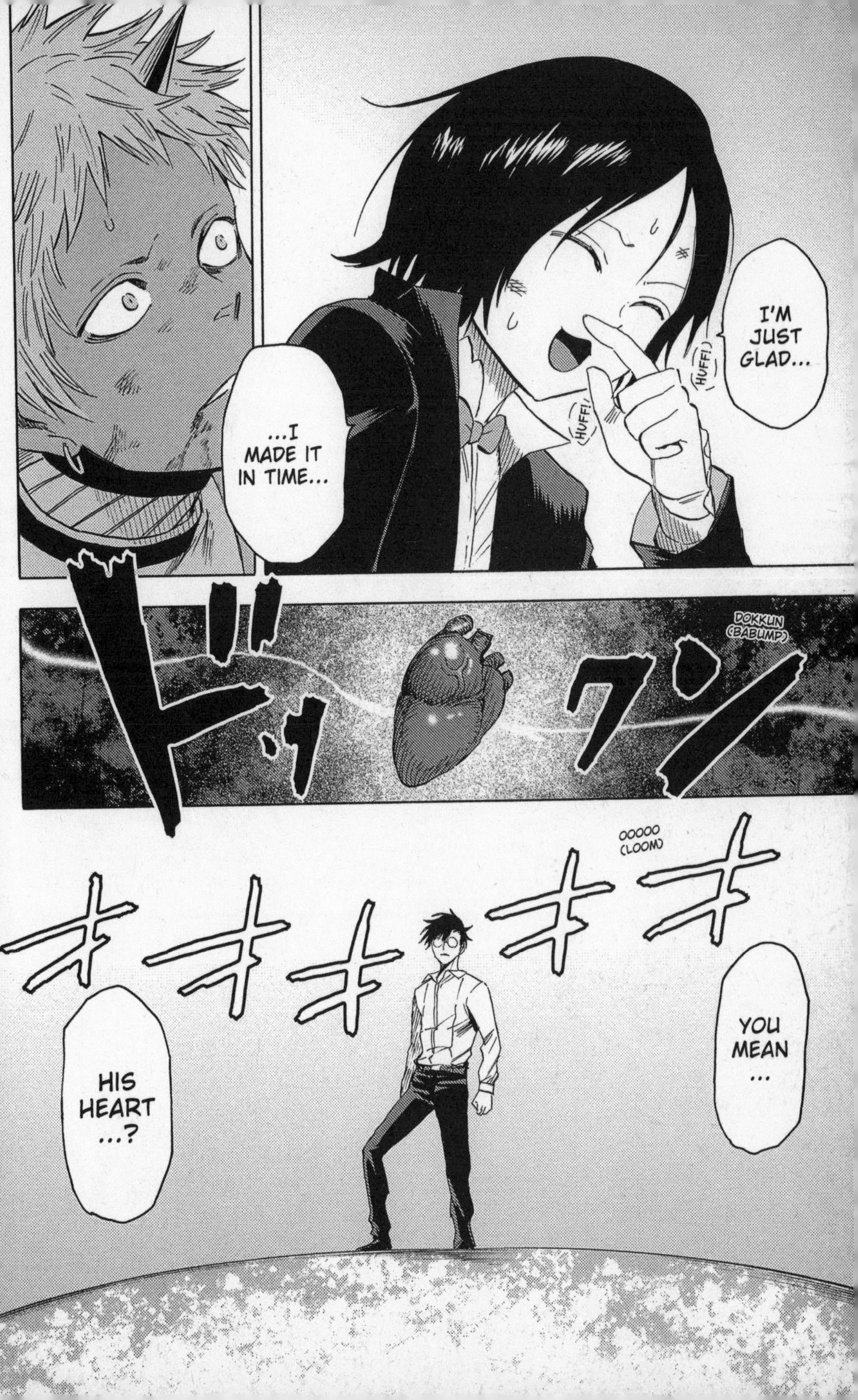

I'M JUST GLAD...
HUFF!
HUFF!
...I MADE IT IN TIME...
DOKKUN (BABUMP)
ドッ クン
OOOOO (LOOM)
オオオオオ
YOU MEAN ...
HIS HEART ...?

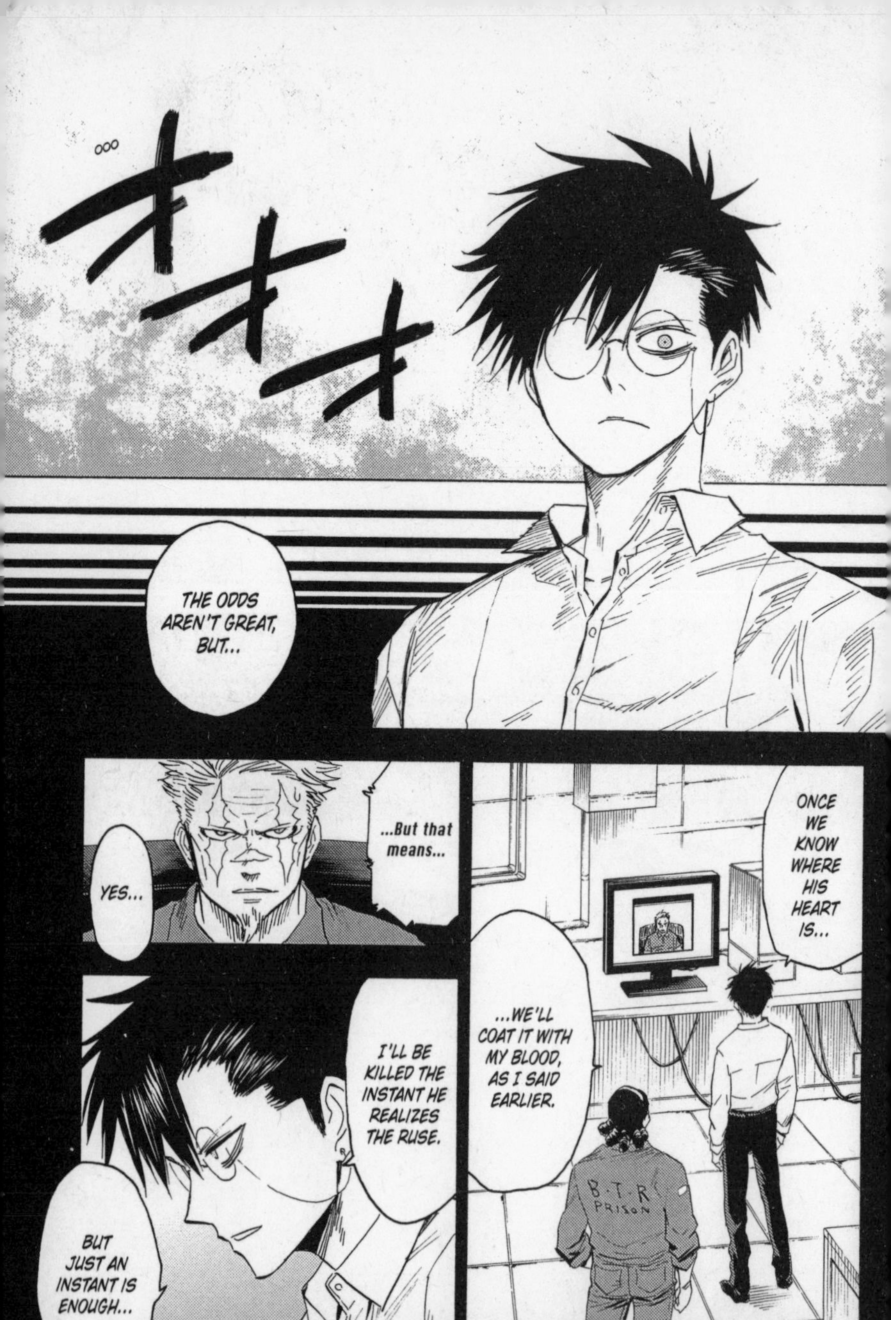

オオオ
OOO
THE ODDS AREN'T GREAT, BUT...
ONCE WE KNOW WHERE HIS HEART IS...
...WE'LL COAT IT WITH MY BLOOD, AS I SAID EARLIER.
B·T·R PRISON
...But that means...
YES...
I'LL BE KILLED THE INSTANT HE REALIZES THE RUSE.
BUT JUST AN INSTANT IS ENOUGH...

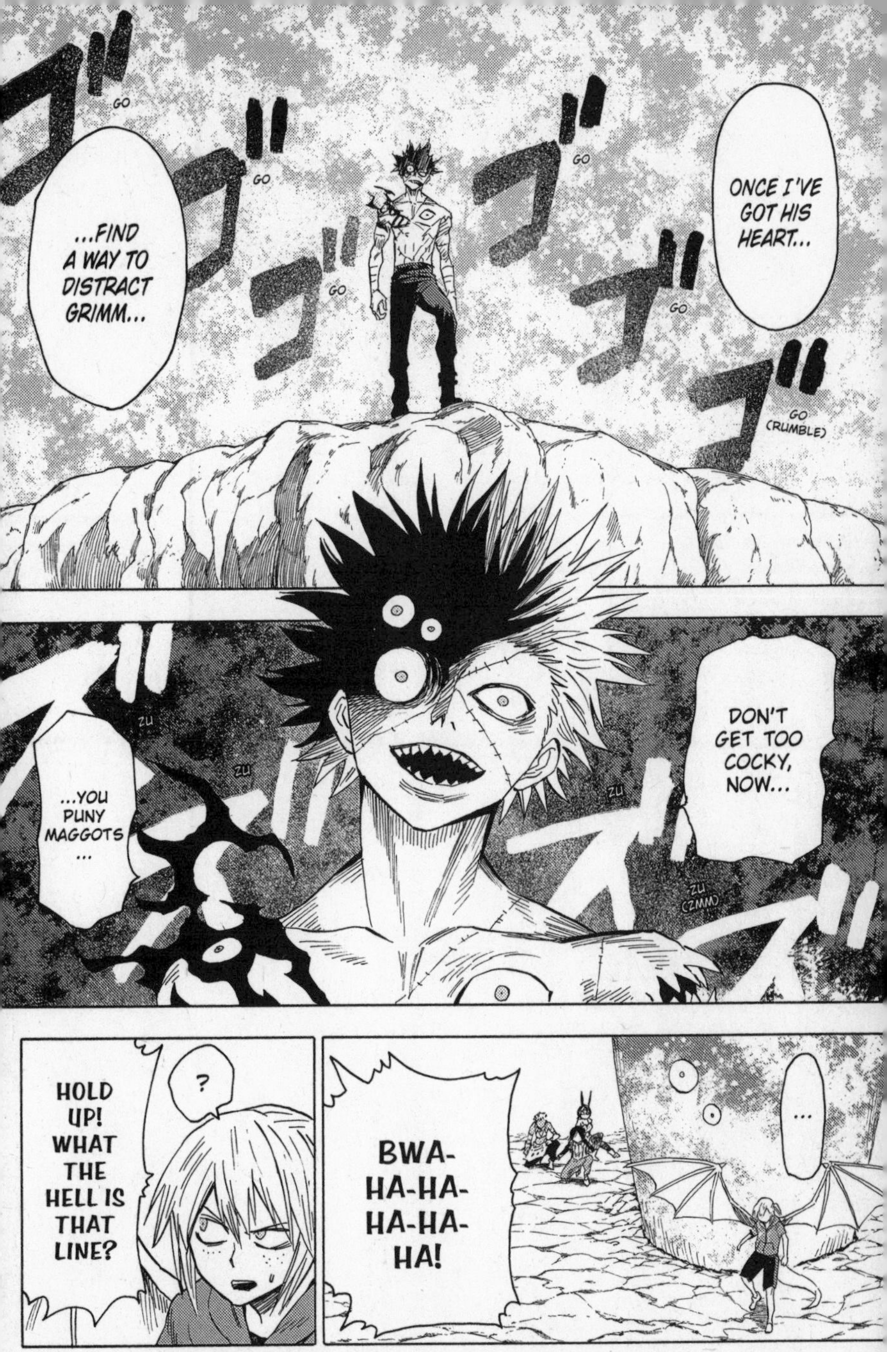
GO
GO
GO
ONCE I'VE GOT HIS HEART...
GO
GO
GO (RUMBLE)
...FIND A WAY TO DISTRACT GRIMM...
DON'T GET TOO COCKY, NOW...
ZU
ZU (ZMM)
ZU
ZU
...YOU PUNY MAGGOTS ...
...
BWA-HA-HA-HA-HA-HA-HA!
?
HOLD UP! WHAT THE HELL IS THAT LINE?

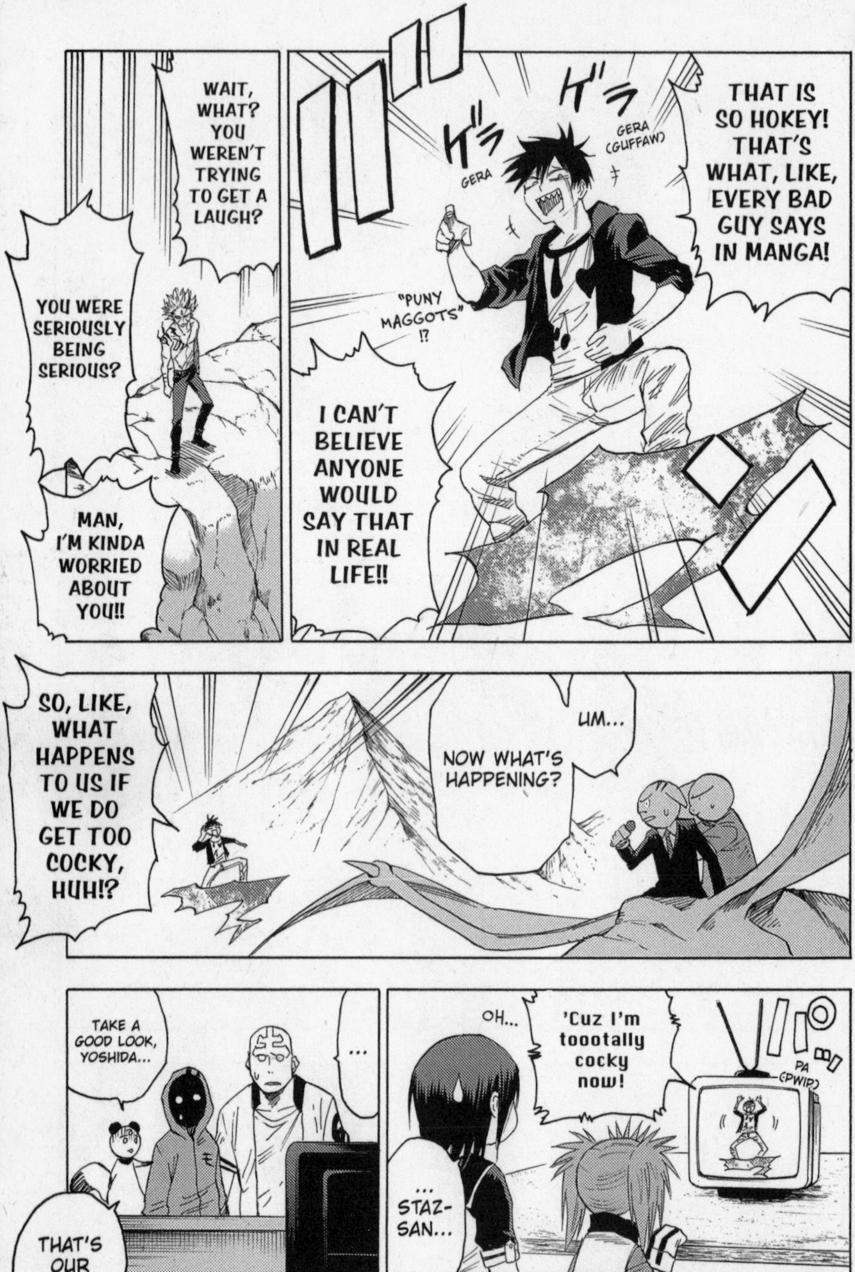
ゲラ
GERA (GUFFAW)
ゲラ
GERA
THAT IS SO HOKEY! THAT'S WHAT, LIKE, EVERY BAD GUY SAYS IN MANGA!
"PUNY MAGGOTS" !?
I CAN'T BELIEVE ANYONE WOULD SAY THAT IN REAL LIFE!!
WAIT, WHAT? YOU WEREN'T TRYING TO GET A LAUGH?
YOU WERE SERIOUSLY BEING SERIOUS?
MAN, I'M KINDA WORRIED ABOUT YOU!!
UM...
NOW WHAT'S HAPPENING?
SO, LIKE, WHAT HAPPENS TO US IF WE DO GET TOO COCKY, HUH!?
PA (PWIP)
'Cuz I'm tooootally cocky now!
OH...
... STAZ-SAN...
...
TAKE A GOOD LOOK, YOSHIDA...
THAT'S OUR BOSS.

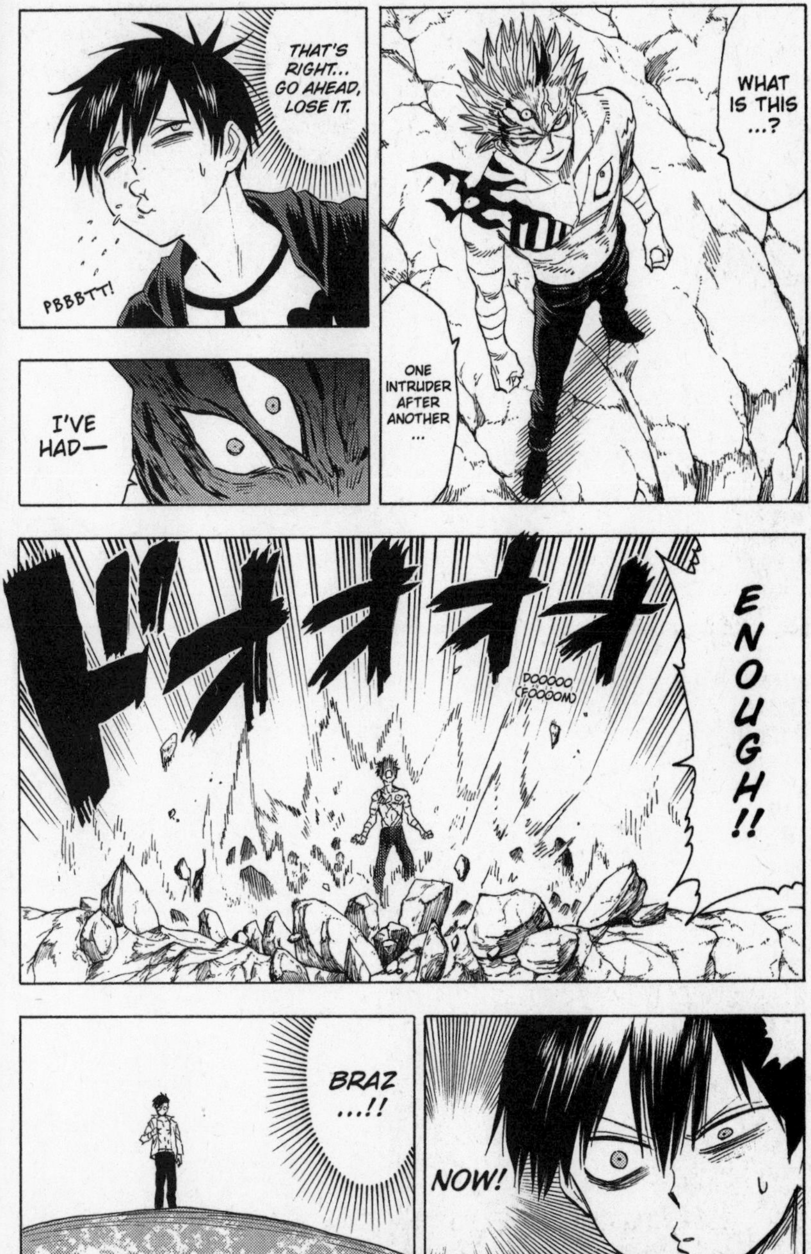
WHAT IS THIS ...?
ONE INTRUDER AFTER ANOTHER ...
THAT'S RIGHT... GO AHEAD, LOSE IT.
PBBBTT!
I'VE HAD—
ENOUGH!!
ドオオオ
DOOOOO (FOOOOM)
NOW!
BRAZ ...!!

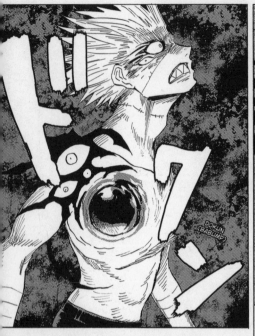

DOKIN
(BABUMP)

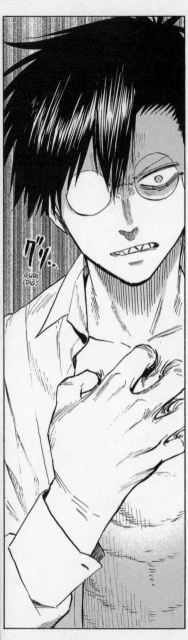

*η"η*…
GURI
(DIG)

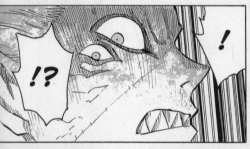

!?          !

...AND...?
THEN WHAT'LL
YOU DO?

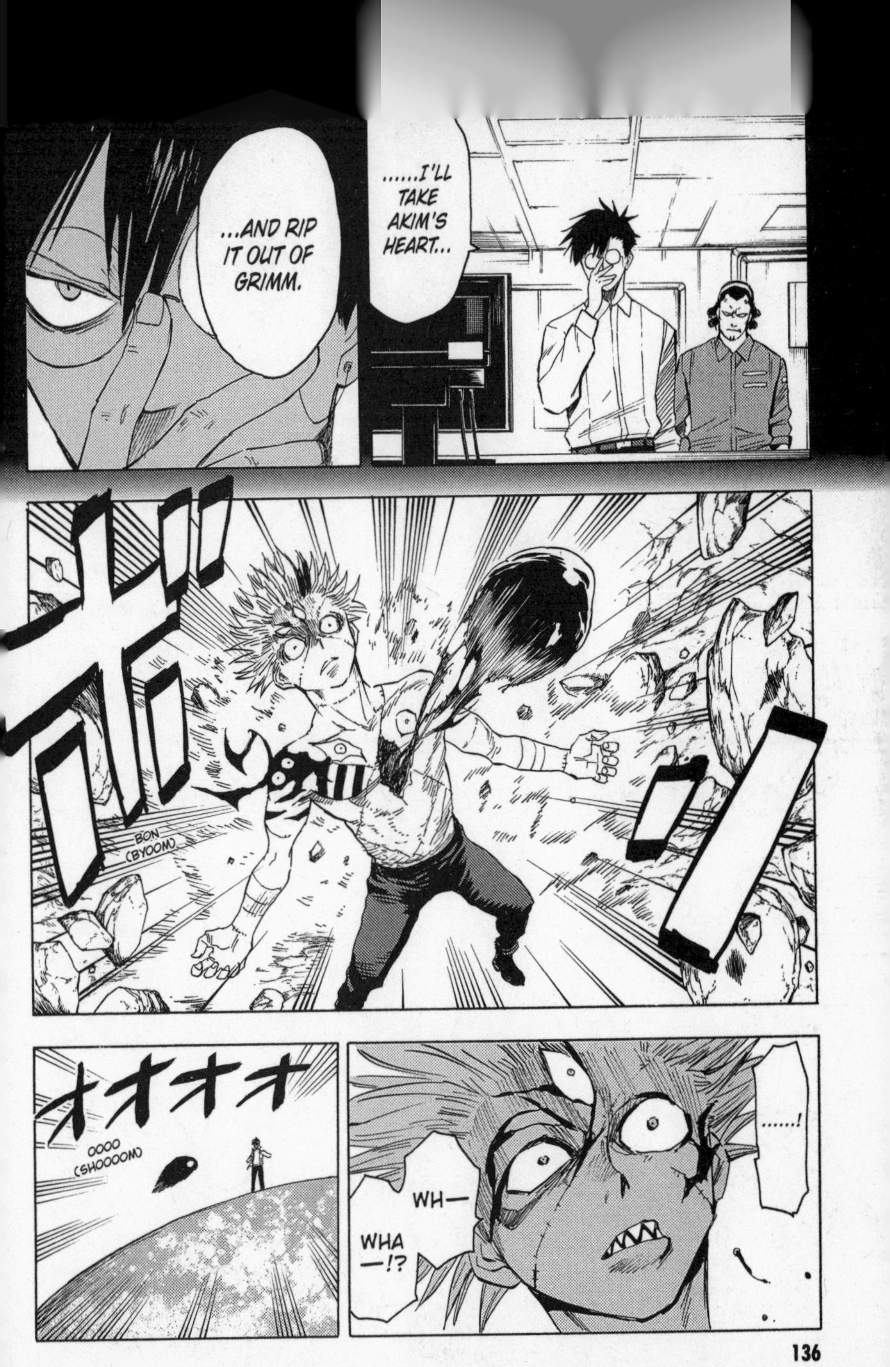
......I'LL TAKE AKIM'S HEART...
...AND RIP IT OUT OF GRIMM.
ボン
BON (BYOOM)
......!
WH—
WHA—!?
オオオオ
OOOO (SHOOOOM)

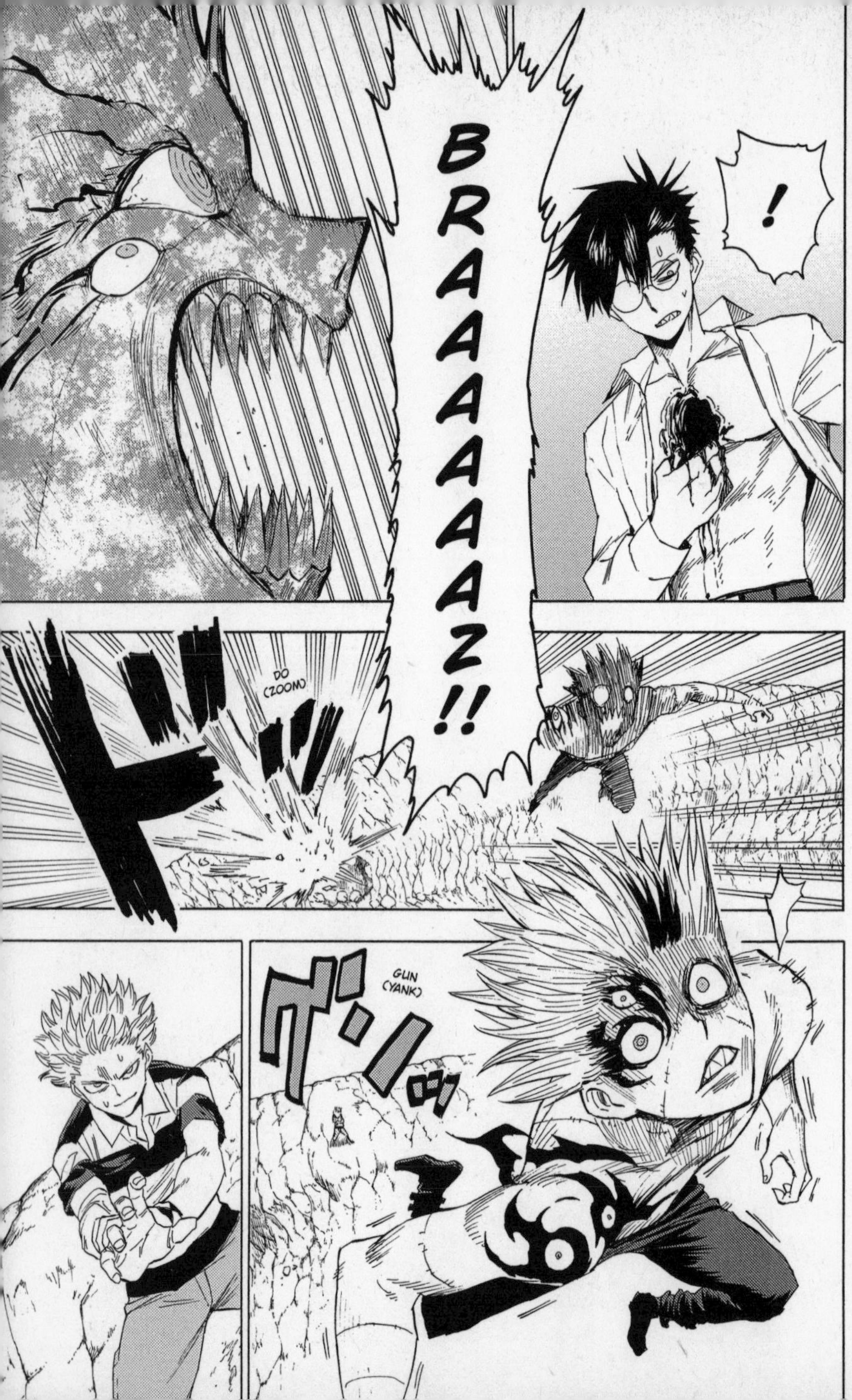
!
BRAAAAAAAZ!!
DO (ZOOM)
GUN (YANK)

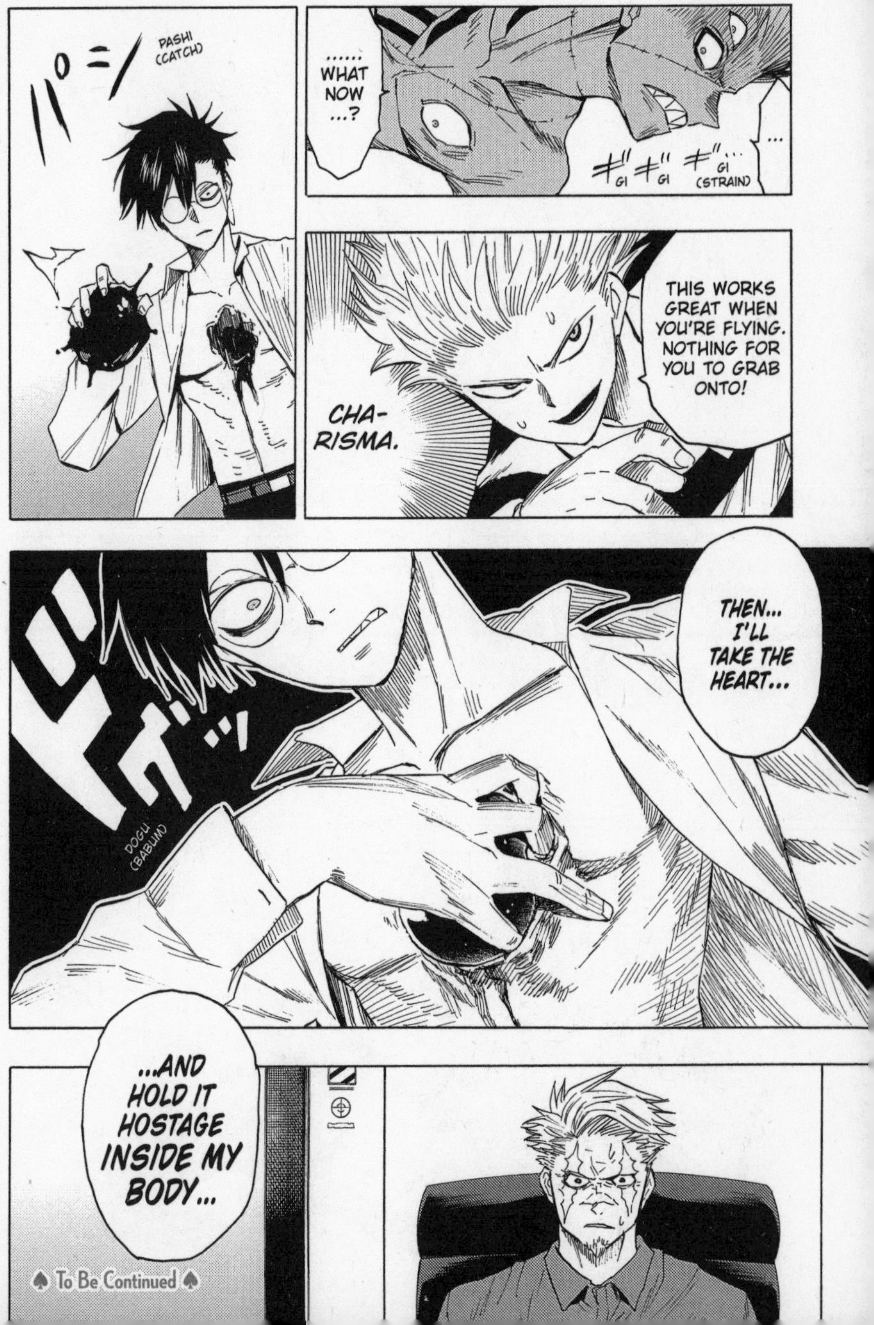
......WHAT NOW ...?
...
GI GI GI (STRAIN)
THIS WORKS GREAT WHEN YOU'RE FLYING. NOTHING FOR YOU TO GRAB ONTO!
CHA-RISMA.
PASHI (CATCH)
THEN... I'LL TAKE THE HEART...
DOGU (BABUM)
...AND HOLD IT HOSTAGE INSIDE MY BODY...
To Be Continued

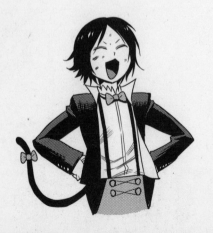

BLOOD LAD

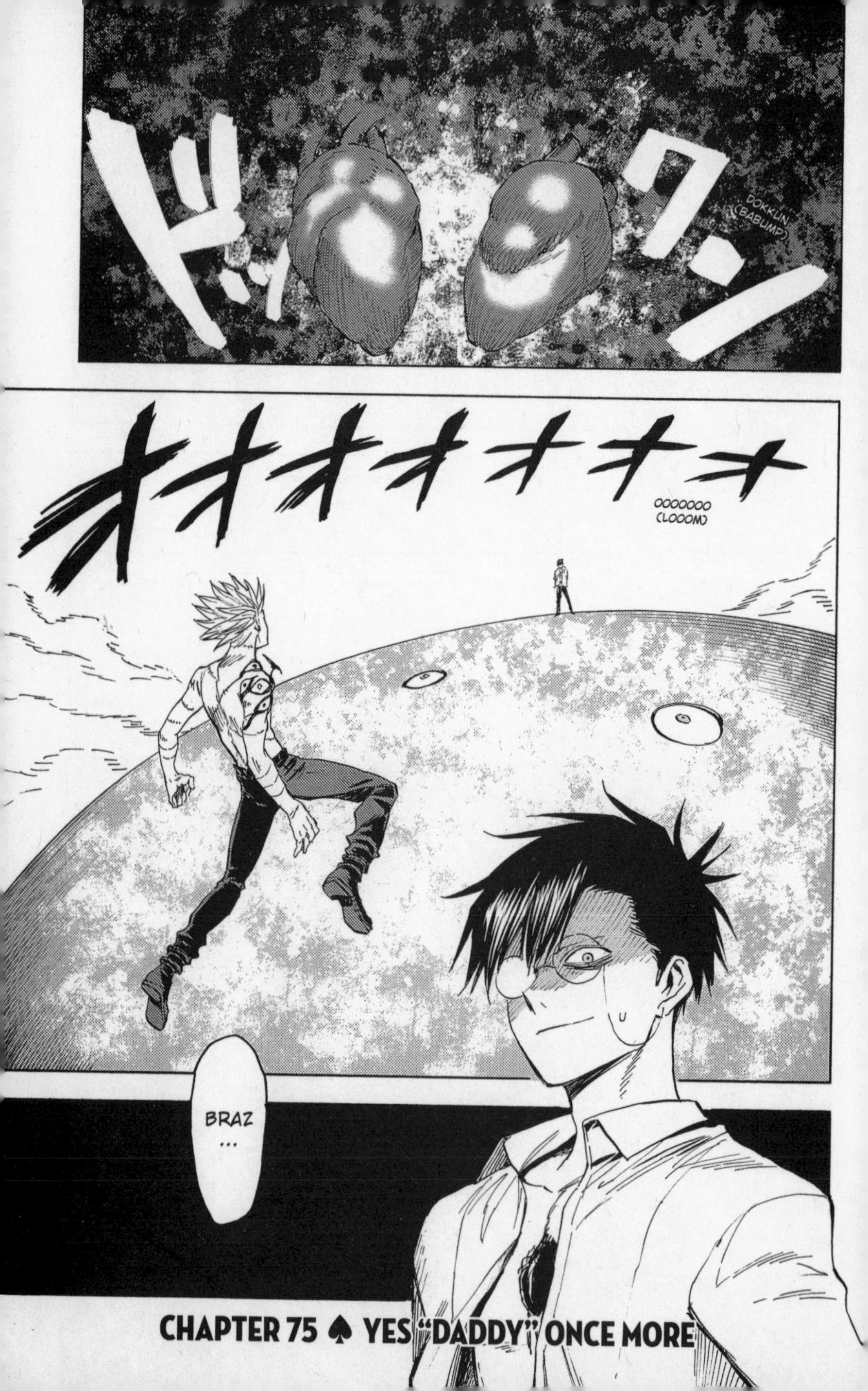
ドクン
DOKKUN (BABUMP)
オオオオオオオオ
OOOOOOO (LOOOM)
BRAZ ...
CHAPTER 75 ♠ YES "DADDY" ONCE MORE

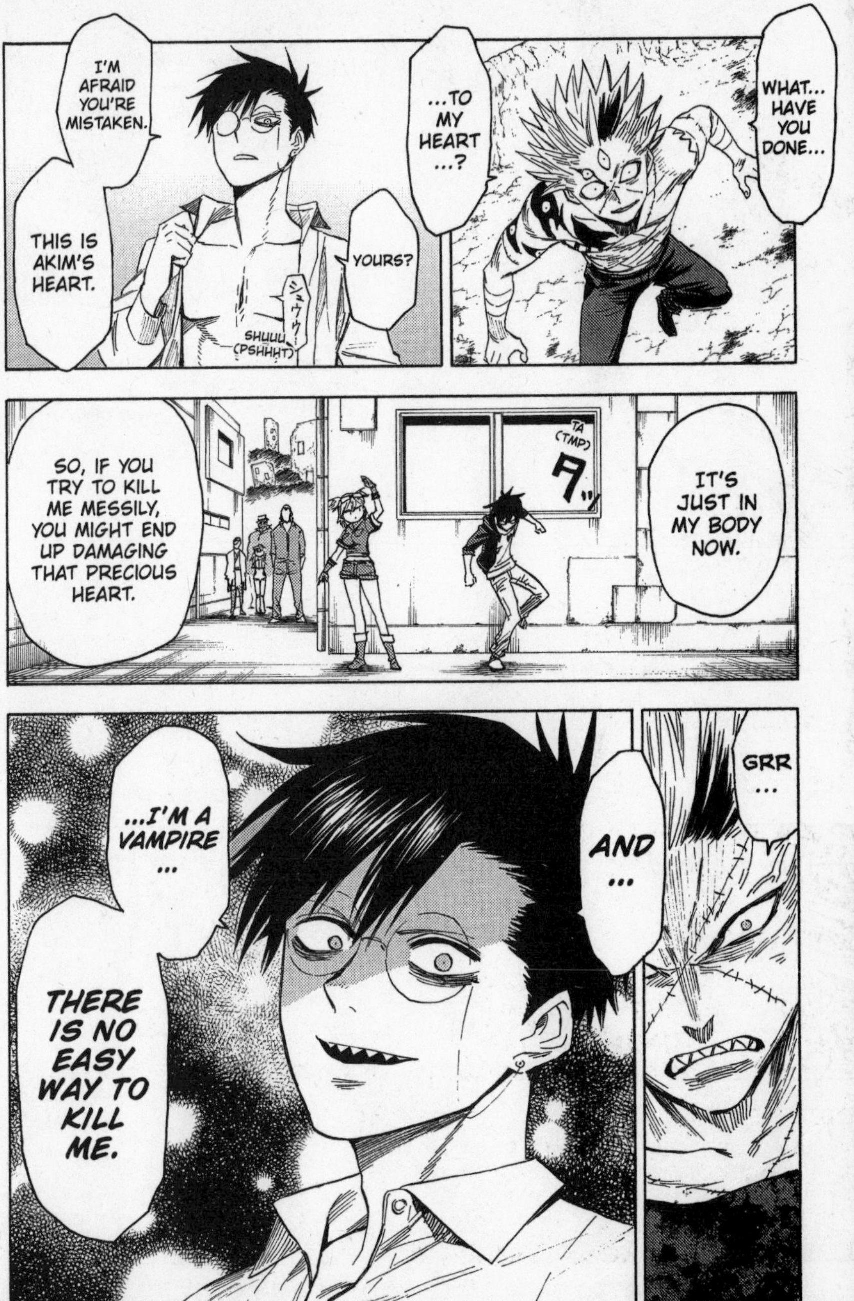
WHAT... HAVE YOU DONE...
...TO MY HEART ...?
YOURS?
I'M AFRAID YOU'RE MISTAKEN.
THIS IS AKIM'S HEART.
シュウウ
SHUUU (PSHHHT)
IT'S JUST IN MY BODY NOW.
タ
TA (TMP)
SO, IF YOU TRY TO KILL ME MESSILY, YOU MIGHT END UP DAMAGING THAT PRECIOUS HEART.
GRR ...
AND ...
...I'M A VAMPIRE ...
THERE IS NO EASY WAY TO KILL ME.

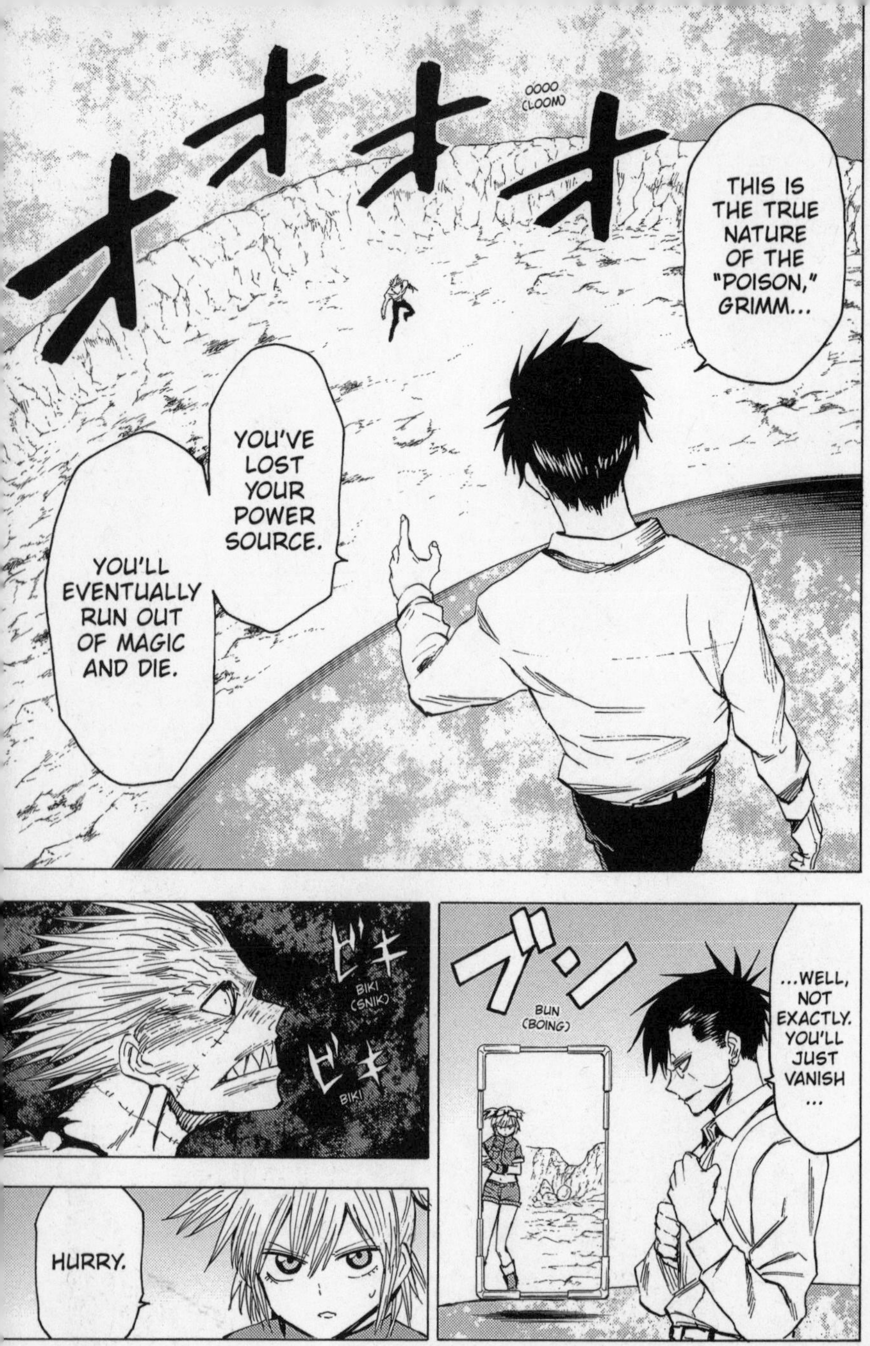
オオオオ
OOOO (LOOM)
THIS IS THE TRUE NATURE OF THE "POISON," GRIMM...
YOU'VE LOST YOUR POWER SOURCE.
YOU'LL EVENTUALLY RUN OUT OF MAGIC AND DIE.
ブン
BUN (BOING)
...WELL, NOT EXACTLY. YOU'LL JUST VANISH ...
ビキ
BIKI (SNIK)
ビキ
BIKI
HURRY.

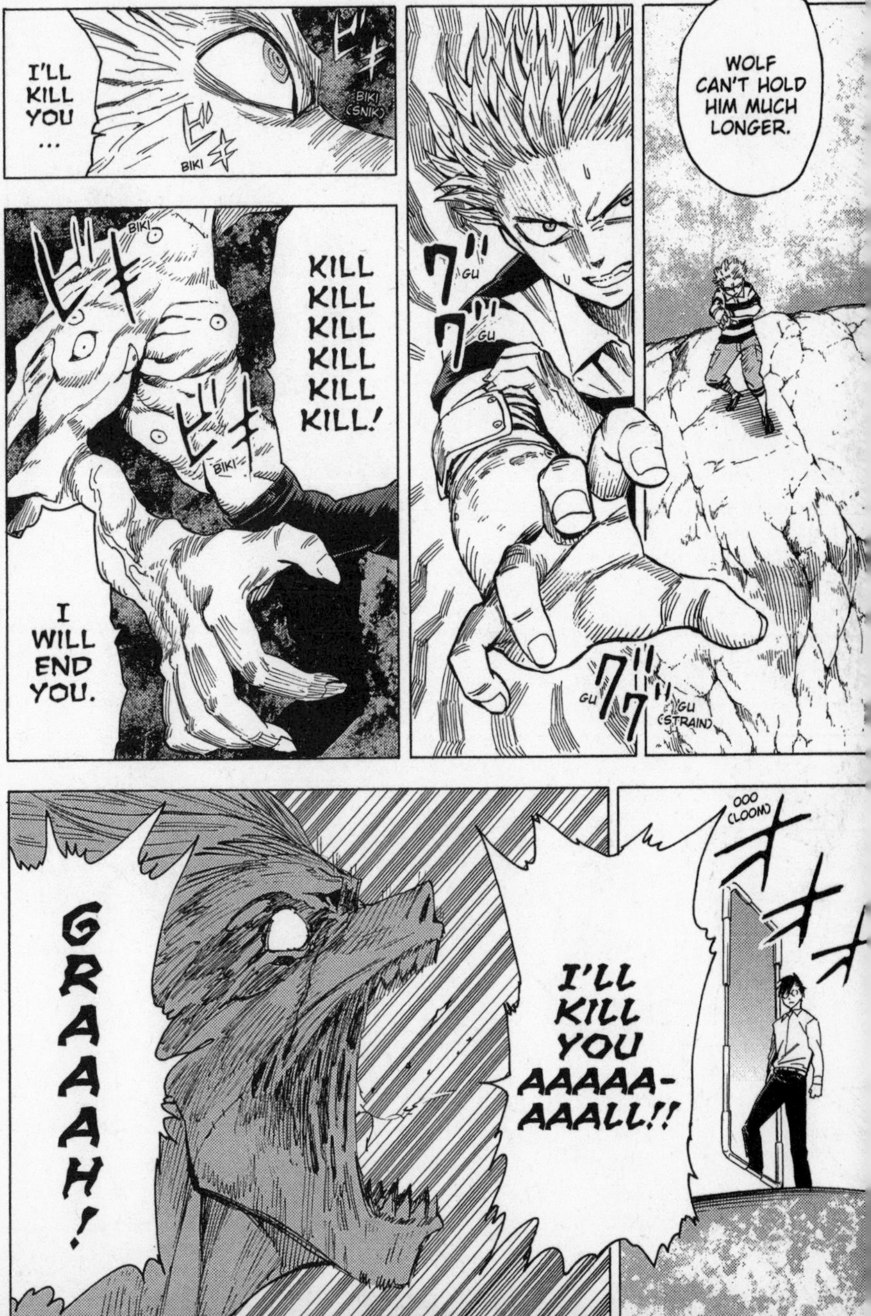
WOLF CAN'T HOLD HIM MUCH LONGER.
GU
GU
GU
GU (STRAIN)
BIKI (SNIK)
BIKI
I'LL KILL YOU ...
BIKI
KILL KILL KILL KILL KILL KILL!
BIKI
I WILL END YOU.
OOO (LOOM)
I'LL KILL YOU AAAAA-AAALL!!
GRAAAH!

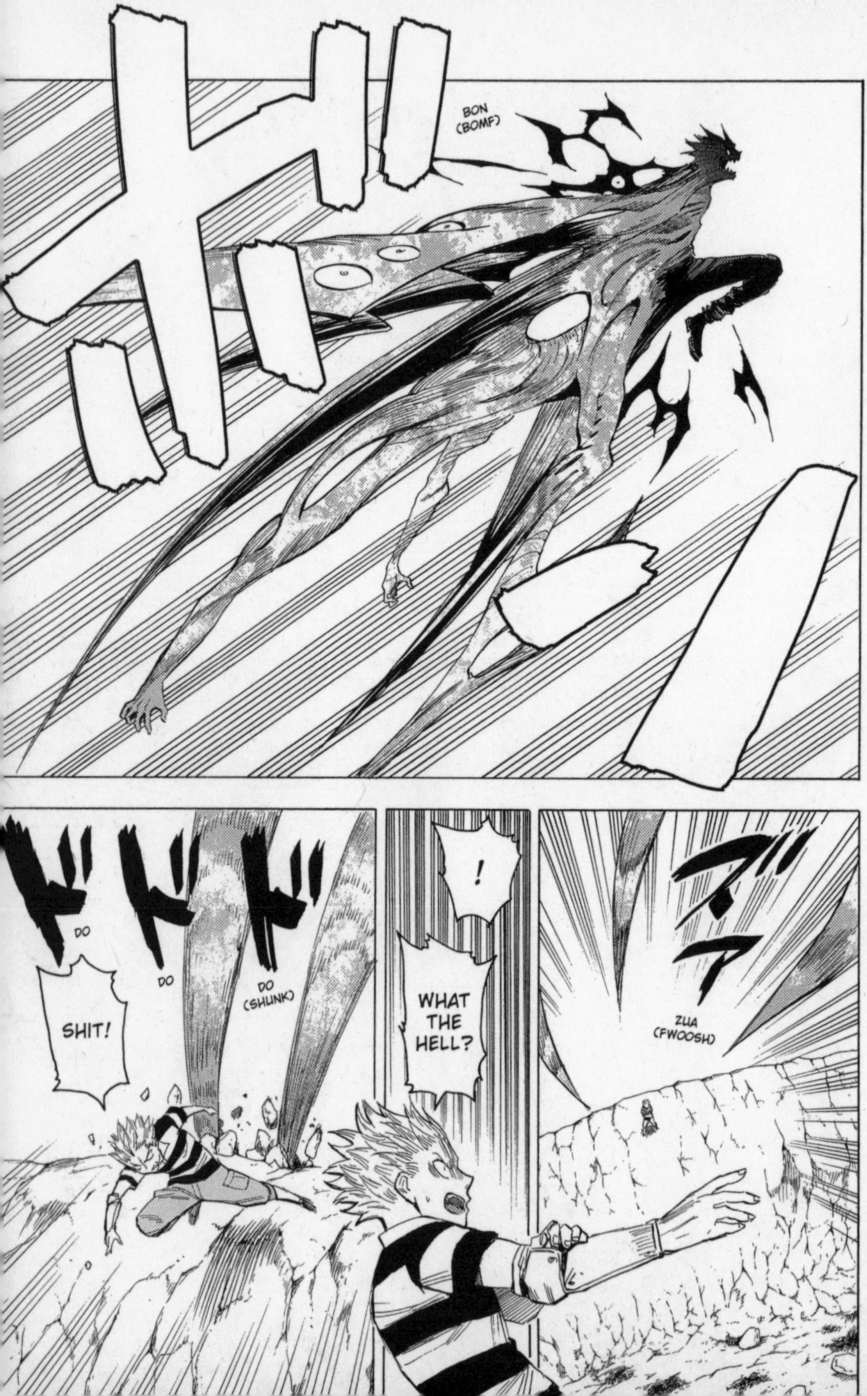
BON
(BOMF)
ZUA
(FWOOSH)
!
WHAT THE HELL?
DO
DO
DO
(SHUNK)
SHIT!

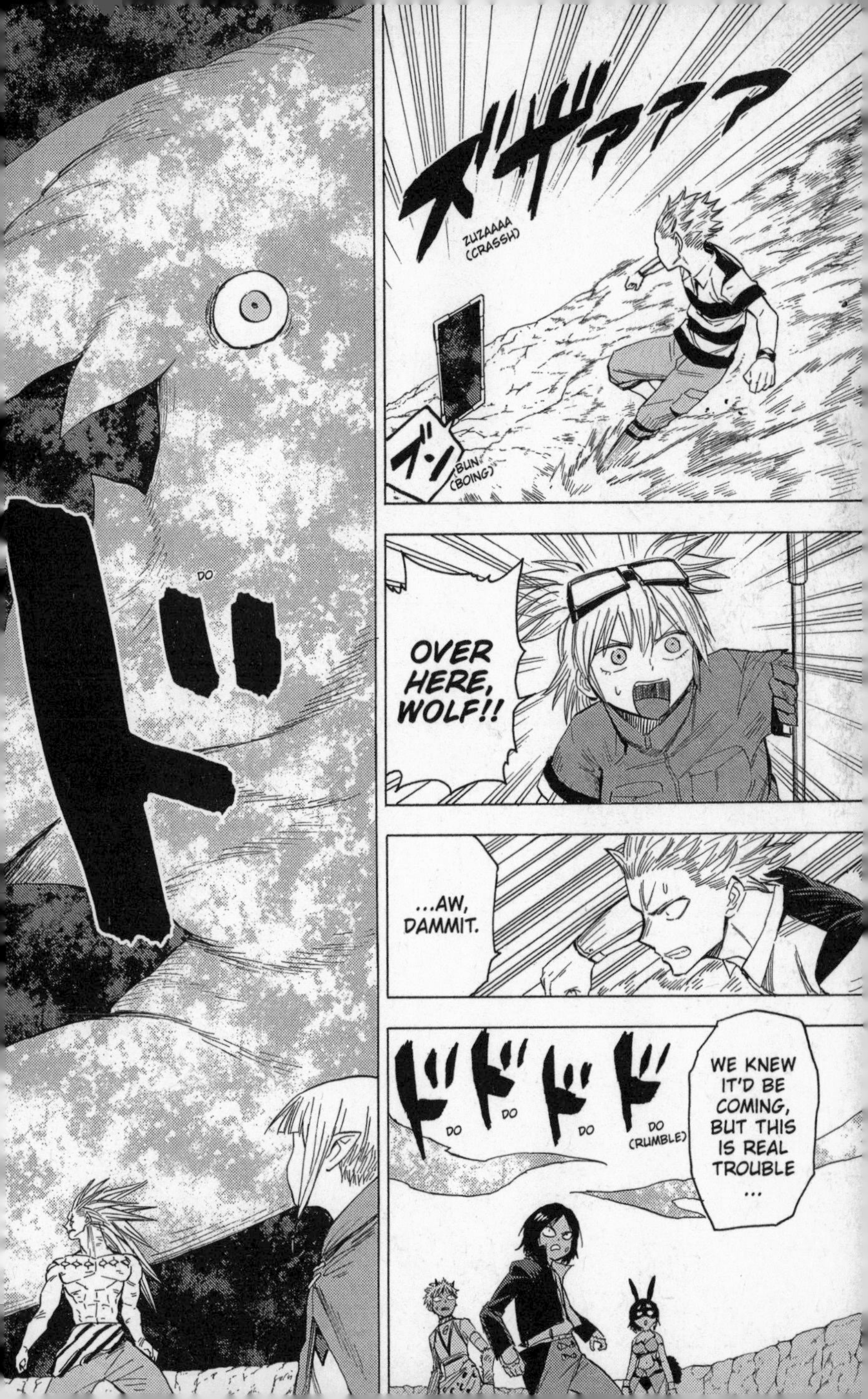
ズザァァァ
ZUZAAAA (CRASSH)
ブン
BUN (BOING)
OVER HERE, WOLF!!
...AW, DAMMIT.
ドドドド
DO DO DO DO (RUMBLE)
WE KNEW IT'D BE COMING, BUT THIS IS REAL TROUBLE...
ドッ
DO

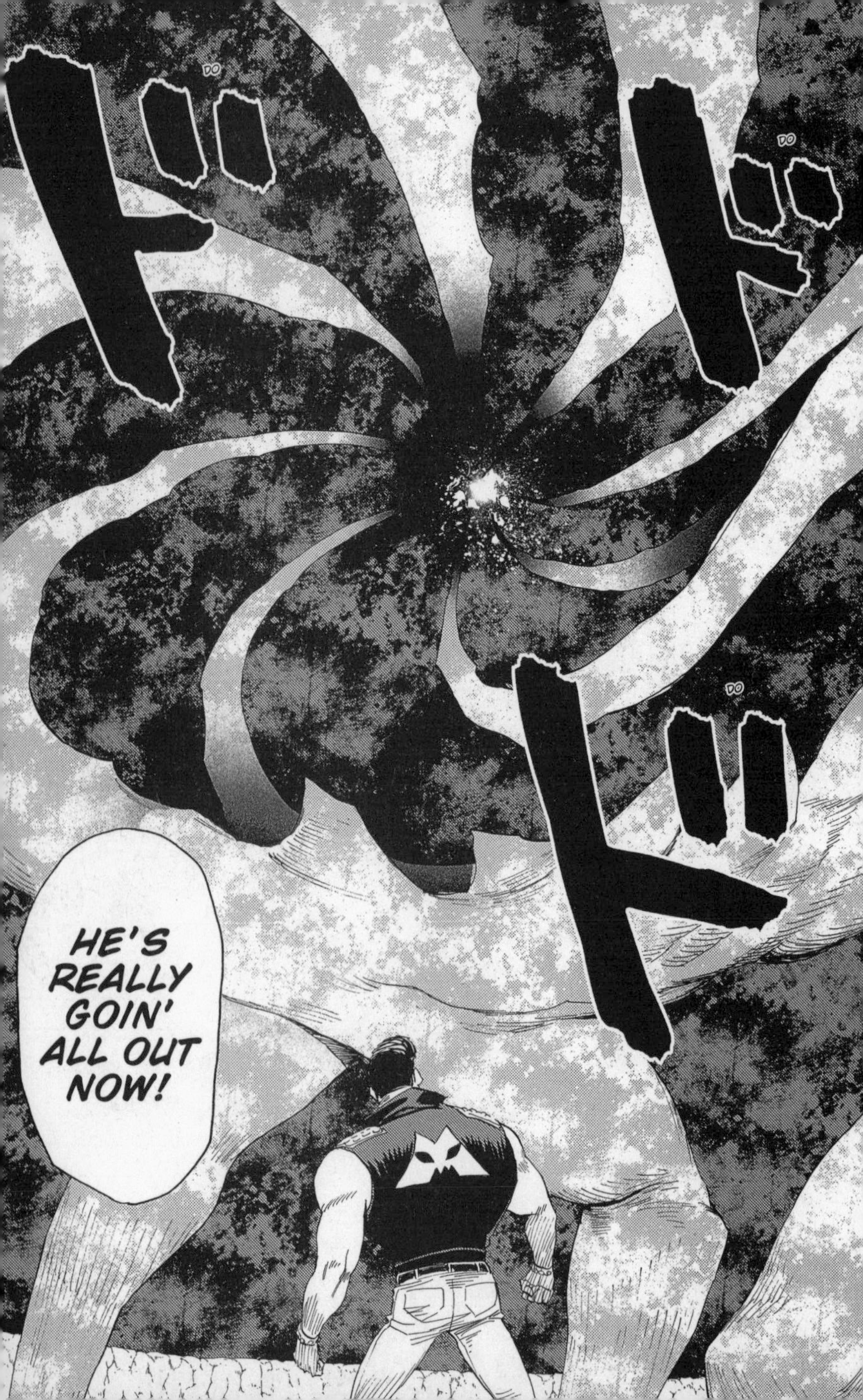
DO
DO
DO
HE'S REALLY GOIN' ALL OUT NOW!

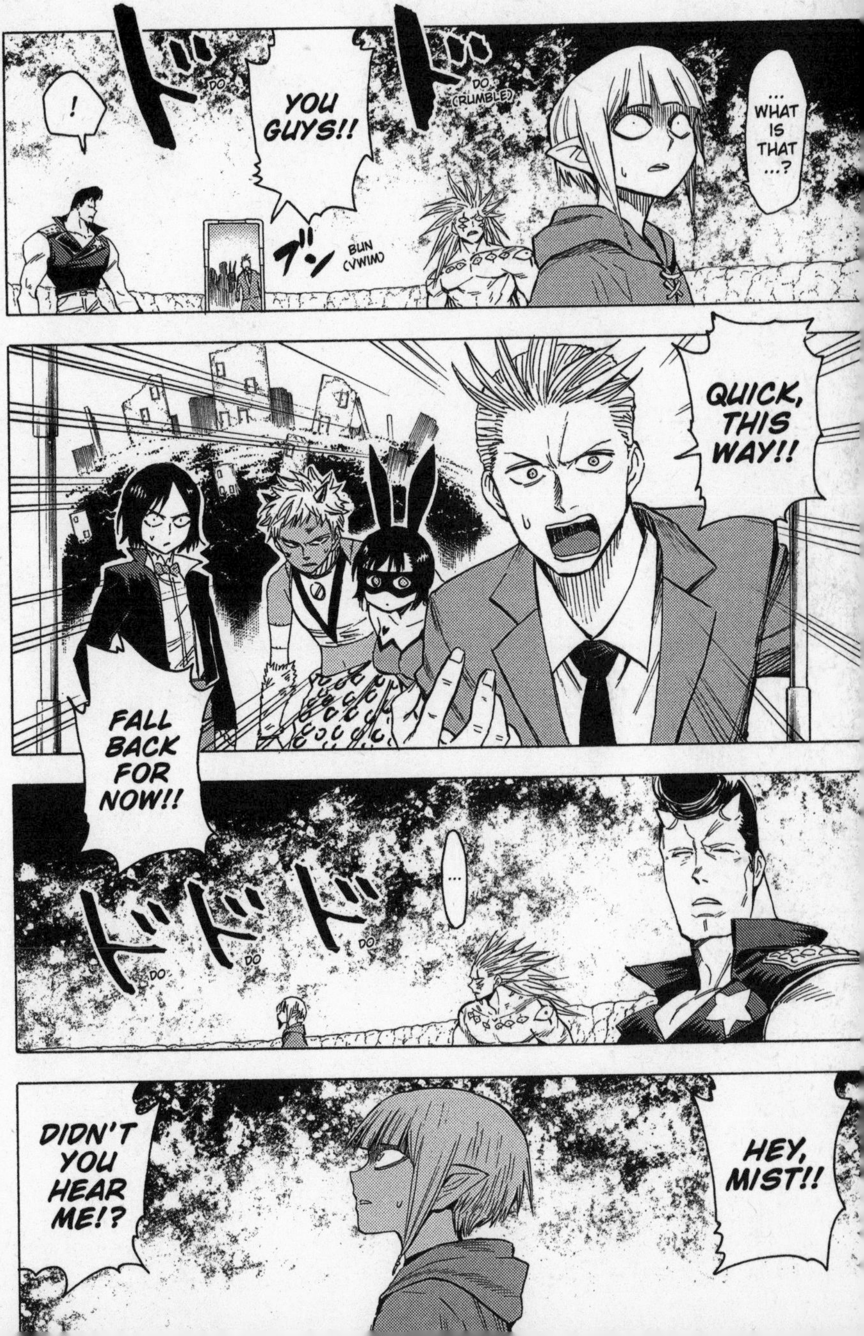
...WHAT IS THAT...?
DO (RUMBLE)
YOU GUYS!!
DO
!
BUN (VWIM)
QUICK, THIS WAY!!
FALL BACK FOR NOW!!
...
DO
DO
DO
HEY, MIST!!
DIDN'T YOU HEAR ME!?

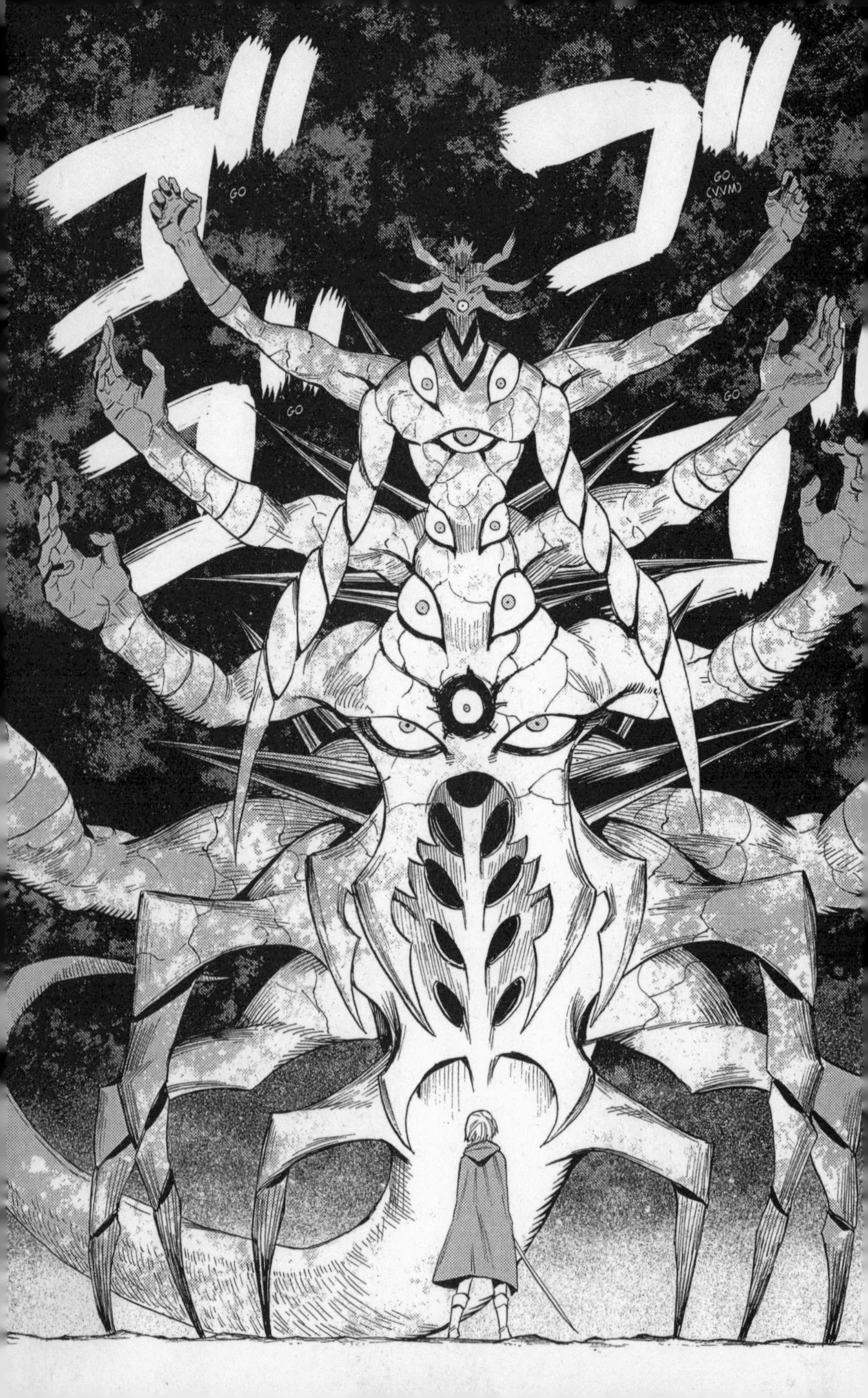
GO (VVM)
GO
GO
GO

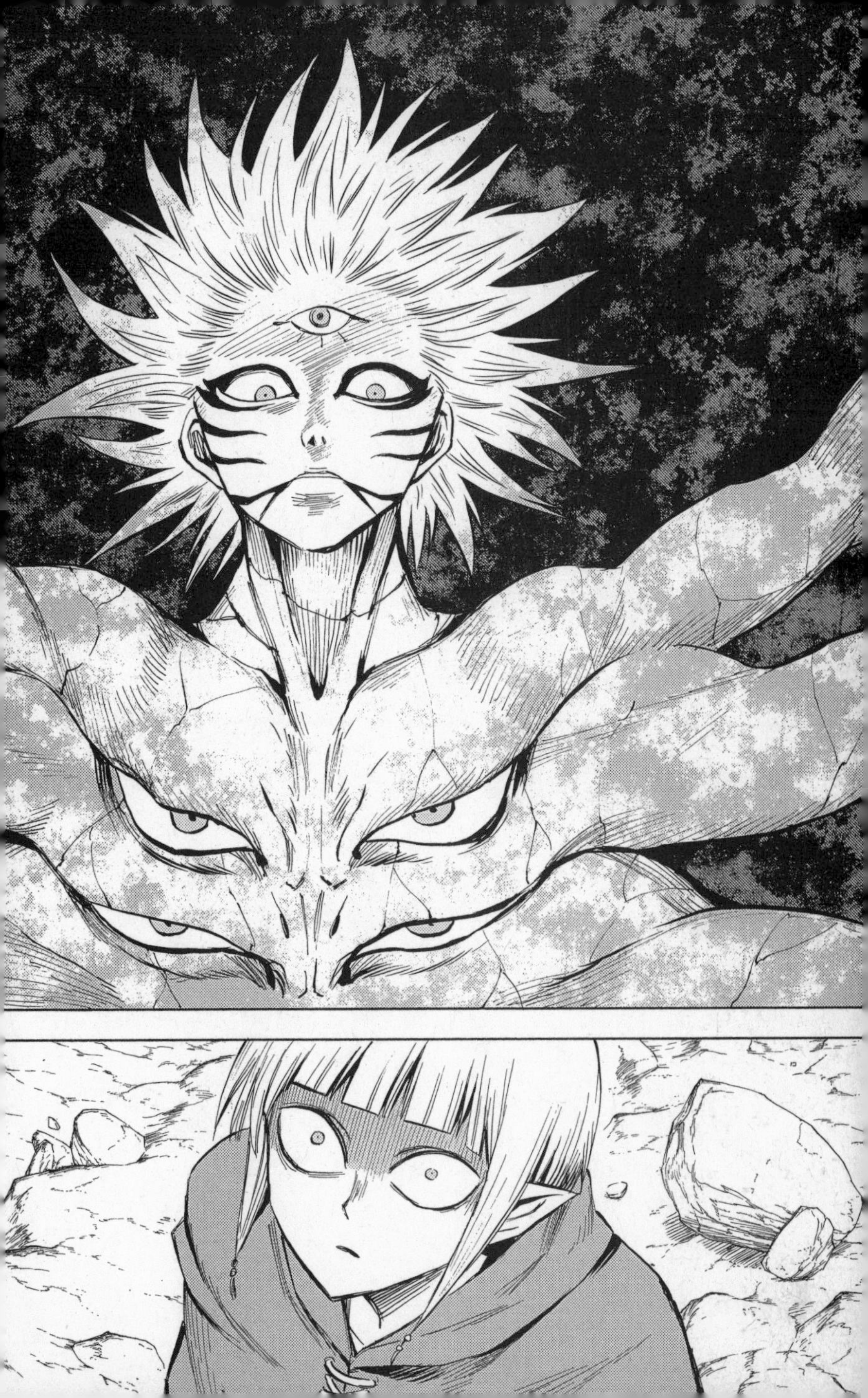

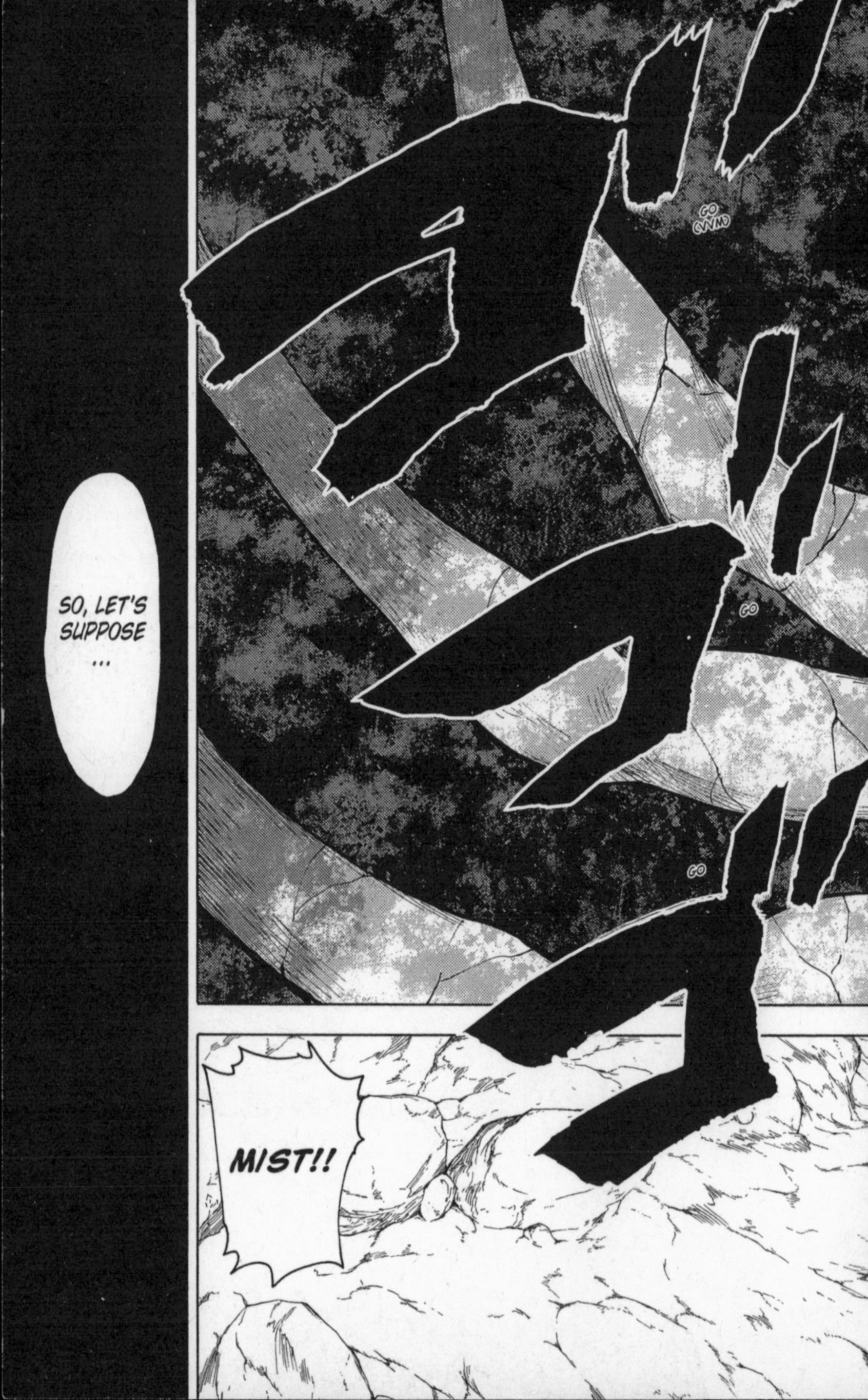
GO
GO
GO
SO, LET'S SUPPOSE ...
MIST!!

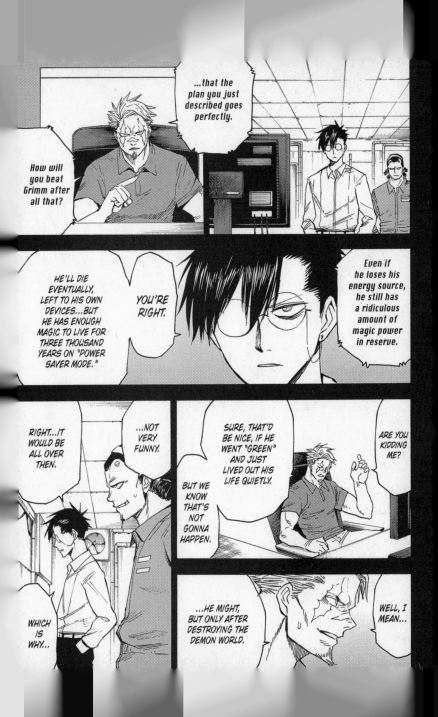

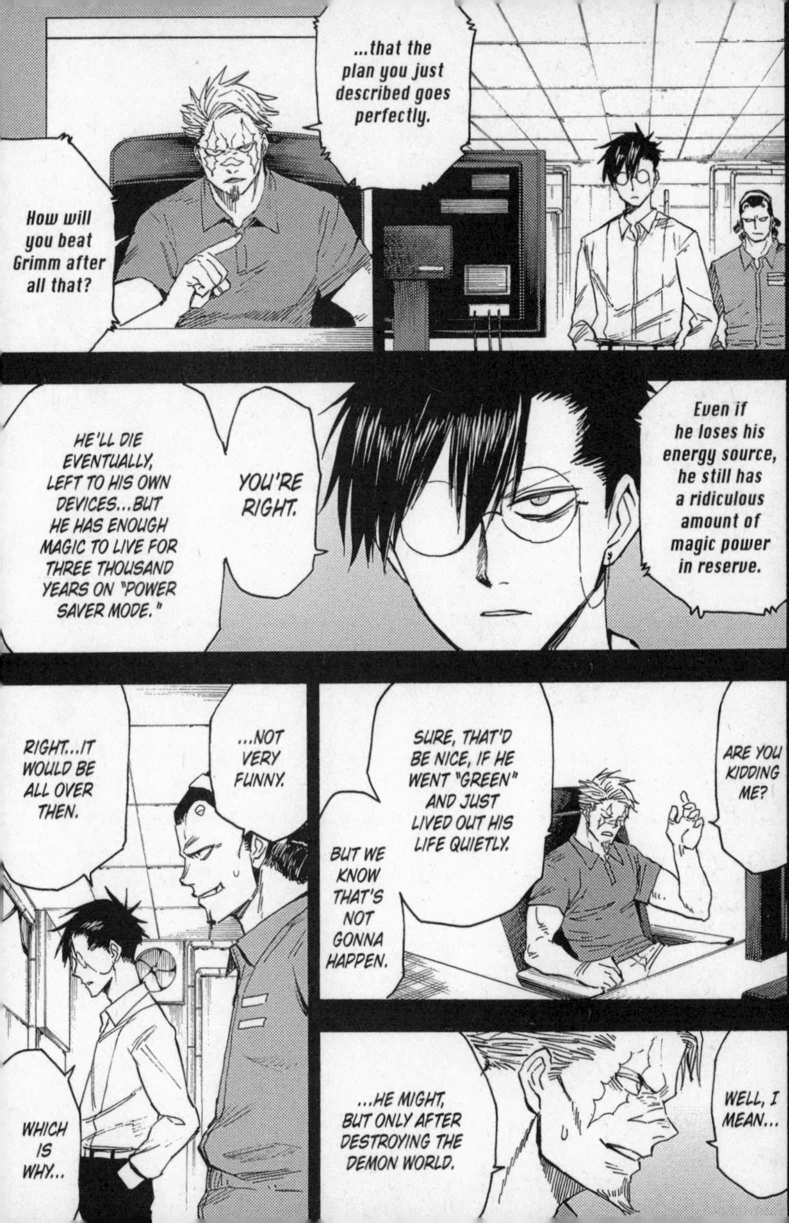
...that the plan you just described goes perfectly.
How will you beat Grimm after all that?
Even if he loses his energy source, he still has a ridiculous amount of magic power in reserve.
YOU'RE RIGHT.
HE'LL DIE EVENTUALLY, LEFT TO HIS OWN DEVICES...BUT HE HAS ENOUGH MAGIC TO LIVE FOR THREE THOUSAND YEARS ON "POWER SAVER MODE."
ARE YOU KIDDING ME?
SURE, THAT'D BE NICE, IF HE WENT "GREEN" AND JUST LIVED OUT HIS LIFE QUIETLY.
BUT WE KNOW THAT'S NOT GONNA HAPPEN.
WELL, I MEAN...
...HE MIGHT, BUT ONLY AFTER DESTROYING THE DEMON WORLD.
...NOT VERY FUNNY.
RIGHT...IT WOULD BE ALL OVER THEN.
WHICH IS WHY...

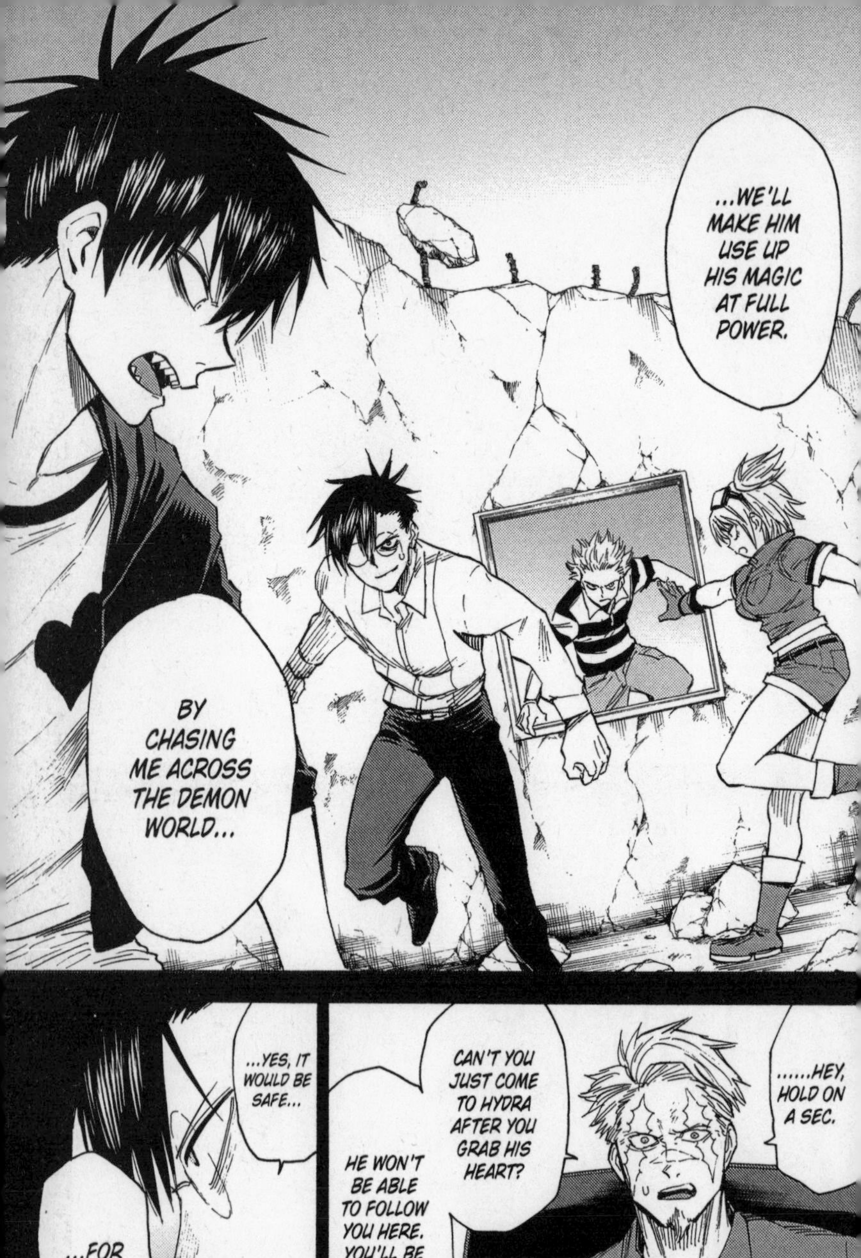
...WE'LL MAKE HIM USE UP HIS MAGIC AT FULL POWER.
BY CHASING ME ACROSS THE DEMON WORLD...
......HEY, HOLD ON A SEC.
CAN'T YOU JUST COME TO HYDRA AFTER YOU GRAB HIS HEART?
HE WON'T BE ABLE TO FOLLOW YOU HERE. YOU'LL BE SAFE.
...YES, IT WOULD BE SAFE...
...FOR ME.

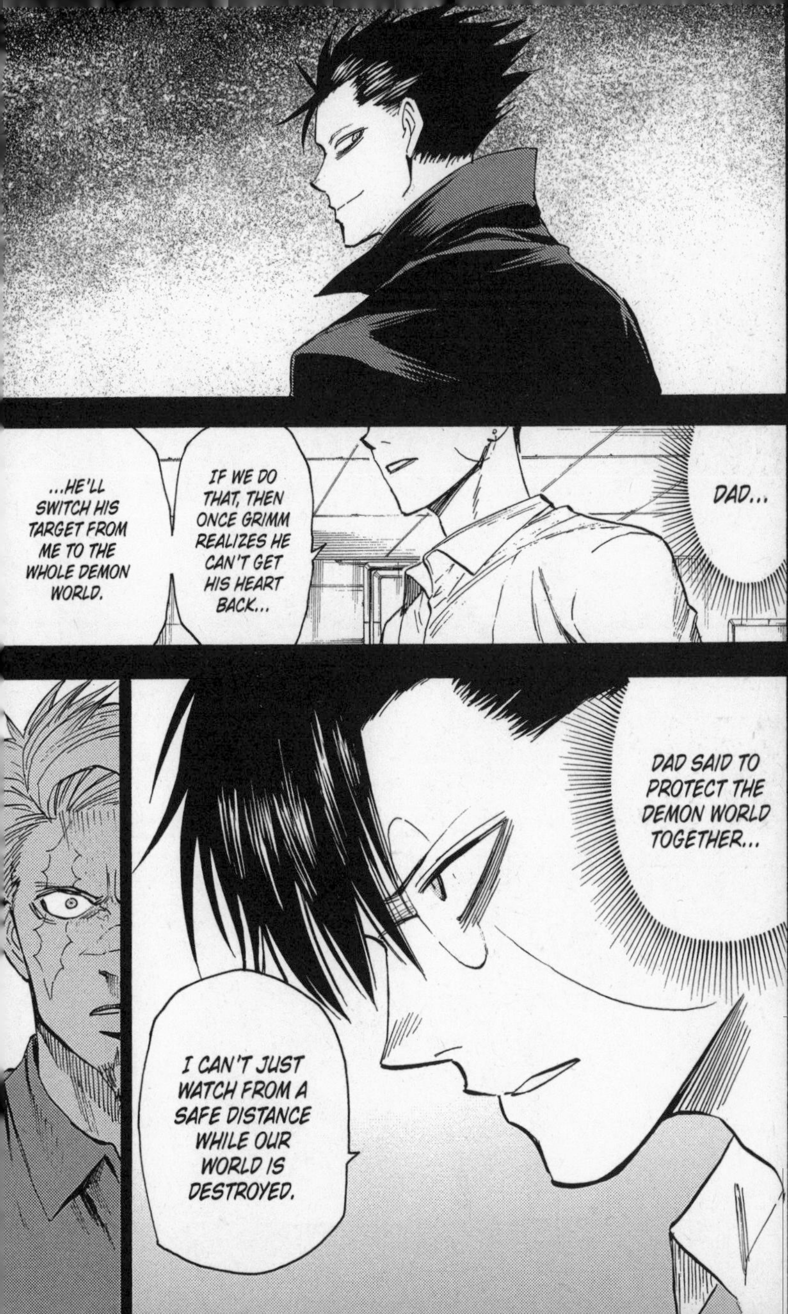
DAD...
IF WE DO THAT, THEN ONCE GRIMM REALIZES HE CAN'T GET HIS HEART BACK...
...HE'LL SWITCH HIS TARGET FROM ME TO THE WHOLE DEMON WORLD.
DAD SAID TO PROTECT THE DEMON WORLD TOGETHER...
I CAN'T JUST WATCH FROM A SAFE DISTANCE WHILE OUR WORLD IS DESTROYED.

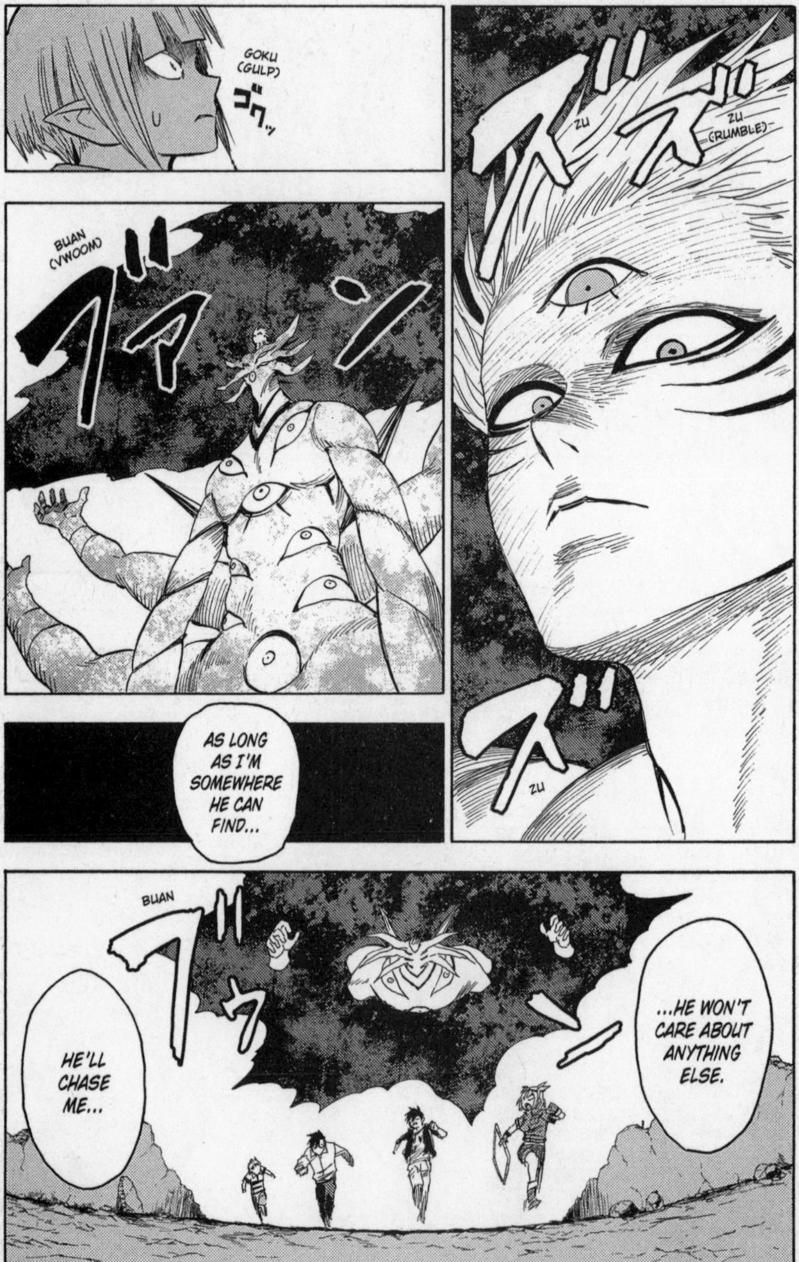
ZU
ZU (RUMBLE)
ZU
GOKU (GULP)
BUAN (VWOOM)
AS LONG AS I'M SOMEWHERE HE CAN FIND...
BUAN
...HE WON'T CARE ABOUT ANYTHING ELSE.
HE'LL CHASE ME...

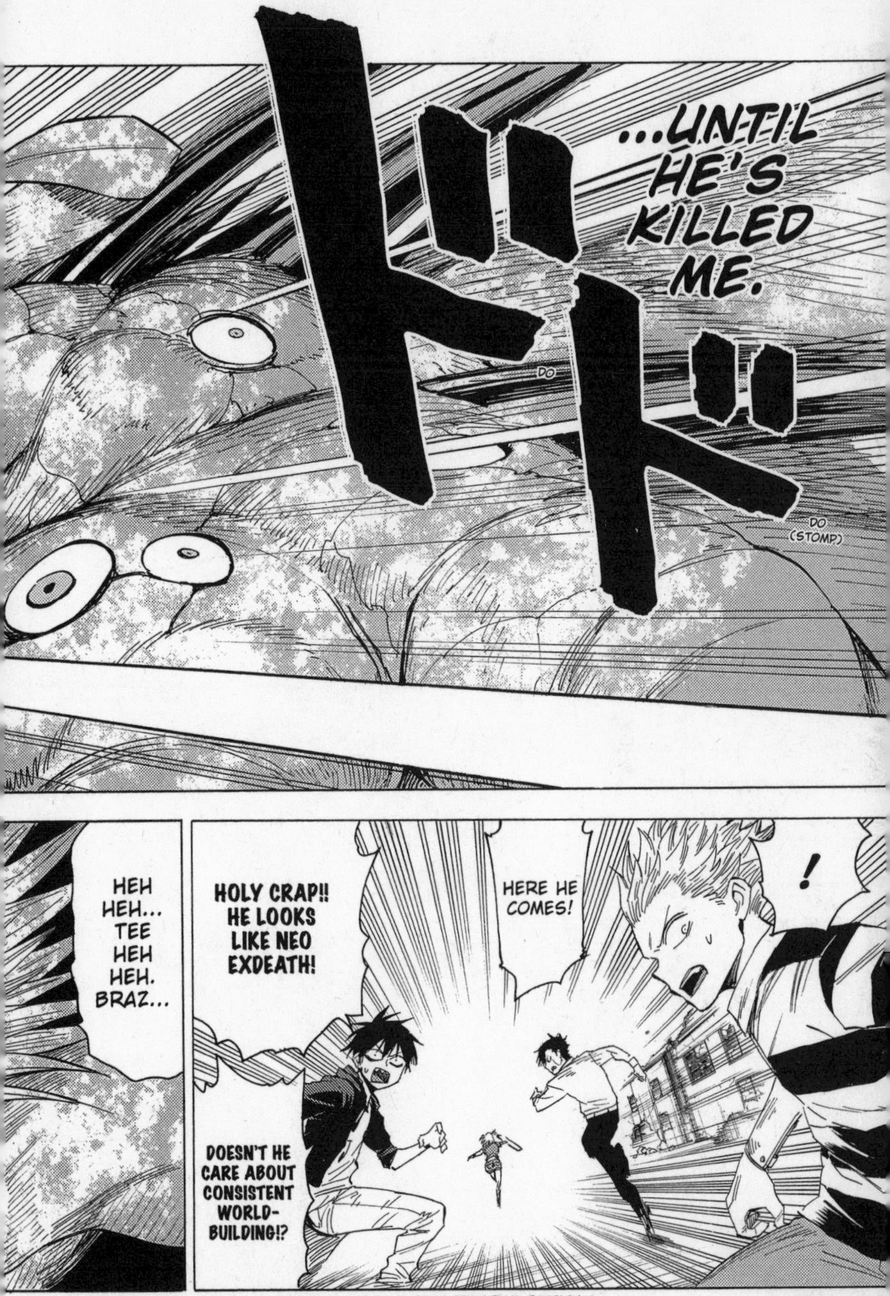
ドド
...UNTIL HE'S KILLED ME.
DO
DO (STOMP)
!
HERE HE COMES!
HOLY CRAP!! HE LOOKS LIKE NEO EXDEATH!
DOESN'T HE CARE ABOUT CONSISTENT WORLD-BUILDING!?
HEH HEH... TEE HEH HEH. BRAZ...

NOTE: NEO EXDEATH IS THE FINAL BOSS FROM FINAL FANTASY V.

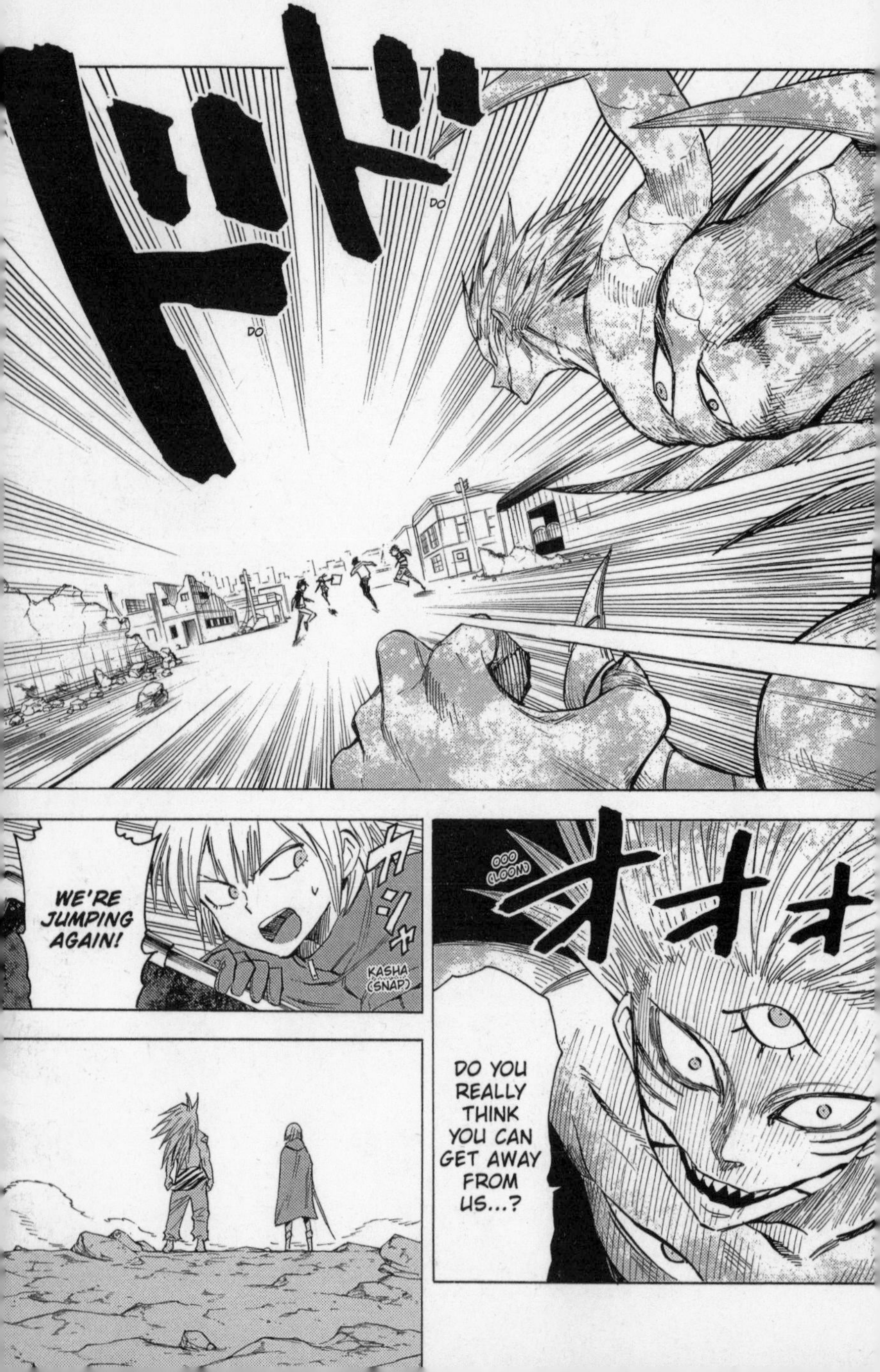
ドッド
DO
DO
オオオ
OOO (LOOM)
DO YOU REALLY THINK YOU CAN GET AWAY FROM US...?
WE'RE JUMPING AGAIN!
カシャ
KASHA (SNAP)

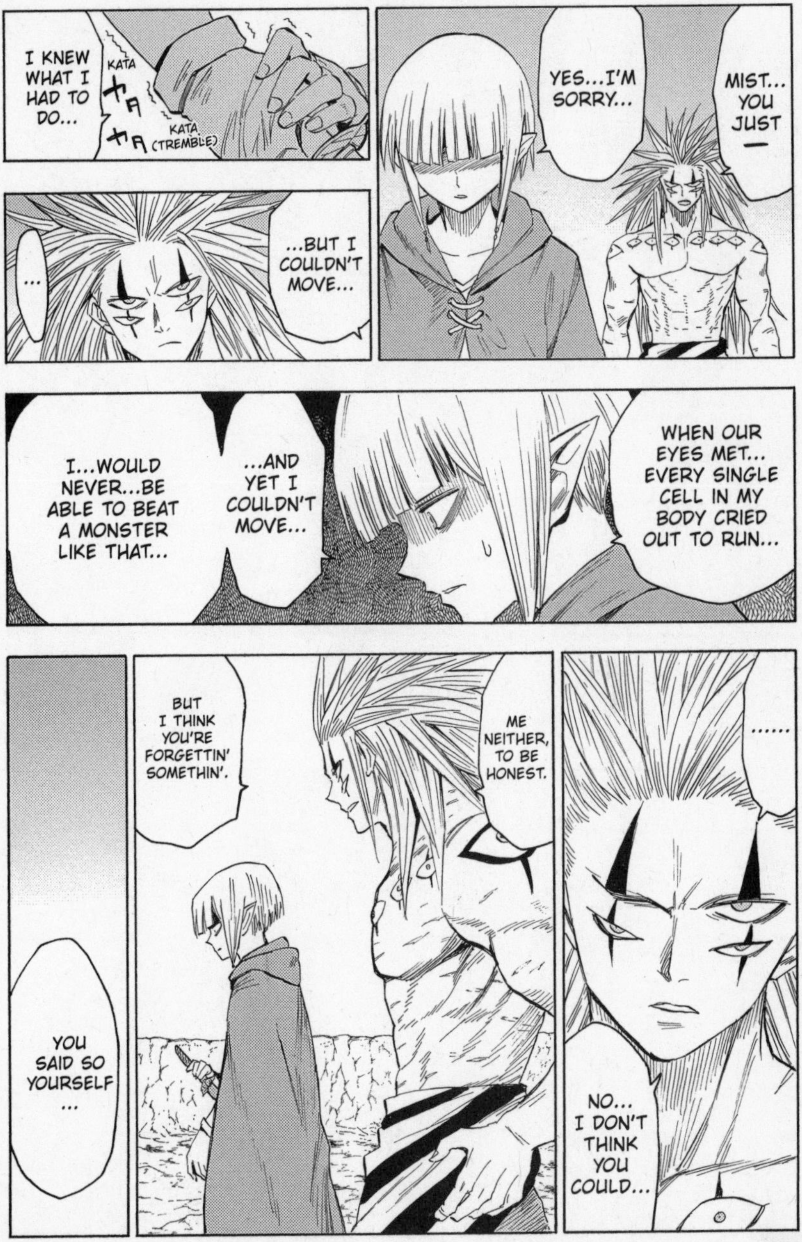
MIST... YOU JUST —
YES...I'M SORRY...
I KNEW WHAT I HAD TO DO...
KATA KATA (TREMBLE)
...BUT I COULDN'T MOVE...
...
WHEN OUR EYES MET... EVERY SINGLE CELL IN MY BODY CRIED OUT TO RUN...
...AND YET I COULDN'T MOVE...
I...WOULD NEVER...BE ABLE TO BEAT A MONSTER LIKE THAT...
......
NO... I DON'T THINK YOU COULD...
ME NEITHER, TO BE HONEST.
BUT I THINK YOU'RE FORGETTIN' SOMETHIN'.
YOU SAID SO YOURSELF ...

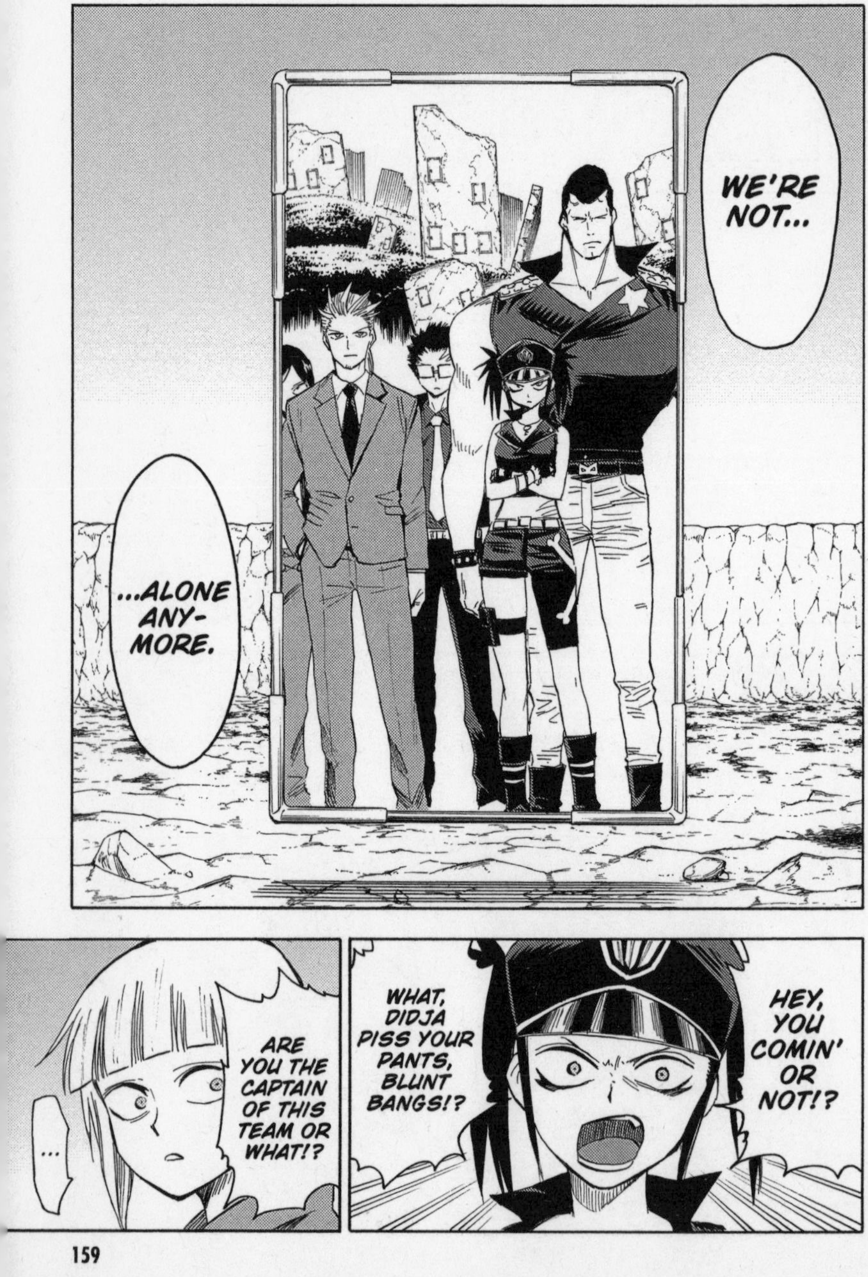
WE'RE NOT...
...ALONE ANYMORE.
HEY, YOU COMIN' OR NOT!?
WHAT, DIDJA PISS YOUR PANTS, BLUNT BANGS!?
ARE YOU THE CAPTAIN OF THIS TEAM OR WHAT!?
...

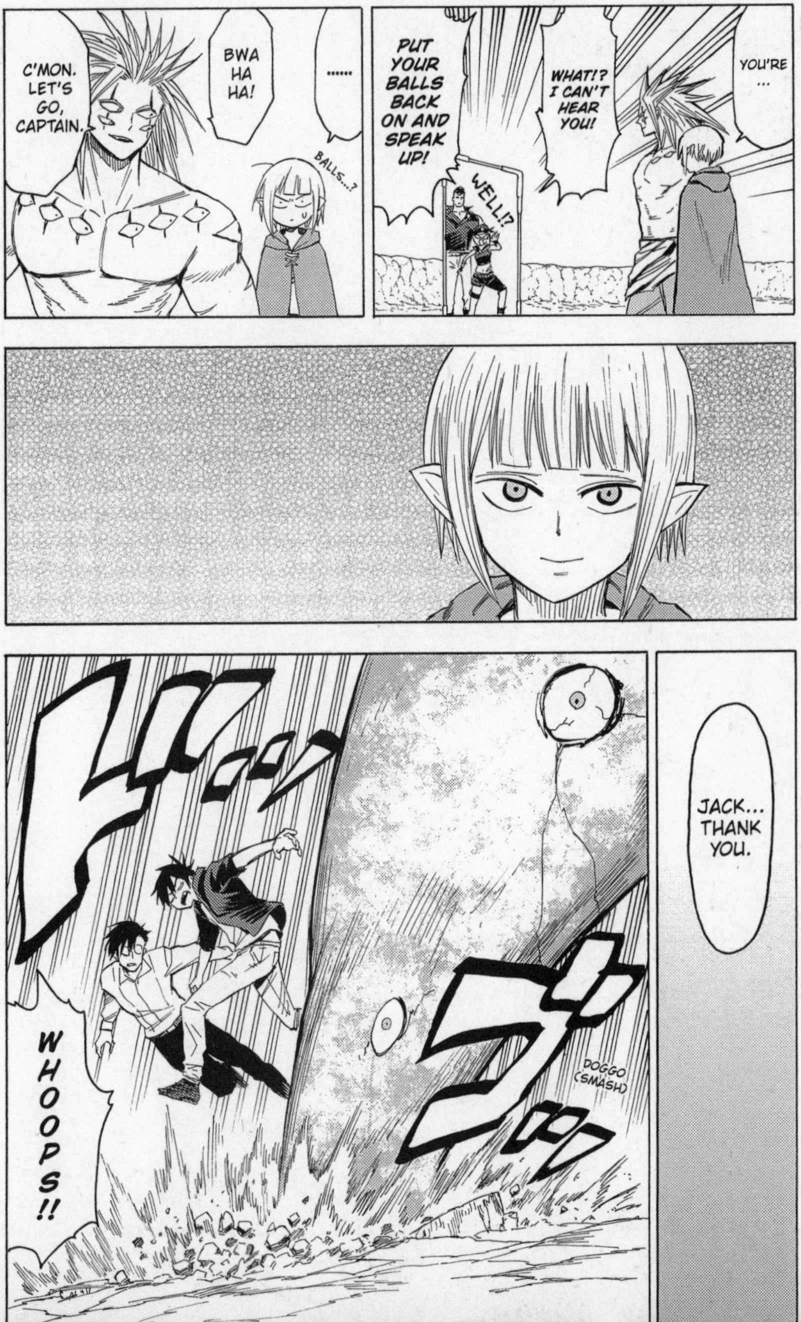
YOU'RE ...
WHAT!? I CAN'T HEAR YOU!
PUT YOUR BALLS BACK ON AND SPEAK UP!
WELL!?
......
BWA HA HA!
C'MON. LET'S GO, CAPTAIN.
BALLS...?
JACK... THANK YOU.
DOGGO (SMASH)
WHOOPS!!

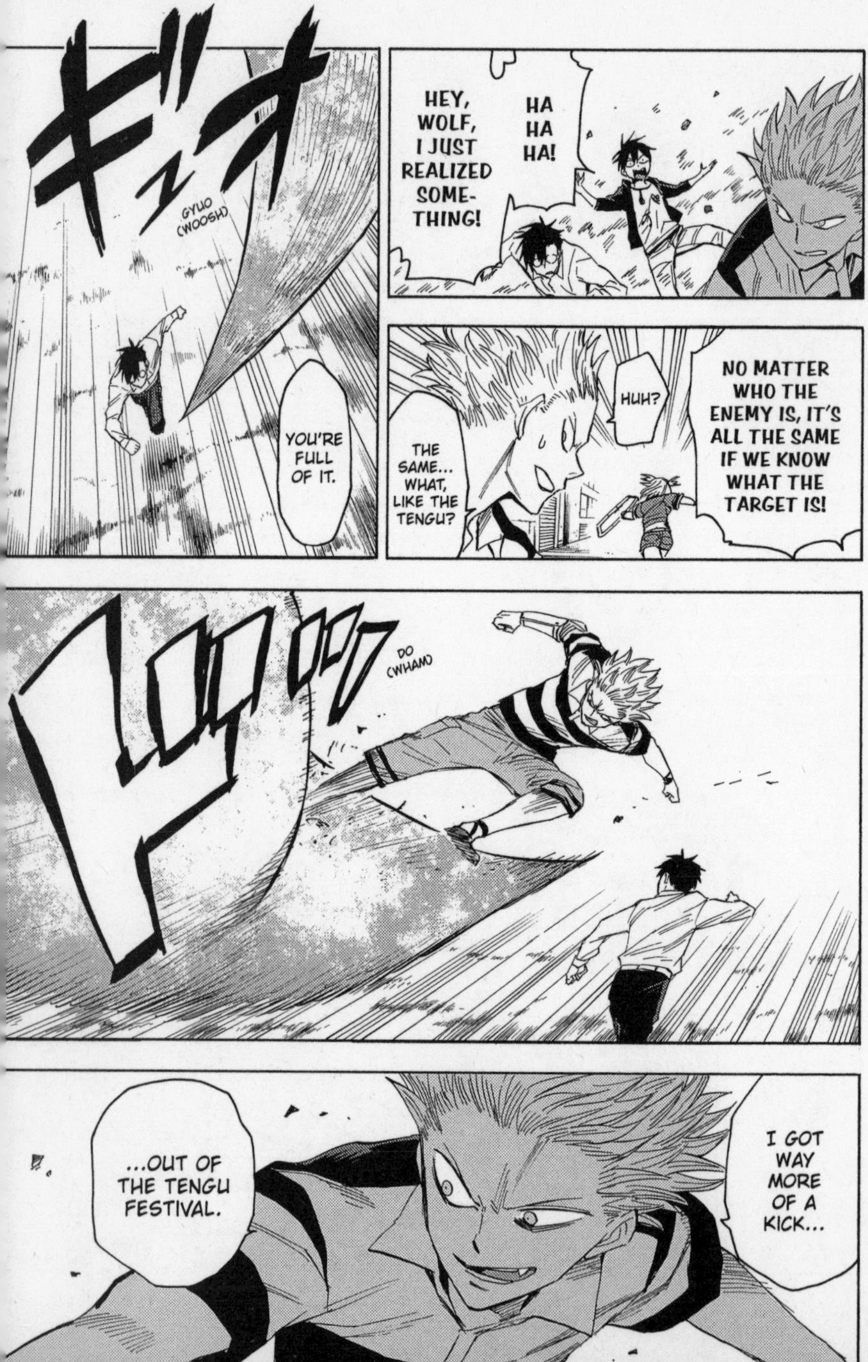
HA HA HA!
HEY, WOLF, I JUST REALIZED SOME-THING!
NO MATTER WHO THE ENEMY IS, IT'S ALL THE SAME IF WE KNOW WHAT THE TARGET IS!
HUH?
THE SAME... WHAT, LIKE THE TENGU?
GYUO (WOOSH)
YOU'RE FULL OF IT.
DO (WHAM)
I GOT WAY MORE OF A KICK...
...OUT OF THE TENGU FESTIVAL.

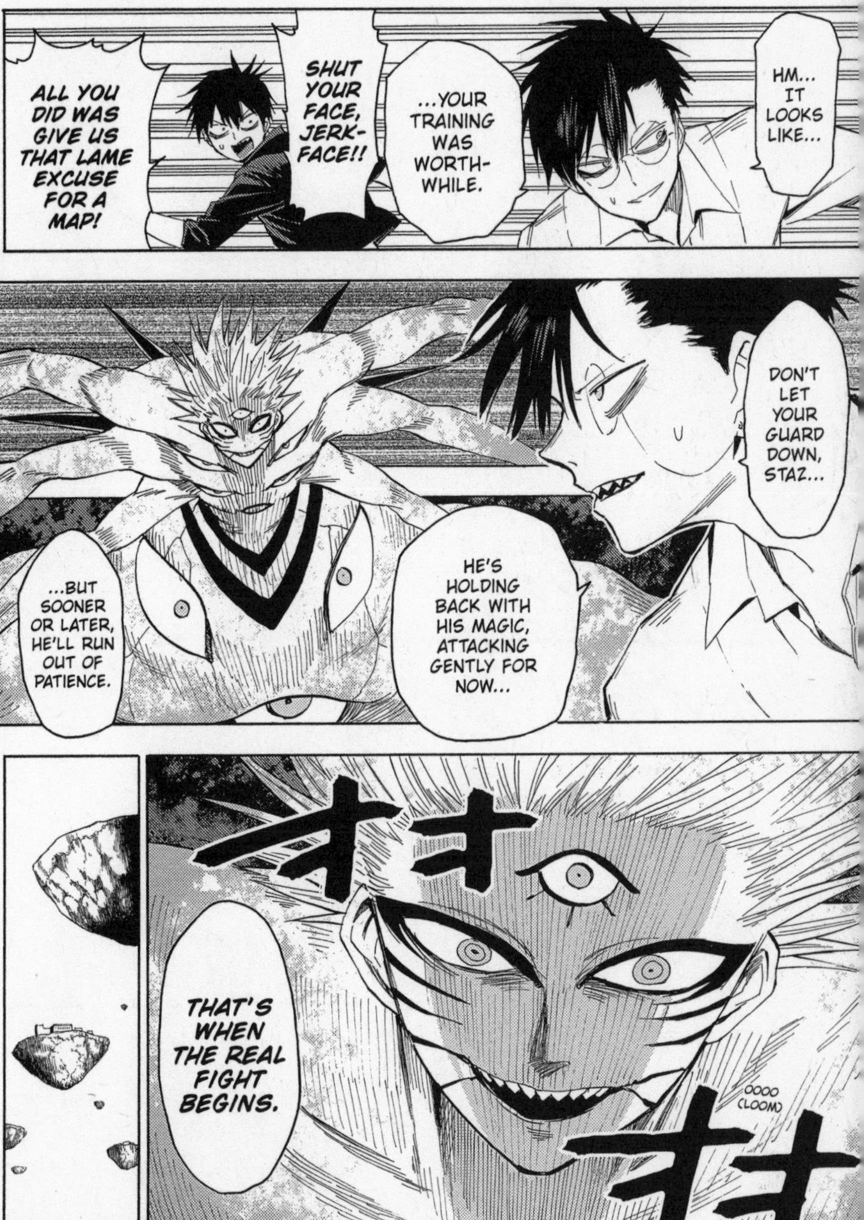
HM... IT LOOKS LIKE...
...YOUR TRAINING WAS WORTH-WHILE.
SHUT YOUR FACE, JERK-FACE!!
ALL YOU DID WAS GIVE US THAT LAME EXCUSE FOR A MAP!
DON'T LET YOUR GUARD DOWN, STAZ...
HE'S HOLDING BACK WITH HIS MAGIC, ATTACKING GENTLY FOR NOW...
...BUT SOONER OR LATER, HE'LL RUN OUT OF PATIENCE.
THAT'S WHEN THE REAL FIGHT BEGINS.
OOOO (LOOM)

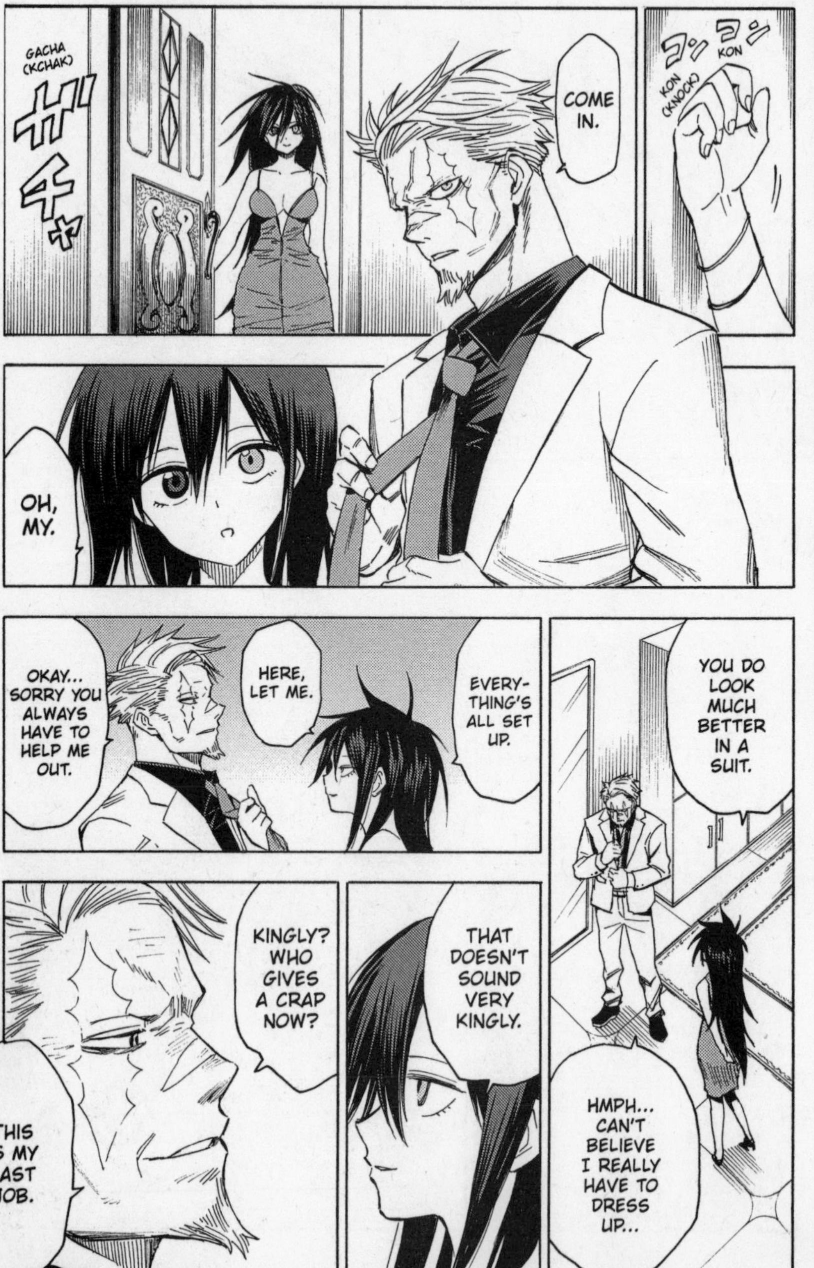
コンコン
KON KON (KNOCK)
COME IN.
ガチャ
GACHA (KCHAK)
OH, MY.
YOU DO LOOK MUCH BETTER IN A SUIT.
HMPH... CAN'T BELIEVE I REALLY HAVE TO DRESS UP...
EVERY-THING'S ALL SET UP.
HERE, LET ME.
OKAY... SORRY YOU ALWAYS HAVE TO HELP ME OUT.
THAT DOESN'T SOUND VERY KINGLY.
KINGLY? WHO GIVES A CRAP NOW?
THIS IS MY LAST JOB.

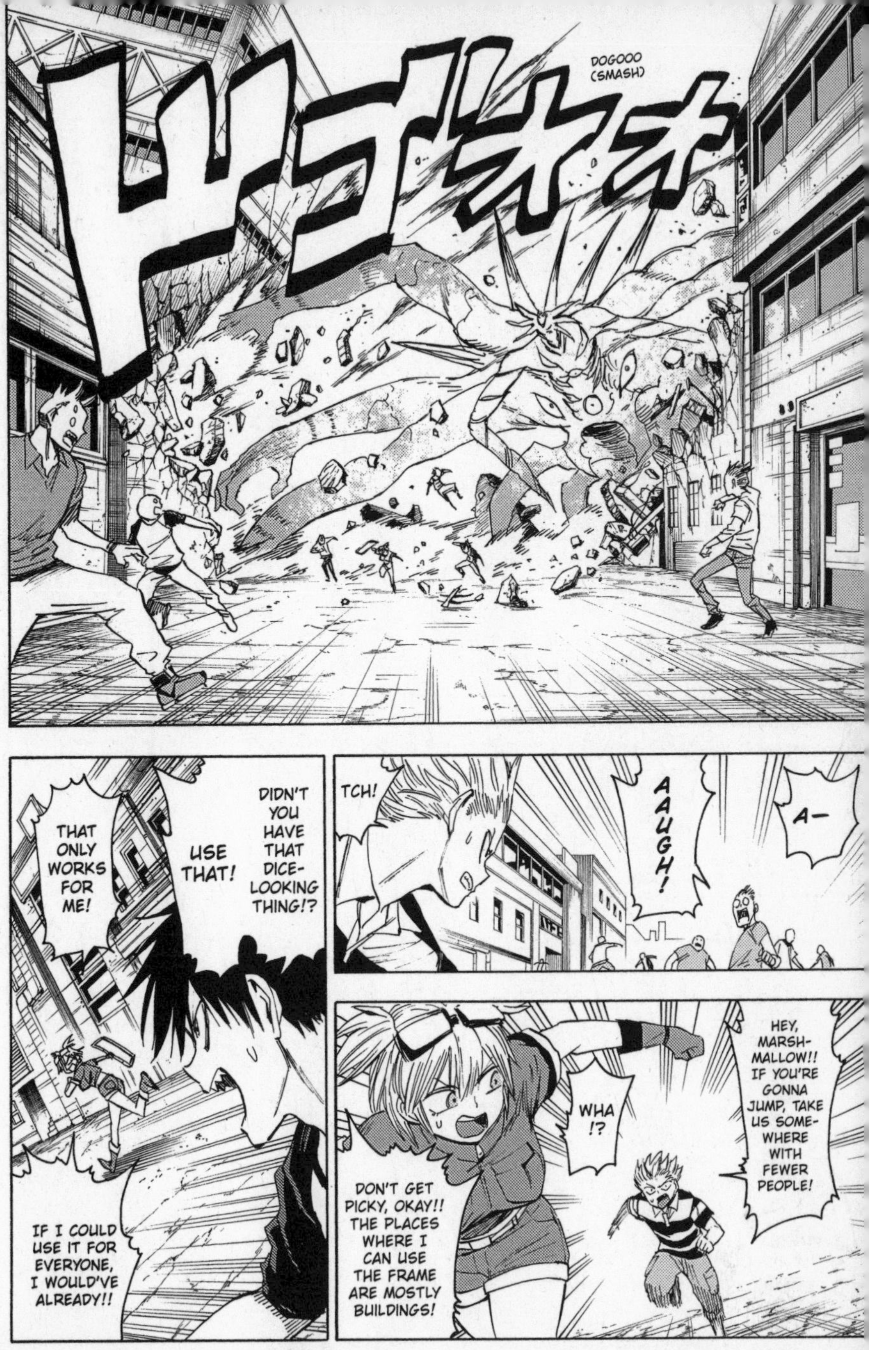
DOGOOO
(SMASH)
A—
AAUGH!
TCH!
HEY, MARSHMALLOW!! IF YOU'RE GONNA JUMP, TAKE US SOMEWHERE WITH FEWER PEOPLE!
WHA!?
DON'T GET PICKY, OKAY!! THE PLACES WHERE I CAN USE THE FRAME ARE MOSTLY BUILDINGS!
DIDN'T YOU HAVE THAT DICE-LOOKING THING!?
USE THAT!
THAT ONLY WORKS FOR ME!
IF I COULD USE IT FOR EVERYONE, I WOULD'VE ALREADY!!

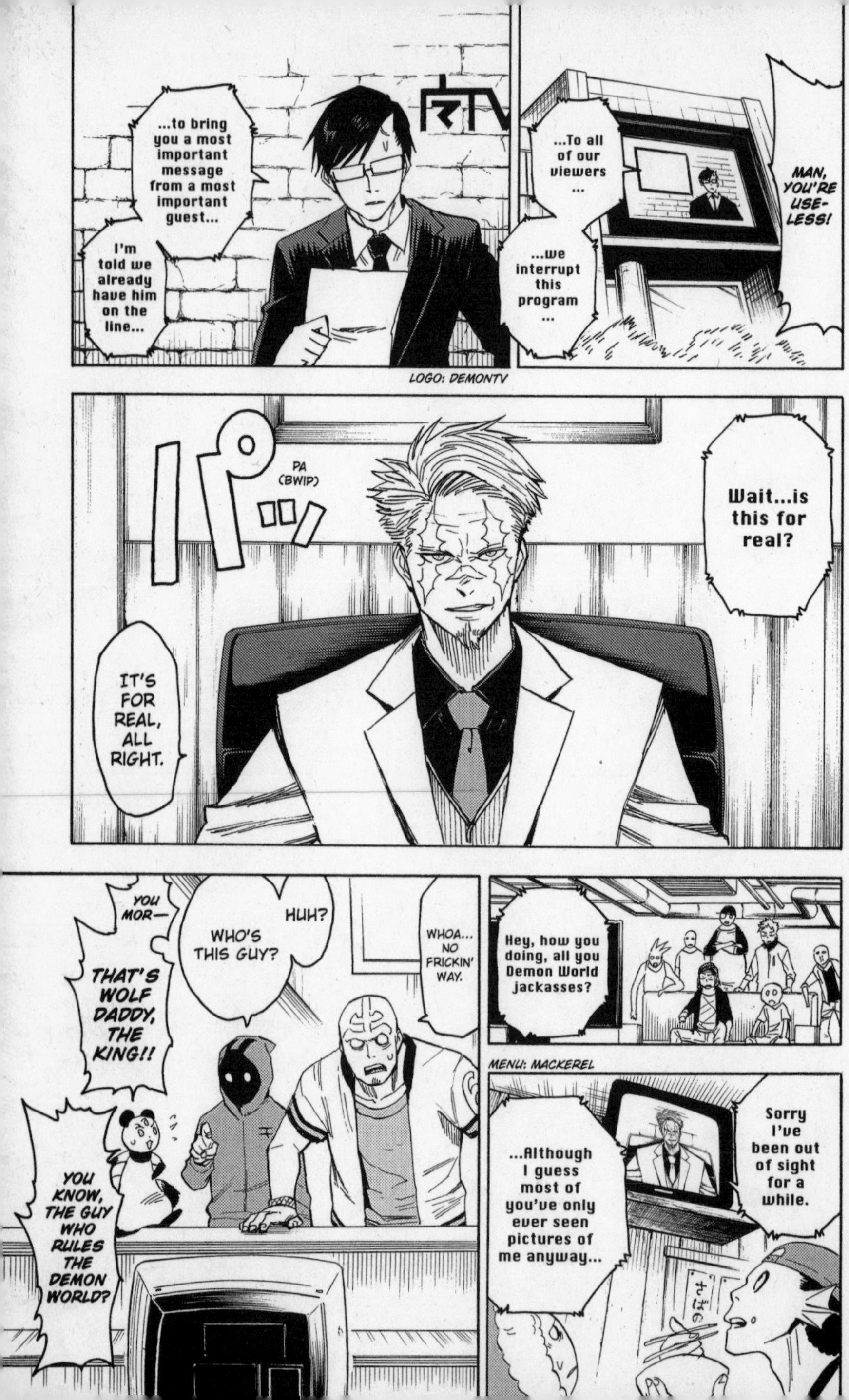
...To all of our viewers ...
...we interrupt this program ...
MAN, YOU'RE USE-LESS!
...to bring you a most important message from a most important guest...
I'm told we already have him on the line...
LOGO: DEMONTV
Wait...is this for real?
PA (BWIP)
IT'S FOR REAL, ALL RIGHT.
Hey, how you doing, all you Demon World jackasses?
MENU: MACKEREL
Sorry I've been out of sight for a while.
...Although I guess most of you've only ever seen pictures of me anyway...
WHOA... NO FRICKIN' WAY.
HUH?
WHO'S THIS GUY?
YOU MOR—
THAT'S WOLF DADDY, THE KING!!
YOU KNOW, THE GUY WHO RULES THE DEMON WORLD?

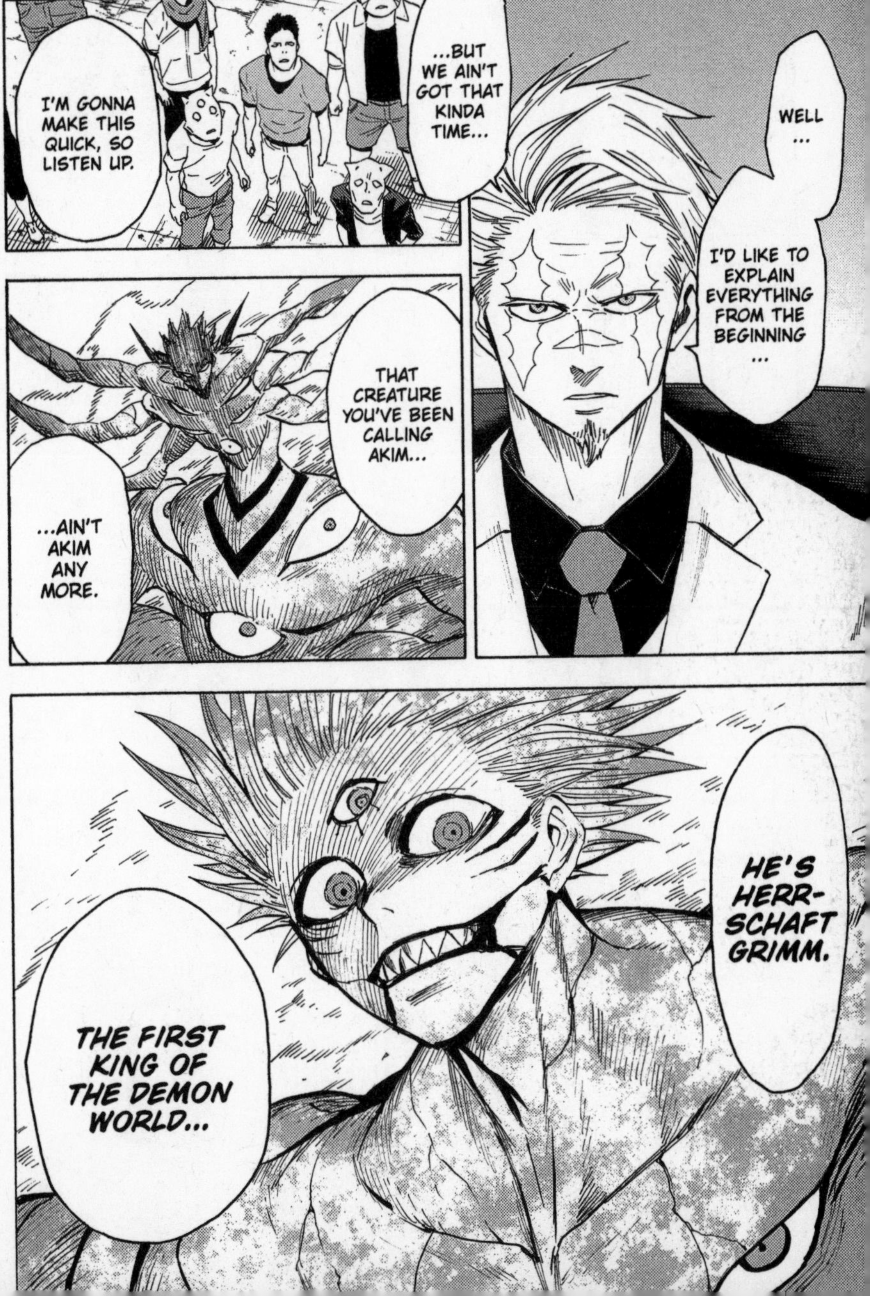
WELL...
I'D LIKE TO EXPLAIN EVERYTHING FROM THE BEGINNING...
...BUT WE AIN'T GOT THAT KINDA TIME...
I'M GONNA MAKE THIS QUICK, SO LISTEN UP.
THAT CREATURE YOU'VE BEEN CALLING AKIM...
...AIN'T AKIM ANY MORE.
HE'S HERR-SCHAFT GRIMM.
THE FIRST KING OF THE DEMON WORLD...

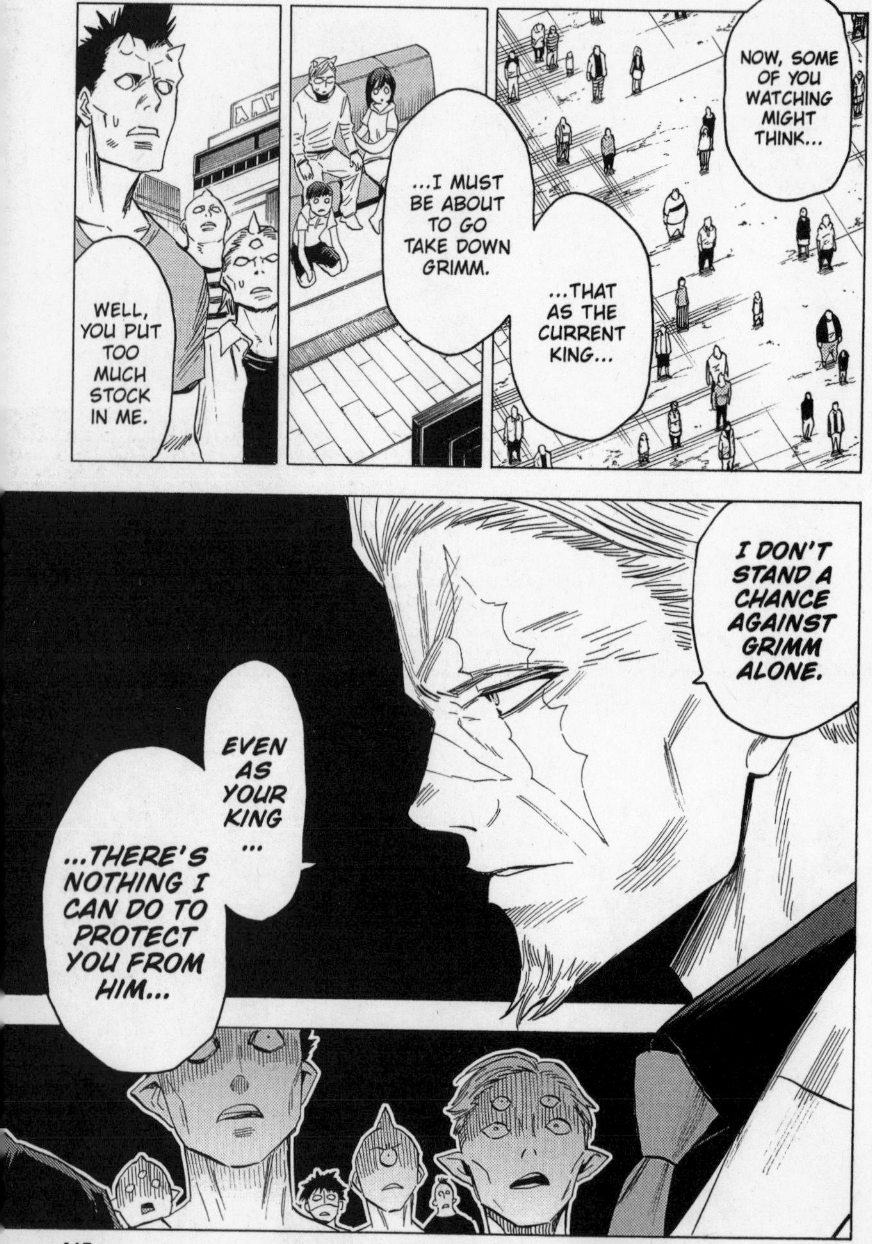
NOW, SOME OF YOU WATCHING MIGHT THINK...
...THAT AS THE CURRENT KING...
...I MUST BE ABOUT TO GO TAKE DOWN GRIMM.
WELL, YOU PUT TOO MUCH STOCK IN ME.
I DON'T STAND A CHANCE AGAINST GRIMM ALONE.
EVEN AS YOUR KING...
...THERE'S NOTHING I CAN DO TO PROTECT YOU FROM HIM...

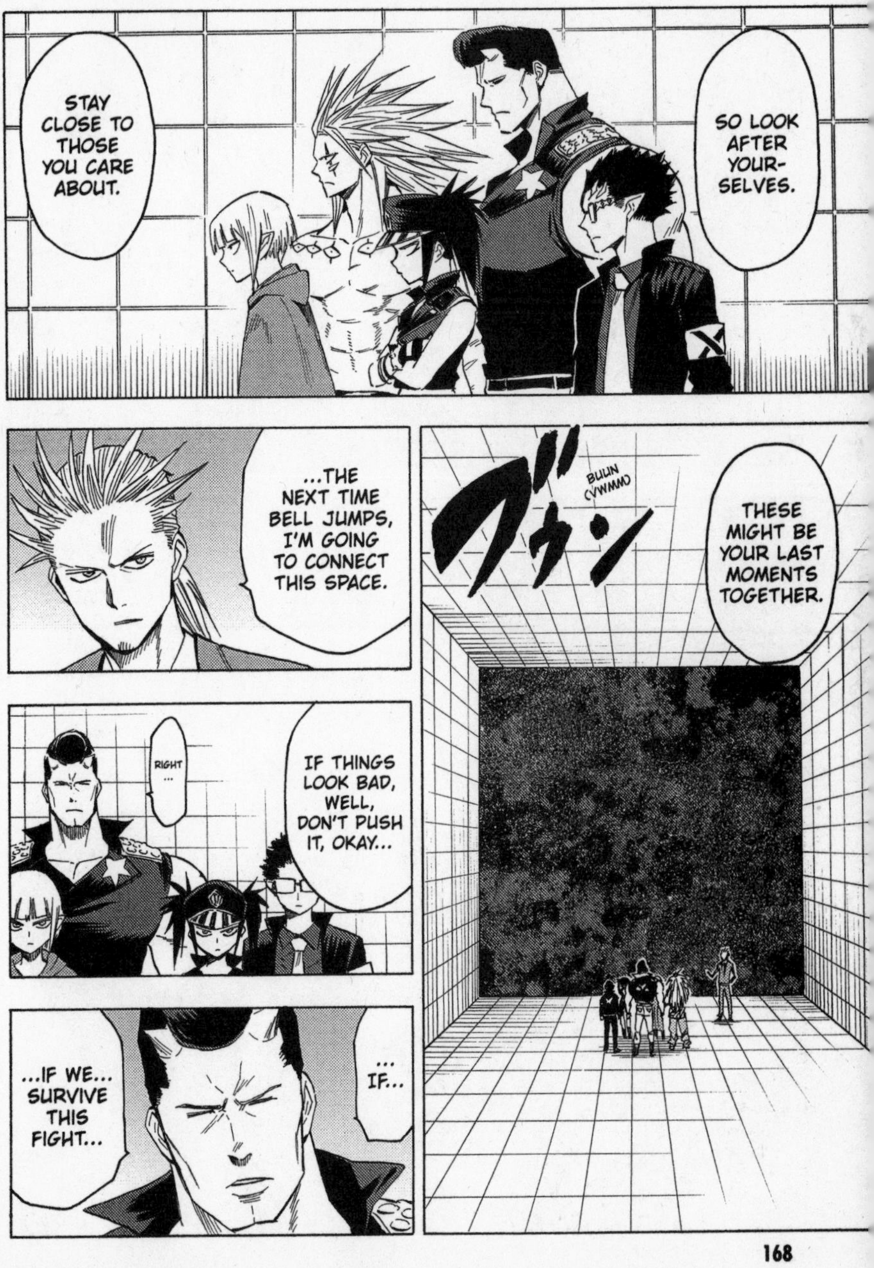
SO LOOK AFTER YOUR-SELVES.
STAY CLOSE TO THOSE YOU CARE ABOUT.
ヴゥン
BUUN (VWMM)
THESE MIGHT BE YOUR LAST MOMENTS TOGETHER.
...THE NEXT TIME BELL JUMPS, I'M GOING TO CONNECT THIS SPACE.
IF THINGS LOOK BAD, WELL, DON'T PUSH IT, OKAY...
RIGHT ...
... IF...
...IF WE... SURVIVE THIS FIGHT...

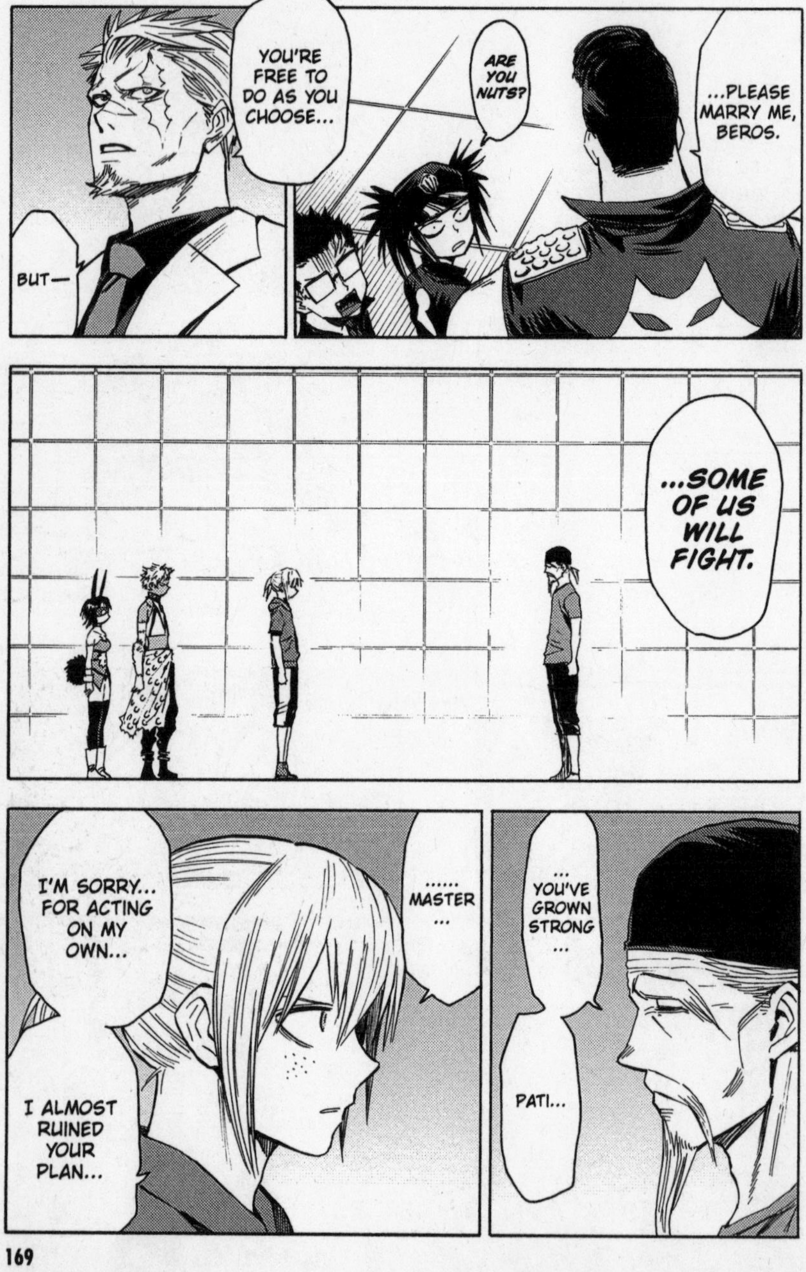
...PLEASE MARRY ME, BEROS.
ARE YOU NUTS?
YOU'RE FREE TO DO AS YOU CHOOSE...
BUT—
...SOME OF US WILL FIGHT.
... YOU'VE GROWN STRONG ...
PATI...
...... MASTER ...
I'M SORRY... FOR ACTING ON MY OWN...
I ALMOST RUINED YOUR PLAN...

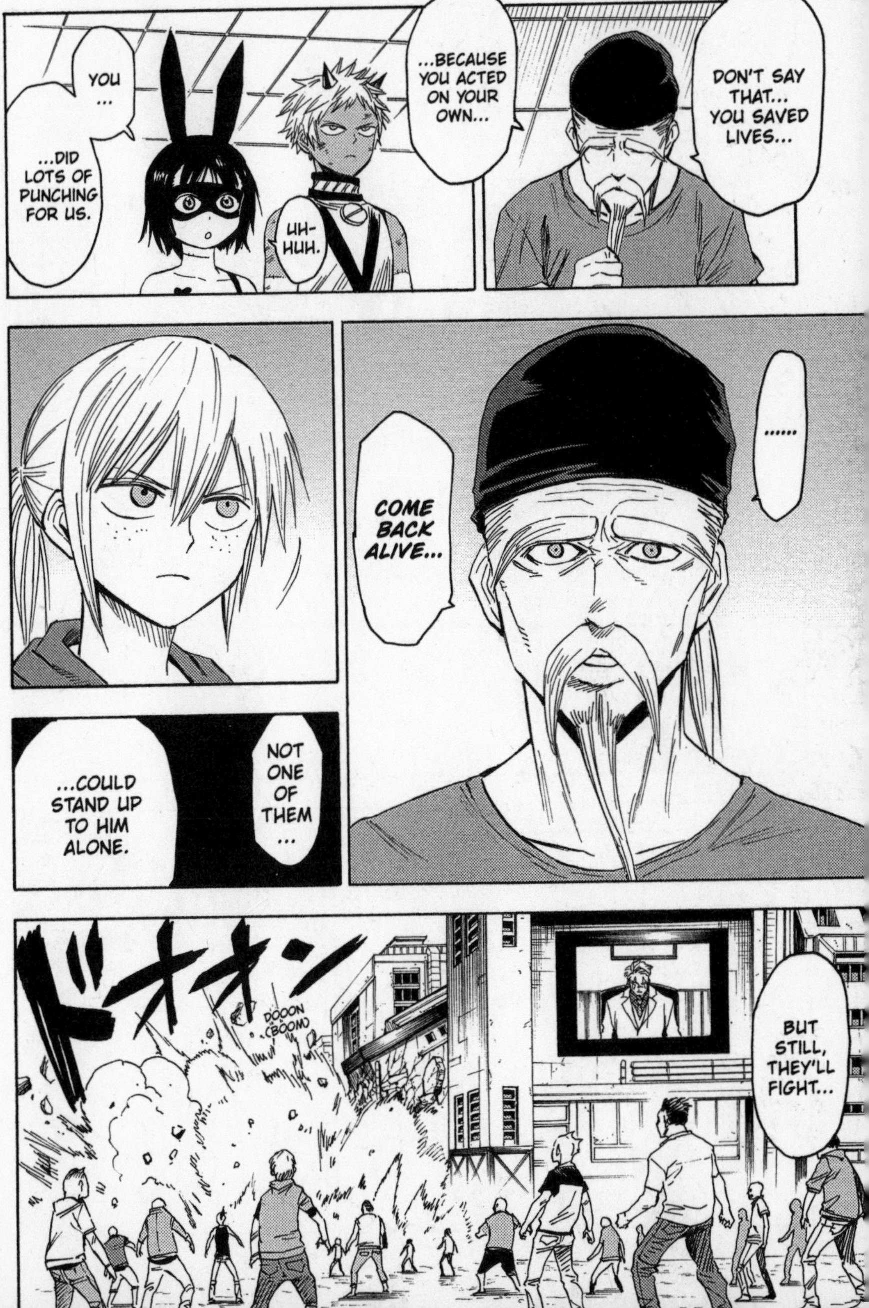
DON'T SAY THAT... YOU SAVED LIVES...
...BECAUSE YOU ACTED ON YOUR OWN...
YOU ...
...DID LOTS OF PUNCHING FOR US.
UH-HUH.
......
COME BACK ALIVE...
NOT ONE OF THEM ...
...COULD STAND UP TO HIM ALONE.
BUT STILL, THEY'LL FIGHT...
ドオオン
DOOON (BOOM)

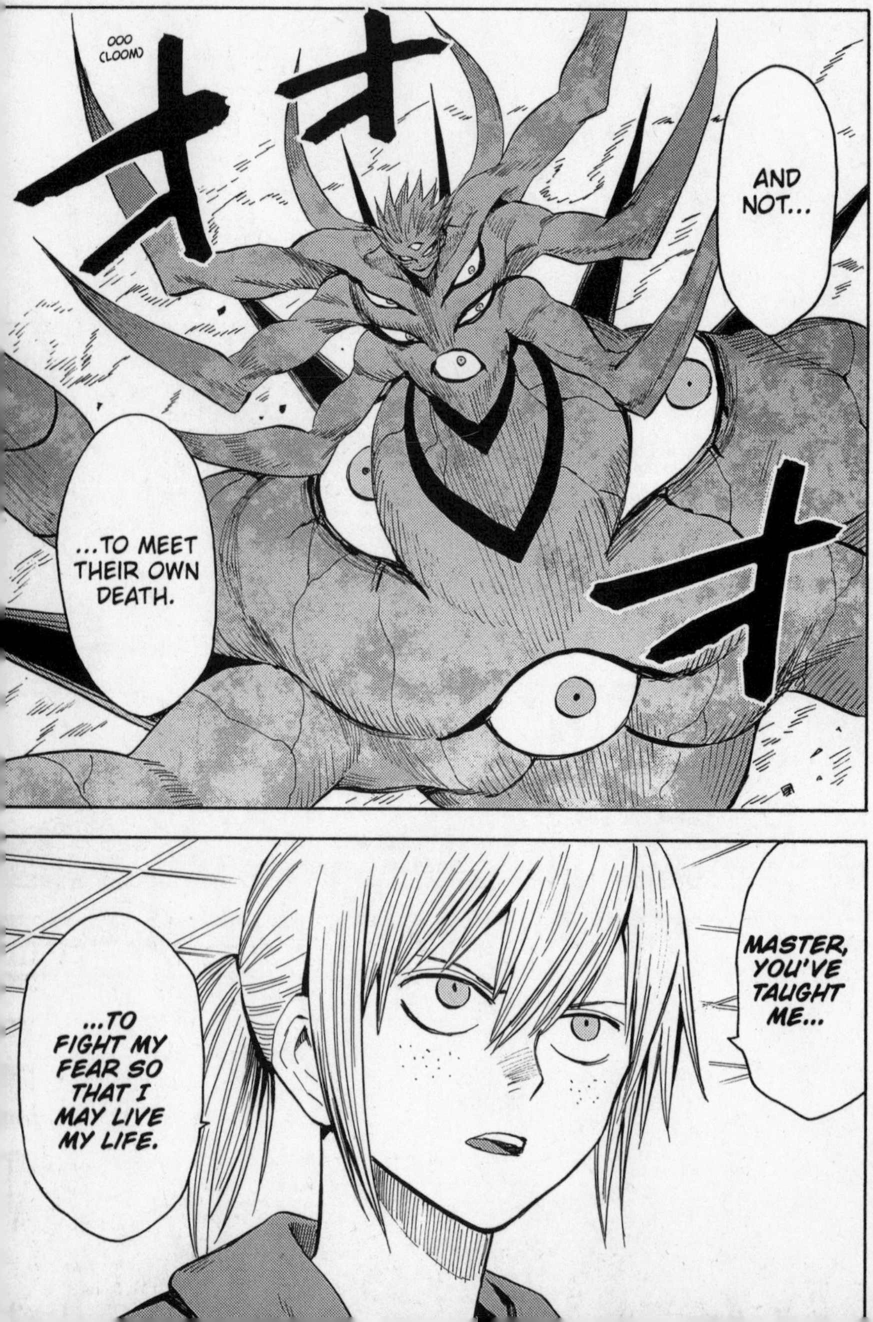
AND NOT...
OOO (LOOM)
...TO MEET THEIR OWN DEATH.
MASTER, YOU'VE TAUGHT ME...
...TO FIGHT MY FEAR SO THAT I MAY LIVE MY LIFE.

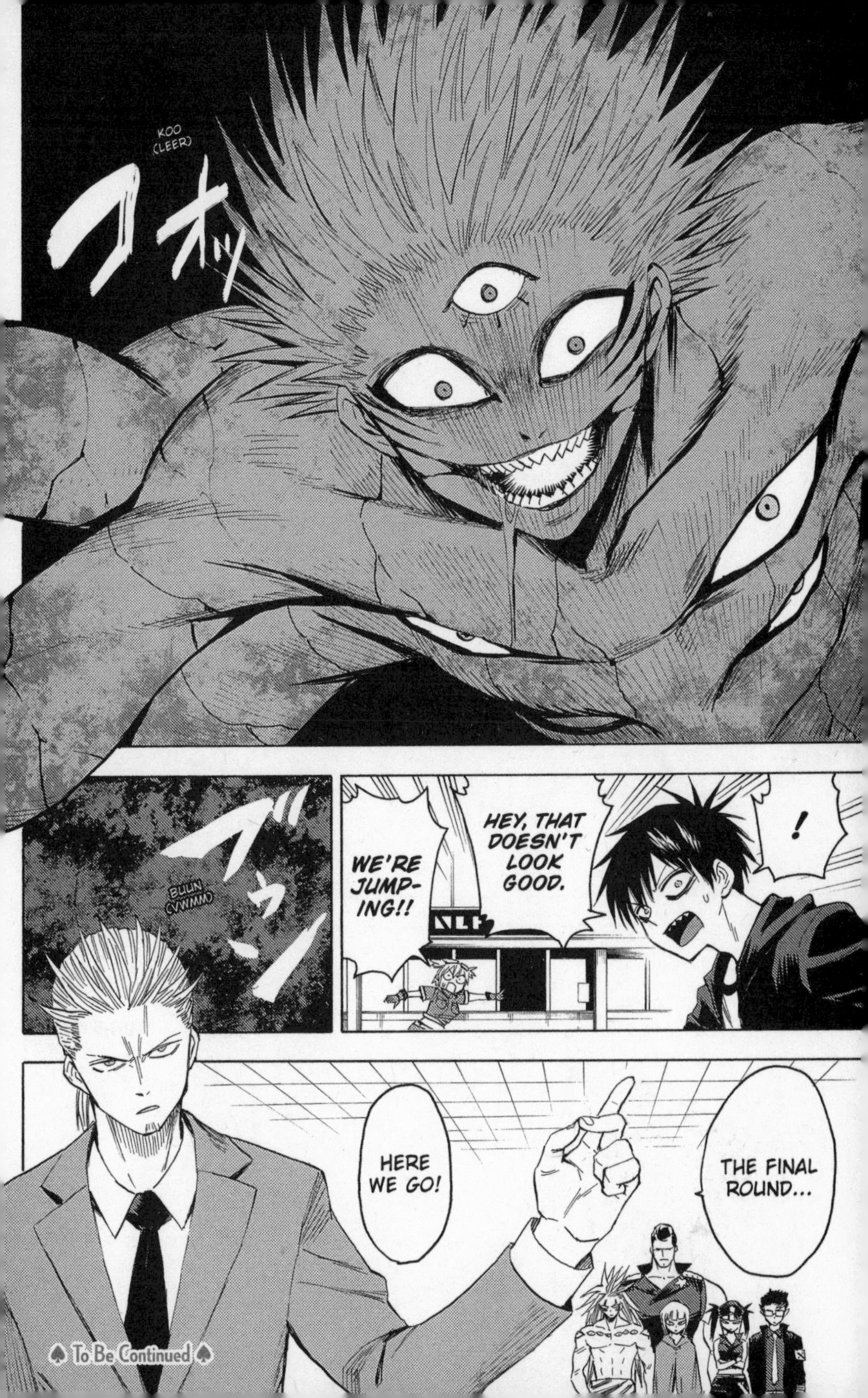
KOO (LEER)
コオッ
!
HEY, THAT DOESN'T LOOK GOOD.
WE'RE JUMP-ING!!
BUUN (VWMM)
ブゥン
THE FINAL ROUND...
HERE WE GO!
To Be Continued

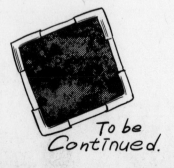

To be
Continued.

BLOOD LAD

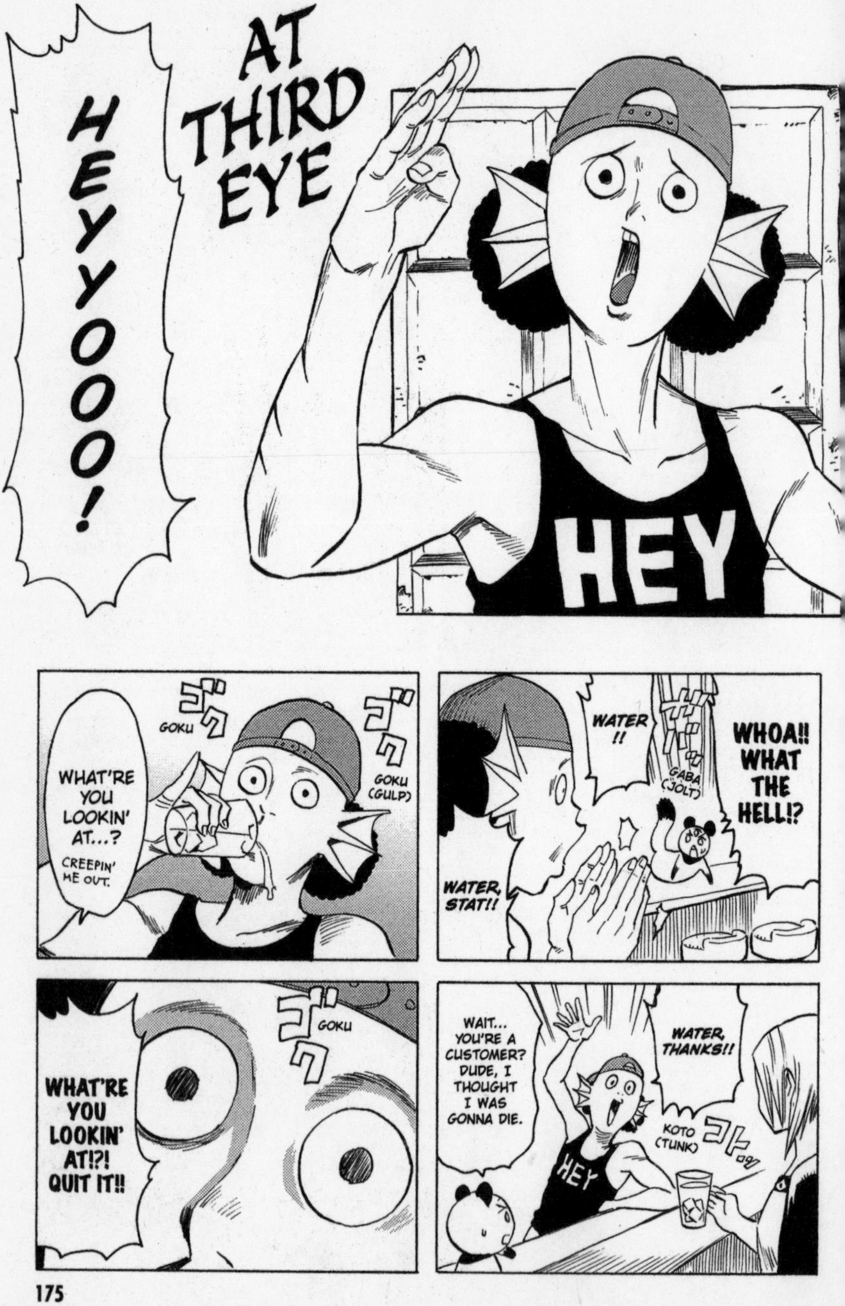
AT THIRD EYE
HEYYOOOO!
WHOA!! WHAT THE HELL!?
WATER !!
GABA (JOLT)
WATER, STAT!!
GOKU
GOKU (GULP)
WHAT'RE YOU LOOKIN' AT...?
CREEPIN' ME OUT.
WATER, THANKS!!
WAIT... YOU'RE A CUSTOMER? DUDE, I THOUGHT I WAS GONNA DIE.
KOTO (TUNK)
GOKU
WHAT'RE YOU LOOKIN' AT!?! QUIT IT!!

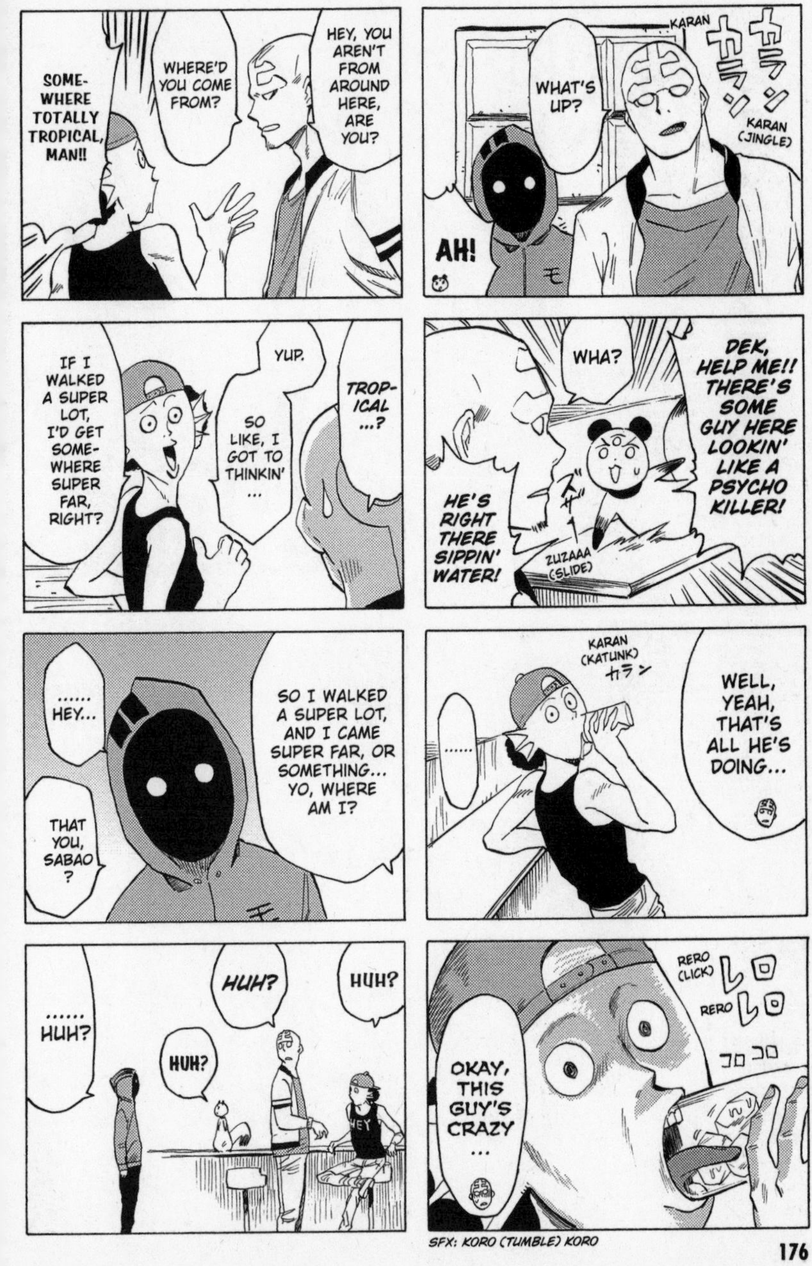
KARAN
カラン
カラン
KARAN (JINGLE)
WHAT'S UP?
AH!
HEY, YOU AREN'T FROM AROUND HERE, ARE YOU?
WHERE'D YOU COME FROM?
SOME-WHERE TOTALLY TROPICAL, MAN!!
DEK, HELP ME!! THERE'S SOME GUY HERE LOOKIN' LIKE A PSYCHO KILLER!
WHA?
ズザー
ZUZAAA (SLIDE)
HE'S RIGHT THERE SIPPIN' WATER!
TROP-ICAL ...?
YUP.
SO LIKE, I GOT TO THINKIN' ...
IF I WALKED A SUPER LOT, I'D GET SOME-WHERE SUPER FAR, RIGHT?
WELL, YEAH, THAT'S ALL HE'S DOING...
KARAN (KATUNK)
カラン
......
SO I WALKED A SUPER LOT, AND I CAME SUPER FAR, OR SOMETHING... YO, WHERE AM I?
......HEY...
THAT YOU, SABAO ?
RERO (LICK)
レロ
RERO
レロ
コロコロ
OKAY, THIS GUY'S CRAZY ...
HUH?
HUH?
HUH?
......HUH?

SFX: KORO (TUMBLE) KORO

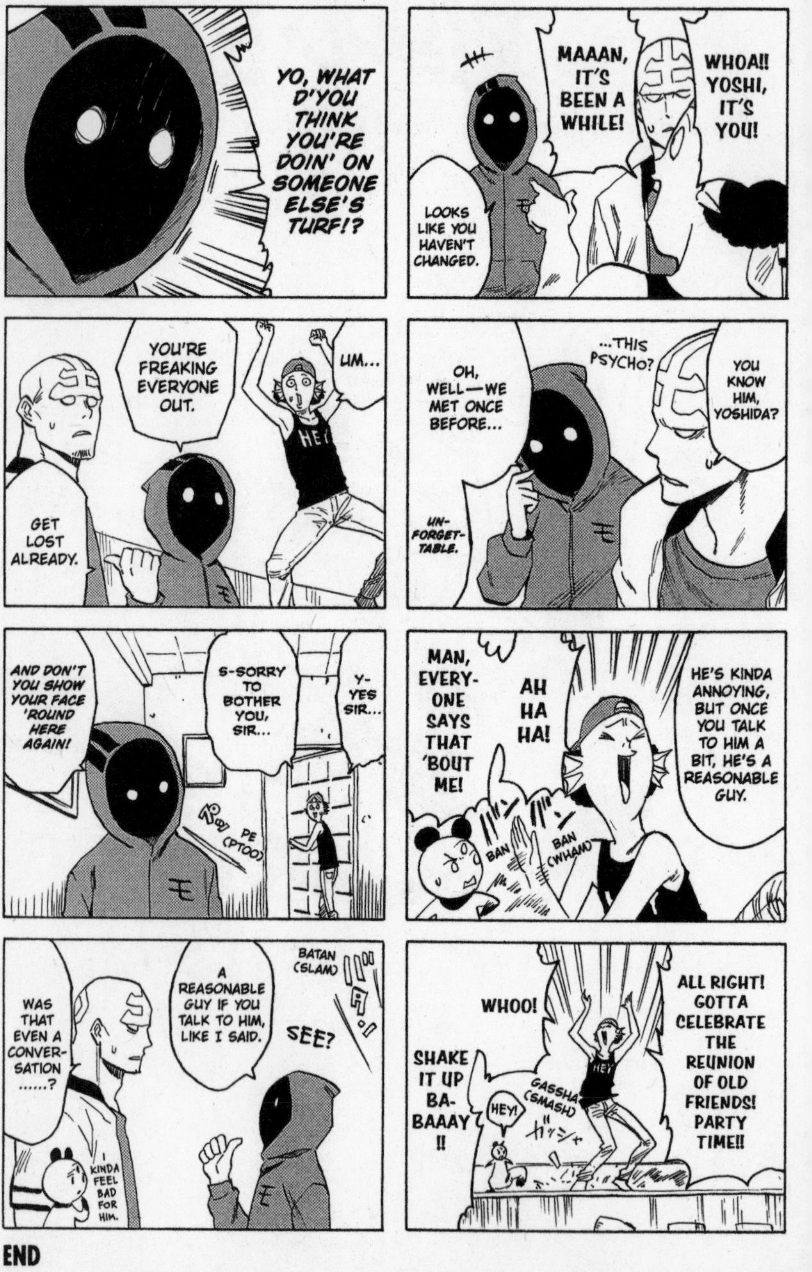
WHOA!! YOSHI, IT'S YOU!
MAAAN, IT'S BEEN A WHILE!
LOOKS LIKE YOU HAVEN'T CHANGED.
YO, WHAT D'YOU THINK YOU'RE DOIN' ON SOMEONE ELSE'S TURF!?
YOU KNOW HIM, YOSHIDA?
...THIS PSYCHO?
OH, WELL—WE MET ONCE BEFORE...
UN-FORGET-TABLE.
UM...
YOU'RE FREAKING EVERYONE OUT.
GET LOST ALREADY.
HE'S KINDA ANNOYING, BUT ONCE YOU TALK TO HIM A BIT, HE'S A REASONABLE GUY.
AH HA HA!
MAN, EVERY-ONE SAYS THAT 'BOUT ME!
BAN (WHAM)
BAN
Y-YES SIR...
S-SORRY TO BOTHER YOU, SIR...
AND DON'T YOU SHOW YOUR FACE 'ROUND HERE AGAIN!
PE (PTOO)
ALL RIGHT! GOTTA CELEBRATE THE REUNION OF OLD FRIENDS! PARTY TIME!!
WHOO!
SHAKE IT UP BA-BAAAY!!
GASSHA (SMASH)
HEY!
BATAN (SLAM)
SEE?
A REASONABLE GUY IF YOU TALK TO HIM, LIKE I SAID.
WAS THAT EVEN A CONVER-SATION......?
I KINDA FEEL BAD FOR HIM.

END

# BLOOD LAD 15

**These images appeared under the jacket of the original edition of *Blood Lad*!**

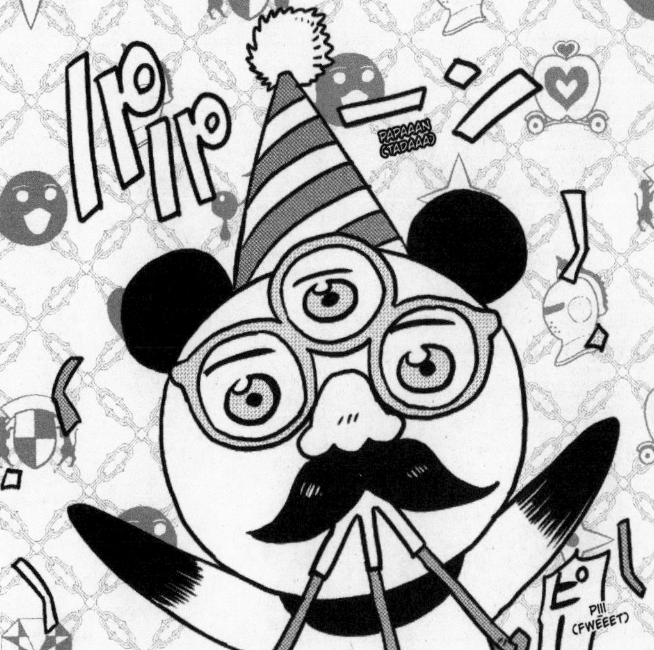
PAPAAAN (TADAAA)
PIII (FWEEET)

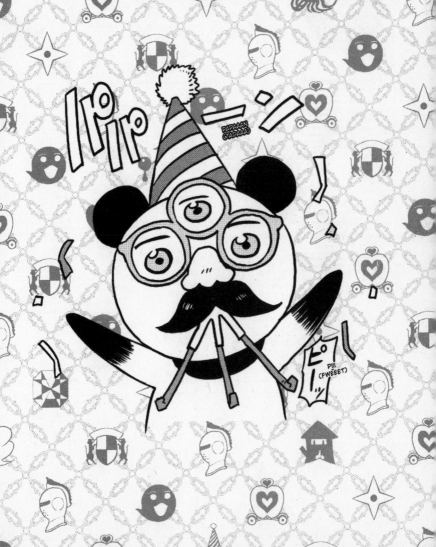

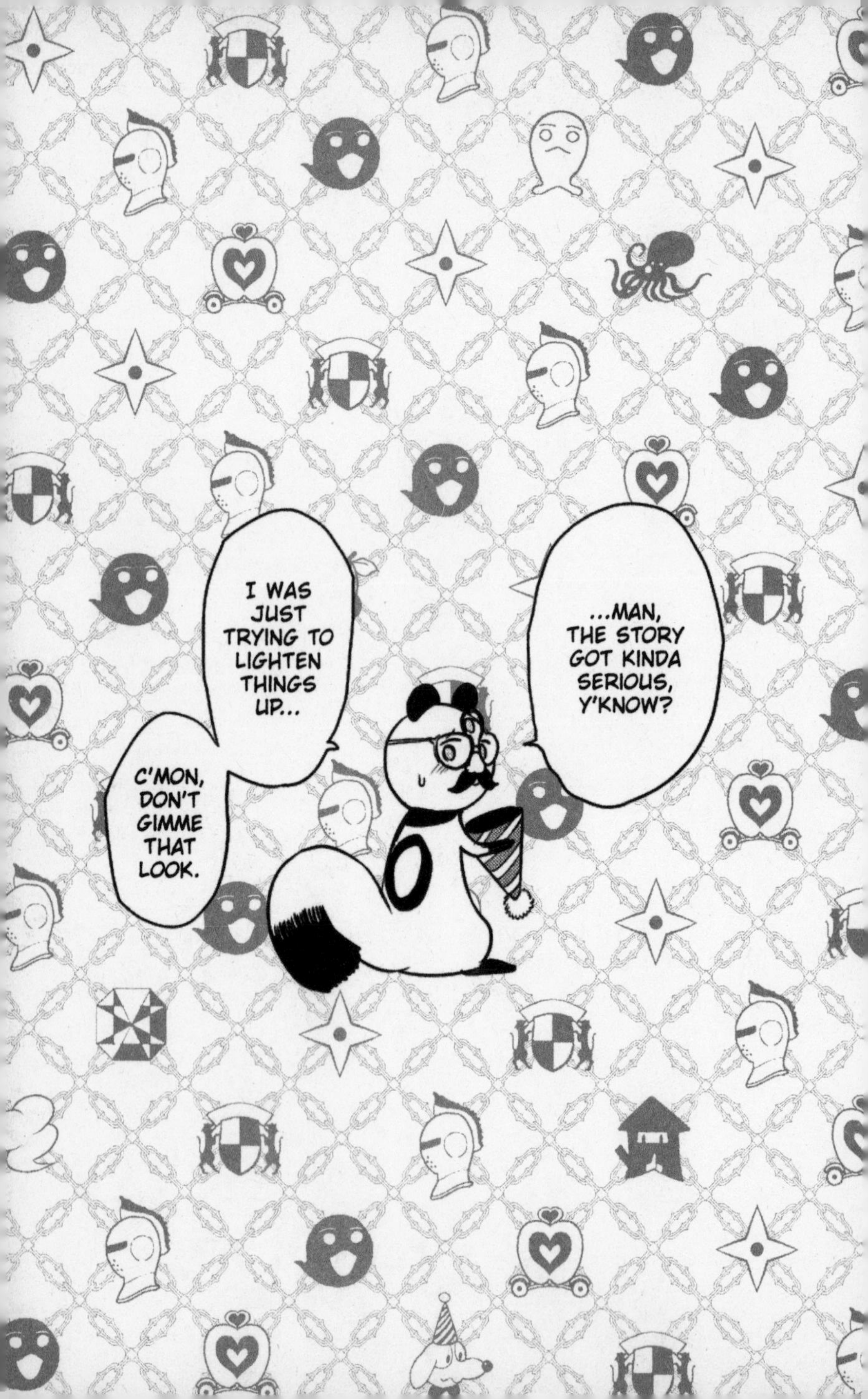
...MAN, THE STORY GOT KINDA SERIOUS, Y'KNOW?
I WAS JUST TRYING TO LIGHTEN THINGS UP...
C'MON, DON'T GIMME THAT LOOK.

BLOOD LAD

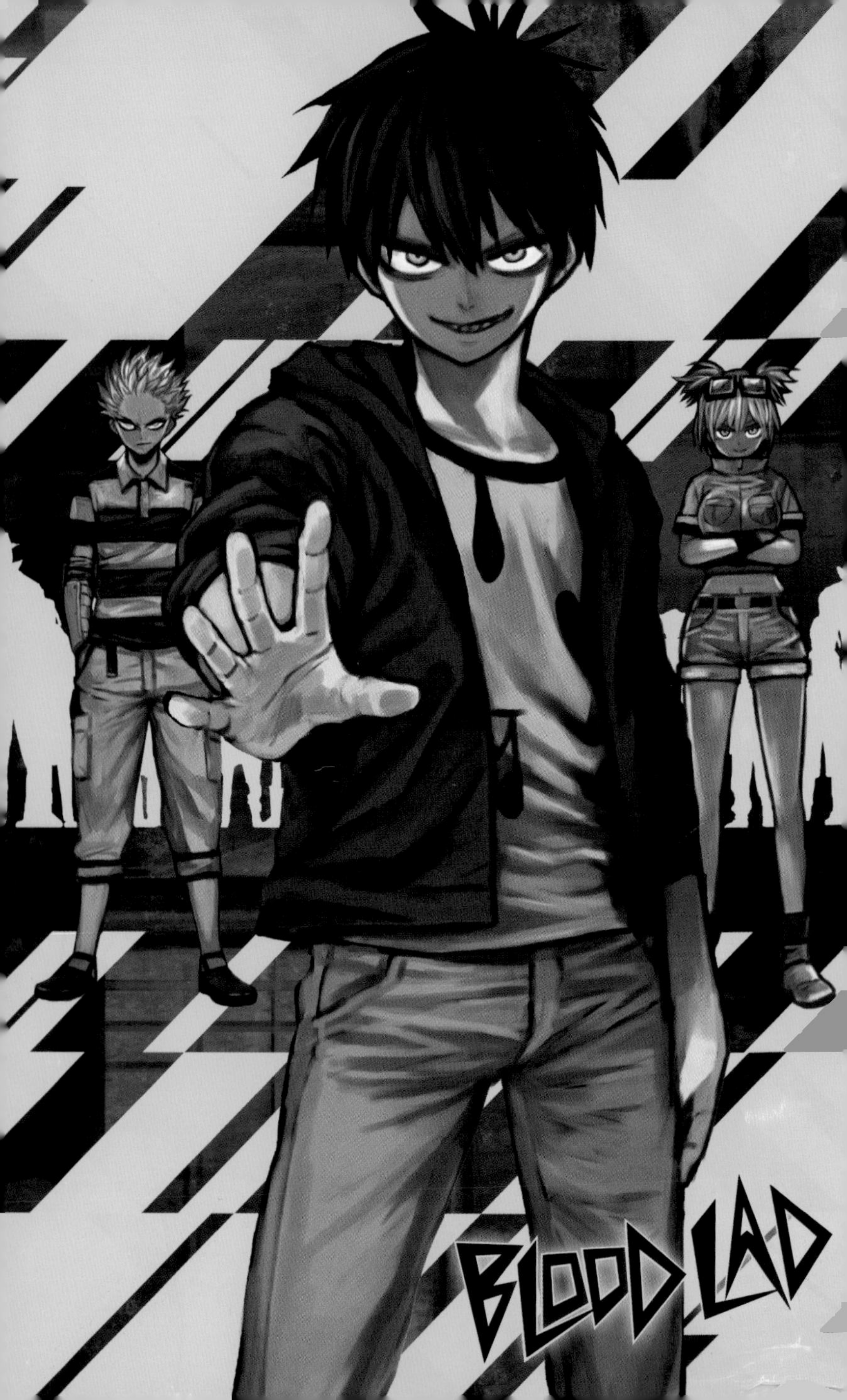
BLOOD LAD

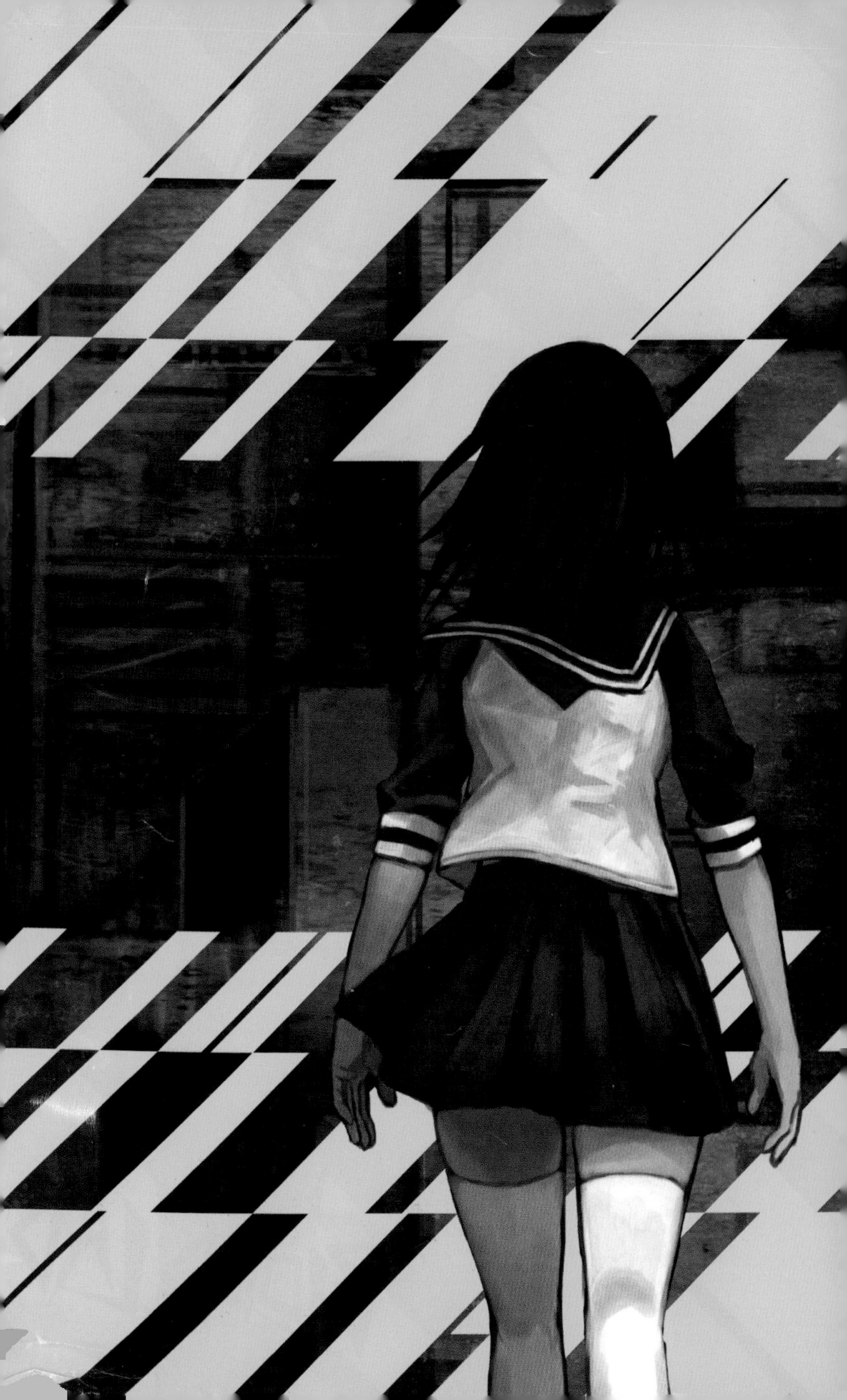

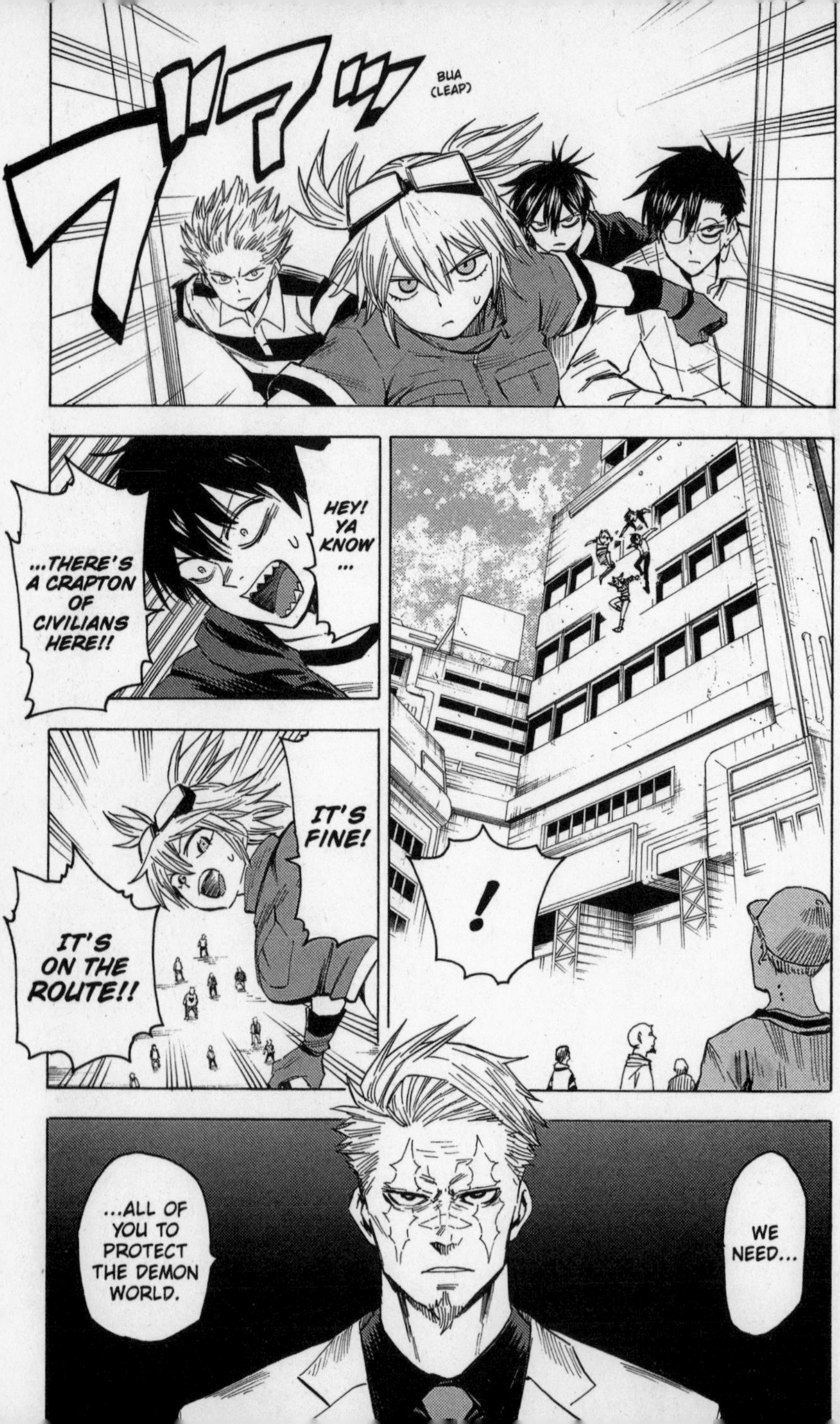
BUA
(LEAP)
!
HEY! YA KNOW ...
...THERE'S A CRAPTON OF CIVILIANS HERE!!
IT'S FINE!
IT'S ON THE ROUTE!!
WE NEED...
...ALL OF YOU TO PROTECT THE DEMON WORLD.

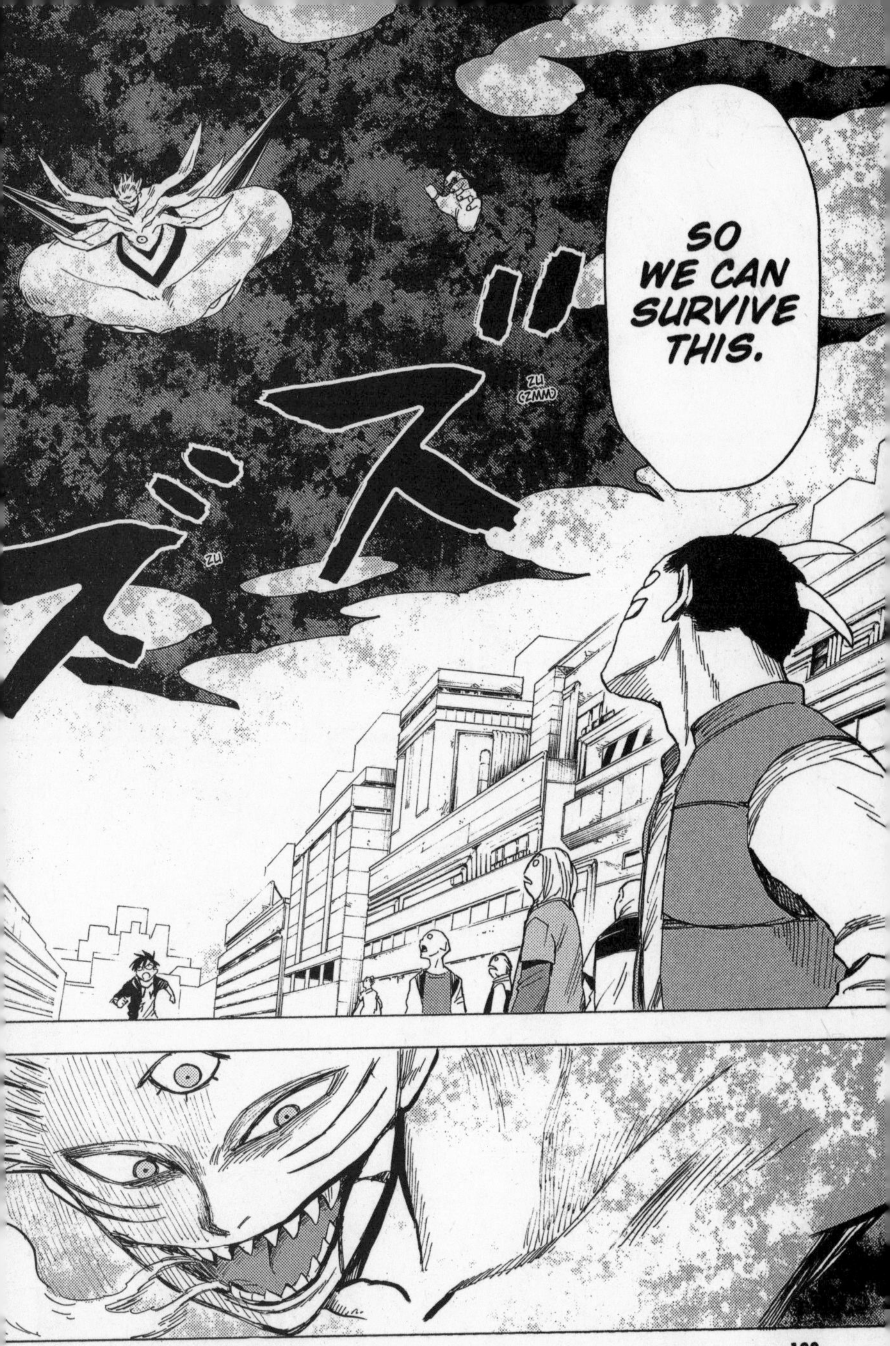
SO WE CAN SURVIVE THIS.
ズ
ZU (ZMMM)
ズ
ZU

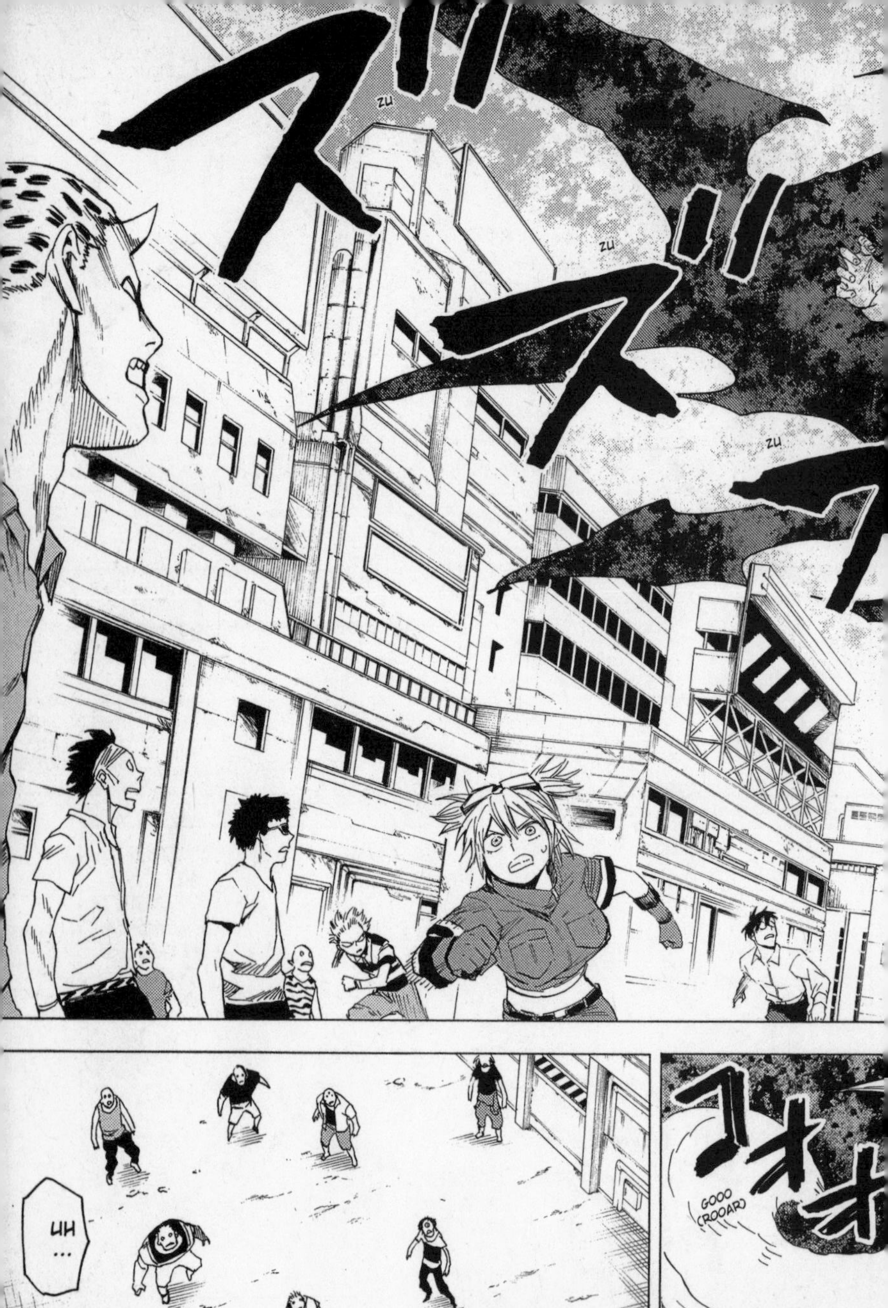

ズ
ZU
ズ
ZU
ズ
ZU
コオオ
GOOO (ROOAR)
UH ...

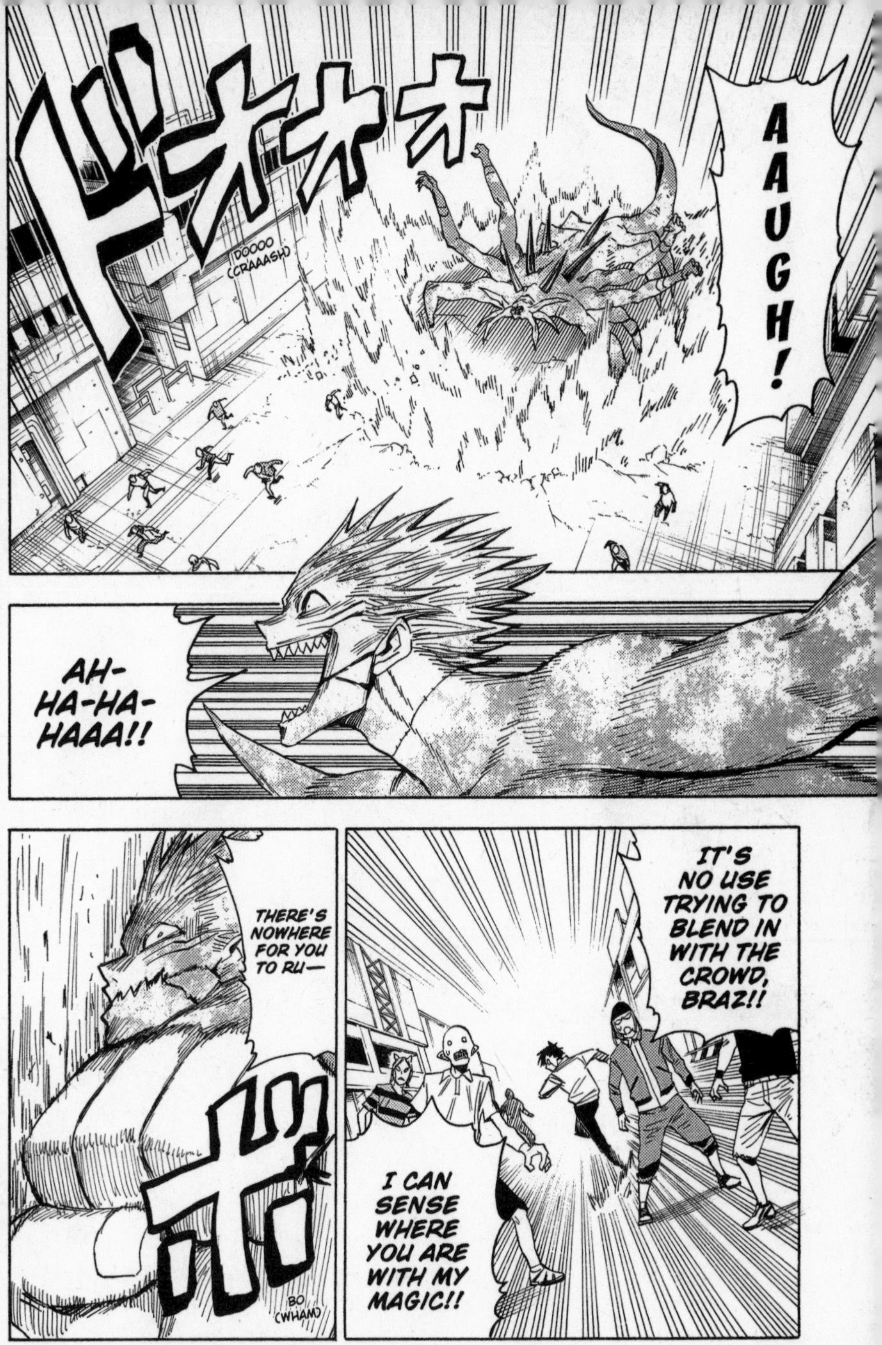
AAAUGH!
DOOOO (CRAAASH)
AH-HA-HA-HAAA!!
IT'S NO USE TRYING TO BLEND IN WITH THE CROWD, BRAZ!!
I CAN SENSE WHERE YOU ARE WITH MY MAGIC!!
THERE'S NOWHERE FOR YOU TO RU—
BO (WHAM)

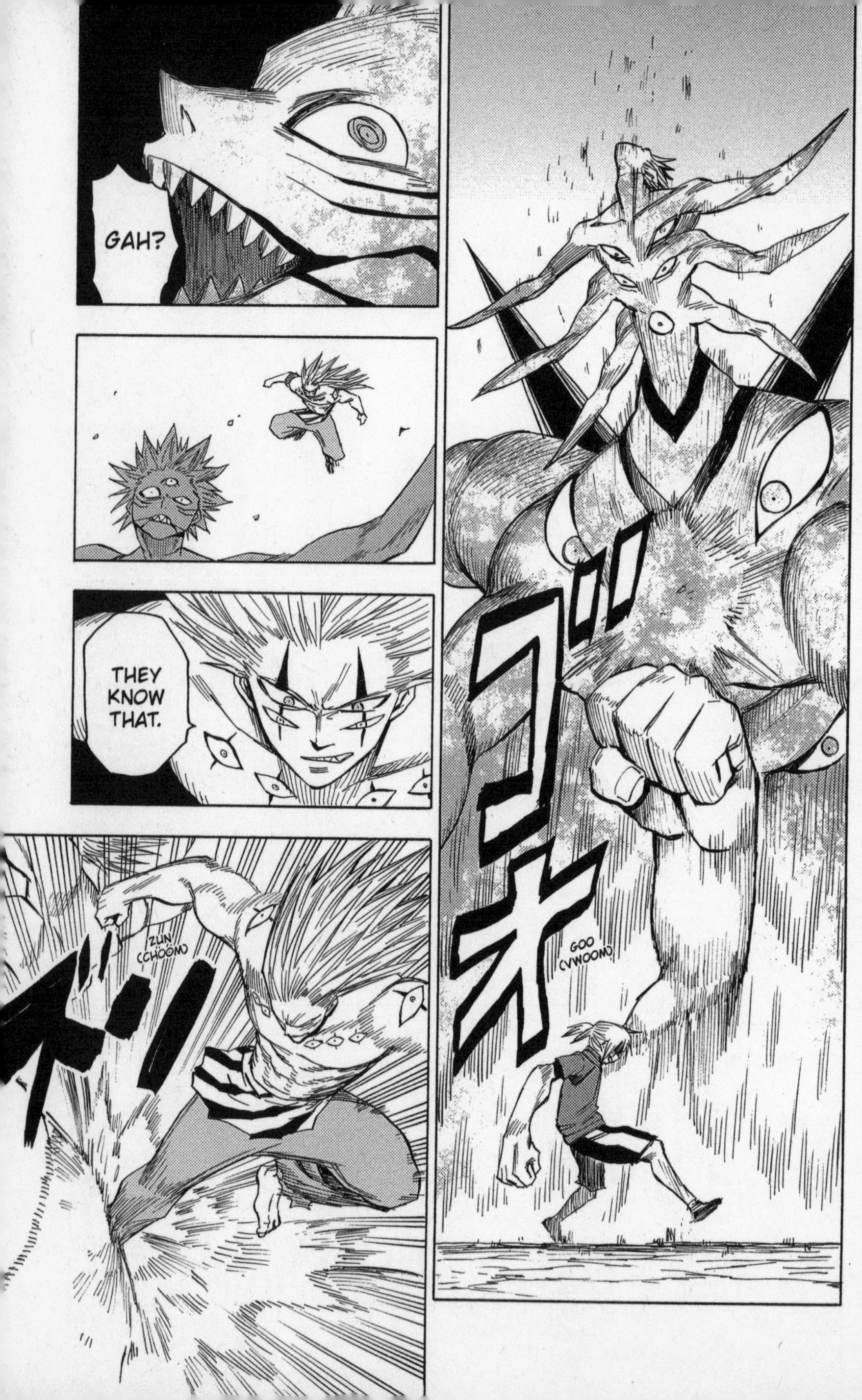
GOO (VWOOM)
GAH?
THEY KNOW THAT.
ZUN (CHOOM)

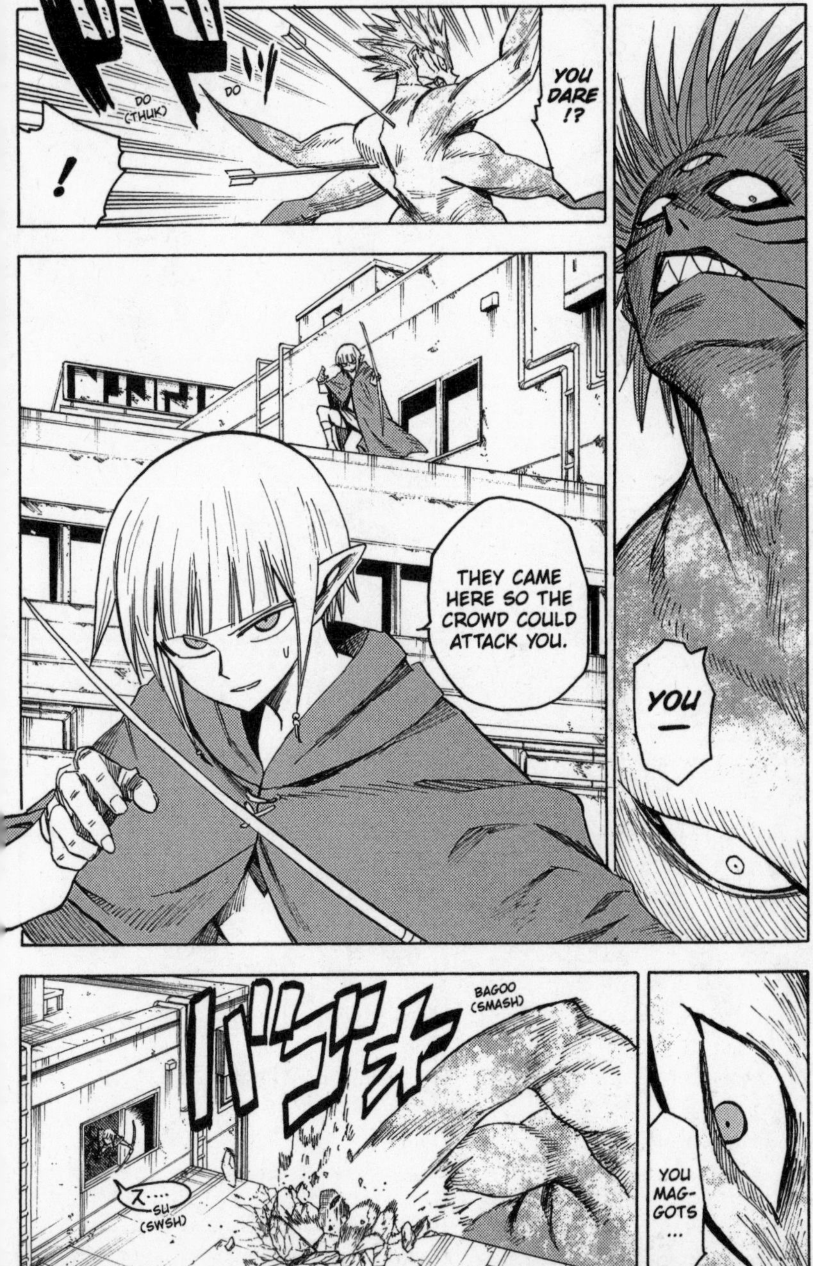
YOU
—
YOU DARE !?
DO
DO (THUK)
!
THEY CAME HERE SO THE CROWD COULD ATTACK YOU.
YOU MAG-GOTS ...
BAGOO (SMASH)
ス…
SU (SWSH)

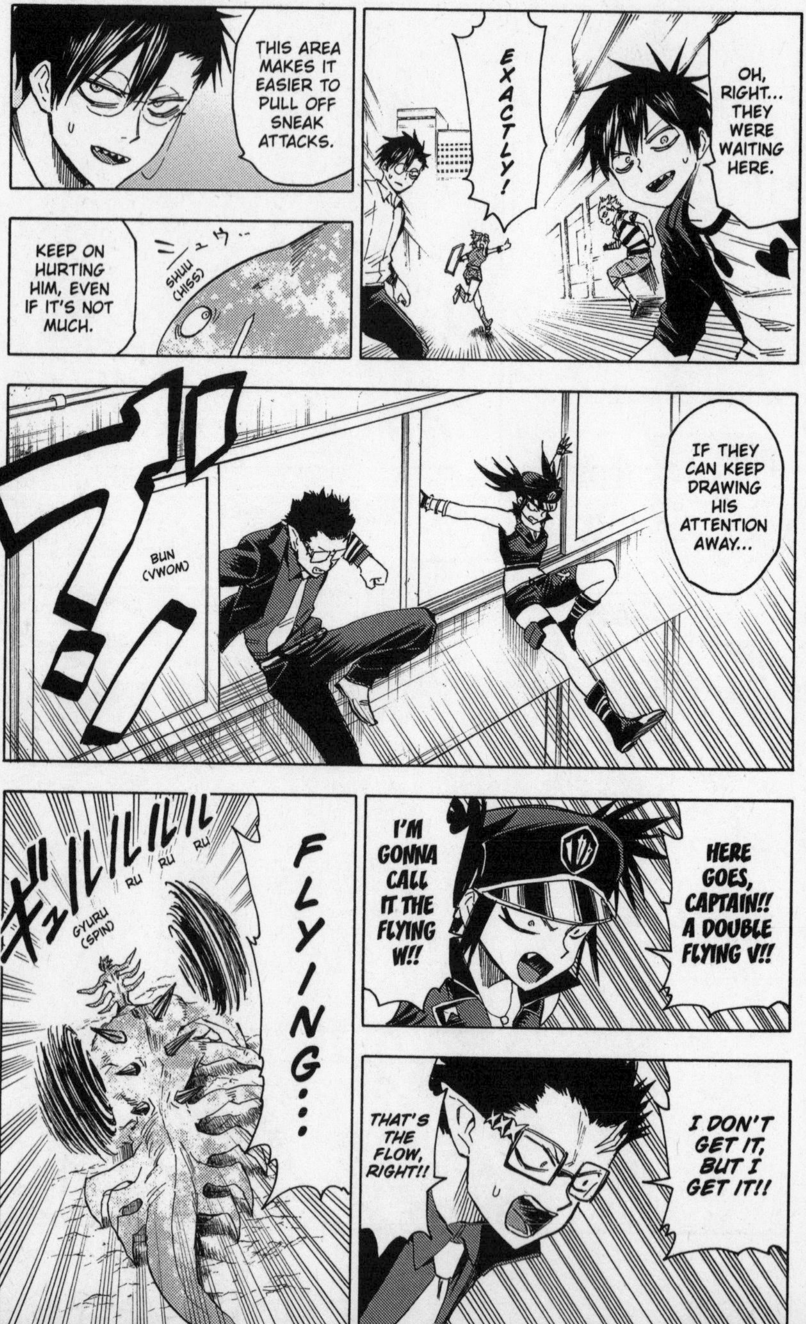
OH, RIGHT... THEY WERE WAITING HERE.
EXACTLY!
THIS AREA MAKES IT EASIER TO PULL OFF SNEAK ATTACKS.
SHUU (HISS)
KEEP ON HURTING HIM, EVEN IF IT'S NOT MUCH.
IF THEY CAN KEEP DRAWING HIS ATTENTION AWAY...
BUN (VWOM)
HERE GOES, CAPTAIN!! A DOUBLE FLYING V!!
I'M GONNA CALL IT THE FLYING W!!
I DON'T GET IT, BUT I GET IT!!
THAT'S THE FLOW, RIGHT!!
FLYING...
RU RU RU
GYURU (SPIN)

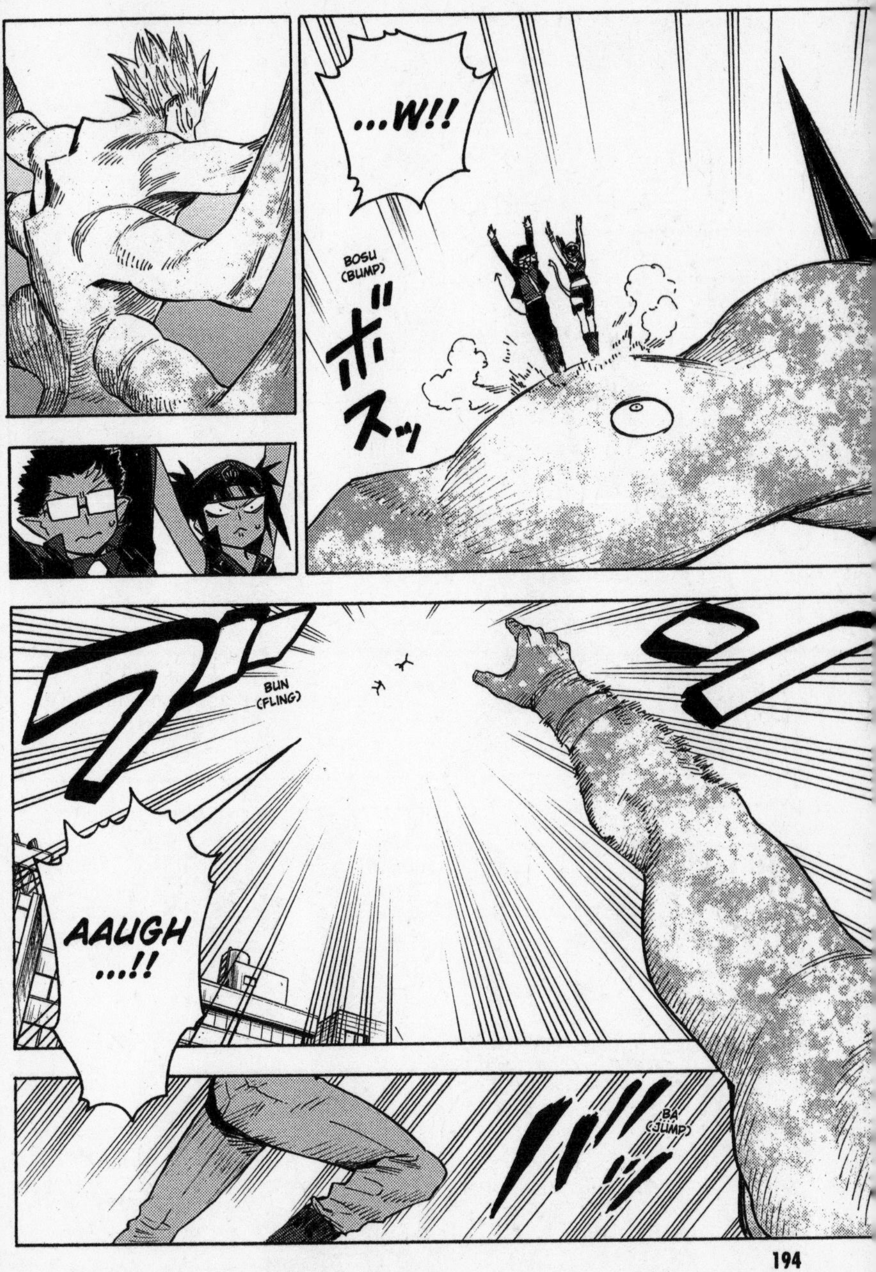
...W!!
BOSU (BUMP)
ボスッ
ロ
BUN (FLING)
ブン
AAUGH ...!!
BA (JUMP)
バッ

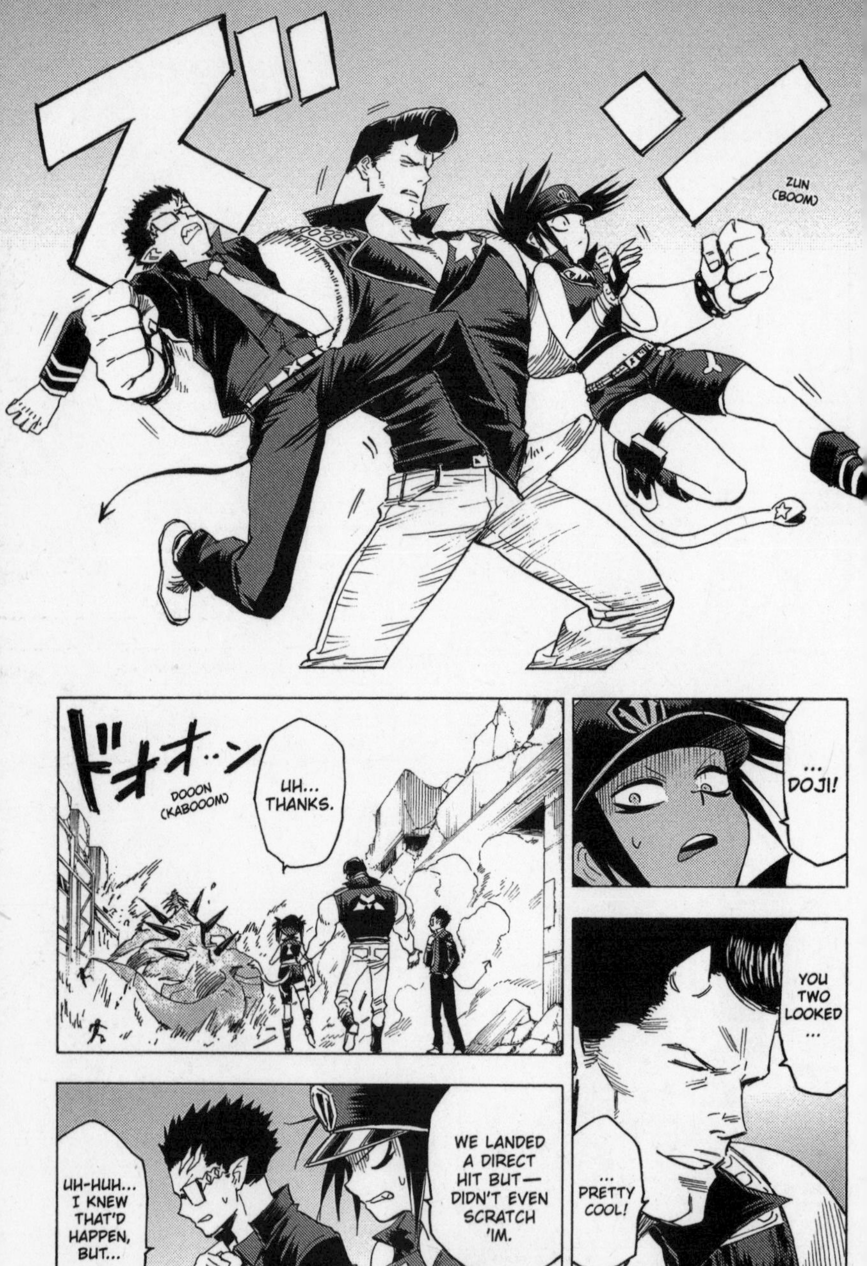
ズーン
ZUN (BOOM)
...DOJI!
ドオォ..ン
DOOON (KABOOOM)
UH... THANKS.
YOU TWO LOOKED ...
...PRETTY COOL!
WE LANDED A DIRECT HIT BUT— DIDN'T EVEN SCRATCH 'IM.
UH-HUH... I KNEW THAT'D HAPPEN, BUT...

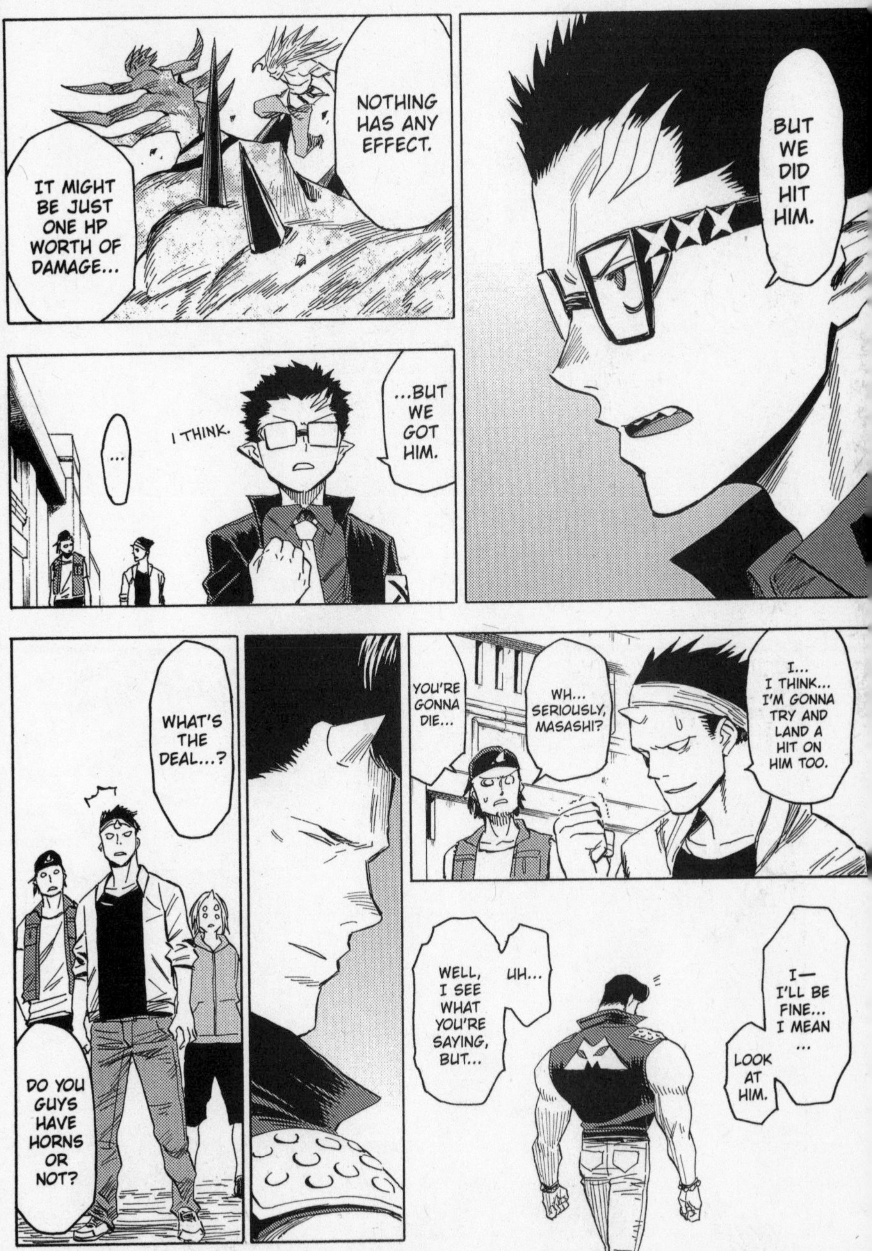
BUT WE DID HIT HIM.
NOTHING HAS ANY EFFECT.
IT MIGHT BE JUST ONE HP WORTH OF DAMAGE...
...BUT WE GOT HIM.
I THINK.
...
I... I THINK... I'M GONNA TRY AND LAND A HIT ON HIM TOO.
WH... SERIOUSLY, MASASHI?
YOU'RE GONNA DIE...
I— I'LL BE FINE... I MEAN...
LOOK AT HIM.
UH...
WELL, I SEE WHAT YOU'RE SAYING, BUT...
WHAT'S THE DEAL...?
DO YOU GUYS HAVE HORNS OR NOT?

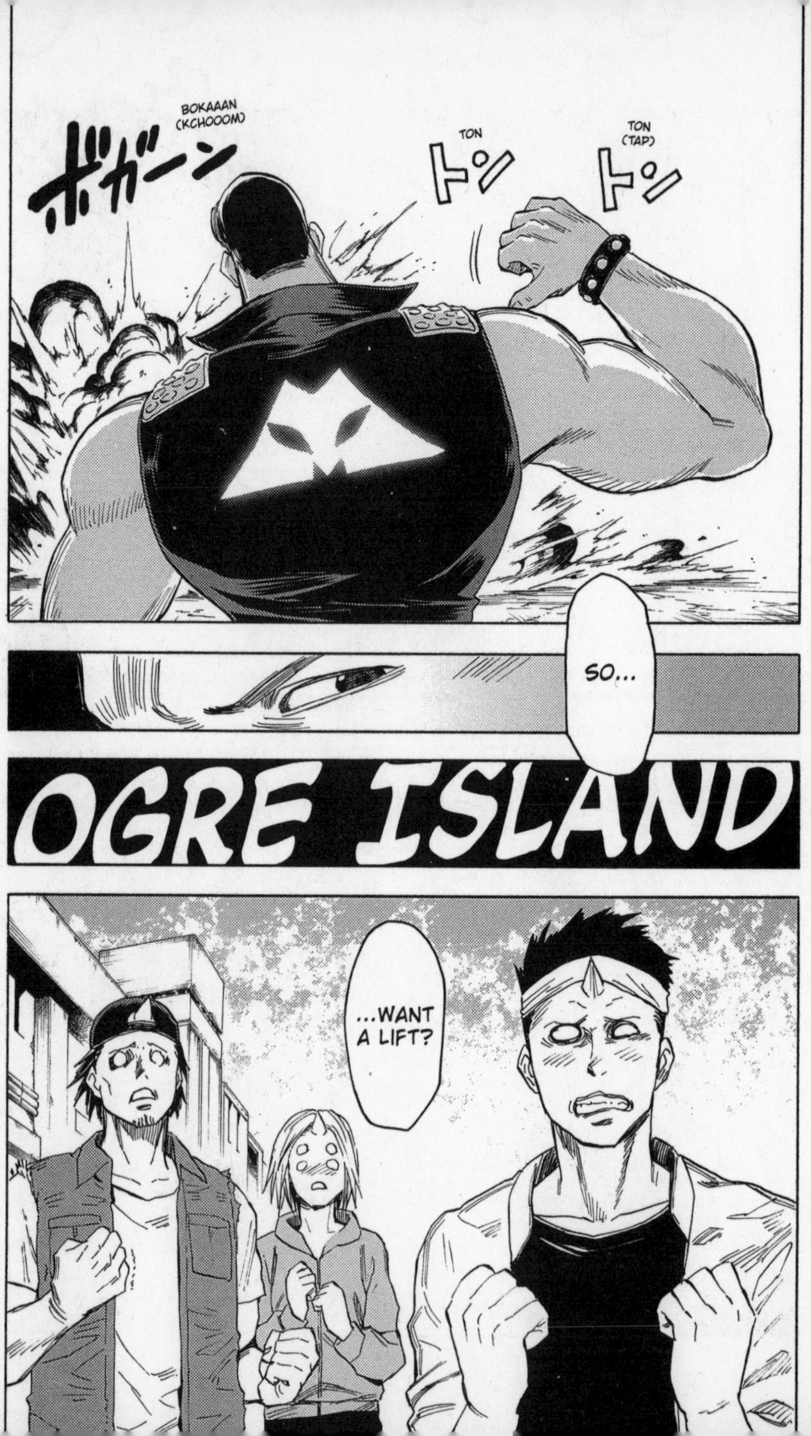

トン
TON (TAP)
トン
TON
ボガーン
BOKAAAN (KCHOOOM)
SO...
OGRE ISLAND
...WANT A LIFT?

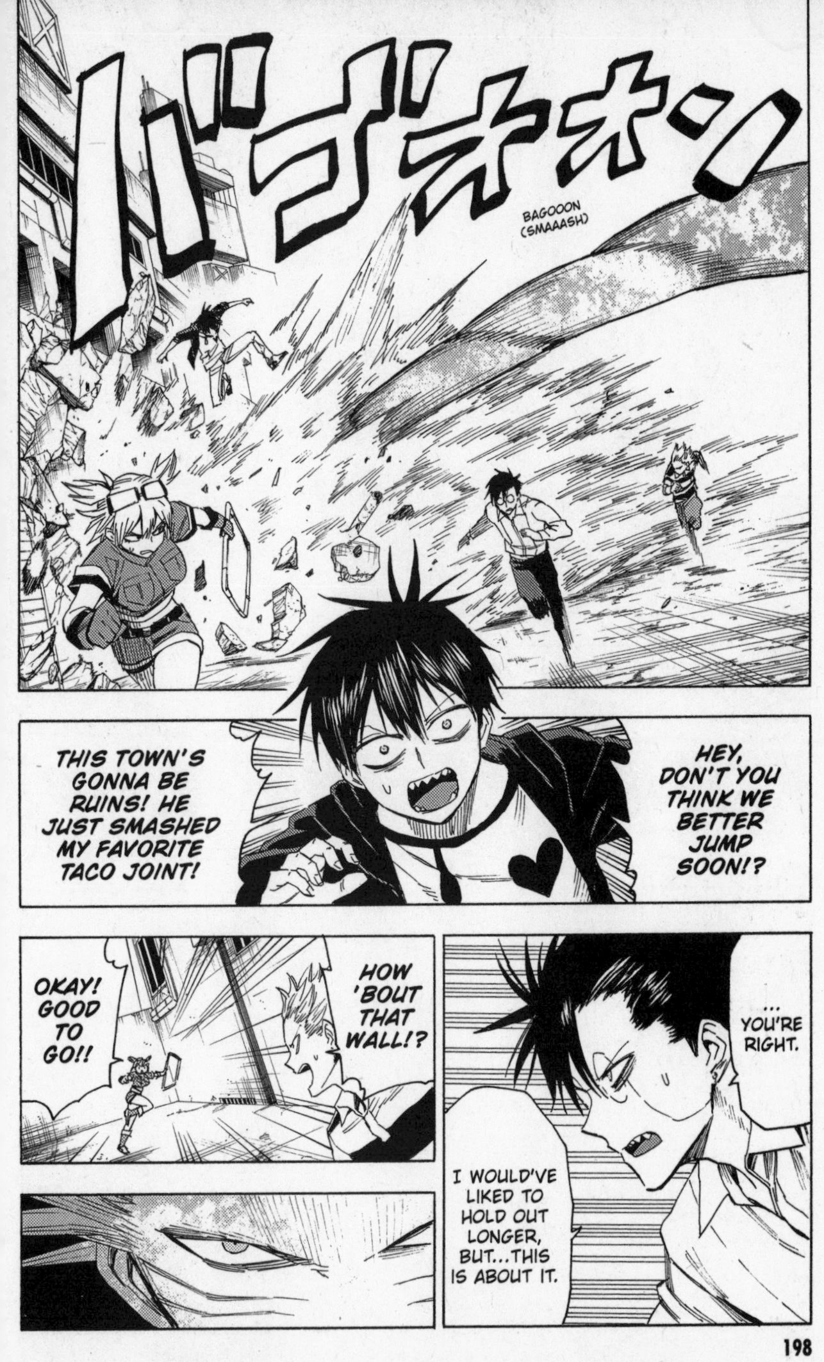

バゴォオン
BAGOOON (SMAAASH)
HEY, DON'T YOU THINK WE BETTER JUMP SOON!?
THIS TOWN'S GONNA BE RUINS! HE JUST SMASHED MY FAVORITE TACO JOINT!
... YOU'RE RIGHT.
I WOULD'VE LIKED TO HOLD OUT LONGER, BUT...THIS IS ABOUT IT.
HOW 'BOUT THAT WALL!?
OKAY! GOOD TO GO!!

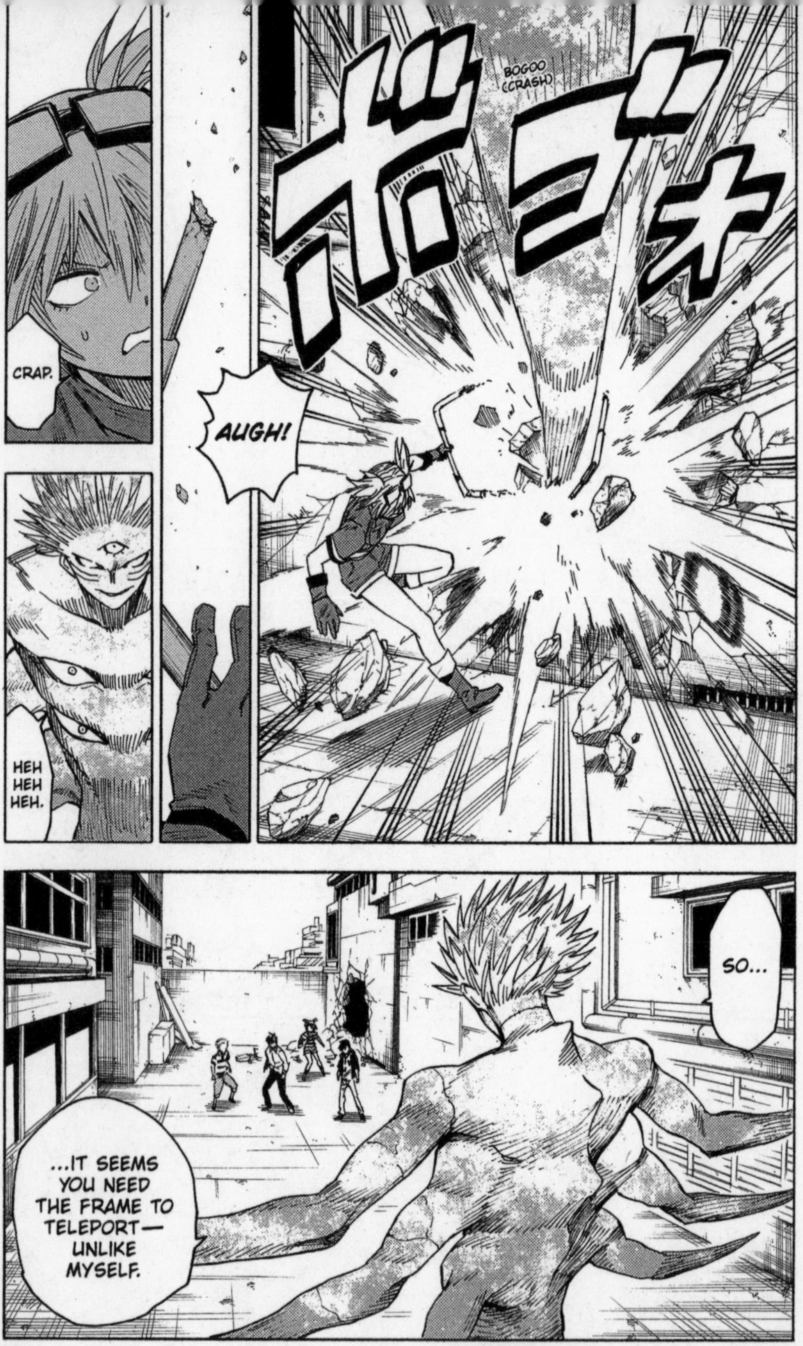
BOGOO (CRASH)
AUGH!
CRAP.
HEH HEH HEH.
SO...
...IT SEEMS YOU NEED THE FRAME TO TELEPORT—UNLIKE MYSELF.

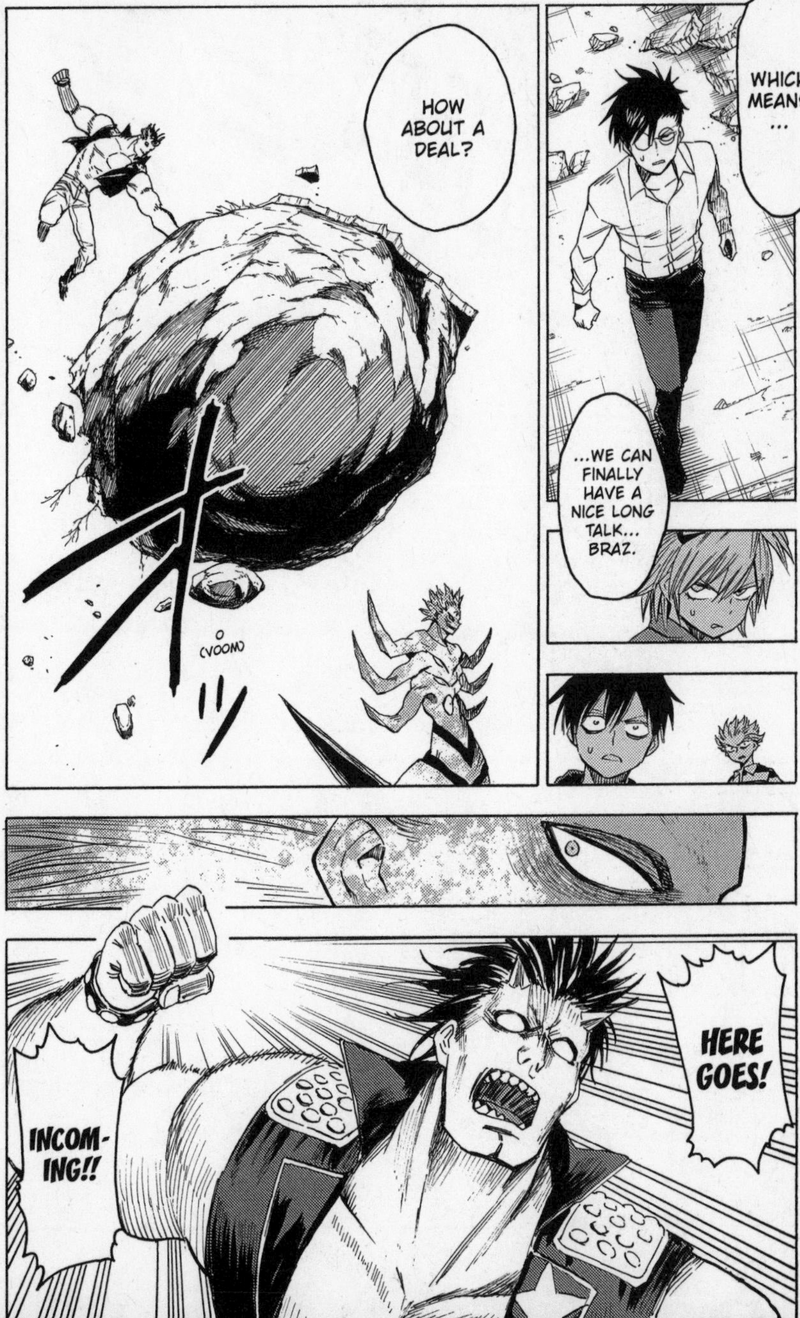
WHICH MEANS ...
...WE CAN FINALLY HAVE A NICE LONG TALK... BRAZ.
HOW ABOUT A DEAL?
(VOOM)
HERE GOES!
INCOM-ING!!

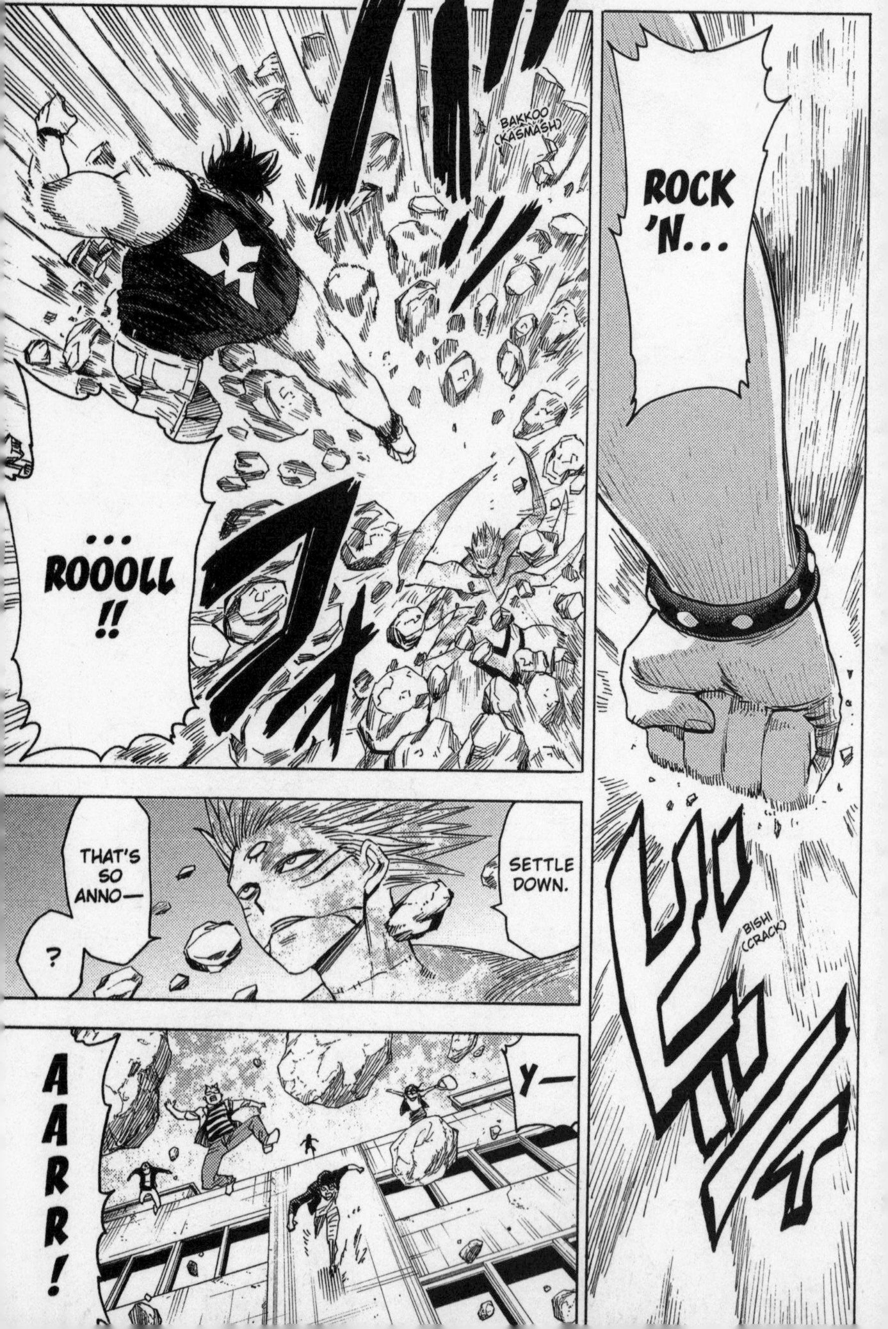
ROCK 'N...
BISHI (CRACK)
BAKKOO (KASMASH)
...ROOOLL!!
SETTLE DOWN.
THAT'S SO ANNO—
?
Y—
AARR!

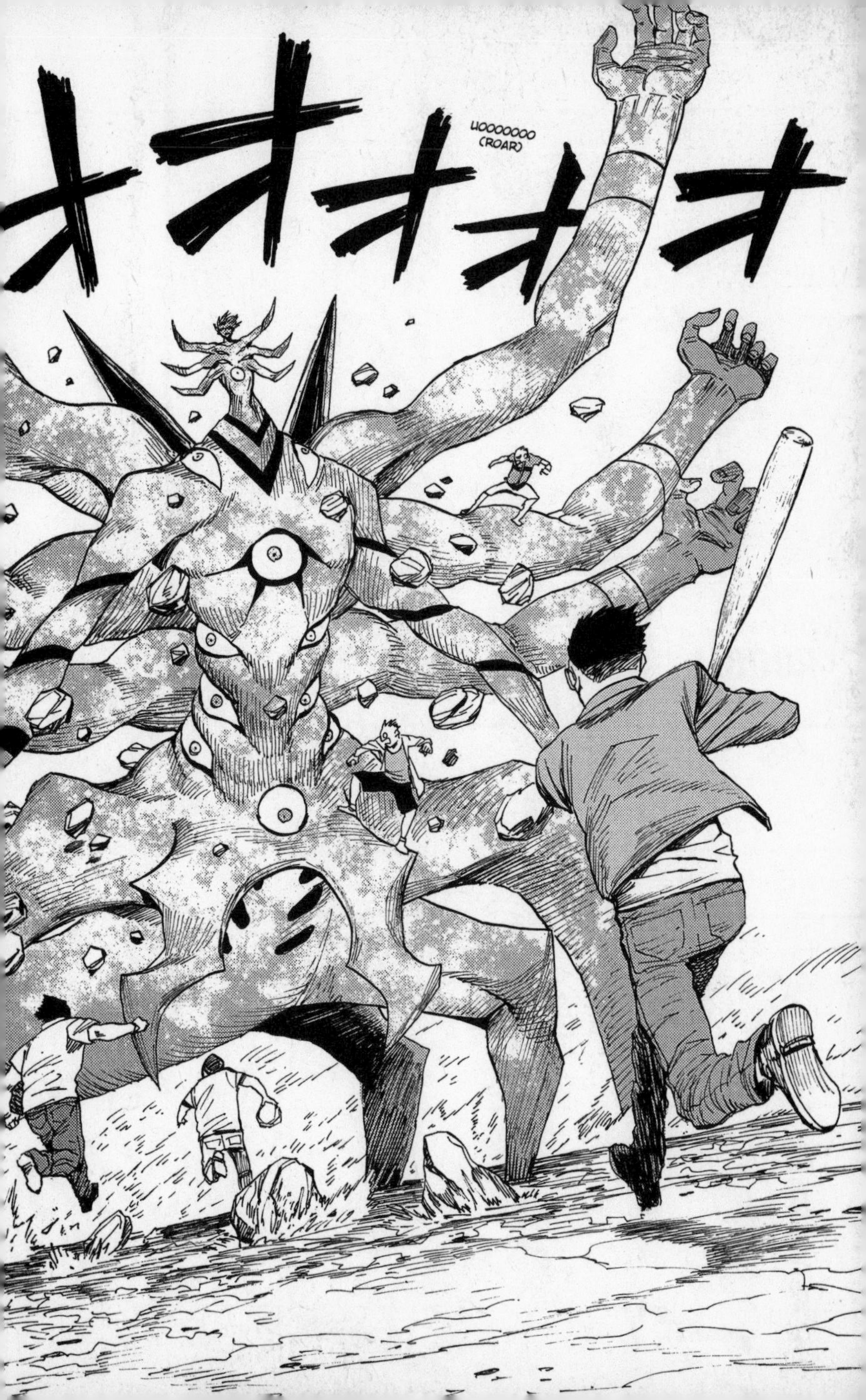
オオオオオ
UOOOOOOO (ROAR)

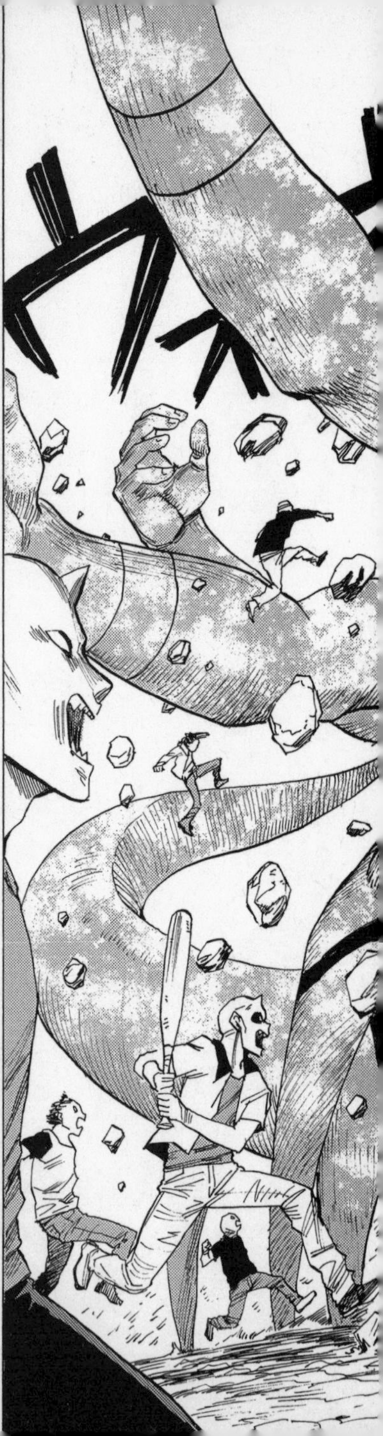

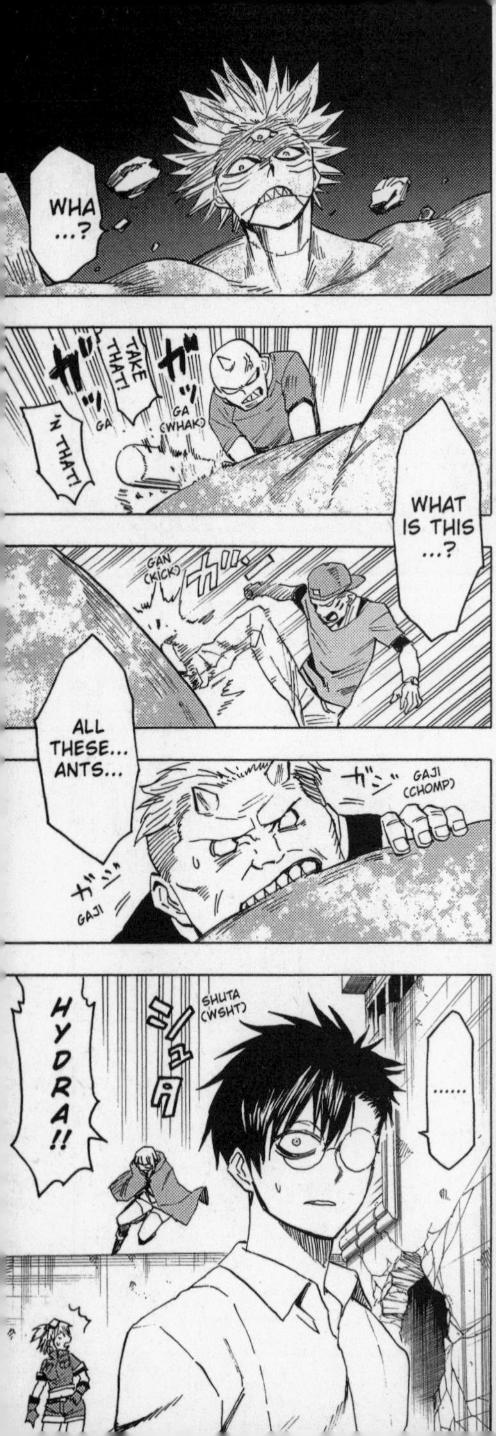
WHA ...?
TAKE THAT!
GA (WHAK)
'N THAT!
GA
WHAT IS THIS ...?
GAN (KICK)
ALL THESE... ANTS...
GAJI (CHOMP)
GAJI
......
SHUTA (WSHT)
HYDRA!!

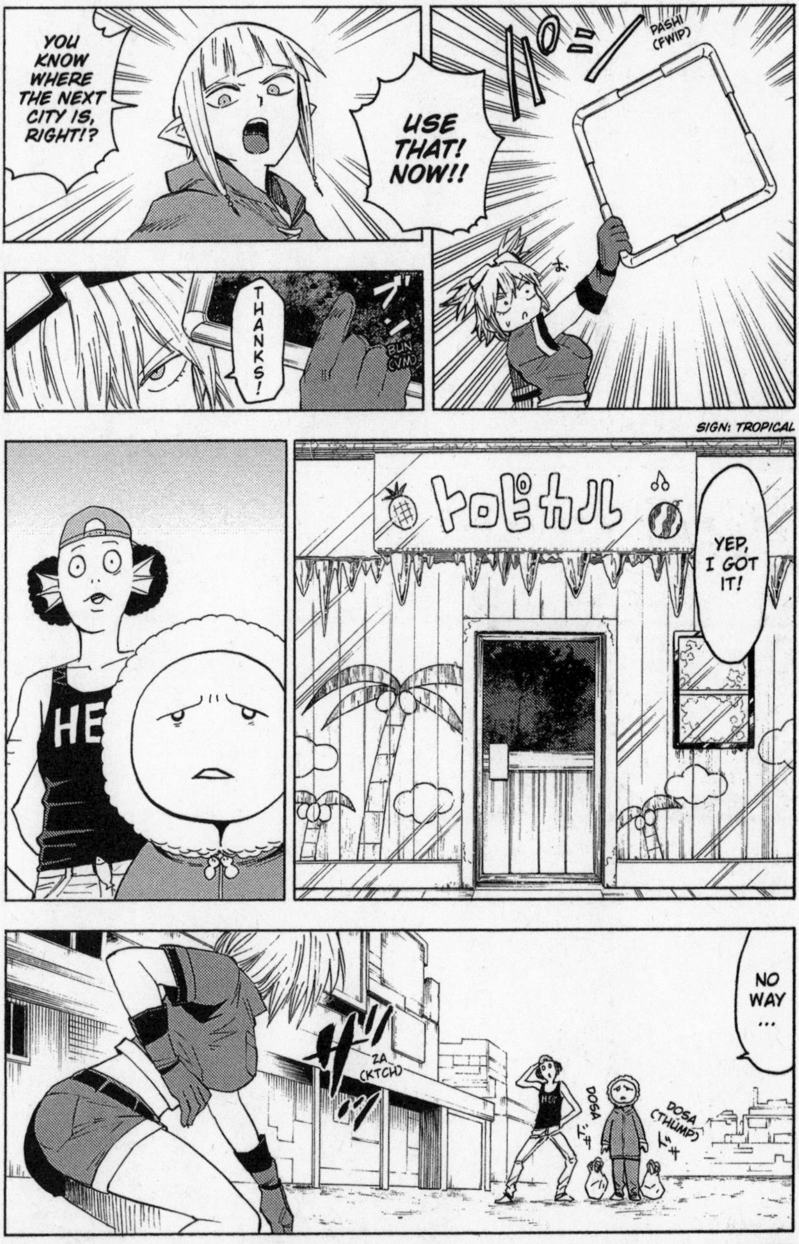
PASHI (FWIP)
YOU KNOW WHERE THE NEXT CITY IS, RIGHT!?
USE THAT! NOW!!
BUN (VM)
THANKS!
SIGN: TROPICAL
トロピカル
YEP, I GOT IT!
NO WAY ...
DOSA (THUMP)
DOSA
ZA (KTCH)

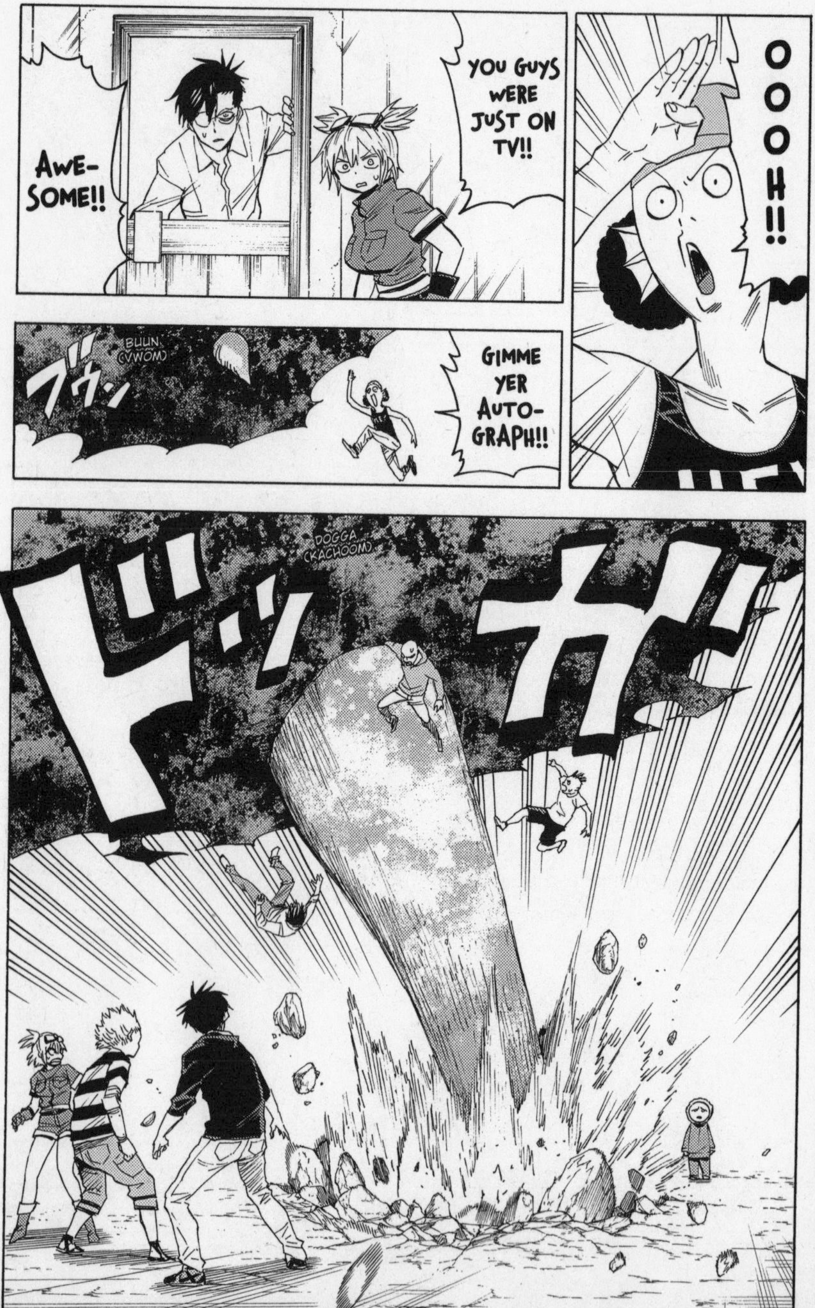
OOOH!!
YOU GUYS WERE JUST ON TV!!
AWE-SOME!!
GIMME YER AUTO-GRAPH!!
ブゥン
BUUN (VWOM)
ドッカ
DOGGA (KACHOOM)

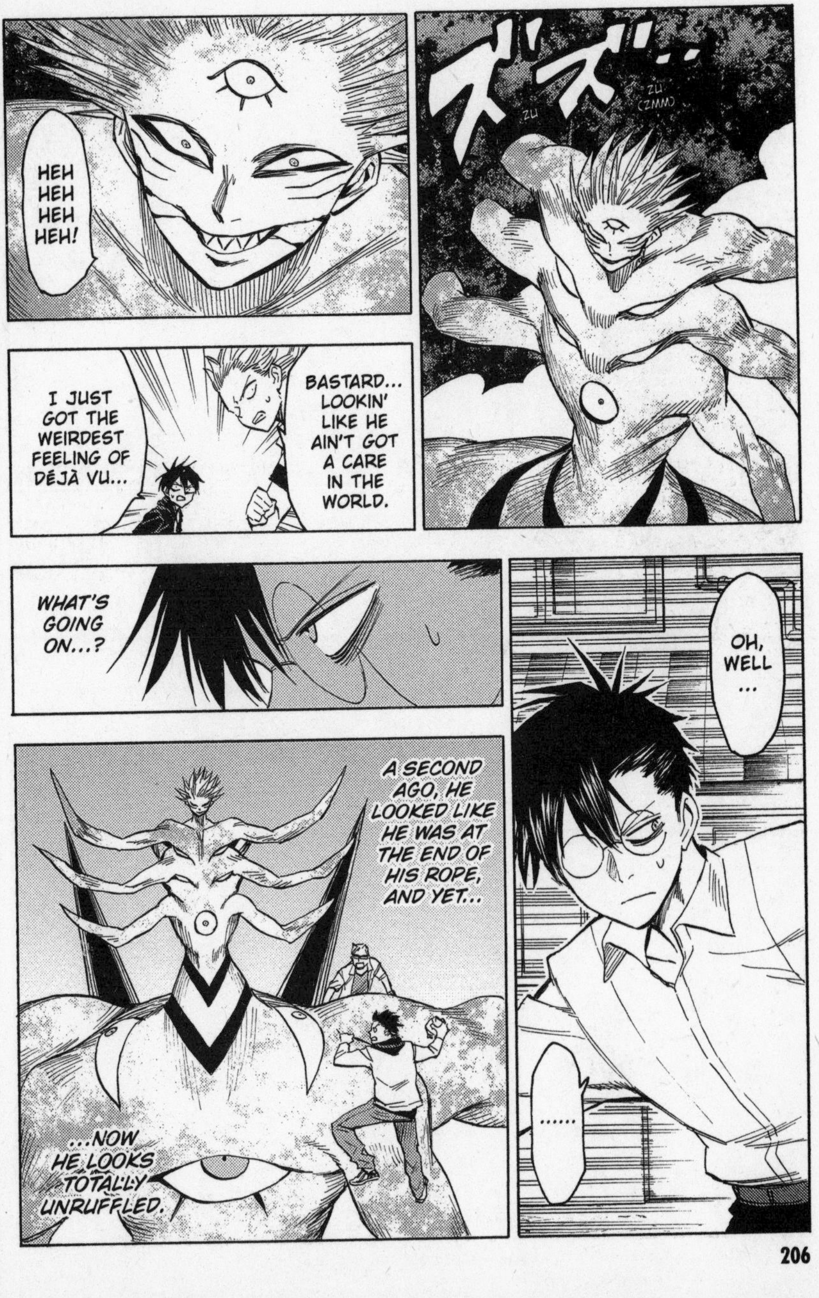

ズズ‥
ZU
ZU (ZMMM)
HEH HEH HEH HEH!
BASTARD... LOOKIN' LIKE HE AIN'T GOT A CARE IN THE WORLD.
I JUST GOT THE WEIRDEST FEELING OF DÉJÀ VU...
OH, WELL ...
......
WHAT'S GOING ON...?
A SECOND AGO, HE LOOKED LIKE HE WAS AT THE END OF HIS ROPE, AND YET...
...NOW HE LOOKS TOTALLY UNRUFFLED.

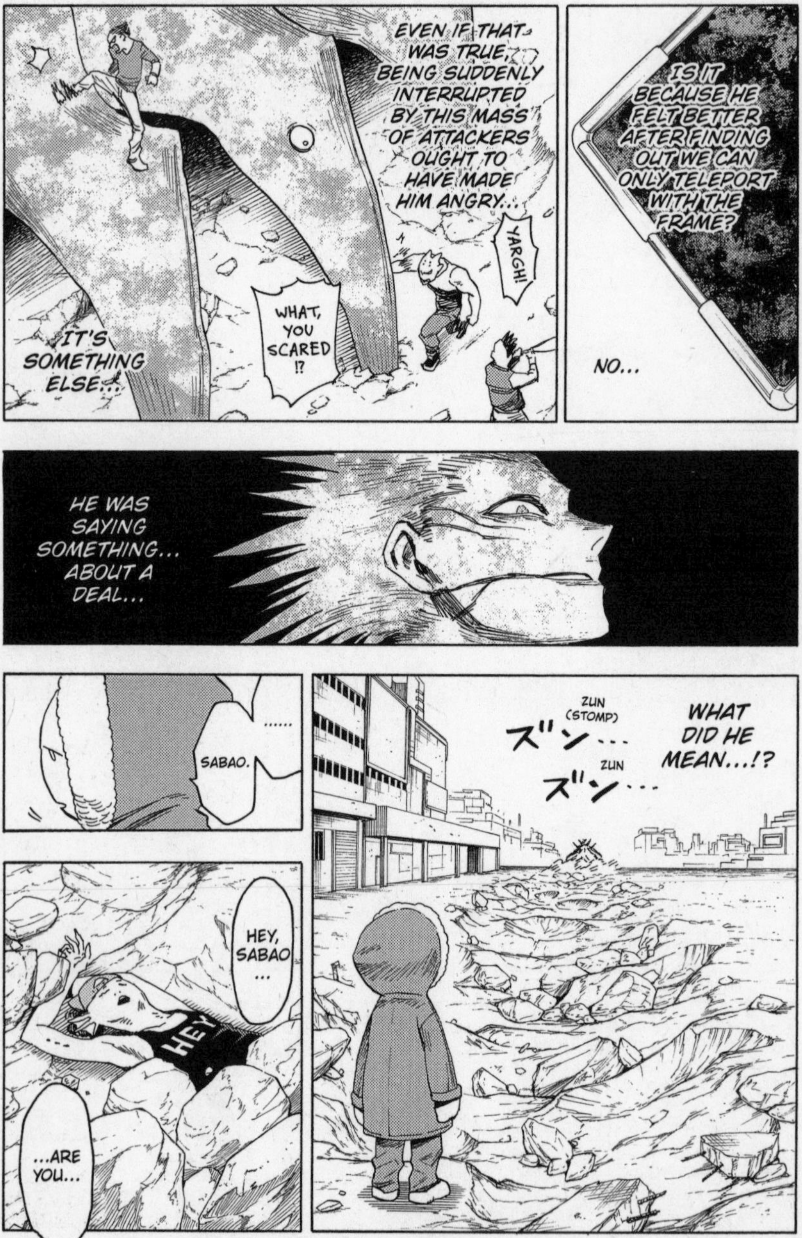
IS IT BECAUSE HE FELT BETTER AFTER FINDING OUT WE CAN ONLY TELEPORT WITH THE FRAME?
NO...
EVEN IF THAT WAS TRUE, BEING SUDDENLY INTERRUPTED BY THIS MASS OF ATTACKERS OUGHT TO HAVE MADE HIM ANGRY...
YARGH!
WHAT, YOU SCARED!?
IT'S SOMETHING ELSE...
HE WAS SAYING SOMETHING... ABOUT A DEAL...
WHAT DID HE MEAN...!?
ZUN (STOMP)
ズン...
ZUN
ズン...
......
SABAO.
HEY, SABAO...
...
...ARE YOU...

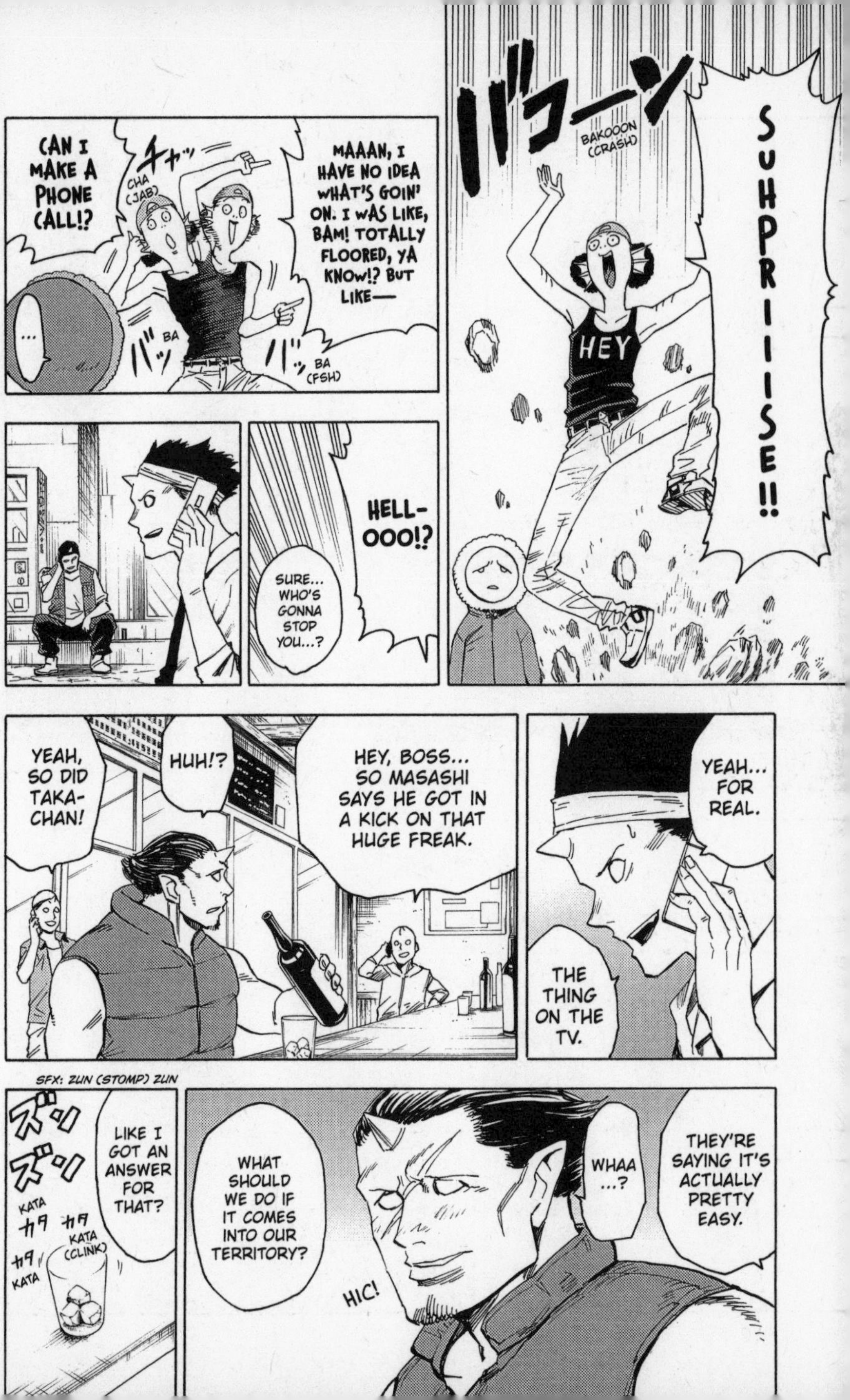
バコーン
BAKOOON (CRASH)
SUHPRIISE!!
MAAAN, I HAVE NO IDEA WHAT'S GOIN' ON. I WAS LIKE, BAM! TOTALLY FLOORED, YA KNOW!? BUT LIKE—
チャッ
CHA (JAB)
CAN I MAKE A PHONE CALL!?
...
バッ
BA
バッ
BA (FSH)
HELL-OOO!?
SURE... WHO'S GONNA STOP YOU...?
YEAH... FOR REAL.
THE THING ON THE TV.
HEY, BOSS... SO MASASHI SAYS HE GOT IN A KICK ON THAT HUGE FREAK.
HUH!?
YEAH, SO DID TAKA-CHAN!
SFX: ZUN (STOMP) ZUN
THEY'RE SAYING IT'S ACTUALLY PRETTY EASY.
WHAA ...?
WHAT SHOULD WE DO IF IT COMES INTO OUR TERRITORY?
HIC!
LIKE I GOT AN ANSWER FOR THAT?
ズン ズン
KATA カタ カタ KATA (CLINK)
カタ KATA

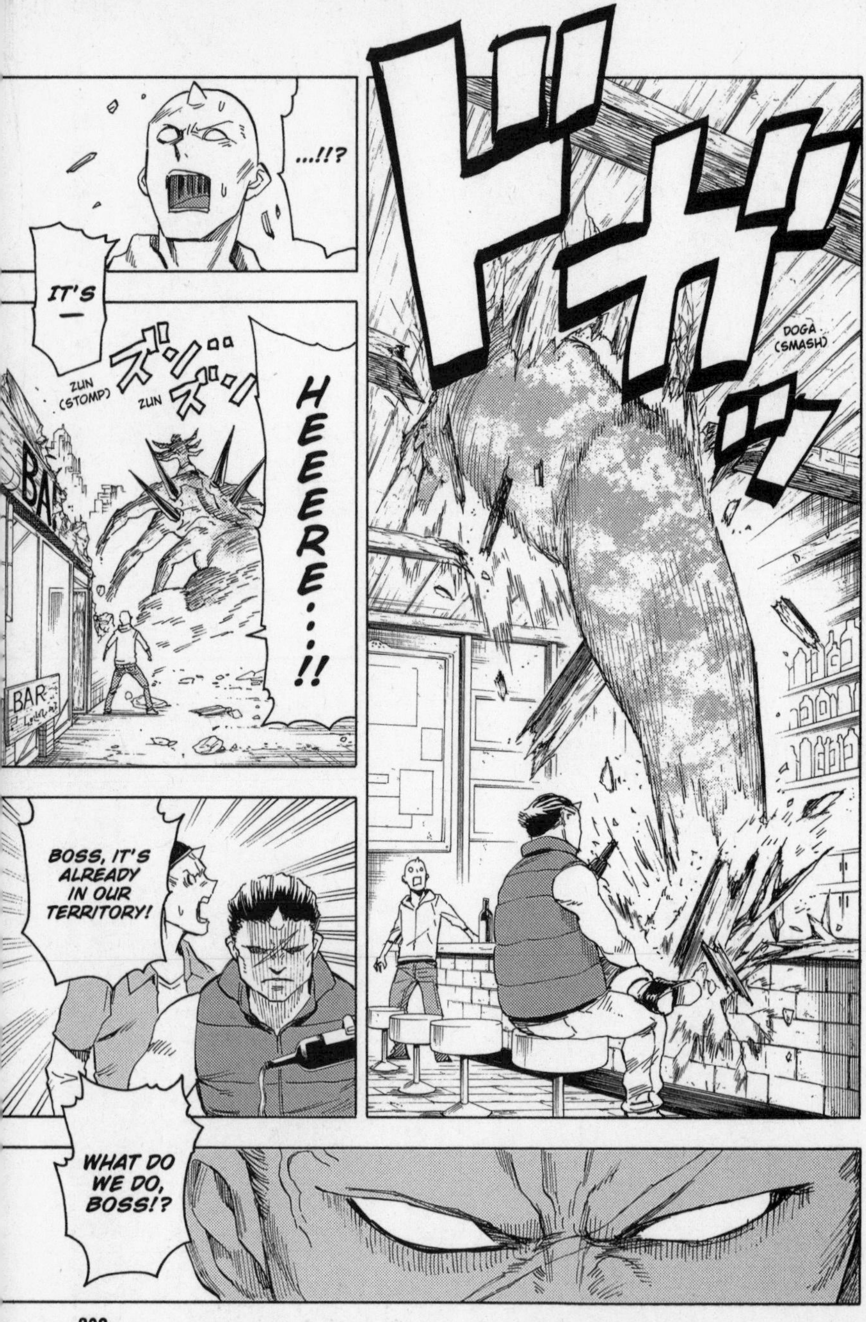
DOGA (SMASH)
...!!?
IT'S —
ZUN (STOMP)
ZUN
HEEEERE...!!
BAR
BAR
BOSS, IT'S ALREADY IN OUR TERRITORY!
WHAT DO WE DO, BOSS!?

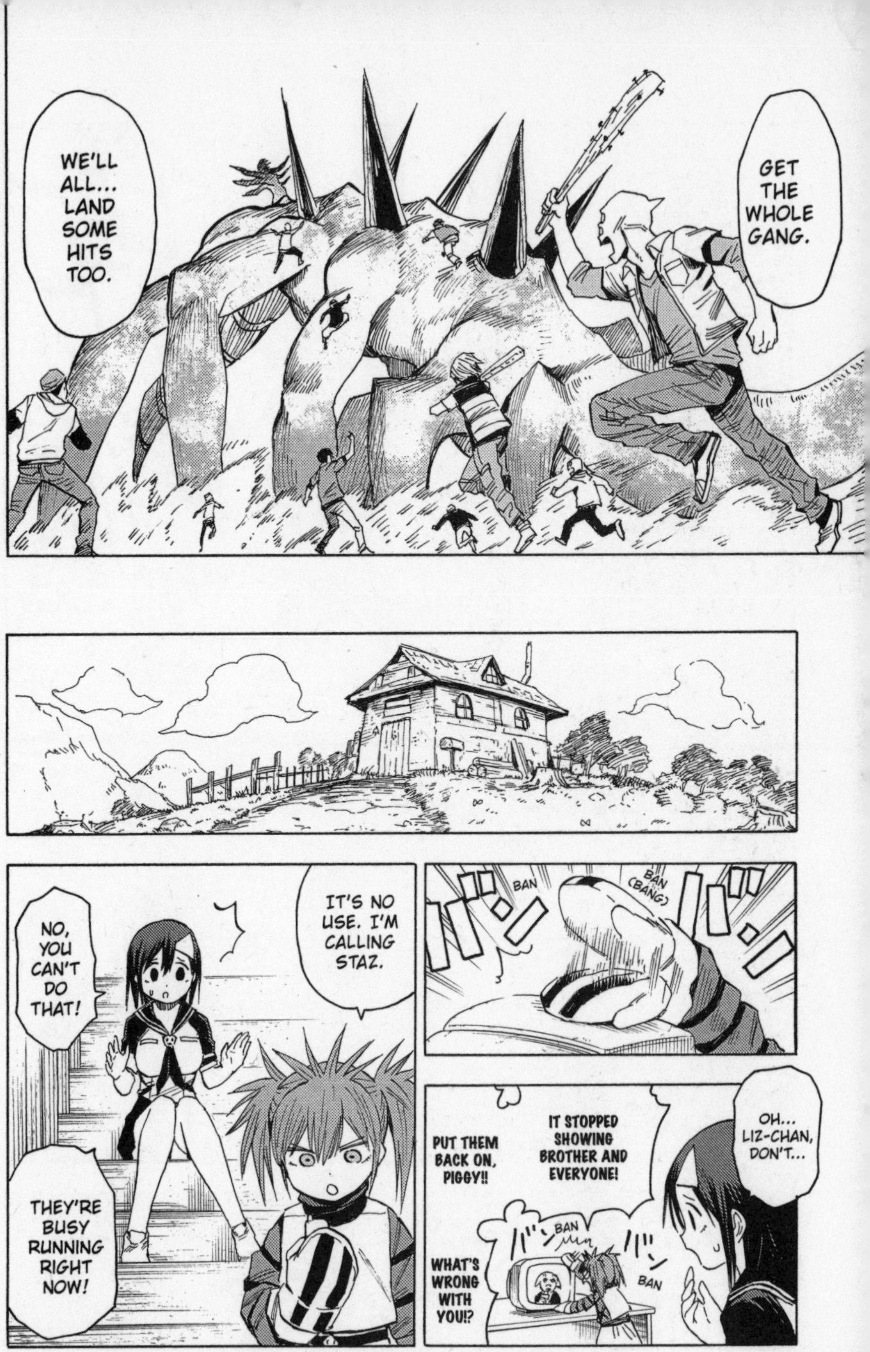
GET THE WHOLE GANG.
WE'LL ALL... LAND SOME HITS TOO.
BAN (BANG)
BAN
OH... LIZ-CHAN, DON'T...
IT STOPPED SHOWING BROTHER AND EVERYONE!
PUT THEM BACK ON, PIGGY!!
BAN
BAN
WHAT'S WRONG WITH YOU!?
IT'S NO USE. I'M CALLING STAZ.
NO, YOU CAN'T DO THAT!
THEY'RE BUSY RUNNING RIGHT NOW!

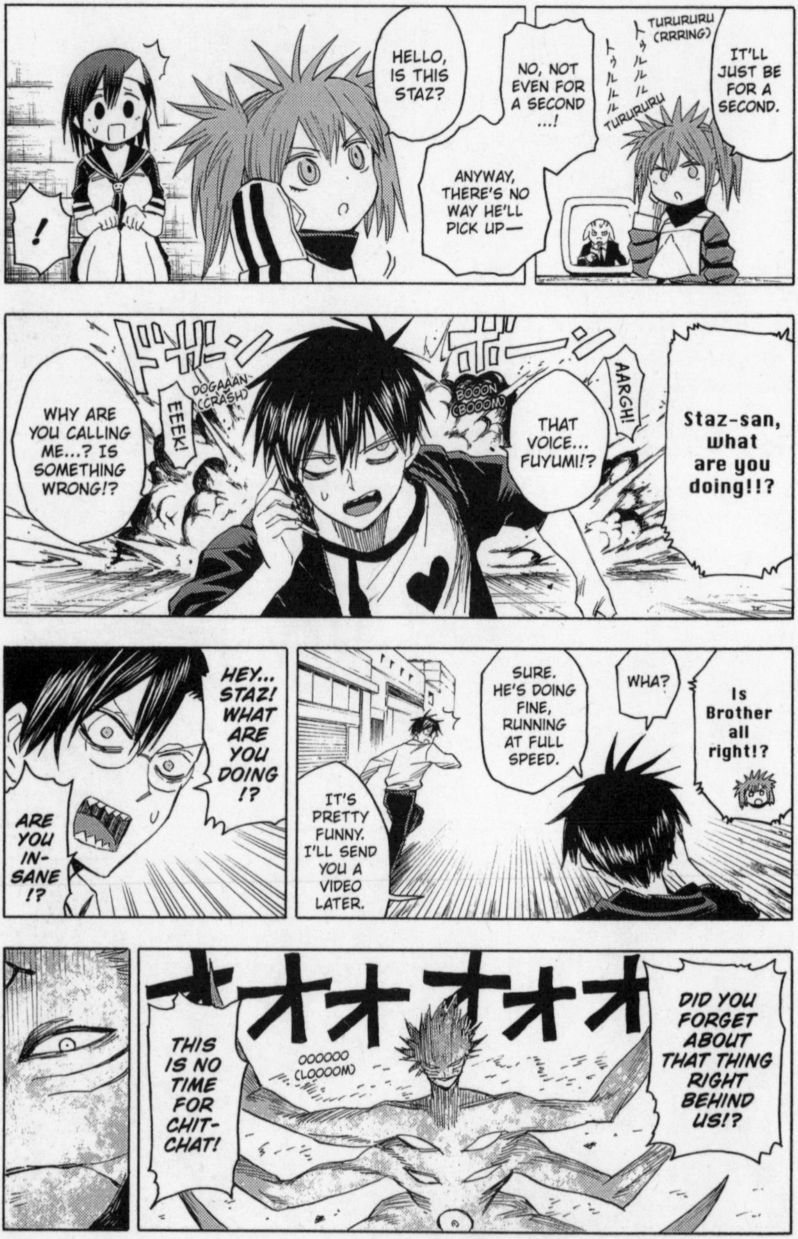
IT'LL JUST BE FOR A SECOND.
TURURURU (RRRING)
TURURURU
NO, NOT EVEN FOR A SECOND ...!
ANYWAY, THERE'S NO WAY HE'LL PICK UP—
HELLO, IS THIS STAZ?
!
Staz-san, what are you doing!!?
AARGH!
THAT VOICE... FUYUMI!?
BOOON (BOOOM)
DOGAAAN (CRASH)
EEEK!
WHY ARE YOU CALLING ME...? IS SOMETHING WRONG!?
Is Brother all right!?
WHA?
SURE. HE'S DOING FINE, RUNNING AT FULL SPEED.
IT'S PRETTY FUNNY. I'LL SEND YOU A VIDEO LATER.
HEY... STAZ! WHAT ARE YOU DOING!?
ARE YOU IN-SANE!?
DID YOU FORGET ABOUT THAT THING RIGHT BEHIND US!?
OOOOOO (LOOOOM)
THIS IS NO TIME FOR CHIT-CHAT!

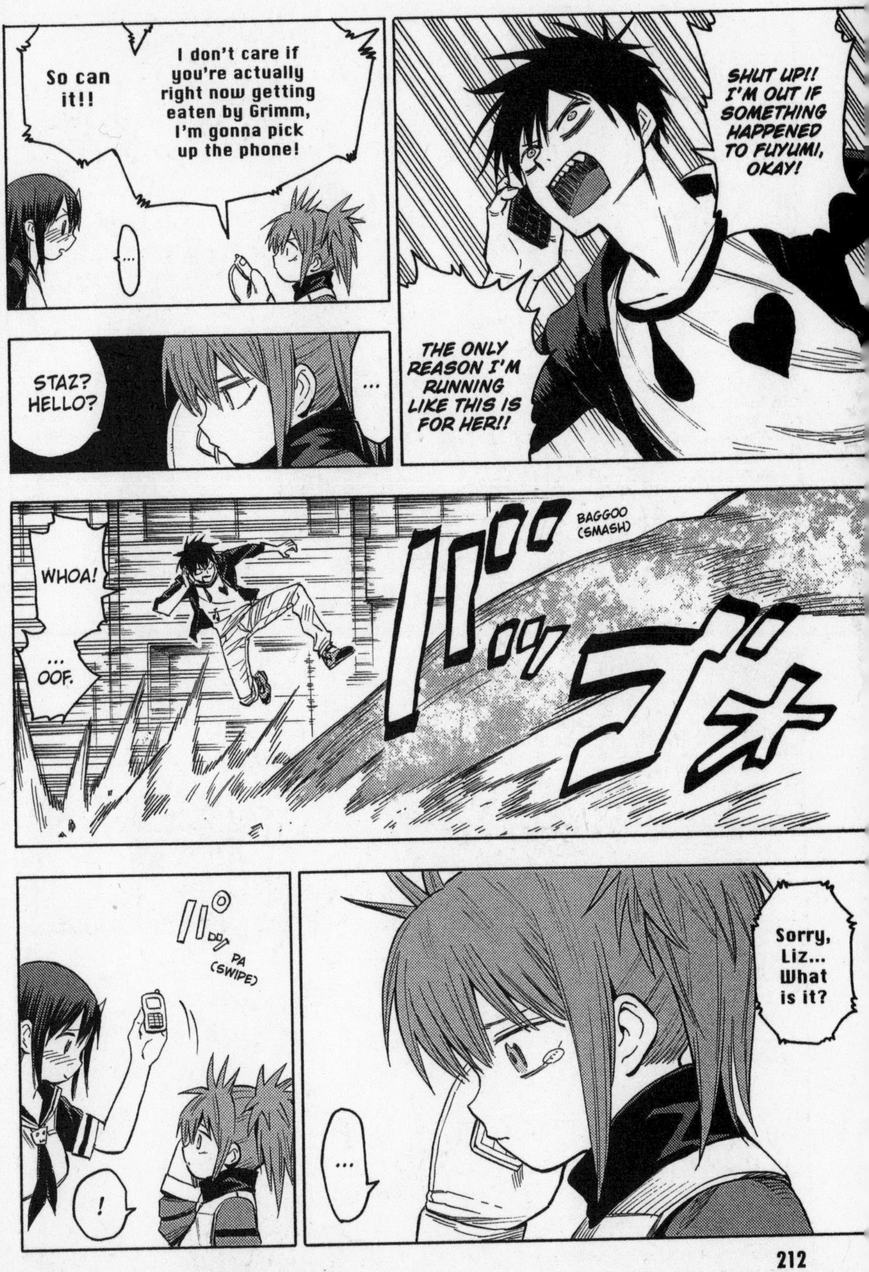
SHUT UP!! I'M OUT IF SOMETHING HAPPENED TO FUYUMI, OKAY!
THE ONLY REASON I'M RUNNING LIKE THIS IS FOR HER!!
I don't care if you're actually right now getting eaten by Grimm, I'm gonna pick up the phone!
So can it!!
...
...
STAZ? HELLO?
BAGGOO (SMASH)
WHOA!
... OOF.
Sorry, Liz... What is it?
...
PA (SWIPE)
!
...

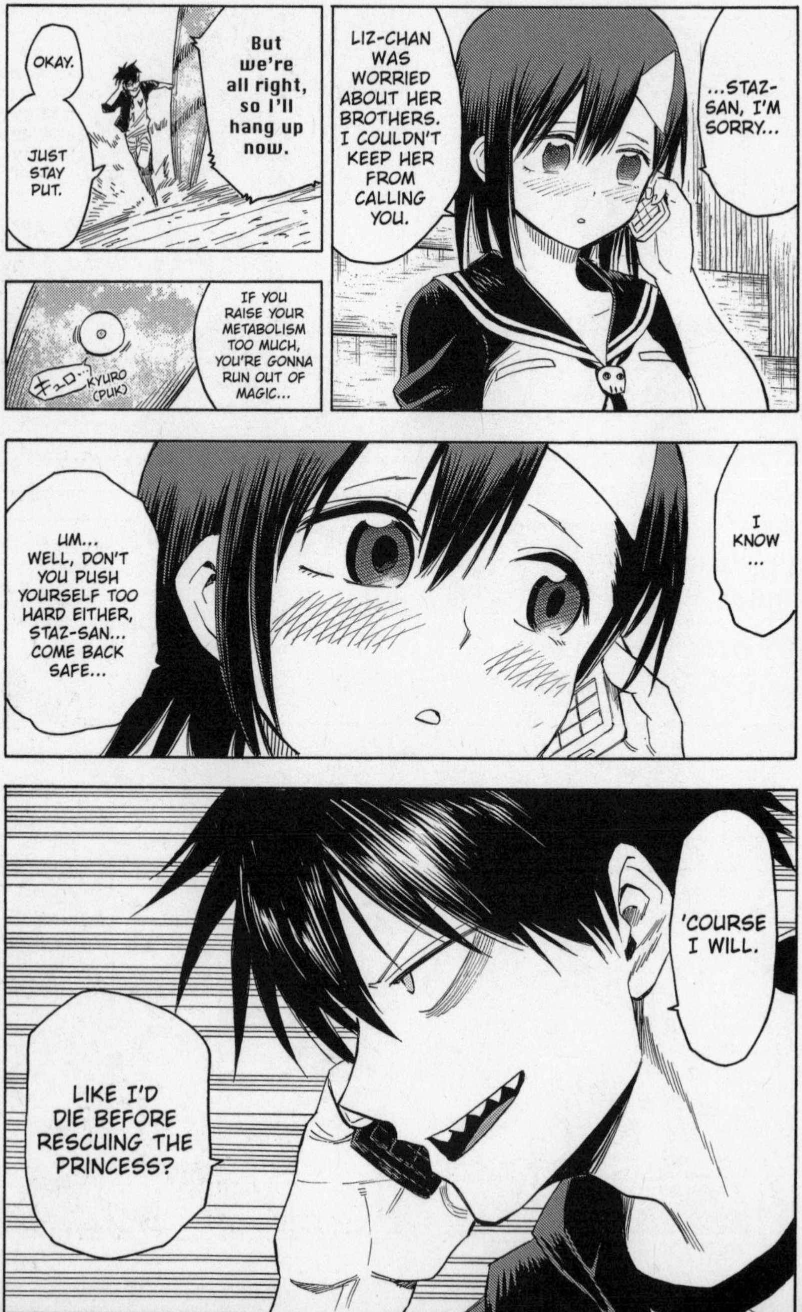
...STAZ-SAN, I'M SORRY...
LIZ-CHAN WAS WORRIED ABOUT HER BROTHERS. I COULDN'T KEEP HER FROM CALLING YOU.
But we're all right, so I'll hang up now.
OKAY.
JUST STAY PUT.
IF YOU RAISE YOUR METABOLISM TOO MUCH, YOU'RE GONNA RUN OUT OF MAGIC...
キュロ… KYURO (PUK)
I KNOW...
UM... WELL, DON'T YOU PUSH YOURSELF TOO HARD EITHER, STAZ-SAN... COME BACK SAFE...
'COURSE I WILL.
LIKE I'D DIE BEFORE RESCUING THE PRINCESS?

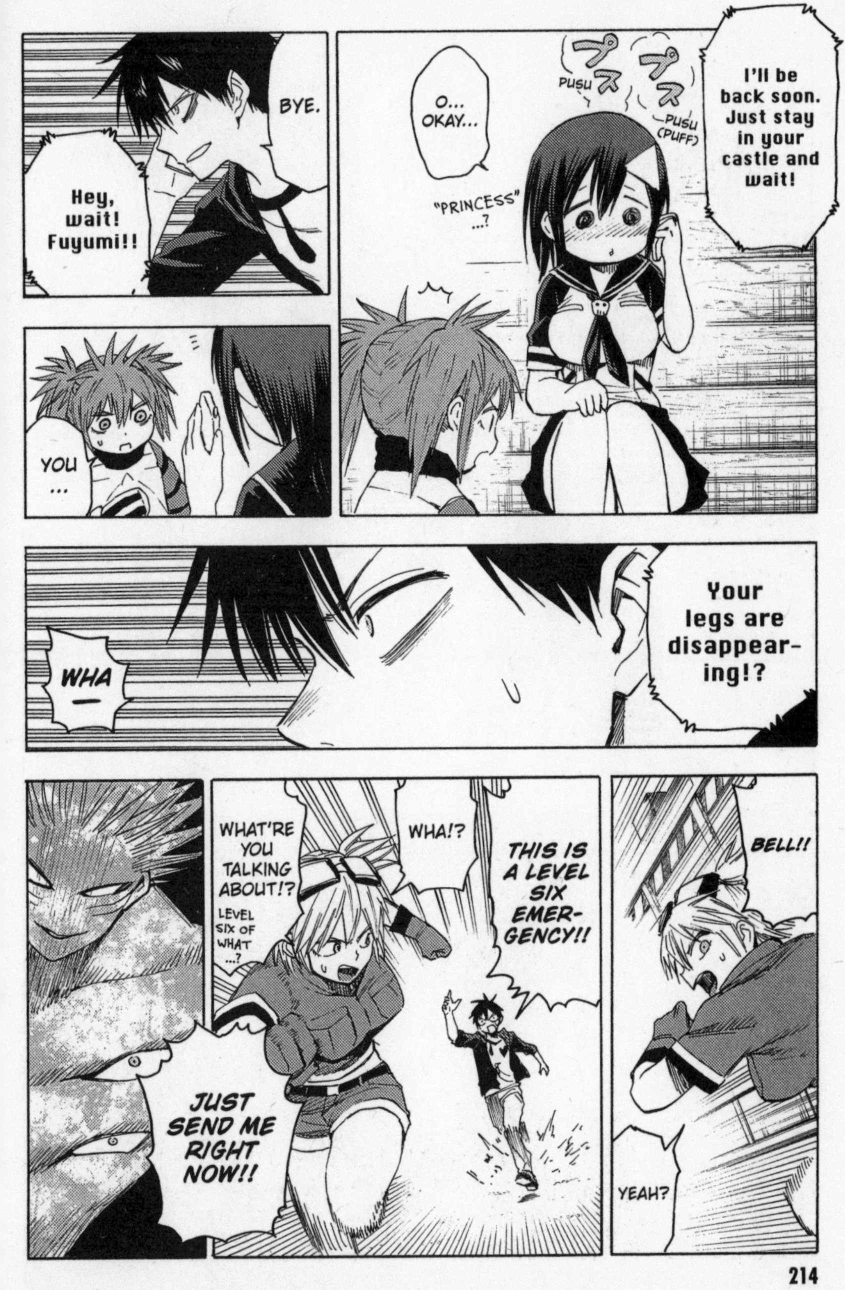
I'll be back soon. Just stay in your castle and wait!
プス PUSU
プス PUSU (PUFF)
O... OKAY...
"PRINCESS" ...?
BYE.
Hey, wait! Fuyumi!!
YOU ...
Your legs are disappear-ing!?
WHA —
BELL!!
YEAH?
WHA!?
THIS IS A LEVEL SIX EMERGENCY!!
WHAT'RE YOU TALKING ABOUT!?
LEVEL SIX OF WHAT ...?
JUST SEND ME RIGHT NOW!!

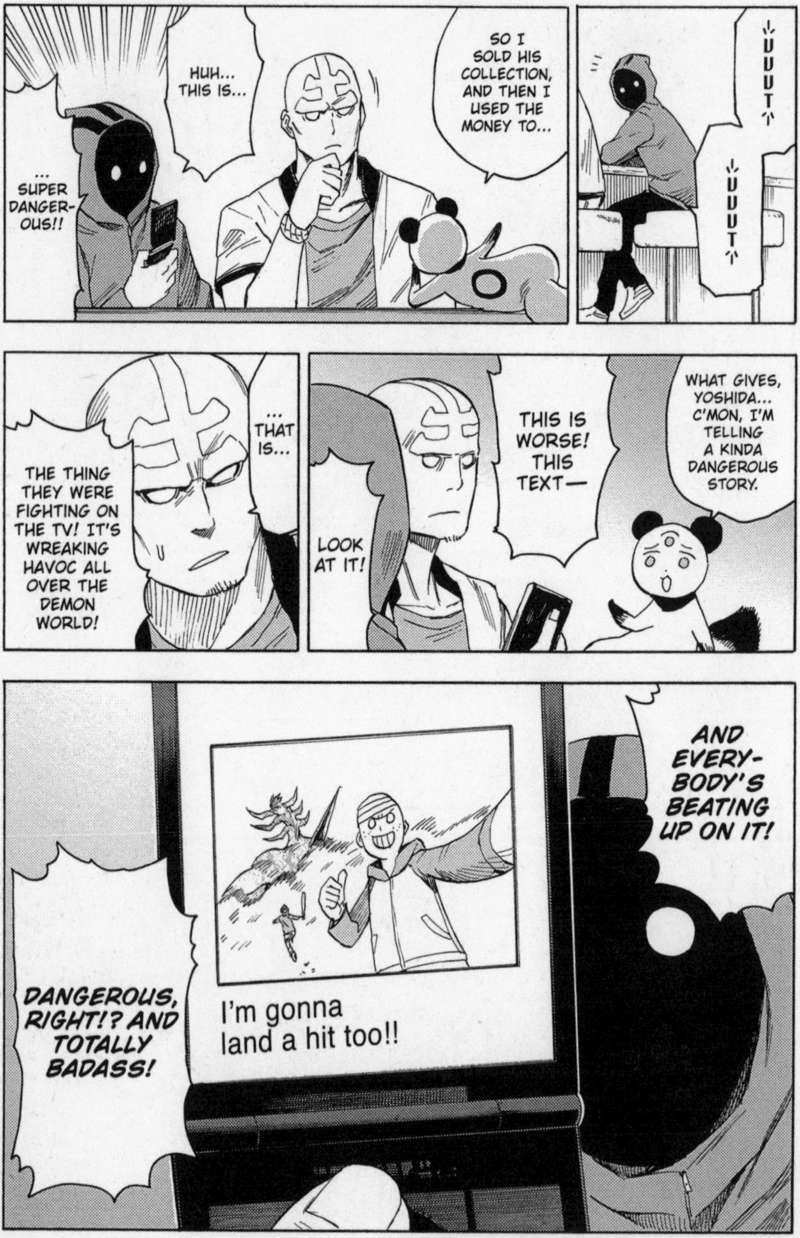
VVVT
VVVT
SO I SOLD HIS COLLECTION, AND THEN I USED THE MONEY TO...
HUH... THIS IS...
... SUPER DANGER-OUS!!
WHAT GIVES, YOSHIDA... C'MON, I'M TELLING A KINDA DANGEROUS STORY.
THIS IS WORSE! THIS TEXT—
LOOK AT IT!
... THAT IS...
THE THING THEY WERE FIGHTING ON THE TV! IT'S WREAKING HAVOC ALL OVER THE DEMON WORLD!
AND EVERY-BODY'S BEATING UP ON IT!
I'm gonna land a hit too!!
DANGEROUS, RIGHT!? AND TOTALLY BADASS!

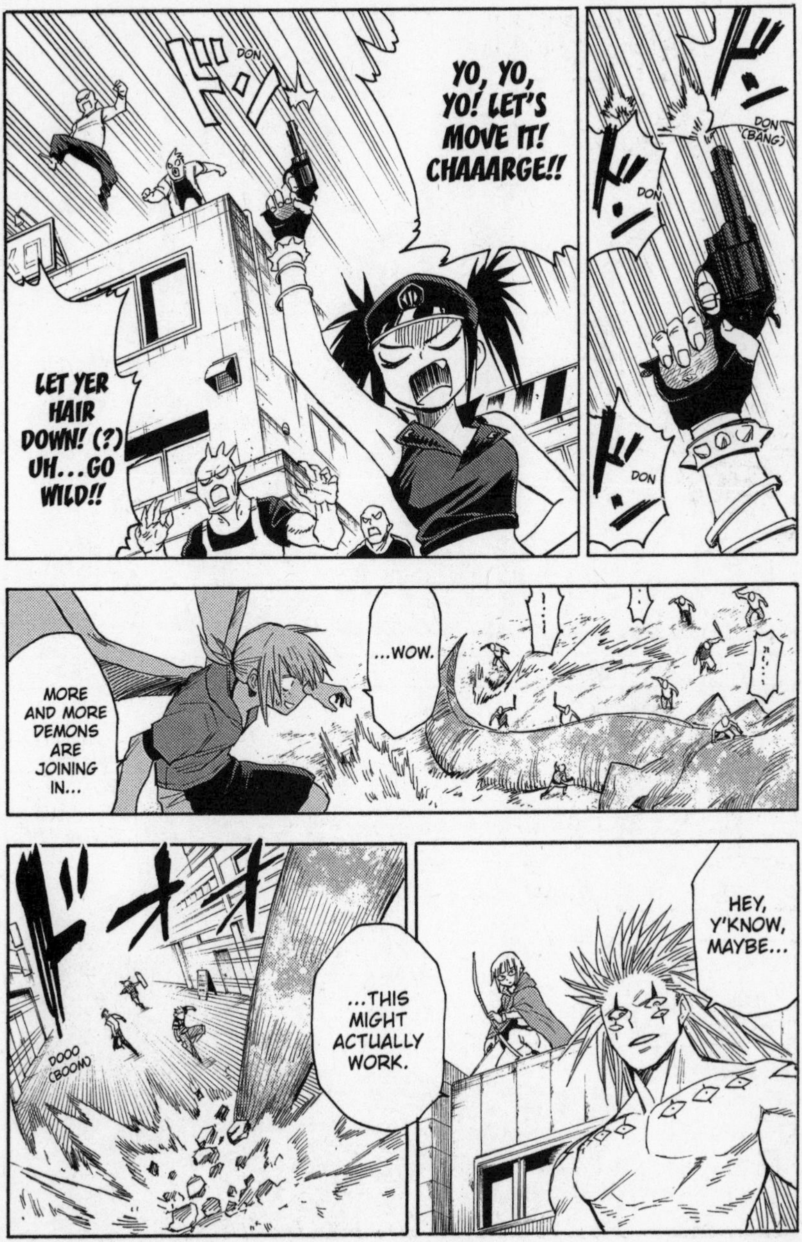
DON
(BANG)
DON
DON
YO, YO, YO! LET'S MOVE IT! CHAAARGE!!
DON
LET YER HAIR DOWN! (?) UH...GO WILD!!
...WOW.
MORE AND MORE DEMONS ARE JOINING IN...
HEY, Y'KNOW, MAYBE...
...THIS MIGHT ACTUALLY WORK.
DOOO (BOOM)

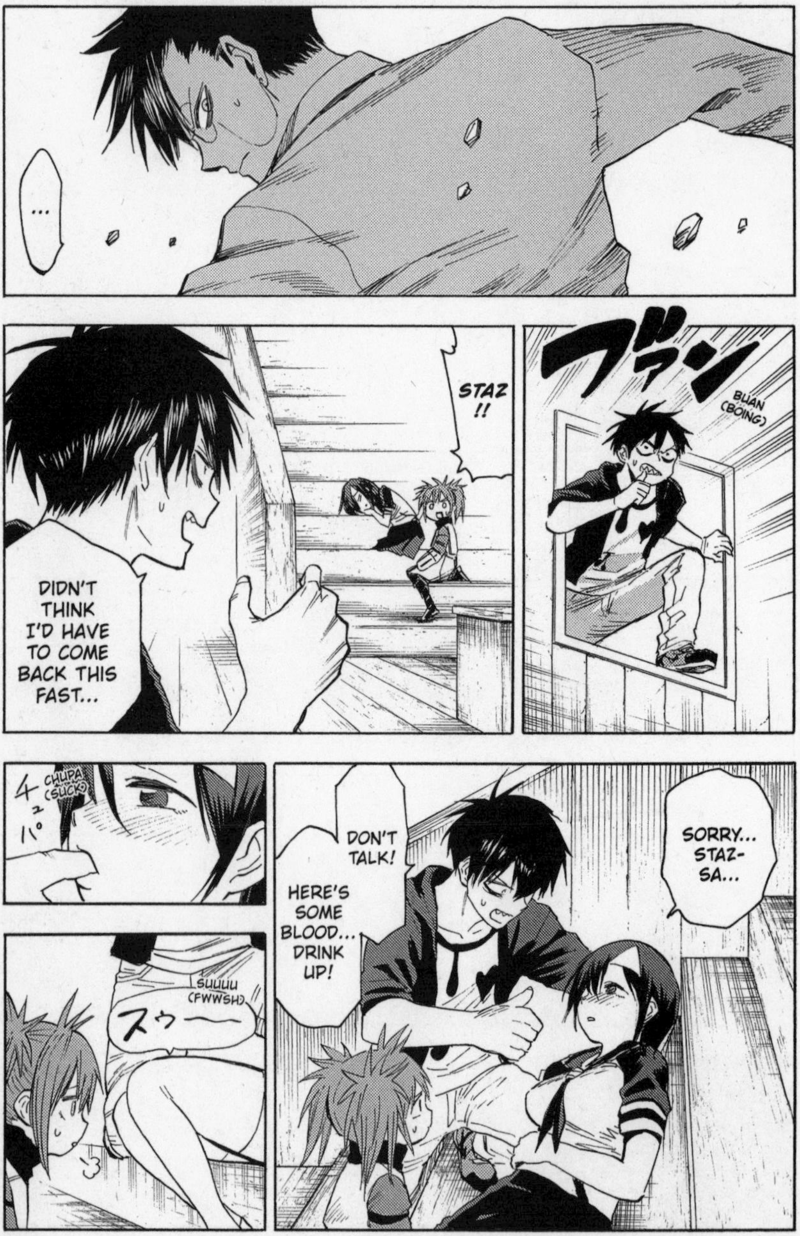
…
ブァン
BUAN (BOING)
STAZ !!
DIDN'T THINK I'D HAVE TO COME BACK THIS FAST…
SORRY… STAZ-SA…
DON'T TALK!
HERE'S SOME BLOOD… DRINK UP!
チュパ
CHUPA (SUCK)
スゥーー
SUUUU (FWWSH)

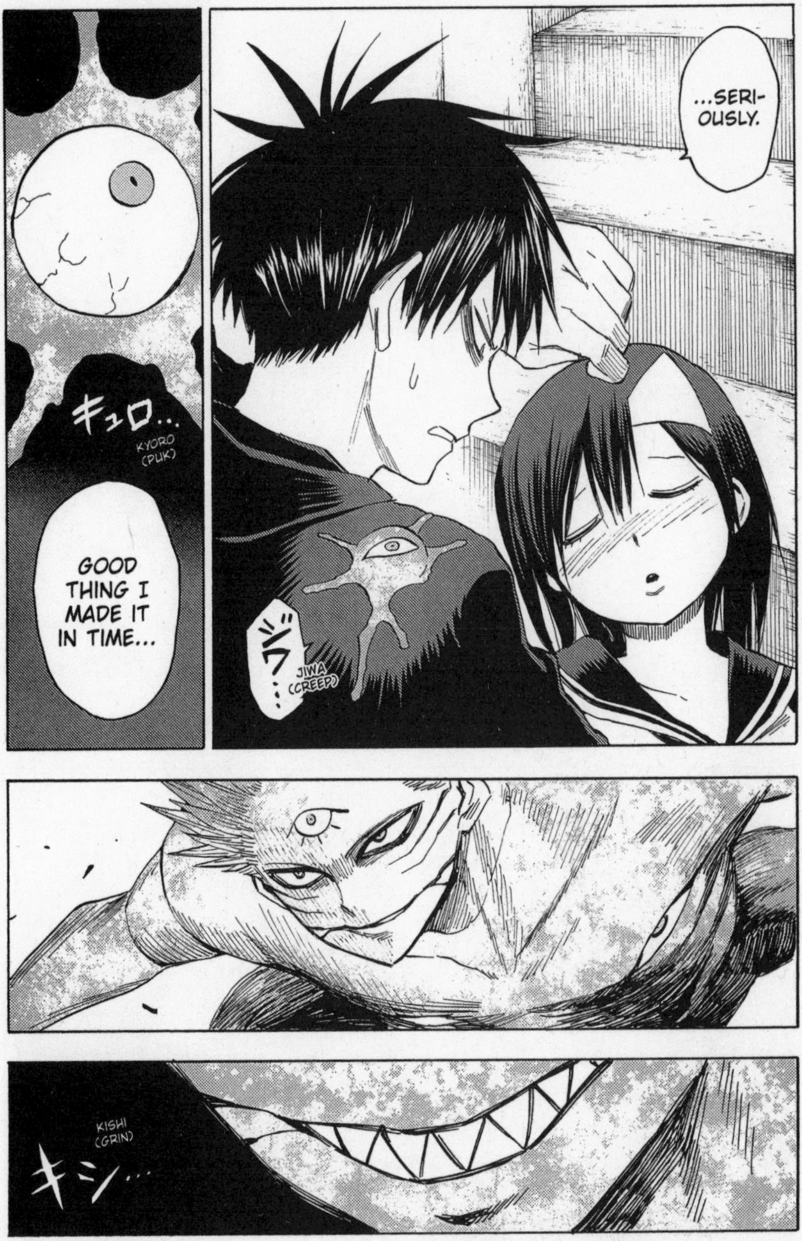
...SERI-OUSLY.
ジワ...
JIWA (CREEP)
キョロ...
KYORO (PUK)
GOOD THING I MADE IT IN TIME...
KISHI (GRIN)
キシ...

♠ To Be Continued ♠

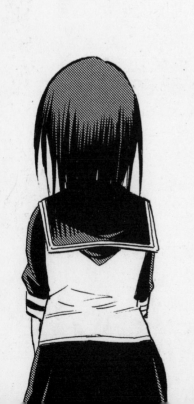

BLOOD LAD

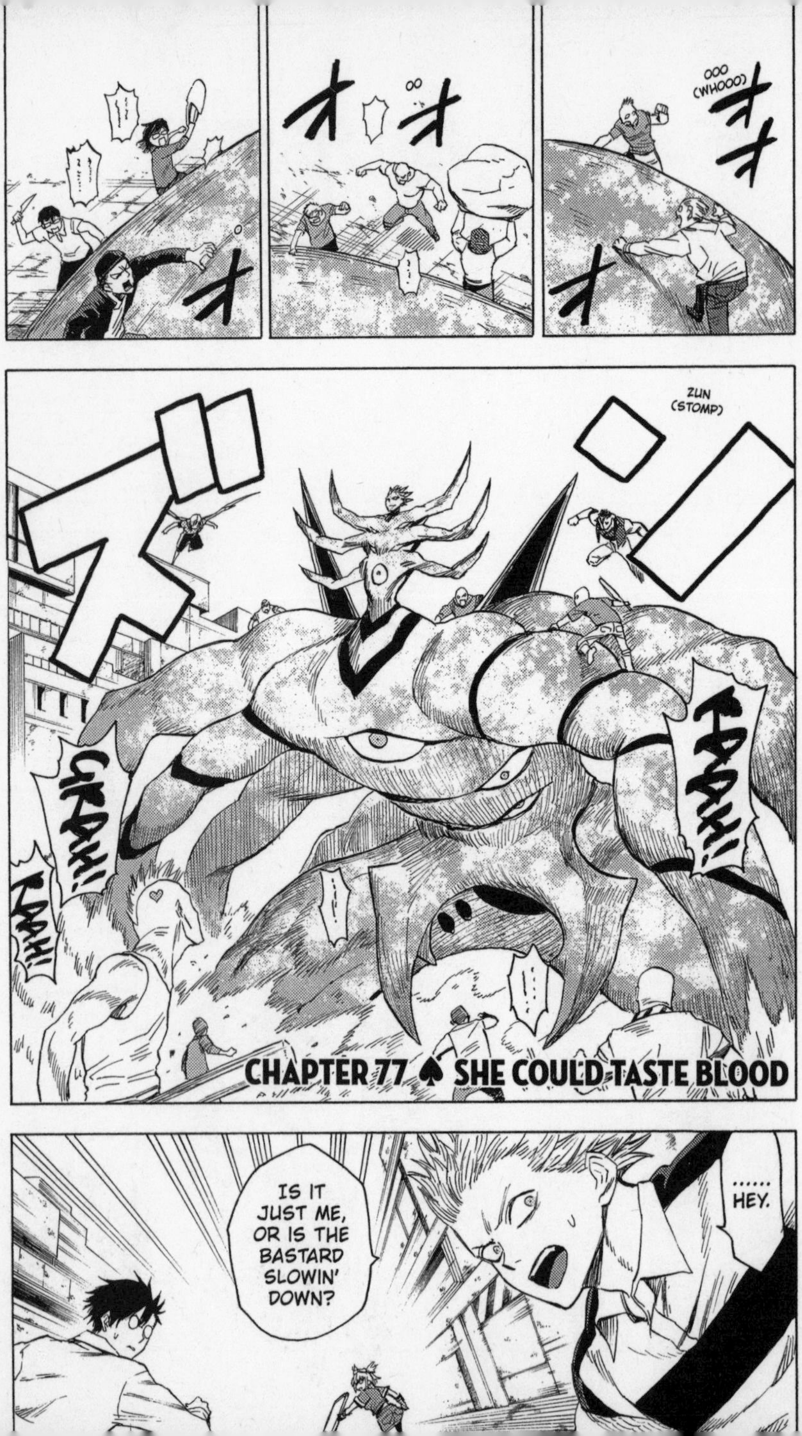
OOO
(WHOOO)
ZUN
(STOMP)
RAAH!
GRAAH!
RAAH!
CHAPTER 77 ♠ SHE COULD TASTE BLOOD
......HEY.
IS IT JUST ME, OR IS THE BASTARD SLOWIN' DOWN?

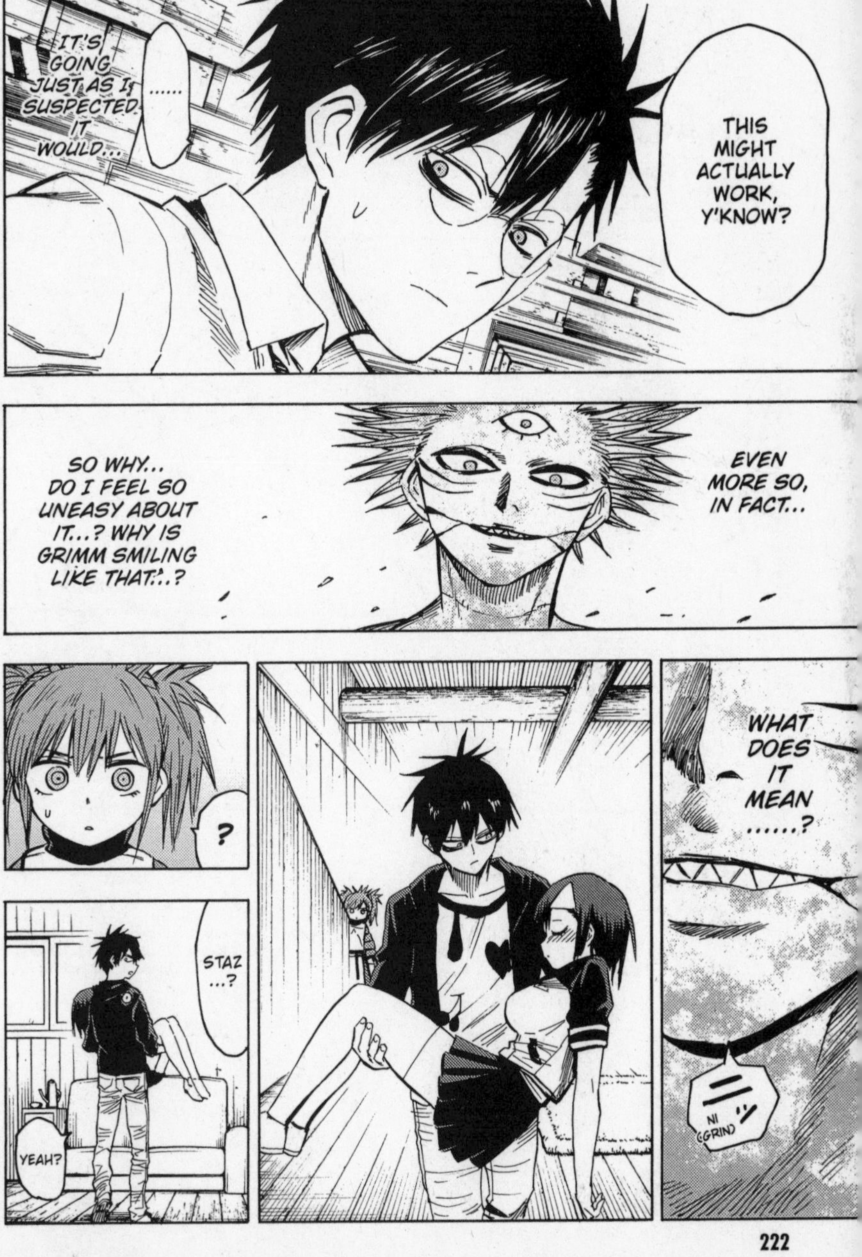
THIS MIGHT ACTUALLY WORK, Y'KNOW?
......
IT'S GOING JUST AS I SUSPECTED IT WOULD...
EVEN MORE SO, IN FACT...
SO WHY... DO I FEEL SO UNEASY ABOUT IT...? WHY IS GRIMM SMILING LIKE THAT...?
WHAT DOES IT MEAN ......?
NI (GRIN)
?
STAZ ...?
YEAH?

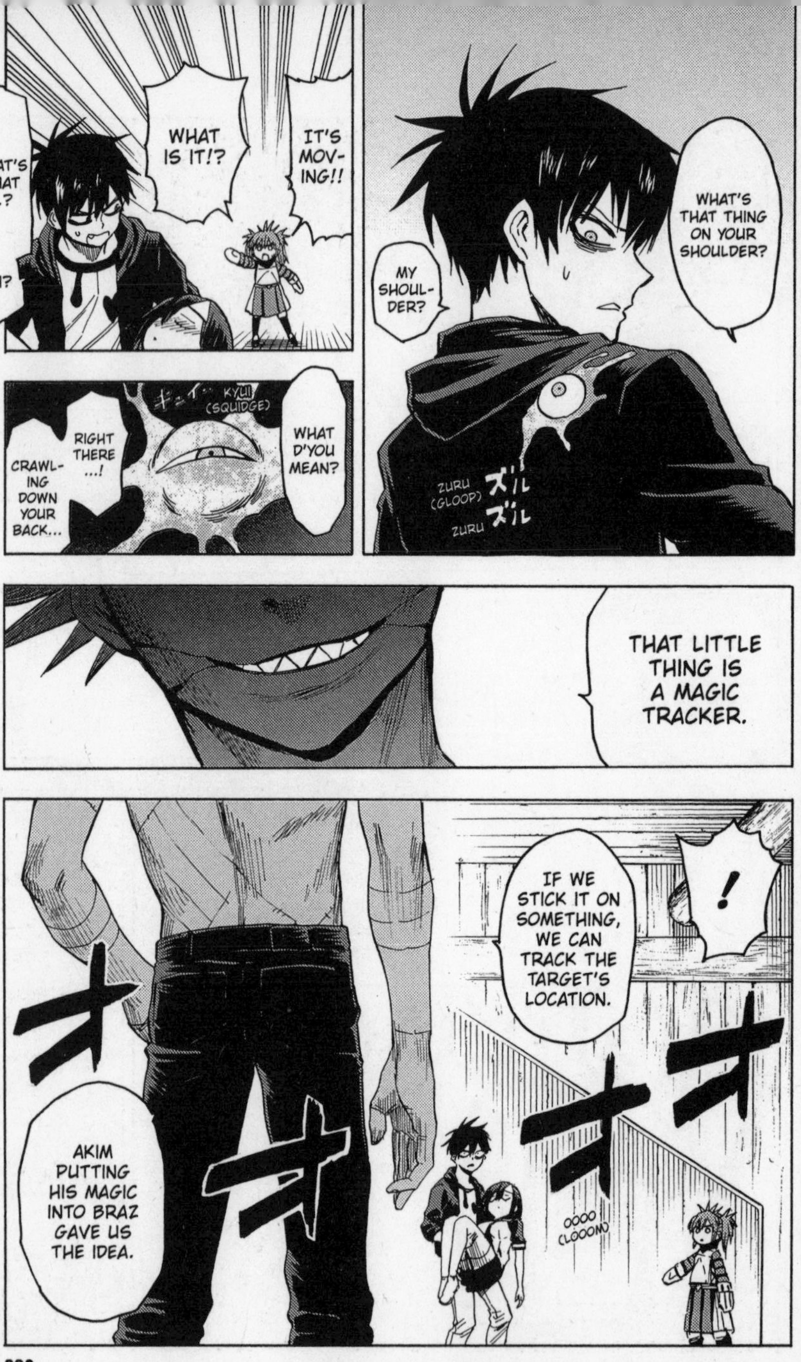
WHAT'S THAT THING ON YOUR SHOULDER?
MY SHOUL-DER?
ZURU ZURU (GLOOP)
IT'S MOV-ING!!
WHAT IS IT!?
WHAT'S WHAT ...?
HUH?
WHAT D'YOU MEAN?
KYUI (SQUIDGE)
RIGHT THERE ...!
CRAWL-ING DOWN YOUR BACK...
THAT LITTLE THING IS A MAGIC TRACKER.
!
IF WE STICK IT ON SOMETHING, WE CAN TRACK THE TARGET'S LOCATION.
OOOO (LOOOM)
AKIM PUTTING HIS MAGIC INTO BRAZ GAVE US THE IDEA.

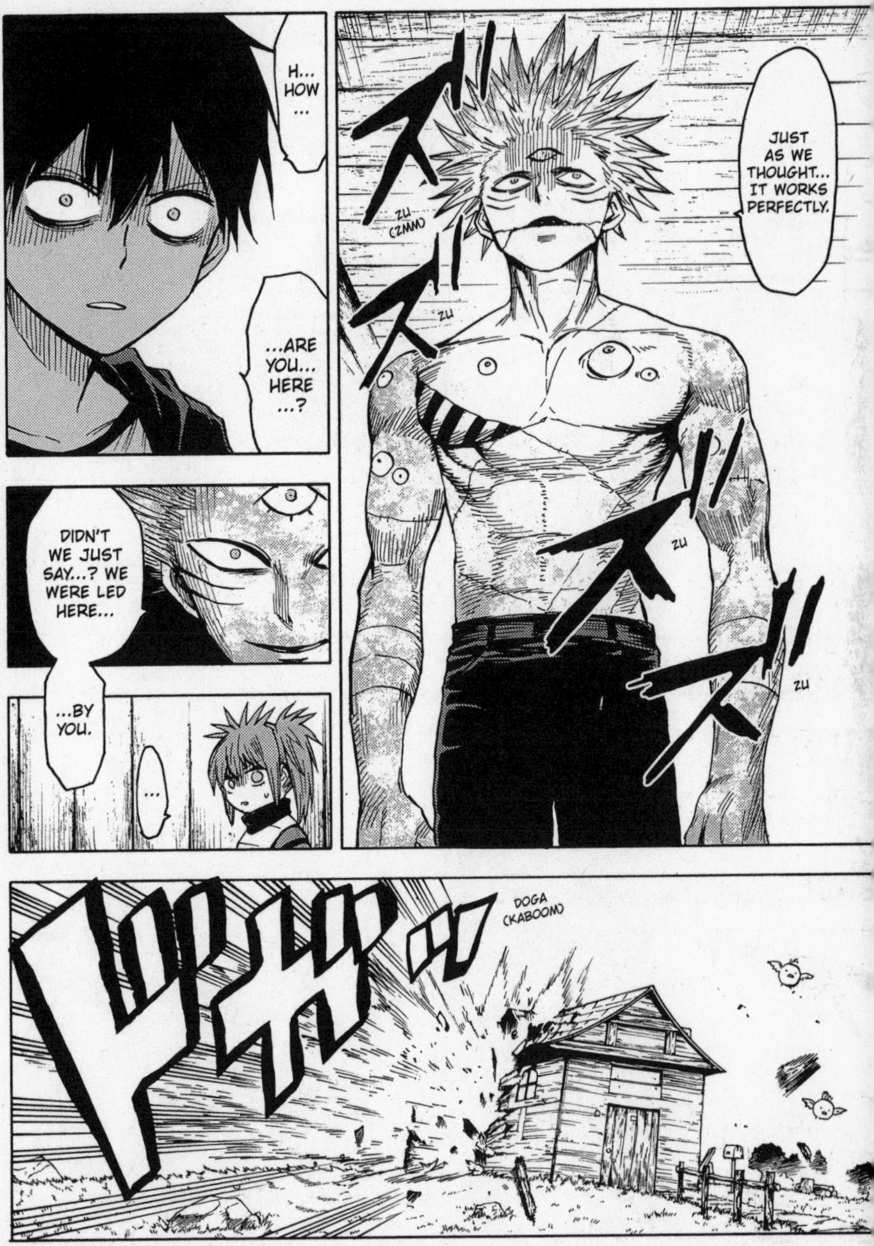
ZU (ZMM)
ZU
JUST AS WE THOUGHT... IT WORKS PERFECTLY.
ZU
ZU
H... HOW ...
...ARE YOU... HERE ...?
DIDN'T WE JUST SAY...? WE WERE LED HERE...
...BY YOU.
...
DOGA (KABOOM)

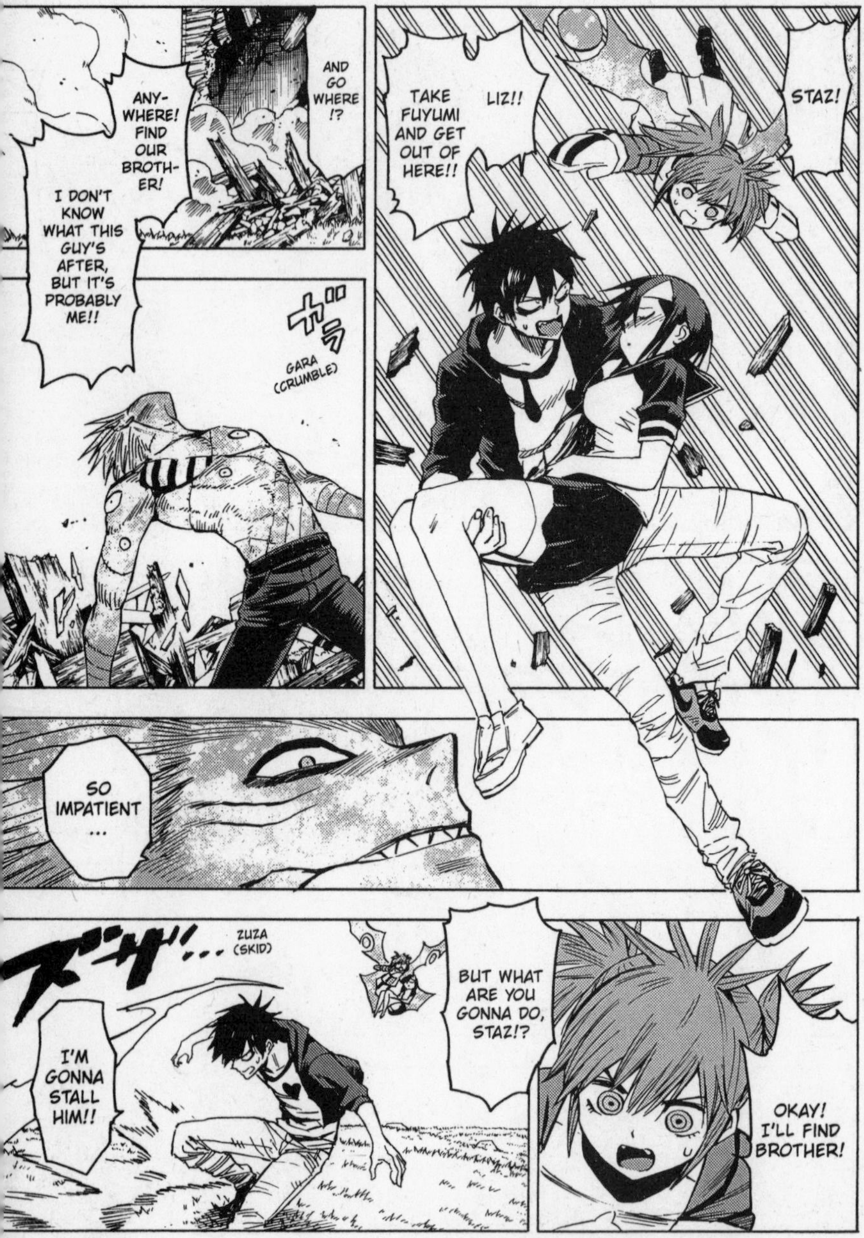
STAZ!
LIZ!!
TAKE FUYUMI AND GET OUT OF HERE!!
AND GO WHERE !?
ANY-WHERE! FIND OUR BROTH-ER!
I DON'T KNOW WHAT THIS GUY'S AFTER, BUT IT'S PROBABLY ME!!
GARA (CRUMBLE)
SO IMPATIENT ...
OKAY! I'LL FIND BROTHER!
BUT WHAT ARE YOU GONNA DO, STAZ!?
ZUZA (SKID)
I'M GONNA STALL HIM!!

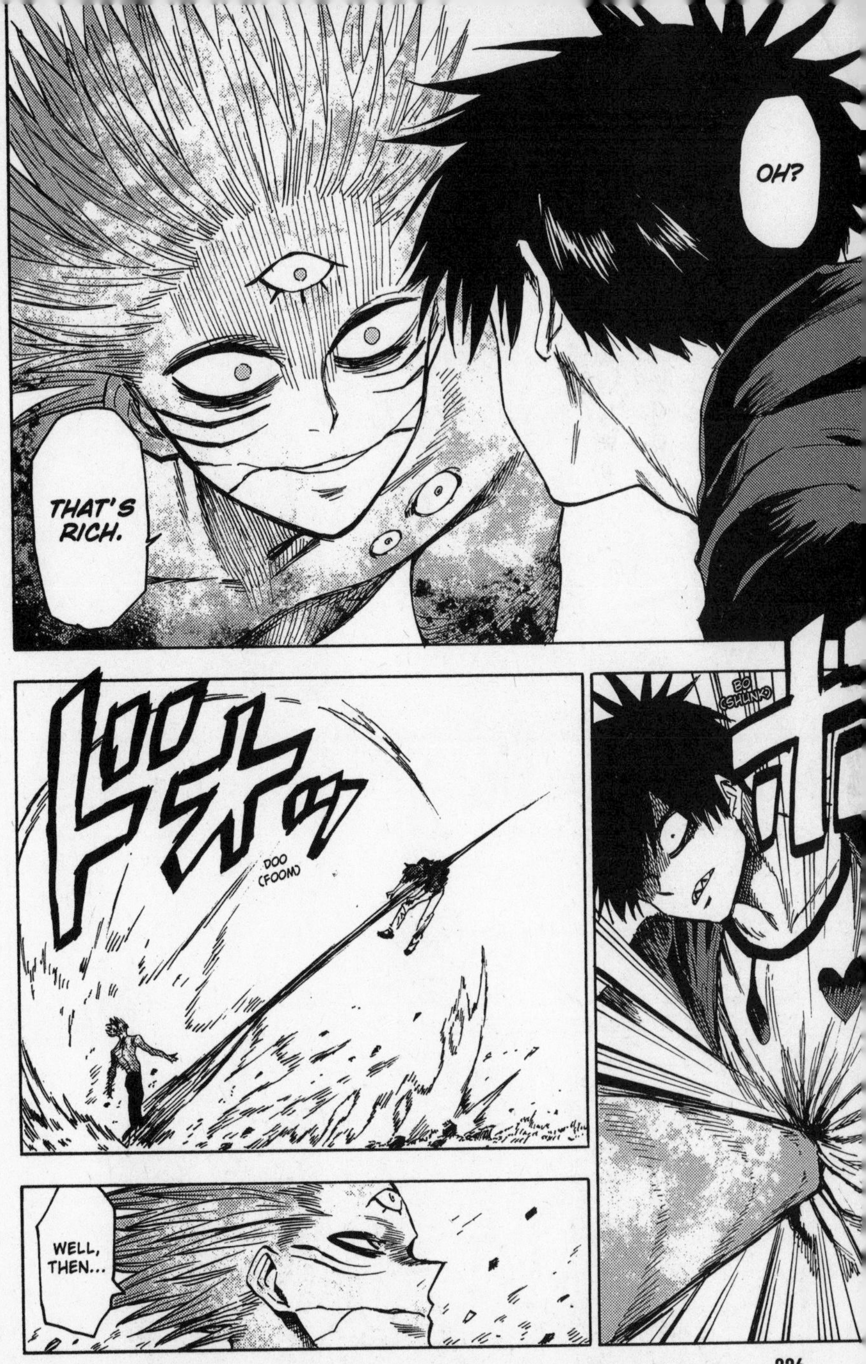
OH?
THAT'S RICH.
BO (SHUNK)
DOO (FOOM)
WELL, THEN...

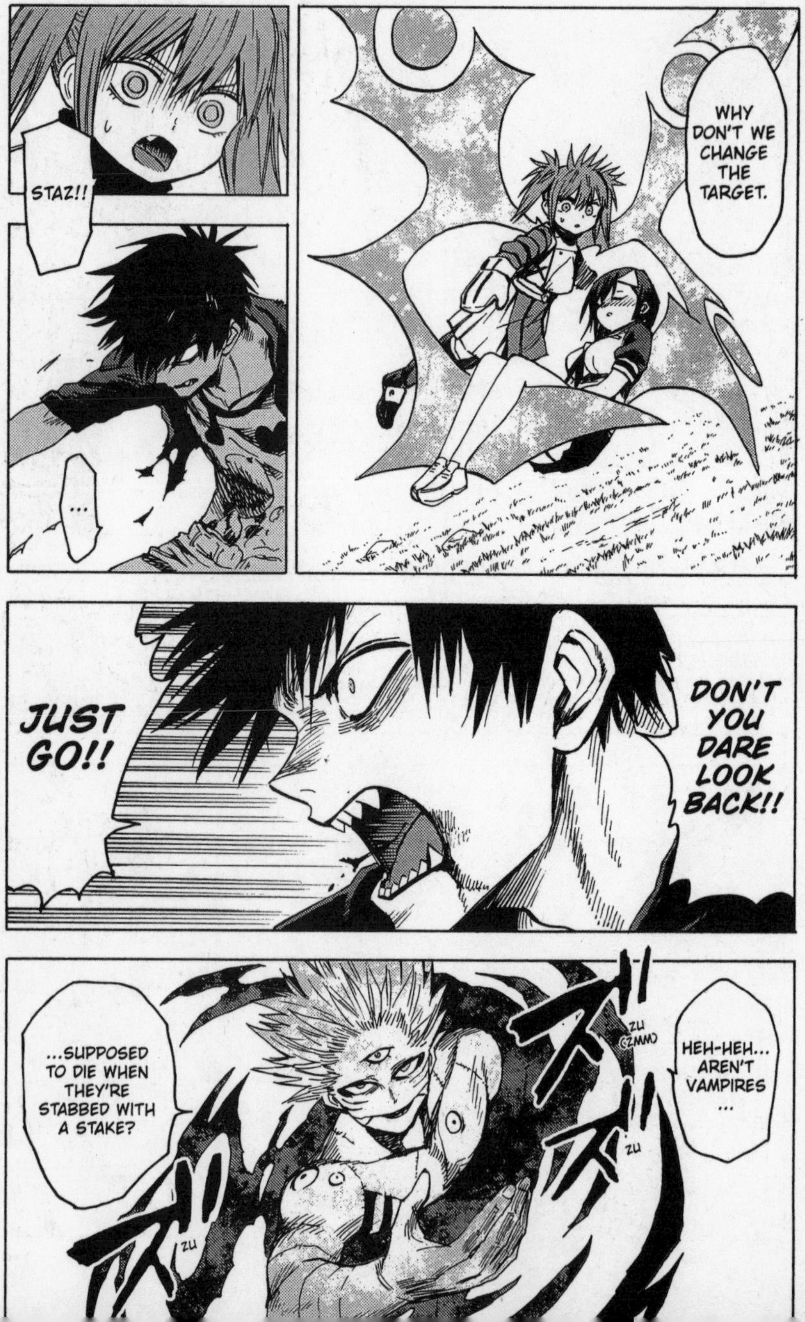
WHY DON'T WE CHANGE THE TARGET.
STAZ!!
...
DON'T YOU DARE LOOK BACK!!
JUST GO!!
HEH-HEH... AREN'T VAMPIRES ...
ZU (ZMM)
ZU
...SUPPOSED TO DIE WHEN THEY'RE STABBED WITH A STAKE?
ZU

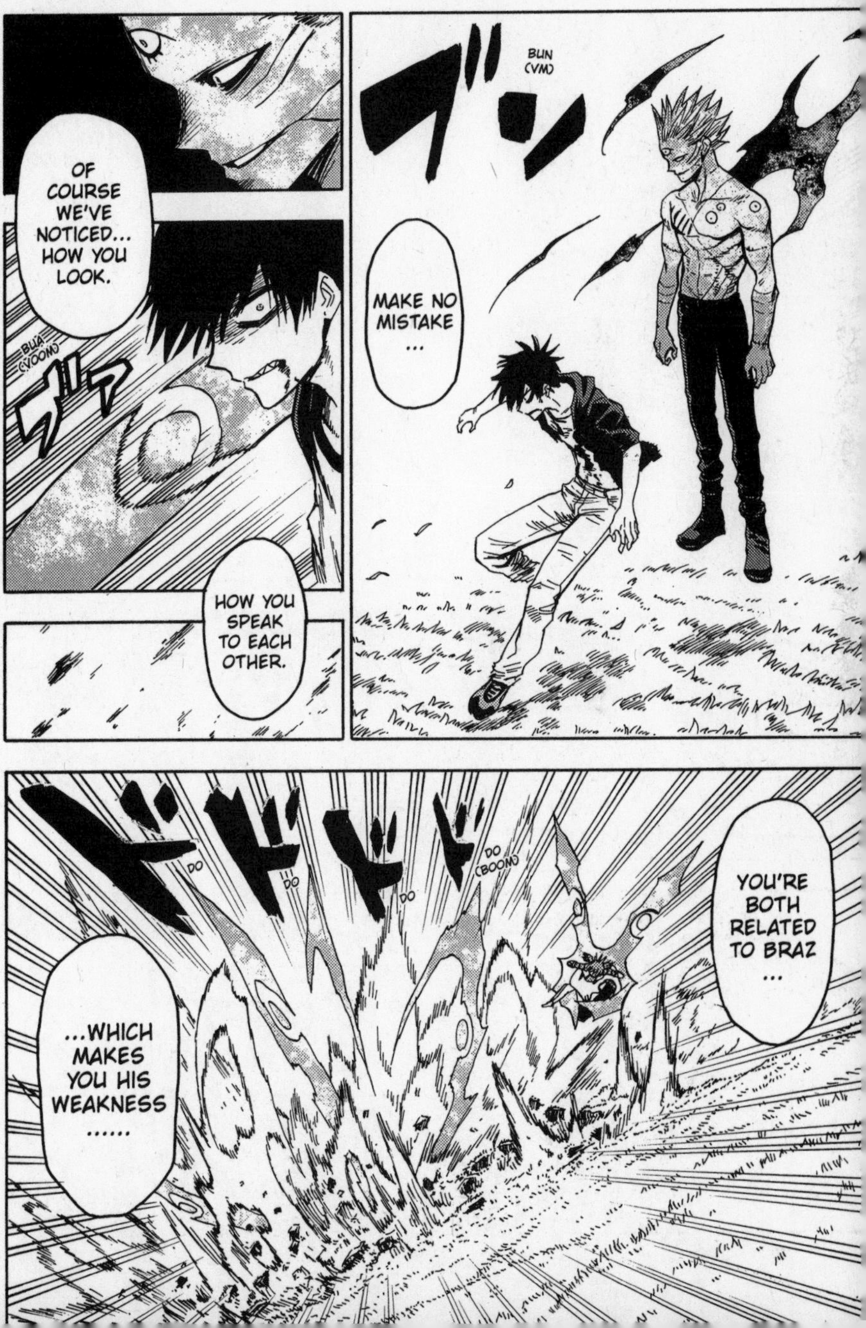
BUN (VM)
MAKE NO MISTAKE ...
OF COURSE WE'VE NOTICED... HOW YOU LOOK.
BUA (VOOM)
HOW YOU SPEAK TO EACH OTHER.
DO (BOOM)
DO
DO
DO
YOU'RE BOTH RELATED TO BRAZ ...
...WHICH MAKES YOU HIS WEAKNESS ......

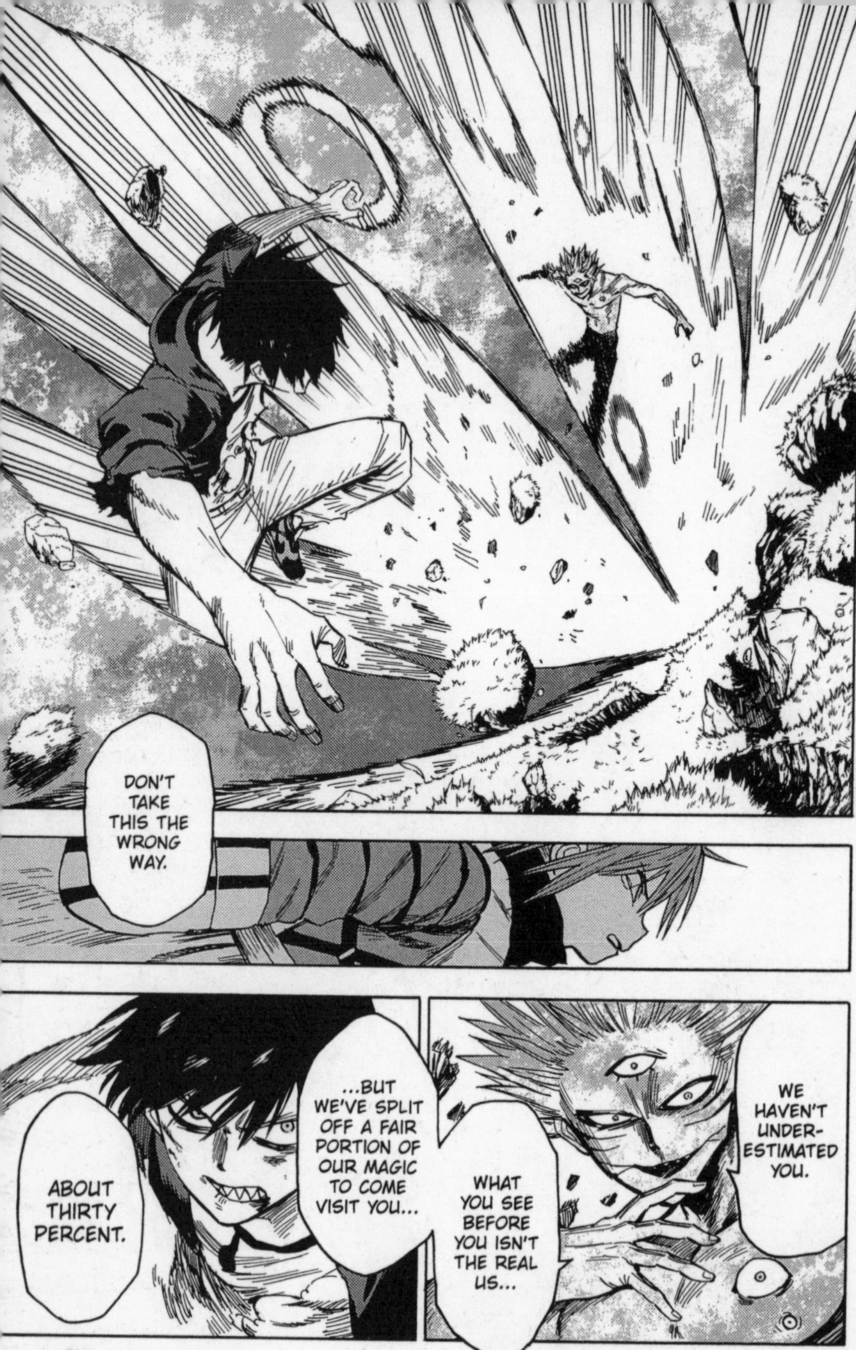
DON'T TAKE THIS THE WRONG WAY.
WE HAVEN'T UNDER-ESTIMATED YOU.
WHAT YOU SEE BEFORE YOU ISN'T THE REAL US...
...BUT WE'VE SPLIT OFF A FAIR PORTION OF OUR MAGIC TO COME VISIT YOU...
ABOUT THIRTY PERCENT.

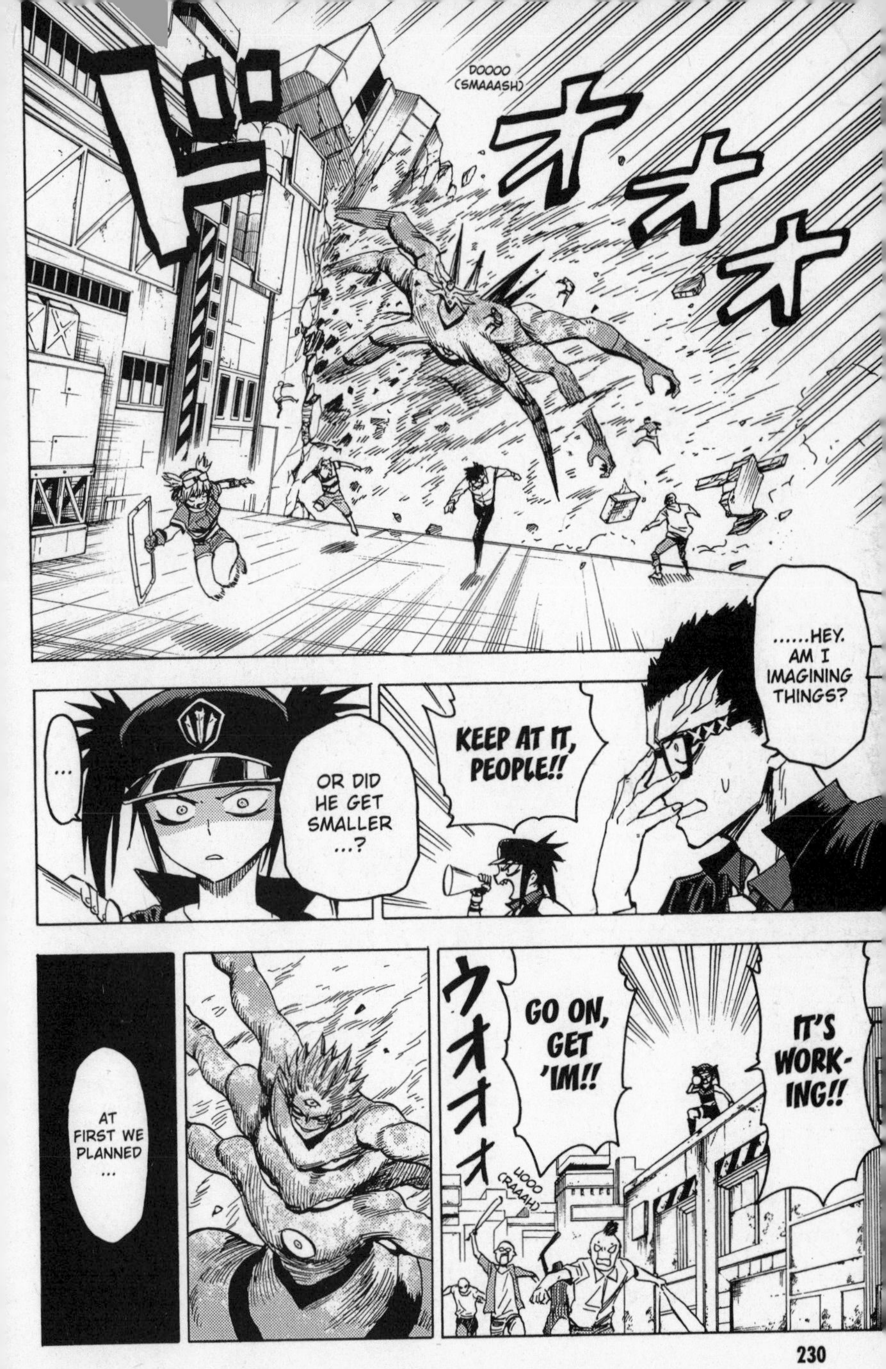

ドオオオ
DOOOO (SMAAASH)
......HEY. AM I IMAGINING THINGS?
KEEP AT IT, PEOPLE!!
OR DID HE GET SMALLER ...?
...
IT'S WORKING!!
GO ON, GET 'IM!!
ウオオオ
UOOO (RAAAH)
AT FIRST WE PLANNED ...

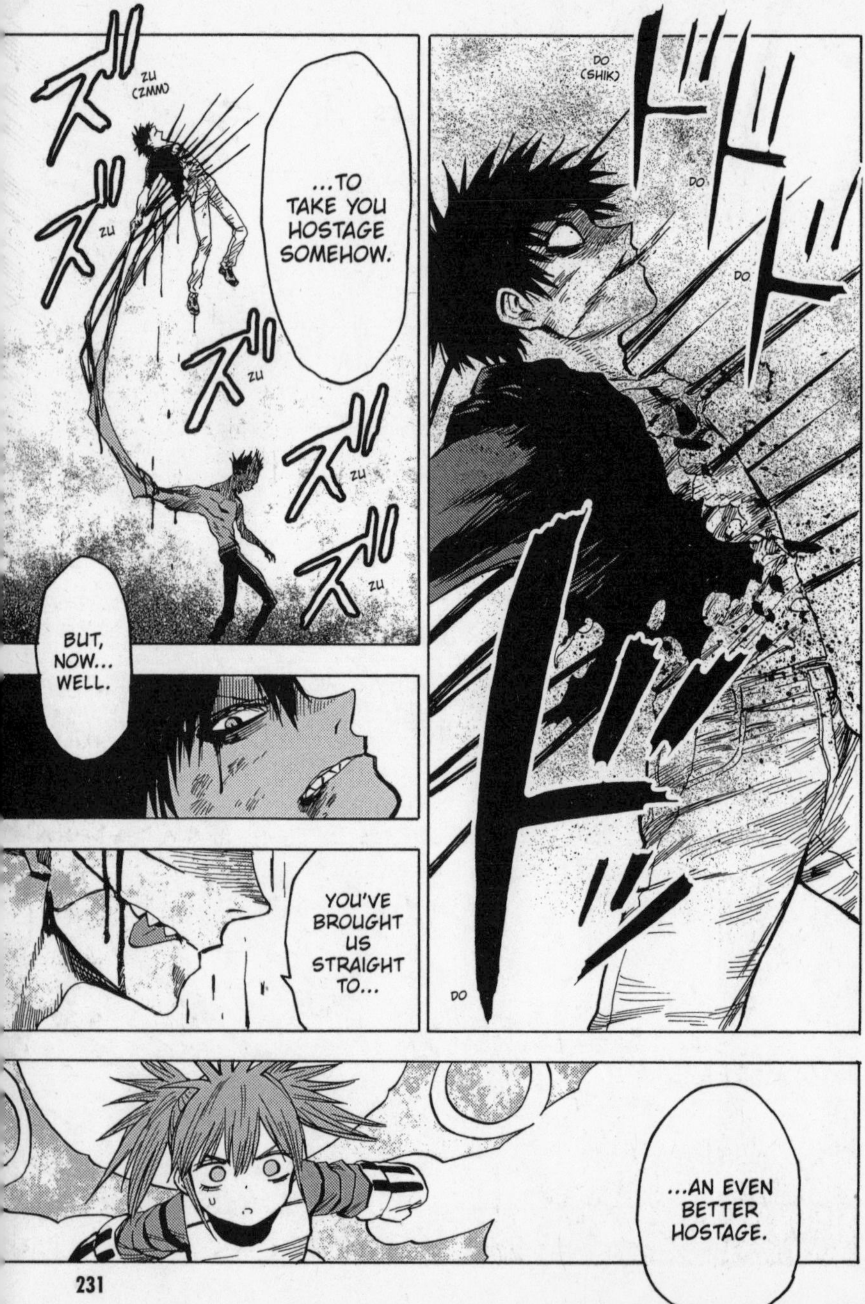
DO (SHIK)
DO
DO
DO
ZU (ZMM)
...TO TAKE YOU HOSTAGE SOMEHOW.
ZU
ZU
ZU
ZU
BUT, NOW... WELL.
YOU'VE BROUGHT US STRAIGHT TO...
...AN EVEN BETTER HOSTAGE.

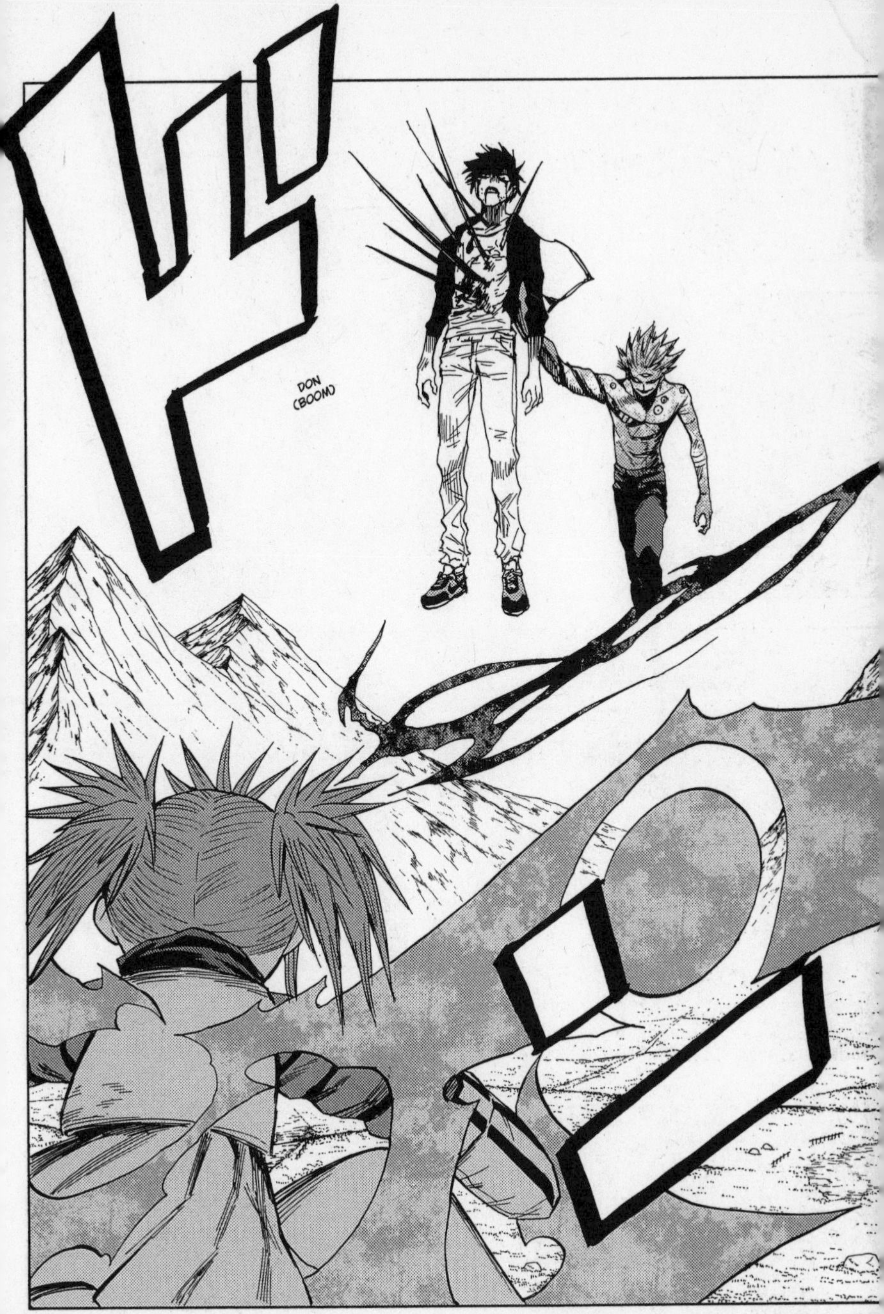
DON
(BOOM)

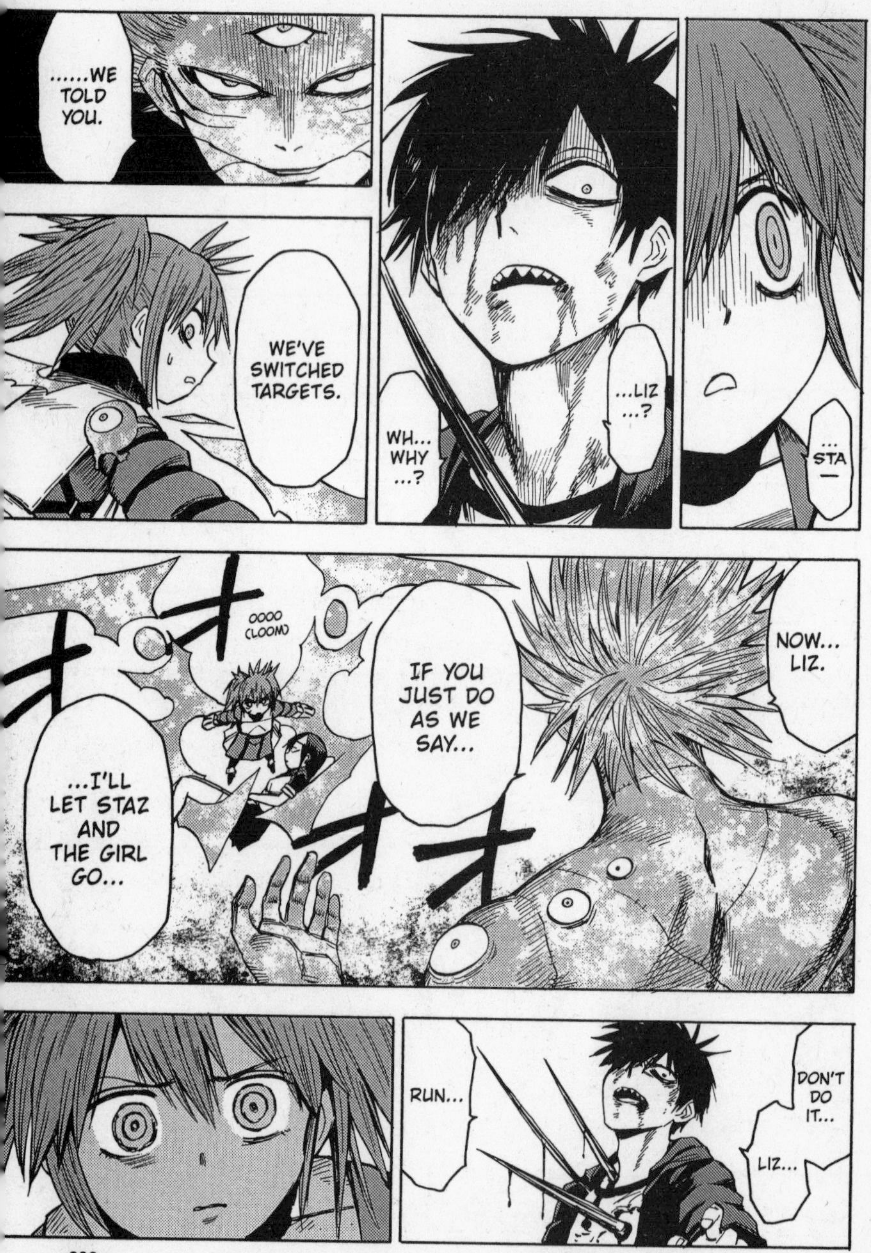
...STA—
...LIZ ...?
WH... WHY ...?
......WE TOLD YOU.
WE'VE SWITCHED TARGETS.
NOW... LIZ.
IF YOU JUST DO AS WE SAY...
OOOO (LOOM)
...I'LL LET STAZ AND THE GIRL GO...
DON'T DO IT...
LIZ...
RUN...

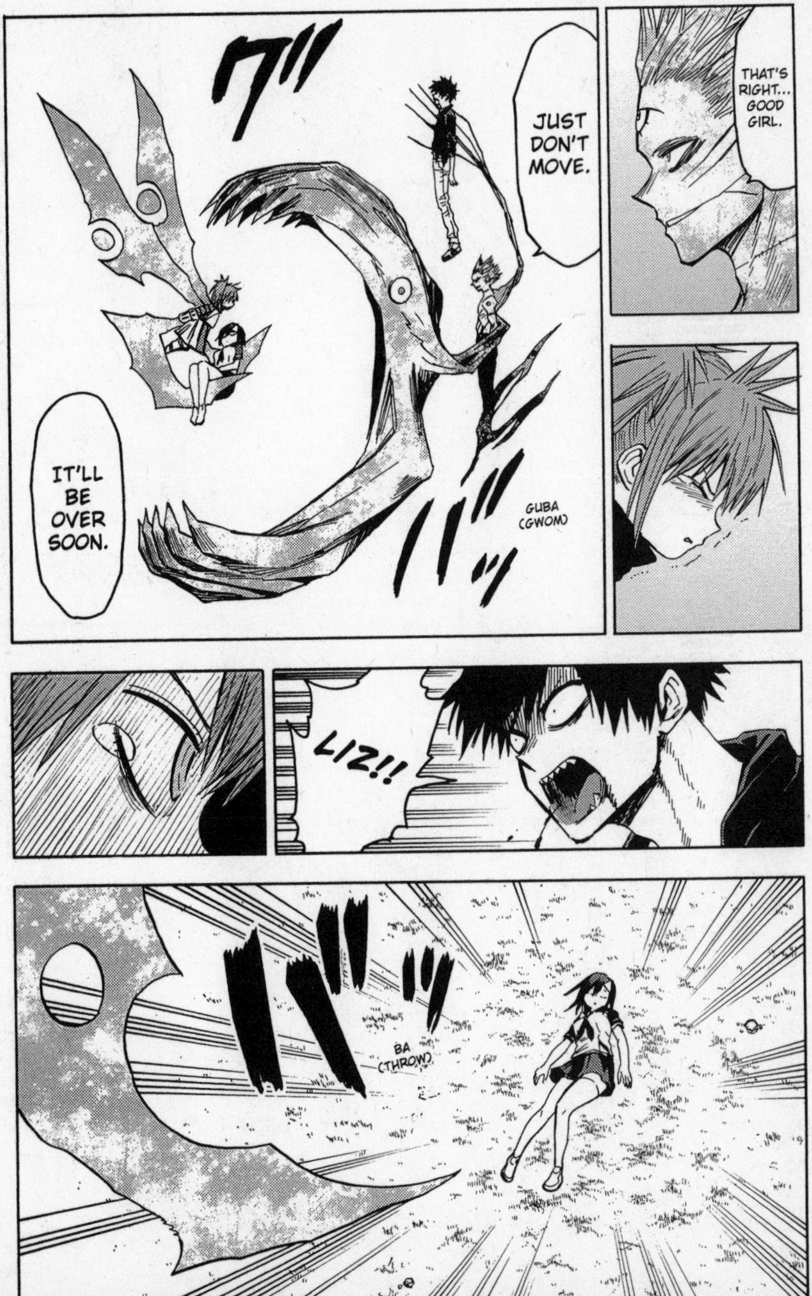
THAT'S RIGHT... GOOD GIRL.
JUST DON'T MOVE.
GUBA (GWOM)
IT'LL BE OVER SOON.
LIZ!!
BA (THROW)

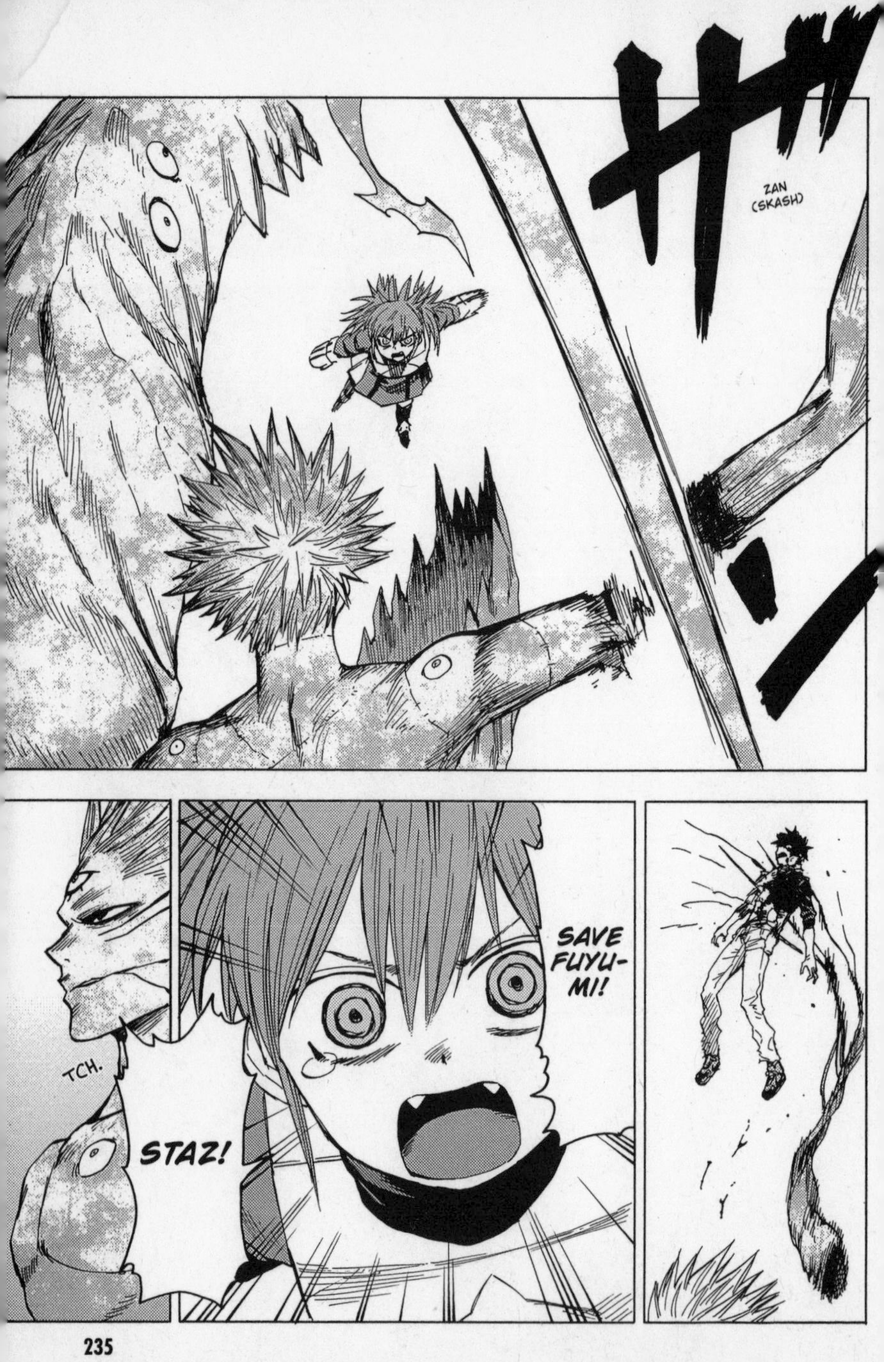
ZAN
(SKASH)
SAVE FUYU-MI!
TCH.
STAZ!

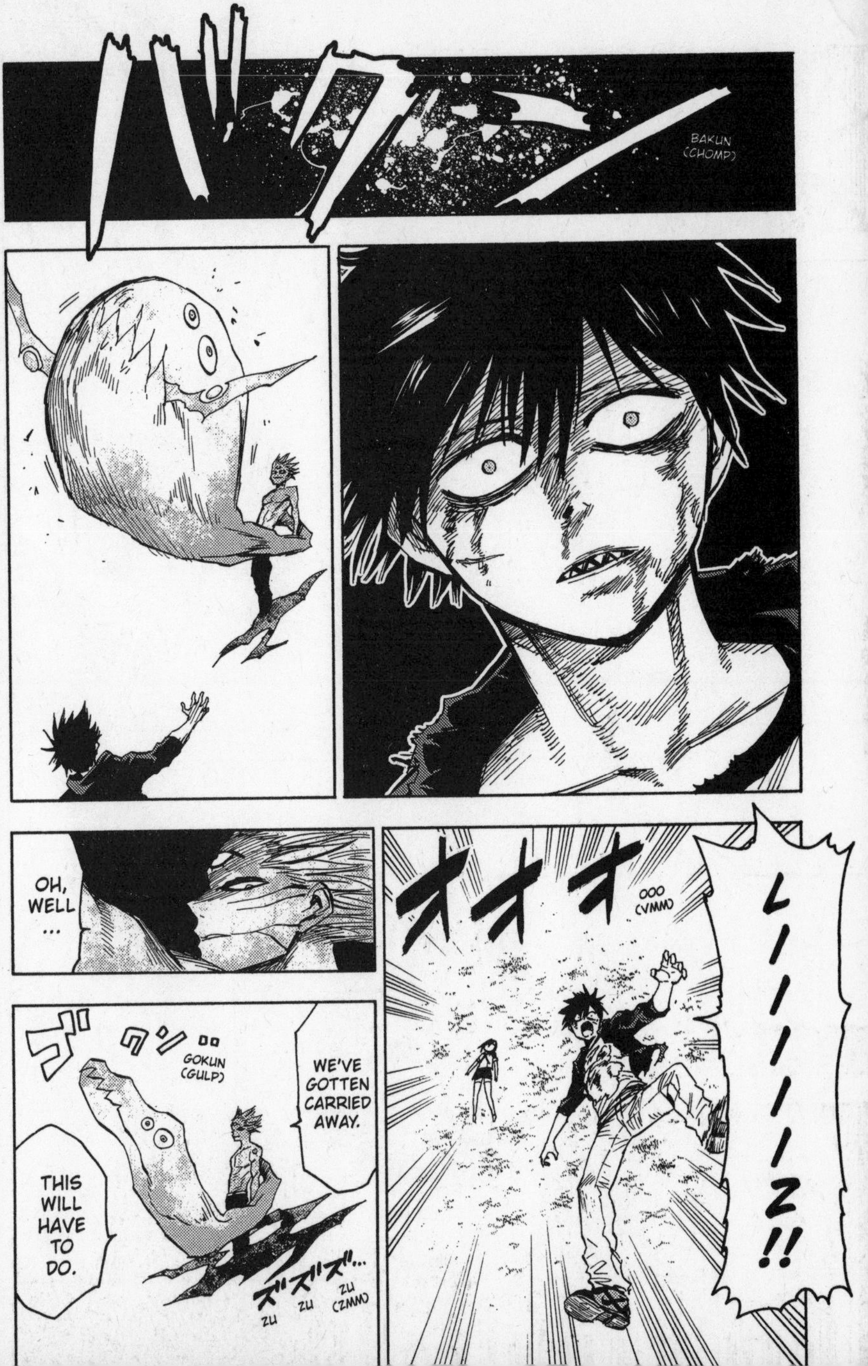

バクン
BAKUN (CHOMP)
オオオ
OOO (VMM)
OH, WELL...
ゴクン
GOKUN (GULP)
WE'VE GOTTEN CARRIED AWAY.
THIS WILL HAVE TO DO.
ズズズ...
ZU ZU ZU (ZMM)

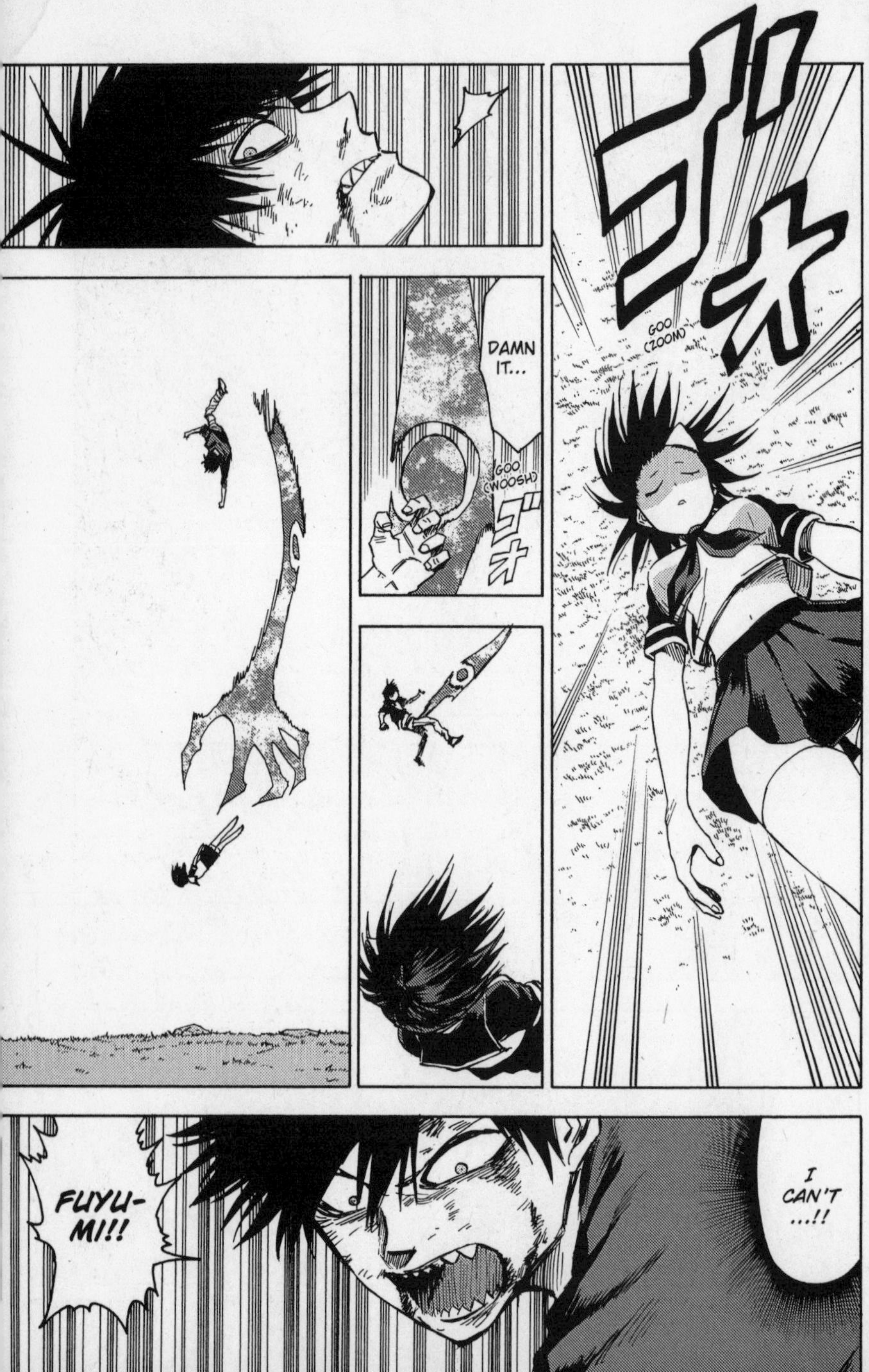
GOO (ZOOM)
DAMN IT...
GOO (WOOSH)
ゴオ
I CAN'T ...!!
FUYU-MI!!

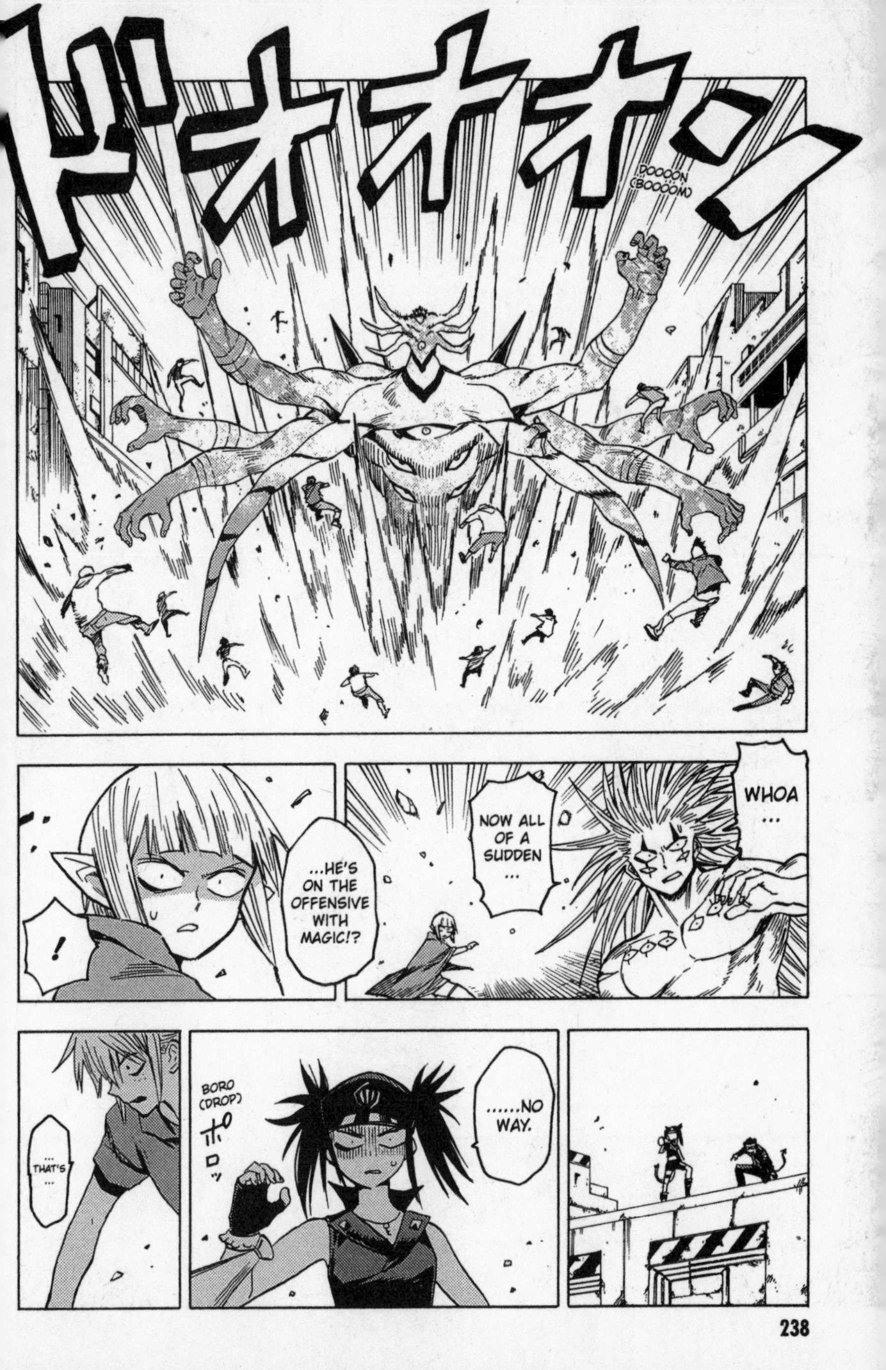
ドオオオン
DOOOON (BOOOM)
WHOA ...
NOW ALL OF A SUDDEN ...
...HE'S ON THE OFFENSIVE WITH MAGIC!?
!
......NO WAY.
BORO (DROP)
ボロッ
... THAT'S ...

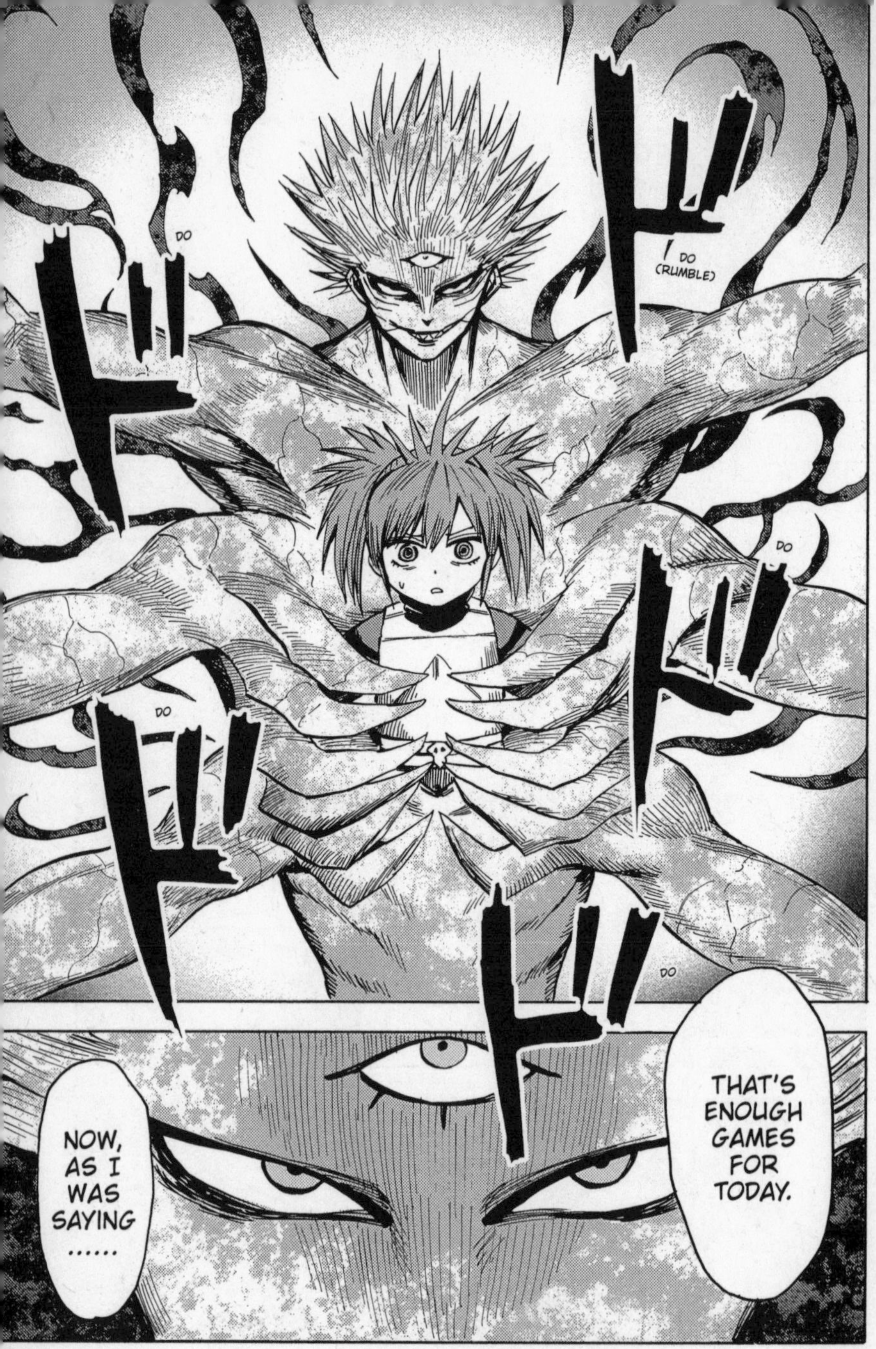
DO (RUMBLE)
DO
DO
DO
DO
THAT'S ENOUGH GAMES FOR TODAY.
NOW, AS I WAS SAYING ......

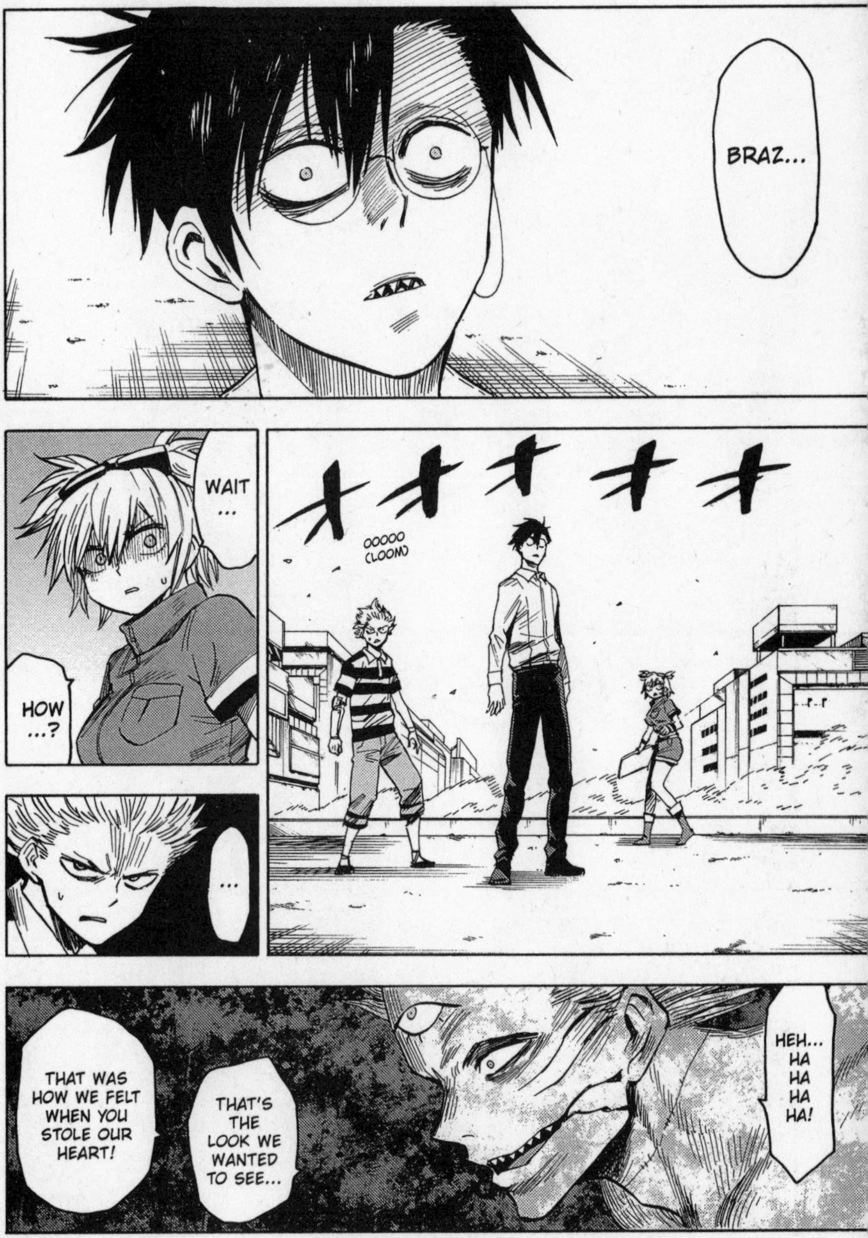
BRAZ...
OOOOO (LOOM)
WAIT ...
HOW ...?
...
HEH... HA HA HA HA!
THAT'S THE LOOK WE WANTED TO SEE...
THAT WAS HOW WE FELT WHEN YOU STOLE OUR HEART!

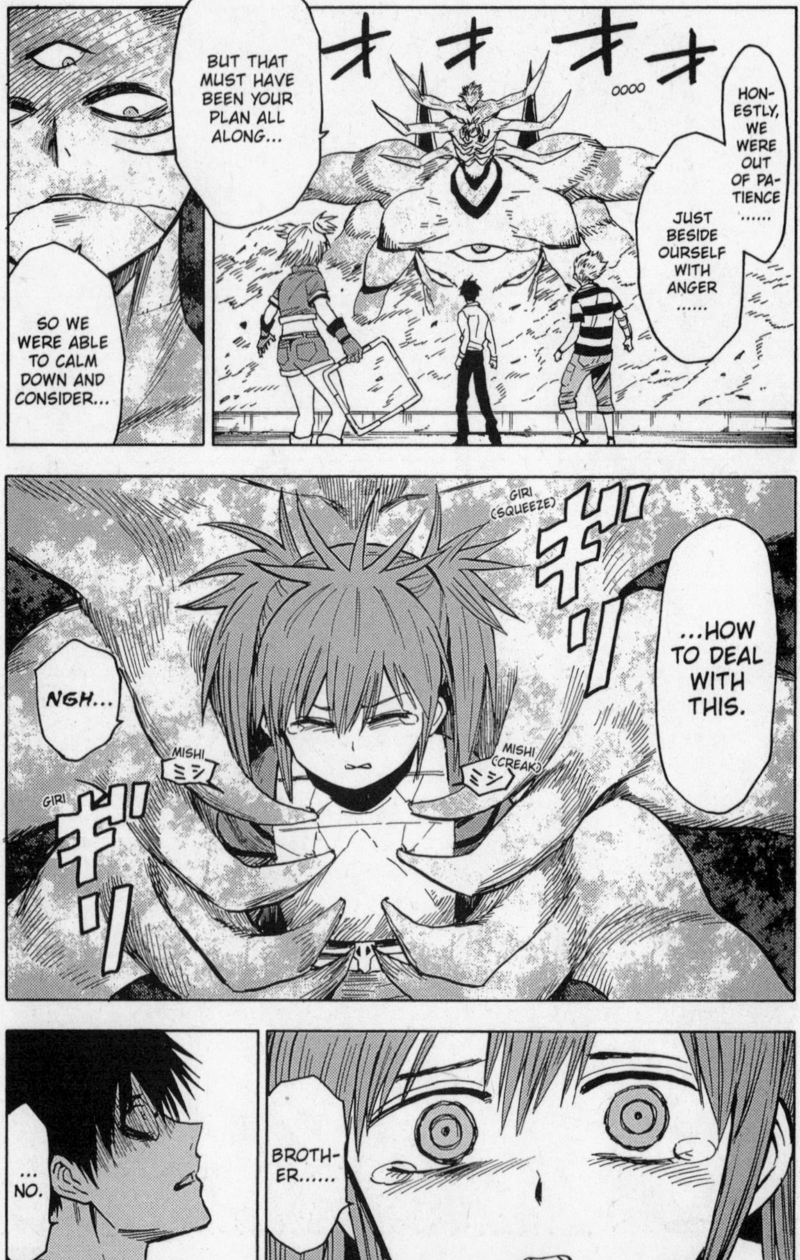
オオオオ
OOOO
HON-ESTLY, WE WERE OUT OF PA-TIENCE ......
JUST BESIDE OURSELF WITH ANGER ......
BUT THAT MUST HAVE BEEN YOUR PLAN ALL ALONG...
SO WE WERE ABLE TO CALM DOWN AND CONSIDER...
GIRI (SQUEEZE)
ギリ
...HOW TO DEAL WITH THIS.
MISHI (CREAK)
ミシ
MISHI
ミシ
NGH...
GIRI
ギリ
BROTH-ER......
... NO.

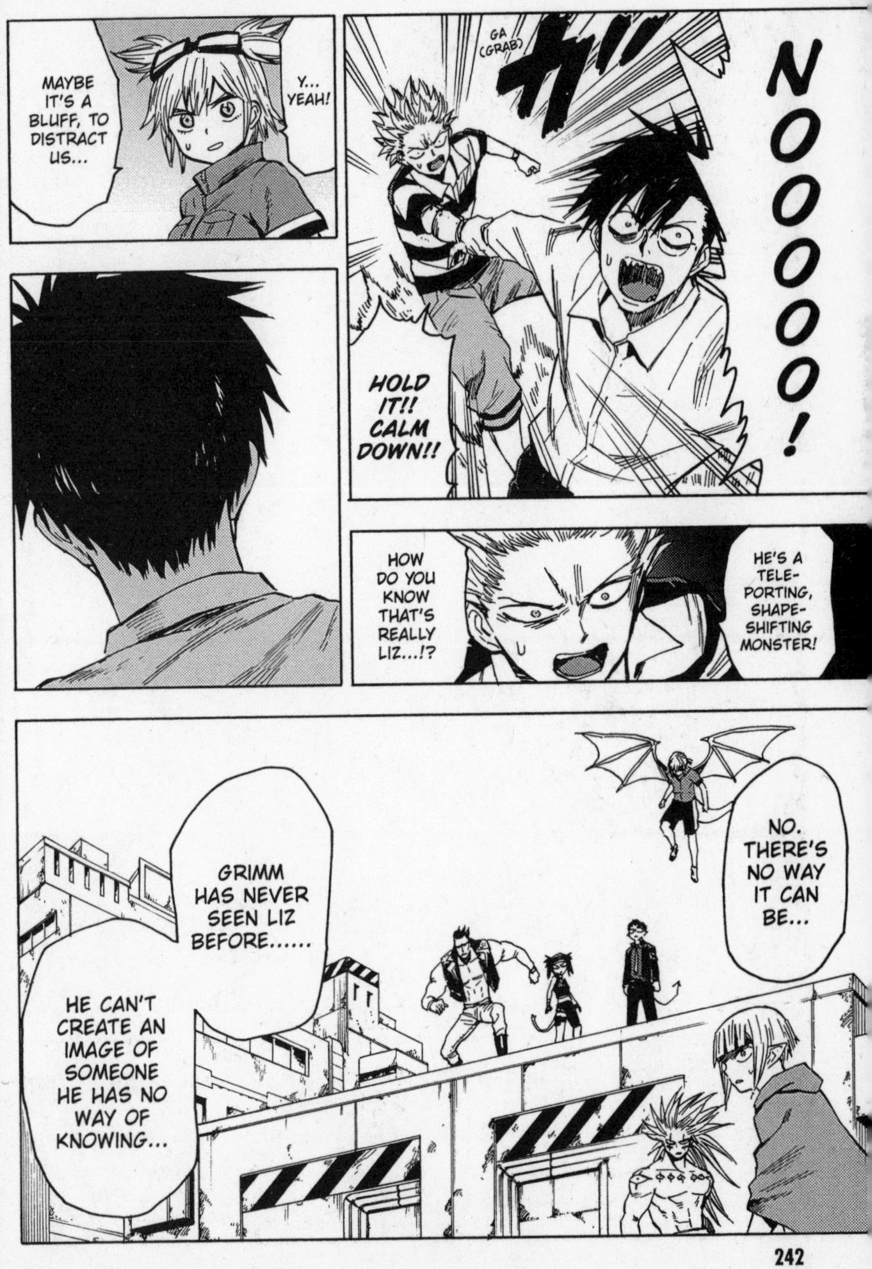
NOOOOOO!
GA (GRAB)
HOLD IT!! CALM DOWN!!
HE'S A TELE-PORTING, SHAPE-SHIFTING MONSTER!
HOW DO YOU KNOW THAT'S REALLY LIZ...!?
MAYBE IT'S A BLUFF, TO DISTRACT US...
Y... YEAH!
NO. THERE'S NO WAY IT CAN BE...
GRIMM HAS NEVER SEEN LIZ BEFORE......
HE CAN'T CREATE AN IMAGE OF SOMEONE HE HAS NO WAY OF KNOWING...

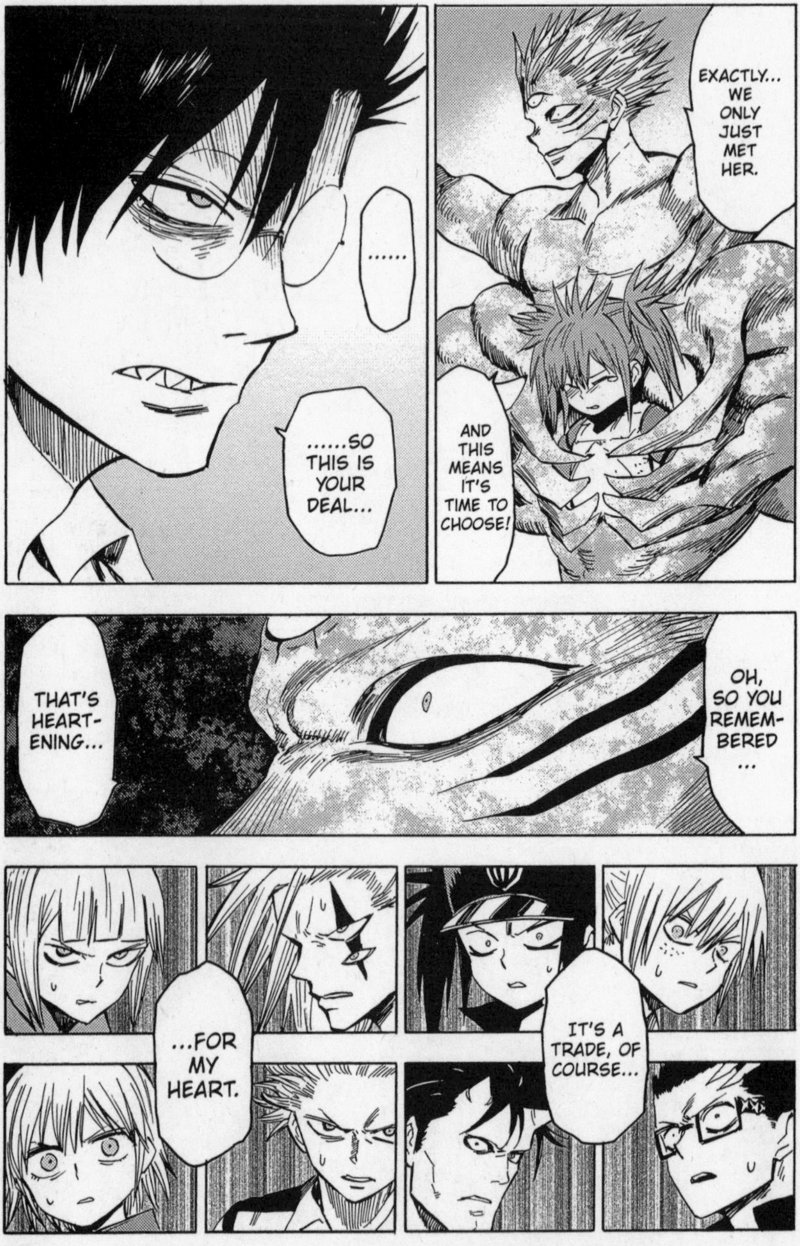
EXACTLY... WE ONLY JUST MET HER.
AND THIS MEANS IT'S TIME TO CHOOSE!
......
......SO THIS IS YOUR DEAL...
OH, SO YOU REMEMBERED...
THAT'S HEARTENING...
IT'S A TRADE, OF COURSE...
...FOR MY HEART.

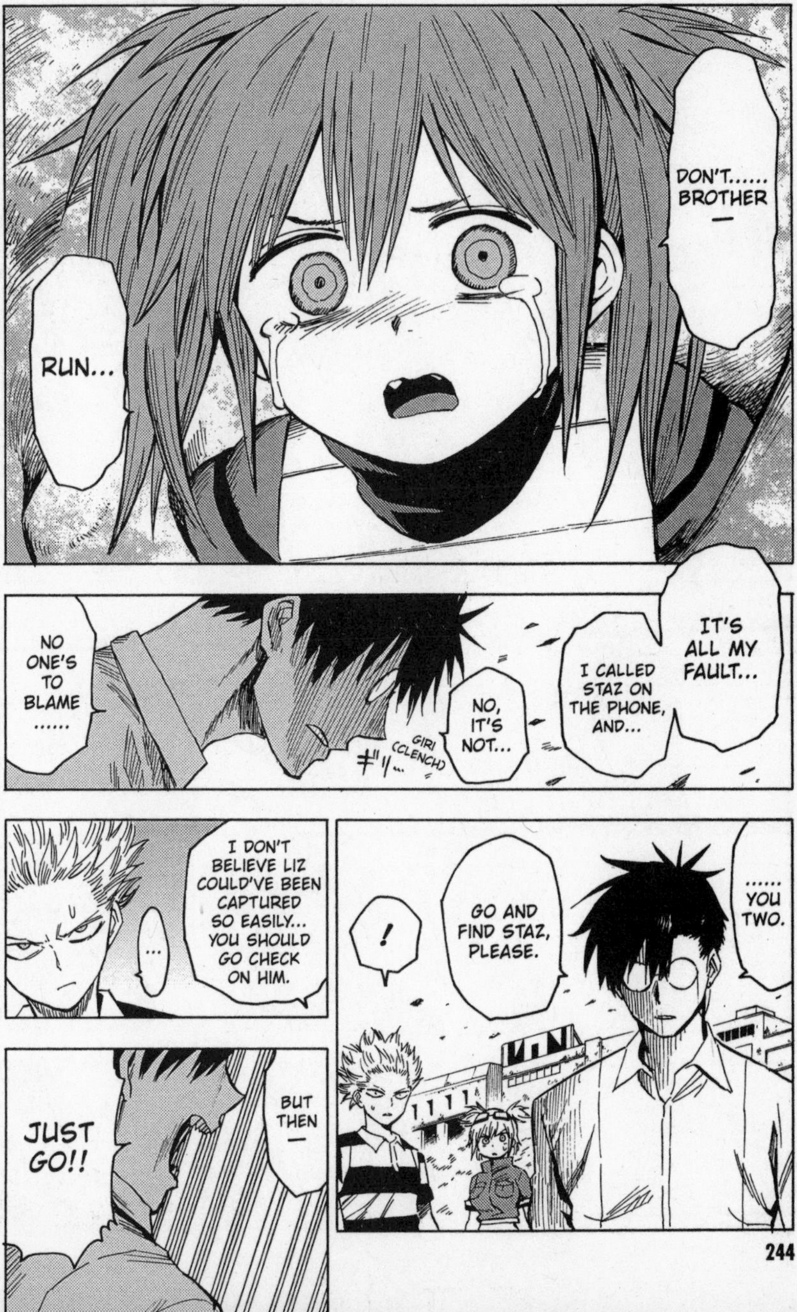
DON'T...... BROTHER —
RUN...
IT'S ALL MY FAULT...
I CALLED STAZ ON THE PHONE, AND...
NO, IT'S NOT...
ギリ…
GIRI (CLENCH)
NO ONE'S TO BLAME ......
...... YOU TWO.
GO AND FIND STAZ, PLEASE.
!
I DON'T BELIEVE LIZ COULD'VE BEEN CAPTURED SO EASILY... YOU SHOULD GO CHECK ON HIM.
...
BUT THEN —
JUST GO!!

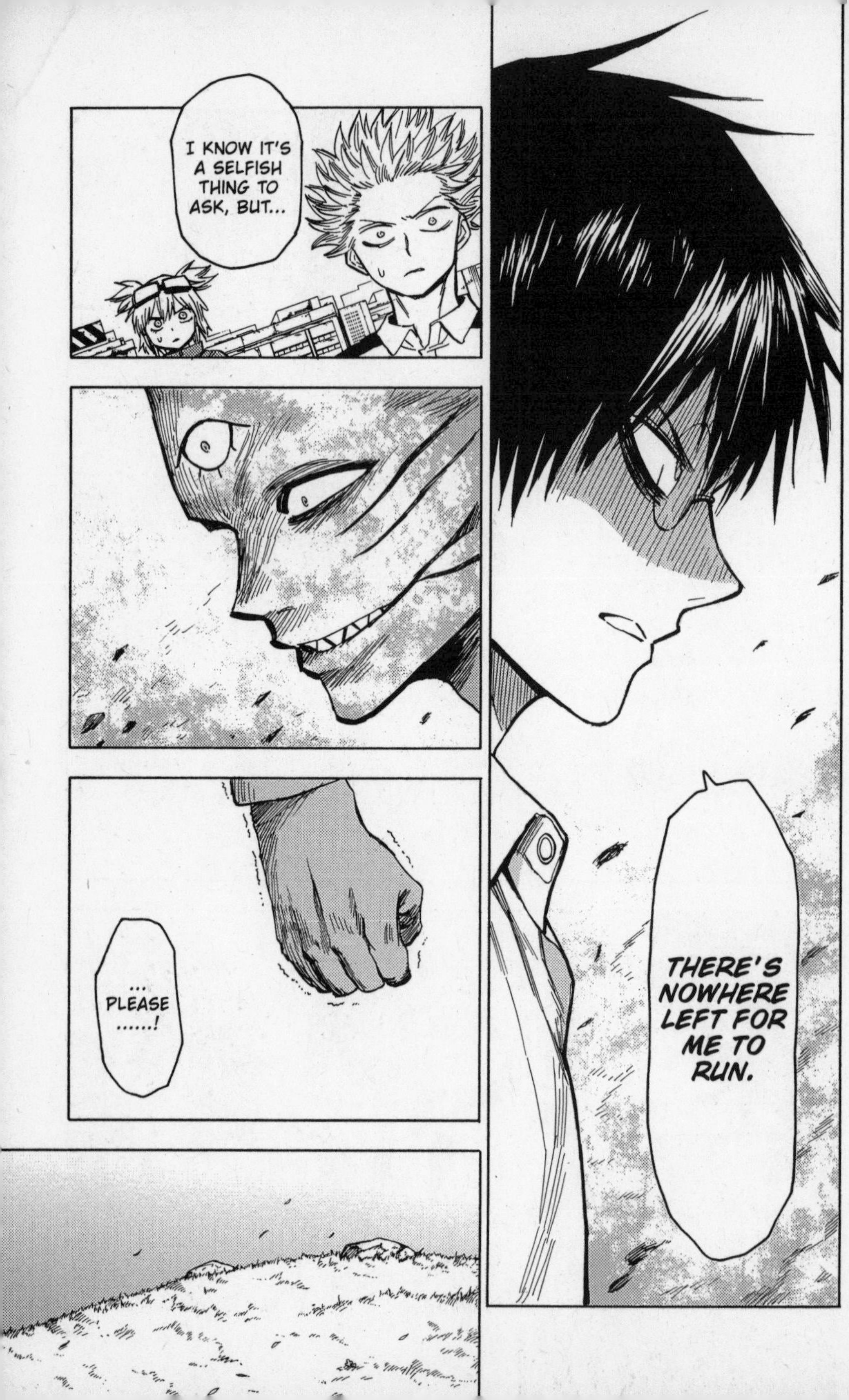
THERE'S NOWHERE LEFT FOR ME TO RUN.
I KNOW IT'S A SELFISH THING TO ASK, BUT...
... PLEASE ......!

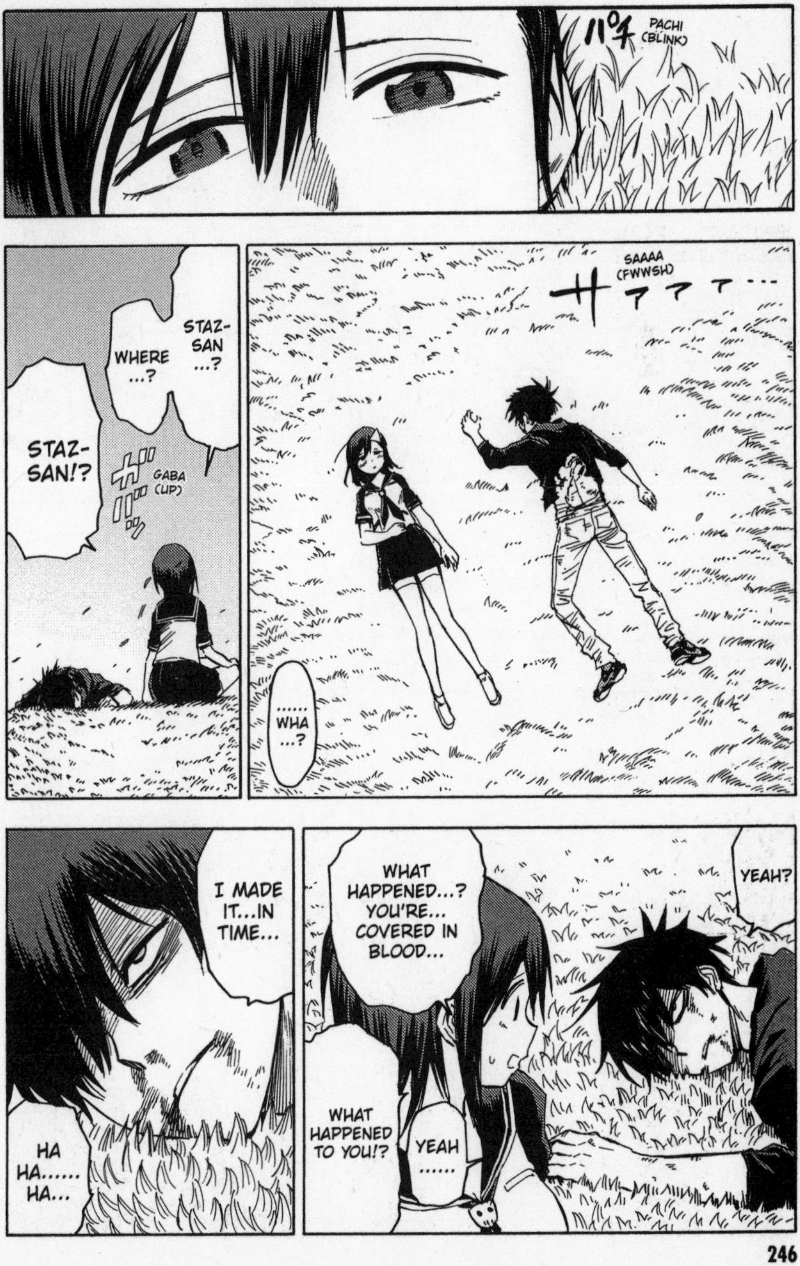

PACHI (BLINK)
SAAAA (FWWSH)
......WHA...?
STAZ-SAN...?
WHERE...?
STAZ-SAN!?
GABA (UP)
YEAH?
WHAT HAPPENED...? YOU'RE... COVERED IN BLOOD...
YEAH......
WHAT HAPPENED TO YOU!?
I MADE IT...IN TIME...
HA HA...... HA...

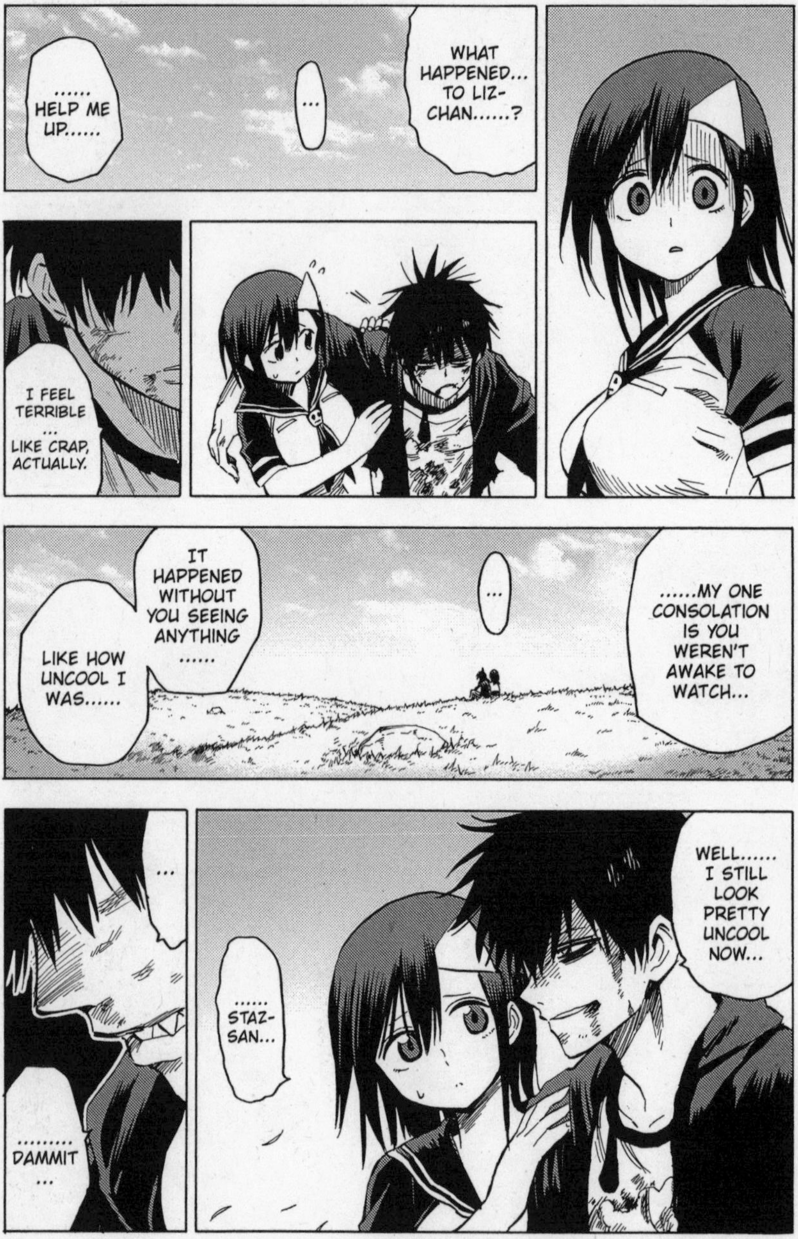
WHAT HAPPENED... TO LIZ-CHAN......?
...
...... HELP ME UP......
I FEEL TERRIBLE ... LIKE CRAP, ACTUALLY.
......MY ONE CONSOLATION IS YOU WEREN'T AWAKE TO WATCH...
...
IT HAPPENED WITHOUT YOU SEEING ANYTHING ......
LIKE HOW UNCOOL I WAS......
WELL...... I STILL LOOK PRETTY UNCOOL NOW...
...... STAZ-SAN...
...
......... DAMMIT ...

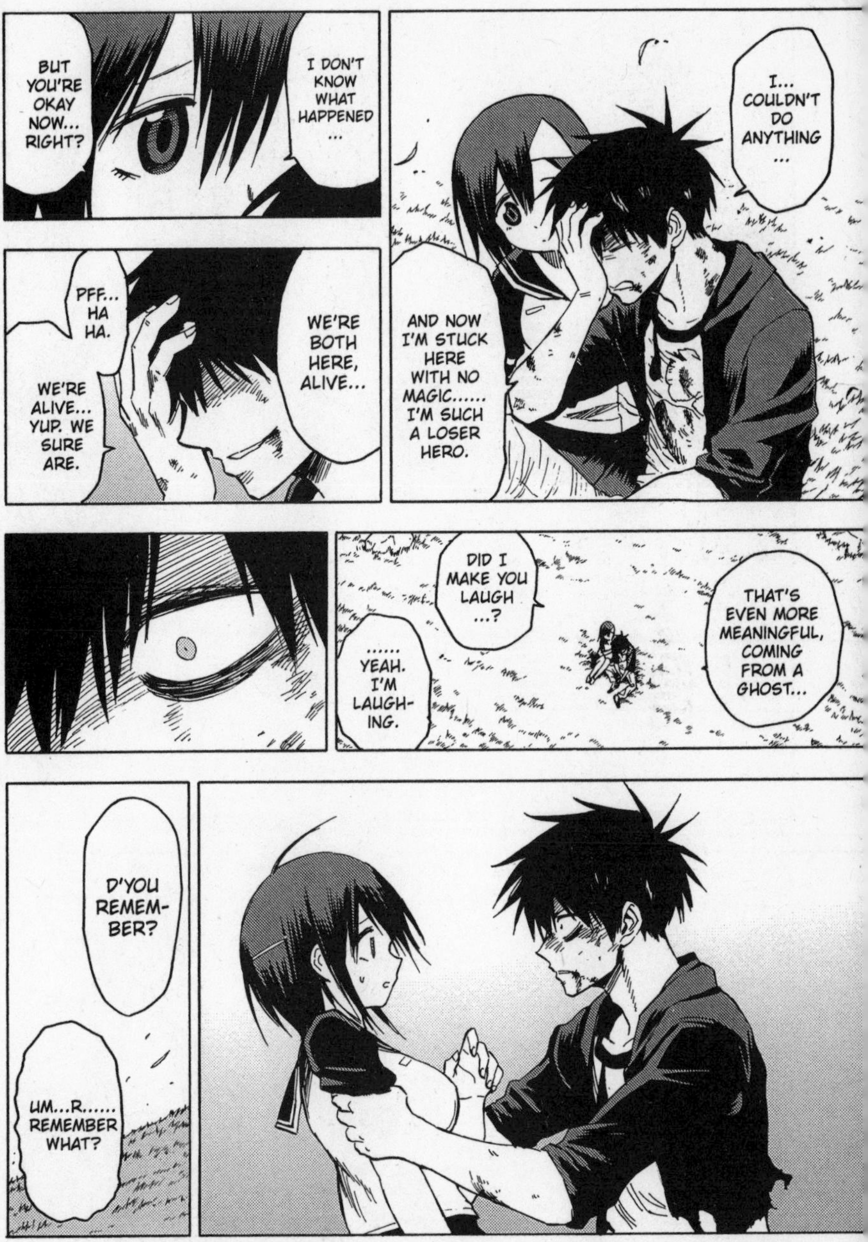
I... COULDN'T DO ANYTHING...
AND NOW I'M STUCK HERE WITH NO MAGIC...... I'M SUCH A LOSER HERO.
I DON'T KNOW WHAT HAPPENED...
BUT YOU'RE OKAY NOW... RIGHT?
WE'RE BOTH HERE, ALIVE...
PFF... HA HA.
WE'RE ALIVE... YUP. WE SURE ARE.
THAT'S EVEN MORE MEANINGFUL, COMING FROM A GHOST...
DID I MAKE YOU LAUGH...?
...... YEAH. I'M LAUGHING.
D'YOU REMEMBER?
UM...R...... REMEMBER WHAT?

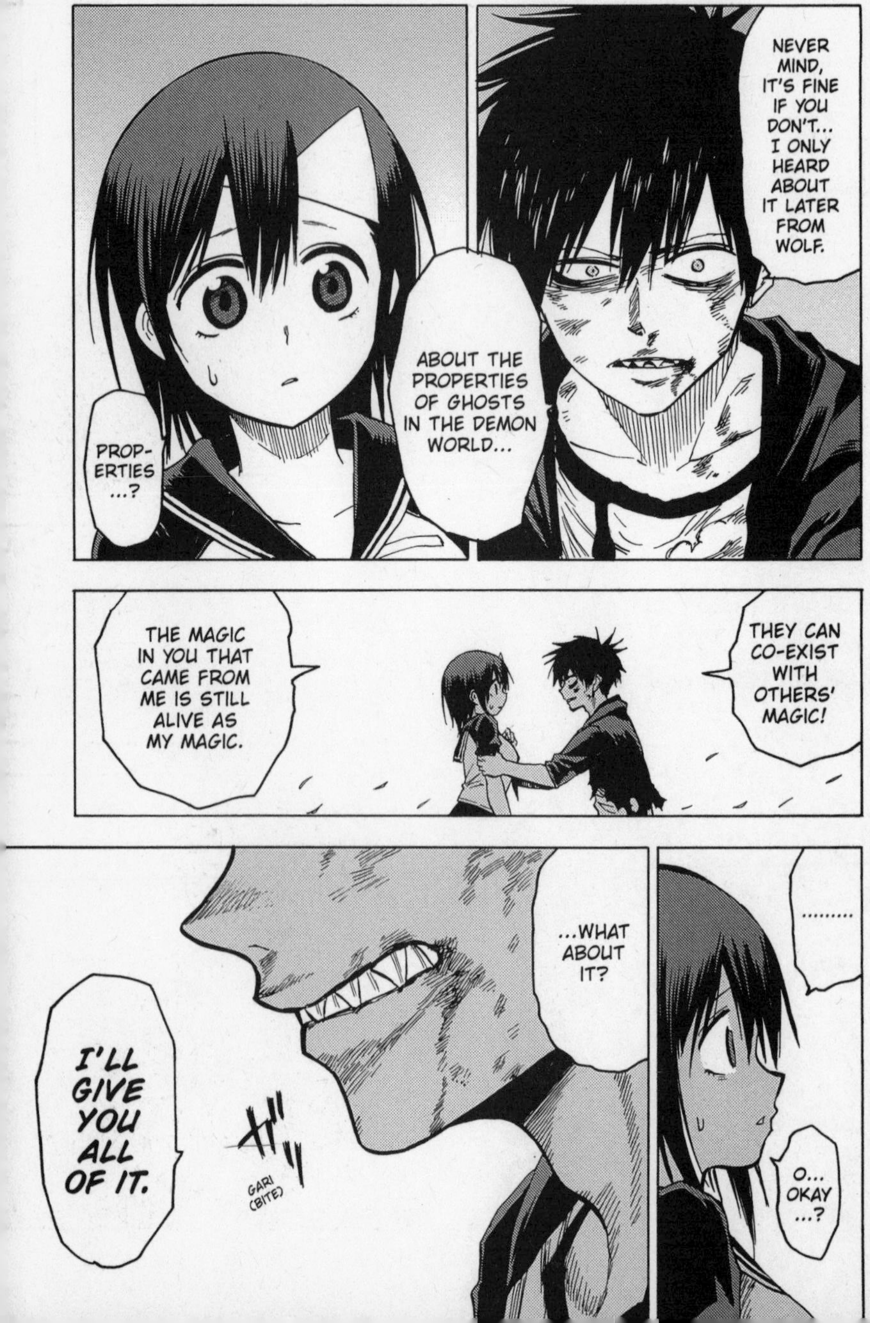
NEVER MIND, IT'S FINE IF YOU DON'T... I ONLY HEARD ABOUT IT LATER FROM WOLF.
ABOUT THE PROPERTIES OF GHOSTS IN THE DEMON WORLD...
PROP-ERTIES...?
THEY CAN CO-EXIST WITH OTHERS' MAGIC!
THE MAGIC IN YOU THAT CAME FROM ME IS STILL ALIVE AS MY MAGIC.
.........
O... OKAY...?
...WHAT ABOUT IT?
I'LL GIVE YOU ALL OF IT.
GARI (BITE)

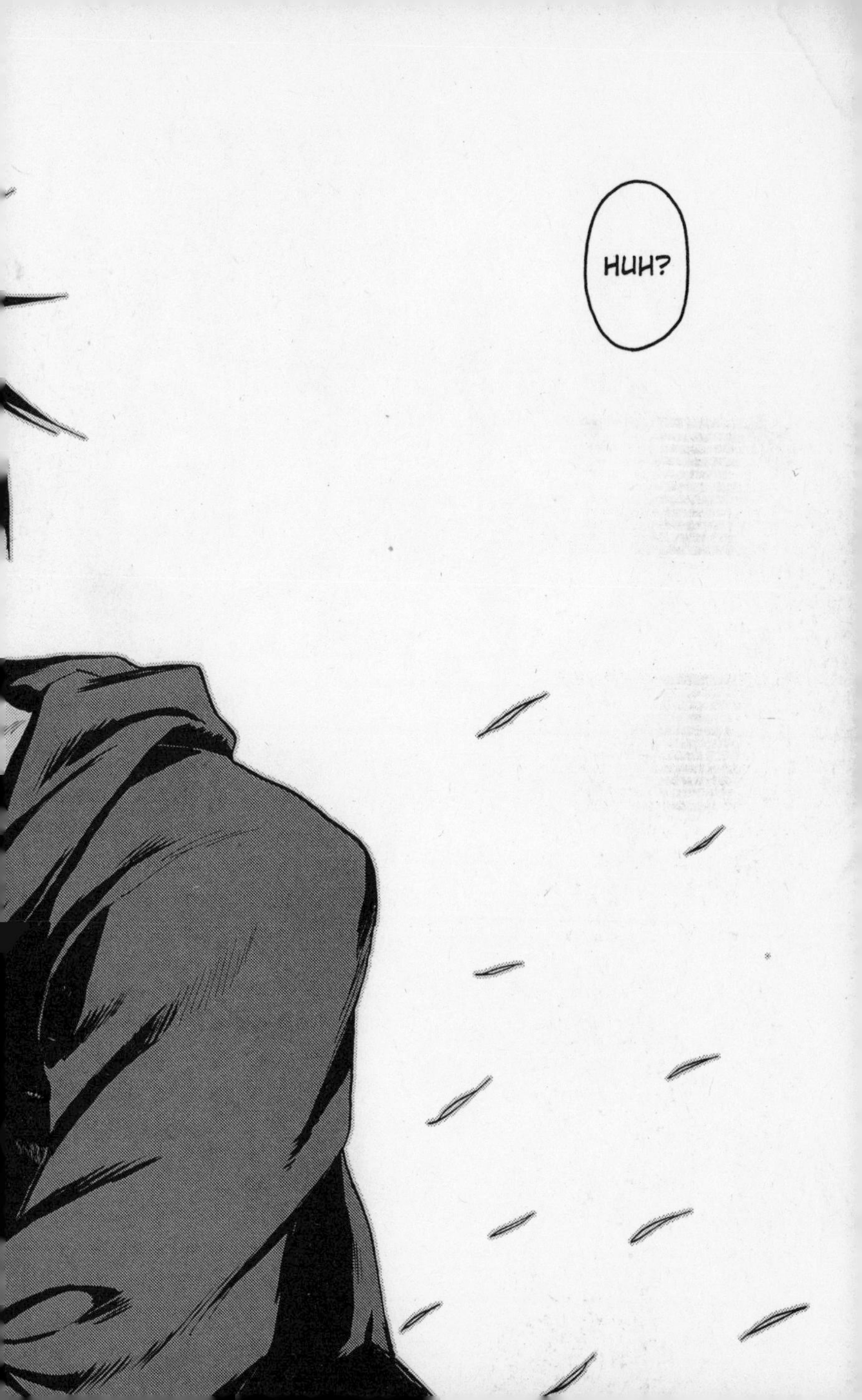
HUH?

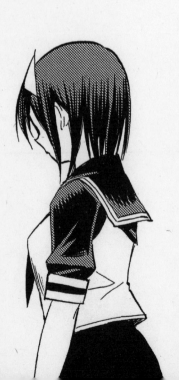

BLOOD LAD

# CHAPTER 78 ♠ THE GIANT ROBOT HE ALWAYS WANTED

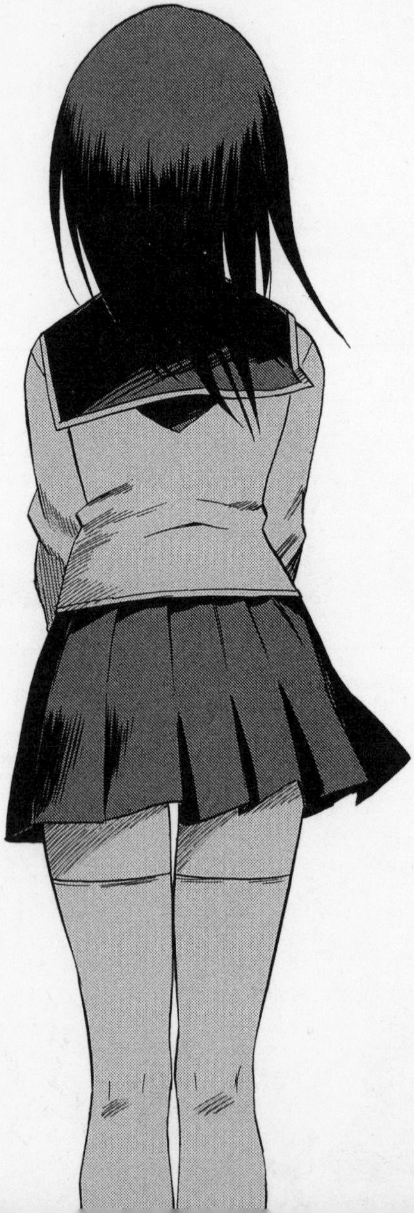

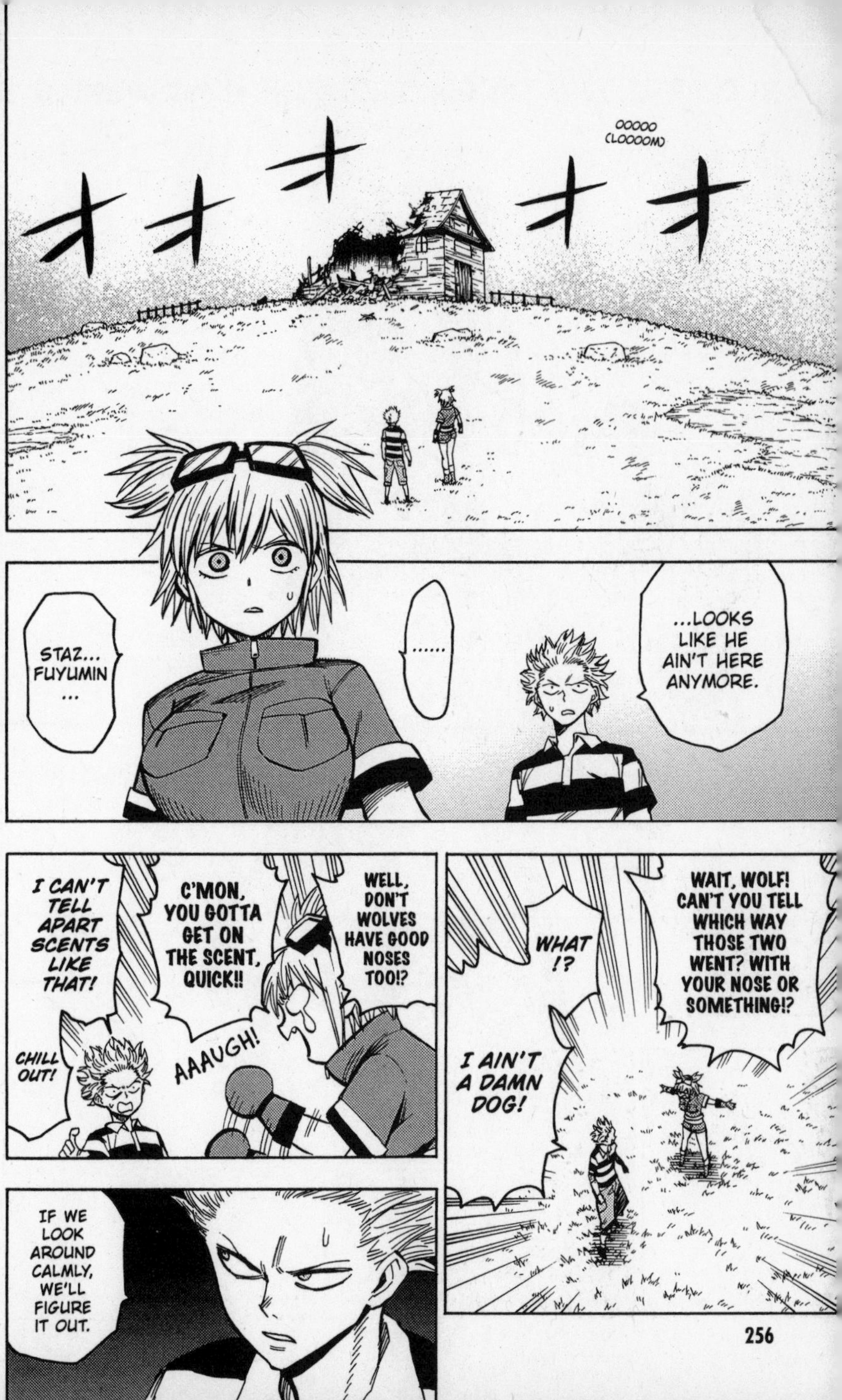
オオオ
OOOOO (LOOOOM)
オオ
...LOOKS LIKE HE AIN'T HERE ANYMORE.
......
STAZ... FUYUMIN ...
WAIT, WOLF! CAN'T YOU TELL WHICH WAY THOSE TWO WENT? WITH YOUR NOSE OR SOMETHING!?
WHAT !?
I AIN'T A DAMN DOG!
WELL, DON'T WOLVES HAVE GOOD NOSES TOO!?
C'MON, YOU GOTTA GET ON THE SCENT, QUICK!!
I CAN'T TELL APART SCENTS LIKE THAT!
AAAUGH!
CHILL OUT!
IF WE LOOK AROUND CALMLY, WE'LL FIGURE IT OUT.

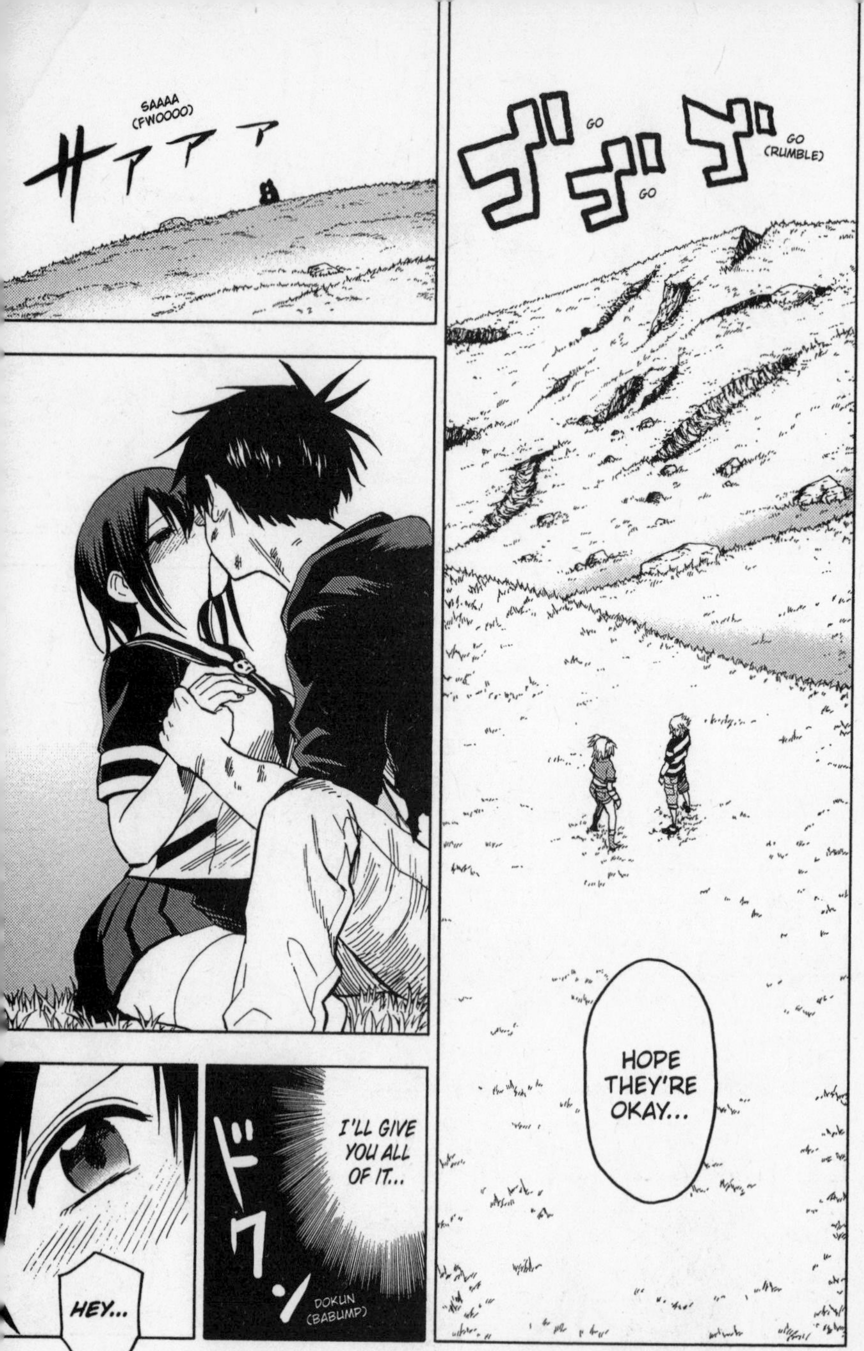
GO
GO
GO (RUMBLE)
HOPE THEY'RE OKAY...
SAAAA (FWOOOO)
I'LL GIVE YOU ALL OF IT...
DOKUN (BABUMP)
HEY...

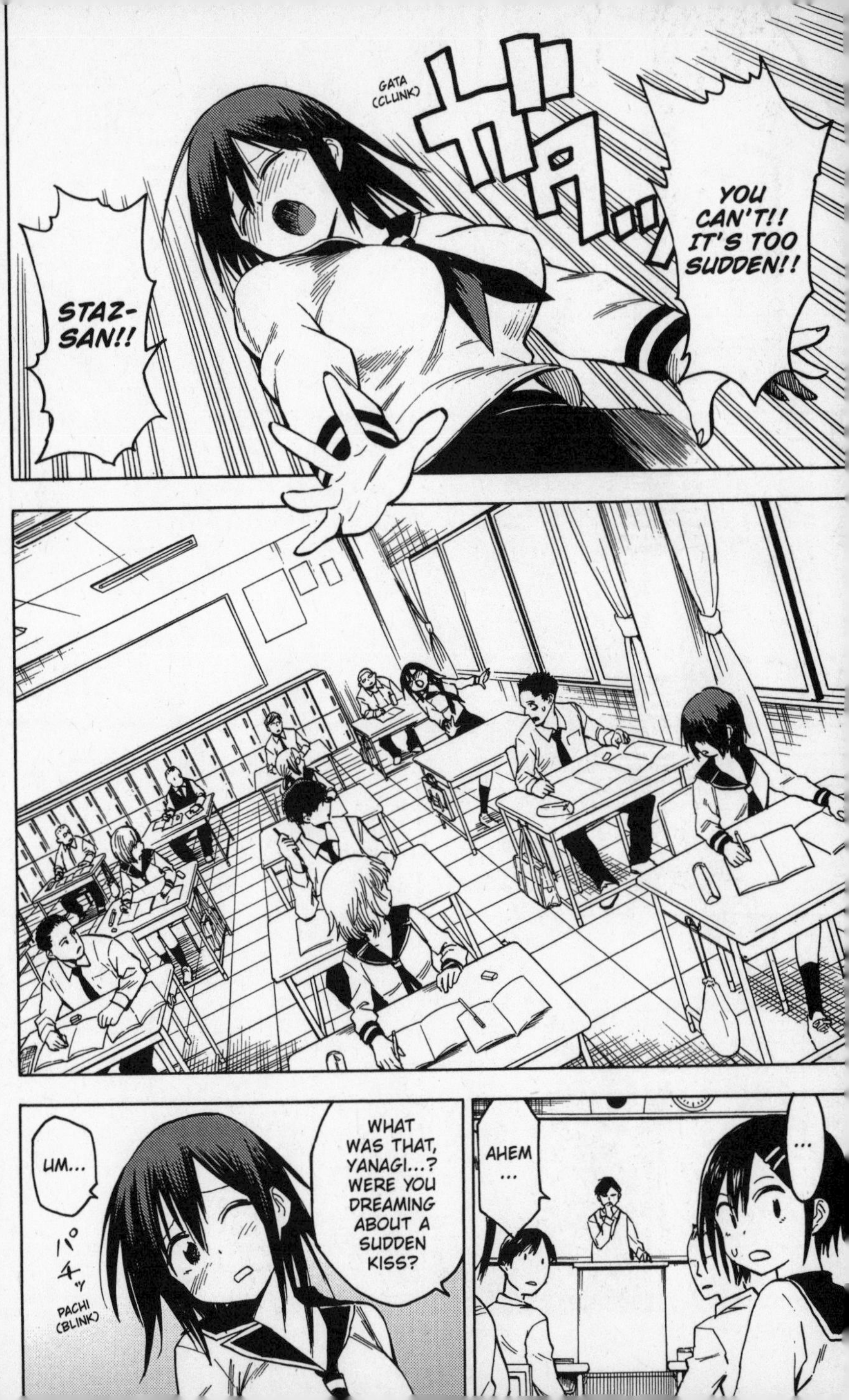

ガタ…
GATA (CLUNK)
YOU CAN'T!! IT'S TOO SUDDEN!!
STAZ-SAN!!
...
AHEM ...
WHAT WAS THAT, YANAGI...? WERE YOU DREAMING ABOUT A SUDDEN KISS?
UM...
パチッ
PACHI (BLINK)

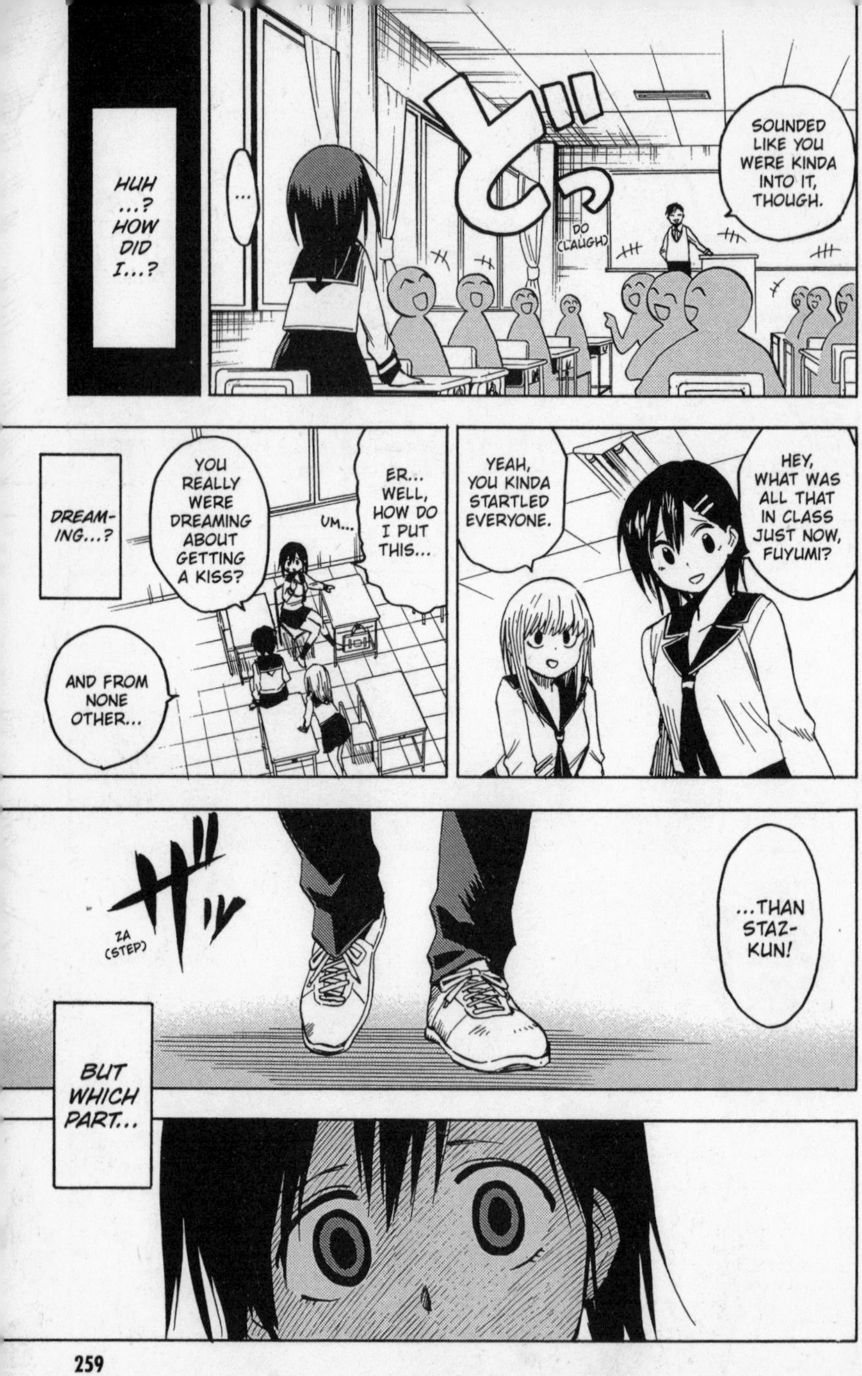
SOUNDED LIKE YOU WERE KINDA INTO IT, THOUGH.
DO (LAUGH)
...
HUH ...? HOW DID I...?
HEY, WHAT WAS ALL THAT IN CLASS JUST NOW, FUYUMI?
YEAH, YOU KINDA STARTLED EVERYONE.
ER... WELL, HOW DO I PUT THIS...
UM...
YOU REALLY WERE DREAMING ABOUT GETTING A KISS?
DREAM-ING...?
AND FROM NONE OTHER...
...THAN STAZ-KUN!
ZA (STEP)
BUT WHICH PART...

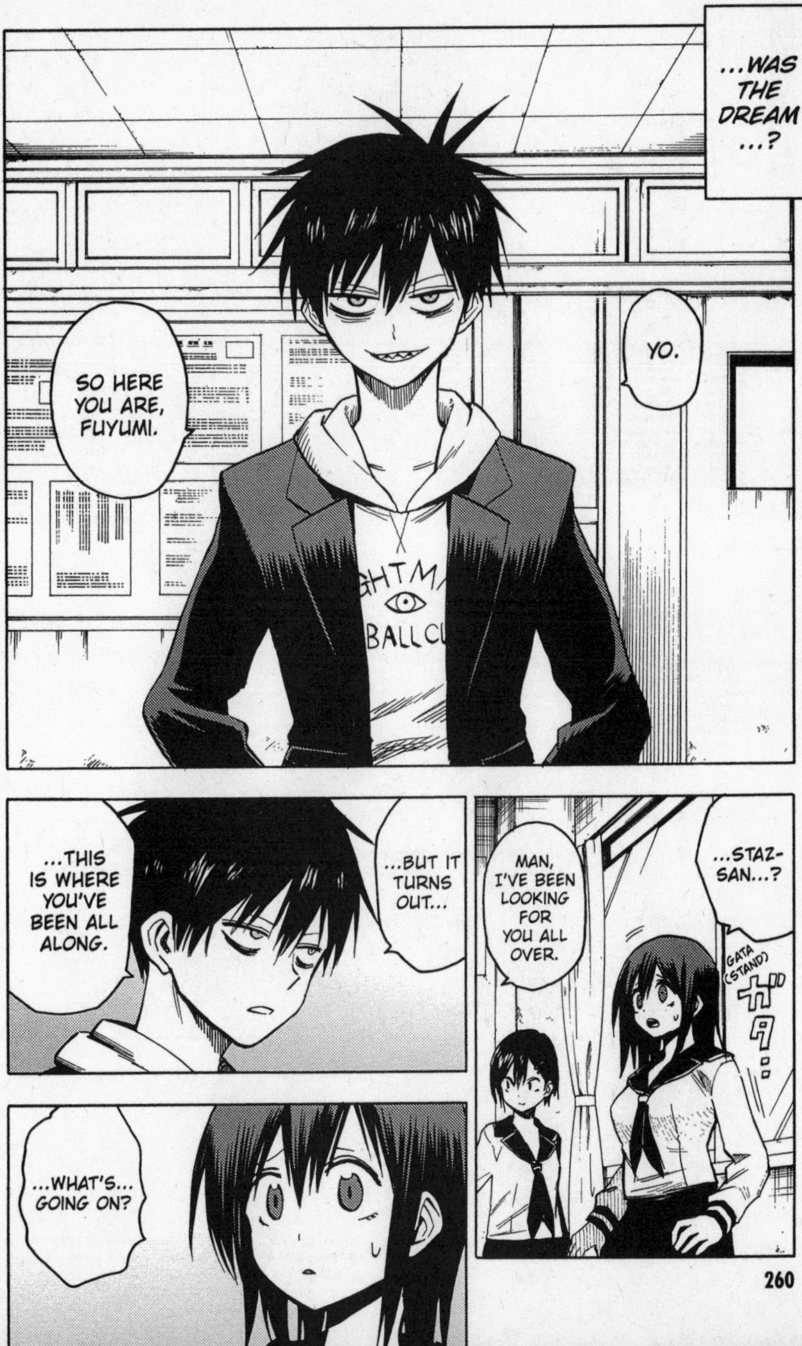
...WAS THE DREAM ...?
YO.
SO HERE YOU ARE, FUYUMI.
...STAZ-SAN...?
GATA (STAND)
ガタ
MAN, I'VE BEEN LOOKING FOR YOU ALL OVER.
...BUT IT TURNS OUT...
...THIS IS WHERE YOU'VE BEEN ALL ALONG.
...WHAT'S... GOING ON?

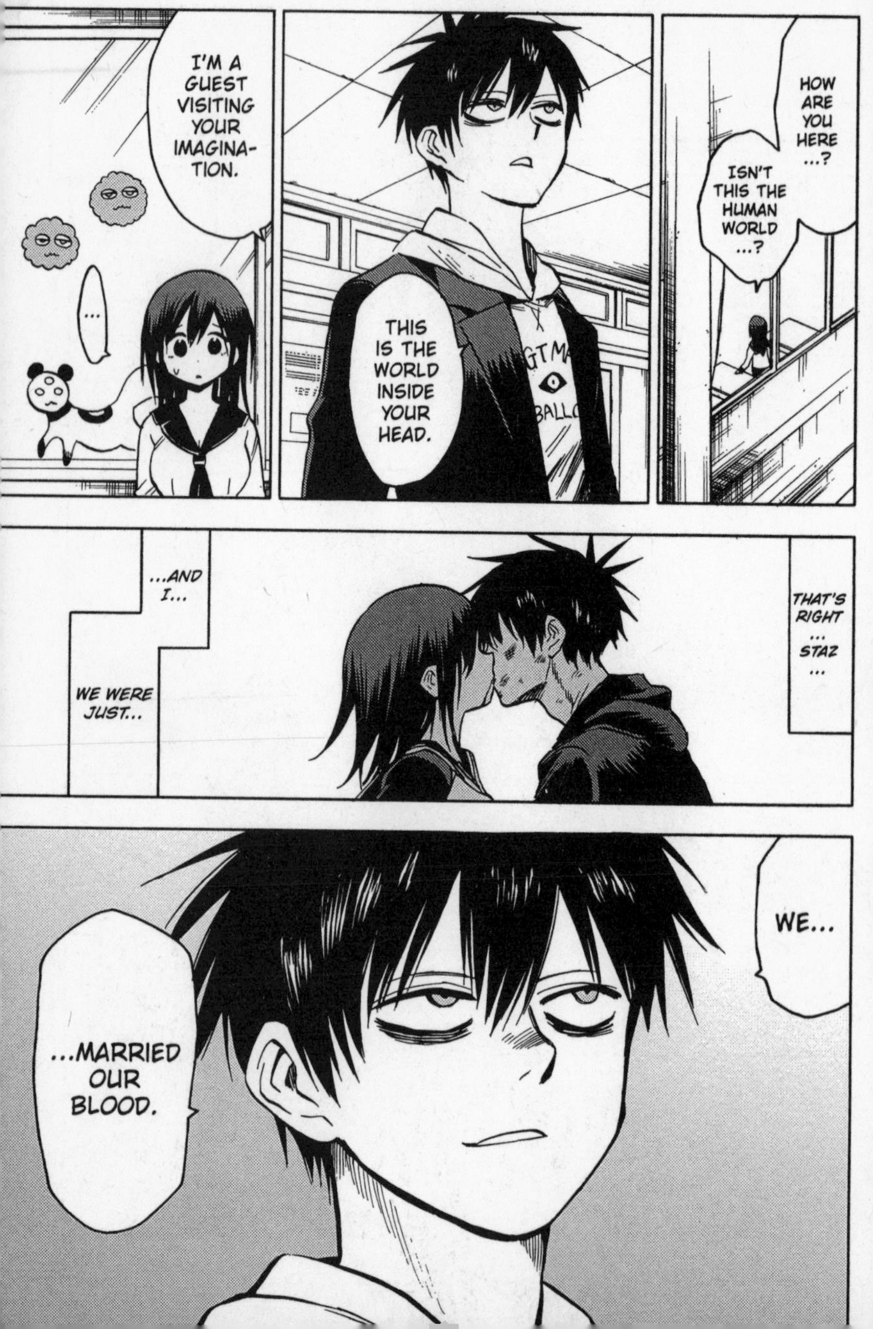
HOW ARE YOU HERE ...?
ISN'T THIS THE HUMAN WORLD ...?
THIS IS THE WORLD INSIDE YOUR HEAD.
I'M A GUEST VISITING YOUR IMAGINA-TION.
...
THAT'S RIGHT ... STAZ ...
...AND I...
WE WERE JUST...
WE...
...MARRIED OUR BLOOD.

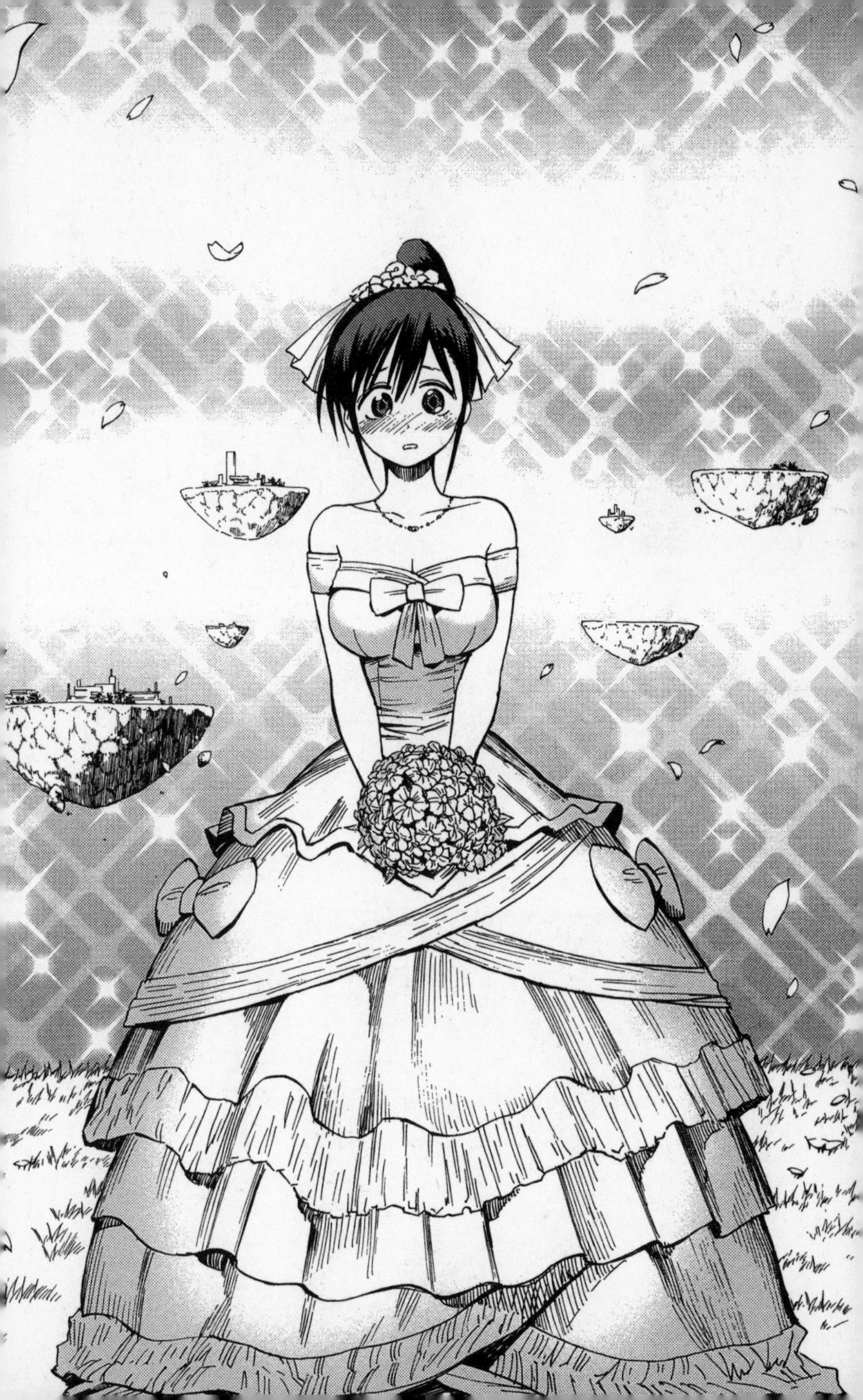

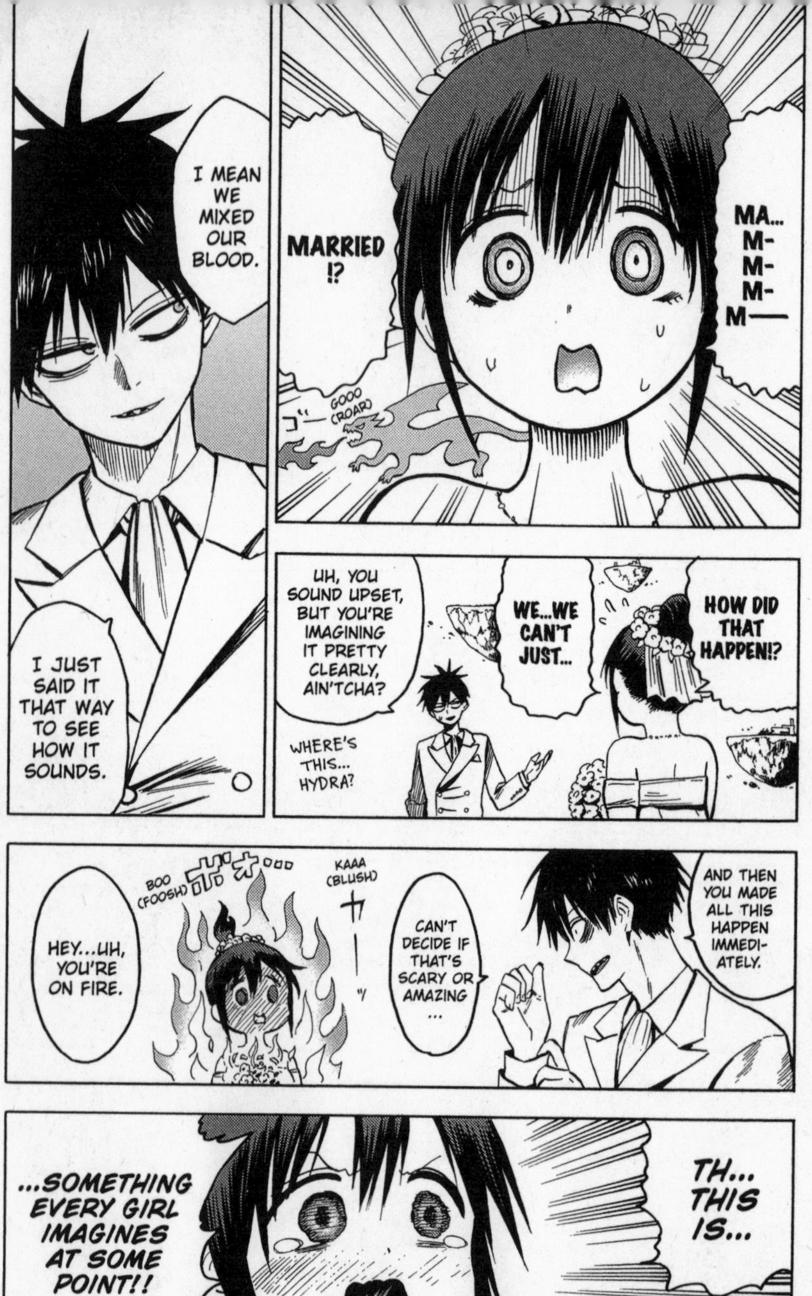
MA... M-M-M-M—
MARRIED!?
GOOO (ROAR)
HOW DID THAT HAPPEN!?
WE...WE CAN'T JUST...
UH, YOU SOUND UPSET, BUT YOU'RE IMAGINING IT PRETTY CLEARLY, AIN'TCHA?
WHERE'S THIS... HYDRA?
I MEAN WE MIXED OUR BLOOD.
I JUST SAID IT THAT WAY TO SEE HOW IT SOUNDS.
AND THEN YOU MADE ALL THIS HAPPEN IMMEDIATELY.
KAAA (BLUSH)
CAN'T DECIDE IF THAT'S SCARY OR AMAZING...
BOO (FOOSH)
HEY...UH, YOU'RE ON FIRE.
TH... THIS IS...
...SOMETHING EVERY GIRL IMAGINES AT SOME POINT!!

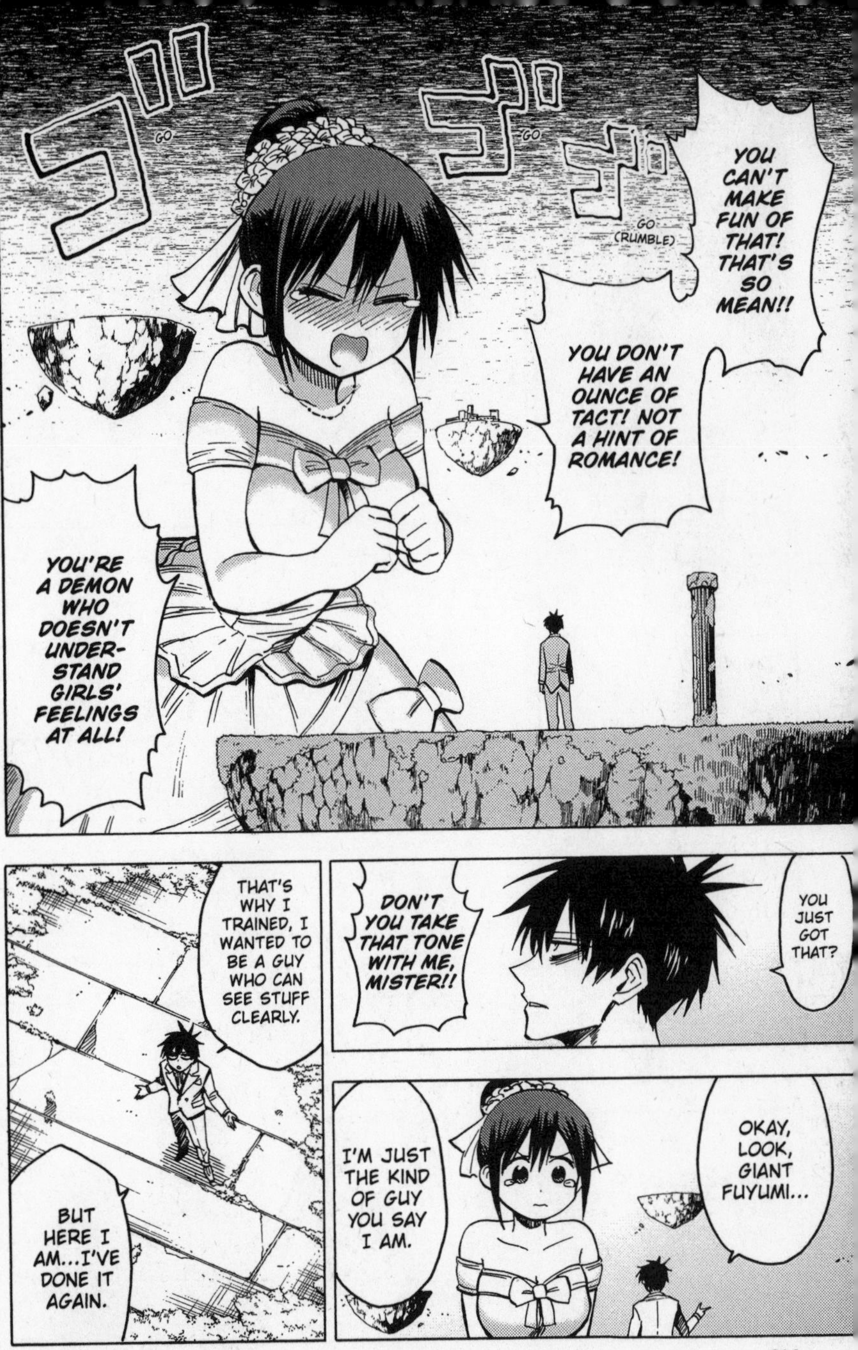
GO
GO
GO (RUMBLE)
YOU CAN'T MAKE FUN OF THAT! THAT'S SO MEAN!!
YOU DON'T HAVE AN OUNCE OF TACT! NOT A HINT OF ROMANCE!
YOU'RE A DEMON WHO DOESN'T UNDER-STAND GIRLS' FEELINGS AT ALL!
YOU JUST GOT THAT?
DON'T YOU TAKE THAT TONE WITH ME, MISTER!!
OKAY, LOOK, GIANT FUYUMI...
I'M JUST THE KIND OF GUY YOU SAY I AM.
THAT'S WHY I TRAINED, I WANTED TO BE A GUY WHO CAN SEE STUFF CLEARLY.
BUT HERE I AM...I'VE DONE IT AGAIN.

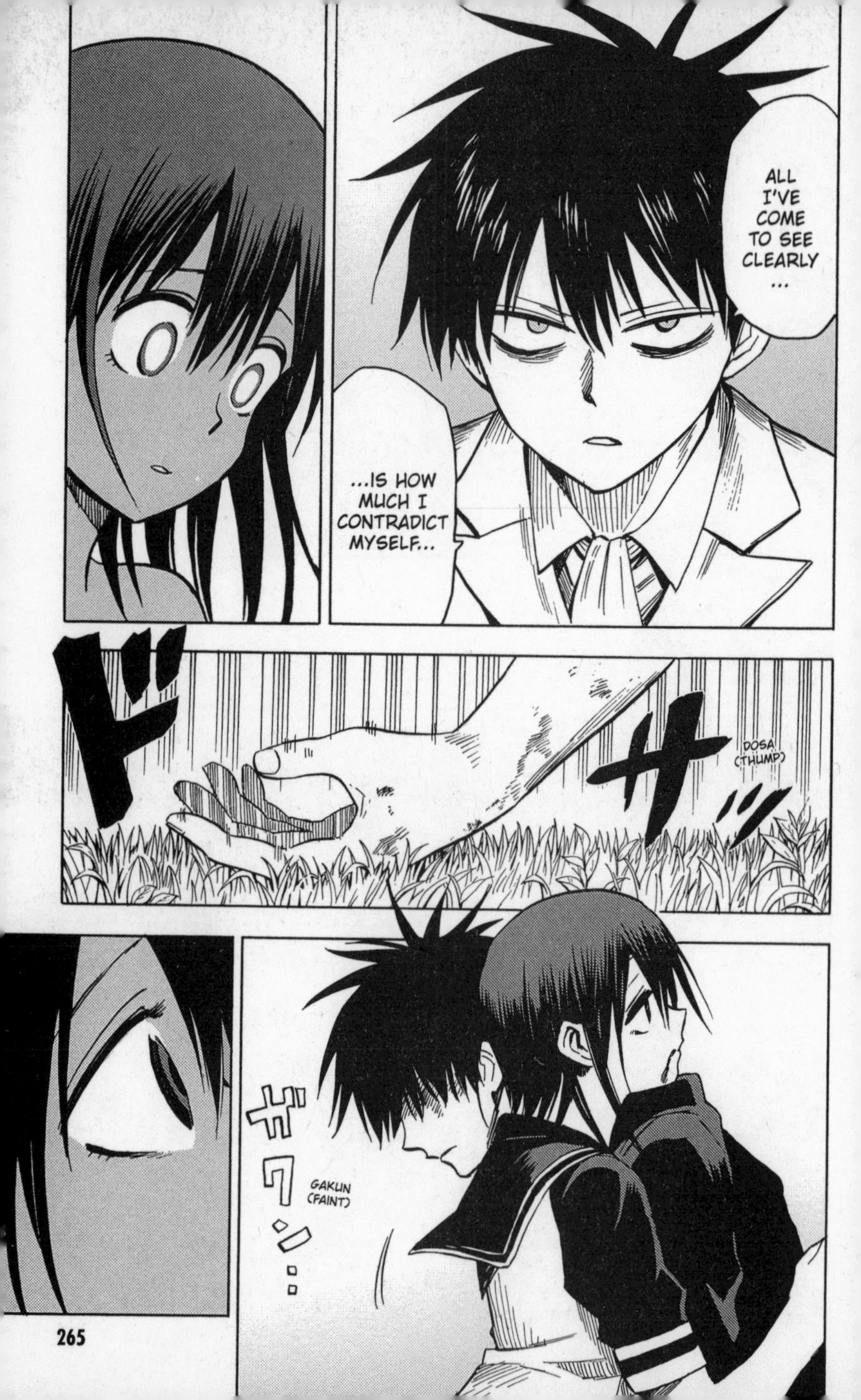
ALL I'VE COME TO SEE CLEARLY ...
...IS HOW MUCH I CONTRADICT MYSELF...
ドサッ
DOSA (THUMP)
ガクン
GAKUN (FAINT)

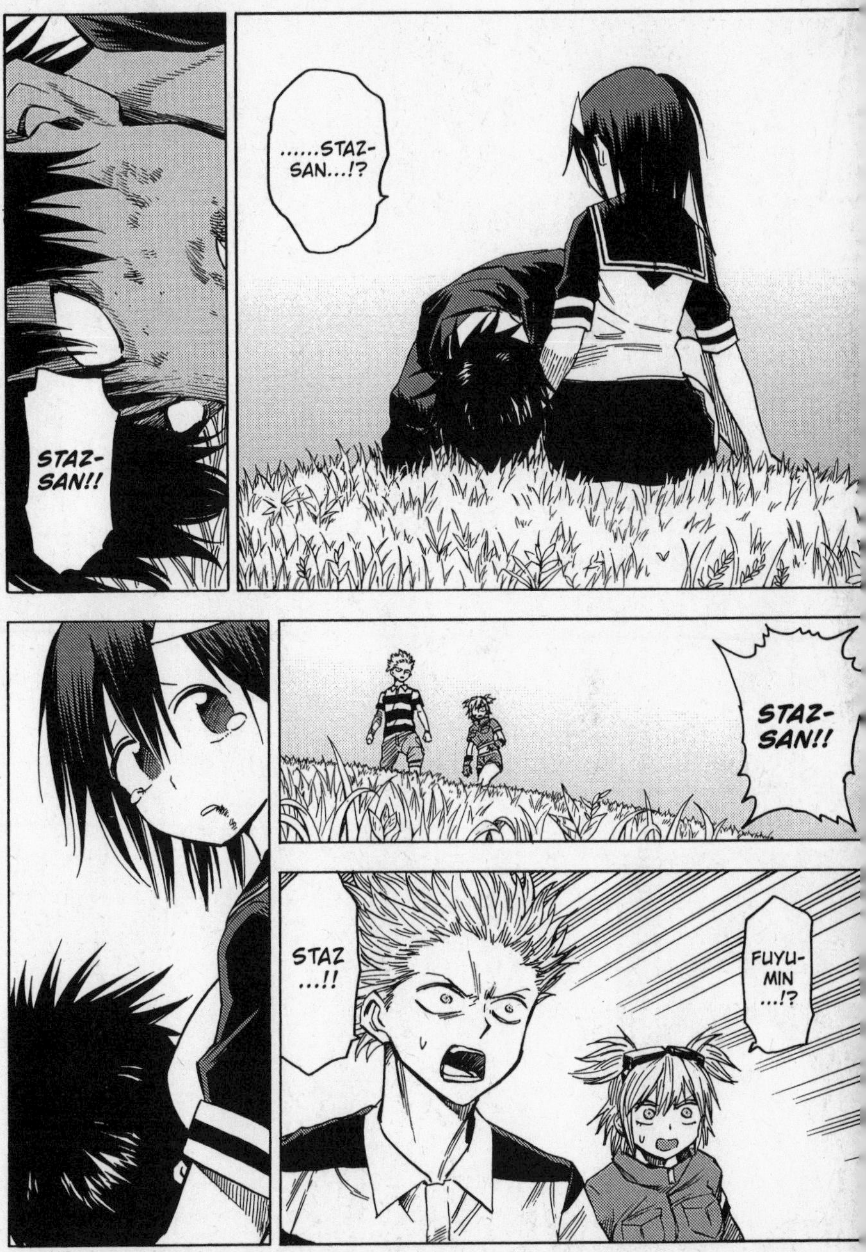
......STAZ-SAN...!?
STAZ-SAN!!
STAZ-SAN!!
FUYU-MIN ...!?
STAZ ...!!

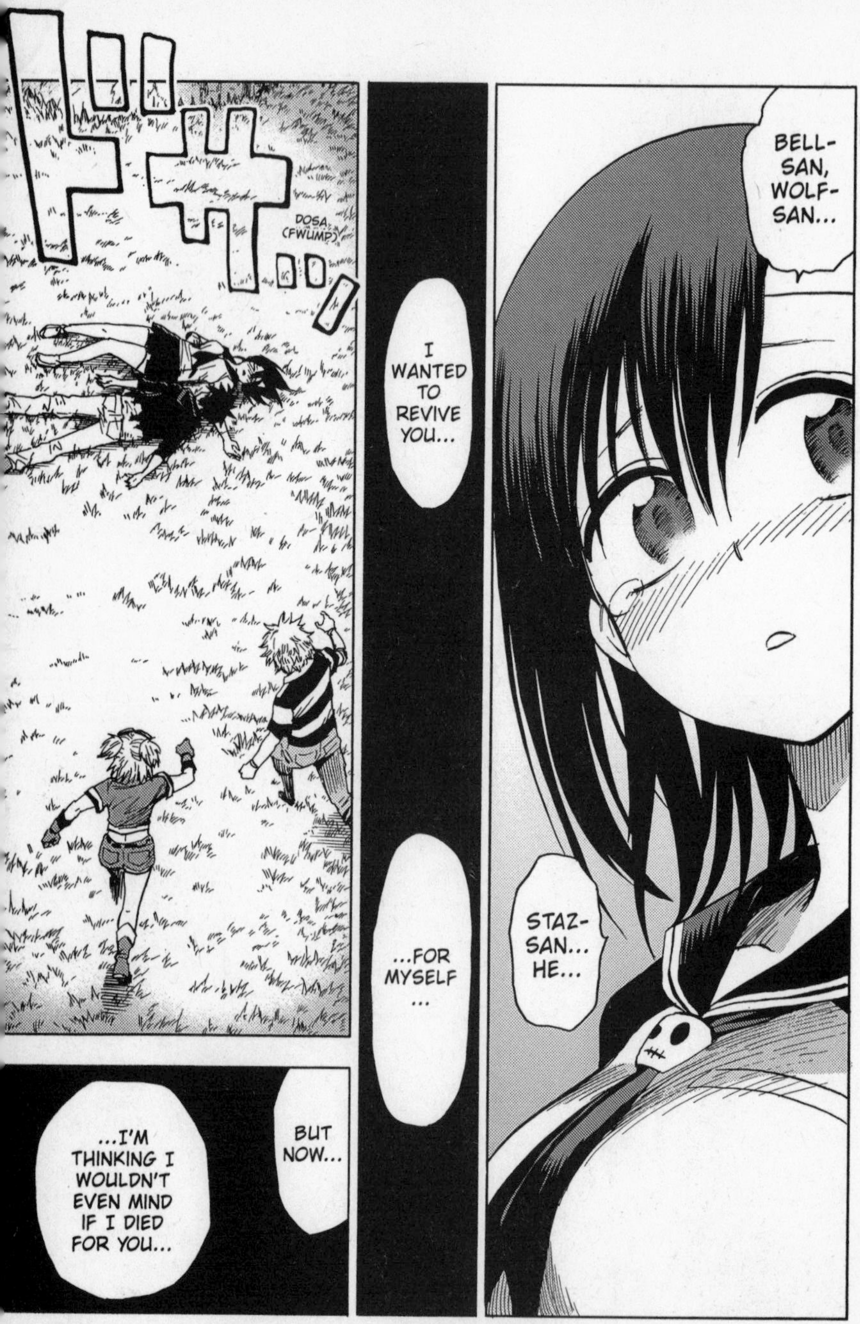
BELL-SAN, WOLF-SAN...
STAZ-SAN... HE...
I WANTED TO REVIVE YOU...
...FOR MYSELF...
DOSA (FWUMP)
BUT NOW...
...I'M THINKING I WOULDN'T EVEN MIND IF I DIED FOR YOU...

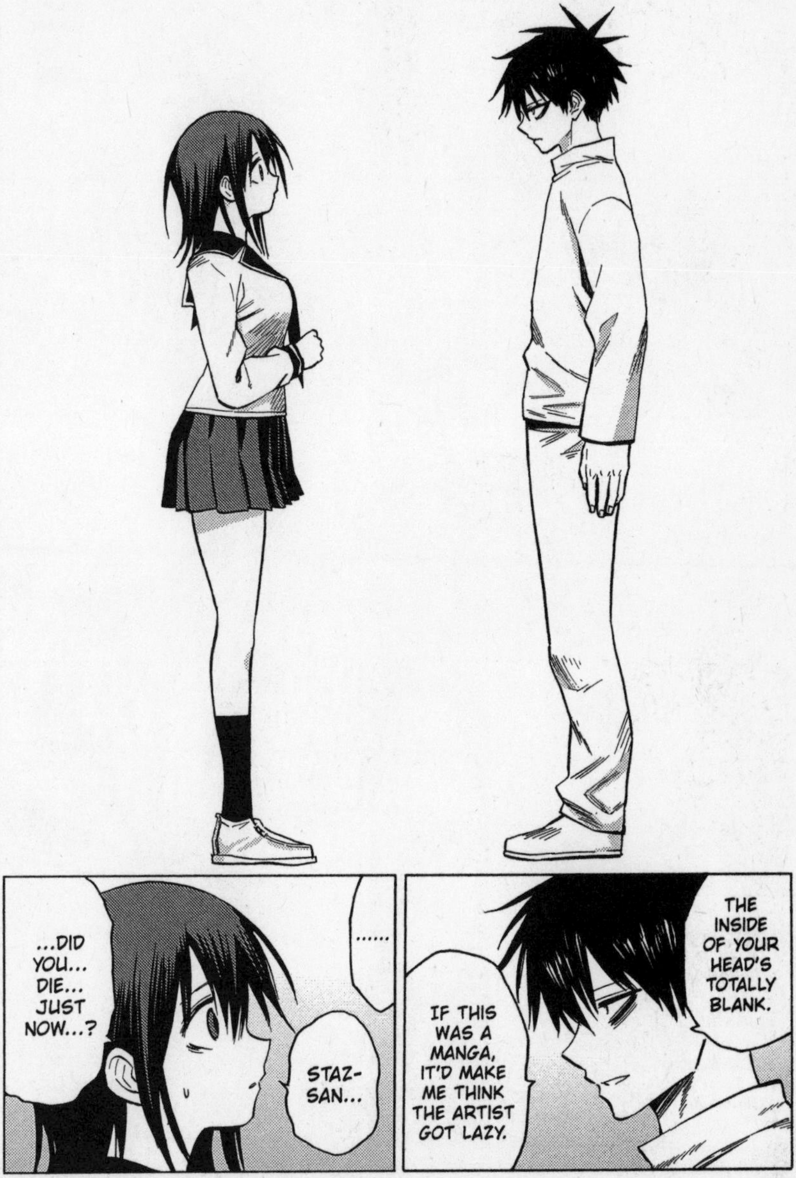
THE INSIDE OF YOUR HEAD'S TOTALLY BLANK.
IF THIS WAS A MANGA, IT'D MAKE ME THINK THE ARTIST GOT LAZY.
......
...DID YOU... DIE... JUST NOW...?
STAZ-SAN...

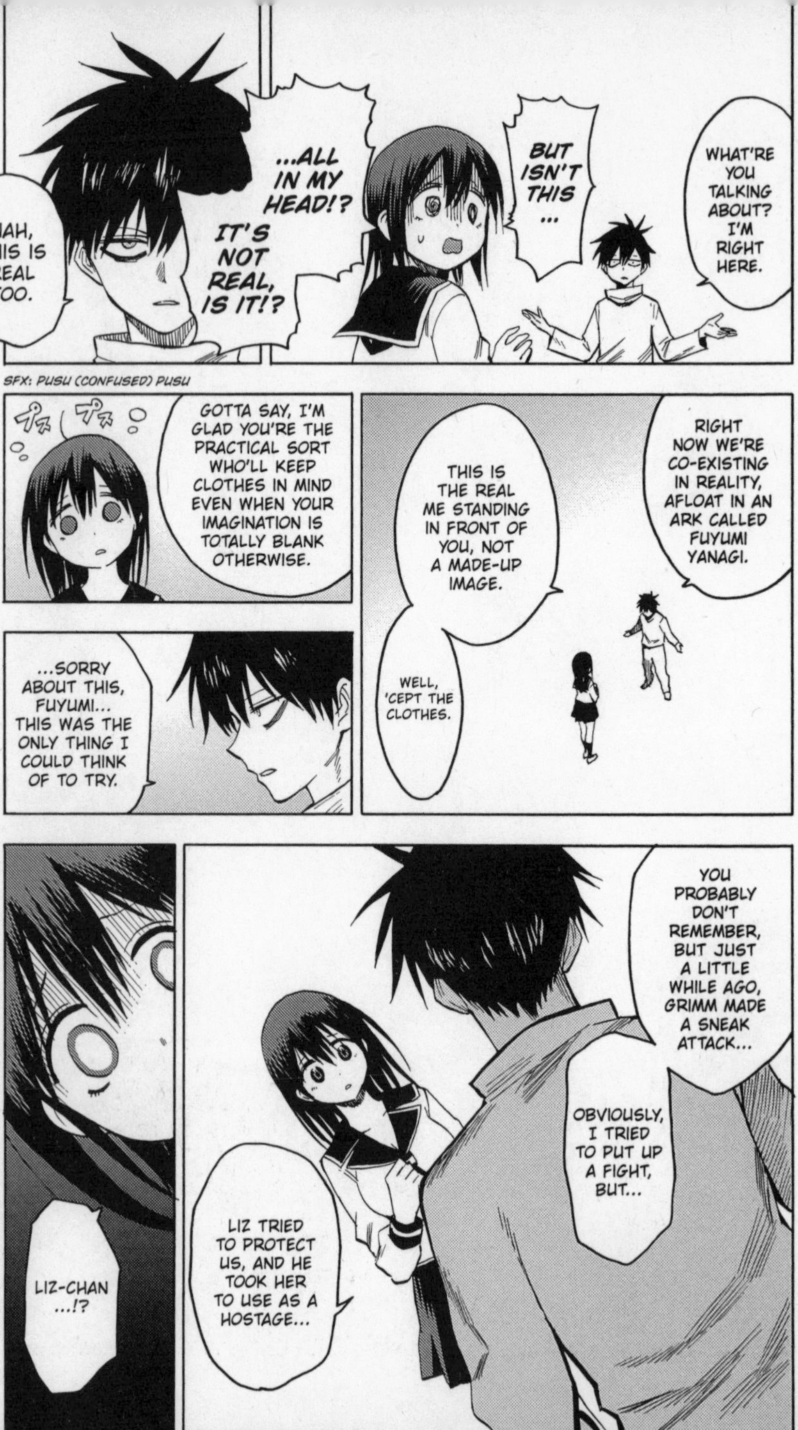
WHAT'RE YOU TALKING ABOUT? I'M RIGHT HERE.
BUT ISN'T THIS ...
...ALL IN MY HEAD!?
IT'S NOT REAL, IS IT!?
NAH, THIS IS REAL TOO.
SFX: PUSU (CONFUSED) PUSU
RIGHT NOW WE'RE CO-EXISTING IN REALITY, AFLOAT IN AN ARK CALLED FUYUMI YANAGI.
THIS IS THE REAL ME STANDING IN FRONT OF YOU, NOT A MADE-UP IMAGE.
WELL, 'CEPT THE CLOTHES.
GOTTA SAY, I'M GLAD YOU'RE THE PRACTICAL SORT WHO'LL KEEP CLOTHES IN MIND EVEN WHEN YOUR IMAGINATION IS TOTALLY BLANK OTHERWISE.
...SORRY ABOUT THIS, FUYUMI... THIS WAS THE ONLY THING I COULD THINK OF TO TRY.
YOU PROBABLY DON'T REMEMBER, BUT JUST A LITTLE WHILE AGO, GRIMM MADE A SNEAK ATTACK...
OBVIOUSLY, I TRIED TO PUT UP A FIGHT, BUT...
LIZ TRIED TO PROTECT US, AND HE TOOK HER TO USE AS A HOSTAGE...
LIZ-CHAN ...!?

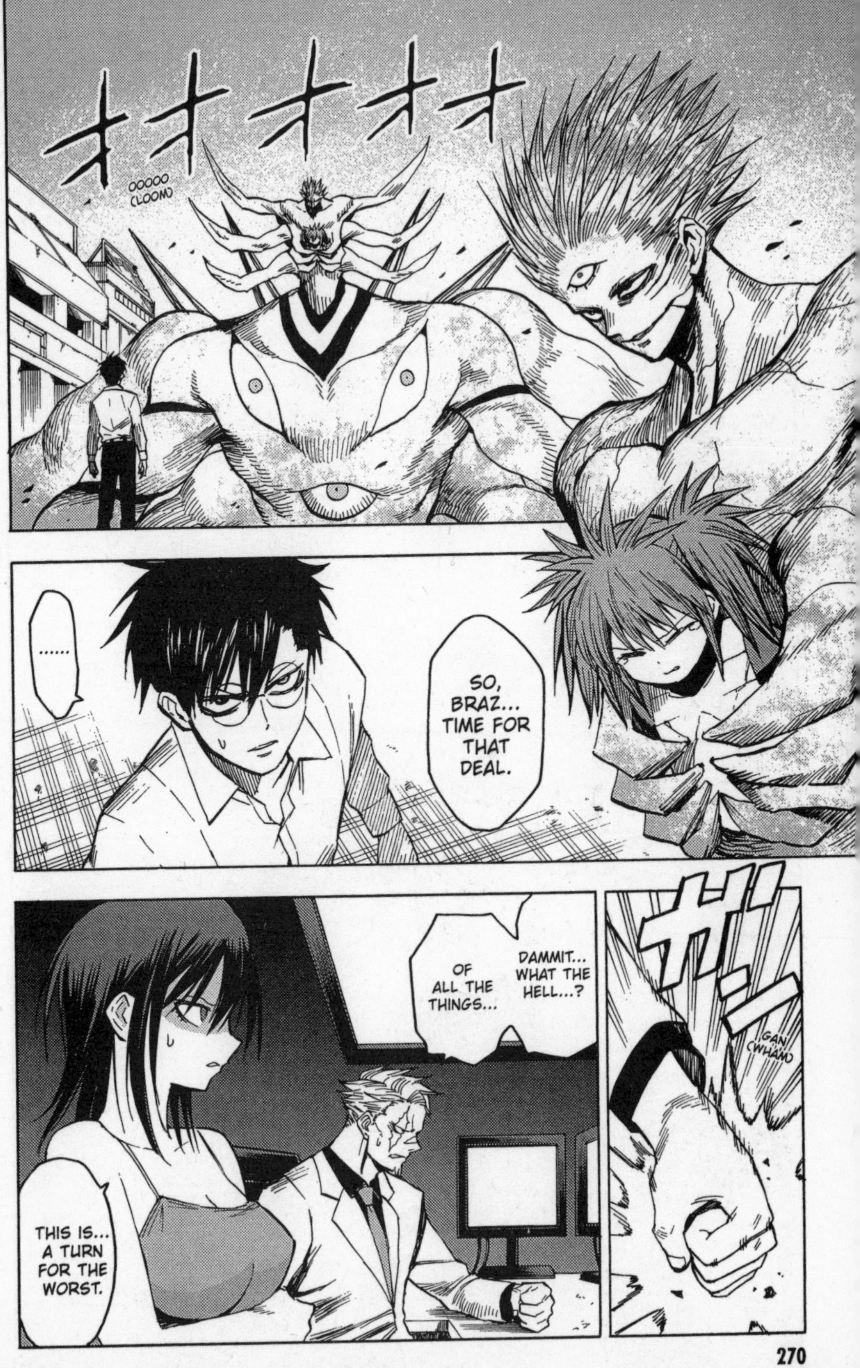

OOOOO (LOOM)
SO, BRAZ... TIME FOR THAT DEAL.
......
DAMMIT... WHAT THE HELL...?
OF ALL THE THINGS...
GAN (WHAM)
THIS IS... A TURN FOR THE WORST.

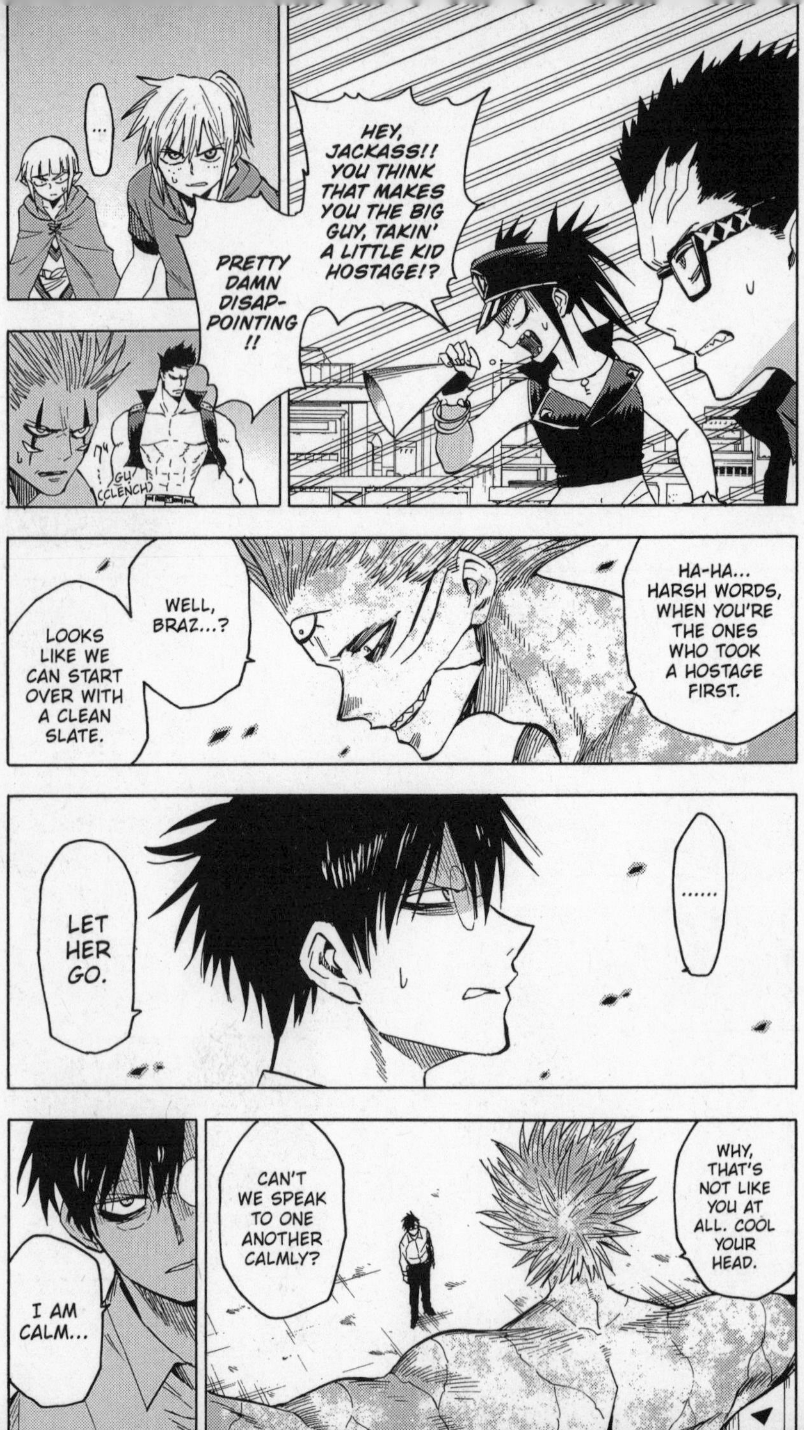
HEY, JACKASS!! YOU THINK THAT MAKES YOU THE BIG GUY, TAKIN' A LITTLE KID HOSTAGE!?
PRETTY DAMN DISAP-POINTING !!
...
GU (CLENCH)
HA-HA... HARSH WORDS, WHEN YOU'RE THE ONES WHO TOOK A HOSTAGE FIRST.
WELL, BRAZ...?
LOOKS LIKE WE CAN START OVER WITH A CLEAN SLATE.
......
LET HER GO.
WHY, THAT'S NOT LIKE YOU AT ALL. COOL YOUR HEAD.
CAN'T WE SPEAK TO ONE ANOTHER CALMLY?
I AM CALM...

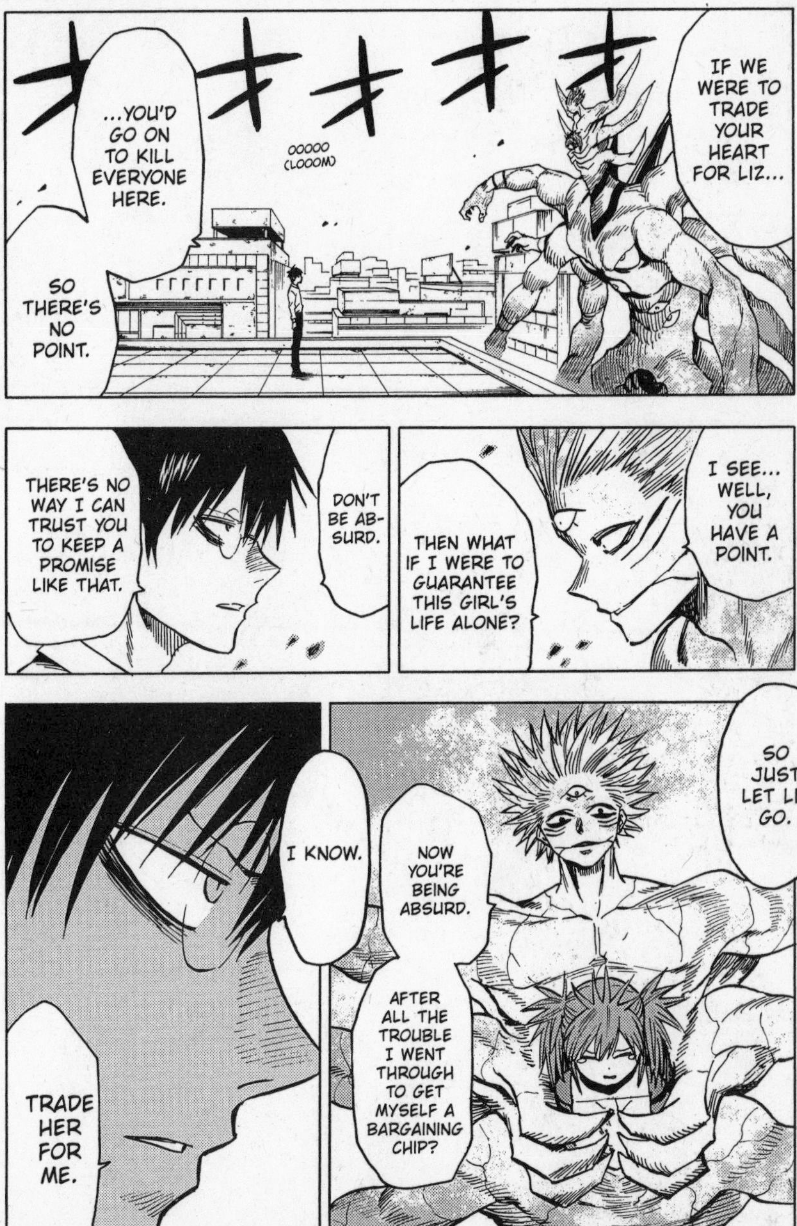
IF WE WERE TO TRADE YOUR HEART FOR LIZ...
オオオオオ
OOOOO (LOOOM)
...YOU'D GO ON TO KILL EVERYONE HERE.
SO THERE'S NO POINT.
I SEE... WELL, YOU HAVE A POINT.
THEN WHAT IF I WERE TO GUARANTEE THIS GIRL'S LIFE ALONE?
DON'T BE AB-SURD.
THERE'S NO WAY I CAN TRUST YOU TO KEEP A PROMISE LIKE THAT.
SO JUST LET LIZ GO.
NOW YOU'RE BEING ABSURD.
AFTER ALL THE TROUBLE I WENT THROUGH TO GET MYSELF A BARGAINING CHIP?
I KNOW.
TRADE HER FOR ME.

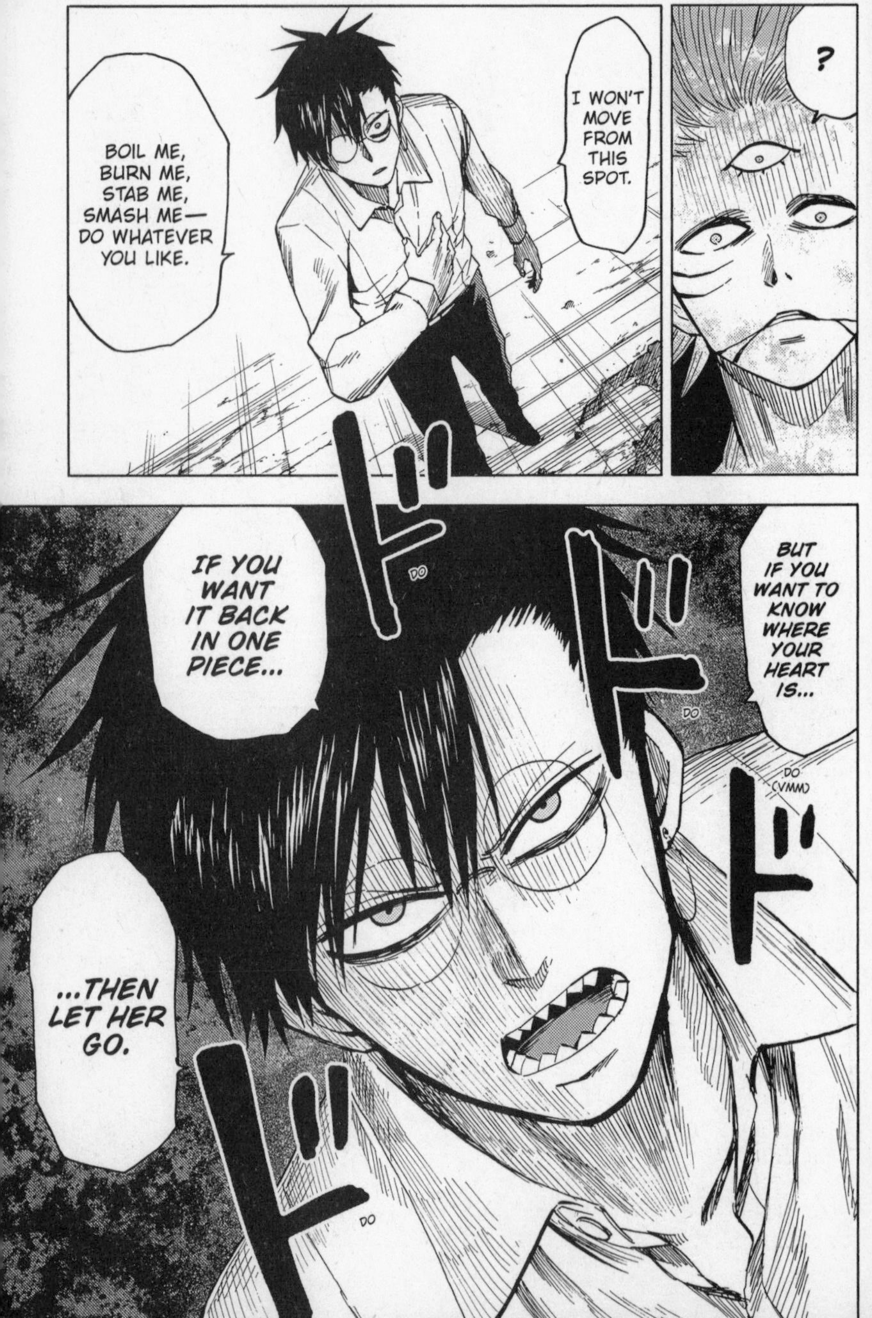
?
I WON'T MOVE FROM THIS SPOT.
BOIL ME, BURN ME, STAB ME, SMASH ME—DO WHATEVER YOU LIKE.
BUT IF YOU WANT TO KNOW WHERE YOUR HEART IS...
DO
DO
IF YOU WANT IT BACK IN ONE PIECE...
DO (VMM)
...THEN LET HER GO.
DO

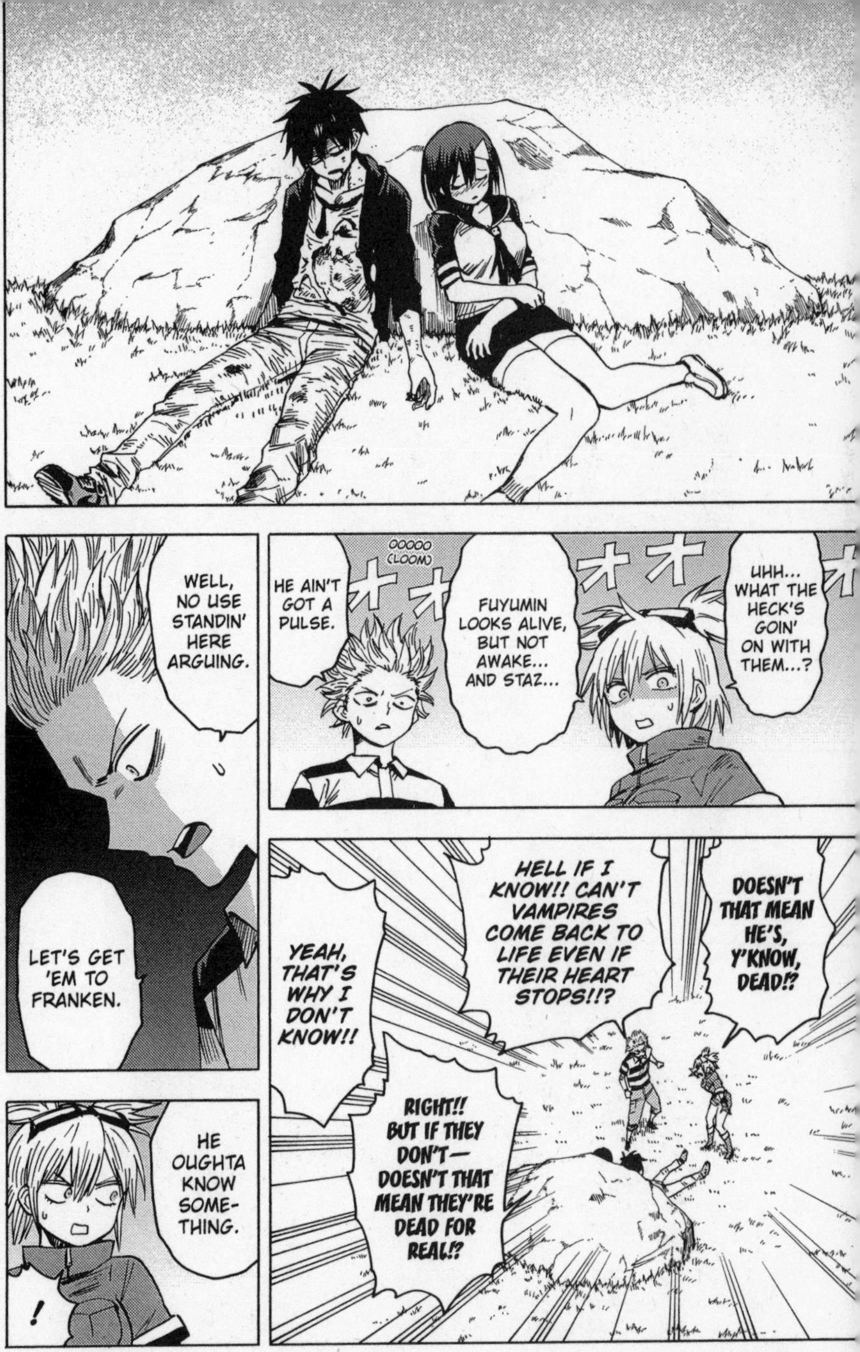
UHH... WHAT THE HECK'S GOIN' ON WITH THEM...?
OOOOO (LOOM)
FUYUMIN LOOKS ALIVE, BUT NOT AWAKE... AND STAZ...
HE AIN'T GOT A PULSE.
DOESN'T THAT MEAN HE'S, Y'KNOW, DEAD!?
HELL IF I KNOW!! CAN'T VAMPIRES COME BACK TO LIFE EVEN IF THEIR HEART STOPS!!?
YEAH, THAT'S WHY I DON'T KNOW!!
RIGHT!! BUT IF THEY DON'T—DOESN'T THAT MEAN THEY'RE DEAD FOR REAL!?
WELL, NO USE STANDIN' HERE ARGUING.
LET'S GET 'EM TO FRANKEN.
HE OUGHTA KNOW SOMETHING.
!

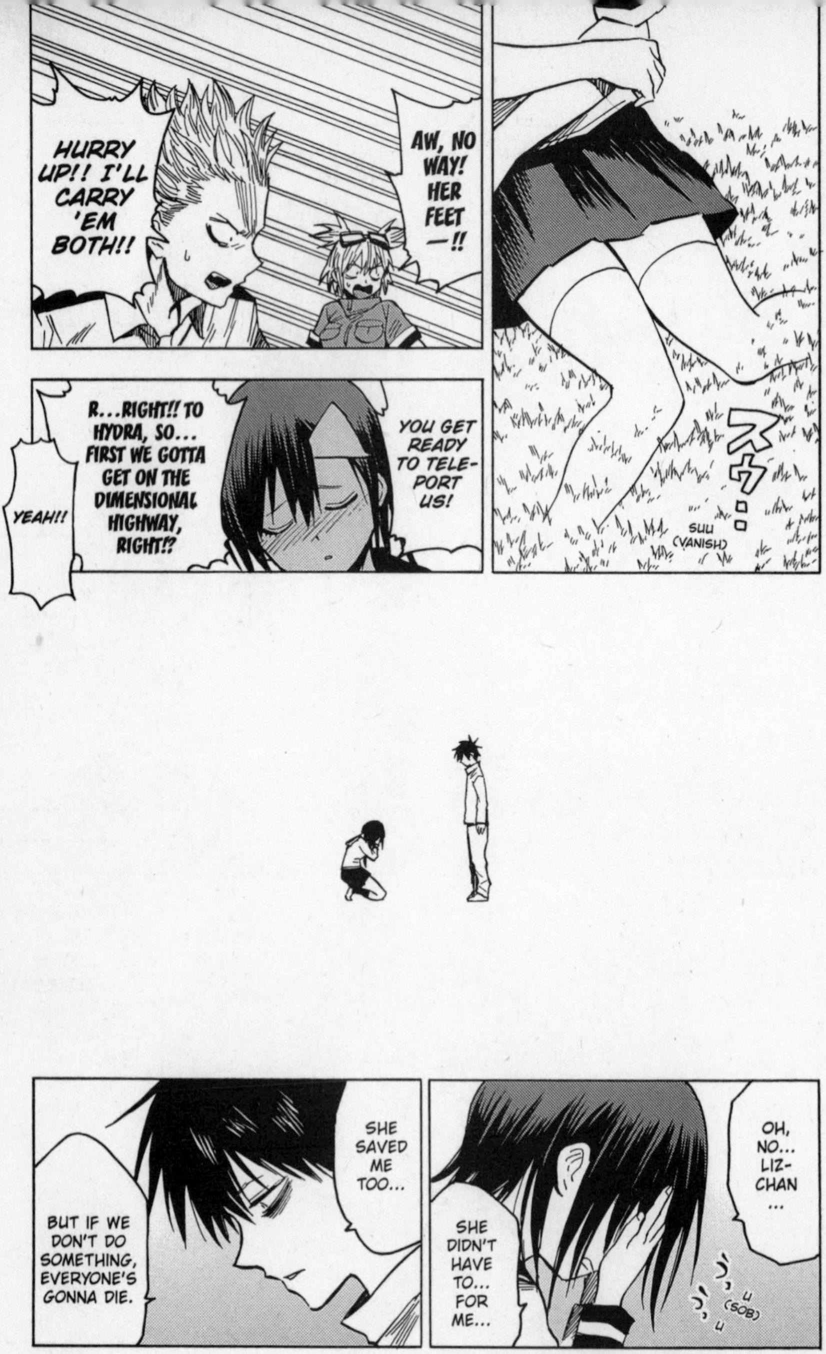
SUU (VANISH)
AW, NO WAY! HER FEET—!!
HURRY UP!! I'LL CARRY 'EM BOTH!!
YOU GET READY TO TELEPORT US!
R...RIGHT!! TO HYDRA, SO... FIRST WE GOTTA GET ON THE DIMENSIONAL HIGHWAY, RIGHT!?
YEAH!!
OH, NO... LIZ-CHAN...
SHE DIDN'T HAVE TO... FOR ME...
(SOB)
SHE SAVED ME TOO...
BUT IF WE DON'T DO SOMETHING, EVERYONE'S GONNA DIE.

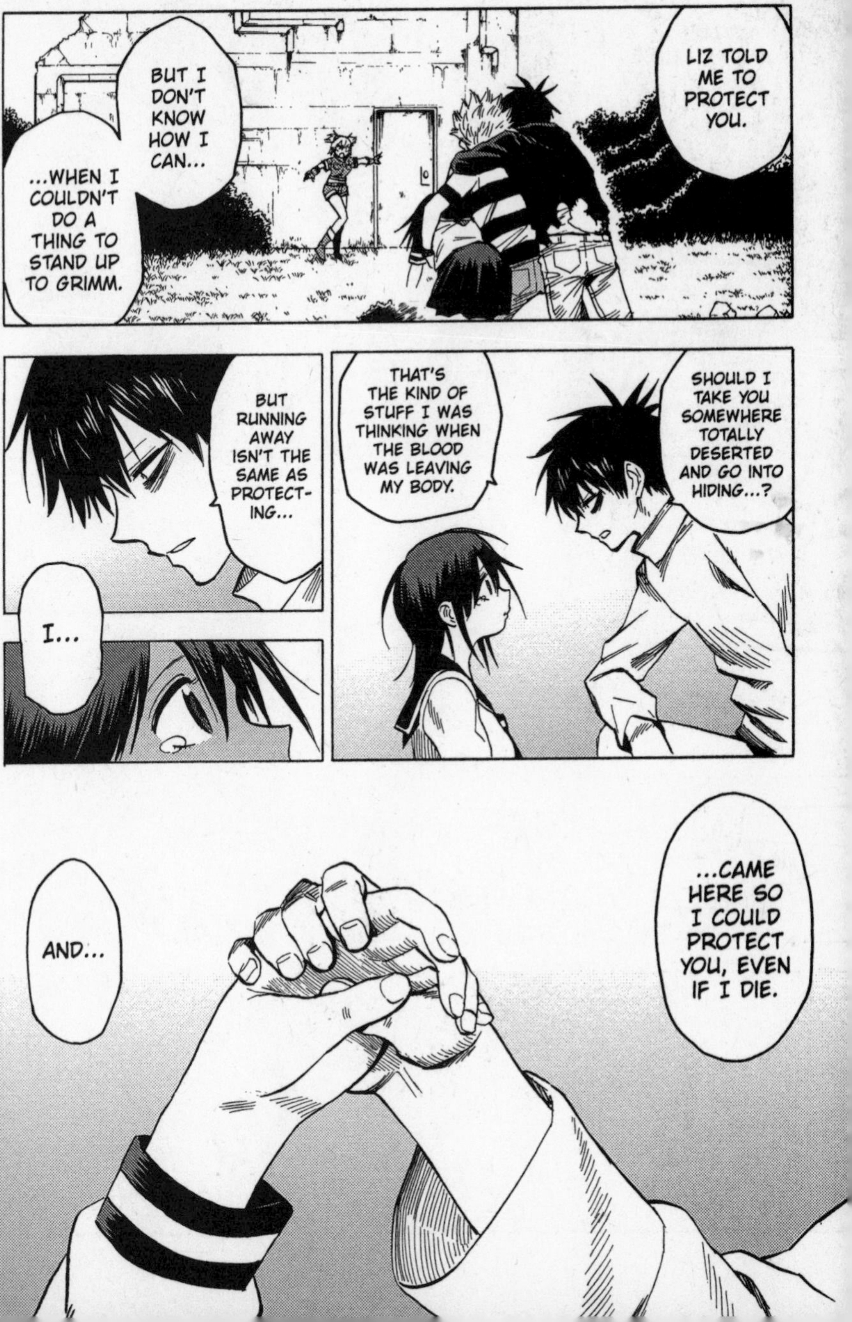
LIZ TOLD ME TO PROTECT YOU.
BUT I DON'T KNOW HOW I CAN...
...WHEN I COULDN'T DO A THING TO STAND UP TO GRIMM.
SHOULD I TAKE YOU SOMEWHERE TOTALLY DESERTED AND GO INTO HIDING...?
THAT'S THE KIND OF STUFF I WAS THINKING WHEN THE BLOOD WAS LEAVING MY BODY.
BUT RUNNING AWAY ISN'T THE SAME AS PROTECTING...
I...
...CAME HERE SO I COULD PROTECT YOU, EVEN IF I DIE.
AND...

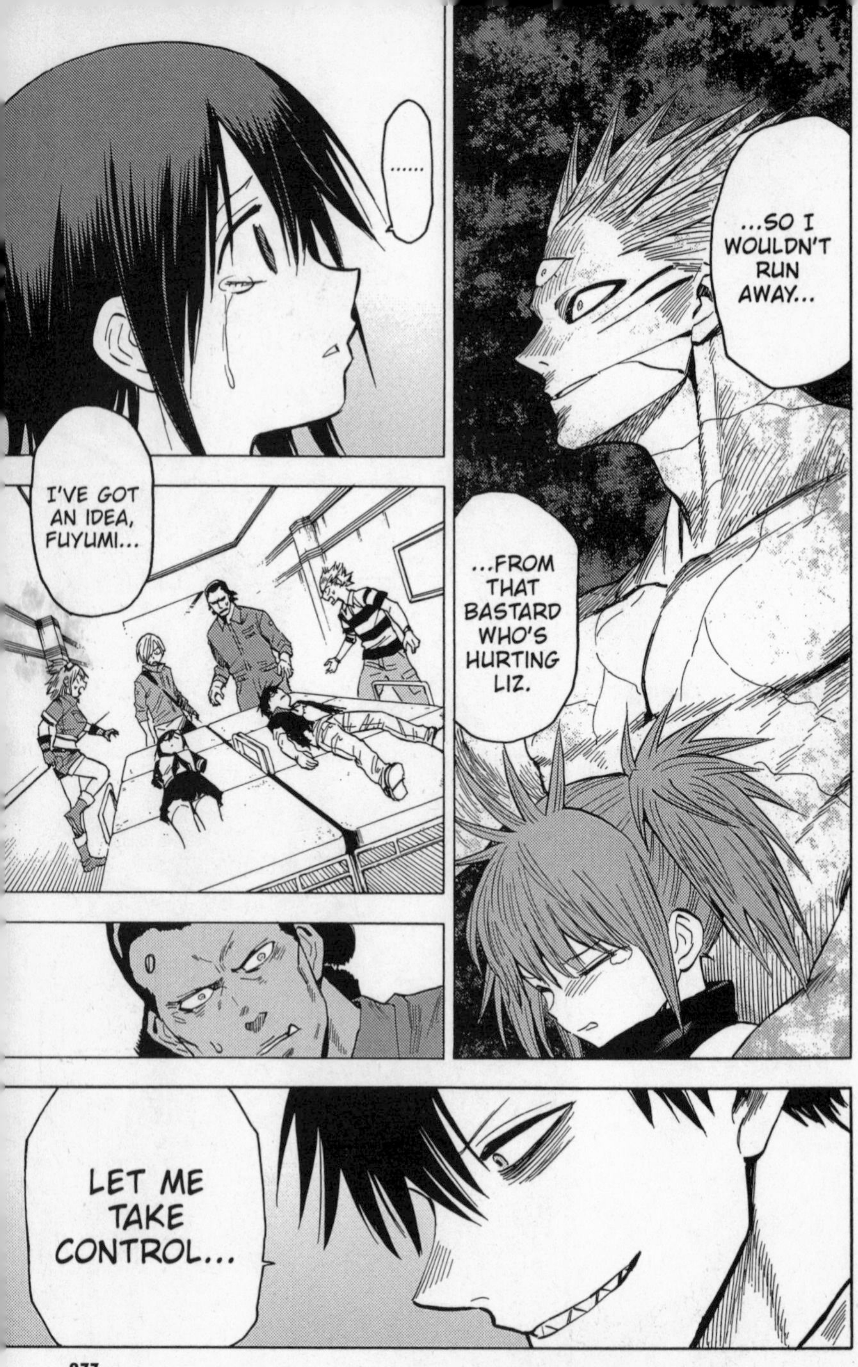
...SO I WOULDN'T RUN AWAY...
...FROM THAT BASTARD WHO'S HURTING LIZ.
......
I'VE GOT AN IDEA, FUYUMI...
LET ME TAKE CONTROL...

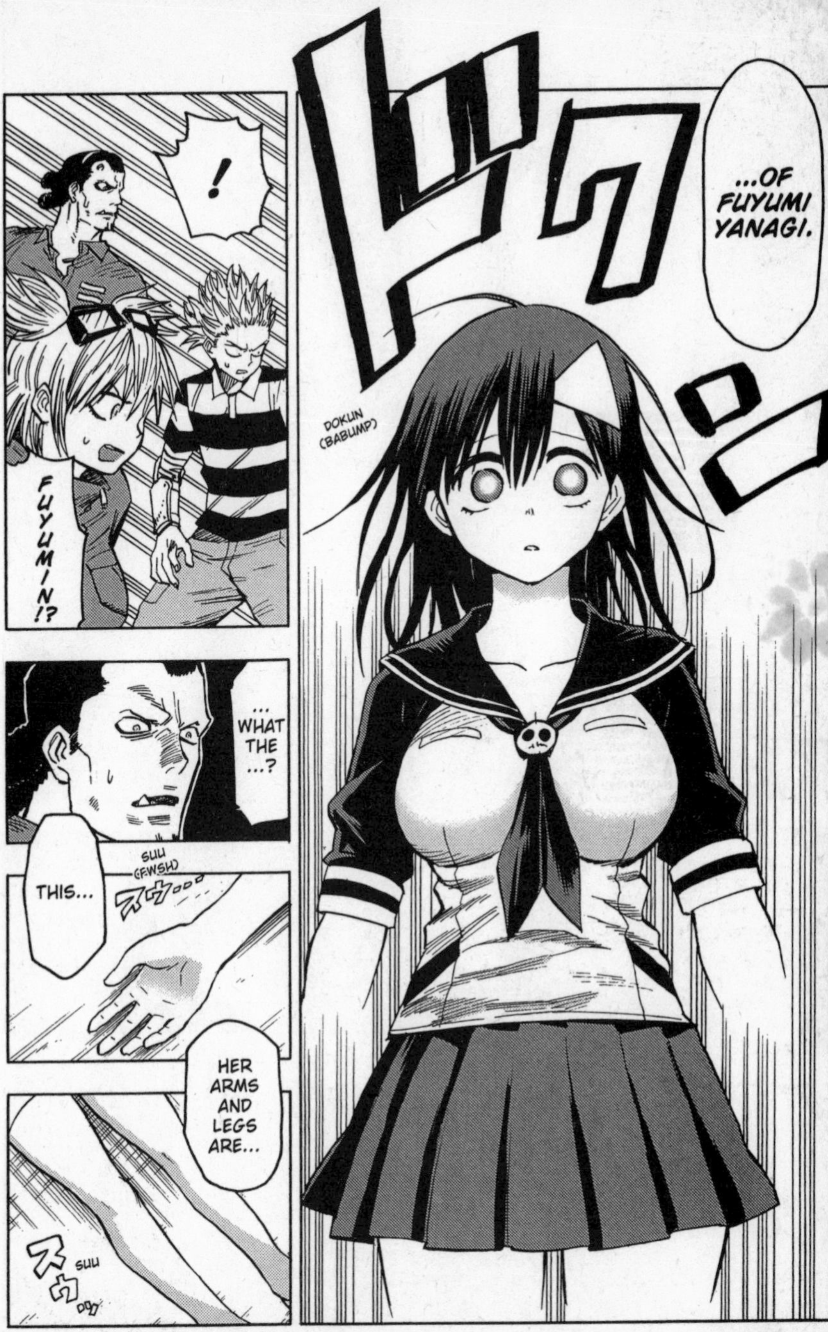
...OF FUYUMI YANAGI.
ドクン
DOKUN (BABUMP)
!
FUYUMIN!?
... WHAT THE ...?
THIS...
スウ...
SUU (FWSH)
HER ARMS AND LEGS ARE...
スウ
SUU

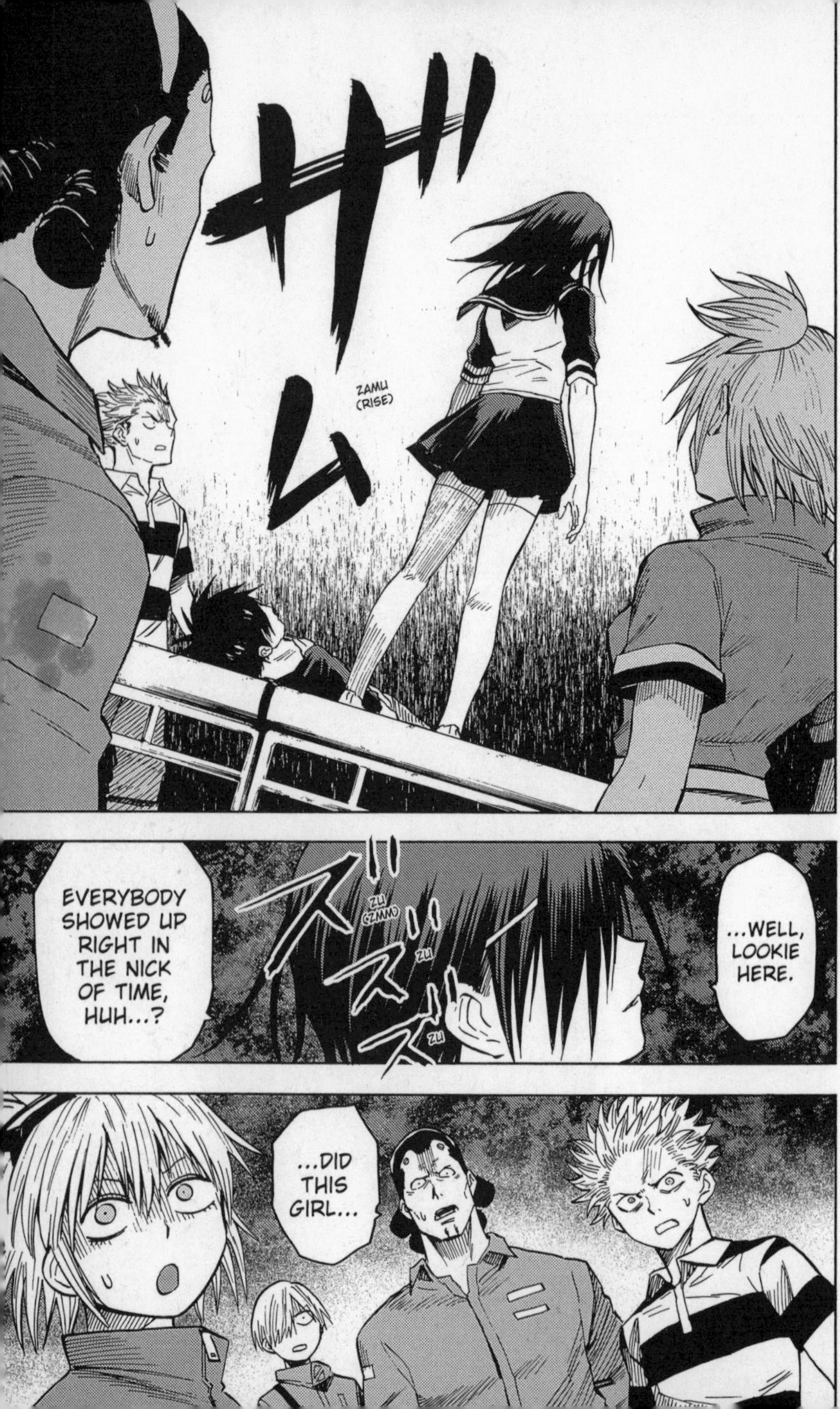
ZAMU (RISE)
...WELL, LOOKIE HERE.
ZU (ZMM)
ZU
ZU
EVERYBODY SHOWED UP RIGHT IN THE NICK OF TIME, HUH...?
...DID THIS GIRL...

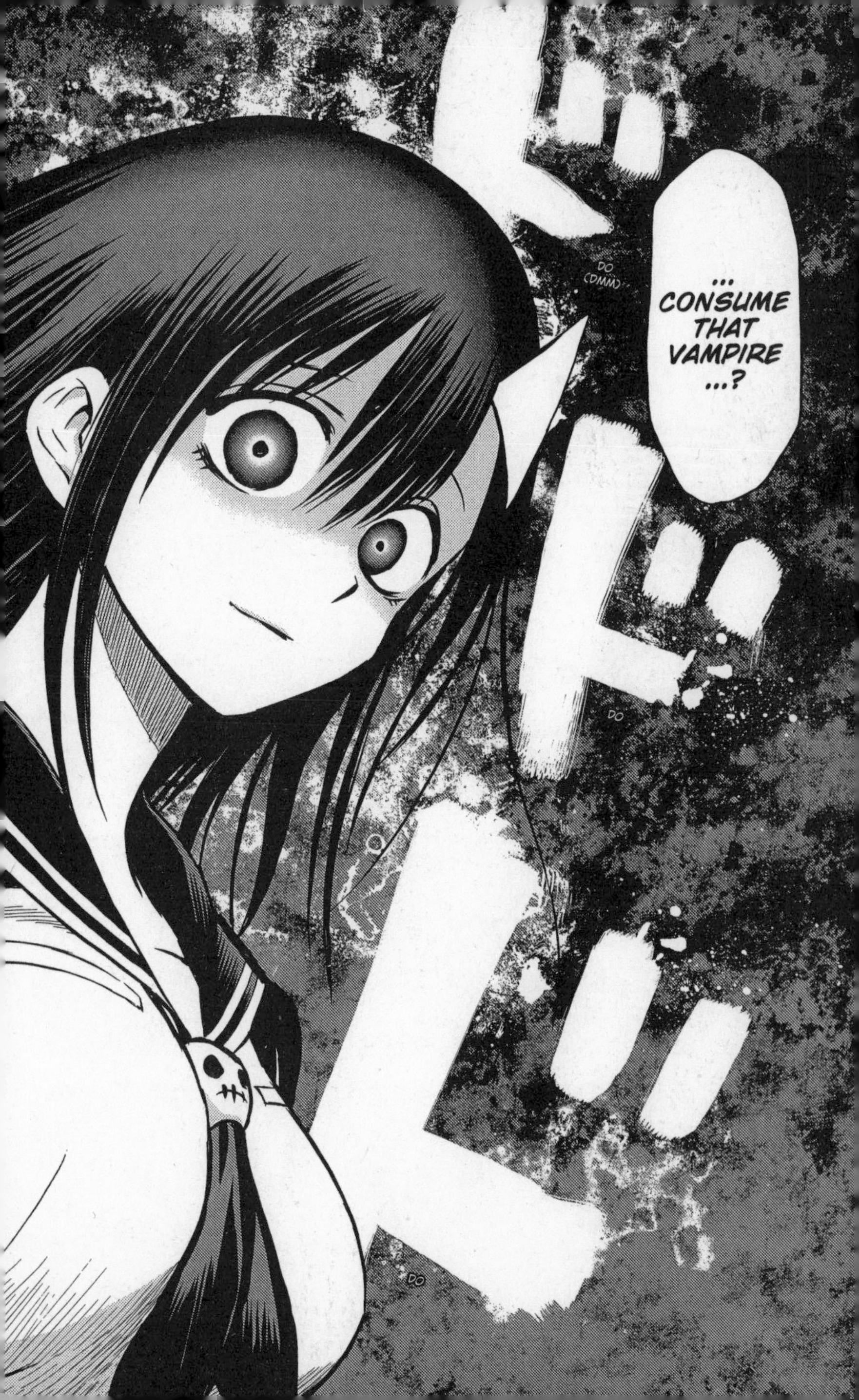

DO (DMM)
... CONSUME THAT VAMPIRE ...?
DO
DO

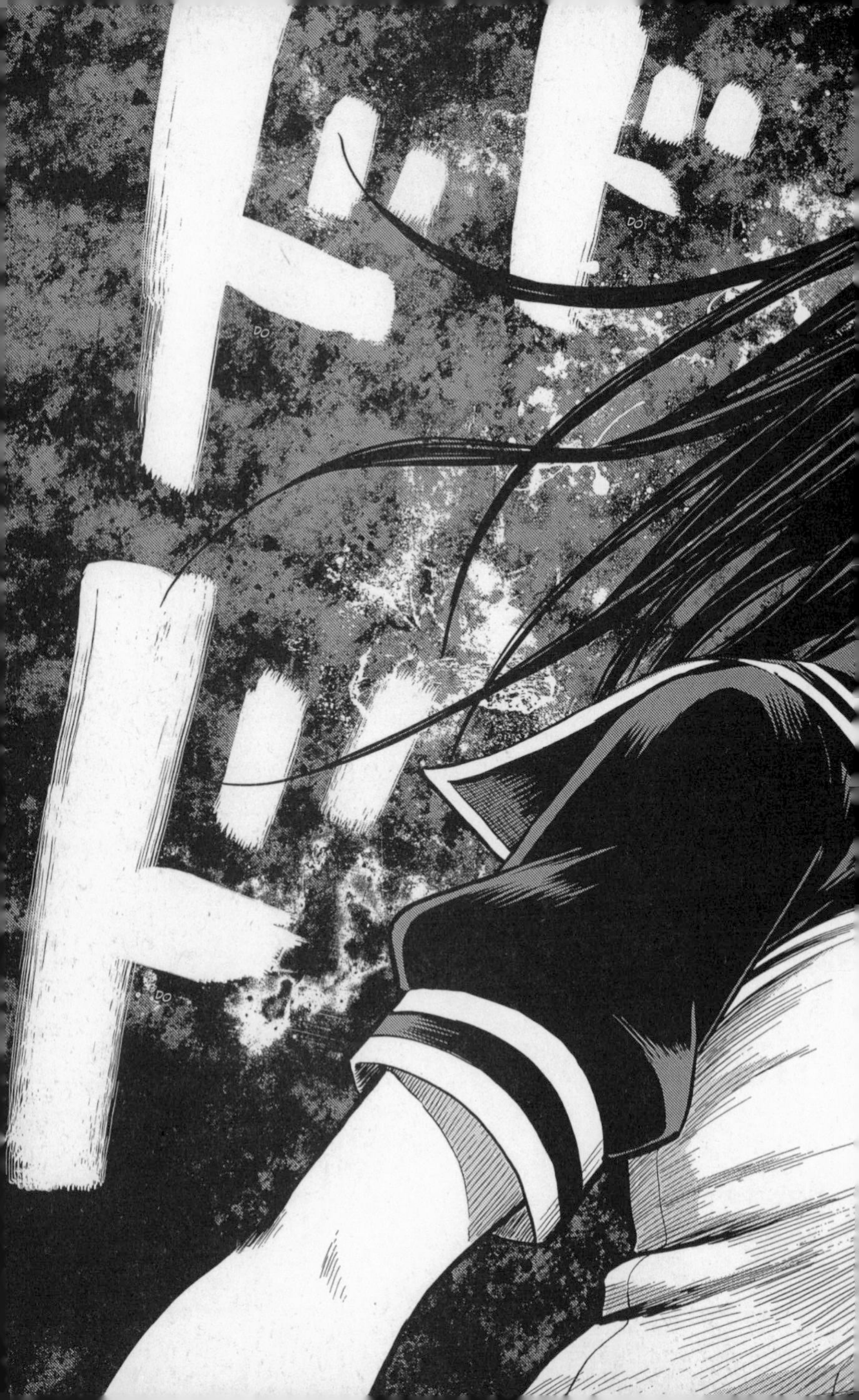
ド
DO
ド
DO
ド
DO

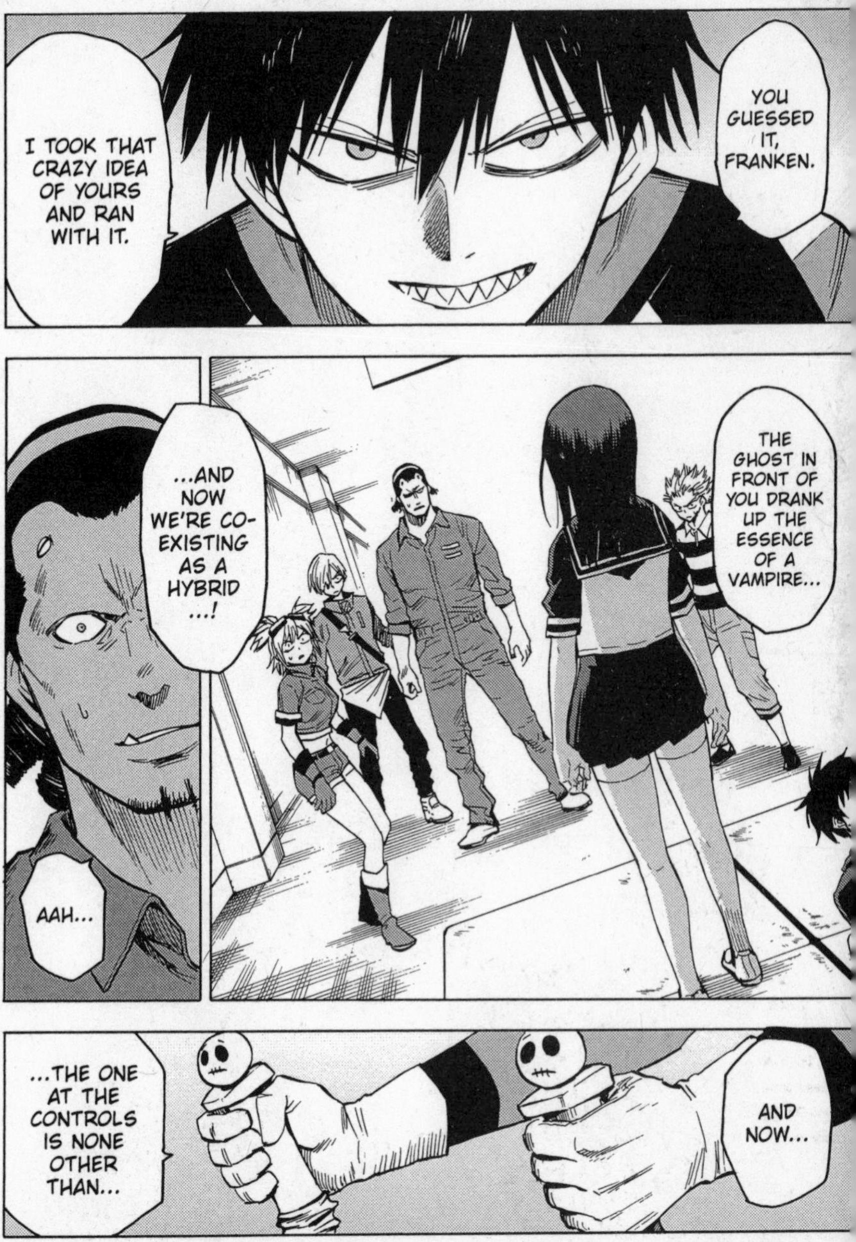
YOU GUESSED IT, FRANKEN.
I TOOK THAT CRAZY IDEA OF YOURS AND RAN WITH IT.
THE GHOST IN FRONT OF YOU DRANK UP THE ESSENCE OF A VAMPIRE...
...AND NOW WE'RE CO-EXISTING AS A HYBRID ...!
AAH...
AND NOW...
...THE ONE AT THE CONTROLS IS NONE OTHER THAN...

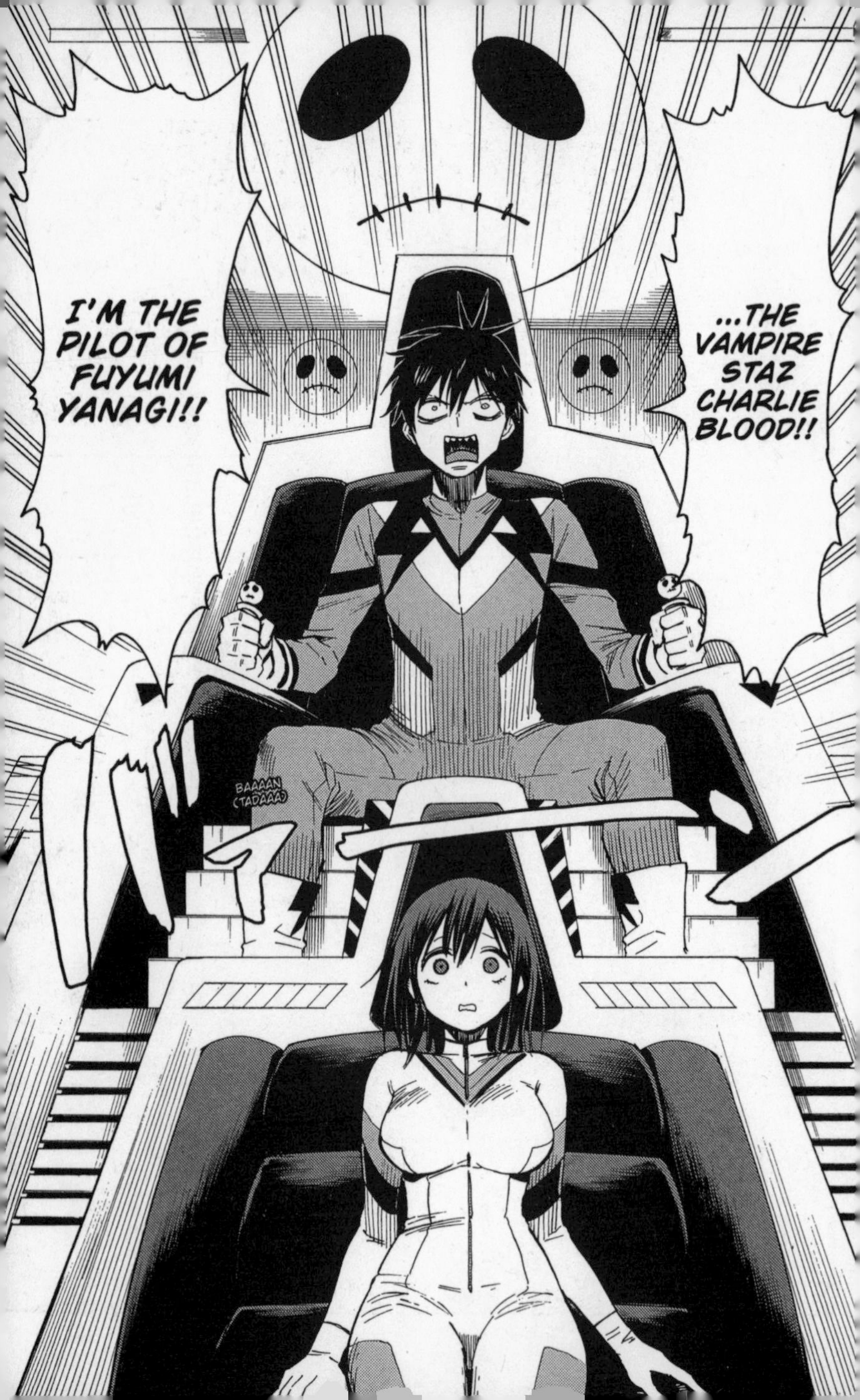
I'M THE PILOT OF FUYUMI YANAGI!!
...THE VAMPIRE STAZ CHARLIE BLOOD!!
BAAAAN (TADAAA)

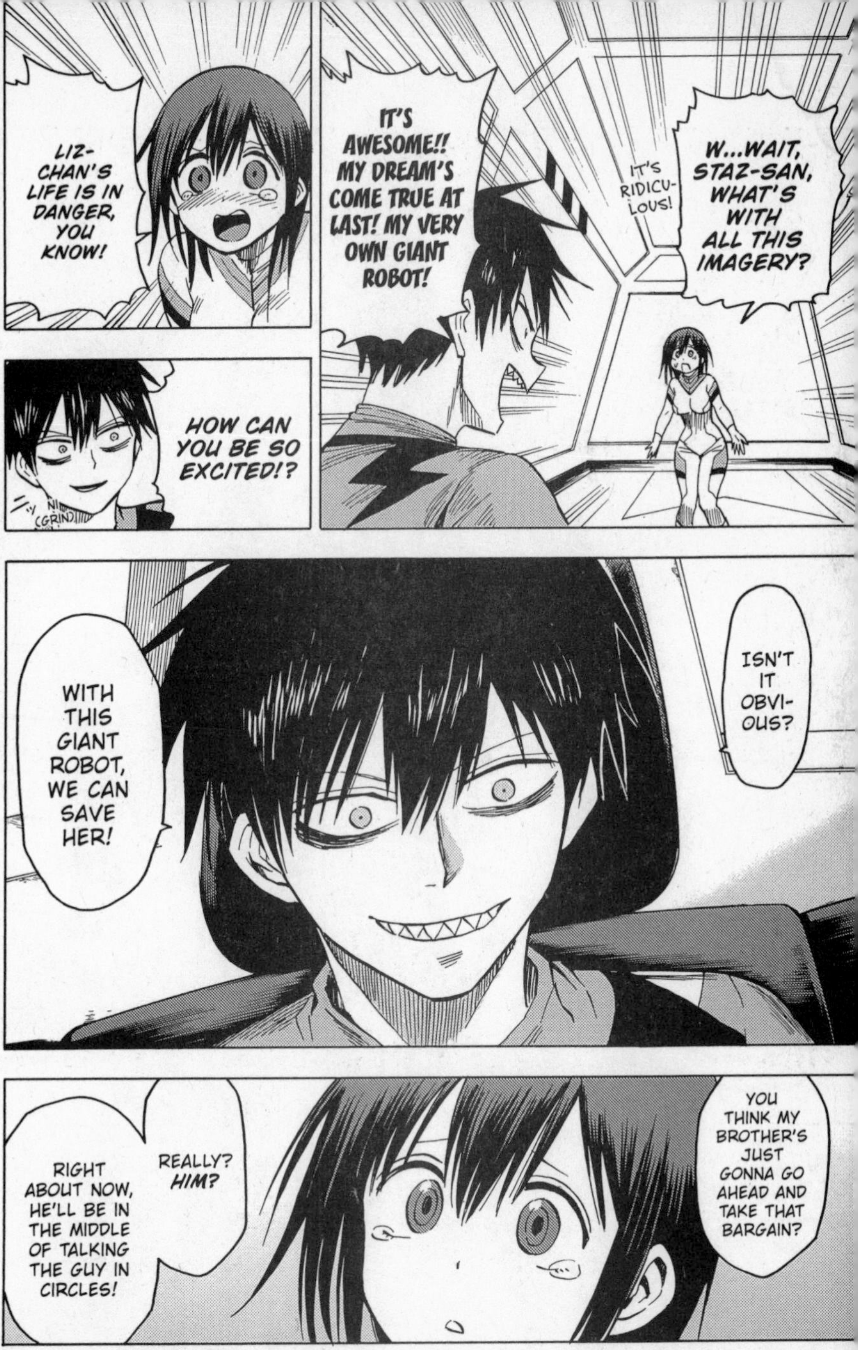
W...WAIT, STAZ-SAN, WHAT'S WITH ALL THIS IMAGERY?
IT'S RIDICULOUS!
IT'S AWESOME!! MY DREAM'S COME TRUE AT LAST! MY VERY OWN GIANT ROBOT!
LIZ-CHAN'S LIFE IS IN DANGER, YOU KNOW!
HOW CAN YOU BE SO EXCITED!?
NI (GRIN)
ISN'T IT OBVIOUS?
WITH THIS GIANT ROBOT, WE CAN SAVE HER!
YOU THINK MY BROTHER'S JUST GONNA GO AHEAD AND TAKE THAT BARGAIN?
REALLY? HIM?
RIGHT ABOUT NOW, HE'LL BE IN THE MIDDLE OF TALKING THE GUY IN CIRCLES!

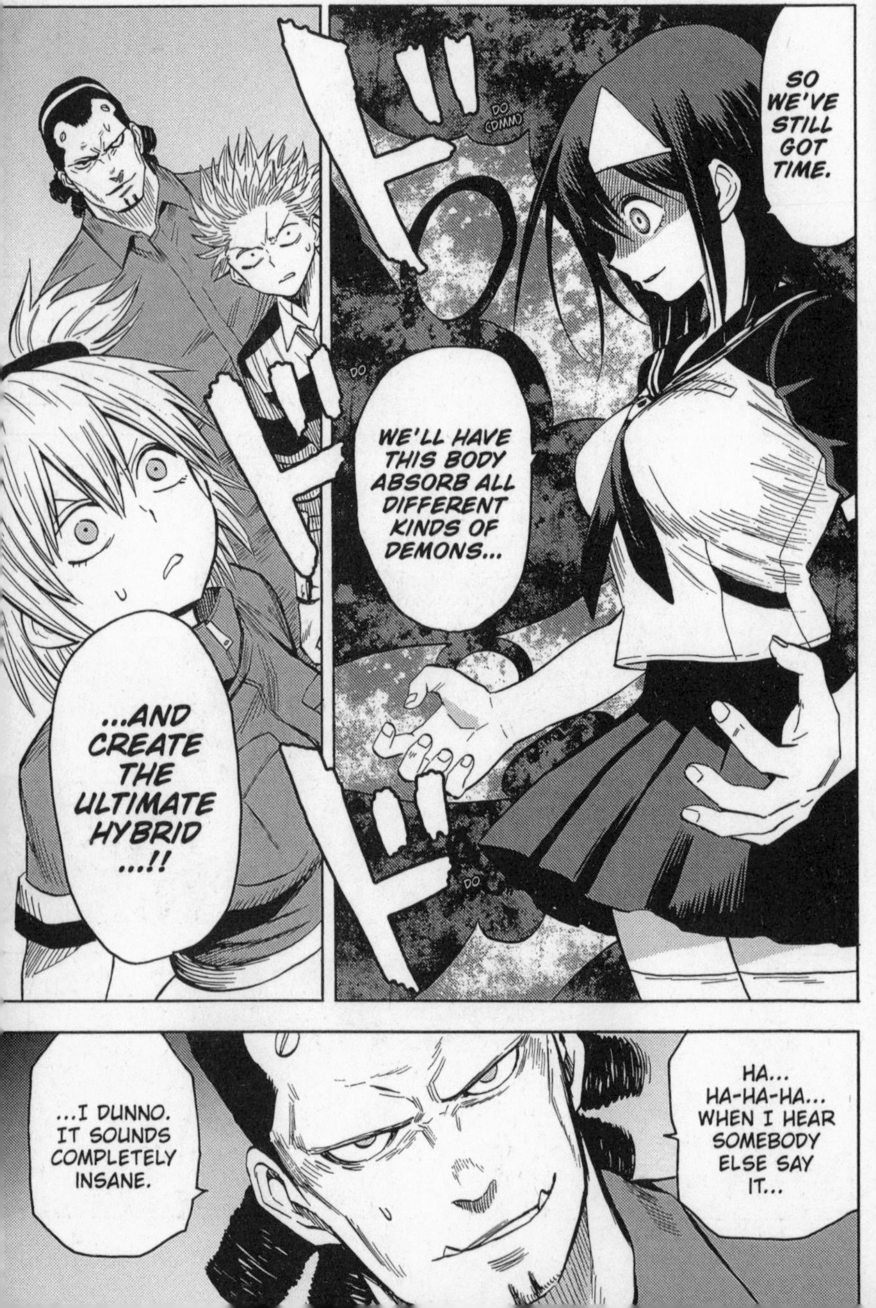
SO WE'VE STILL GOT TIME.
DO (DMM)
DO
WE'LL HAVE THIS BODY ABSORB ALL DIFFERENT KINDS OF DEMONS...
DO
...AND CREATE THE ULTIMATE HYBRID ...!!
HA... HA-HA-HA... WHEN I HEAR SOMEBODY ELSE SAY IT...
...I DUNNO. IT SOUNDS COMPLETELY INSANE.

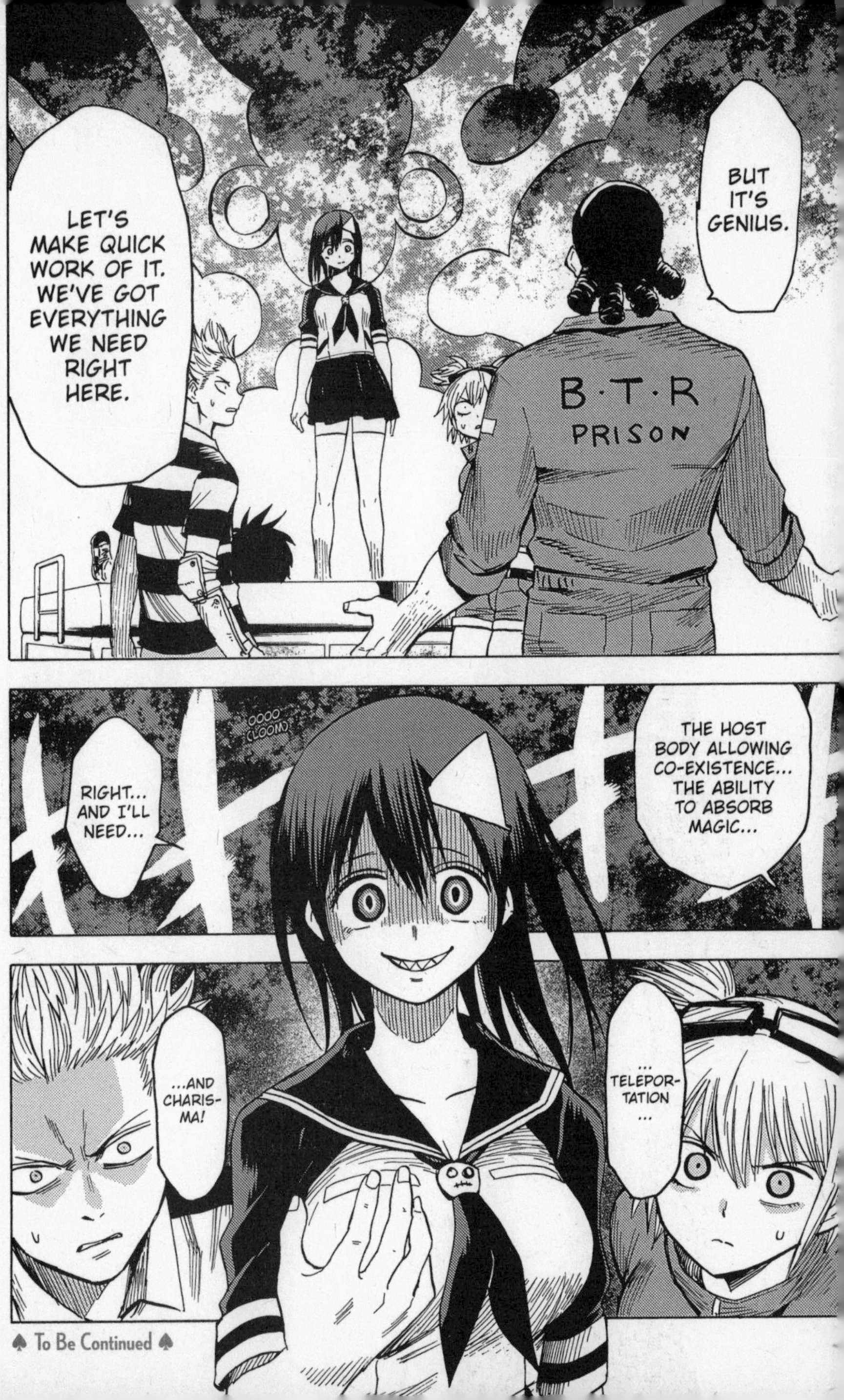
BUT IT'S GENIUS.
LET'S MAKE QUICK WORK OF IT. WE'VE GOT EVERYTHING WE NEED RIGHT HERE.
B·T·R PRISON
THE HOST BODY ALLOWING CO-EXISTENCE... THE ABILITY TO ABSORB MAGIC...
OOOO (LOOM)
RIGHT... AND I'LL NEED...
...TELEPORTATION...
...AND CHARISMA!
To Be Continued

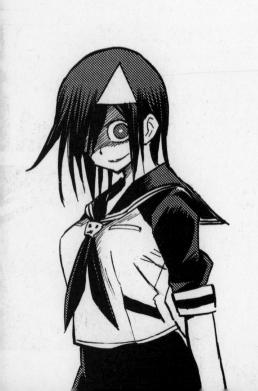

BLOOD LAD

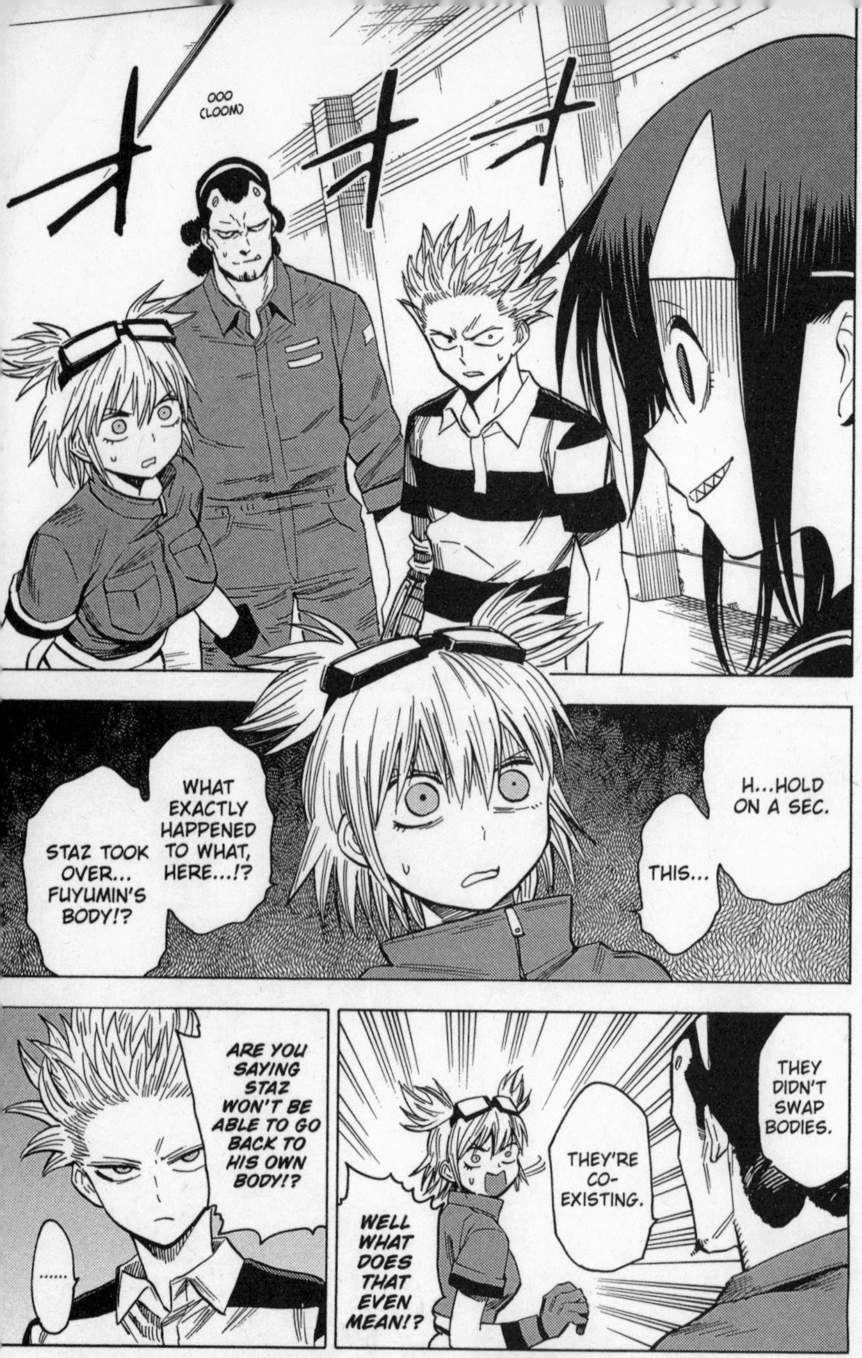
OOO (LOOM)
H...HOLD ON A SEC.
THIS...
WHAT EXACTLY HAPPENED TO WHAT, HERE...!?
STAZ TOOK OVER... FUYUMIN'S BODY!?
THEY DIDN'T SWAP BODIES.
THEY'RE CO-EXISTING.
WELL WHAT DOES THAT EVEN MEAN!?
ARE YOU SAYING STAZ WON'T BE ABLE TO GO BACK TO HIS OWN BODY!?
......

## CHAPTER 79 ♠ FUYUMI YANAGI THE DEMON

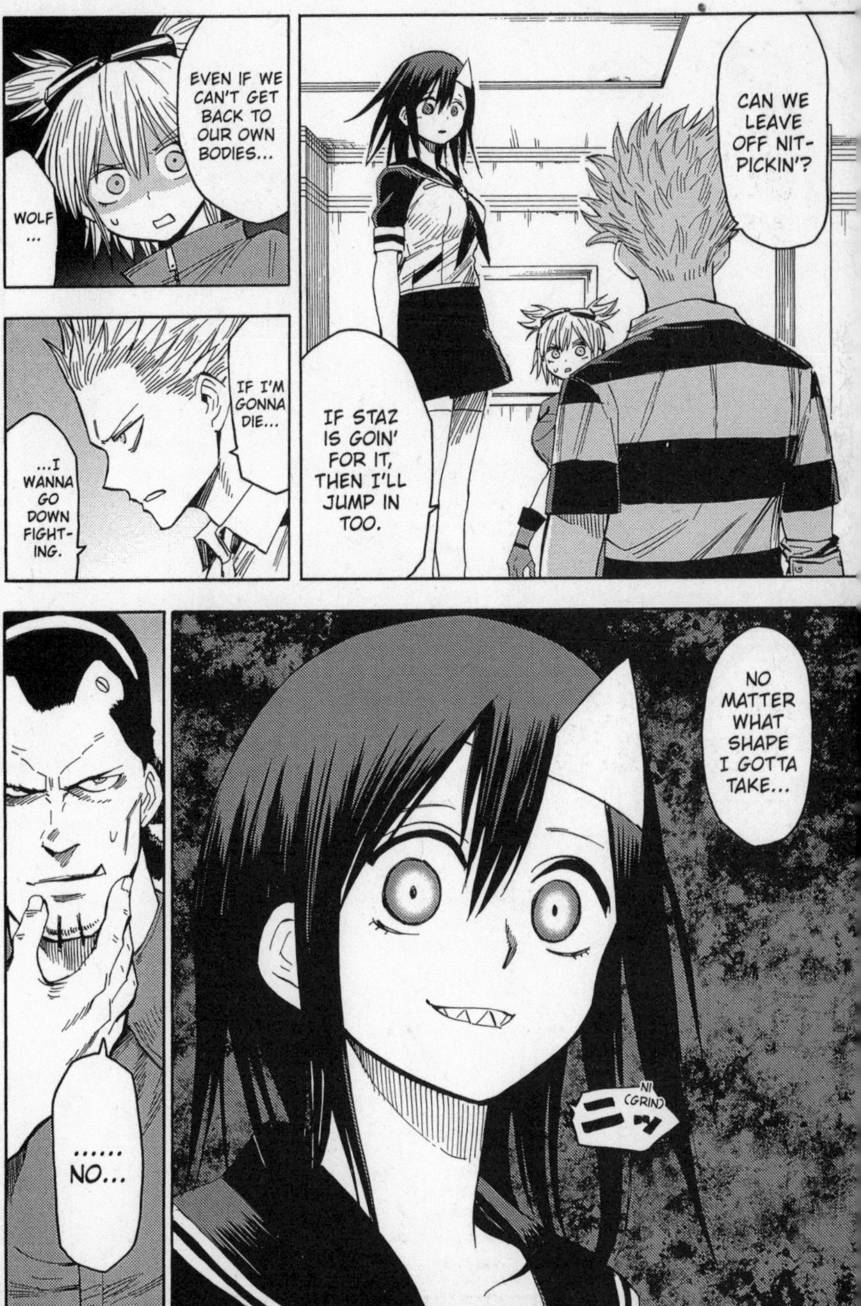
CAN WE LEAVE OFF NIT-PICKIN'?
IF STAZ IS GOIN' FOR IT, THEN I'LL JUMP IN TOO.
EVEN IF WE CAN'T GET BACK TO OUR OWN BODIES...
WOLF...
IF I'M GONNA DIE...
...I WANNA GO DOWN FIGHT-ING.
NO MATTER WHAT SHAPE I GOTTA TAKE...
NI (GRIN)
...... NO...

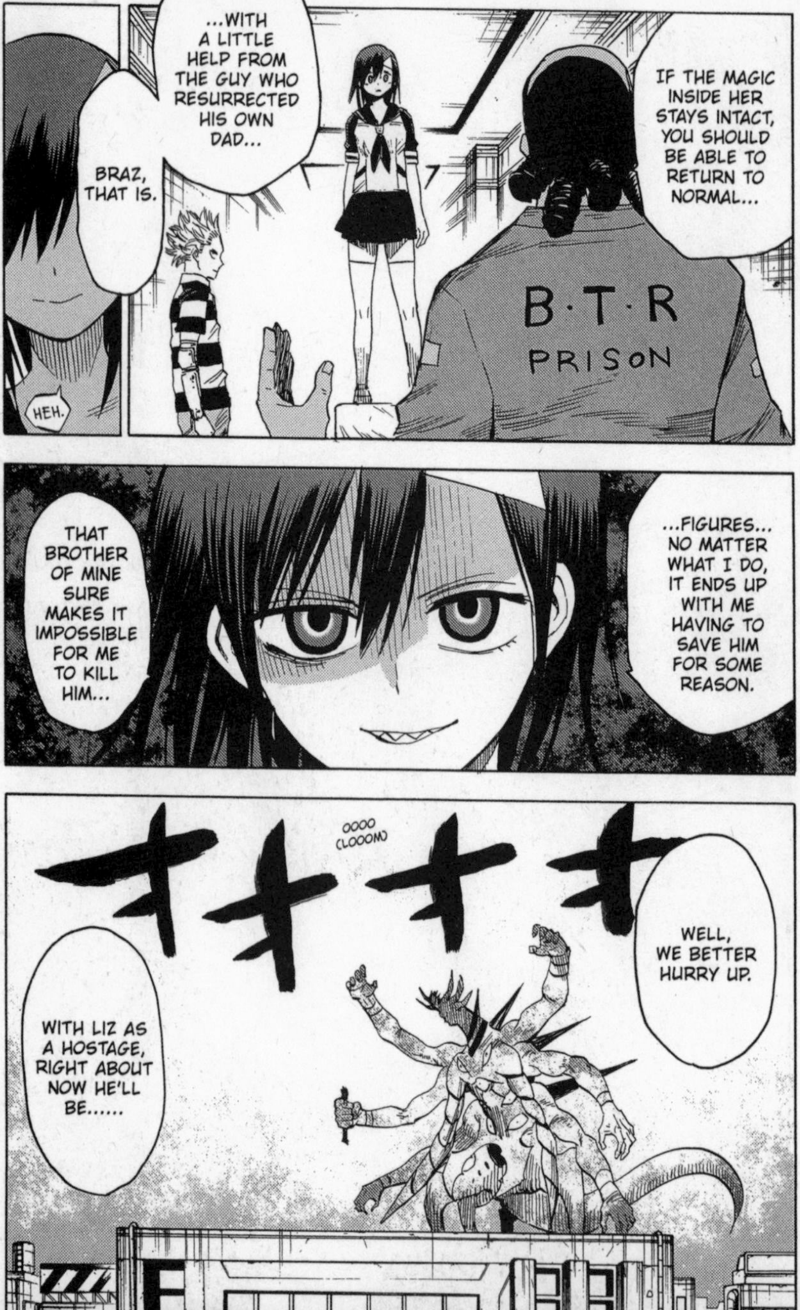
IF THE MAGIC INSIDE HER STAYS INTACT, YOU SHOULD BE ABLE TO RETURN TO NORMAL...
B·T·R PRISON
...WITH A LITTLE HELP FROM THE GUY WHO RESURRECTED HIS OWN DAD...
BRAZ, THAT IS.
HEH.
...FIGURES... NO MATTER WHAT I DO, IT ENDS UP WITH ME HAVING TO SAVE HIM FOR SOME REASON.
THAT BROTHER OF MINE SURE MAKES IT IMPOSSIBLE FOR ME TO KILL HIM...
OOOO (LOOOM)
WELL, WE BETTER HURRY UP.
WITH LIZ AS A HOSTAGE, RIGHT ABOUT NOW HE'LL BE......

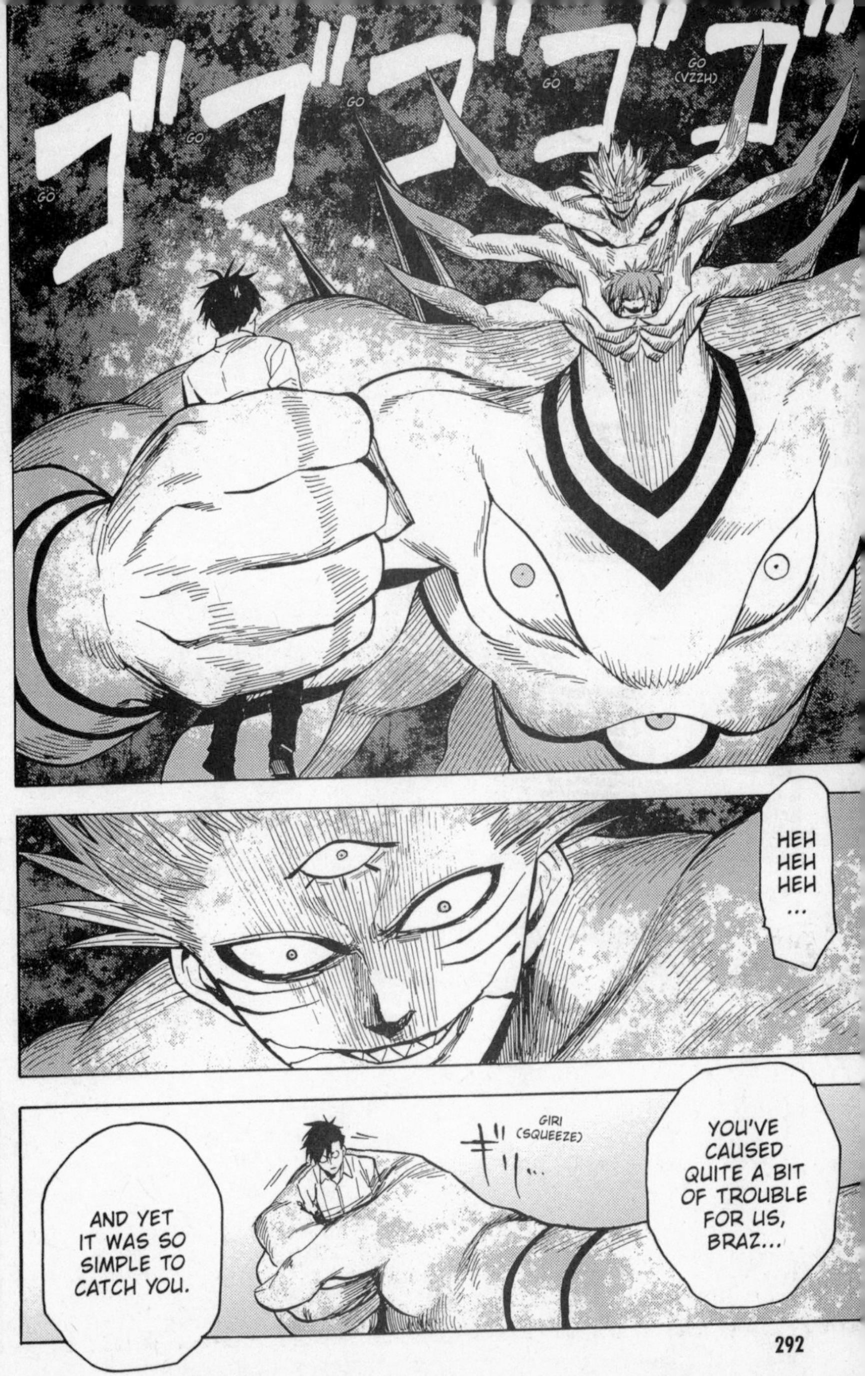
GO (VZZH)
GO
GO
GO
GO
HEH HEH HEH ...
YOU'VE CAUSED QUITE A BIT OF TROUBLE FOR US, BRAZ...
GIRI (SQUEEZE)
AND YET IT WAS SO SIMPLE TO CATCH YOU.

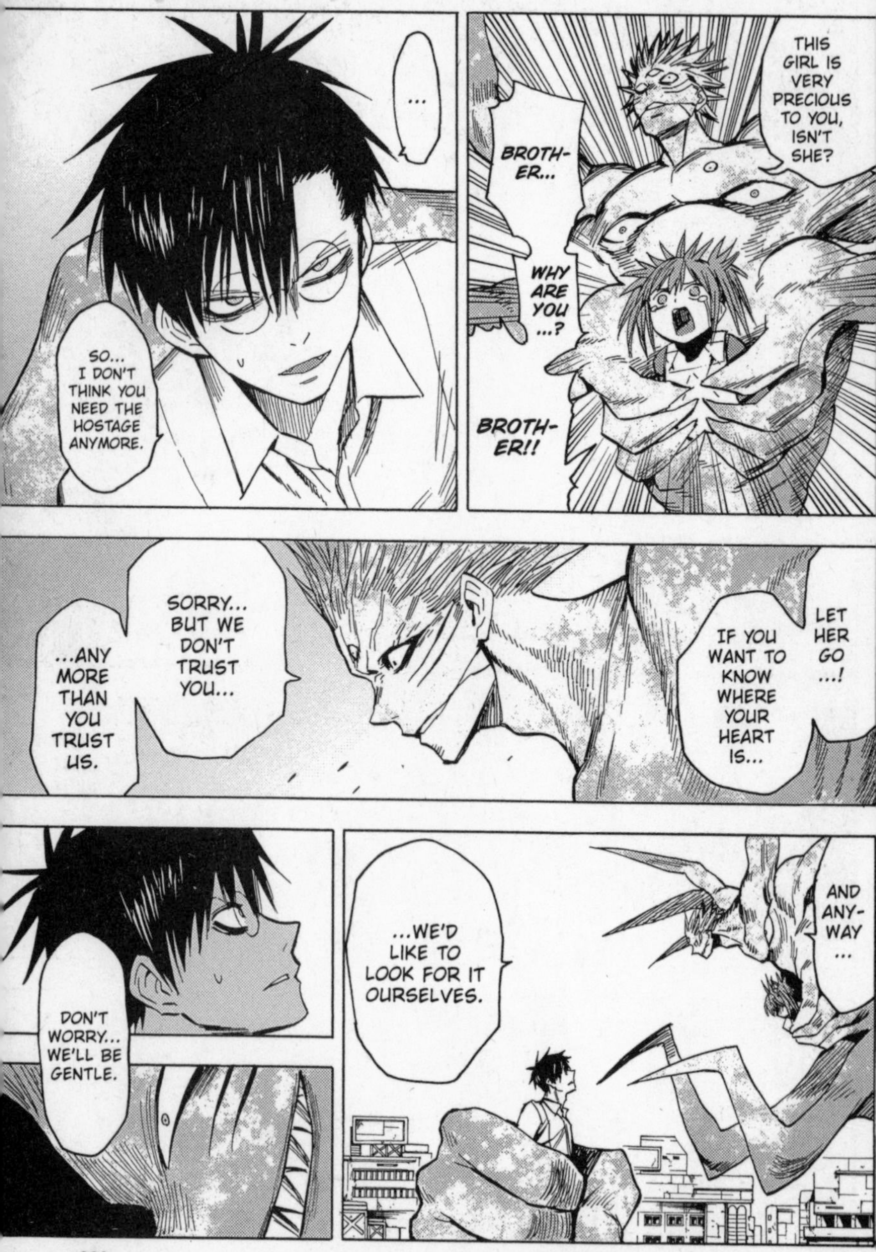
THIS GIRL IS VERY PRECIOUS TO YOU, ISN'T SHE?
BROTHER...
WHY ARE YOU ...?
BROTHER!!
...
SO... I DON'T THINK YOU NEED THE HOSTAGE ANYMORE.
LET HER GO ...!
IF YOU WANT TO KNOW WHERE YOUR HEART IS...
SORRY... BUT WE DON'T TRUST YOU...
...ANY MORE THAN YOU TRUST US.
AND ANYWAY...
...WE'D LIKE TO LOOK FOR IT OURSELVES.
DON'T WORRY... WE'LL BE GENTLE.

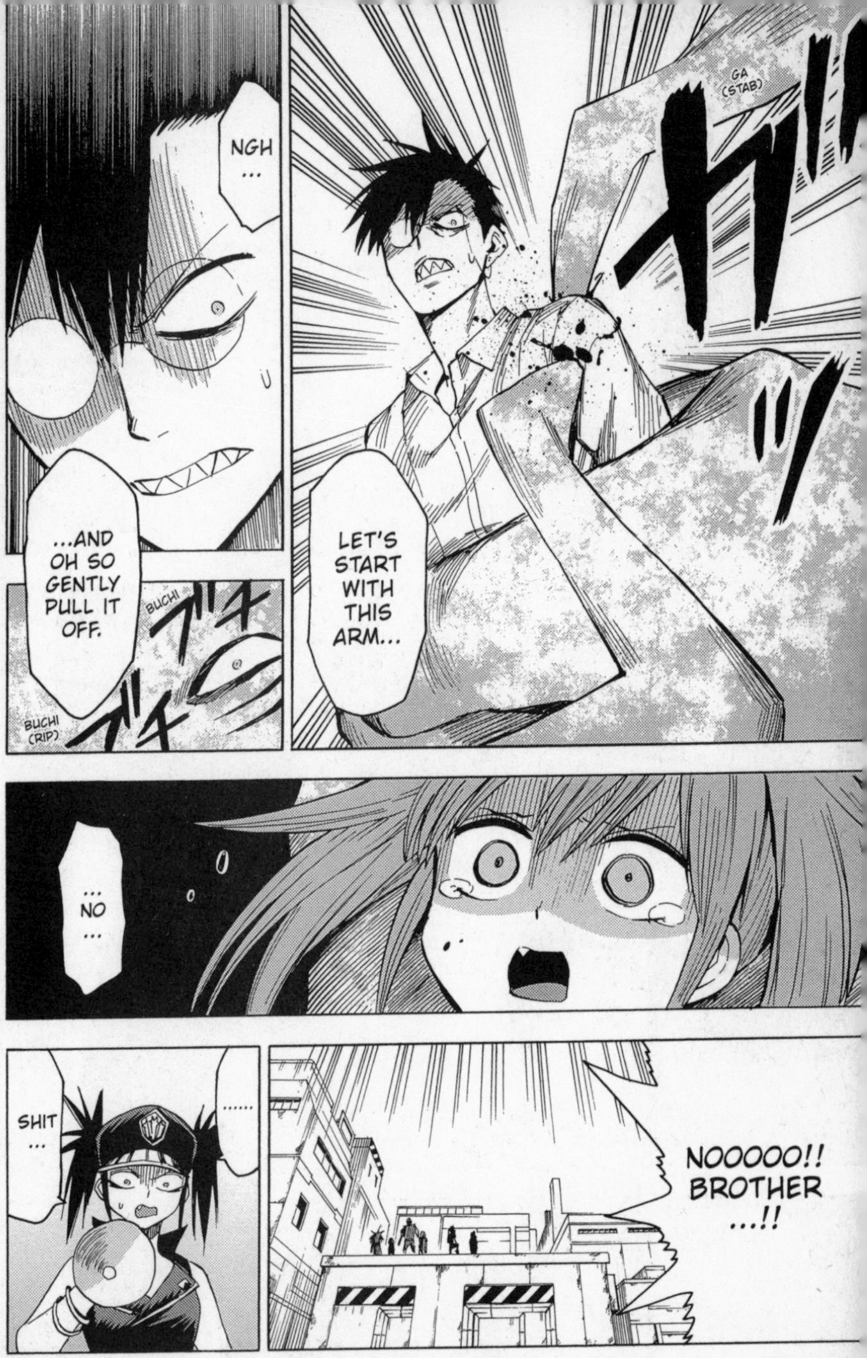
GA (STAB)
LET'S START WITH THIS ARM...
NGH ...
...AND OH SO GENTLY PULL IT OFF.
BUCHI
BUCHI (RIP)
... NO ...
NOOOOO!! BROTHER ...!!
......
SHIT ...

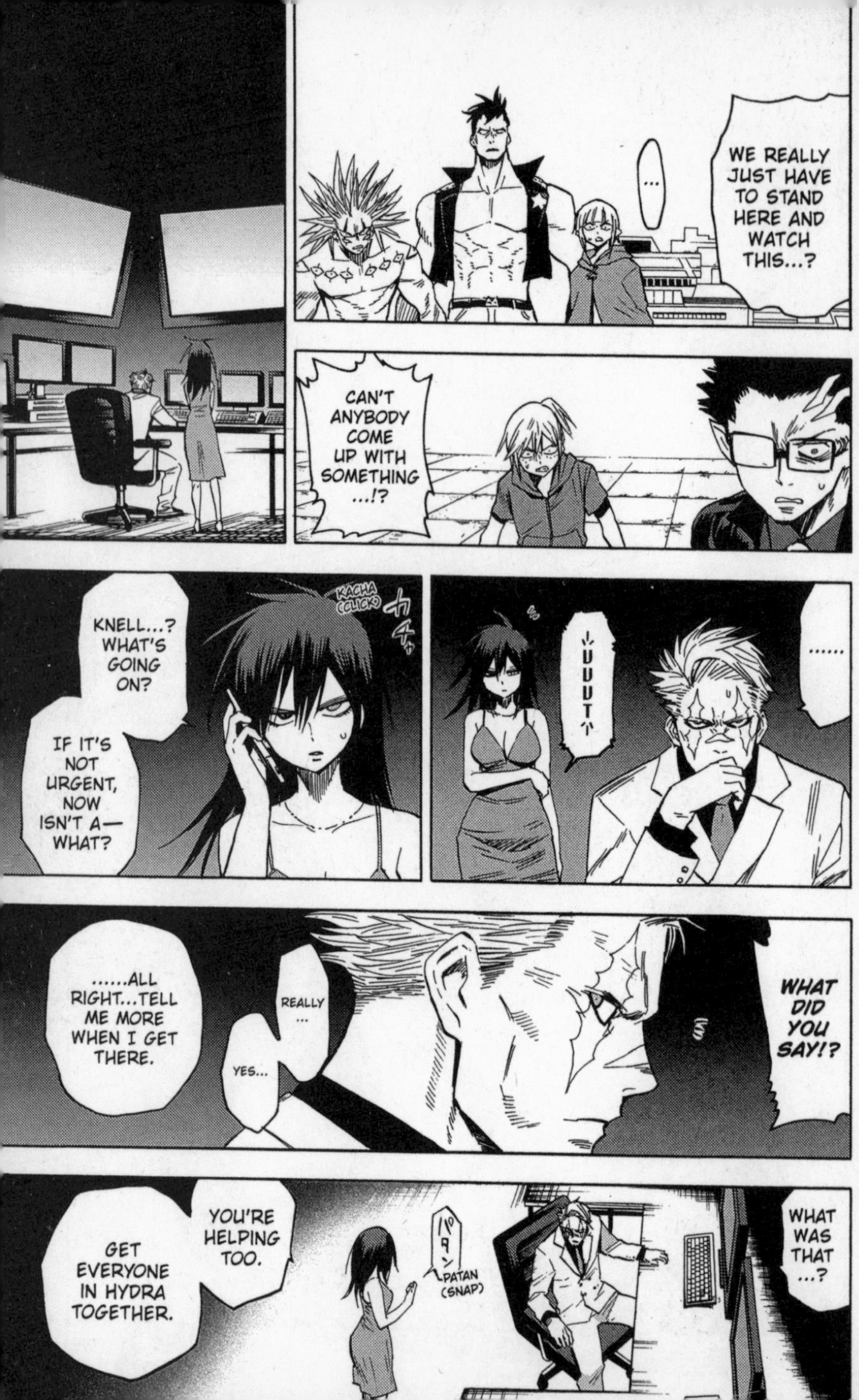
WE REALLY JUST HAVE TO STAND HERE AND WATCH THIS...?
...
CAN'T ANYBODY COME UP WITH SOMETHING ...!?
......
-BUUUT-
カチャ
KACHA (CLICK)
KNELL...? WHAT'S GOING ON?
IF IT'S NOT URGENT, NOW ISN'T A— WHAT?
WHAT DID YOU SAY!?
REALLY ...
YES...
......ALL RIGHT...TELL ME MORE WHEN I GET THERE.
WHAT WAS THAT ...?
パタン
PATAN (SNAP)
YOU'RE HELPING TOO.
GET EVERYONE IN HYDRA TOGETHER.

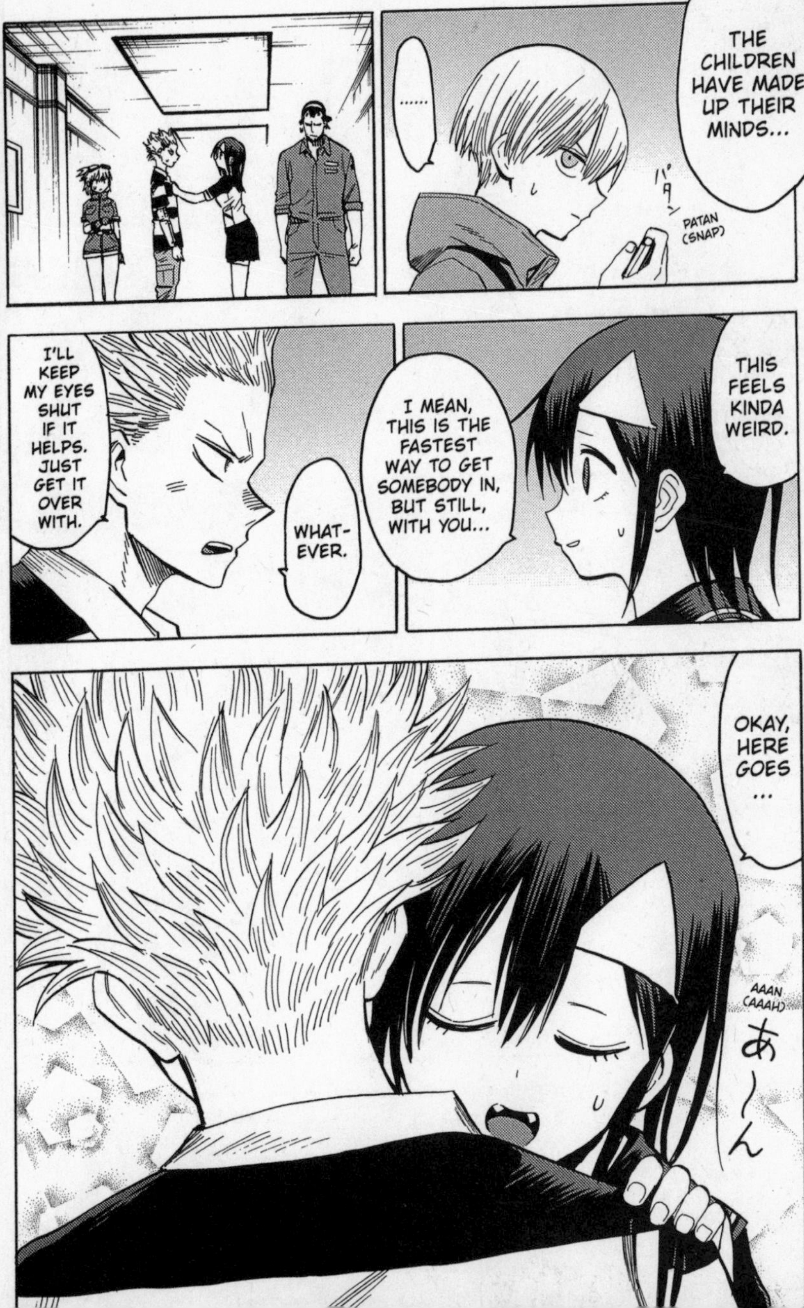
THE CHILDREN HAVE MADE UP THEIR MINDS...
......
パタン
PATAN (SNAP)
THIS FEELS KINDA WEIRD.
I MEAN, THIS IS THE FASTEST WAY TO GET SOMEBODY IN, BUT STILL, WITH YOU...
WHAT-EVER.
I'LL KEEP MY EYES SHUT IF IT HELPS. JUST GET IT OVER WITH.
OKAY, HERE GOES...
AAAN (AAAH)
あ〜ん

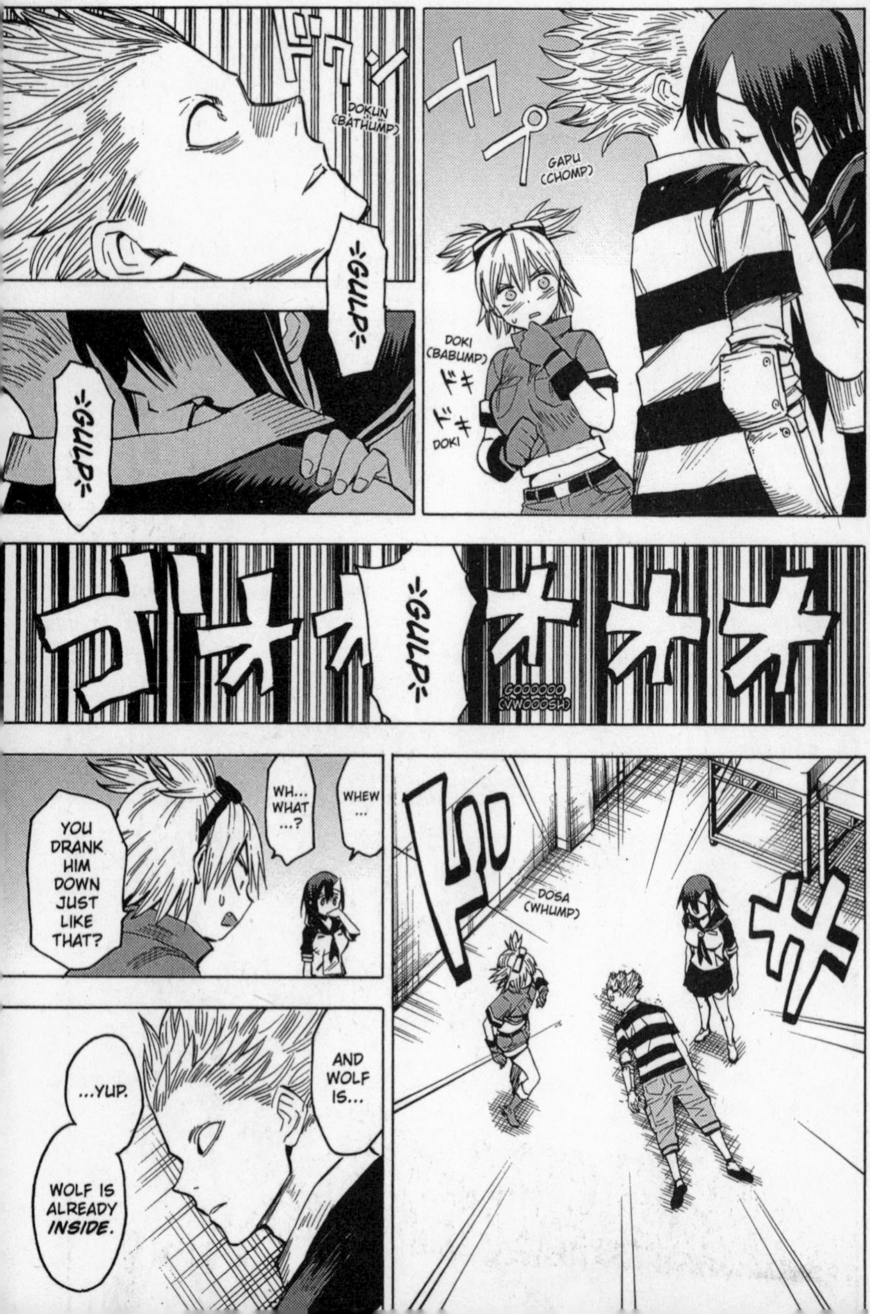
GAPU (CHOMP)
DOKI (BABUMP)
DOKI
DOKUN (BATHUMP)
GULP
GULP
GULP
GOOOOOO (VWOOOSH)
DOSA (WHUMP)
WHEW...
WH... WHAT...?
YOU DRANK HIM DOWN JUST LIKE THAT?
AND WOLF IS...
...YUP.
WOLF IS ALREADY *INSIDE*.

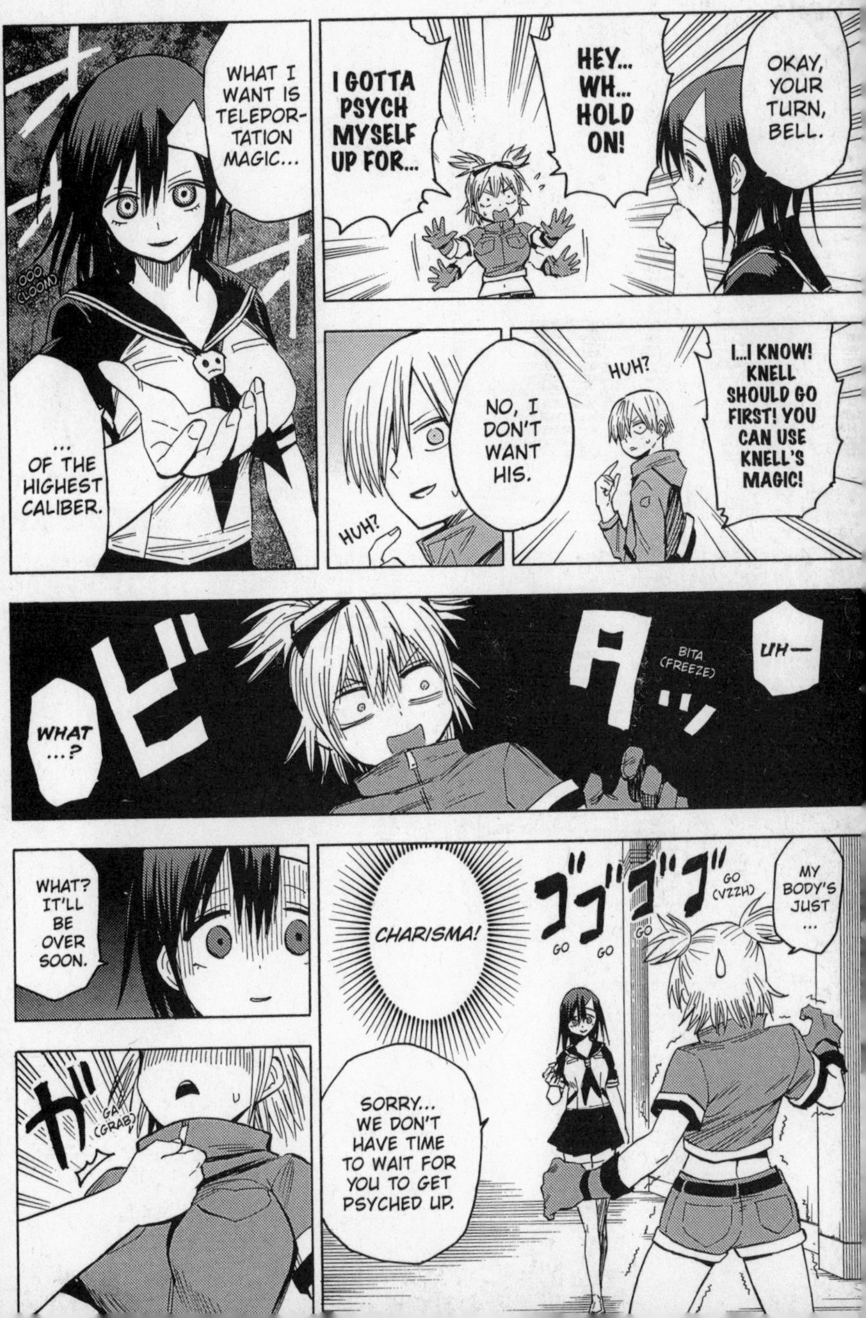
OKAY, YOUR TURN, BELL.
HEY... WH... HOLD ON!
I GOTTA PSYCH MYSELF UP FOR...
I...I KNOW! KNELL SHOULD GO FIRST! YOU CAN USE KNELL'S MAGIC!
HUH?
NO, I DON'T WANT HIS.
HUH?
WHAT I WANT IS TELEPORTATION MAGIC...
OOO (LOOM)
... OF THE HIGHEST CALIBER.
UH—
BITA (FREEZE)
WHAT ...?
MY BODY'S JUST ...
GO (VZZH)
GO GO GO
CHARISMA!
SORRY... WE DON'T HAVE TIME TO WAIT FOR YOU TO GET PSYCHED UP.
WHAT? IT'LL BE OVER SOON.
GA (GRAB)

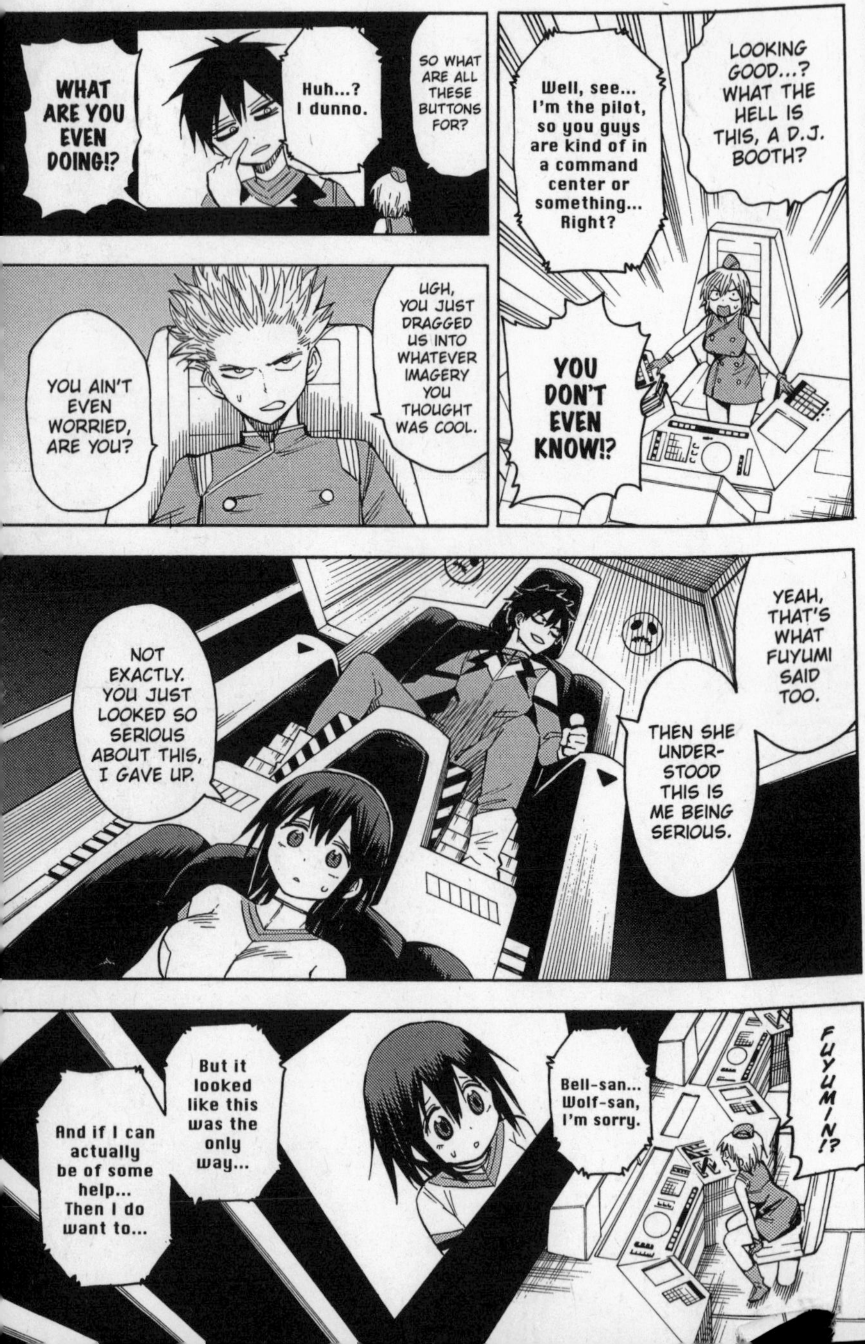
LOOKING GOOD...? WHAT THE HELL IS THIS, A D.J. BOOTH?
Well, see... I'm the pilot, so you guys are kind of in a command center or something... Right?
YOU DON'T EVEN KNOW!?
SO WHAT ARE ALL THESE BUTTONS FOR?
Huh...? I dunno.
WHAT ARE YOU EVEN DOING!?
UGH, YOU JUST DRAGGED US INTO WHATEVER IMAGERY YOU THOUGHT WAS COOL.
YOU AIN'T EVEN WORRIED, ARE YOU?
YEAH, THAT'S WHAT FUYUMI SAID TOO.
THEN SHE UNDERSTOOD THIS IS ME BEING SERIOUS.
NOT EXACTLY. YOU JUST LOOKED SO SERIOUS ABOUT THIS, I GAVE UP.
FUYUMIN!?
Bell-san... Wolf-san, I'm sorry.
But it looked like this was the only way...
And if I can actually be of some help... Then I do want to...

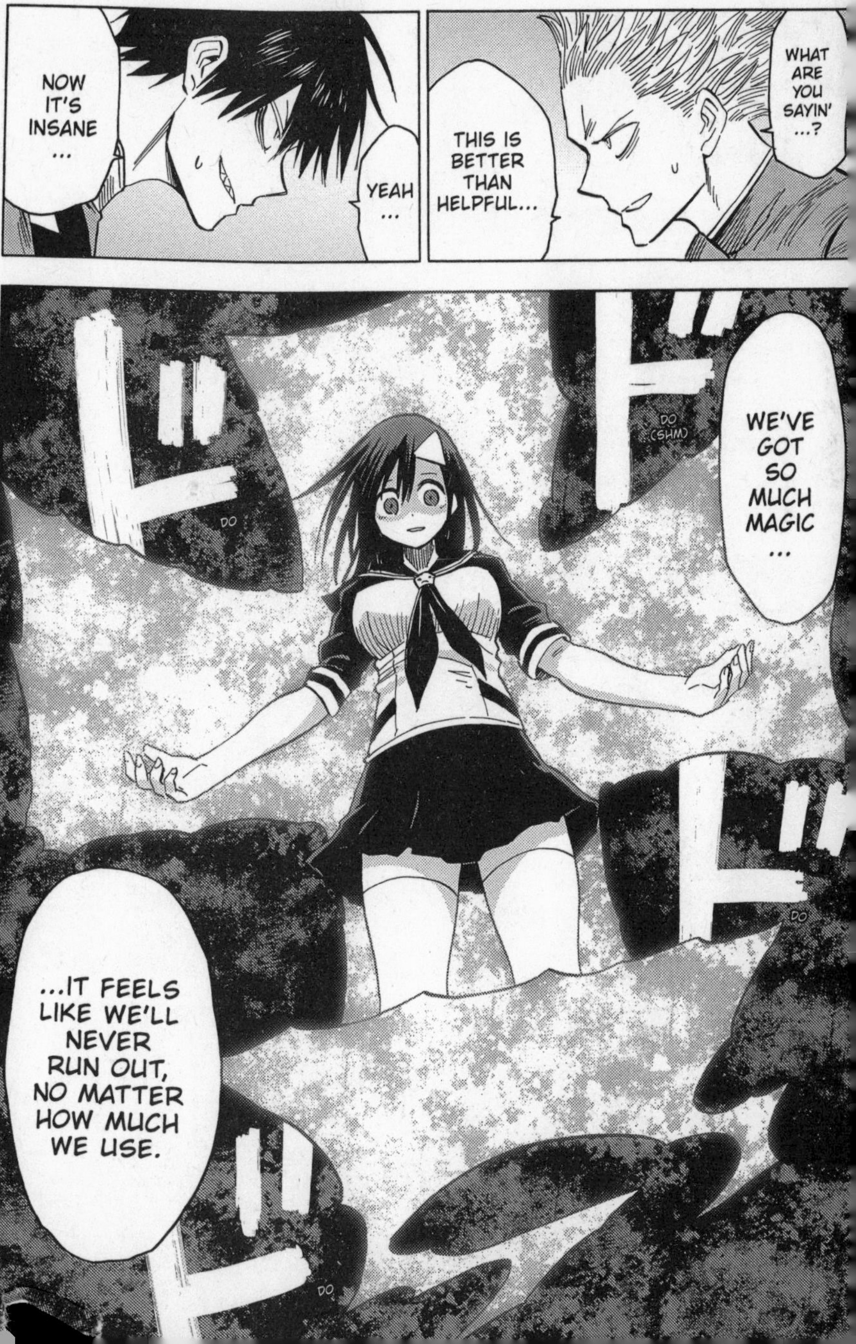
WHAT ARE YOU SAYIN' ...?
THIS IS BETTER THAN HELPFUL...
YEAH ...
NOW IT'S INSANE ...
WE'VE GOT SO MUCH MAGIC ...
DO (SHM)
DO
DO
...IT FEELS LIKE WE'LL NEVER RUN OUT, NO MATTER HOW MUCH WE USE.
DO

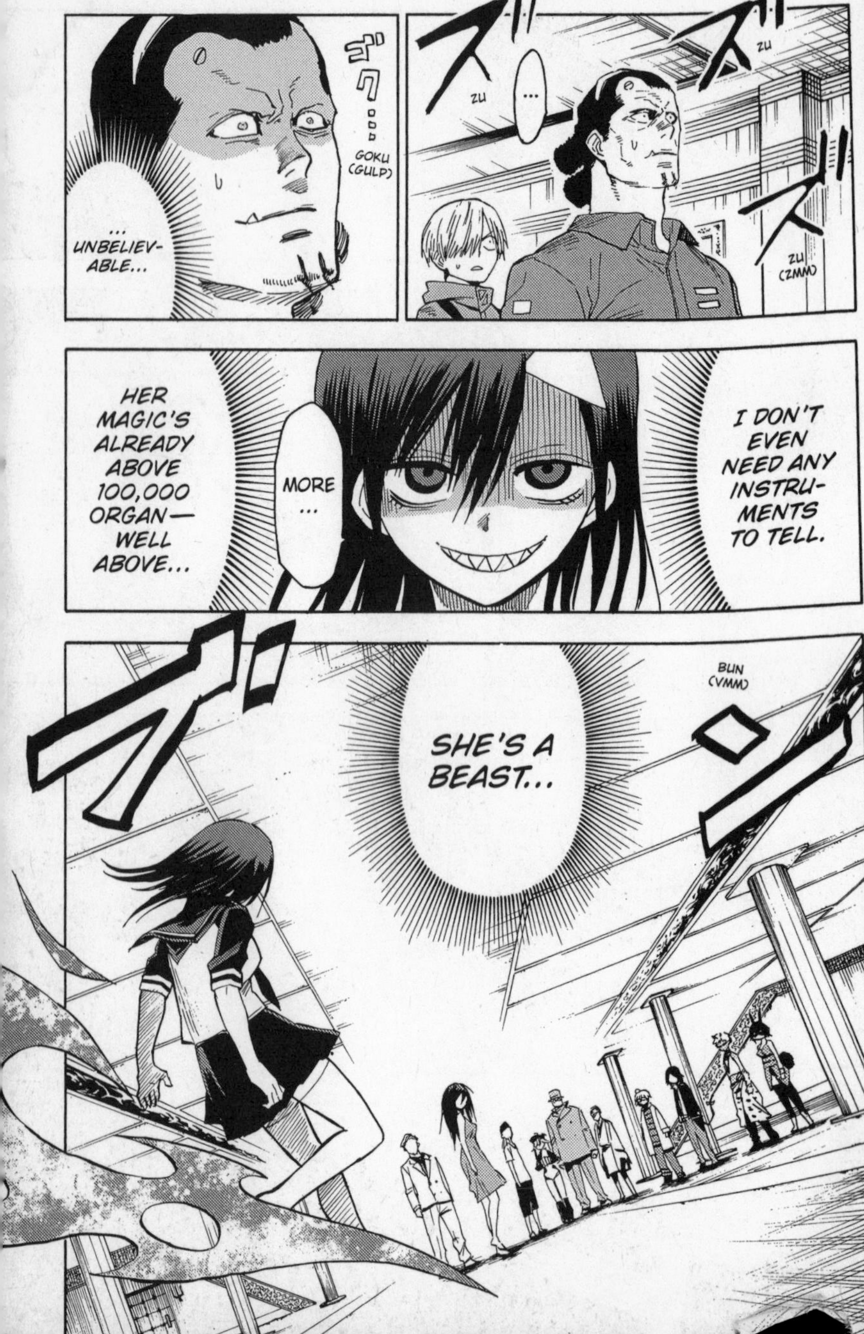
ZU
...
ZU
ZU (ZMM)
GOKU (GULP)
... UNBELIEV-ABLE...
I DON'T EVEN NEED ANY INSTRU-MENTS TO TELL.
MORE...
HER MAGIC'S ALREADY ABOVE 100,000 ORGAN— WELL ABOVE...
BUN (VMM)
SHE'S A BEAST...

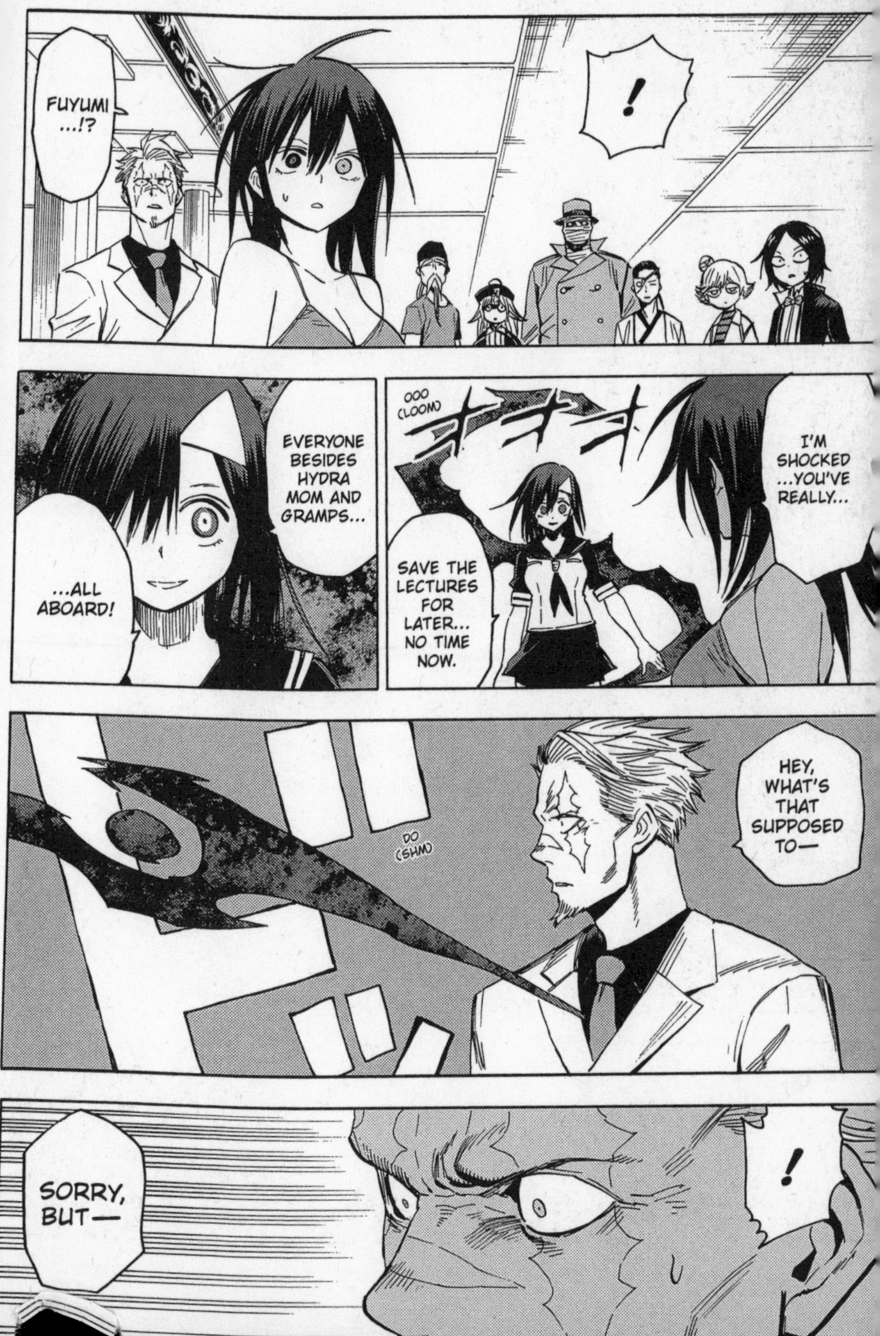
!
FUYUMI ...!?
I'M SHOCKED ...YOU'VE REALLY...
OOO (LOOM)
SAVE THE LECTURES FOR LATER... NO TIME NOW.
EVERYONE BESIDES HYDRA MOM AND GRAMPS...
...ALL ABOARD!
HEY, WHAT'S THAT SUPPOSED TO—
DO (SHM)
!
SORRY, BUT—

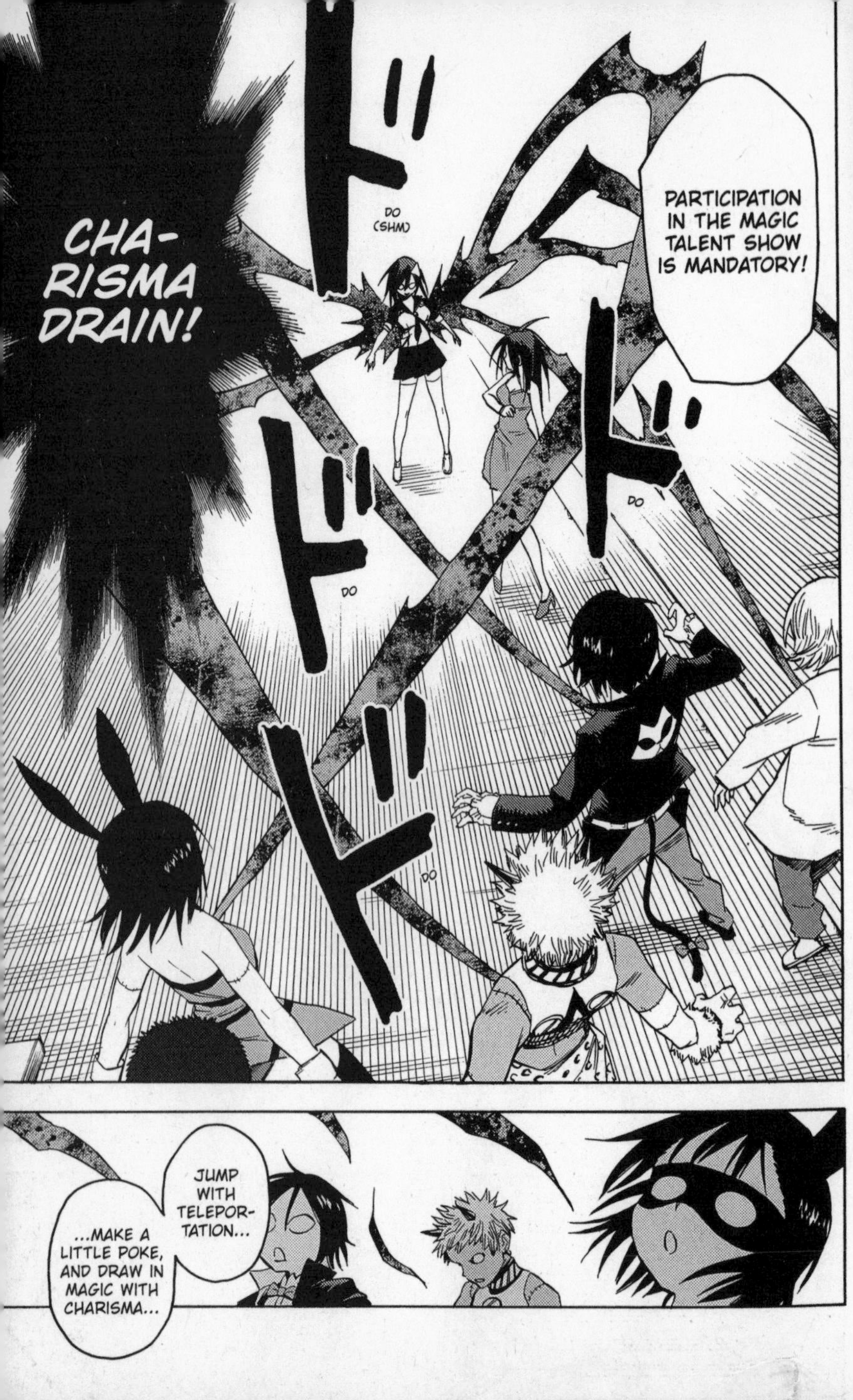
PARTICIPATION IN THE MAGIC TALENT SHOW IS MANDATORY!
DO (SHM)
CHA-RISMA DRAIN!
DO
DO
DO
JUMP WITH TELEPORTATION...
...MAKE A LITTLE POKE, AND DRAW IN MAGIC WITH CHARISMA...

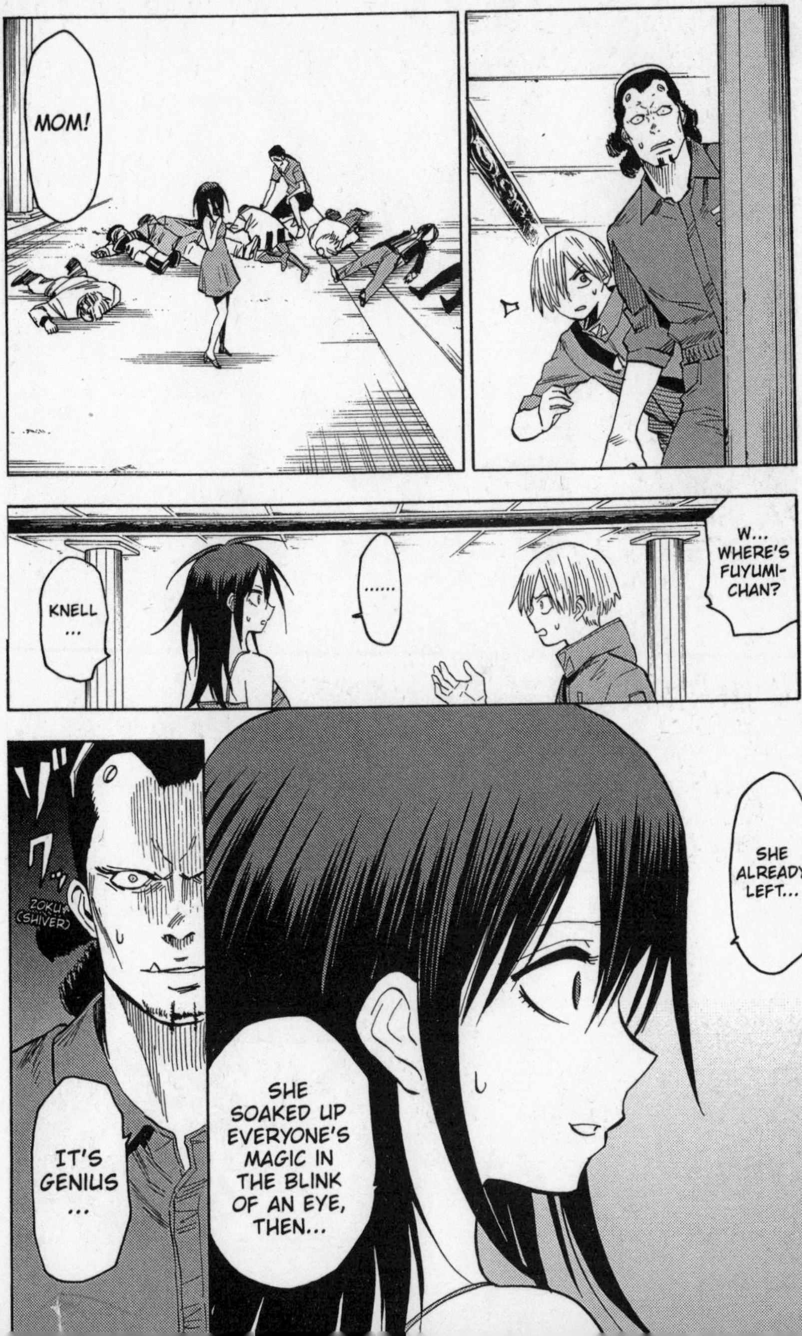
MOM!
W... WHERE'S FUYUMI-CHAN?
......
KNELL ...
SHE ALREADY LEFT...
SHE SOAKED UP EVERYONE'S MAGIC IN THE BLINK OF AN EYE, THEN...
ZOKU (SHIVER)
IT'S GENIUS ...

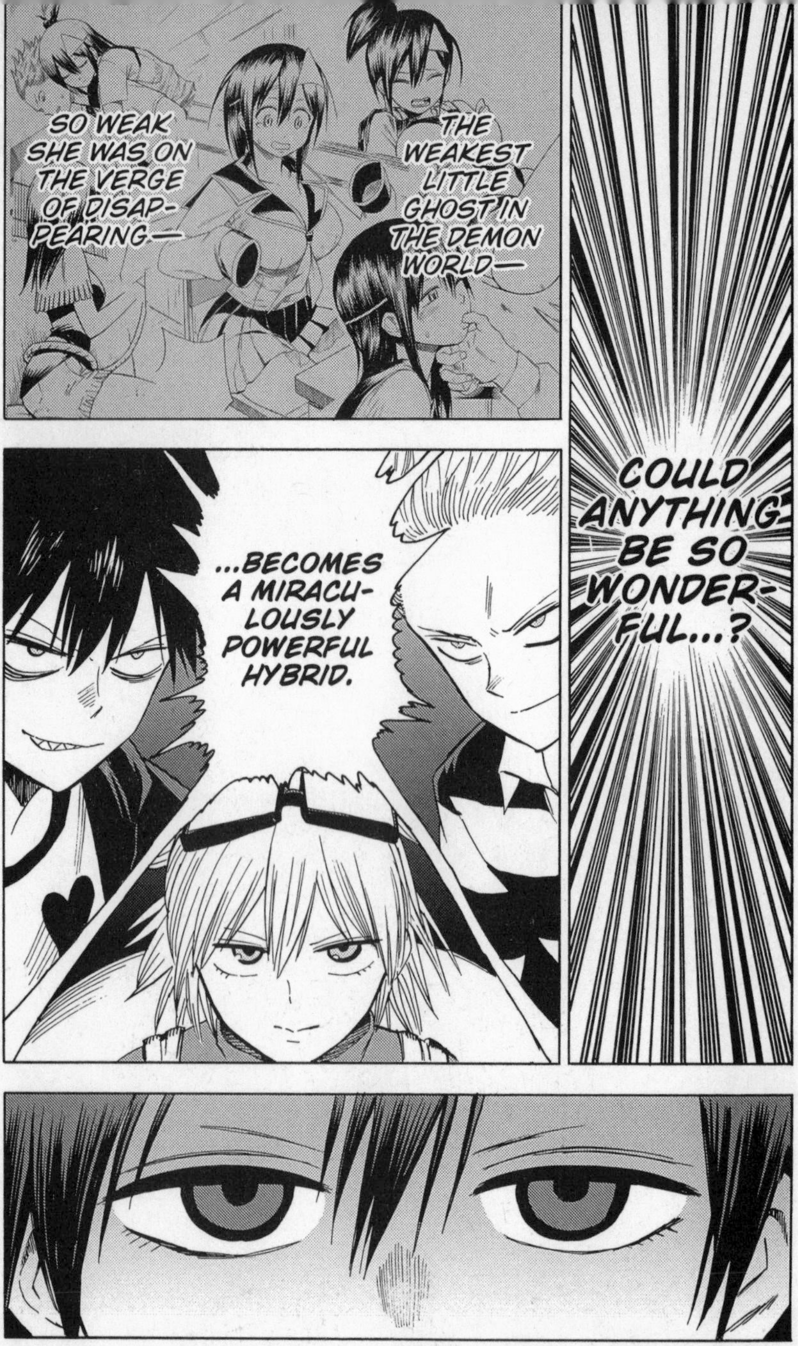
COULD ANYTHING BE SO WONDER-FUL...?
THE WEAKEST LITTLE GHOST IN THE DEMON WORLD—
SO WEAK SHE WAS ON THE VERGE OF DISAP-PEARING—
...BECOMES A MIRACU-LOUSLY POWERFUL HYBRID.

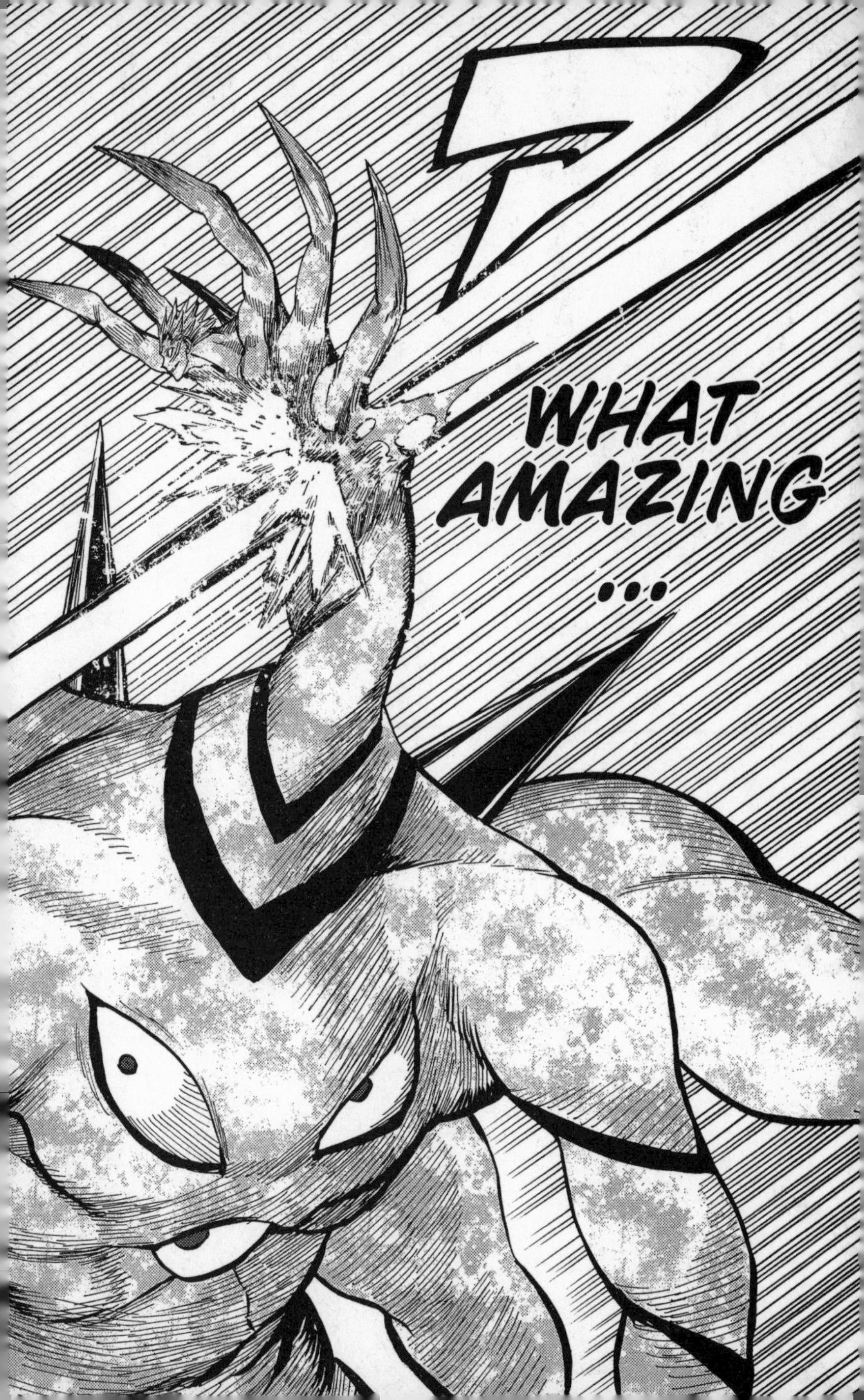
WHAT AMAZING ...

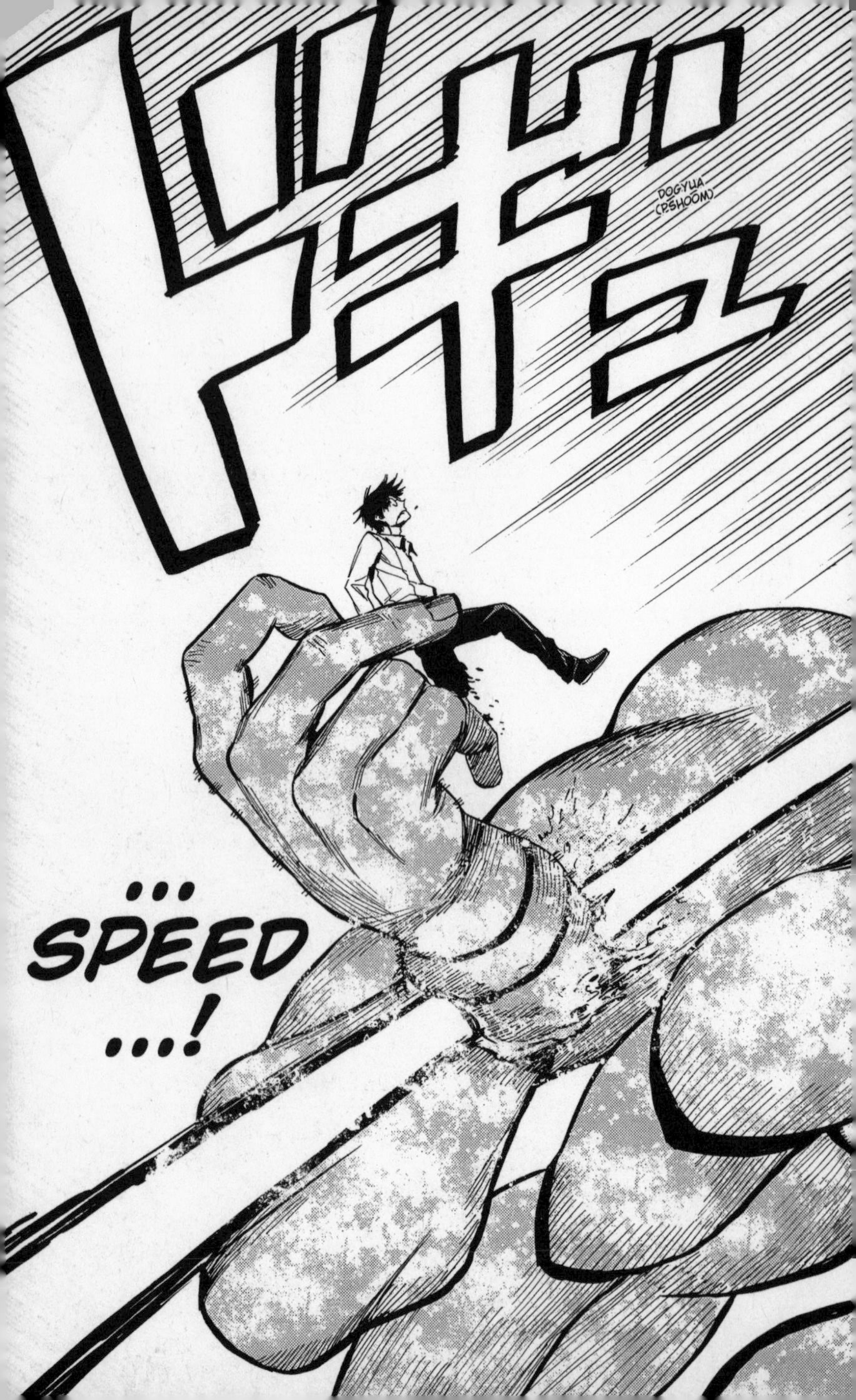
DOGYUA (P-SHOOM)
...SPEED ...!

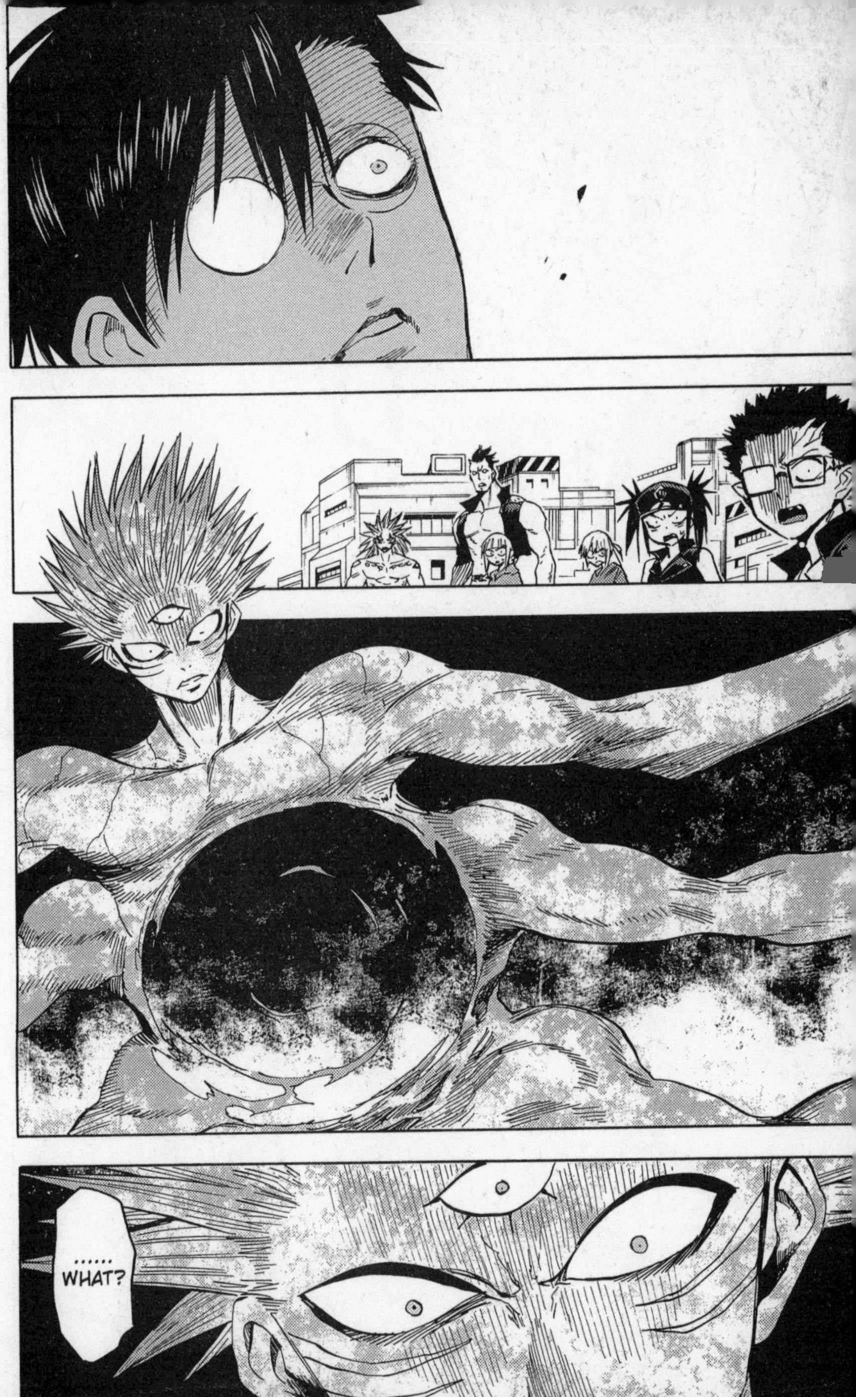

......
WHAT?

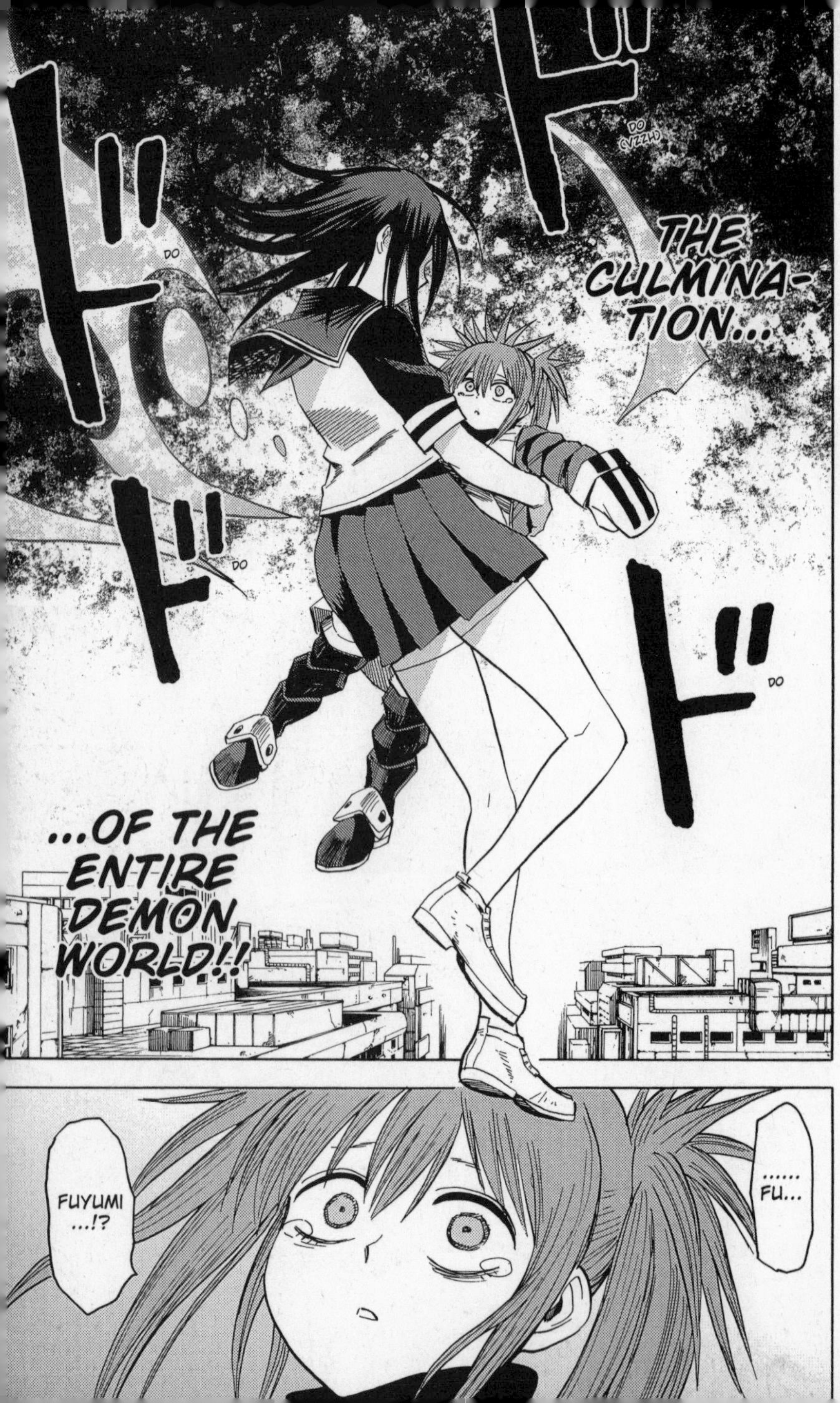
ド
DO (VZZH)
THE CULMINATION...
ドド
DO
ドド
DO
ドド
DO
ドド
DO
...OF THE ENTIRE DEMON WORLD!!
......FU...
FUYUMI ...!?

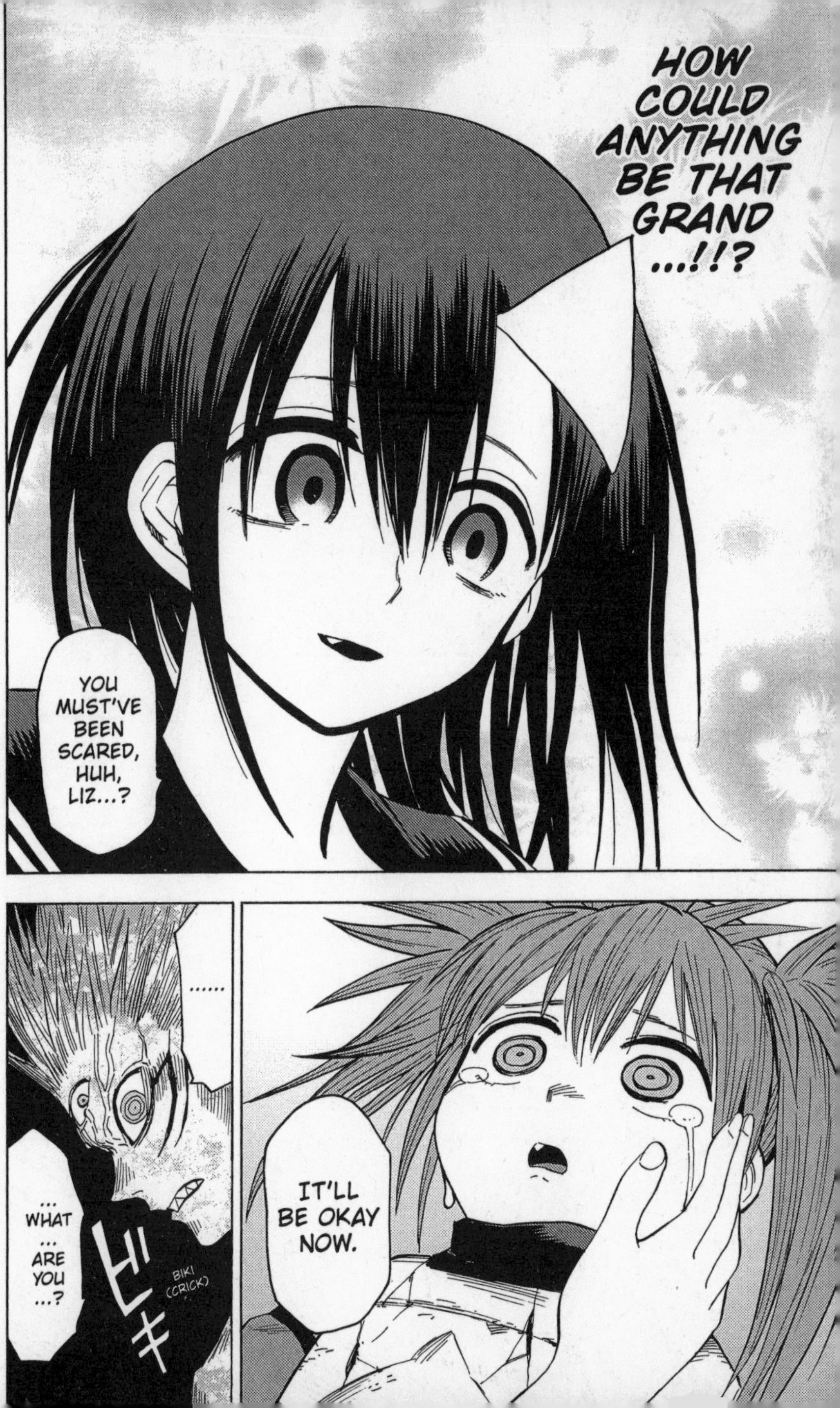
HOW COULD ANYTHING BE THAT GRAND ...!!?
YOU MUST'VE BEEN SCARED, HUH, LIZ...?
IT'LL BE OKAY NOW.
......
... WHAT ... ARE YOU ...?
BIKI (CRICK)

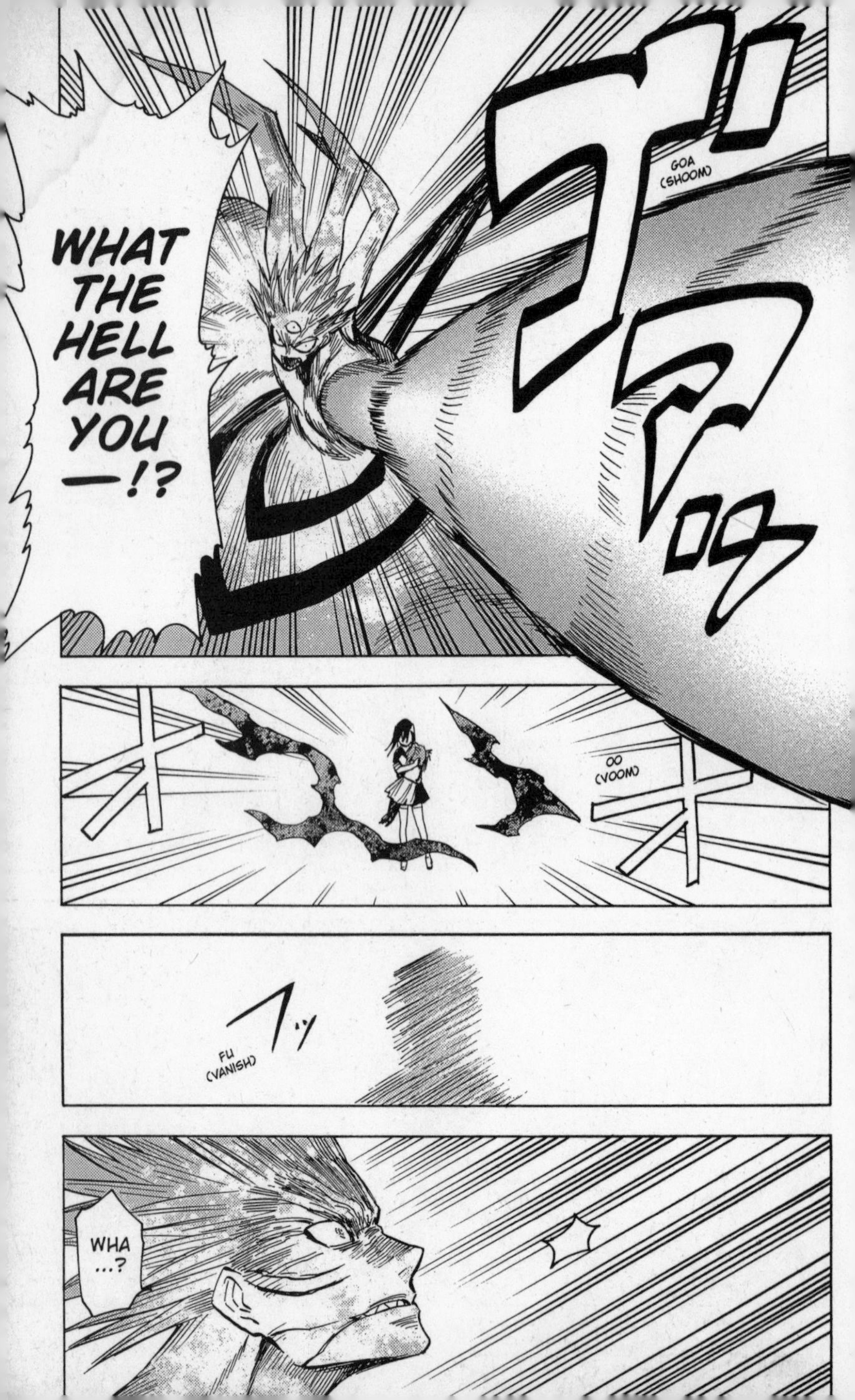
GOA (SHOOM)
WHAT THE HELL ARE YOU—!?
OO (VOOM)
FU (VANISH)
WHA ...?

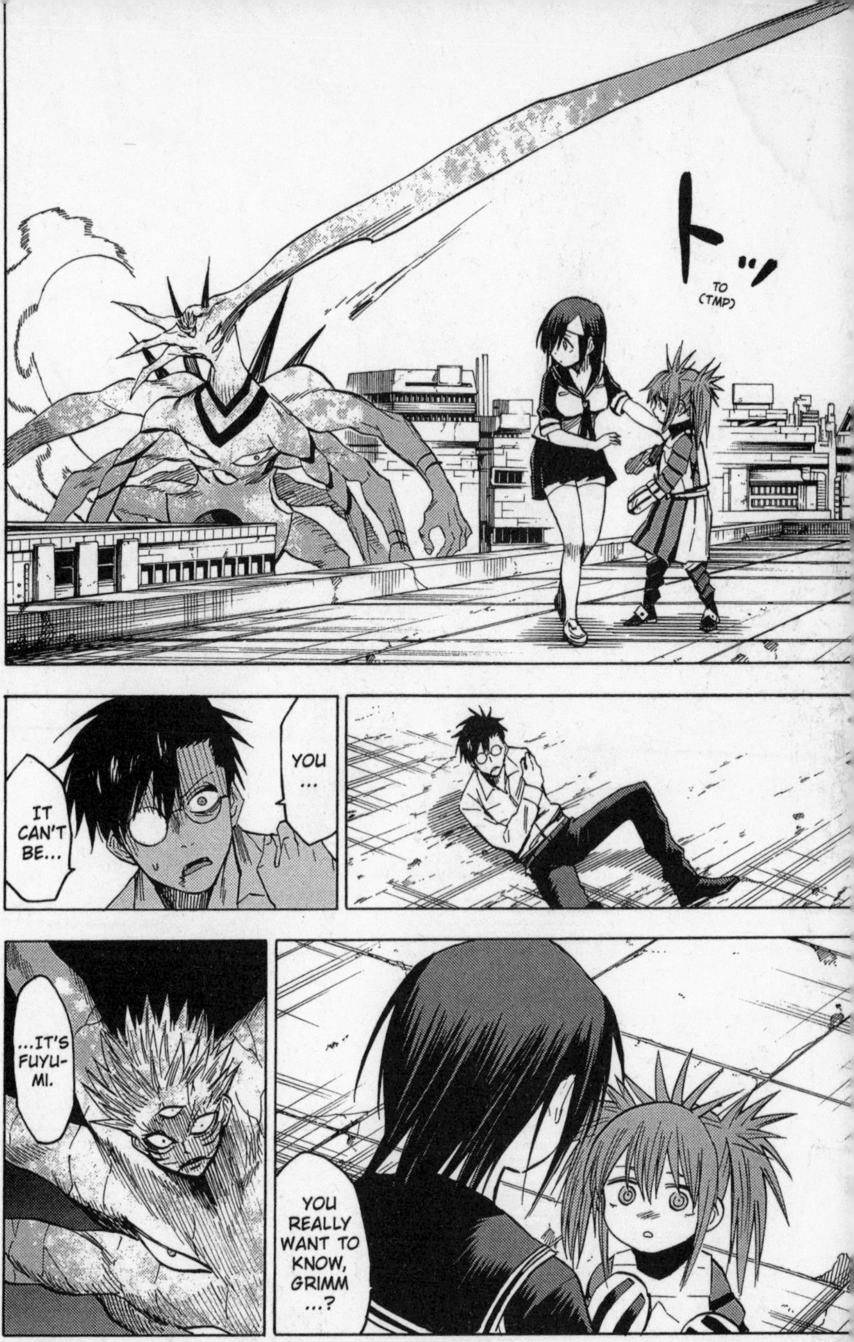
トッ
TO (TMP)
YOU ...
IT CAN'T BE...
YOU REALLY WANT TO KNOW, GRIMM ...?
...IT'S FUYU-MI.

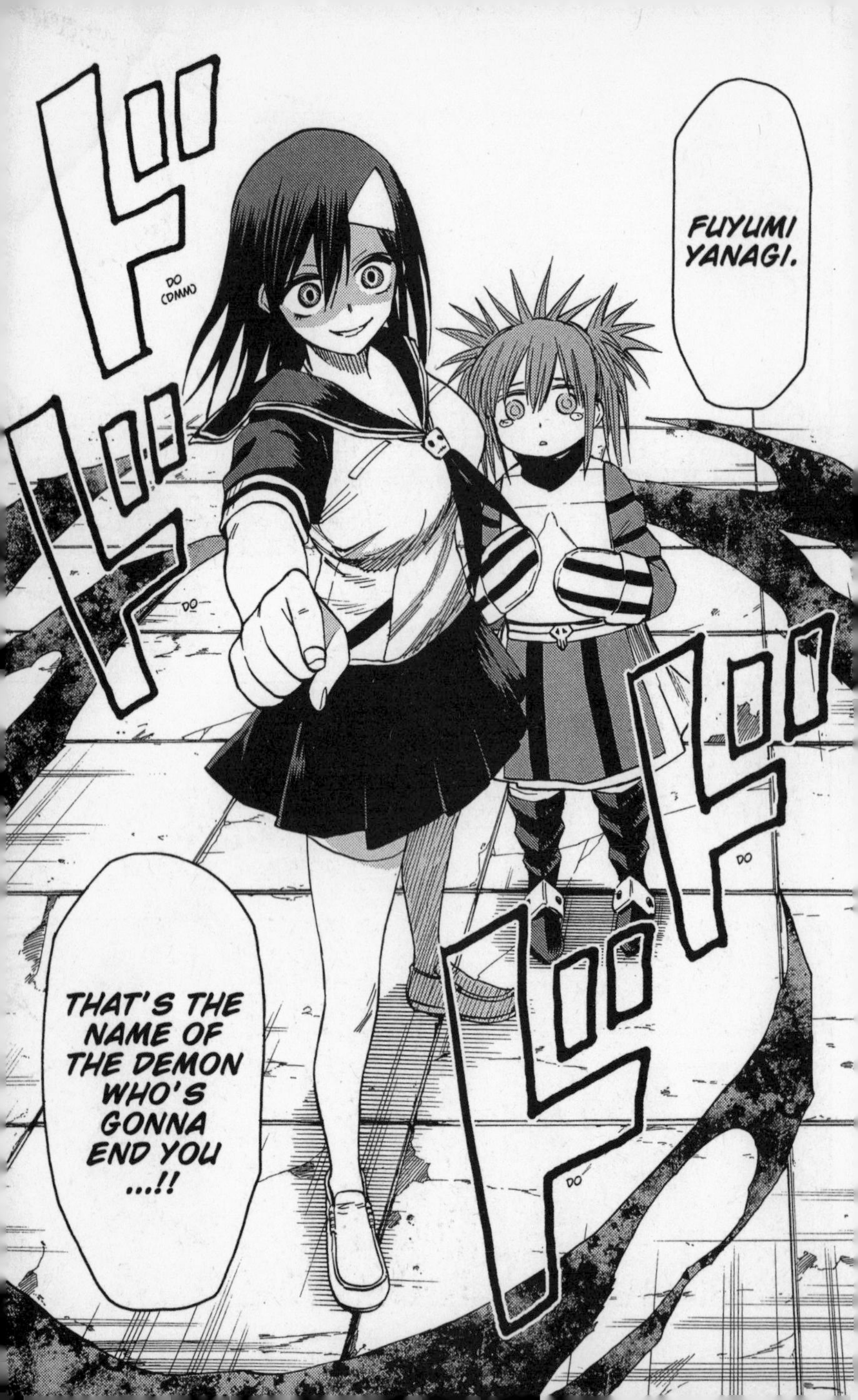
FUYUMI YANAGI.
DO (OMM)
DO
THAT'S THE NAME OF THE DEMON WHO'S GONNA END YOU ...!!
DO
DO

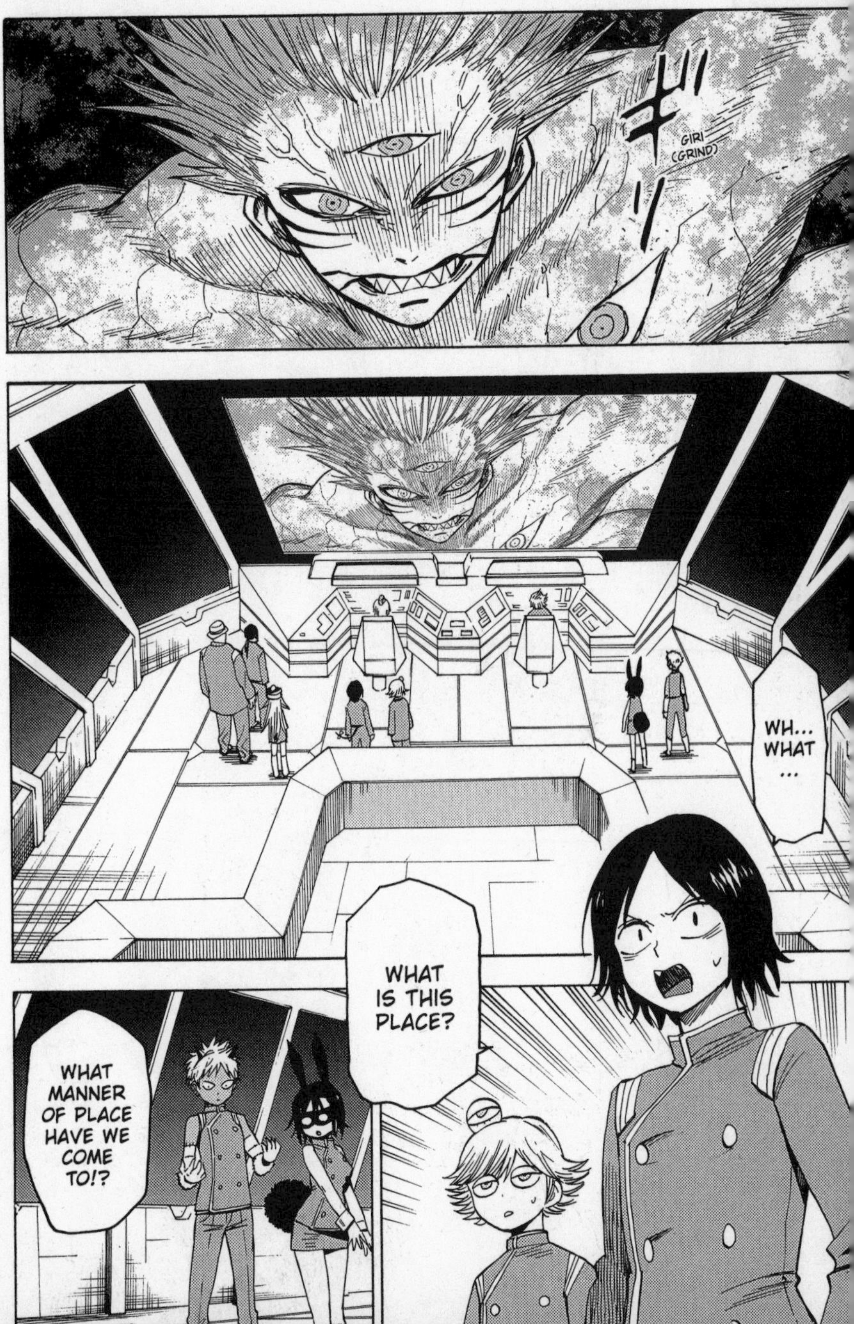
ギリ
GIRI (GRIND)
WH... WHAT ...
WHAT IS THIS PLACE?
WHAT MANNER OF PLACE HAVE WE COME TO!?

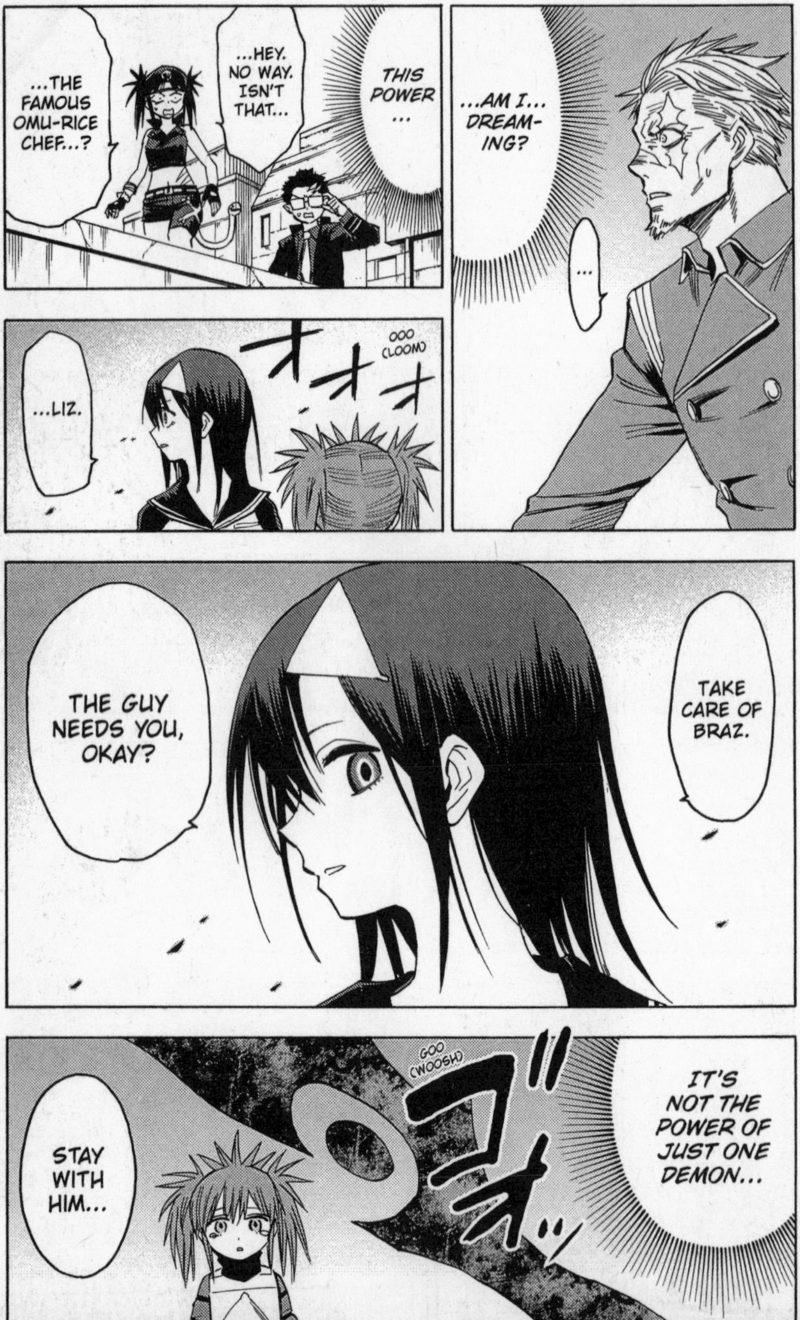
...AM I... DREAMING?
...
THIS POWER ...
...HEY. NO WAY. ISN'T THAT...
...THE FAMOUS OMU-RICE CHEF...?
OOO (LOOM)
...LIZ.
TAKE CARE OF BRAZ.
THE GUY NEEDS YOU, OKAY?
IT'S NOT THE POWER OF JUST ONE DEMON...
GOO (WOOSH)
STAY WITH HIM...

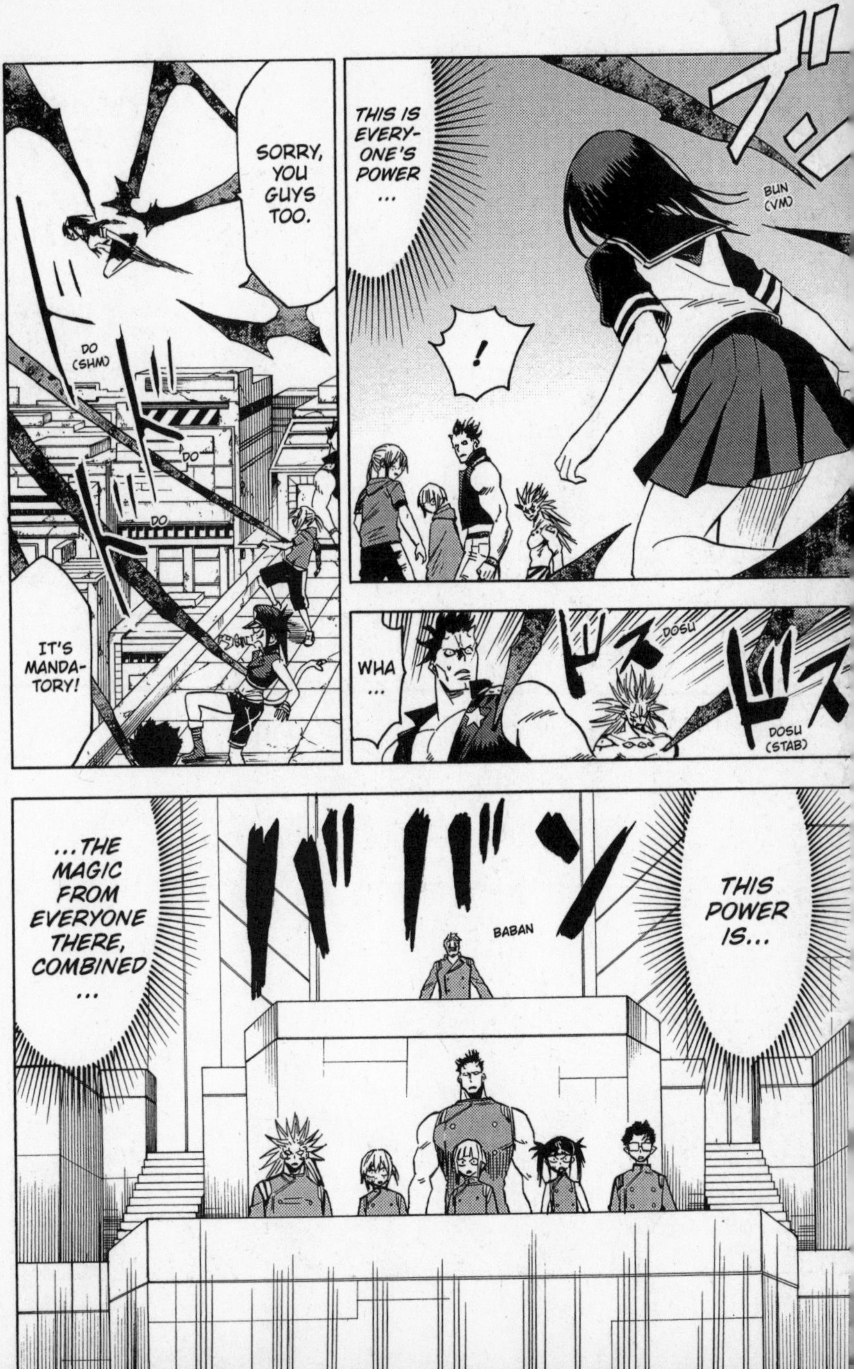
BUN (VM)
THIS IS EVERY-ONE'S POWER ...
!
DOSU
DOSU (STAB)
WHA ...
SORRY, YOU GUYS TOO.
DO (SHM)
DO
DO
IT'S MANDA-TORY!
THIS POWER IS...
BABAN
...THE MAGIC FROM EVERYONE THERE, COMBINED ...

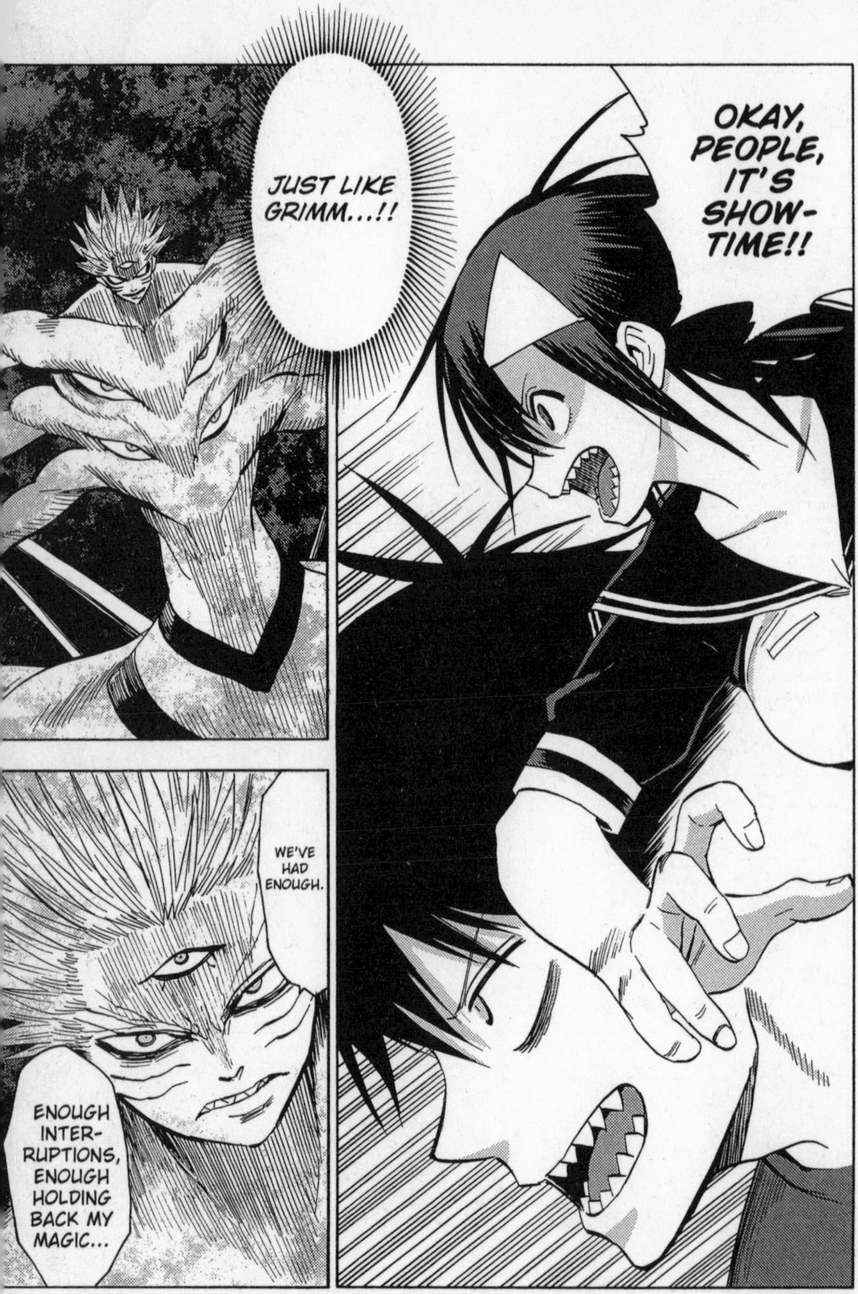
OKAY, PEOPLE, IT'S SHOW-TIME!!
JUST LIKE GRIMM...!!
WE'VE HAD ENOUGH.
ENOUGH INTER-RUPTIONS, ENOUGH HOLDING BACK MY MAGIC...

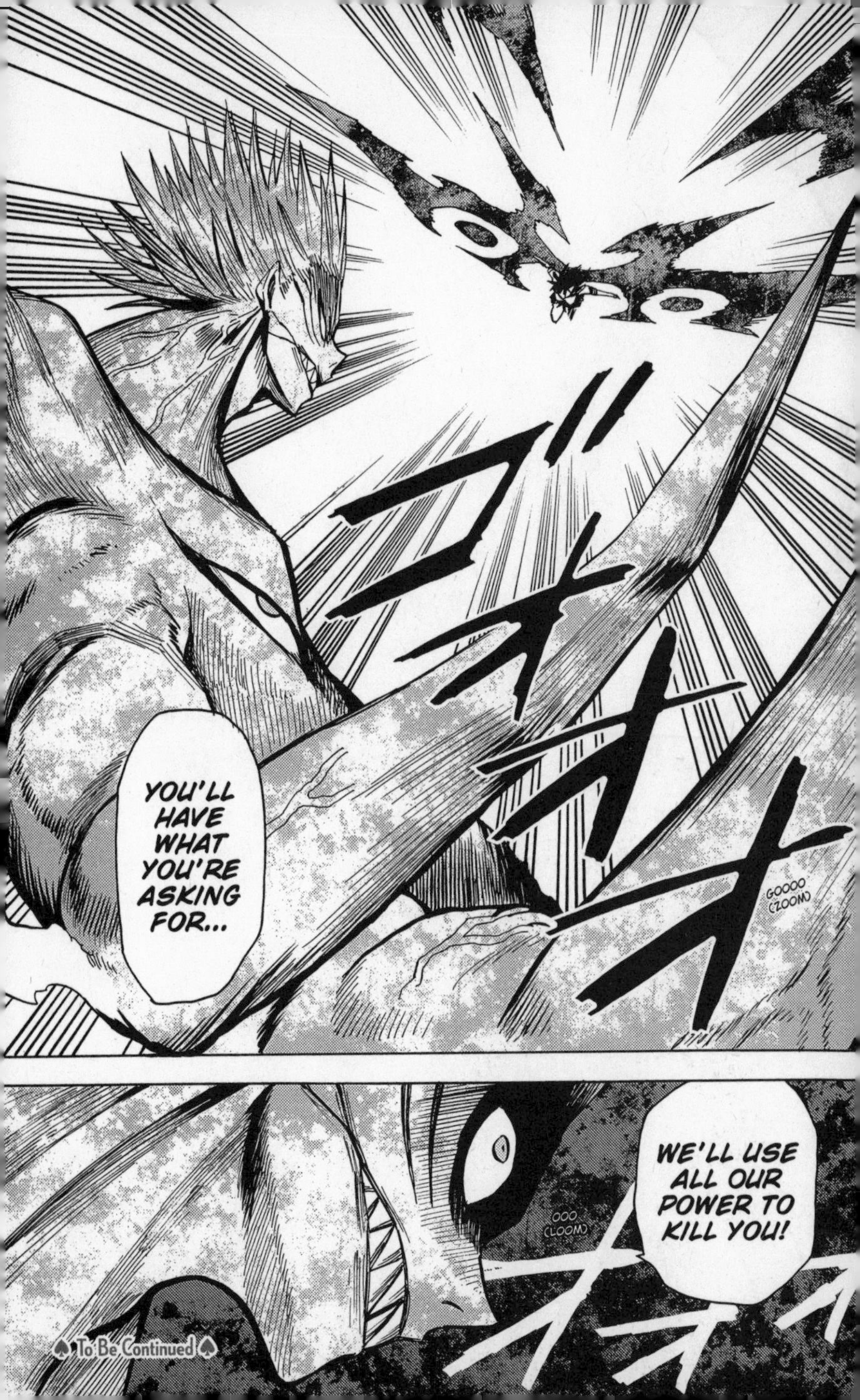
YOU'LL HAVE WHAT YOU'RE ASKING FOR...
GOOOO (ZOOM)
WE'LL USE ALL OUR POWER TO KILL YOU!
OOO (LOOM)
To Be Continued

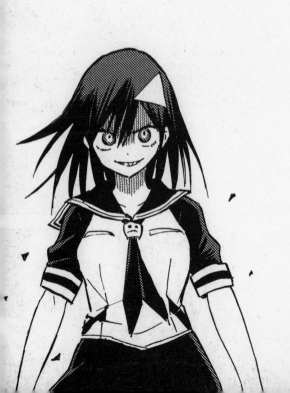

BLOOD LAD

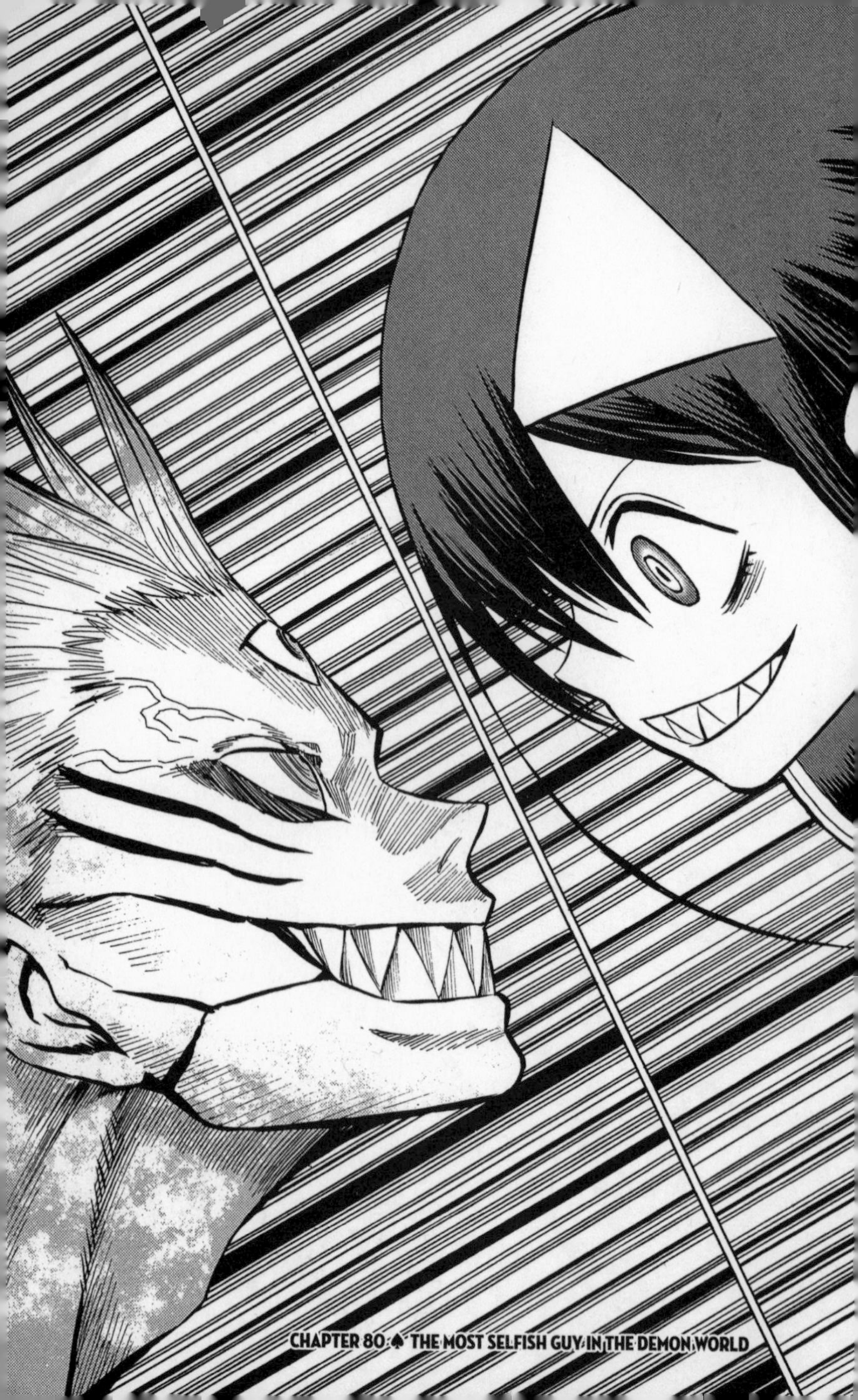

## CHAPTER 80 ♠ THE MOST SELFISH GUY IN THE DEMON WORLD

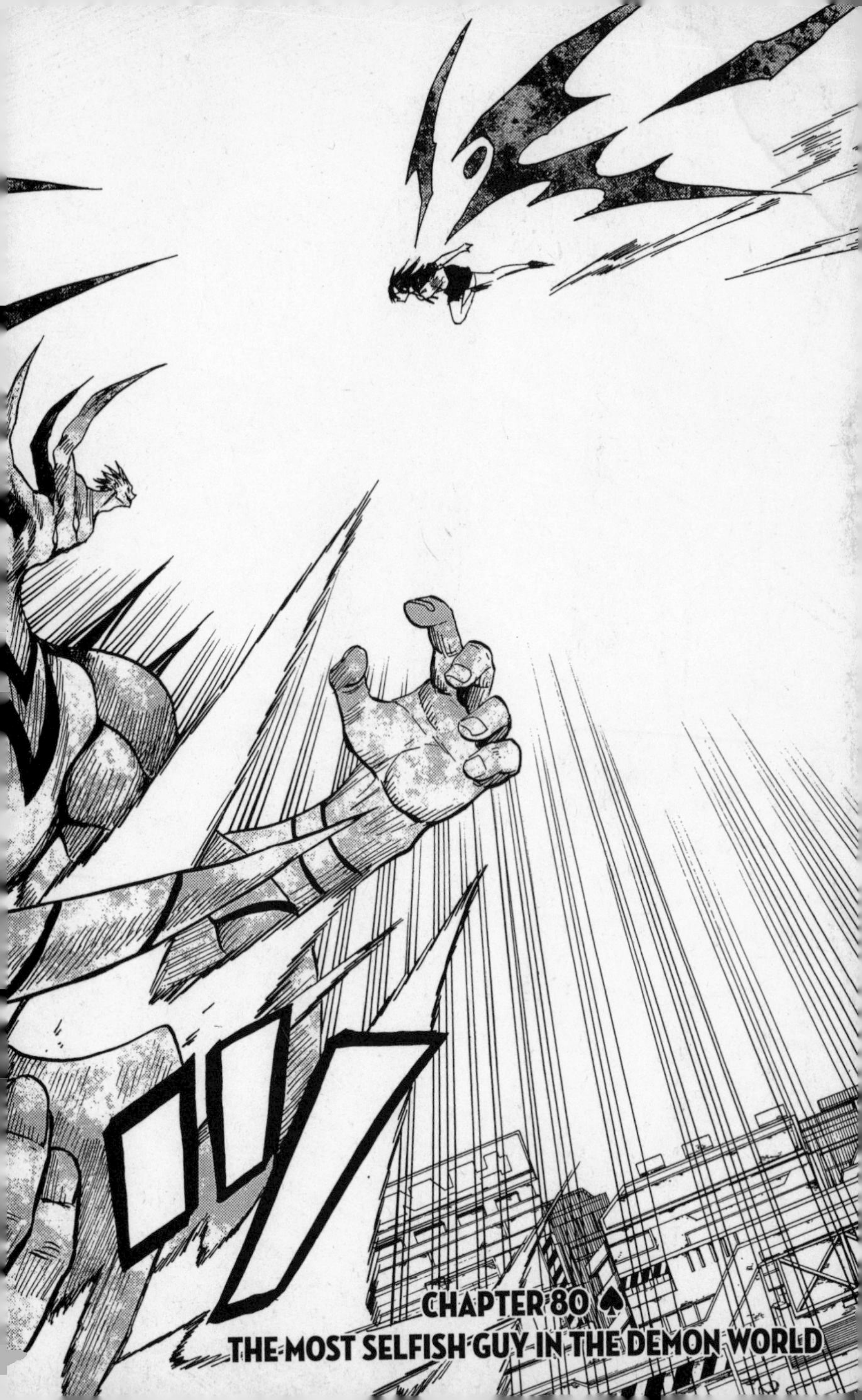

# CHAPTER 80 ♠ THE MOST SELFISH GUY IN THE DEMON WORLD

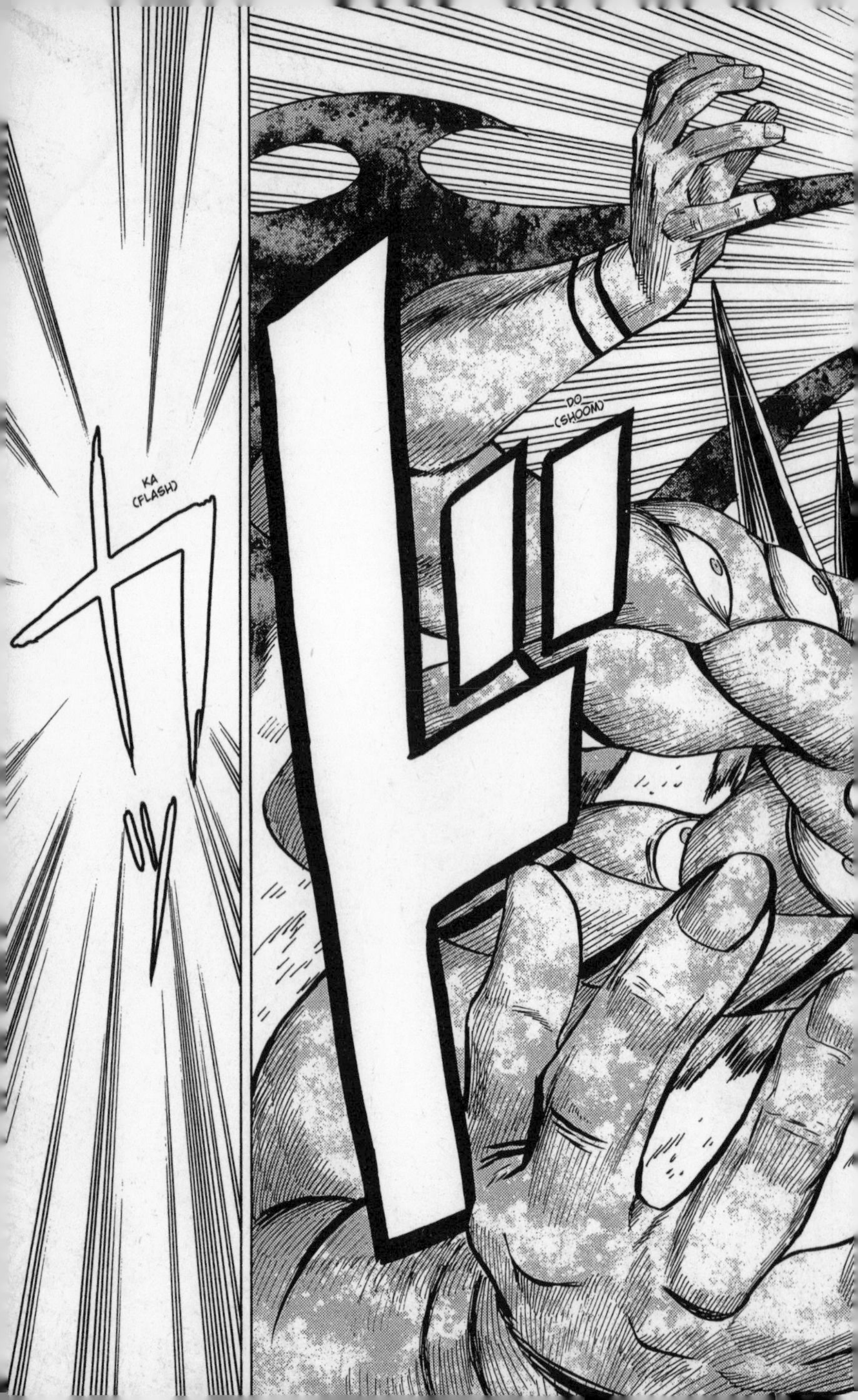
DO
(SHOOM)
KA
(FLASH)

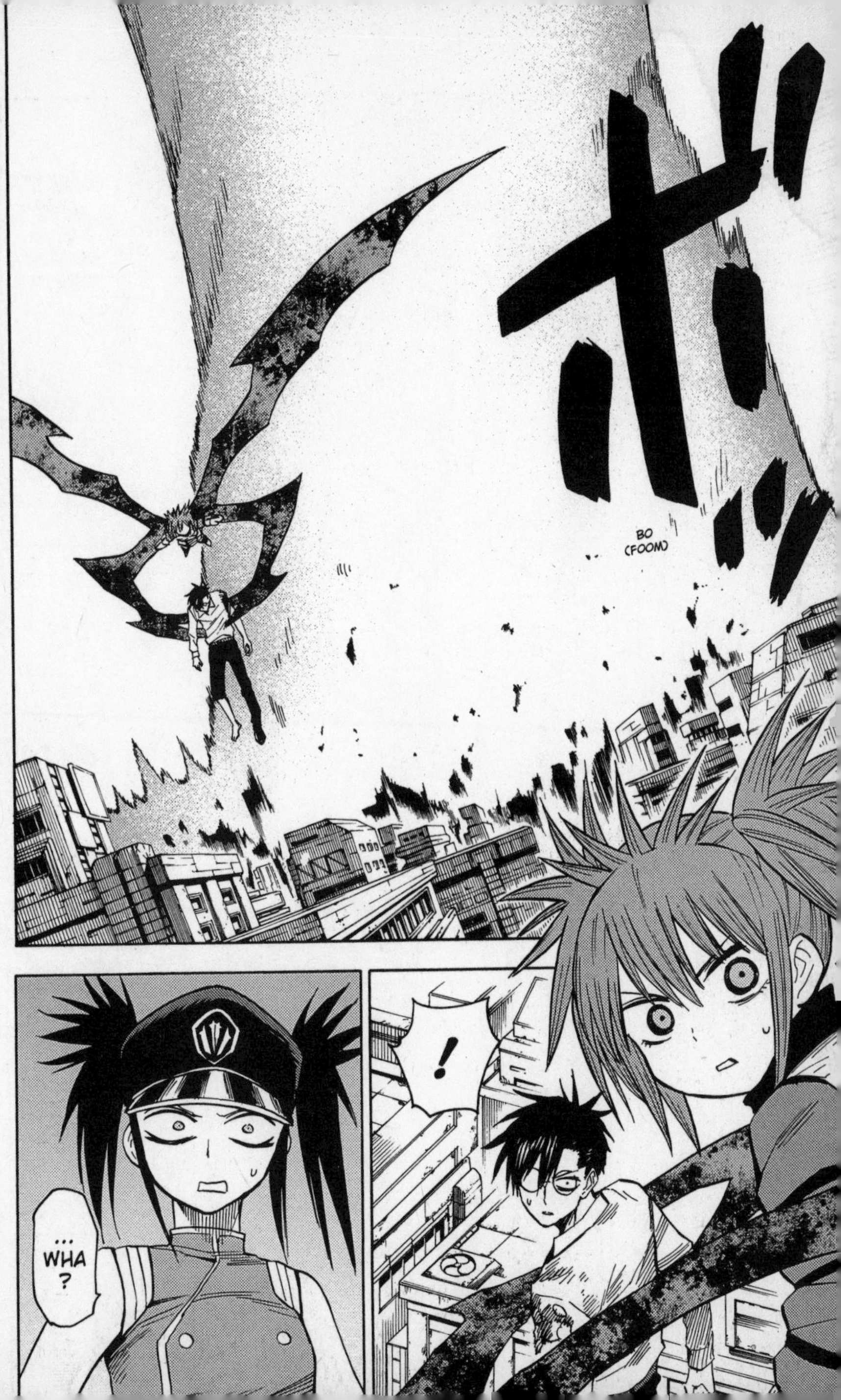
BO
(FOOM)
!
...WHA?

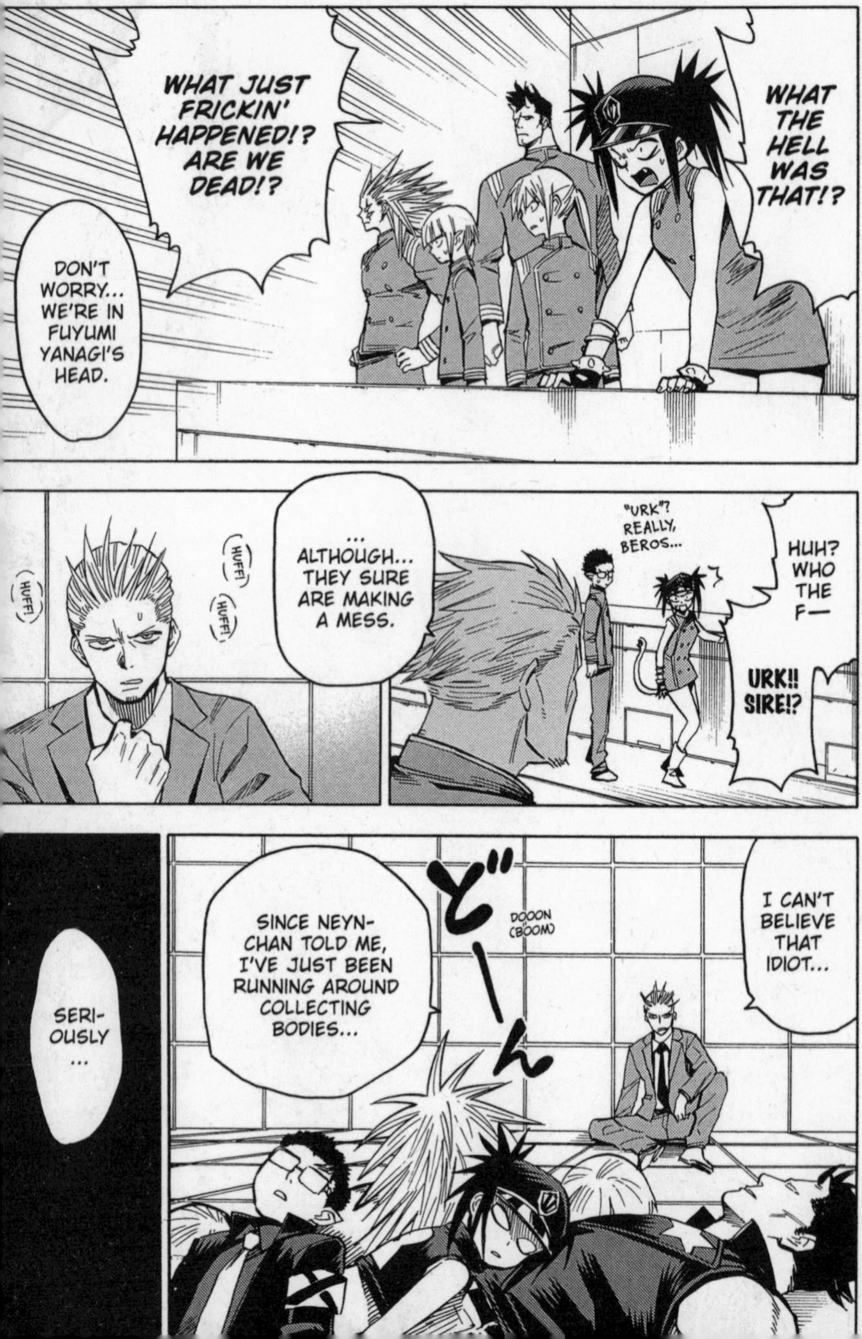
WHAT THE HELL WAS THAT!?
WHAT JUST FRICKIN' HAPPENED!? ARE WE DEAD!?
DON'T WORRY... WE'RE IN FUYUMI YANAGI'S HEAD.
HUH? WHO THE F—
URK!! SIRE!?
"URK"? REALLY, BEROS...
... ALTHOUGH... THEY SURE ARE MAKING A MESS.
HUFF!
HUFF!
HUFF!
I CAN'T BELIEVE THAT IDIOT...
どーん
DOOON (BOOM)
SINCE NEYN-CHAN TOLD ME, I'VE JUST BEEN RUNNING AROUND COLLECTING BODIES...
SERIOUSLY...

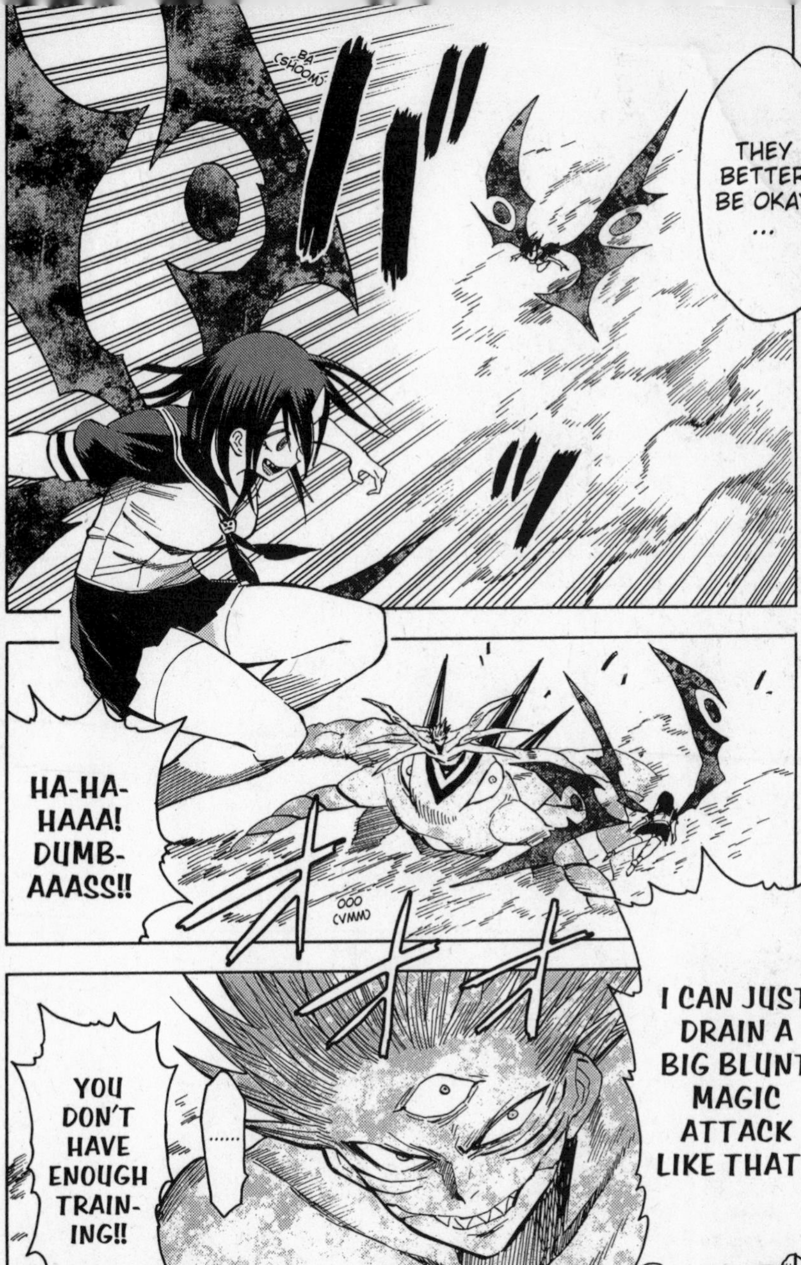
THEY BETTER BE OKAY ...
BA (SHOOM)
HA-HA-HAAA! DUMB-AAASS!!
OOO (VMM)
I CAN JUST DRAIN A BIG BLUNT MAGIC ATTACK LIKE THAT!!
......
YOU DON'T HAVE ENOUGH TRAIN-ING!!

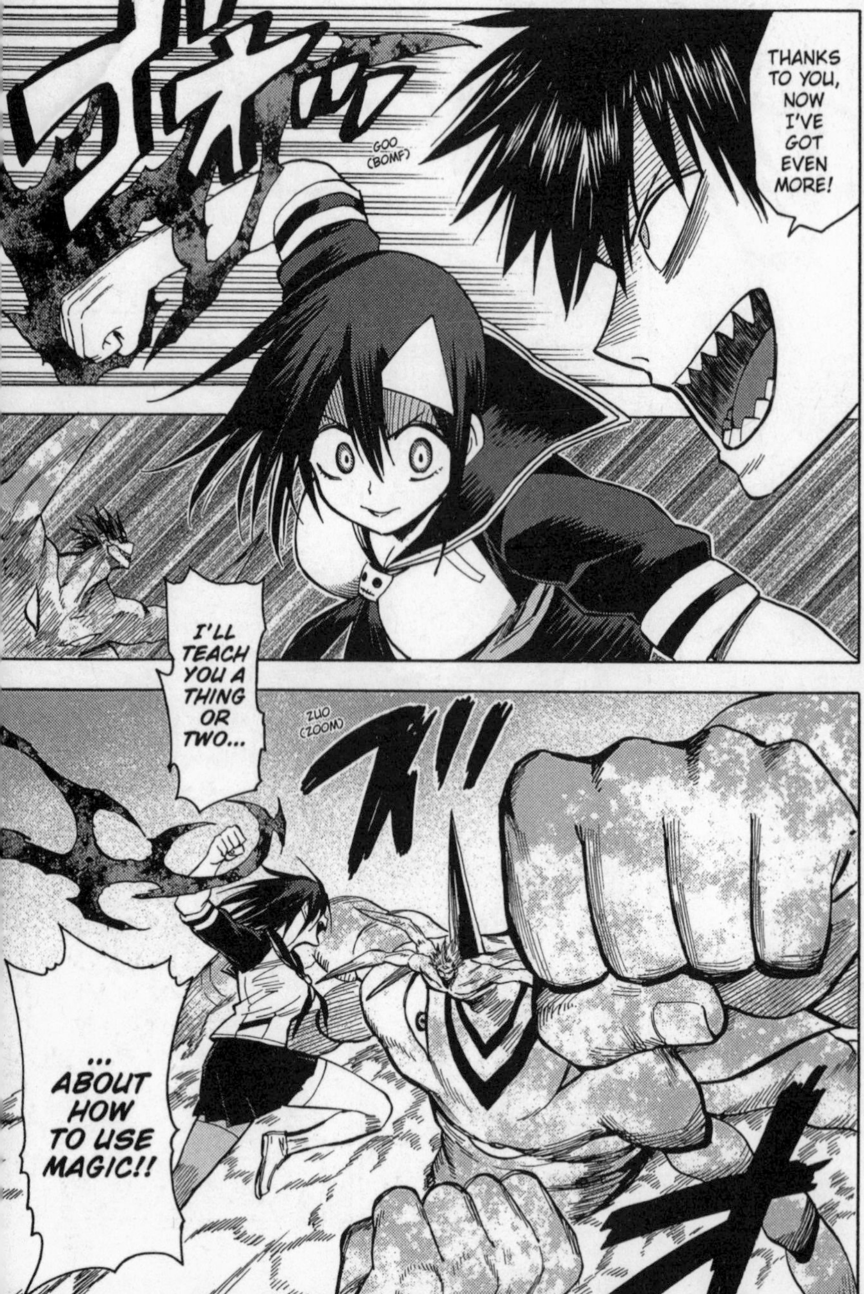
THANKS TO YOU, NOW I'VE GOT EVEN MORE!
GOO (BOMF)
I'LL TEACH YOU A THING OR TWO...
ZUO (ZOOM)
... ABOUT HOW TO USE MAGIC!!

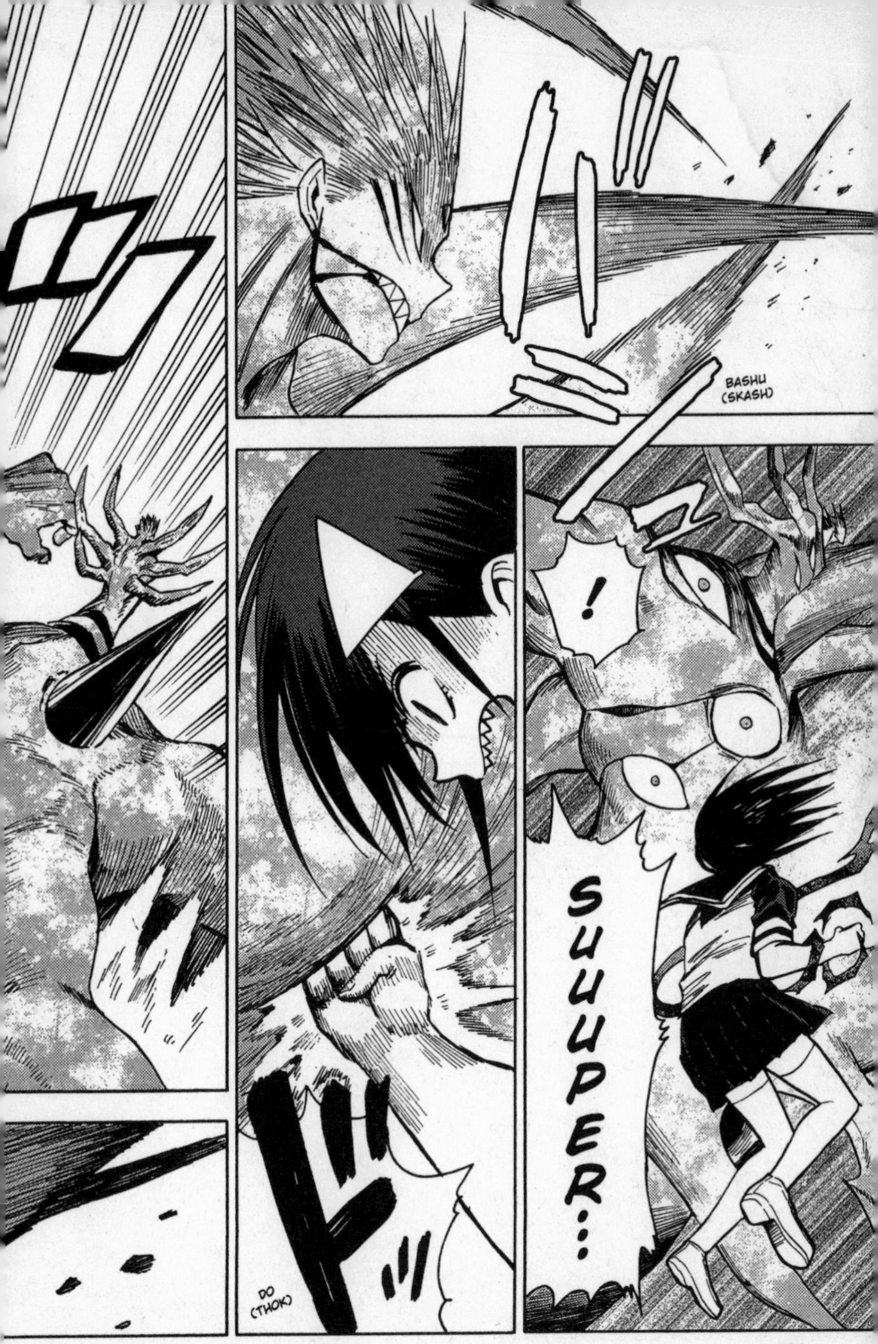
BASHU
(SKASH)
!
SUUUPER...
DO
(THOK)

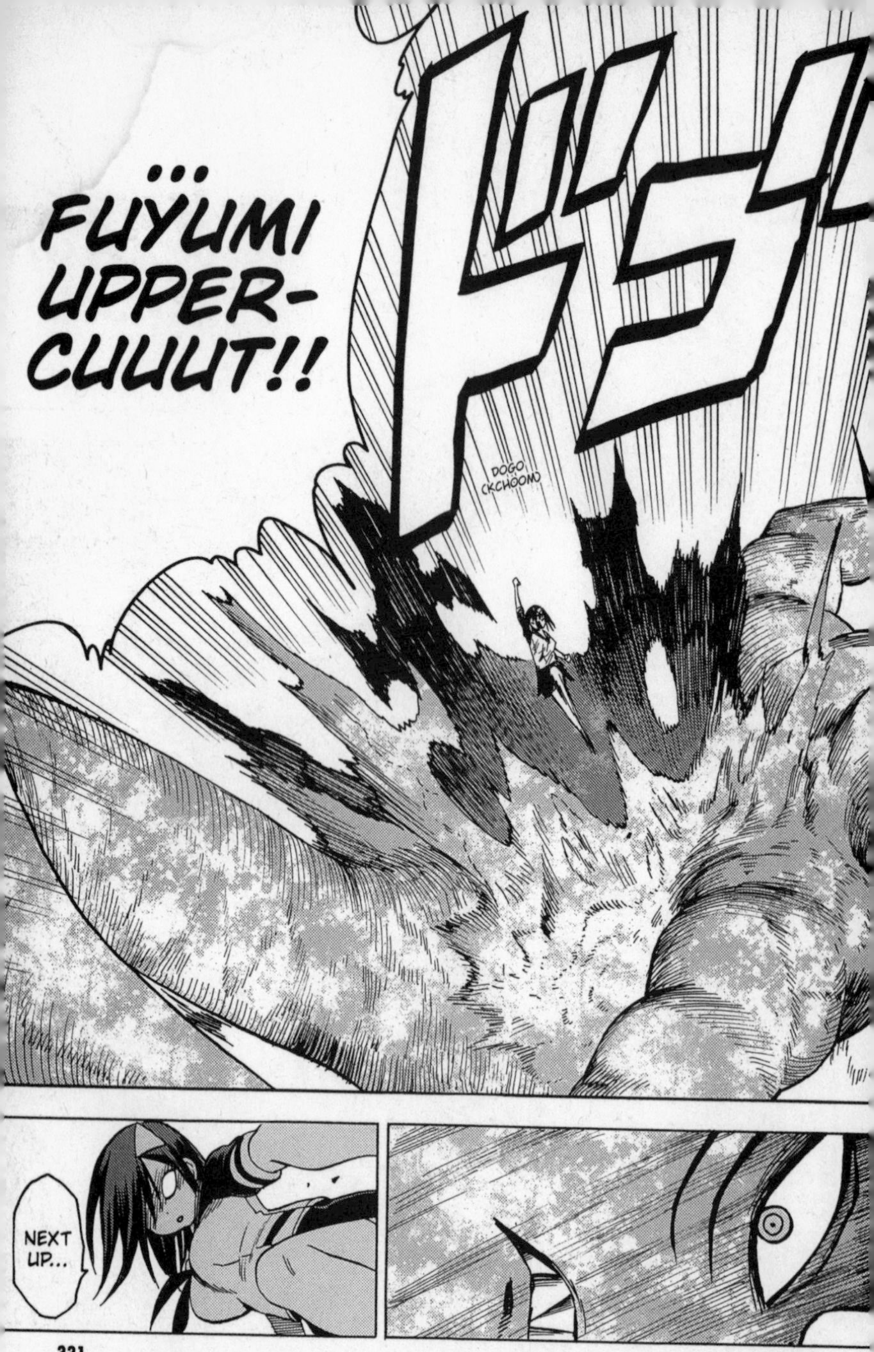
...FUYUMI UPPER-CUUUT!!
DOGO
(KCHOOM)
NEXT UP...

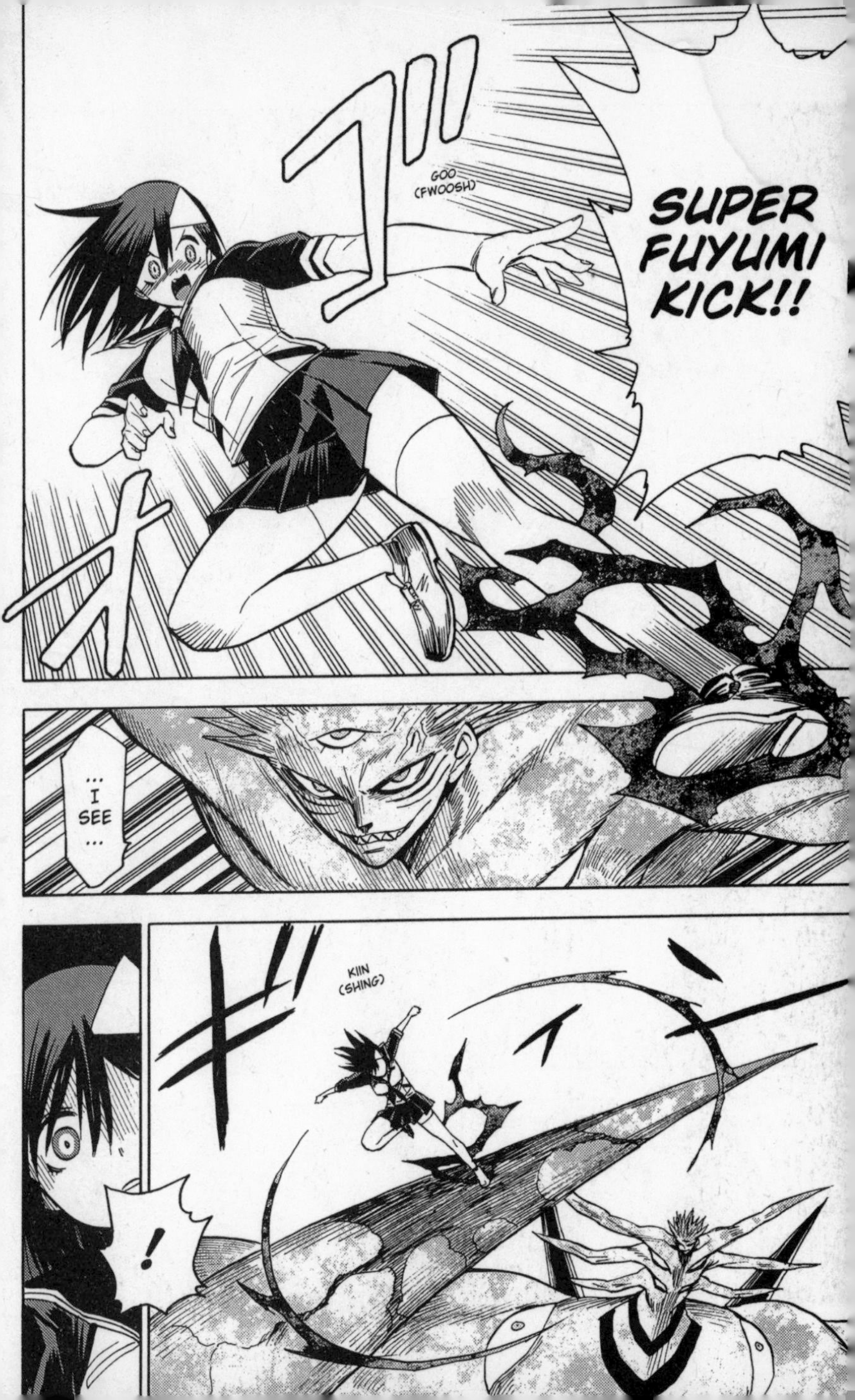
SUPER FUYUMI KICK!!
GOO (FWOOSH)
... I SEE ...
KIIN (SHING)
!

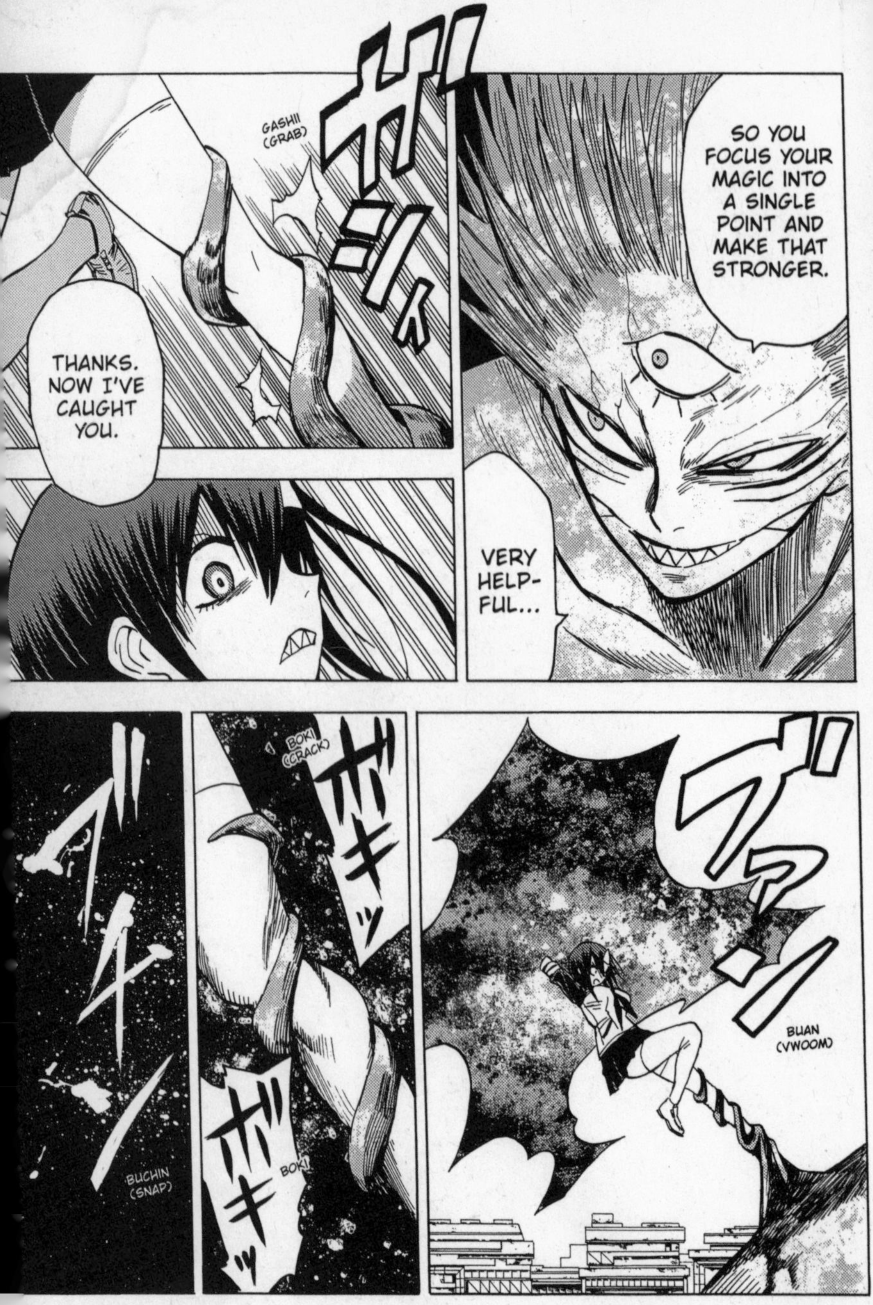
SO YOU FOCUS YOUR MAGIC INTO A SINGLE POINT AND MAKE THAT STRONGER.
VERY HELP-FUL...
GASHII (GRAB)
THANKS. NOW I'VE CAUGHT YOU.
BUAN (VWOOM)
BOKI (CRACK)
BOKI
BUCHIN (SNAP)

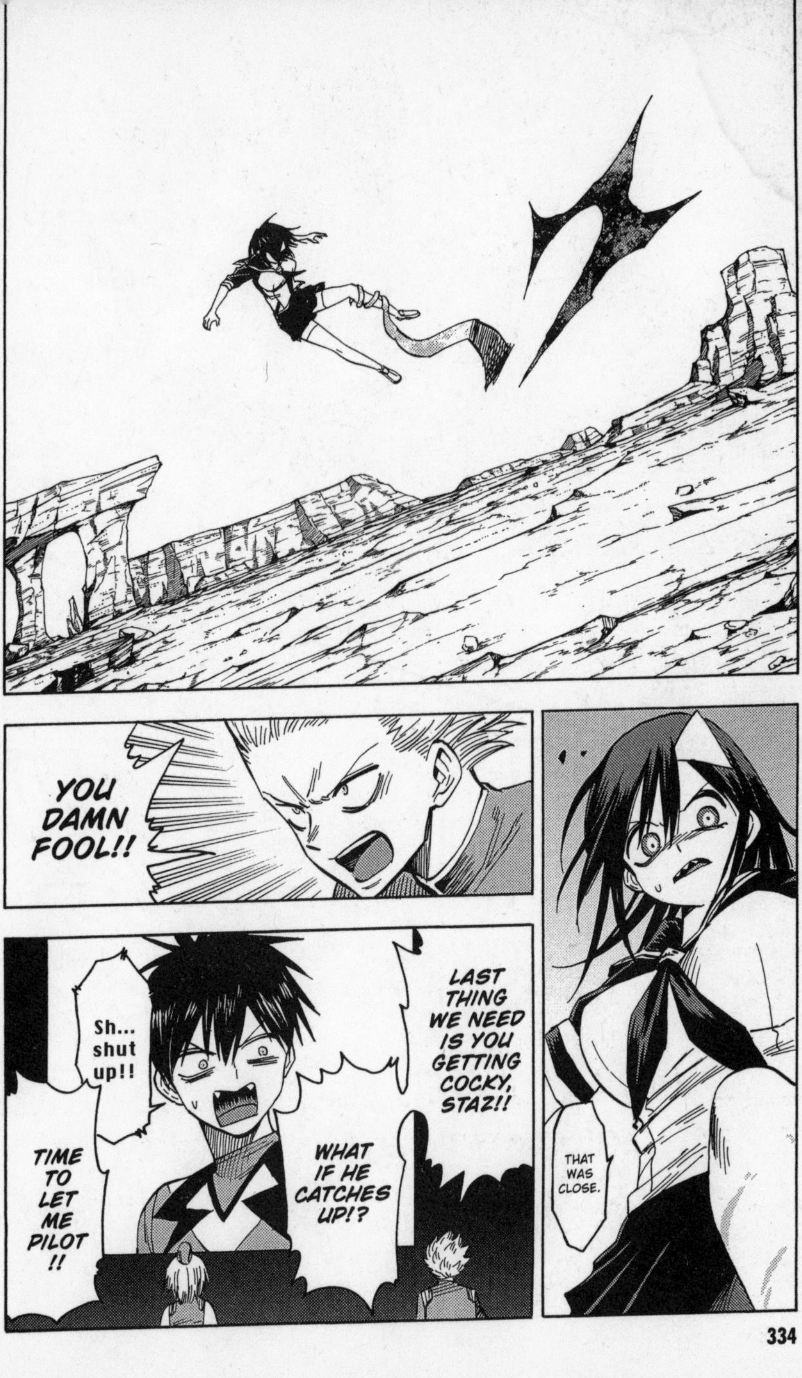
THAT WAS CLOSE.
YOU DAMN FOOL!!
LAST THING WE NEED IS YOU GETTING COCKY, STAZ!!
WHAT IF HE CATCHES UP!?
Sh... shut up!!
TIME TO LET ME PILOT!!

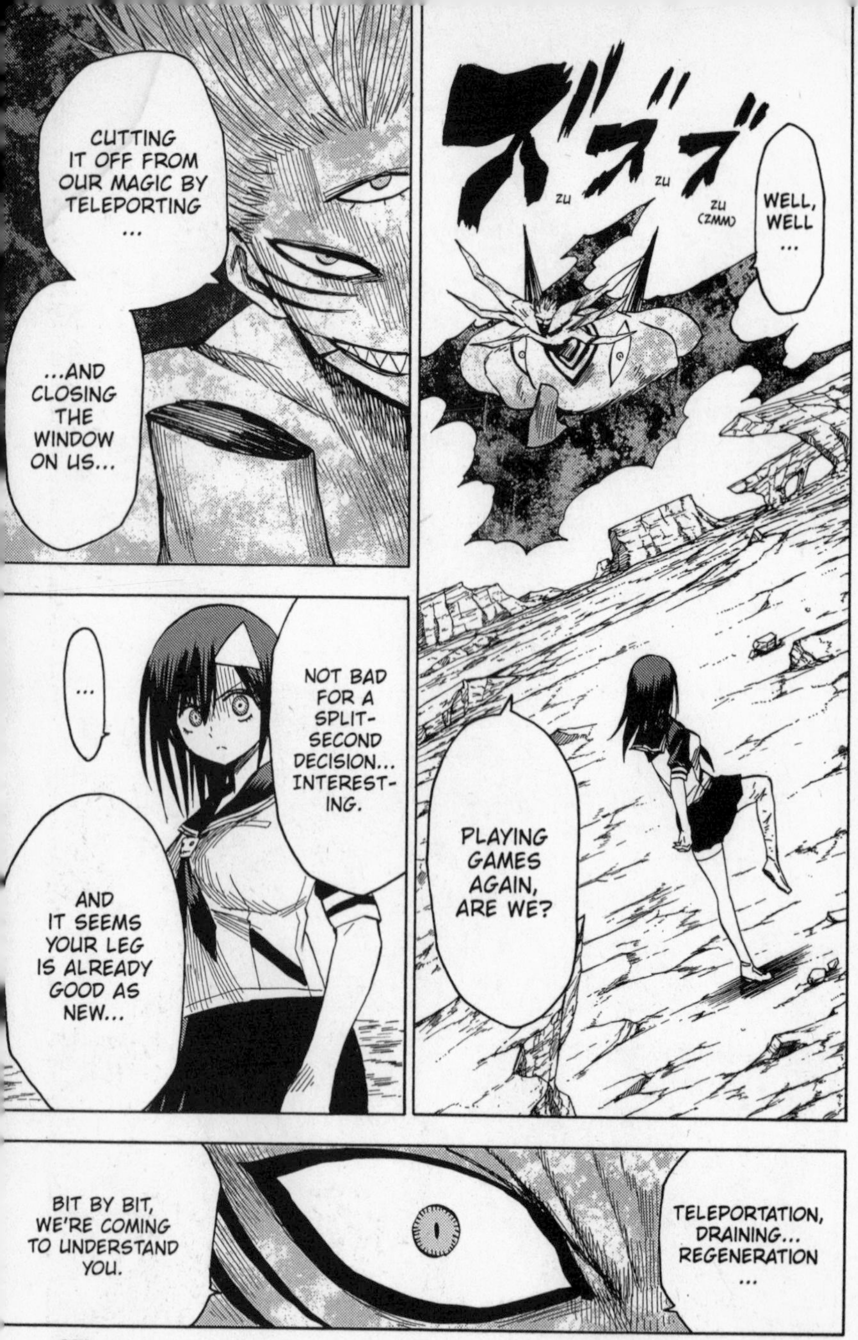
ZU ZU ZU (ZMM)
WELL, WELL ...
PLAYING GAMES AGAIN, ARE WE?
CUTTING IT OFF FROM OUR MAGIC BY TELEPORTING ...
...AND CLOSING THE WINDOW ON US...
NOT BAD FOR A SPLIT-SECOND DECISION... INTERESTING.
...
AND IT SEEMS YOUR LEG IS ALREADY GOOD AS NEW...
TELEPORTATION, DRAINING... REGENERATION ...
BIT BY BIT, WE'RE COMING TO UNDERSTAND YOU.

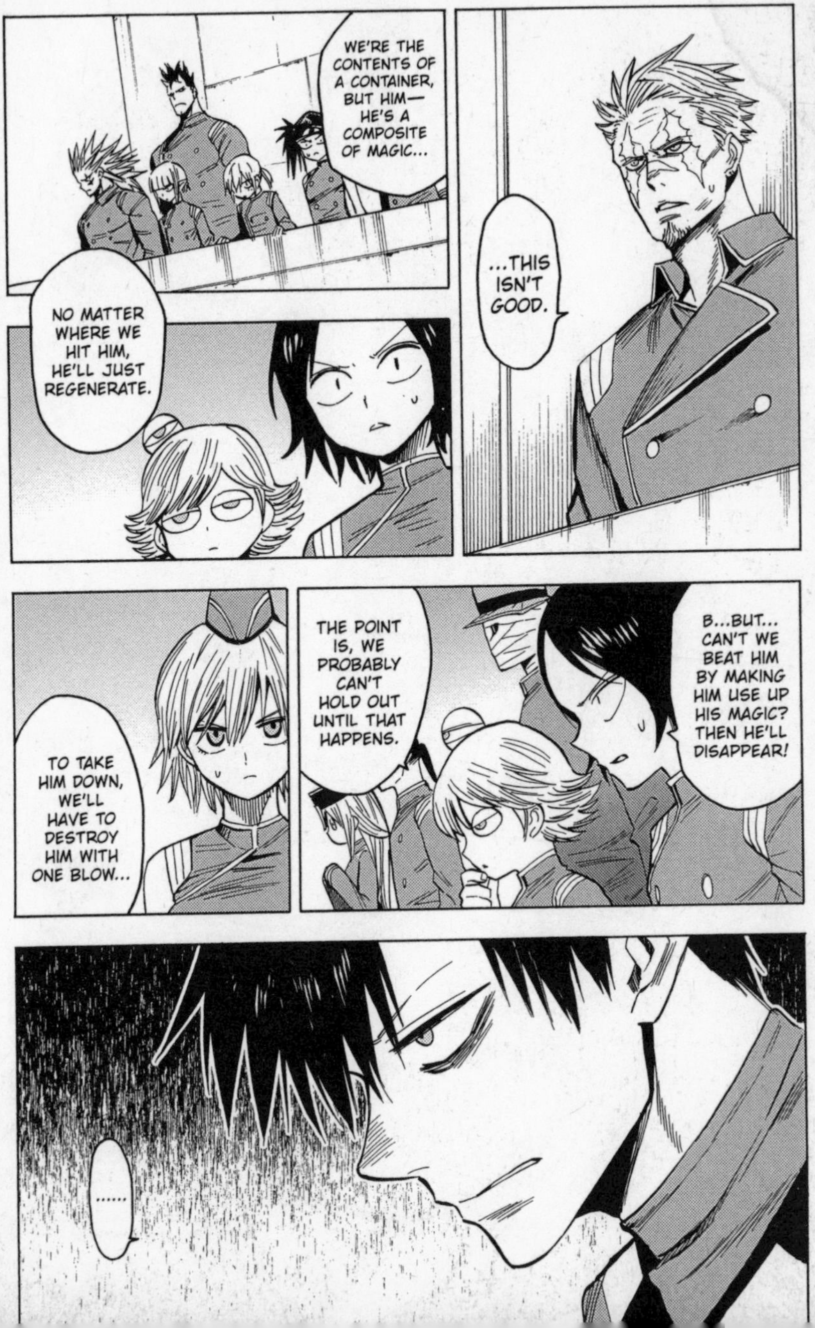
...THIS ISN'T GOOD.
WE'RE THE CONTENTS OF A CONTAINER, BUT HIM—HE'S A COMPOSITE OF MAGIC...
NO MATTER WHERE WE HIT HIM, HE'LL JUST REGENERATE.
B...BUT... CAN'T WE BEAT HIM BY MAKING HIM USE UP HIS MAGIC? THEN HE'LL DISAPPEAR!
THE POINT IS, WE PROBABLY CAN'T HOLD OUT UNTIL THAT HAPPENS.
TO TAKE HIM DOWN, WE'LL HAVE TO DESTROY HIM WITH ONE BLOW...
......

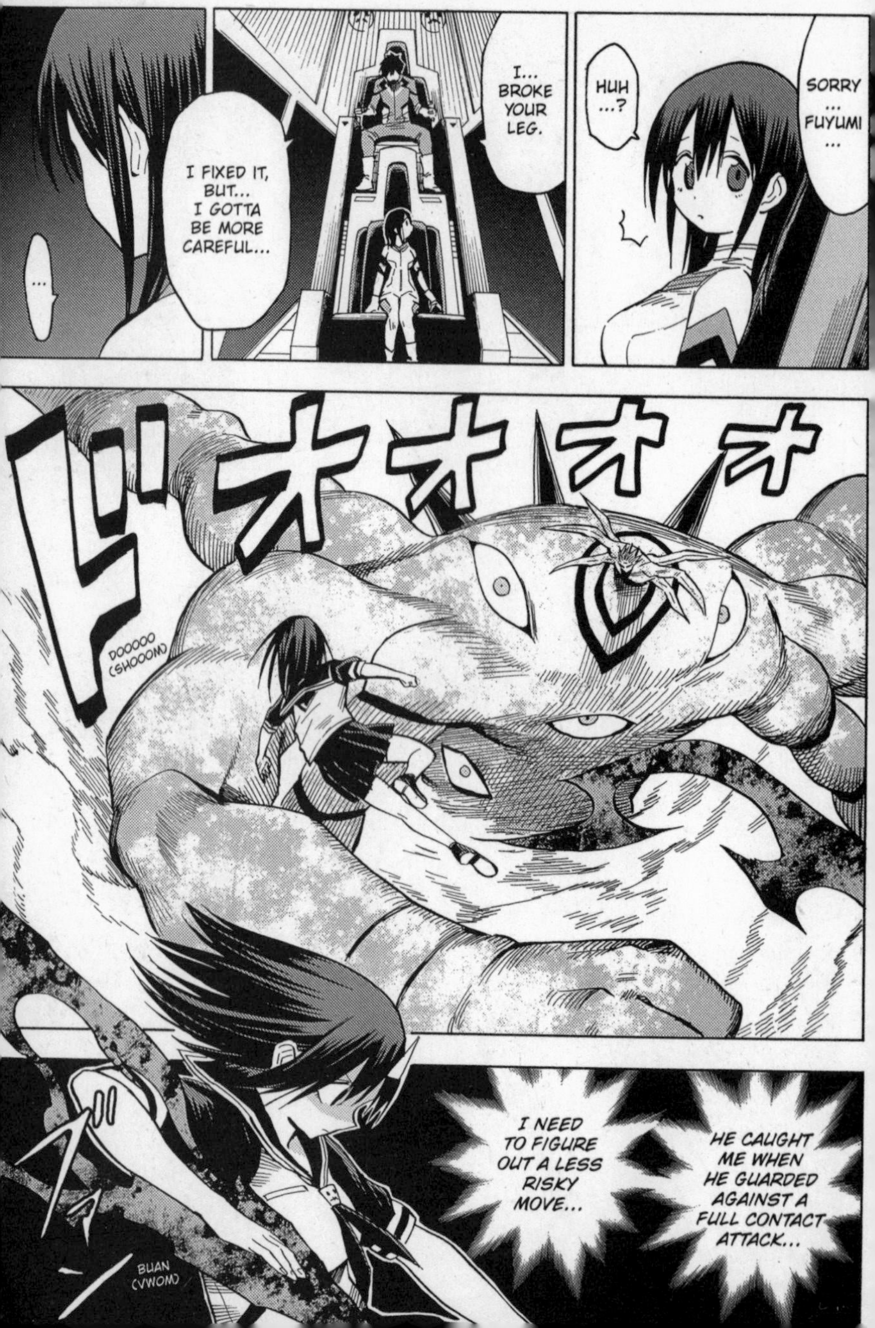

SORRY ... FUYUMI ...
HUH ...?
I... BROKE YOUR LEG.
I FIXED IT, BUT... I GOTTA BE MORE CAREFUL...
...
ドオオオ
DOOOOO (SHOOOM)
HE CAUGHT ME WHEN HE GUARDED AGAINST A FULL CONTACT ATTACK...
I NEED TO FIGURE OUT A LESS RISKY MOVE...
BUAN (VWOM)

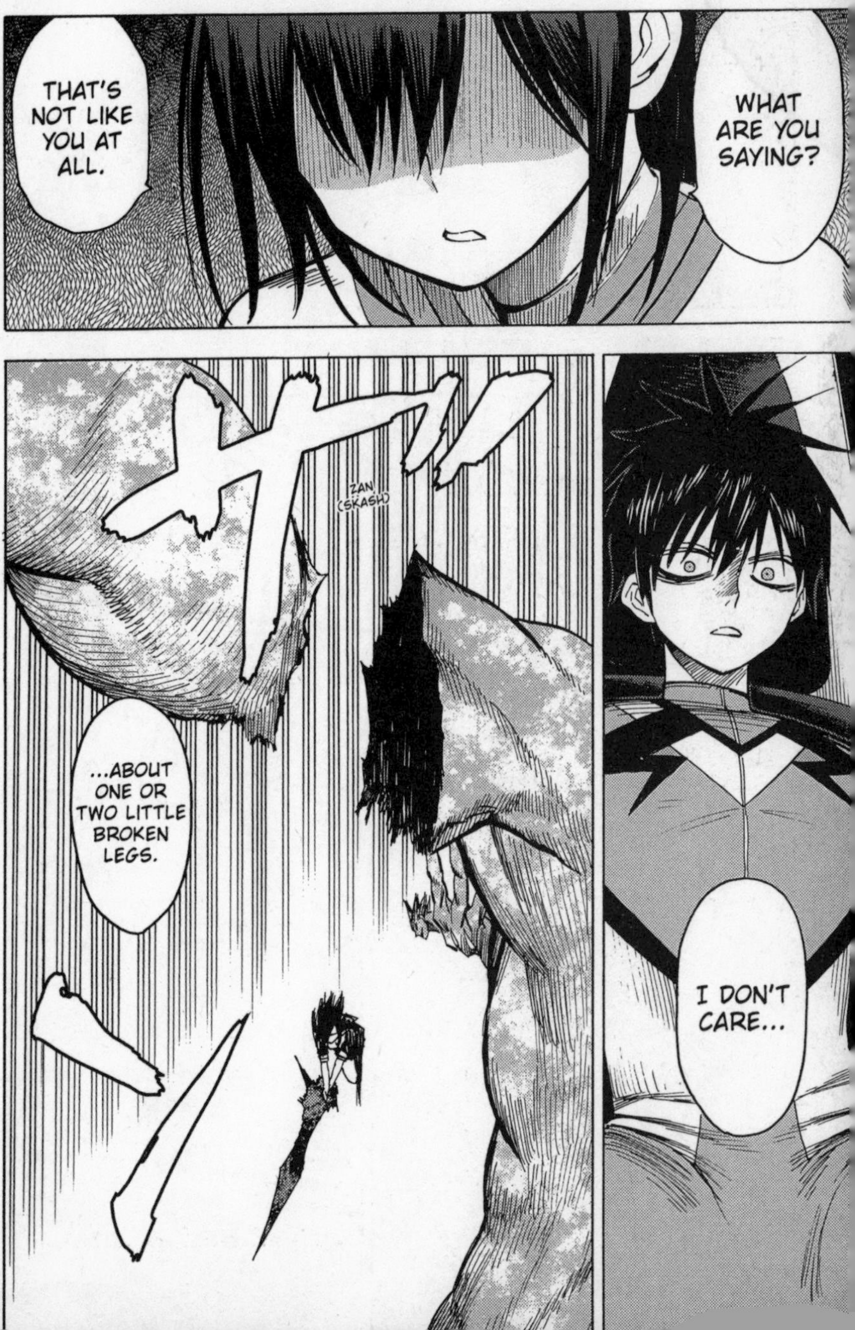
WHAT ARE YOU SAYING?
THAT'S NOT LIKE YOU AT ALL.
I DON'T CARE...
ZAN (SKASH)
...ABOUT ONE OR TWO LITTLE BROKEN LEGS.

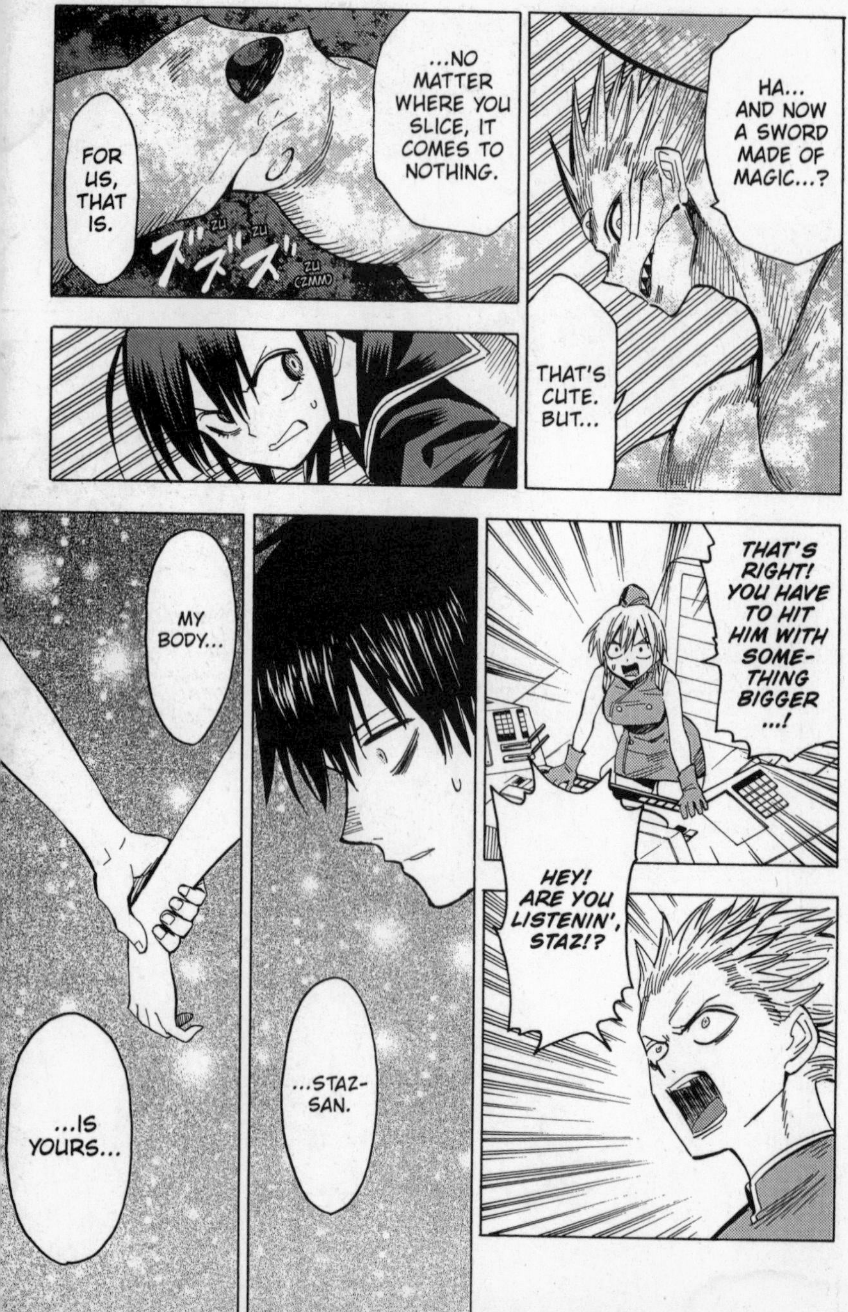
HA... AND NOW A SWORD MADE OF MAGIC...?
THAT'S CUTE. BUT...
...NO MATTER WHERE YOU SLICE, IT COMES TO NOTHING.
FOR US, THAT IS.
ズズズ
ZU ZU ZU (ZMMM)
THAT'S RIGHT! YOU HAVE TO HIT HIM WITH SOME-THING BIGGER...!
HEY! ARE YOU LISTENIN', STAZ!?
...STAZ-SAN.
MY BODY...
...IS YOURS...

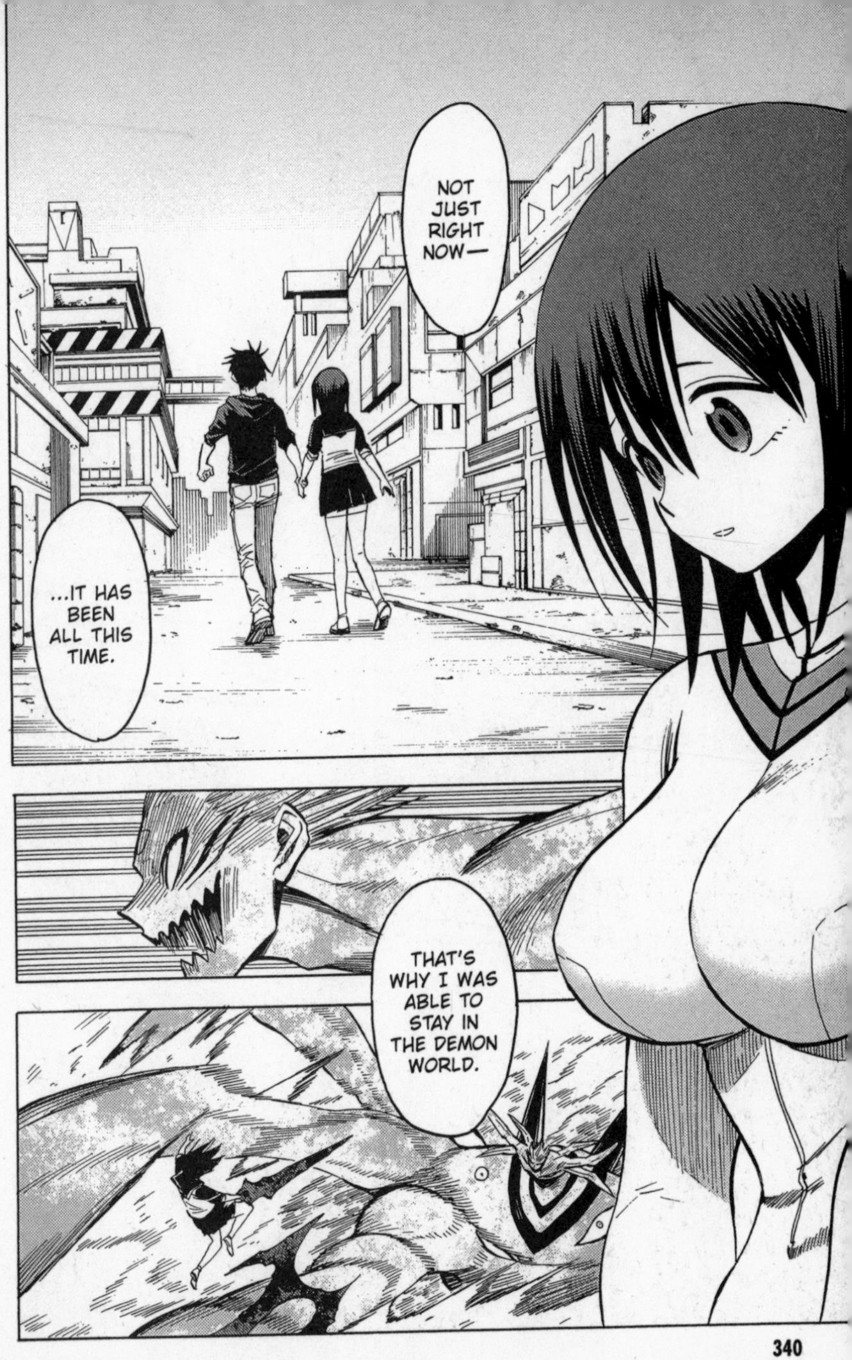
NOT JUST RIGHT NOW—
...IT HAS BEEN ALL THIS TIME.
THAT'S WHY I WAS ABLE TO STAY IN THE DEMON WORLD.

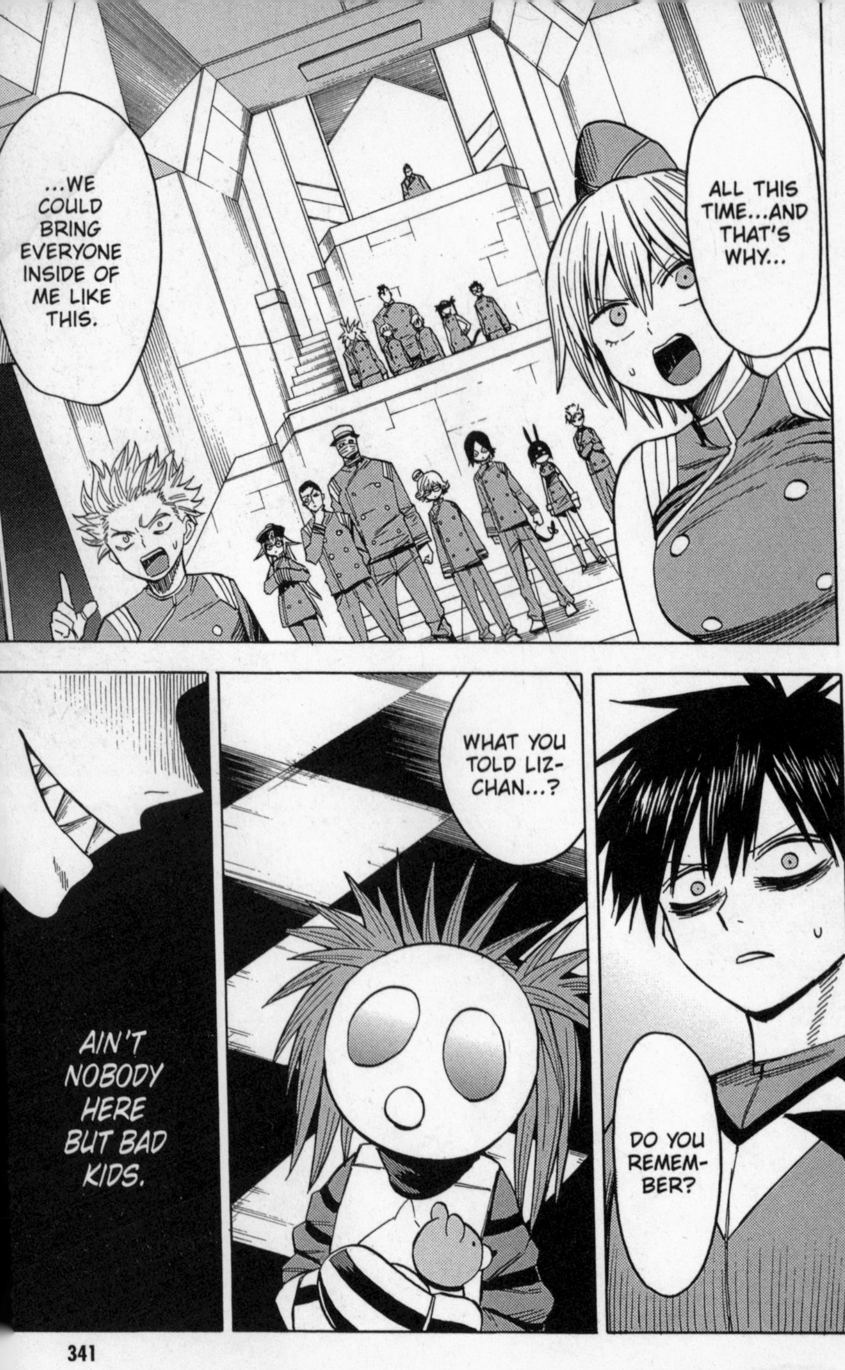
ALL THIS TIME...AND THAT'S WHY...
...WE COULD BRING EVERYONE INSIDE OF ME LIKE THIS.
DO YOU REMEM-BER?
WHAT YOU TOLD LIZ-CHAN...?
AIN'T NOBODY HERE BUT BAD KIDS.

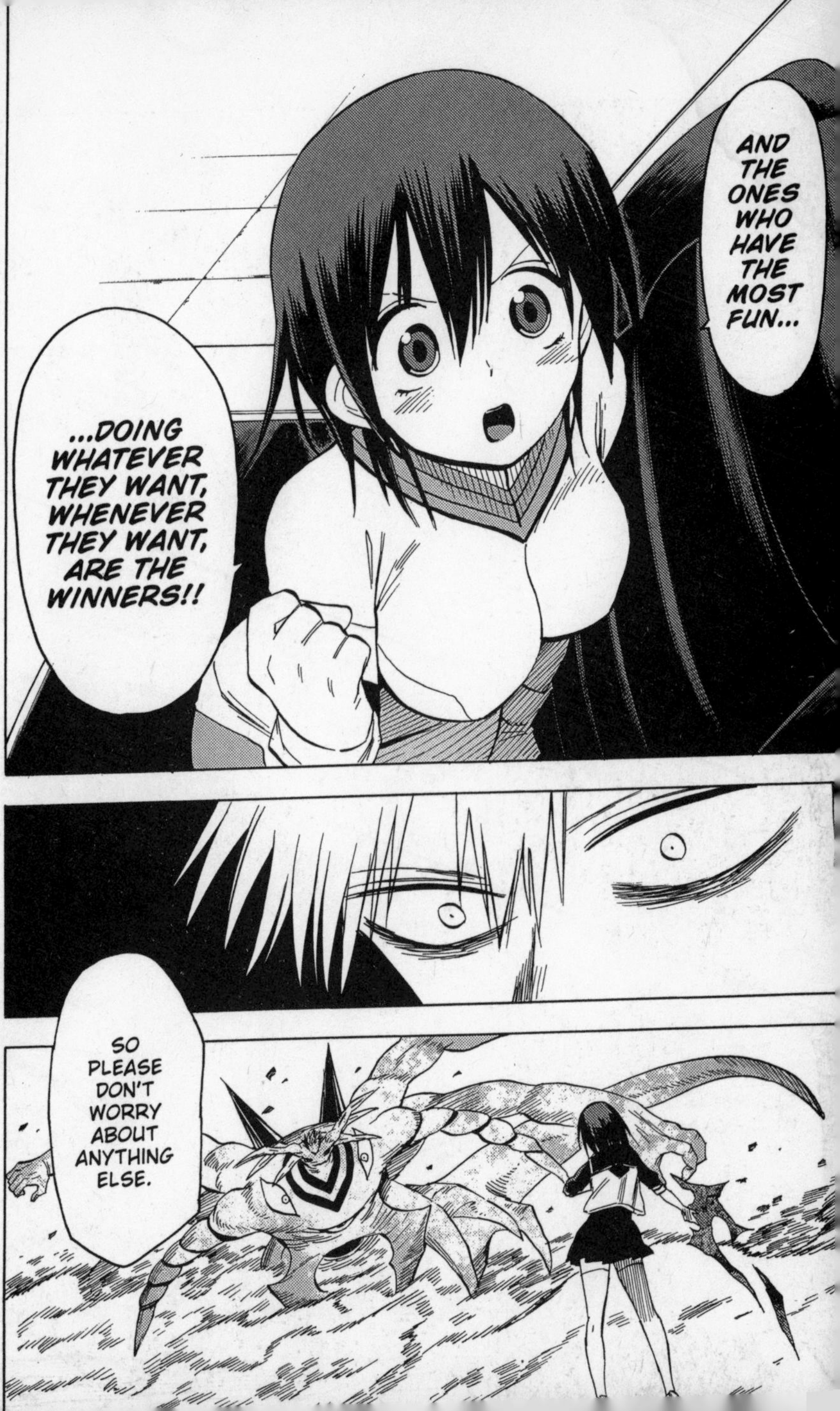
AND THE ONES WHO HAVE THE MOST FUN...
...DOING WHATEVER THEY WANT, WHENEVER THEY WANT, ARE THE WINNERS!!
SO PLEASE DON'T WORRY ABOUT ANYTHING ELSE.

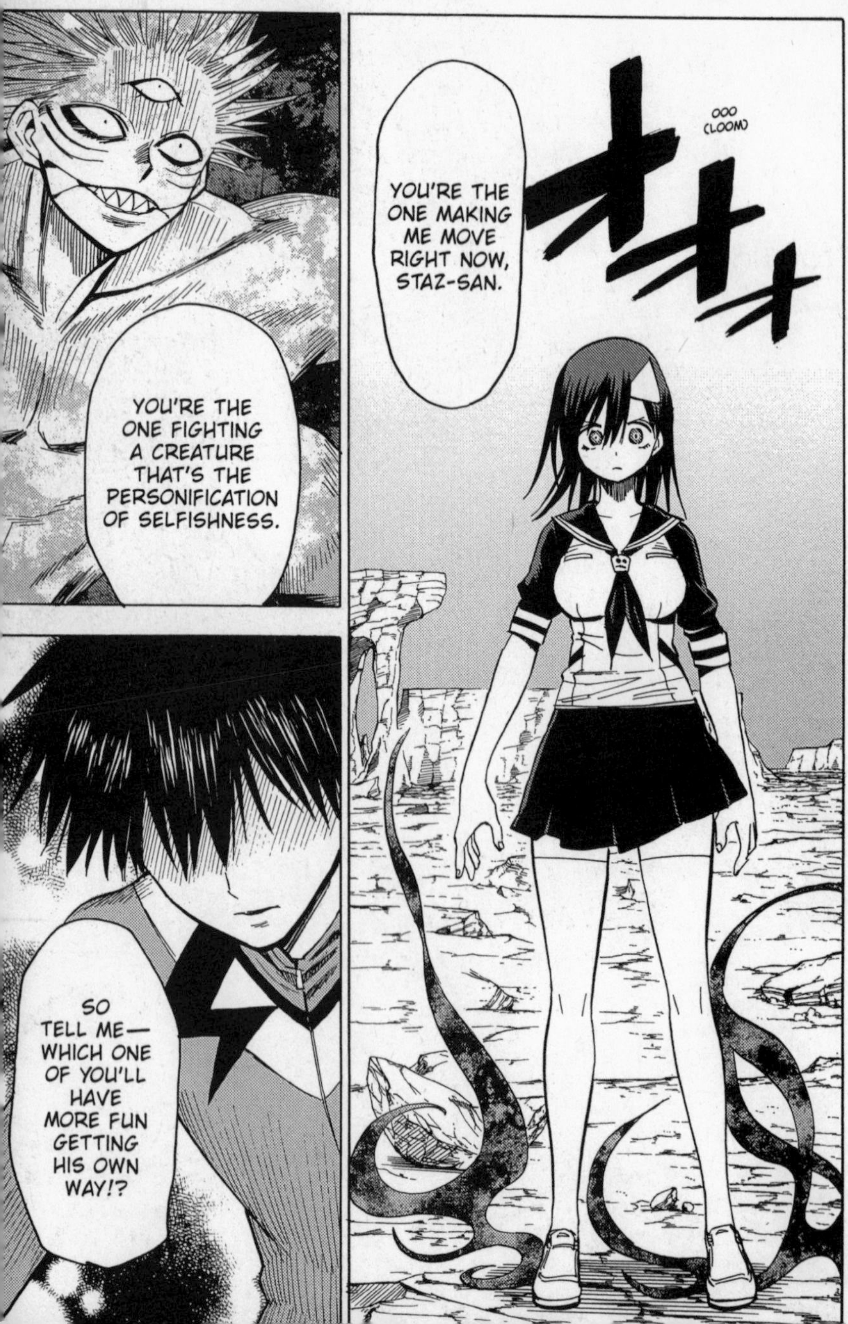
OOO (LOOM)
YOU'RE THE ONE MAKING ME MOVE RIGHT NOW, STAZ-SAN.
YOU'RE THE ONE FIGHTING A CREATURE THAT'S THE PERSONIFICATION OF SELFISHNESS.
SO TELL ME—WHICH ONE OF YOU'LL HAVE MORE FUN GETTING HIS OWN WAY!?

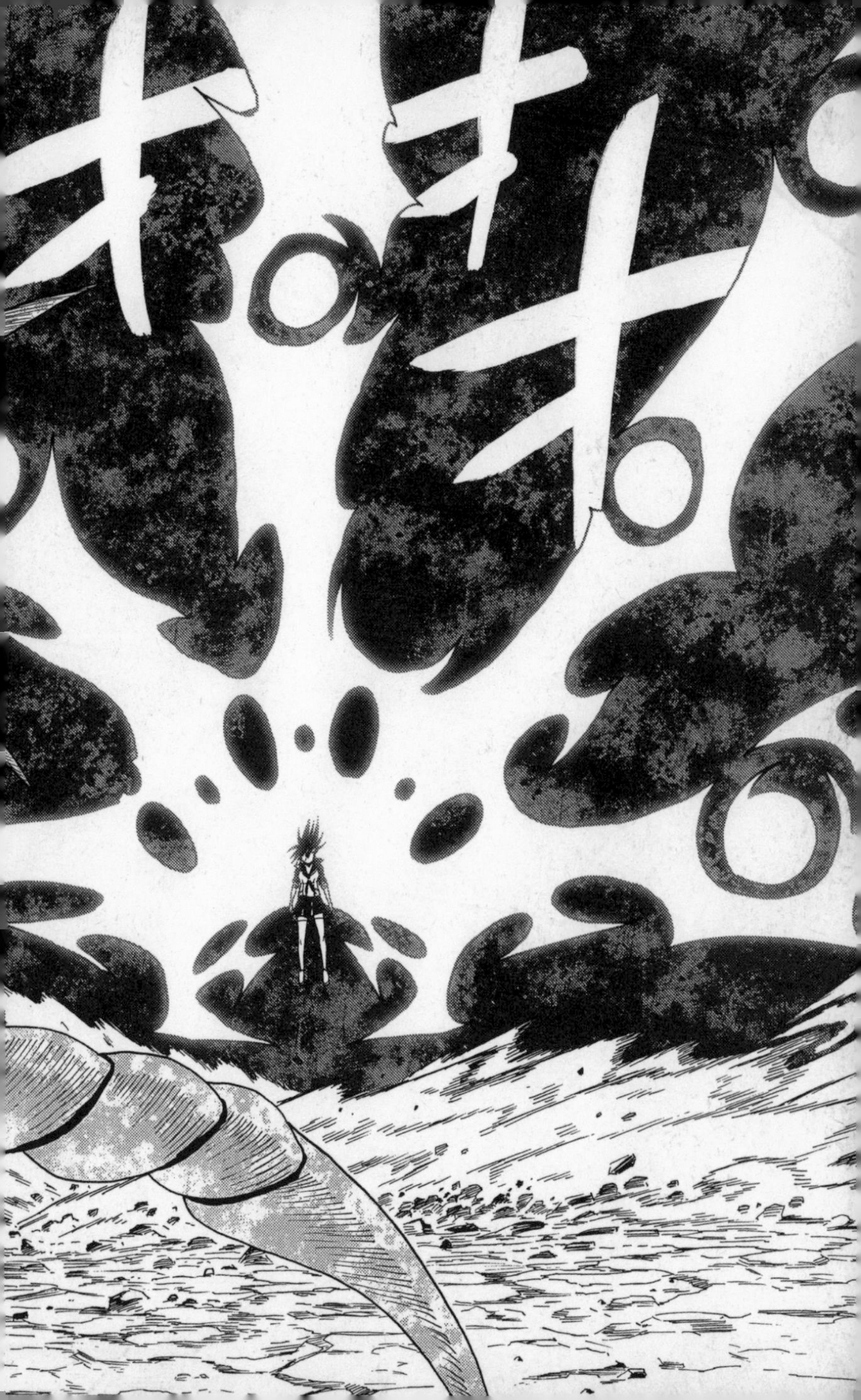

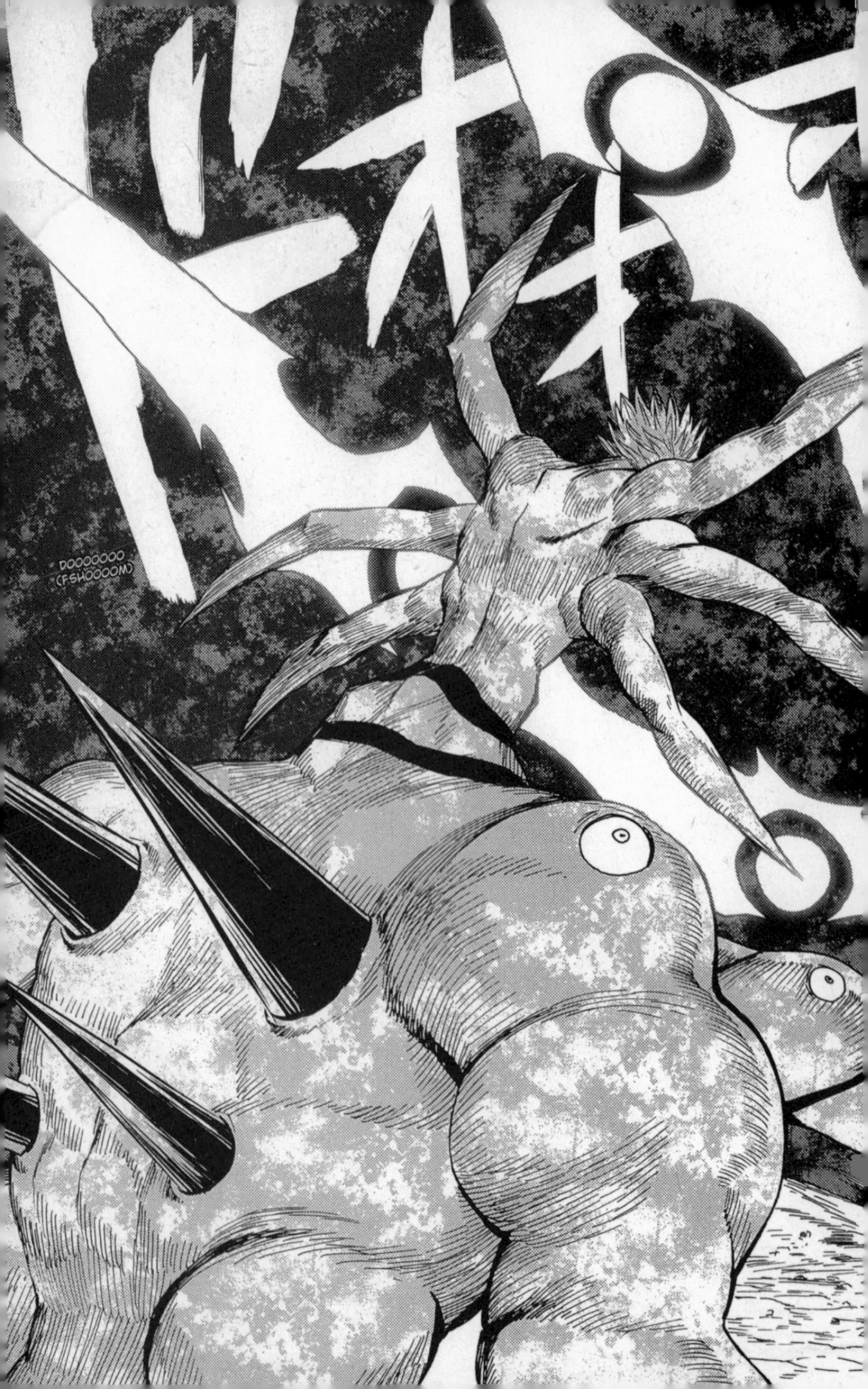
DOOOOOOO
(FSHOOOOM)

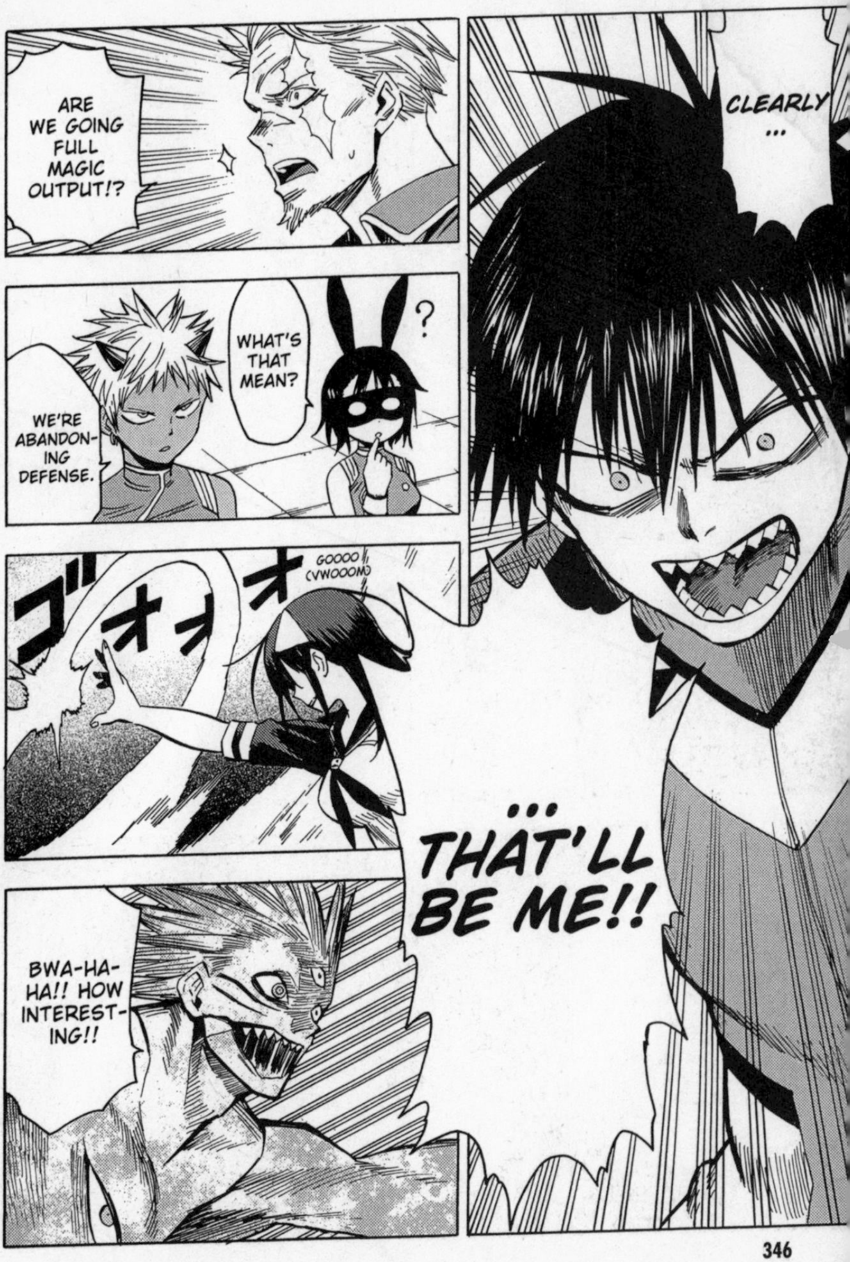
CLEARLY ...
... THÄT'LL BE ME!!
ARE WE GOING FULL MAGIC OUTPUT!?
WHAT'S THAT MEAN?
?
WE'RE ABANDON-ING DEFENSE.
ゴオォオ
GOOOO (VWOOOM)
BWA-HA-HA!! HOW INTEREST-ING!!

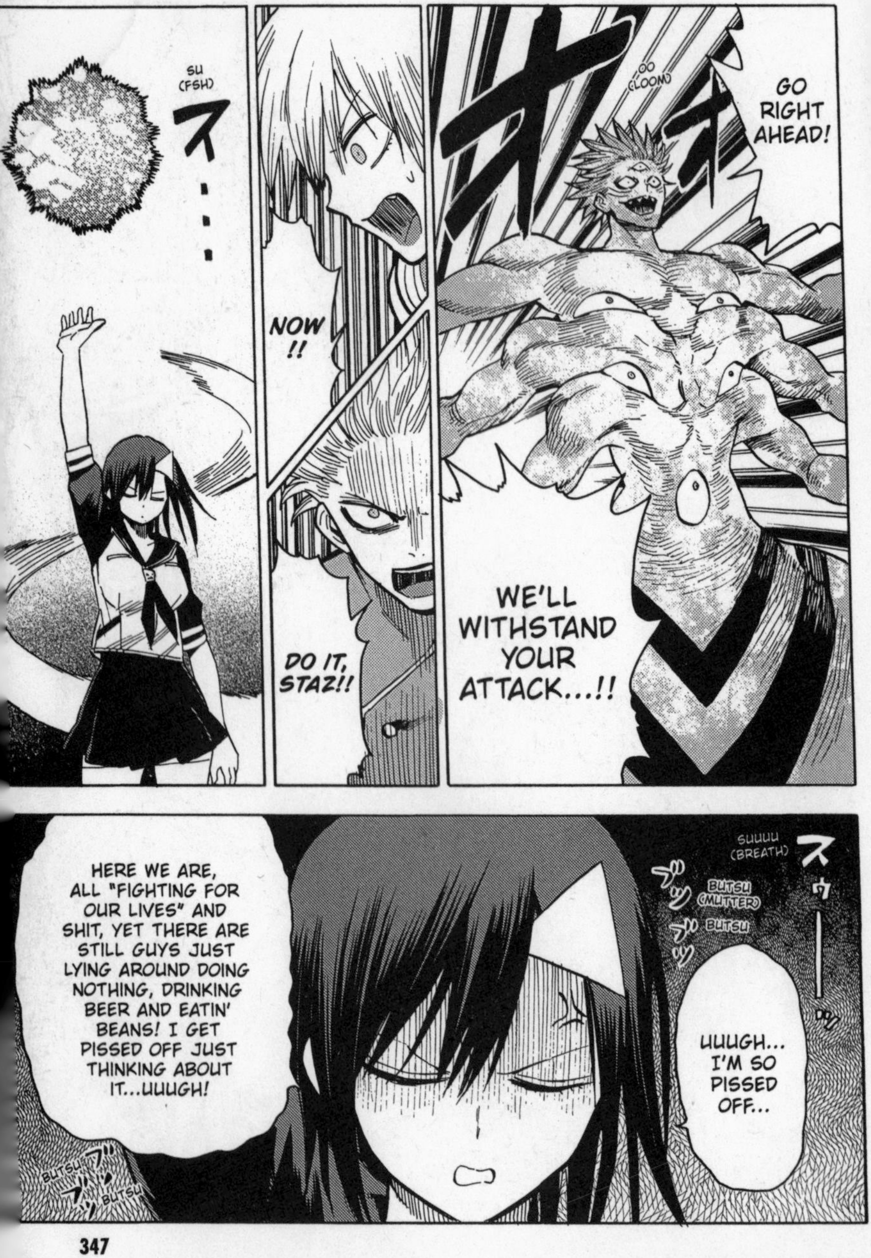
OO (LOOM)
GO RIGHT AHEAD!
WE'LL WITHSTAND YOUR ATTACK...!!
NOW!!
DO IT, STAZ!!
SU (FSH)
SUUUU (BREATH)
BUTSU (MUTTER)
BUTSU
UUUGH... I'M SO PISSED OFF...
HERE WE ARE, ALL "FIGHTING FOR OUR LIVES" AND SHIT, YET THERE ARE STILL GUYS JUST LYING AROUND DOING NOTHING, DRINKING BEER AND EATIN' BEANS! I GET PISSED OFF JUST THINKING ABOUT IT...UUUGH!
BUTSU
BUTSU

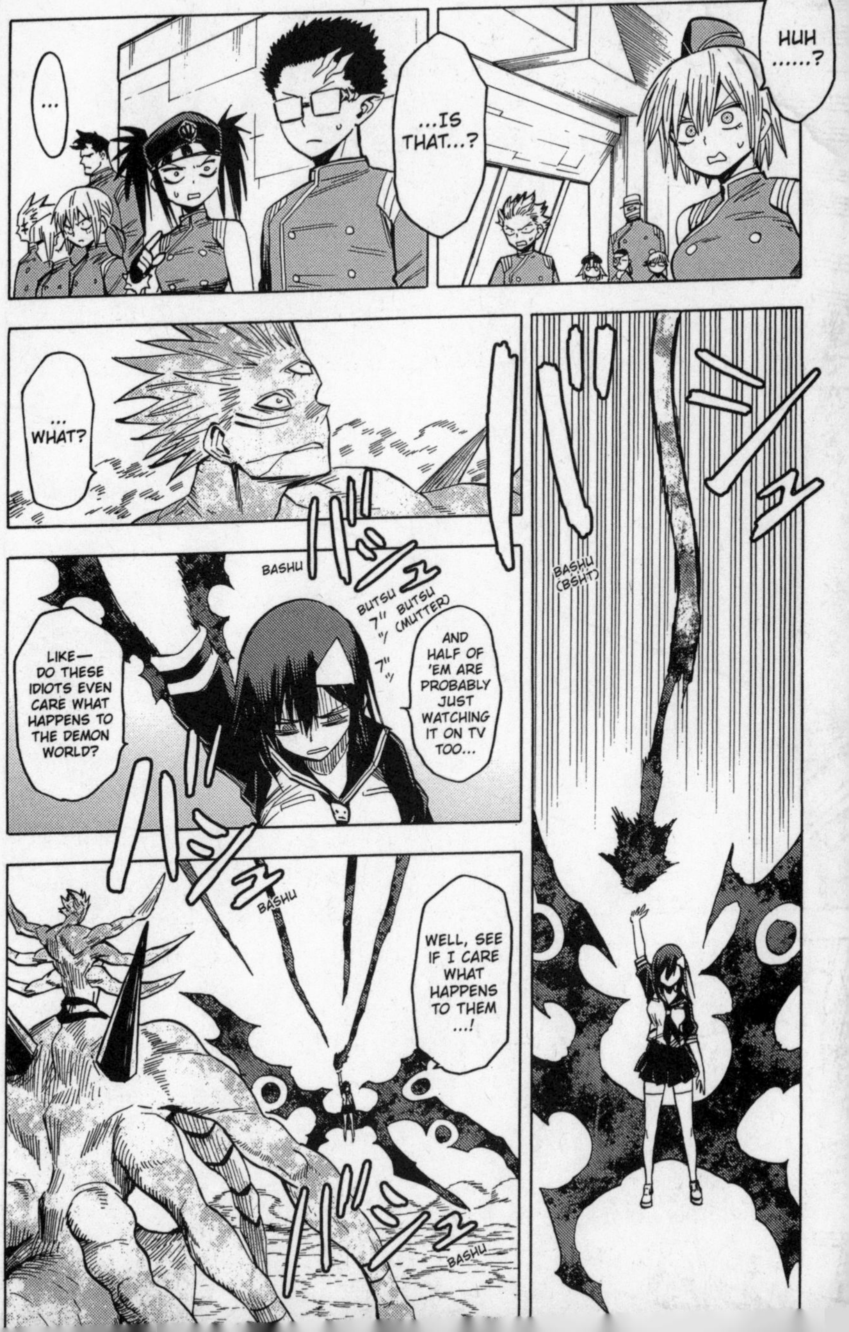
HUH ......?
...IS THAT...?
...
BASHU (BSHT)
... WHAT?
BASHU
BUTSU BUTSU (MUTTER)
AND HALF OF 'EM ARE PROBABLY JUST WATCHING IT ON TV TOO...
LIKE— DO THESE IDIOTS EVEN CARE WHAT HAPPENS TO THE DEMON WORLD?
BASHU
WELL, SEE IF I CARE WHAT HAPPENS TO THEM ...!
BASHU

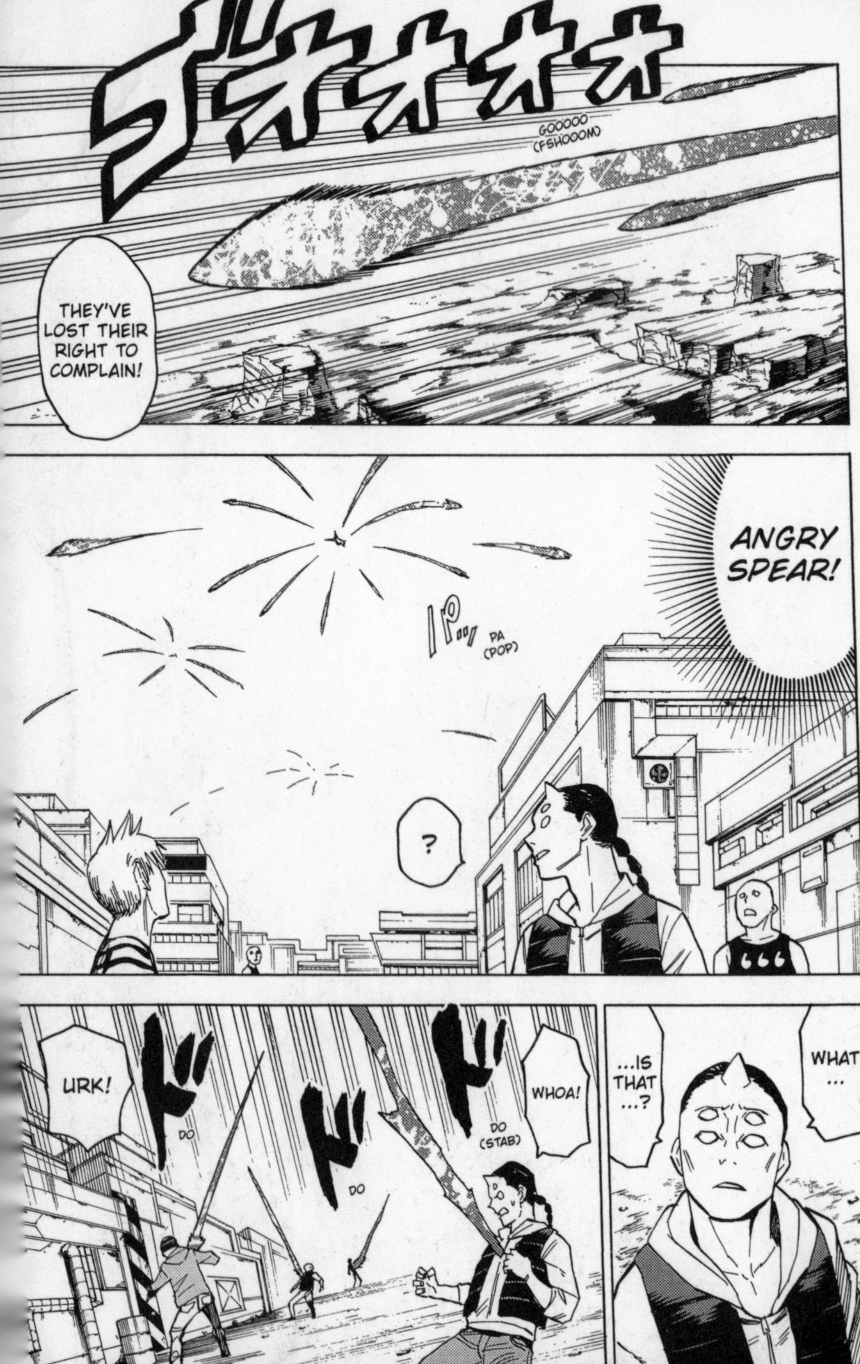
GOOOOO
(FSHOOOM)
THEY'VE LOST THEIR RIGHT TO COMPLAIN!
ANGRY SPEAR!
PA
(POP)
?
WHAT ...
...IS THAT ...?
WHOA!
DO
(STAB)
DO
DO
URK!

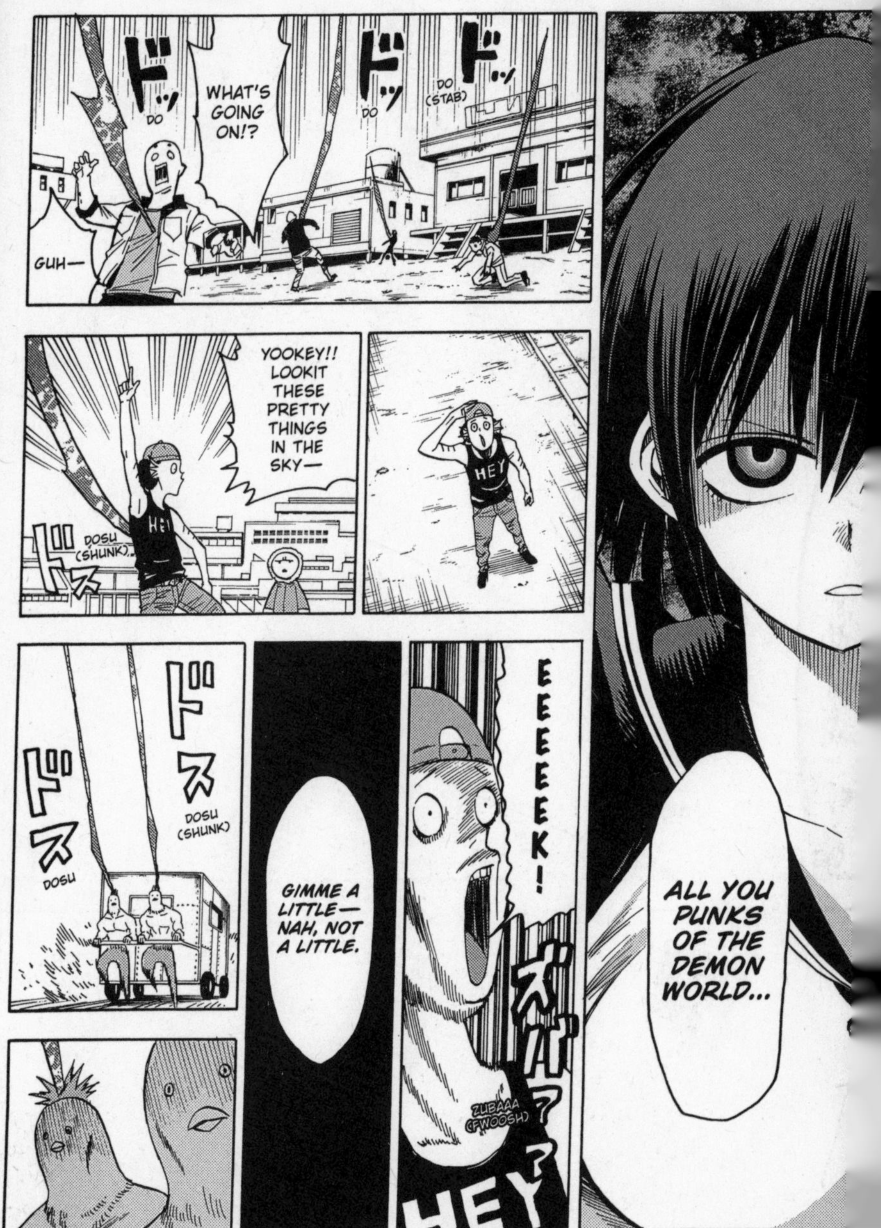
ALL YOU PUNKS OF THE DEMON WORLD...
DO
WHAT'S GOING ON!?
DO
DO (STAB)
GUH—
YOOKEY!! LOOKIT THESE PRETTY THINGS IN THE SKY—
DOSU (SHUNK)
EEEEEEEK!
ZUBAAA (FWOOSH)
HEY
GIMME A LITTLE— NAH, NOT A LITTLE.
DOSU (SHUNK)
DOSU
HEY

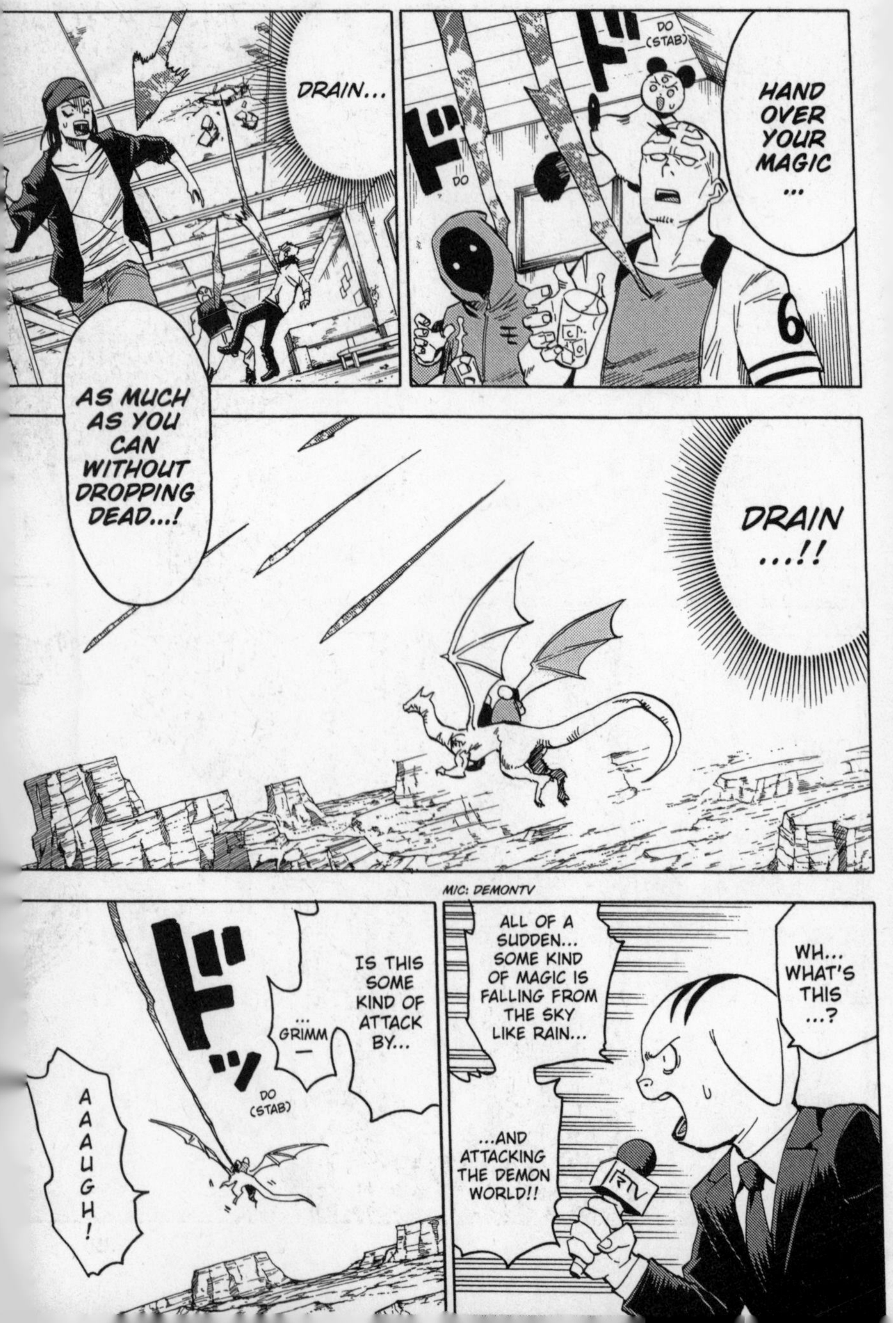
DO (STAB)
DO
HAND OVER YOUR MAGIC ...
DRAIN...
AS MUCH AS YOU CAN WITHOUT DROPPING DEAD...!
DRAIN ...!!
MIC: DEMONTV
WH... WHAT'S THIS ...?
ALL OF A SUDDEN... SOME KIND OF MAGIC IS FALLING FROM THE SKY LIKE RAIN...
...AND ATTACKING THE DEMON WORLD!!
IS THIS SOME KIND OF ATTACK BY...
... GRIMM—
DO (STAB)
AAAUGH!

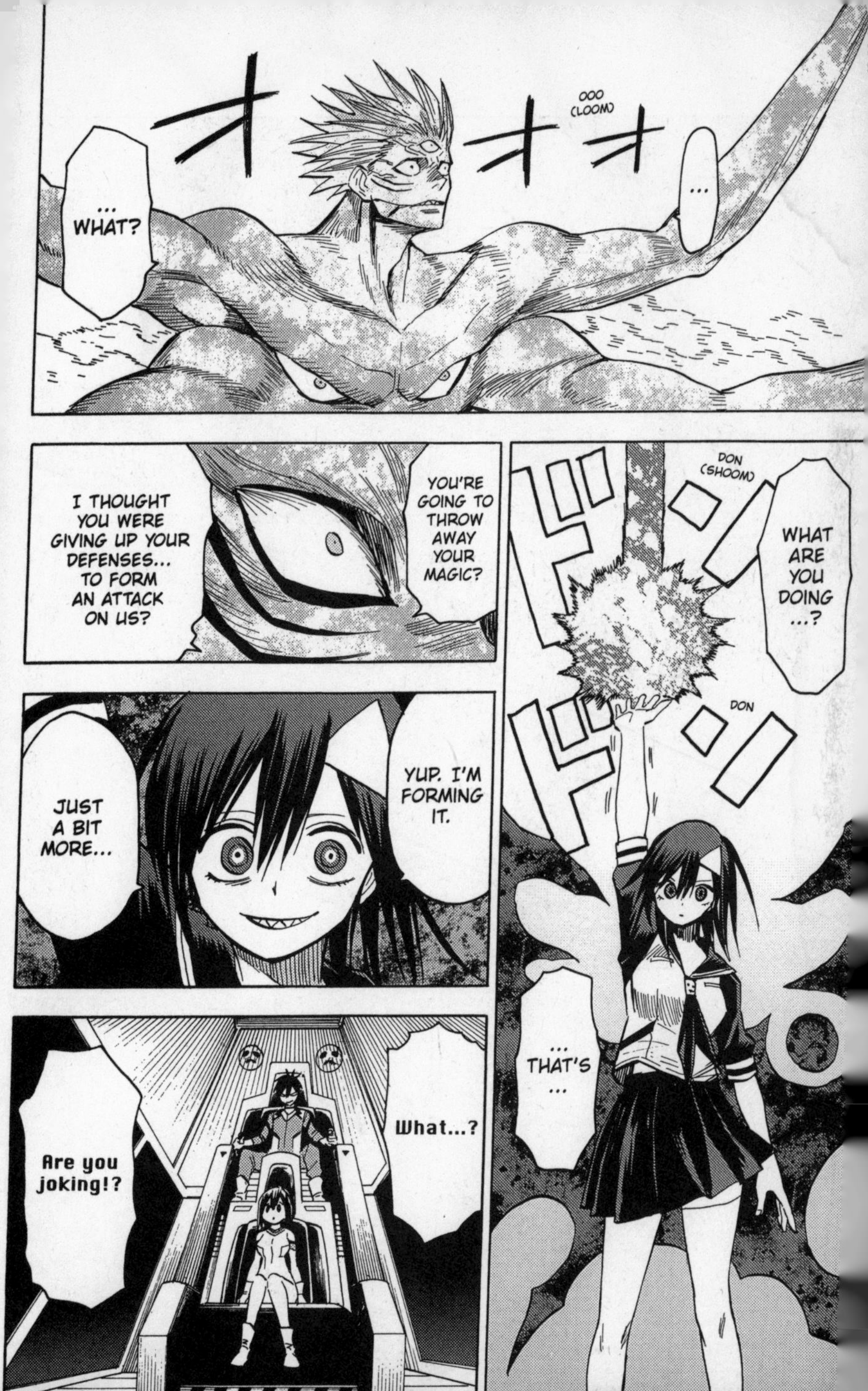
OOO (LOOM)
...
... WHAT?
DON (SHOOM)
WHAT ARE YOU DOING ...?
DON
... THAT'S ...
YOU'RE GOING TO THROW AWAY YOUR MAGIC?
I THOUGHT YOU WERE GIVING UP YOUR DEFENSES... TO FORM AN ATTACK ON US?
YUP. I'M FORMING IT.
JUST A BIT MORE...
What...?
Are you joking!?

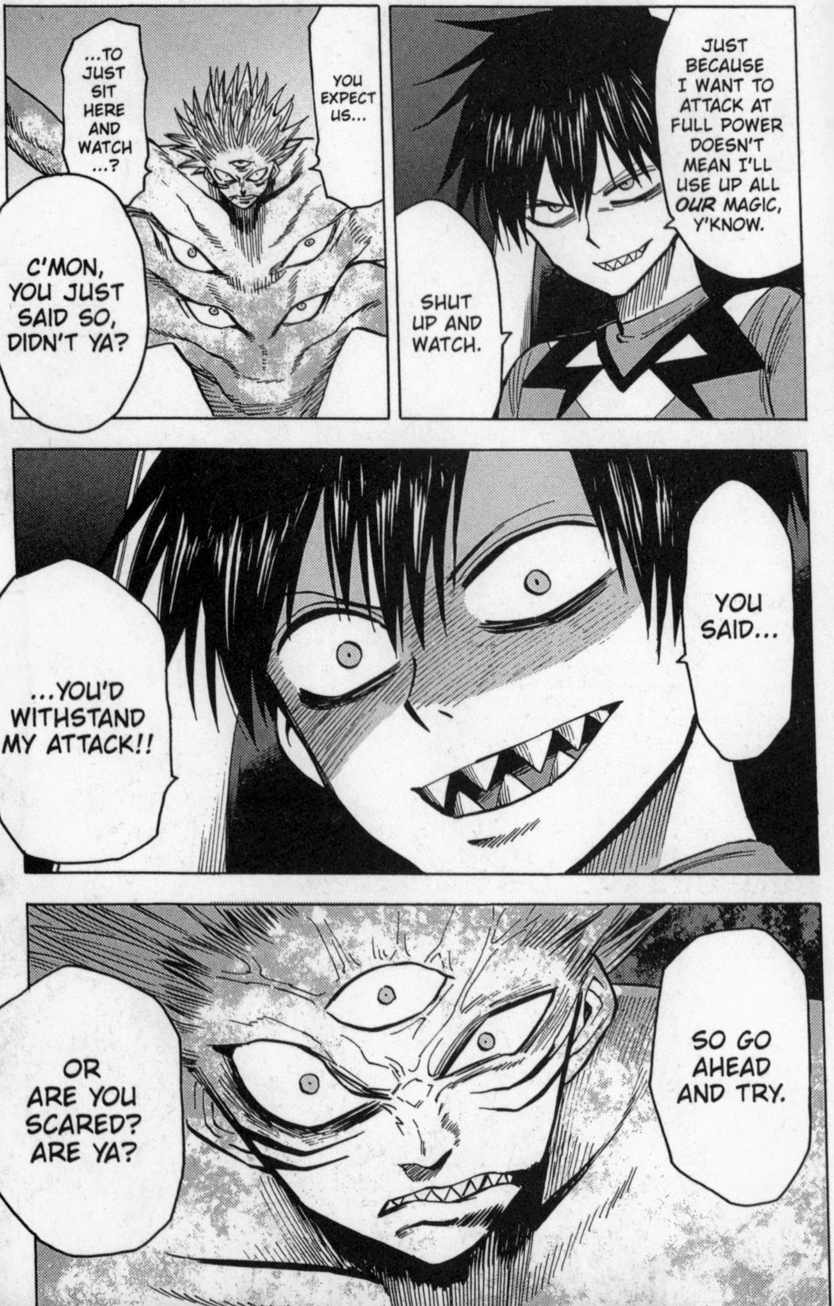
JUST BECAUSE I WANT TO ATTACK AT FULL POWER DOESN'T MEAN I'LL USE UP ALL *OUR* MAGIC, Y'KNOW.
SHUT UP AND WATCH.
YOU EXPECT US...
...TO JUST SIT HERE AND WATCH ...?
C'MON, YOU JUST SAID SO, DIDN'T YA?
YOU SAID...
...YOU'D WITHSTAND MY ATTACK!!
SO GO AHEAD AND TRY.
OR ARE YOU SCARED? ARE YA?

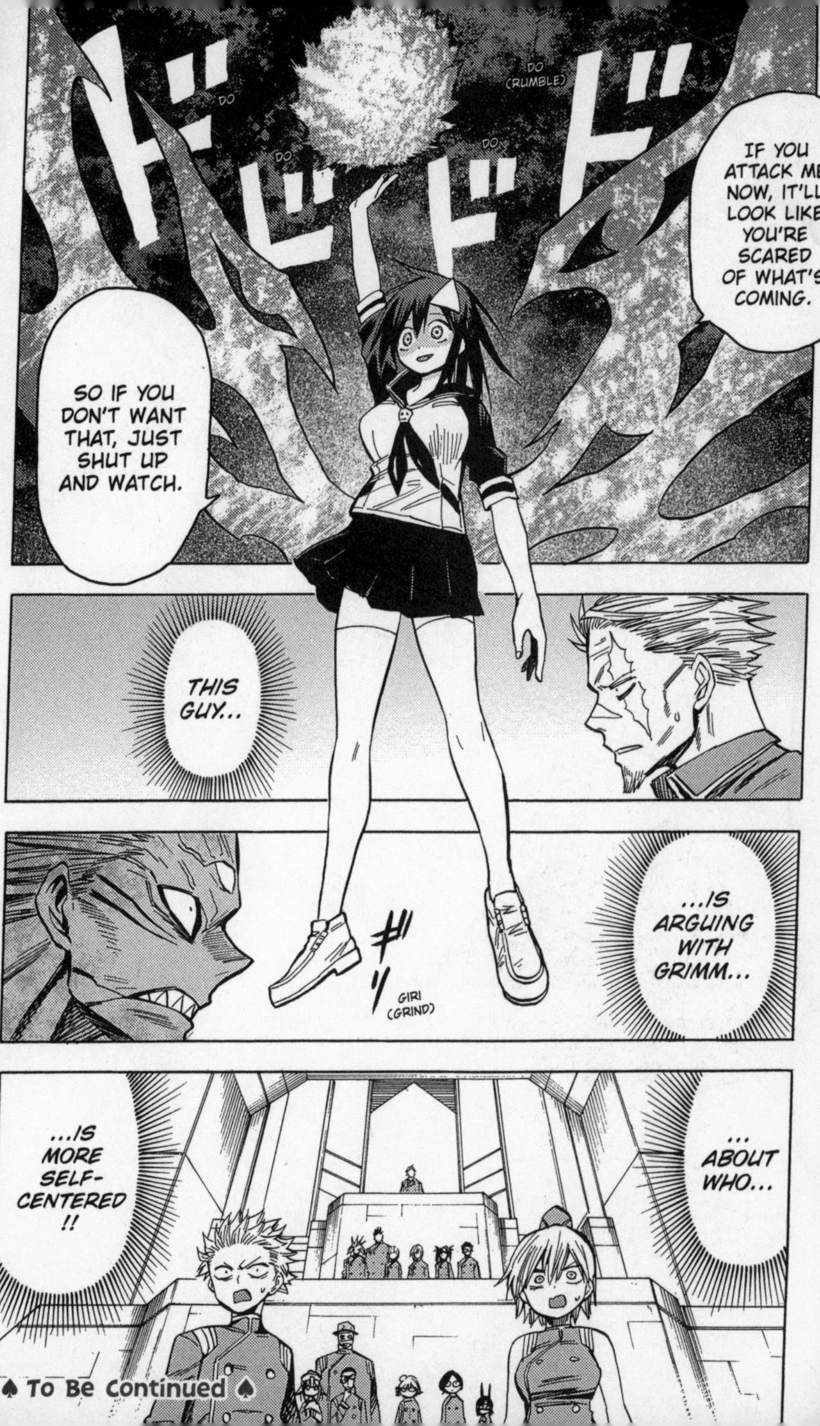
IF YOU ATTACK ME NOW, IT'LL LOOK LIKE YOU'RE SCARED OF WHAT'S COMING.
DO (RUMBLE)
DO
DO
DO
SO IF YOU DON'T WANT THAT, JUST SHUT UP AND WATCH.
THIS GUY...
...IS ARGUING WITH GRIMM...
GIRI (GRIND)
... ABOUT WHO...
...IS MORE SELF-CENTERED !!
♠ To Be Continued ♠

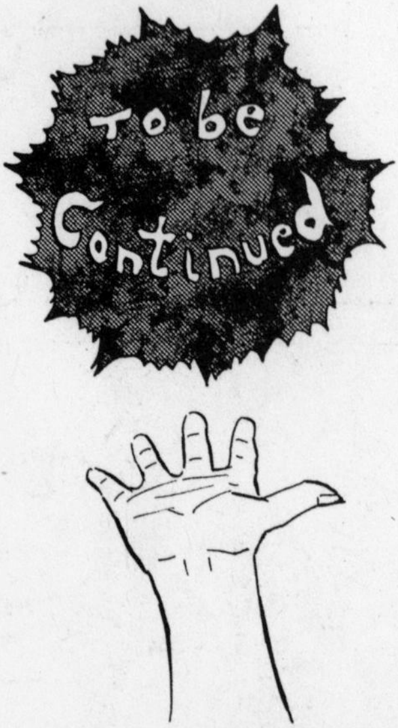
To be Continued

BLOOD LAD

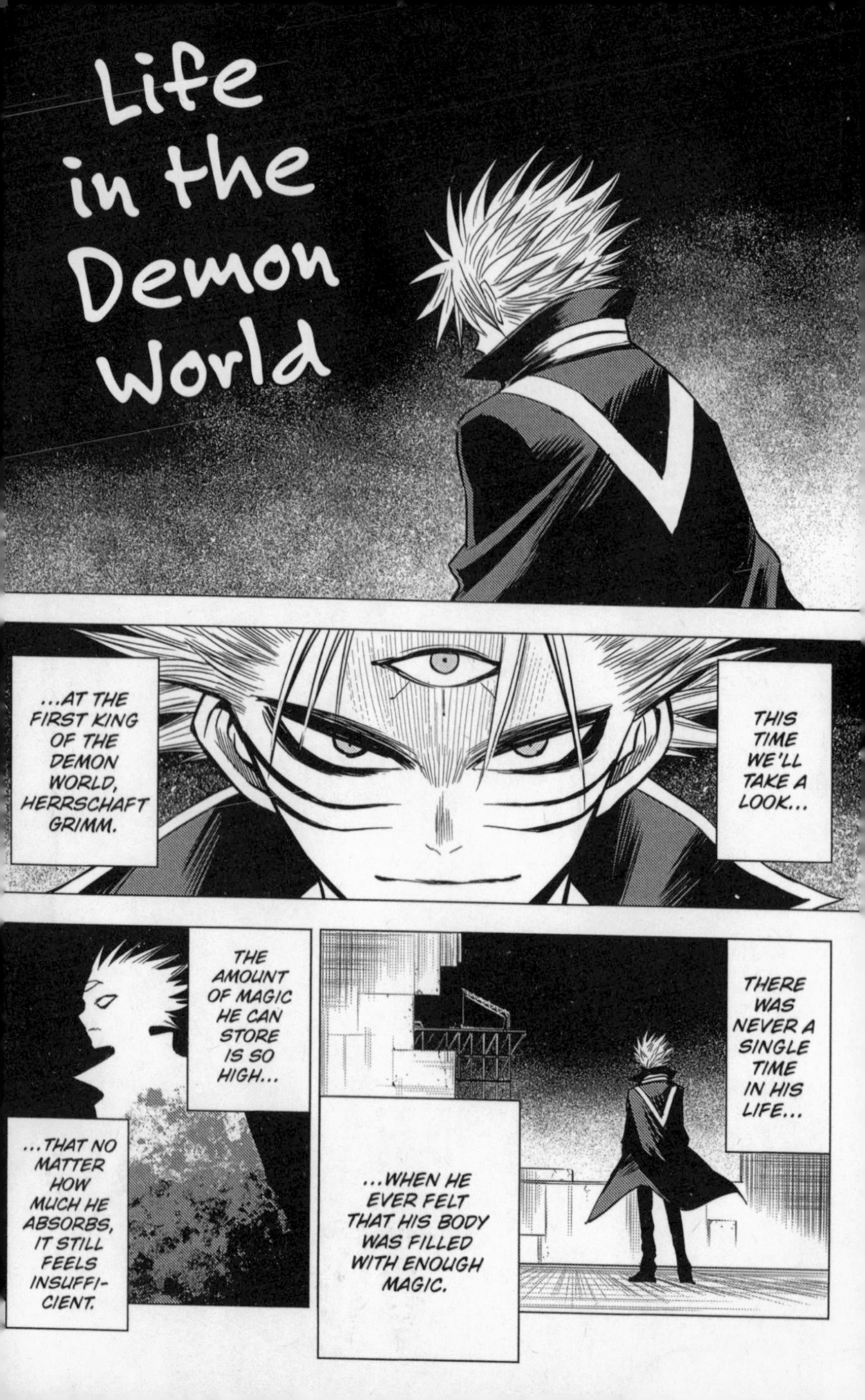
Life in the Demon World
THIS TIME WE'LL TAKE A LOOK...
...AT THE FIRST KING OF THE DEMON WORLD, HERRSCHAFT GRIMM.
THERE WAS NEVER A SINGLE TIME IN HIS LIFE...
...WHEN HE EVER FELT THAT HIS BODY WAS FILLED WITH ENOUGH MAGIC.
THE AMOUNT OF MAGIC HE CAN STORE IS SO HIGH...
...THAT NO MATTER HOW MUCH HE ABSORBS, IT STILL FEELS INSUFFI-CIENT.

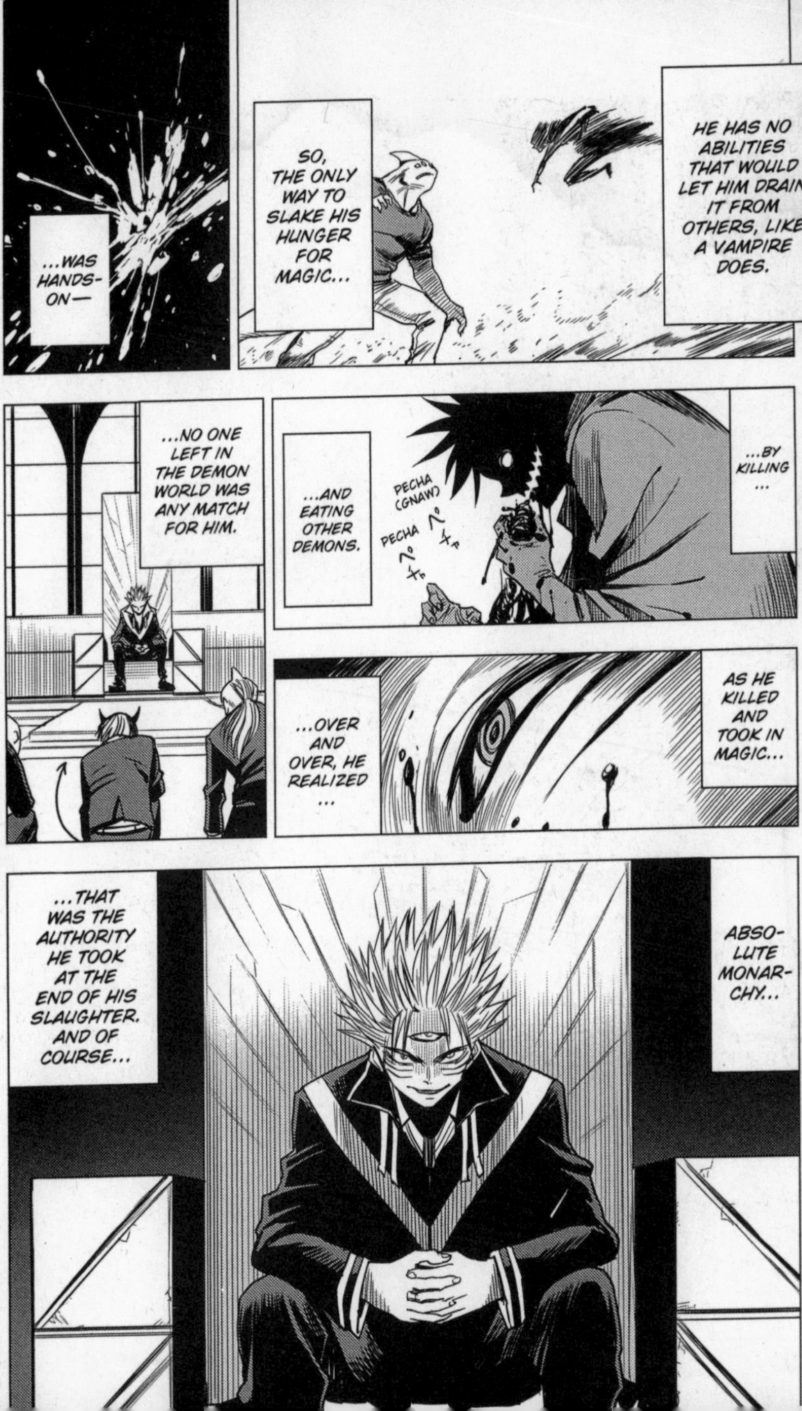
HE HAS NO ABILITIES THAT WOULD LET HIM DRAIN IT FROM OTHERS, LIKE A VAMPIRE DOES.
SO, THE ONLY WAY TO SLAKE HIS HUNGER FOR MAGIC...
...WAS HANDS-ON—
...BY KILLING...
PECHA (GNAW)
PECHA
...AND EATING OTHER DEMONS.
AS HE KILLED AND TOOK IN MAGIC...
...OVER AND OVER, HE REALIZED...
...NO ONE LEFT IN THE DEMON WORLD WAS ANY MATCH FOR HIM.
ABSO-LUTE MONAR-CHY...
...THAT WAS THE AUTHORITY HE TOOK AT THE END OF HIS SLAUGHTER. AND OF COURSE...

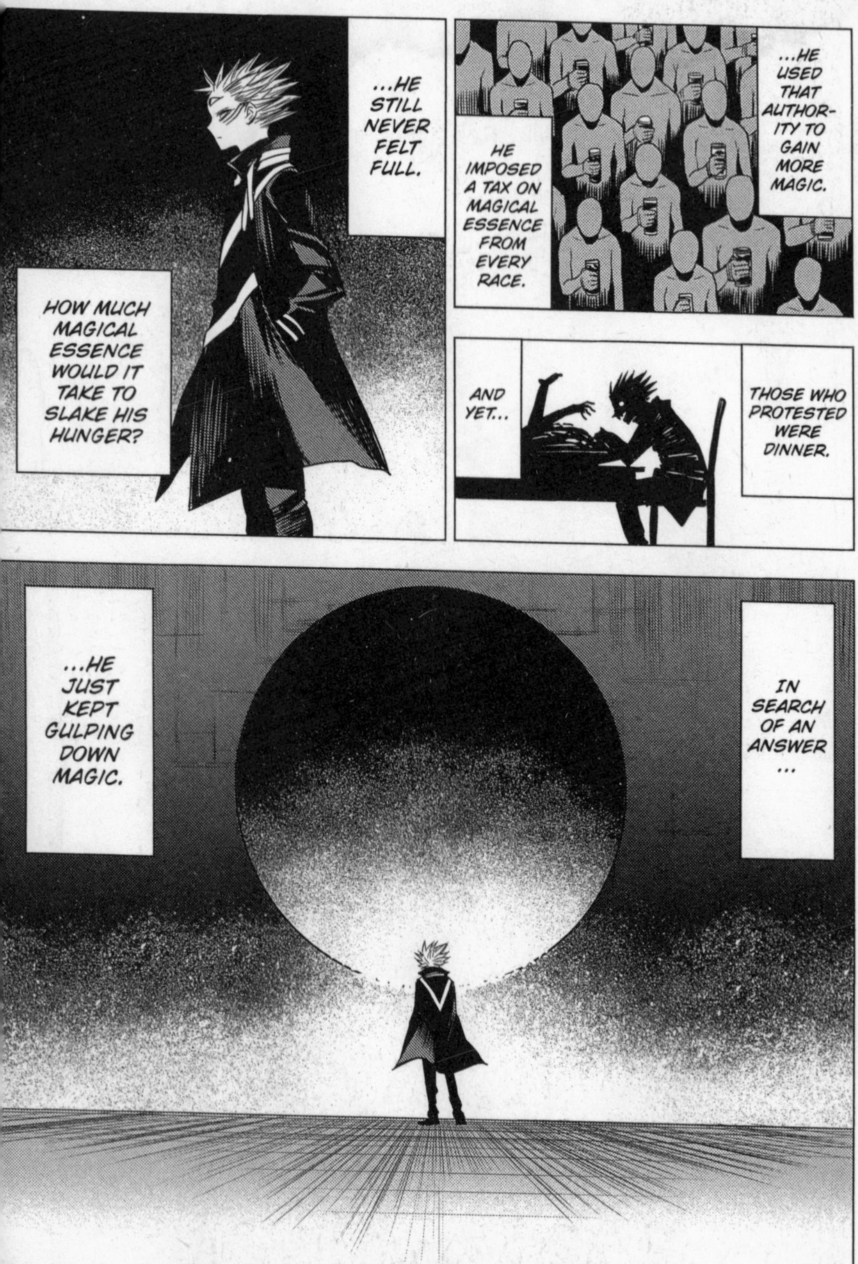
...HE USED THAT AUTHORITY TO GAIN MORE MAGIC.
HE IMPOSED A TAX ON MAGICAL ESSENCE FROM EVERY RACE.
THOSE WHO PROTESTED WERE DINNER.
AND YET...
...HE STILL NEVER FELT FULL.
HOW MUCH MAGICAL ESSENCE WOULD IT TAKE TO SLAKE HIS HUNGER?
IN SEARCH OF AN ANSWER...
...HE JUST KEPT GULPING DOWN MAGIC.

END

# BLOOD LAD 16

These images appeared under the jacket of the original edition of *Blood Lad*!

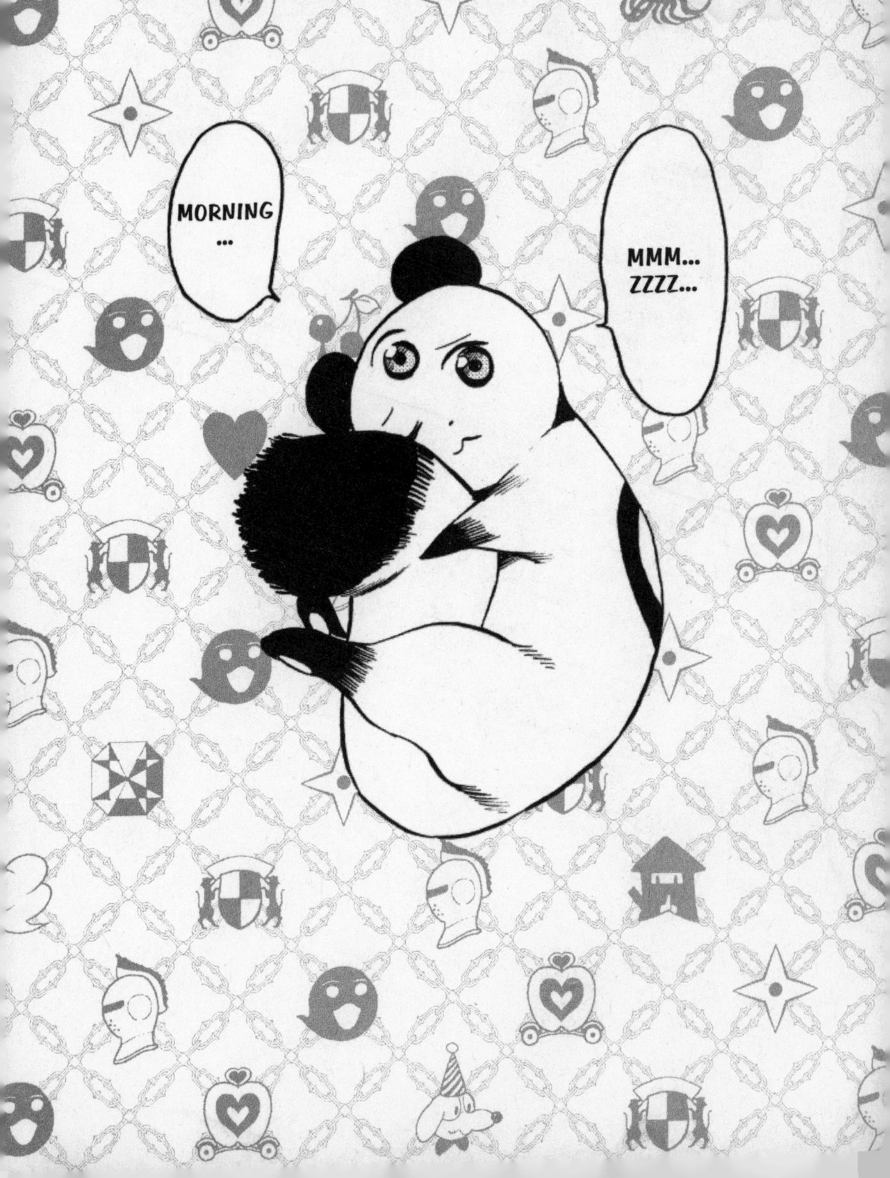

MMM... ZZZZ...
MORNING ...

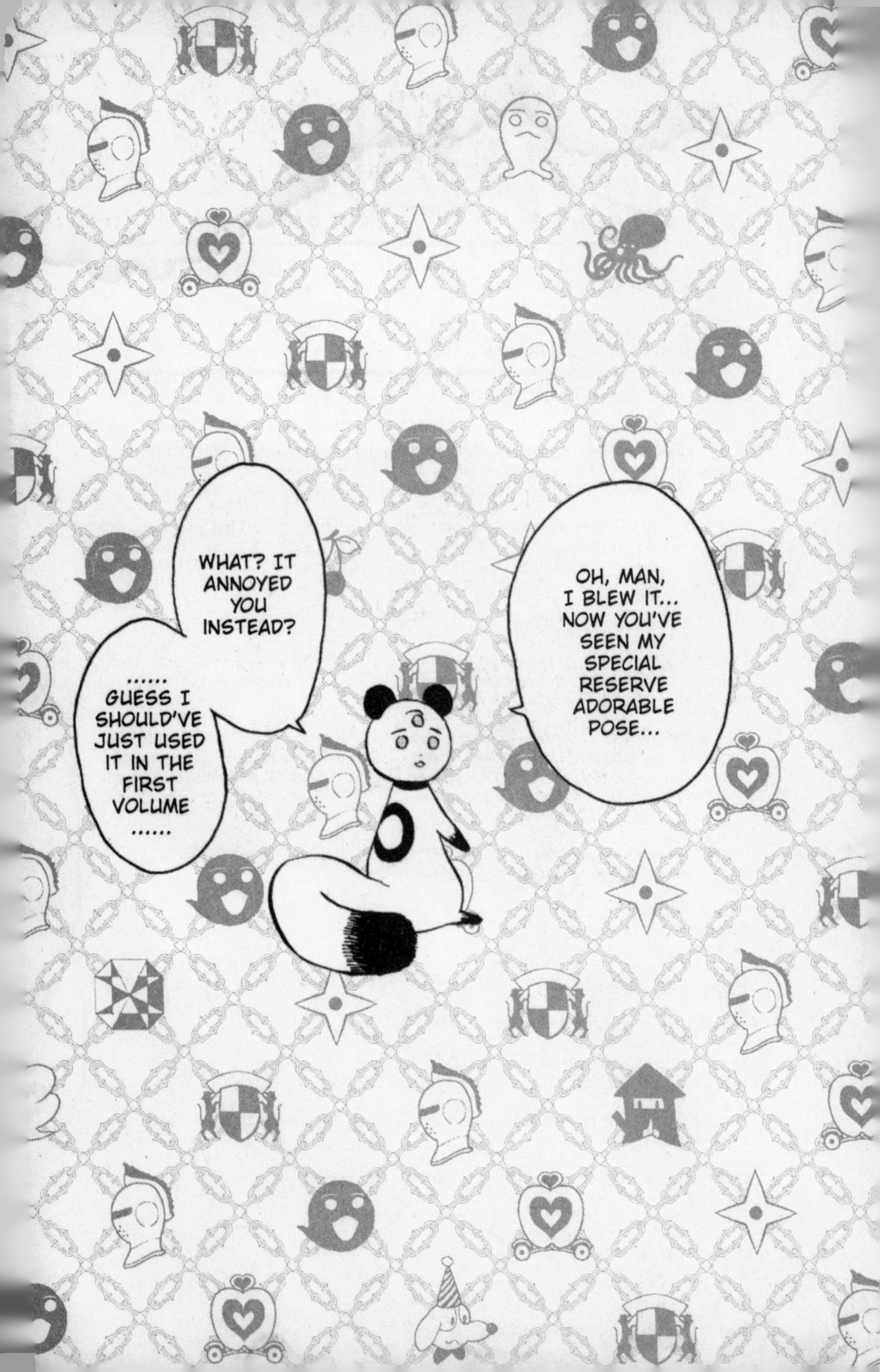
OH, MAN, I BLEW IT... NOW YOU'VE SEEN MY SPECIAL RESERVE ADORABLE POSE...
WHAT? IT ANNOYED YOU INSTEAD?
...... GUESS I SHOULD'VE JUST USED IT IN THE FIRST VOLUME ......

Translation: Melissa

Lettering: Alexis E

BLOOD LAD Volumes 15 and 16 © Yuuki KODAMA 2015, 2016. First published in Japan in 2015, 2016 by KADOKAWA CORPORATION, Tokyo. English translation rights arranged with KADOKAWA CORPORATION, Tokyo, through TUTTLE-MORI AGENCY, INC., Tokyo.

English translation © 2017 by Yen Press, LLC

Yen Press
1290 Avenue of the Americas
New York, NY 10104

Visit us at yenpress.com
facebook.com/yenpress
twitter.com/yenpress
yenpress.tumblr.com
instagram.com/yenpress

First Yen Press Edition: March 2017

Yen Press is an imprint of Yen Press, LLC.
The Yen Press name and logo are trademarks of Yen Press, LLC.

The publisher is not responsible for websites (or their content) that are not owned by the publisher.

Library of Congress Control Number: 2014504627

ISBN: 978-0-316-46922-7

10 9 8 7 6 5 4 3 2 1

BVG

Printed in the United States of America